# THE PHILOSOPHY OF
# C. I. LEWIS

## THE LIBRARY OF LIVING PHILOSOPHERS

PAUL ARTHUR SCHILPP, *Editor*

*Already Published:*

THE PHILOSOPHY OF JOHN DEWEY (1939)

THE PHILOSOPHY OF GEORGE SANTAYANA (1940)

THE PHILOSOPHY OF ALFRED NORTH WHITEHEAD (1941)

THE PHILOSOPHY OF G. E. MOORE (1942)

THE PHILOSOPHY OF BERTRAND RUSSELL (1944)

THE PHILOSOPHY OF ERNST CASSIRER (1949)

ALBERT EINSTEIN: PHILOSOPHER-SCIENTIST (1949)

THE PHILOSOPHY OF SARVEPALLI RADHAKRISHNAN (1952)

THE PHILOSOPHY OF KARL JASPERS (1957)

THE PHILOSOPHY OF C. D. BROAD (1959)

THE PHILOSOPHY OF RUDOLF CARNAP (1963)

THE PHILOSOPHY OF MARTIN BUBER (1967)

THE PHILOSOPHY OF C. I. LEWIS (1968)

*In Preparation:*

THE PHILOSOPHY OF KARL R. POPPER

THE PHILOSOPHY OF GABRIEL MARCEL

*Other volumes to be announced later*

Clarence Lewis

THE LIBRARY OF LIVING PHILOSOPHERS

VOLUME XIII

# THE

# PHILOSOPHY

## OF

# C. I. LEWIS

EDITED BY

## PAUL ARTHUR SCHILPP

NORTHWESTERN UNIVERSITY &
SOUTHERN ILLINOIS UNIVERSITY

LA SALLE, ILLINOIS • OPEN COURT • ESTABLISHED 1887

LONDON • CAMBRIDGE UNIVERSITY PRESS

# THE PHILOSOPHY OF C. I. LEWIS

*Printed in the United States of America*

# GENERAL INTRODUCTION*
## TO
## "THE LIBRARY OF LIVING PHILOSOPHERS"

According to the late F. C. S. Schiller, the greatest obstacle to fruitful discussion in philosophy is "the curious etiquette which apparently taboos the asking of questions about a philosopher's meaning while he is alive." The "interminable controversies which fill the histories of philosophy," he goes on to say, "could have been ended at once by asking the living philosophers a few searching questions."

The confident optimism of this last remark undoubtedly goes too far. Living thinkers have often been asked "a few searching questions," but their answers have not stopped "interminable controversies" about their real meaning. It is none the less true that there would be far greater clarity of understanding than is now often the case, if more such searching questions had been directed to great thinkers while they were still alive.

This, at any rate, is the basic thought behind the present undertaking. The volumes of *The Library of Living Philosophers* can in no sense take the place of the major writings of great and original thinkers. Students who would know the philosophies of such men as John Dewey, George Santayana, Alfred North Whitehead, G. E. Moore, Bertrand Russell, Ernst Cassirer, Karl Jaspers, Rudolf Carnap, Martin Buber, *et al.*, will still need to read the writings of these men. There is no substitute for first-hand contact with the original thought of the philosopher himself. Least of all does this *Library* pretend to be such a substitute. The *Library* in fact will spare neither effort nor expense in offering to the student the best possible guide to the published writings of a given thinker. We shall attempt to meet this aim by providing at the end of each volume in our series a complete bibliography of the published work of the philosopher in question. Nor should one overlook the fact that the essays in each volume cannot but finally lead to this same goal. The interpretative and critical discussions of the various phases of a great thinker's work and, most of all, the reply of the thinker himself, are bound to lead the reader to the works of the philosopher himself.

At the same time, there is no denying the fact that different experts find different ideas in the writings of the same philosopher. This is as true of the appreciative interpreter and grateful disciple as it is of the critical opponent. Nor can it be denied that such differences of reading and of interpretation on the part of other experts often leave the neophyte

* This *General Introduction*, setting forth the underlying conception of this *Library*, is purposely reprinted in each volume (with only very minor changes).

aghast before the whole maze of widely varying and even opposing
interpretations. Who is right and whose interpretation shall he accept?
When the doctors disagree among themselves, what is the poor student to
do? If, in desperation, he decides that all of the interpreters are probably
wrong and that the only thing for him to do is to go back to the original
writings of the philosopher himself and then make his own decision—un-
influenced (as if this were possible) by the interpretation of any one
else—the result is not that he has actually come to the meaning of the
original philosopher himself, but rather that he has set up one more
interpretation, which may differ to a greater or lesser degree from the
interpretations already existing. It is clear that in this direction lies
chaos, just the kind of chaos which Schiller has so graphically and inim-
itably described.[1]

It is curious that until now no way of escaping this difficulty has been
seriously considered. It has not occurred to students of philosophy that
one effective way of meeting the problem at least partially is to put these
varying interpretations and critiques before the philosopher while he is
still alive and to ask him to act at one and the same time as both
defendant and judge. If the world's great living philosophers can be
induced to co-operate in an enterprise whereby their own work can, at
least to some extent, be saved from becoming merely "dessicated lecture-
fodder," which on the one hand "provides innocuous sustenance for
ruminant professors," and, on the other hand, gives an opportunity to
such ruminants and their understudies to "speculate safely, endlessly, and
fruitlessly, about what a philosopher must have meant" (Schiller), they
will have taken a long step toward making their intentions clearly com-
prehensible.

With this in mind, *The Library of Living Philosophers* expects to
publish at more or less regular intervals a volume on each of the greater
among the world's living philosophers. In each case it will be the purpose
of the editor of the *Library* to bring together in the volume the interpretations and criticisms of a wide range of that particular thinker's scholarly contemporaries, each of whom will be given a free hand to discuss the
specific phase of the thinker's work which has been assigned to him. All
contributed essays will finally be submitted to the philosopher with
whose work and thought they are concerned, for his careful perusal and
reply. And, although it would be expecting too much to imagine that
the philosopher's reply will be able to stop all differences of interpretation and of critique, this should at least serve the purpose of stopping

---

[1] In his essay on "Must Philosophers Disagree?" in the volume by the same title
(Macmillan, London, 1934), from which the above quotations were taken.

certain of the grosser and more general kinds of misinterpretations. If no further gain than this were to come from the present and projected volumes of this *Library*, it would seem to be fully justified.

In carrying out this principal purpose of the *Library*, the editor announces that (insofar as humanly possible) each volume will conform to the following pattern:

*First,* a series of expository and critical articles written by the leading exponents and opponents of the philosopher's thought;

*Second,* the reply to the critics and commentators by the philosopher himself;

*Third,* an intellectual autobiography of the thinker whenever this can be secured; in any case an authoritative and authorized biography; and

*Fourth,* a bibliography of writings of the philosopher to provide a ready instrument to give access to his writings and thought.

The editor has deemed it desirable to secure the services of an Advisory Board of philosophers to aid him in the selection of the subjects of future volumes. The names of the seven prominent American philosophers who have consented to serve appear below. To each of them the editor expresses his sincere gratitude.

Future volumes in this series will appear in as rapid succession as is feasible in view of the scholarly nature of this *Library*. The next volume in this series will be devoted to the philosophy of Karl R. Popper.

Through the generosity of the Edward C. Hegeler Foundation, the publication of each new volume of the *Library* is assured on completion of the manuscript. However, funds are still required for editorial purposes in order to place the entire project of *The Library of Living Philosophers* on a sound financial foundation. The *Library* would be deeply grateful, therefore, for gifts and donations. Moreover, since November 6th, 1947, any gifts or donations made to The Library of Living Philosophers, Inc., are deductible by the donors in arriving at their taxable net income in conformity with the Internal Revenue Code of the Treasury Department of the United States of America.

DEPARTMENTS OF PHILOSOPHY
NORTHWESTERN UNIVERSITY AND
SOUTHERN ILLINOIS UNIVERSITY

P. A. S.
*Editor*

## ADVISORY BOARD

## ACKNOWLEDGMENTS
*by the editor*

The editor hereby gratefully acknowledges his obligation and sincere gratitude to all the publishers of Professor Lewis' books and publications for their kind and uniform courtesy in permitting us to quote—sometimes at some length—from Professor Lewis' writings.

PAUL A. SCHILPP

# TABLE OF CONTENTS

# PREFACE

When Professor Clarence Irving Lewis passed away in Menlo Park, California, in February 1964, those of us who had both been greatly influenced by his thought and were also concerned with *The Philosophy of C. I. Lewis* in this "Library of Living Philosophers," had at least one consolation: the manuscripts for the volume were in our hands in their totality; we had not only Professor Lewis' "Autobiographic Notes" and the twenty-six contributed essays from his disciples and critics, but also Professor Lewis' own "Reply" to those essays as well as a complete Bibliography of his writings.

The passing of a great and original mind is always a great loss to humanity; this is as true of Lewis' leaving us. But those of us who had been in contact with him in recent years had known all along that he was actually living on 'borrowed time'; so that his passing was not the great shock which otherwise it would have been. At the same time we feel a sense of great regret that this volume could not have appeared during his life-time.

The readers of our Carnap volume will already have learned of our deep sorrow at the untimely loss of Paul Henle of the University of Michigan and Arthur Pap of Yale University who contributed distinguished essays to both the Carnap and the Lewis volumes.

Many of the contributors to this volume may register a sense of disappointment at Professor Lewis' formal "Reply" to their respective essays. This is understandable. But it must be recorded here that, at the time Professor Lewis got those essays, his health was greatly impaired and consequently he did the very best he could under the circumstances. Moreover, it is not always the length of a reply which is important, but rather the clarity and incisiveness of it. And, seen from this point of view, Professor Lewis' "Reply" leaves little to be desired. Insofar as his physical strength permitted, he gave complete and whole-hearted co-operation to this enterprise from the very moment when he had agreed to a volume on his philosophy in this "Library." For this we desire even here once more to express our sincere appreciation. The same goes for the very kind and courteous co-operation received, since the passing of Professor Lewis, from his widow, Mrs. Mabel M. Lewis, and from his son, Mr. Andrew Lewis.

It also was no surprise to the editor to find how many philosophers were not merely willing but anxious to participate in this undertaking.

Nothing could have constituted a better proof of the wide influence of Lewis' thinking than the almost universal readiness for such participation. The editor's sincere gratitude is here expressed to every one of our contributors, whose essays demonstrate how seriously they took this assignment.

Gratitude and appreciation is due also to the Hegeler Foundation of LaSalle, Illinois, for a small grant covering some secretarial expenses. But most appreciation must go to that great team of Editorial Consultants of The Open Court Publishing Company, Professor and Mrs. Eugene Freeman, who have spared neither time nor effort to make this volume as nearly letter-perfect as was humanly possible. Without their unstinted labors the editor's own task would have been infinitely more difficult and involved. He finds it difficult, therefore, to express to them his full sense of sincere and heart-felt appreciation.

For the first time in now almost 29 years this "Library" has received a major grant for editorial expenses and purposes, when the National Foundation for the Humanities, Washington, D.C., awarded our "Library" a one-year grant of $15,260.00. This grant has made it possible for the Editor to give his undivided attention to the work on the volumes of this "Library" at least during the summer of 1967.

Paul Arthur Schilpp

Carbondale, Illinois
June 27, 1967

# C. I. LEWIS

# AUTOBIOGRAPHY

For Professor Schilpp

*Vale atque vade—sed non praesente*

C. L.

68 Yale Road, Menlo Park, Calif.
Nov. 5, 1961

Dear Professor Schilpp,

I enclose copy for one alteration I should like to make in my autobiographic notes.

Recently I entertained a visiting colleague who inquired about your projected Lewis volume.

It is not my business to speak of that; and I should like you to know my settled policy in case of such inquiry. I make it clear that I do not feel concerned about the date of its appearance. But on inquiry, I say that I have read the contributions and my part of it is in your hands. Any other or further questions, I evade and manage to allow no basis for inference about them.

Yours very truly
Clarence Lewis

FACSIMILE REPRODUCTION OF LEWIS' HANDWRITING

# AUTOBIOGRAPHY

I WOULD gladly omit autobiography: it is too much like taking off the mask while still on stage. But our editor calls for such, and how should I excuse myself when so many others are interrupting their work to give attention to mine! However if it is intellectual biography which is called for, let me confess at once that I do not know how to write one. Ideas grow, for one thing, and one keeps no files of them with dates on the back. And for another, how should I set down briefly what I have found it impossible to satisfy myself in saying at book length? All I can provide here will be something relating to external circumstances and a little gossip. If that affords some clue to whatever philosophical bias my writings may be thought to exhibit, I shall have done my best to satisfy any just claim upon me.

Both by inheritance and in temperament, I am, I think, an up-country New England Yankee. I was born in 1883, in Stoneham, Massachusetts, and my boyhood was divided between small Massachusetts towns and the White Mountain region of New Hampshire. It was the New Hampshire environment to which I responded. The mountains and the deep woods have always called to me; and I know in my bones why those from whom I come chose the wilder and less settled places.

My father was a shoemaker; a quiet thoughtful man, and with a social conscience. He was sure to have convictions concerning any matter of social betterment; and despite habitual modesty and reticence, he would speak out about them. Throughout his life he was devoted to good causes. His first such allegiance had been to the temperance movement of the eighteen-seventies; and his efforts in support of that had been well received in his community. But his advocacy, at a little later date, of the aims of the Knights of Labor did not meet with similar approval. Difficult as it may be for us to understand it now, that early trade-union movement aroused a bitterness not far from that which presently affects the issue of communism. My father's defense of that, and a local strike in which he figured, cost him much—his job, the home in which his savings were invested and, because his name was put on a 'blacklist', the possibility of finding work at his trade in any nearby community. It was only after some years of poverty and struggle that he became established elsewhere.

This period had begun before I was old enough to understand such matters: I knew only that times were hard and it was difficult to make ends meet. And from the time that I could discuss with my father the things which interested him, it was Fabian socialism ("evolutionary, not revolutionary") which had come to have first place in his allegiance. He was not one to thrust convictions on others—"Every man according to his own conscience"—but of course I imbibed them. Beginning at an absurdly early age, I read *The Voice*—organ of the Prohibition Party— and such books as Edward Bellamy's *Looking Backward* and Marx's *Capital*. And I went with my father to listen to Samuel Gompers, trade-union leader, and to a meeting with Eugene Debs, about whom the moderate socialists rallied in the nineties.

My mother was a vital young woman—nineteen when I was born— of simple faith and with the love of life. She met the hard years with ready courage, determined that, whatever might come, her children should have a healthy and normal childhood. She helped my father and me in making and tending the large garden which supplied our table in summer and stores for the winter months. Among the best and most vivid of my childhood recollections is the picture of her singing at her work. I grew up convinced that there were high things to be won, and that, with courage, self-reliance and hard work, it would always be possible to attain whatever one put first. And that college training for me should be included among such first things, there was never any question, however obscure the practicalities of that might be.

Before high-school years, I had already learned to earn money on the farms in summer and by doing odd-jobs for the neighbors at other times. And I now began to work also, afternoons and Saturdays, alongside my father in the shoe factory. The money earned was my own, to spend without supervision. But by the time I was ready for college, enough had been put by for early bills; and I felt sure that, for the rest, it would be possible to earn my way.

In those days (1902) college entrance requirements were more demanding than they are now. Harvard, where I wished to enter, required a total of twelve three-hour written examinations; six ordinarily taken at the close of the third high-school year, and six the year following. And in passing I would pay my deep respects to the New England high schools of that period (I know little of those elsewhere), in which there was always a "college course" organized for the meeting of such requirements. My own program included four years of English rhetoric, literature and composition, four years of Latin, three of Greek, a one-year "condensed" course in French, two years each of algebra, geometry, and history, and a one-year course in laboratory physics. We were also taught to read music and to sing—this began in grammar school—and once a week the whole high school (nobody excused) joined in choral singing for an hour. The instruction—in the Haverhill, Massachusetts, High School—was good. I recall with gratitude the man who taught us geometry without a text, merely assigning next day's theorems with a hint or two; and the physics teacher who put in our hands "One Thousand Questions in Physics," coördinated these with laboratory work and, after laying out the apparatus and explaining the experiment, merely looked in occasionally to get us out of trouble or find out why results had come out wrong. Also the teacher of French who, largely by sheer push and feigned impatience, brought us in one year to the point where we were reading simple French novels for the fun of it. (That was easier after Latin, of course.) All of our group who took the Harvard examinations passed them, and some received advanced credit toward the A.B. In my case the debt was particularly heavy: what with the four hours a day which I was spending in the shoe factory, I should hardly have been able to meet college-entrance requirements without the insight and skill of such teaching. I should like to think that instruction so effectively organized and carried out is still available to youngsters preparing for college in our public high schools; but I doubt that it is. I also wish that they might do their high-school work in the expectation of meeting such objective and impersonal requirements; but I doubt that also.

I was already bent upon philosophy before I entered college. Preoccupation with that is not something which I chose, either then or later: somehow it was inevitable for me. At about the age of thirteen, I had found myself beset with puzzles which, as far as I could discern, came out of the blue and had no antecedents. Some contrast between the convictions of my father and those which came first with my mother may have played a part. In any case, I fell into a torment of thinking, unaware that, for example, wonderment whether the universe went on unendingly and there could never be a better telescope which would not find more stars, had ever troubled anyone before. I discovered, so to say, the flux of Heraclitus with no inkling of the Logos; the paradoxes of Zeno with no mathematical conception of infinite progressions or compact series; and Kant's antinomies without the distinction of phenomena from things-in-themselves. In addition, I developed doubts of all the orthodoxies; and such conundrums would not let me be. At first, I kept these matters to myself, fearful that occupation with them represented some outrageous idiosyncrasy on my part. But in the summer when I was fifteen I encountered, on the upland farm in Jackson, New Hampshire, where I was working, a little old lady who drew me out

and encouraged discussion by confessing that she also was a heretic. I
can still see her sprightly figure and little smile as we would sit on the
porch at the end of the day, watching the mountains turn to black
shadows in the twilight and comparing notes about the universe. It was
an unforgettable kindness to an adolescent boy, and marked a stage in
my development.

Up to that time I did not know the meaning of the word 'philosophy'; and I cannot now remember whether it was she or some other
who advised that there were books on such topics. But it was shortly
thereafter that I got Marshall's *History of Greek Philosophy* from the
public library and discovered, to my chagrin, that all my best ideas
had been anticipated. It was my first professional disappointment, and
quite the most grievous. I looked into some other philosophical works
also, including the Zeller books on Greek Philosophy and Herbert
Spencer's *First Principles*. In spite of my total unpreparedness, I took
some profit from reading Spencer. The general idea of evolution was
not new to me, but he impressed me as using better common sense than
Marx. Also it might have its measure of truth to say that, in this first
volume of his Synthetic Philosophy, Spencer is a naïve cosmologist,
untroubled by the tradition of antecedent philosophy; and that aspect
of his writing was pat to my own predicament. I remember also that,
in my senior high-school course on the history of ancient Greece and
Rome, I was assigned the topic of Greek Philosophy for an hour's
presentation to the class—the teacher called it a seminar. (I was spurred
to best efforts on that occasion by the fact that the preceding such
'seminar' had been assigned to the young lady who, five years later,
became my wife. I do not remember her topic, but it was a livelier one
than philosophy.) After that, what other vocation could I choose!

It was the Harvard of Eliot and the free-elective system which I
entered in the fall of 1902; the Harvard whose Yard still held much
open space and was bounded by rough granite posts with wooden string-
ers between. ("We do not sit on the fence," I was told; "They do that
at Yale.") The environs of the college still were marked with the
touch of country; Norton's Pond, the small brook which flowed through
what is now Shady Hill Square, the low wooden bridge which spanned
the Charles, and the Washington Elm which still stood on the Common
at a point now in the middle of Garden Street.

It was also the Harvard which, then as now, always kept in mind the
forty percent of its students who were, like myself, wholly or partly
dependent on their own earnings. One could enroll for as many as six
courses without addition to the regular tuition fee—one hundred fifty
dollars for the college year, and no part of it required in advance.

This six-course permission allowed completion of degree requirements in three years. My room-mate and I had a study and bedroom in old Foxcroft House; sixty-two dollars and fifty cents each for the year. And at one of the eating-halls—Randall—meals were served à la carte, with staple items held to inordinately low prices—two cents for a glass of milk, a penny for two slices of bread, and four cents for a plate of beans. Employment as waiters at Randall was also reserved for students. I found that there were other odd-jobs to be had in and around the university, and gradually settled into some of the more reliable of them. During the summers, farm work was now replaced by better-paid employment in hotels of the White Mountain region. By such means, and with the remission, on two occasions, of a part of my tuition fees, I was able to complete the three years of residence required for the A.B.

The free-elective system, whatever its defects, was most congenial to an independent-minded youth who knew—or thought he knew—his own objectives. After one year spent mainly in elementary courses, my time was about equally divided between English, economics and philosophy. In English, I studied with Charles Townsend Copeland, Barrett Wendell, and Dean Briggs. In economics, it was Taussig, Ripley, and Carver. And my philosophy teachers were Royce, James, Münsterberg, Palmer, and Woods. (Perry was not yet at Harvard, and I did not meet Santayana until my graduate years.)

In my third and final year, I took the famous course in metaphysics which James and Royce divided between them and in which each gave some attention to shortcomings of the other's views. It was immense. James, I thought, scored the most points, but Royce won on a technical knockout. James's quick thrusts and parries, his striking aperçus, and his stubborn sense of mundane fact were not well matched against Royce's ponderous and indefatigable cogency. Royce became then, and remained thereafter, my ideal of a philosopher.

It also impressed me that James and Royce had more in common—particularly the voluntaristic strain—than either of them recognized; and I was later gratified by Royce's reference to what he called his "absolute pragmatism." I should be glad to think that the "conceptual pragmatism" of *Mind and the World-Order* had its roots in that same ground; indeed the general tenor of my own philosophic thinking may have taken shape under the influence of that course.

Since those years, I have been surprised to find, among those who sat under James, the opinion that he was not a good teacher. He was nondidactic and unsystematic, but—so I have been told—because he believed that prepared lectures were unsuited to meetings with advanced students and thought they were entitled to a more spontaneous give and take. Certainly that accords with his practice in this course: although the class was too large for a discussion group, there were frequent interpositions from the floor, and spirited colloquies around the desk after class.

It is also a surprise to me that, among Royce's students, there is so little recollection of his unobtrusive but pervasive humor. To be sure, this hardly finds expression in his writing; and since his whimsies were always delivered 'dead pan', they escaped a certain percentage of the audience who could not believe that anything so orotundly pronounced could be intentionally funny. I recall his illustration of a certain aspect of the problem of appearance and reality, by the story of two little girls sitting by the road at play. In a reflective moment, the younger of the two asks; "Lucy, what makes the sky blue?" To which Lucy replies: "Why, you ignorant little thing; don't you know there ain't no such a thing as the sky? There's just only the air, and it comes right down to the earth." After pondering this, however, the little one is dissatisfied: "But Lucy, if there ain't no such a thing as the sky, what is it that ain't?" Nor am I likely to forget the episode of my consulting Royce about the incompatibility I seemed to find between something Russell wrote in his book on Leibnitz and his later expressed views in *Principles of Mathematics*. I was mortified to have Royce respond, "But you don't suppose they were written by the same man!" But after a moment he laughed and added, "The man who wrote the book on Leibnitz and the author of *Principles of Mathematics* have nothing in common but a certain cheery dogmatism."

It was in connection with this James-Royce course also that I had the privilege of sitting at table with a number of graduate students enrolled in it. Morris Cohen was the leading spirit in that group; and where Morris was, there was never any paucity of discussion. We regularly reargued points of the morning's lecture; and it was for me an educational experience second to none in my undergraduate years.

From the beginning of my work at Harvard, I had felt that I could not manage more than the required three years of college. But now as the end approached I reconsidered, being aware that there were things still to do without which my education must be less than well rounded. Experience has corroborated that judgment: I have ever since felt handicapped by the lack of further training in mathematics, a more extended and more varied acquaintance with the sciences, and any real facility in German. In some part, these omissions were made up for by later study; but this would have been the time to do it, and I knew it then. My program, however, had been onerous and crowded. I had, perforce, become a fairly good broken-field runner in the matter of meeting financial obstacles, and had acquired skills, such as tutoring, which brought more money with less encroachment on my time. Still, I found myself with mounting fatigue from such efforts: I decided to stick to the original intention. But now, what next? I was prepared for no vocation in which I could find satisfaction. Nothing but more philosophy—I was clear—could meet my urge. Why not, then, straight into the graduate school, in spite of the continued rigors which that would involve? The answer, implausible as it may seem, is that I did not then understand that graduate study was the regular and reliable approach to university teaching. I had been impressed—justifiably of course—by the outstanding quality of the men under whom I had studied, and had come to suppose that entrance to the profession required demonstration of something like genius. The 'Ph.D. factory' aspect of the matter had escaped me.

Finally, I took appointment to teach English, for the year 1905-06, at the Quincy, Massachusetts, High School. It was a miserable experience: the pupils assigned to me were from the "commercial course," many of them there only until the law would allow them to be gainfully employed. It was the low point of my career. The sole item worth recording was the accidental meeting with Professor Palmer on a train one day. Characteristically, he drew me out concerning my present circumstances and future plans. In consequence, I gained, for the first time, a clear view of the road ahead if I were to enter upon the teaching of philosophy. However, I was, by sheer good fortune, appointed as Instructor in English Language, at the University of Colorado, for the year following. It seems that I had been awarded the A.B. with "honorable mention in Philosophy and English." I was unaware of this, not having attended Commencement or collected my diploma. But this information had been given to the delegate from the University of Colorado, at the Harvard office; and that, together with an interview, settled the matter.

This appointment meant for me swift rebound from the low point to one of the high points. Boulder, Colorado, lying close under the eastern escarpment of the Rockies and bounded by the huge 'flatiron' crags uplifted from the ancient sea-bed, is one of the beautiful little cities of the West—much smaller then than now. The locale satisfied my atavistic cravings. And the Colorado of 1906 was not too far off from its frontier days for persistence of the pioneer flavor. It was still the fashion to tote a gun when one entered the mountain region. I found the student body very congenial. There was a good sprinkling of boys who had come in from the ranches or the mines with small resources, to earn their education as I had done; some of these after an interval of work to accumulate needed funds, and near to my own age. (When I first went to the Registrar's office for information, they automatically handed me a card for entering freshmen.) And the head of my department, George Coffin Taylor, was a prince of men.

In accepting this appointment, there was that young lady back in New England, Mabel Maxwell Graves, whom I have mentioned and who figured in my plans. At the Christmas recess, having determined that I could expect reappointment at Colorado at the end of the college year, I made the trip East, and we were married on New Year's, 1907. On a cold clear winter's day, we set up housekeeping in a little apartment so close to the mountains that their shadow fell across the window at two-thirty in the afternoon.

Professor Walter Libby was the whole philosophy department at Colorado—and he made as good a one-man band as could be asked for. Work as his assistant was now added to my duties, supplementing my meager salary and allowing me a small part in what I wanted most to do. We remained in Boulder until June of 1908, and our first son, Irving, was born there. I had expected to postpone graduate study until a later time and begin with more nearly adequate funds. But in this I found that I had counted without my wife: she said, "We shall never do it any younger"; and with that the die was cast.

I left Colorado with a premonition of nostalgia; glad to have had a glimpse of the old West and the quality of the folks who made it. As I read it, the outstanding characteristics were self-reliant independence and the mutual respect of those who had proved themselves to themselves and their capacity to meet, singly or together, whatever might come. As students, they were uncommonly respectful of the instructor's office but, in or out of class, they met him man to man. For pretense—except for fun—they felt no need and had no use. But when fun was the order of the day, this same absence of self-doubt and of any uneasiness before others could show itself in their capacity for spontaneous exuberance.

There are a couple of stories to illustrate. One day a year, the University held open-house for any who might wish to come. The offices and halls were open, with someone in attendance to give information. There were games, and a barbecue. Self-elected and sizable delegations from the various towns attended, with their high-school athletes and perhaps the town band. Some of these delegations identified themselves for purposes of rivalry; one nearby community by straw hats with the legend "Longmont against the World." And there was the incident of my unwilling rescue of the baby burro. The burro—in case there should be any who do not know—is not only the most stubborn but also the most intelligent animal on four feet. And an infant burro has a ridiculously outsize head, dainty little hoofs, and a greasy curly coat with an outrageous odor. It was the hour when students were converging on the campus for class, and some of them were amusing themselves with this stray infant. They had formed a ring around him, and wherever he tried to get out they closed up to block him. They broke the ring to let me pass; and instantly the burro stuck that head with its long ears under my arm. Nothing I could do would disengage him more than momentarily; I was obliged to promenade so down the walk and run the gauntlet of observations which, if you cannot guess them, I refuse to recite.

It was in the fall of 1908 that I enrolled again at Harvard. The obvious question is, "Why Harvard again, instead of another institution for the sake of diversity?" But perhaps the answer is equally obvious: Royce, Palmer, Münsterberg, Santayana, and Perry. (James had retired in 1907.) Also I knew how I could hope to provide for a wife and infant son in Cambridge; and that assignment I must start upon without preamble.

Once more, it was necessary to complete the program in the shortest possible time; and my thesis was in fact presented for the Ph.D. in the spring of 1910. (Royce celebrated my headlong pursuit of my degree with one of his drolleries. Such theses are presented at Harvard unbound; to bind them in advance of acceptance is a presumption. Springbinders and other such contrivances were unknown at that date; and my thesis was tied into the cover with a shoelace. When he picked it up to initiate my oral examination on the contents of it, Royce observed, "So far as I remember, this is the first thesis ever presented to us on a shoestring.") The title was "The Place of Intuition in Knowledge": beyond that I can say little about it; my own copy was lost in 1920; and except for the impression that it contained some germ of what later appeared in *Mind and the World-Order,* I remember little of it.

In the first graduate year, I studied Plato with Santayana, and Kant with Perry. In the Kant course, Perry required weekly summaries of sections read; and I then and there became convinced that no one would be likely to achieve real grasp of the *Critique of Pure Reason* without such step-by-step outlining of Kant's argument. If my own students of Kant over a period of thirty years have rebelled against this task, but come to recognize the rewarding character of it, let them blame—and thank—Perry, from whom I learned to set this requirement. I also repeated metaphysics with Royce, and sat with Perry's seminar in epistemology. It was in connection with these last two that trains of thought begun in the James-Royce course, three years earlier, were renewed and now began to take more definite shape.

This, it should be remembered, was the period in which objective or 'absolute' idealism—unquestionably dominant in British and American philosophy up to the turn of the century—was challenged, not only by pragmatism but by the New Realist movement represented by G. E. Moore and Russell in England and just then finding its first formulation in America, with Perry and Montague as prime expositors. (Perry's first public statement of it, *Realism as Polemic and Program of Reform*, was printed in 1910.) With Royce next door and Perry in the chair, Perry's seminar was the liveliest in which I ever have participated. It was about equally divided between those who leaned toward idealism and those who leaned the other way, but the latter had rather the better of it. Personally, I found myself in the middle, being clear that I could not accept the idealist metaphysics but equally clear that the opposition were arguing against Berkeley, rather than against the idealism of Royce or the Bradley-Bosanquet school, and that they often failed to discern the point and weight of the idealistic argument and the epistemological bases of it. Such contributions as I offered were likely to be aimed at redressing the balance.

What was being overlooked, I thought, were certain considerations which both parties should agree upon. For idealism, pragmatism, and realism, all three, it was the nature of knowledge and its relation to its object which figured as the central problem. And all three of them might be said to take off from the Jamesian dictum, "The real is what it is known as": they merely took off in different directions. Absolute idealism proceeded to qualify by the observation that the real cannot be identified with what it is known as by the finite and fallible knower, but only with what it *would be* known as if the cognitive intent of the knower, in this act of knowing, were to be completely satisfied. It is such ideally correct and adequate knowing only which could be fully congruent with the reality projected as its actual object.

So far, the absolute idealist reads knowledge up to its immanent ideal —which, as he admits or even insists, is never to be finitely attained. By contrast, the pragmatism of James and Dewey tends to read knowledge down to the mundane limitations of the human animal and his restricted and practical objectives. And the New Realism, which identifies "the idea, so far as it is a knowing of this object" with "this object so far as it is known by this idea," is mainly questioning the implicative intent of the act of knowing and insisting upon the something-more-than-that-and-independent-of-it character of the actuality upon which this knowing is directed. But this view failed to answer such arguments as that of Royce in his lengthy examination of the distinction and the connection between "internal meaning" and "external meaning," or the Bradley-Bosanquet point that the metaphysical character of the object as infinitely specific is an implicit postulate of the attempt to know it:

the answer to every question we can ask about it is contained in the
reality of it, and co-terminous with that. And this whole-of-the-truth-
about-it must include the relation of it to everything else: short of that, it
is not determinate as just the individual thing that it is. Hence, to know
this thing as real would be to know the all-that-is. (That this object is
that which exists uniquely at time $T_1$–$T_2$ in locus $S_1$–$S_2$, does not
touch that point; such descriptive identification does not extend to the
'what' of 'that which' exists then and there, and does not satisfy the
aim of knowledge, but is merely a directive for obtaining such
knowledge.)

As I have said, such arguments did not convince me, but I did not
like to see them set aside without—as I thought—adequate understanding
of their point and without, in fact, any satisfactory answer to it. I also
thought that, within the area in which the controversy was mainly
waged, we could have it both ways—provided requisite distinctions are
made. Absolute truth and the validity of such knowledge of the real as
is achievable by humans, are two different things. The validity of acceptable empirical beliefs concerns a relation of them to their given premises;
to the data on which they must be judged. Truth is, by contrast, a
metaphysical notion—in current jargon, semantic.

It was the besetting sin of James's pragmatism to confuse validity
with truth; and of Dewey's to avoid the issue by the near absence of any
clear distinction of the two. James's "human truth," by suggesting that
the best we can do in the way of knowledge is good enough, and that
unchanging truth is a transcendental myth, subtly belittles the human
cognitive enterprise and its unchanging goal. Even Dewey's more judicious phrase, "warranted assertability,"—obviously descriptive of *valid*
or *justified* belief, but often functioning as substitute for 'truth'—holds
some danger of offering those short-range problems which are solved
by achieving some more comfortable adjustment as paradigm for human
knowledge, and suggesting that verification is a matter of muddling
through.

If I had known more of Peirce at the time, I should have felt confirmed in my failure to go along with James and Dewey on such points.
As it was, I thought that Royce did rather better with respect to them
than the pragmatists. By reminding us of controlling consideration by
reference to which the changing beliefs of man in history—e.g., in the
history of science—are marked as intellectual advance, and not merely
as altered reactions to altered problems; and by emphasizing that,
though beliefs can and must change, the criteria by which they are to be
assessed are permanent; Royce offered a more salutary depiction of our

cognitive human nature, and avoided short-changing us with respect to its enduring motivations.

In any case, once we have learned the necessary lesson of empiricism —that empirical knowledge can never be assured with complete and theoretical certainty, and hence that its validity does not guarantee its truth—there is no longer any contrariety between the pragmatic insistence that the vital function of knowledge is the justified advice of action and that beliefs are to be attested by their "working," and the idealistic insistence upon rationality as the permanent critique of cognitive validity, and upon the ideal of an absolute truth which would completely meet both pragmatic and rational criteria and stand as the implicit limit which knowledge should continually approach.

However, I did agree with Perry's main contention: the idealistic premises do not establish the idealistic metaphysical conclusion. There was no justification in them for reification of the cognitive ideal as absolute mind. The idealists had reverted to a metaphysical *non sequitur* against which they should have taken warning from Kant: they had mistaken a valid regulative ideal for a constitutive metaphysical principle. The considerations which they legitimately stressed might justify a pragmatic "as if," but not the postulate of transcendental reality. I had left idealistic metaphysics permanently behind. But I had done so with the conviction that, if its theses had not been proved, neither had they been disproved. Its critics had won a shadow victory by capturing ground it did not hold and failing to attack where it was strongest. And no successor philosophic movement strikes me as having anything like equal depth and breadth. It remains as one of the most profound and impressive answers to perennial philosophic questions, though now largely neglected and forgotten. I wonder if we shall not someday see revival of it.

There was only one other matter of sufficient import in these graduate years to call for inclusion of it here: my developing interest in symbolic logic. That began with Royce's course in the subject. Royce's command of, and interest in, mathematics and the logic of mathematics went far beyond anything which his published writings might suggest. In this course we were required to become acquainted not only with the Boolean algebra and Schröder and Peano but also with the number theory of Dedekind and with Cantor's conceptions relating to the transfinite numbers. Modern geometry, and the logical and methodological considerations pertinent to that, were also drawn to our attention. We spent as much time mastering Huntington's little book, *The Continuum as a Type of Order*, as upon the fundamentals of symbolic logic. Needless to say, it was a tough course; but no better preparation for exactly what, as it turned out, was to ensue in the development of exact logic could well have been devised.

As it happened, I also assisted Royce in this course, two years after taking it. I had received the Ph.D. in June, 1910; but there was no job. The department appointed me to assist for as much of my time as the rules allowed; and Royce said, "I think you may do better assisting in logic than in metaphysics." (He was not, in fact, completely happy over my metaphysical heresies, and had told me at the time when my thesis was presented, "I thought that you had been principally influenced by Perry, but I find he thinks that you have been principally influenced by me: between us, we decided that perhaps this thesis is original.") At the outset of this assisting in logic, I asked Royce to outline further study for me, to patch up my inadequate command of mathematics. My spare time during that year was about equally divided between that and two other projects; better acquaintance with Fichte, Hegel, and other major philosophies of the nineteenth century, including especially the left-wing Hegelian movement; and the studying through of volume I of *Principia Mathematica* which had just been published. Under the pretext that he had ordered a copy before receiving a complimentary one, Royce put it in my hands. It was study of that which set off such work as I have done in logic.

In the fall of 1911, I went to the University of California as Instructor in Philosophy. Or as it should be put, Palmer sent me there. If it was Royce and Perry who had presided over my intellectual development, it was Palmer who had stood *in loco parentis* in my slightly desperate financial and more personal affairs. It was only Palmer who ventured to correct my faults: the concluding sentence of a little talk on the topic of my brusquerie still stays in my mind: "Remember, you must always build a golden bridge for your opponent to retreat over." (But that art I have never learned.) And in placing novice Ph.D.'s, it was Palmer, more often than any other member of the Harvard department, who, as he put it, always considered first the requirements of the place and then selected the man best fitted to them. He seemed to know half the college presidents and heads of philosophy departments in the country; and there was no escaping Palmer's astute persuasiveness.

At Berkeley, I soon wished to conduct a course in symbolic logic—or "advanced logic" as it was more likely to be listed in those days. But the undergraduates who would make up my class could not well proceed without a text. And there was no text; nothing except the little book of Couturat, *L'algèbre de la logique* (not translated until 1914) and an even slighter book by A. T. Shearman. Eventually it occurred to me that perhaps I might fill this gap myself. Also, the University of California was just then projecting a series of publications in anticipation of its semicentennial celebration. That would take care of the cost of bringing out a book which, as I felt sure, no commercial publisher would undertake.

In the light of what has developed since, I should not expect to be plausible if I attempted to convey the extent to which both mathematicians and philosophers looked down the nose at symbolic logic in those years. Most mathematicians dismissed it as philosophy, and in any case too simple to interest a grown-up mathematician. And the philosophers were sure it was principally a mathematical recreation and, as logic, merely a hard and roundabout way of arriving at results already obvious. But I had felt certain as soon as I looked into volume I of *Principia Mathematica* that publication of that would redress this matter: here was an obviously monumental work by two authors of otherwise established reputation. It was also one which few would be able to read at first; and even fewer would easily proceed to the point where they would grasp the demonstration of the substantive points it was written to corroborate. And how can one speak otherwise than with admiration of a work so impressive, which he ought to understand but doesn't!

I worked hard on the *Survey of Symbolic Logic.* Outlining the historic development of the subject, in Chapter I, took a year of additional research and writing. Another six months was spent on putting into shape my own system of Strict Implication; and the rest of the book took about another year. Providing clear copy for the printer would make a saga by itself: two "Hammond Mathematical" typewriters were used, one of them altered by the company for the purpose; and a series of typists resigned the task of helping me. But I have always wished I could meet and thank the monotype operator who set the copy at the New Era Press. I have never seen any other printer's proof so clean: no more than a dozen errors in the whole of it. That was fortunate because, after the galley proofs, I neither saw nor heard anything further of the book until a bound copy reached me at an Army post in Virginia.

From the time of first looking into *Principia Mathematica,* I had felt that the exclusively extensional logic and the relation of 'material implication', on which the whole development was based, was defective as a paradigm of logical deduction, and theoretically oblique. I also thought that the reasons for this restriction to functions of extension lay in a series of historical accidents, in the earlier development from Boole to Schröder, rather than reflecting full consideration of the matter on the part of anybody. In the *Survey,* Chapter V, I presented the different calculus of propositions to which my cogitations had led. Some short papers on the topic had already been printed; but these were premature and contained errors. In the *Survey* also, I made an error with respect to one postulate. But this was quickly pointed out by Dr. E. L. Post, of Columbia University, and, fortunately, the required emendation could be indicated very briefly. On seeing it, Post most courteously suggested that his proof of the error and my emendation be printed together; and that was done. However, the development of Strict Implication which I should wish to be regarded as final is that contained in Chapter VI and Appendix II of *Symbolic Logic*, written in coöperation with Cooper Harold Langford.

When we sent that book to print, I felt that there was a decision for me to make. I was glad to have done such work in the subject as fell within my interest and purview; and I remained, and still remain, deeply concerned about the issues just suggested which pertain to the logic of *intension* and the relation of concepts, as against functions of denotation and the relation of classes. Such issues, I conceive, have import for the more general questions concerning the contrast between the normative at large—or the a priori and analytic—and the descriptive and contingent. But my primary interest had always been in such questions of logical theory and the import of it for the theory of knowledge and other philosophic problems. The logic of mathematics and the mathematics of logic were of subordinate interest only. The literature of the subject was, moreover, growing at such a pace that I could no longer hope to keep up with it and have time for like attention to any other philosophic field. And there were such other things in which my interest was now greater. Since that time, I have tried to follow—at a distance—the more important developments in symbolic logic, and have read with care such papers as pertain to my own work, or otherwise relate to a logic dealing with the *intensional*. But, with two exceptions, I have made no further studies which will find their way to print.[1]

But in rounding out what relates to logic, I have got ahead of my story here. In 1920, I was invited to return to Harvard, as Lecturer in Philosophy for one year, and after that, as Assistant Professor. Once more, my wife and I left the West with reluctance; and when, in later years, there have been opportunities to reverse the direction, we have felt the same conflict over again. But for one who grew up under Royce and James and Perry, no other position in philosophy could have quite the same meaning as one at Harvard. We remained there—with

---

[1] A short article, "Notes on the Logic of Intension," was contributed to *Structure Method and Meaning*, Essays in Honor of Henry M. Sheffer, ed. P. Henle, H. M. Kallen, and S. K. Langer, and an even briefer "Final Note on System S2" was added as an appendix to the recent new edition of *Symbolic Logic*, by Lewis and Langford.

sabbatical and vacation periods spent as often as possible in California—until the retirement year of 1953.

At the time of this 1920 appointment, the Harvard department was concerned about the manuscript remains of Charles S. Peirce which had been brought to the Harvard Library. There was obviously some expectation that I would be interested in them—and I was. The large room in which they were stored became my study, and I practically lived with them for two years. They seemed to include everything Peirce had ever written—with the notable exception that there was no final draft of anything he had ever published. One could easily conclude that Peirce had no wastebasket, and had never discovered such conveniences as files. By far the greater part of these papers were simply loose sheets, now piled on shelves and tables and around the room. Such earlier attempts as had been made to introduce order into this chaos had amounted to no more than a good beginning. It quickly became apparent that merely to bring together what belonged together would involve examination of the greater part of them, page by page.

I had no understood duties in the matter; and the business of settling into the work of the department and developing my courses was the first obligation. But I used such time at the university as was not otherwise occupied in becoming acquainted with these Peirce materials and, little by little, identifying and putting together what might turn out to be pieces of continuous writing. I never went beyond that in dealing with these manuscripts. It became evident that final ordering, and eventual selection of portions which ought to be published, would require a labor of years; and I was not willing, at this period in my life, to make that kind of work my first obligation. The more mechanical and clerical part of it was taken over by other hands—I have now forgotten the details of that—and the final selection and editing by Paul Weiss and Charles Hartshorne resulted in the *Collected Papers,* publication of which was begun in 1931. As one who should know, I wish to express my admiration of their patience, their good judgment, and their achievement.

The only part of this matter which belongs here is the rich reward I drew from the little that I did. I suppose there were few pages of this material which I did not handle and on each page read something. When I found myself interested, of course I read further. It is a strange way to become acquainted with the mind of another man, but not a bad one. It leaves no precipitate of scholarly command, but it is like receiving a thousand suggestions, on a hundred topics, which eventually round out to a total impression. And I think of few other minds than Peirce's from which one might better choose to receive such a kaleidoscopic succession of scintillations. Indeed, I suspect that in his case it might be the scintillations which are most profitable. There would be few of us who could read any five pages together out of Peirce without somewhere dissenting, but perhaps none of us who would not, from any five pages, draw something of profit.

This experience served to revive earlier trains of thought, particularly such as found their initiation under James's tutelage. And in Peirce basic ideas were often more roundly developed than in James, and in ways which jumped with my own bent of thinking. It finally dawned upon me, with some surprise, that as nearly as my own conceptions could be classified, they were pragmatic; somewhere between James and the absolute pragmatism of Royce; a little to one side of Dewey's naturalism and what he speaks of as "logic." When *Mind and the World-Order* was published in 1929, I ventured to label its general point of view "conceptual pragmatism."

Materials toward that had been accumulating since 1920. It has always been my habit to spend some portion of every day which allows it at my desk, and set down whatever I find on top of my mind in such hours. Such writing is, so to say, irresponsible. I take hold of whatever topic engages me by whatever handle comes nearest to my hand. This writing may run to a few pages only, or it may be more or less consecutive for days on end. What is so formulated is likely to grow and develop. But in any case, what is so written off never finds its way to print, and is seldom referred to afterward. The mere writing of it down has filed it also where it will be more easily recoverable if pertinent; and I can never repeat myself without revision anyway. Such materials are behind everything which is sent to print, though in every case the last stage of good order and consecutiveness is a separate and onerous task. In this instance, what I had on hand was notably added to in the summer of 1924, while conducting classes at the University of Chicago. After that, I was ready for the next-to-final draft, and it went to print in 1928.

At the time when *Mind and the World-Order* was reprinted, I read it again for the first time in years. On the whole, I was less dissatisfied than I had expected to be. No one could write again just as he wrote thirty years before, but there is nothing in the book which I would now recant. There are two points only over which I have any real regret. I wish I had done differently, and more circumspectly, what relates to the topic of the ultimate data of knowledge found in experience. When that topic recurred, in *An Analysis of Knowledge and Valuation,* I approached it with a different strategy of exposition, in terms of "expressive language." (But perhaps I made myself no clearer there: those who refer to that discussion frequently fail to remark points for the sake of which the manner of presentation was altered, and confuse "expressive statements" with "terminating judgments.")

After thirty years of debating questions of the given element in experience, I come to think that an accurate and well-expressed phenomenology of the perceptual is the most difficult—the most nearly impossible—enterprise to which epistemology is committed. But we cannot fob it off and begin the story of empirical knowledge with chat about 'accepted sentences' of observation. Wishing to include a last word on that topic (or—let me be cautious—perhaps next-to-last) , I interpolate here from an old note, not written for print:

An experience is *presentational* insofar as there are identifiable aspects or characters or items constituent in it which are as they are, incorrigibly to us, and for which there are correlative expectancies, established by past experience, such that, in the instance in question, they could be verified or falsified by further experience. Such established expectancies, correlative with identifiable constituents in presentational experience, are too evident to require argument—not only in the case of man but in other of the higher animals also. They are, plainly, the root of empirical knowledge.

Insofar as such correlative expectancies could be elicited by attention, any presentational experience is *cognitive*. Where they are merely implicit, though operative in the determination of behavior, they could be called precognitive. A cognitive presentational experience is a *perception* provided the correlated expectations which find their cues in constituents of it are testable but entertained with confidence in advance of test.

For any perceptual experience, there will be such verifiable or falsifiable expectations, elicitable by attention to it; and there will be identifiable aspects, characters, or items of it as presentational which operate as cues to such expectation or *perceptual belief*. The identifiable cue, or cues, I would call the *given* element in the perceptual experience; and the expectation which goes with it I would call an *interpretation* of it with respect to the given cue or cues.

The explicit identification of such given elements in experience, and recognition of the correlative expectancies as being such, is always the work of abstractive attention (analysis?) directed upon the perceptual experience, whether in common-sense knowing or in any philosophic examination of knowledge.

The common-sense identification of the visual, auditory, olfactory, tactile, and other cues operative in  instigating perceptual beliefs, is as old as *homo sapiens* himself. They are the 'data of sense' which did not wait upon any philosophic sophistication for their recognition. There is no verifiable content of any perceptual belief except expectations thus common-sensibly correlated with such given cues. Also, the distinction of veridical from erroneous perceptual beliefs, so cued, did not wait upon epistemological sophistication for its recognition and critical attention to it.

Philosophic examination of perception may go further, in a variety of directions. But if it belies these outstanding features of presentational experience, then I think it will fare worse.

The second regret I have in retrospect concerns the manner in which the concluding chapter of the book addresses its point—the point, namely, that it requires no assumption of the uniformity of nature, nor any other—unless as acknowledgment of that for which there is no conceivable alternative—to secure the validity of logic in general and induction in particular. We need only to observe our own unavoidable modes of dealing with the disordered and kaleidoscopic procession of experience as it comes, in order to secure the point. Given such basic bent of the human mind, and the manner in which we denominate things 'real', no experience we can by any stretch imagine could be so formless as to escape the net of logical and categorial order requisite to intelligibility. And it is by reason of that fact that logic and principles of our categorizing are 'necessary' truths, not analytic of our particular conceptual meanings merely, but analytic of our entertaining concepts with intention to apply them or—in particular instances—refuse application of them. Such 'necessary' truth imposes—*ipso facto*—no limitation on what conceivably could happen or conceivably could present itself to us. What should defy intelligibility would be 'unreal'; 'illusory'. The mind needs no Timean demiurge; and the patterns it imposes need no templates in a Platonic heaven: we bring them with us in our meeting with experience. I have no thought of retracting any of this: I wish only that my discussion in the book had less the air of 'proving', and more that of simply calling attention to: I come to think that matters so fundamental are, just by being thus fundamental, beyond the reach of anything appropriately to be regarded as proof.

In the period following *Mind and the World-Order* and *Symbolic Logic*, I first turned to studies directed upon ethics. From the early years of my teaching I had thought of ethics as the most important branch of philosophy; and a course labelled "Social Ethics" had been included in my program as often as circumstances permitted. Developing convictions on the subject had now reached the point where I wished to devote the hours at my desk to preliminary writing of them out. But so proceeding, I found that they refused to take direction, and what I got down on paper kept reverting to epistemological considerations. Eventually I began to see why. A somewhat incidental reason was the distraction represented by critical discussions of the content of *Mind and the World-Order* which were beginning to appear in the journals; and the publication of books by other authors devoted to the same topics and presenting views more or less congruent with, but also more or less divergent from, my own. In the book, I had made no clear separation of the more metaphysical questions from the more epistemological considerations. Meeting such comment and debating with myself over divergent views, shifted somewhat the axis of my thinking, and it began

to organize itself more sharply and more systematically in terms of what
was pertinent to the epistemological issues by themselves. Incident to
this there was another strain of reflection also. The conceptualism of
"conceptualistic pragmatism" and the conceptualism likewise implicit
in Strict Implication began to consolidate and formulate itself as a
distinct topic. But the most important impediment to these studies in
ethics was that I shortly came to recognize that the ethical conceptions
of which I was convinced required the premise that objective and valid
valuations represent a species of empirical knowledge. And that thesis
had found no development in anything I had so far published.

The confluence of these considerations accounts for my putting aside
the projected ethical studies, and also accounts for the plan and content
of *An Analysis of Knowledge and Valuation,* to which I presently
turned. The writing—and rewriting—of that occupied the whole period
up to 1945. In the central portion—Book II—attempt was made to develop more systematically the theory of empirical knowledge. The considerations of logical theory, relevant to analytic knowledge, are
intrinsically antecedent and needed for support of the more purely
epistemological argument: they were put in Book I. I now think that
I overdid this business of separating the logical from the epistemological,
and that in result the connection between Book I and Book II was
never well made. I do not know how I should have done it better, but
I am sure it should be better done.

However, from my own point of view, it is the content of Book III,
on Valuation, to which the whole converges; with the intent to
establish the thesis already mentioned—that valuation is a form of
empirical knowledge, and value-judgments are valid or invalid, empirically testable, and true or false. The issue concerned is, of course,
precisely that currently debated as cognitivism versus noncognitivism
in ethics. But at the same time that it has acquired this name, discussion
of it has, I think, become wildly confused by failure to observe essential
connections and essential distinctions. First, there is quite general failure
to observe that this issue concerns not merely ethics, or ethical and
other types of value-assessment, but the whole area of the normative,
including logical determinations of consistency and cogency or the opposite, as well as any assurance which can be claimed for truth in logic
itself. It likewise extends to any correctness and justification which can
be claimed for beliefs in general. Second, there is failure to distinguish
what are strictly valuations from judgment of right and wrong in
general. And third, there is failure to mark the distinction of value as
a predicate of external actualities from value as ascribable to experience
itself—and so ascribable in more than one mode.

Something of the direction in which I think that I must move here may be indicated in the little book with the large title, *The Ground and Nature of the Right;* and the third section of *Our Social Inheritance* is also pertinent. ——

The intention has been to revise this—eliminating as many occurrences of 'I' as possible—and to add something by way of conclusion. But the Editor writes, indicating that he would like to have it now. And after all, autobiographic notes do not conclude; having come to matters of present engagement, they terminate. I send it as it is.

C. I. Lewis

Menlo Park, California
January 13, 1960

1

*Victor Lowe*

# LEWIS' CONCEPTION OF PHILOSOPHY

## I. *Introduction: How a Conception of Philosophy May be Criticized*

THE writing of a critical essay on any aspect of Lewis' philosophy is a task which demands unusual caution, for both general and particular reasons. Only an incurable optimist can read published interchanges between philosophers year after year without concluding that at least half of the criticisms which they make of one another's work rest upon misunderstandings. The polite explanation of these failures in the critical process is that the men are talking about somewhat different problems. Probably they are; and possibly that happens because they are different types of men, addressing themselves to philosophical discussion in contrasting ways which they are determined to maintain. When a Whitehead writes, ". . . in the real world it is more important that a proposition be interesting than that it be true,"[1] there will be readers whose orientation enables them to agree, and others who simply must disagree. And among the latter some may be able, imaginatively, to catch Whitehead's point, while others will be unable to see why anyone should say such a thing except from perversity. In sum, the existence of emphatically different orientations of mind is a fact which I want to recognize before attempting any contribution to a volume such as this.

When the critic's topic is *X*'s conception of philosophy, unrecognized differences of this sort will be fatal, but recognized ones may be valuable; for the general question at issue is, what orientation toward the field commonly called 'philosophy' is most profitable for human intellects. Lewis has a conception of philosophy, and he has put forward what he calls "the reflective method" as "the proper method of philosophy."[2] How well it fits this billing is the question for the critical part of my essay.

[1] A. N. Whitehead, *Process and Reality* (New York: The Macmillan Co., 1929), Part III, Chap. IV, Sec. II. Hereafter cited as PR.

[2] C. I. Lewis, *Mind and the World-Order* (New York: Charles Scribner's Sons, 1929), Chap. I. Hereafter cited as MWO.

In the light of what I have said, how is this question discussible? Its discussion requires us to assume that it is possible for an honest philosophy reader of fair imaginative power to envision another's way of philosophizing, in the main truly, even when this way is quite different from the one which he himself would practice. Inability to see the other's position as expressing something other than perversity, signifies unimaginativeness. But man is an imaginative animal, and when that power is not overcome by the aggressive impulses which easily develop in the members of a competitive profession, our assumption is reasonable. In the present case, we are helped by the fact that Lewis' conception of philosophy, apart from the important pragmatic element in it, makes philosophizing the process of bringing to clear consciousness and formulating coherently the categories of thought which we—the philosopher and his natural audience—find ourselves actually using. Now every self-conscious thinker, of whatever school, does this to some extent. Philosophy must at least be this, whatever else it may be—unless it is only a game. Thus the reflective method includes *a* proper method of philosophy—one that goes back to Socrates.

Turning then to the definite article, we may doubt that it should ever be attached to "proper method of philosophy," and yet seek *the best conception* of philosophy. I do not believe—though Lewis seems to—that there is one way of philosophizing which would give the greatest intellectual profit to all if they would but devote themselves to it. One need only observe one's colleagues! One's students also exhibit minds that are naturally bent, some toward using one philosophical procedure, some toward using another. It is hard to say how deep the causes of all this may lie; the differences themselves have been noted for centuries. However, above a certain level of obtuseness, they strike me as only differences in degrees of suitability and vital appeal, and so in what a particular mind can profitably and easily adopt for itself. Hence, as imaginative creatures, those who practice one method may hope to sketch an overall conception of philosophy which includes other methods and objectives—a conception answering to the various abiding intellectual interests, not satisfied in and by the special sciences, which men in various degrees possess.

It is out of the question to construct such a conception within the limits of this essay. I shall, however, after an exposition designed to show what is distinctive and important about Lewis' conception of philosophy and how he himself (as I believe) supplements it, indicate another valuable way of reflecting on our categories, and consider the contrast between reflection and the alternative which Lewis notes and rejects—speculation. This procedure will incidentally provide concrete content for the conviction which I have already expressed—that neither Lewis' nor any other single method of philosophy is the one and only proper method. Most of my criticisms will concern the branch of philosophy for which, as he observed,[3] the claim that his method is adequate was a fairly novel one: metaphysics.[4]

So often it is just his special merit as a philosopher that makes it hardest to get inside the thought of a contemporary. I think that Lewis has in an unusual degree a fundamental simplicity of thought, unhappily lacking in most professional thinkers. The general problems which he has taken on are standard professional problems—the definition of the summum bonum, the modes of meaning of terms, the nature of the a priori, and so on. It is the familiar thicket of side-issues that is noticeably absent. In his professional education this man has never lost something which, though it is undefinable, I suggest to myself by calling it a tough Yankee hold upon broad practical facts and purposes—not only in his statement of philosophical issues, but also and especially in his getting at the considerations which must be decisive if anything is to be *settled*. We may find some dubious concomitants of this virtue: a pragmatism which needs qualification, and a casting of almost all philosophic discussion in epistemological terms. Nevertheless, Lewis' practical root-of-the-matter simplicity is an unusual virtue in philosophic arguments—a most refreshing one to come across today. And it is terribly hard for us to stick with. I have often found that a difficulty which I had with some part of his work was but a complication of my own making.

It is my impression that the roots of Lewis' reflective method lie much more in the man than in what he read—Kant perhaps excepted— or in what he was taught at Harvard. His adherence to it seems to me plain in the critical reaction which he made to Russell's concept of

[3] MWO, pp. 3 f.

[4] As I write, the only extended presentation of his conception of philosophy which Lewis has published is the first chapter of MWO. Elucidation of his view is a rather brash undertaking, because there he presented a clear and magnificent statement. I want to single out certain aspects of his conception for critical scrutiny, but I cannot hope to do justice to that chapter; I must urge my reader to read it. There is added point in doing so, because in the present state of philosophy it shares with a sharply contrasting essay on philosophic method—I mean the opening chapter on Speculative Philosophy, in Whitehead's *Process and Reality* (which by a fine coincidence also came out of Harvard University in the year 1929) —something of the unfortunate status of a classic.

In view of the use which I shall make of Whitehead's thought later in this essay, it may be appropriate to remark that I have sometimes found myself tagged as a Whiteheadian, and to warn the reader against doing that. Lewis as well as Whitehead was my teacher. Neither one, so far as I can tell, has had substantially more influence on me than the other.

material implication at the very beginning of his philosophic career. I take it that at least by 1921, when he published "The Structure of Logic and its Relation to Other Systems," his reflections on the grounds of truth in logic had carried him to a general doctrine of philosophic method[5] which he has tried to practice ever since. I think he has followed it quite closely. Whether its inception owed anything, and if so, what, to his earlier study of the post-Kantian German idealists, and what before that to his chief teacher, Josiah Royce—all such questions, interesting but not imperative, I leave to more competent persons.

## II. *Lewis' General Conception of Philosophy*

The chief clue to Lewis' conception of philosophy—a clue which is almost, if not quite, complete—I find in the very first sentence of his statement of "underlying convictions" in *Mind and the World-Order*.[6] "It is—I take it—a distinguishing character of philosophy that it is everybody's business." That is, "everyone both can and must be his own philosopher." Must be, and can be; both are of crucial importance.

His explanation of the "must" is that "philosophy [unlike science and technology] deals with ends, not means"—and the individual may not delegate to others determination of "the valid ends of life." However philosophy may have begun in the race or in the individual, its primary interest for the adult today, and its urgency at any time, do not derive from curiosity about "the universe begetting us" (Whitehead's phrase). Though Lewis makes room for 'metaphysical' reflection in connection with science, and does not suppose that the normative branches of philosophy are the whole of it, he does seem to locate its center in the questions which flow directly from the individual's responsibility for the conduct of his life. I doubt that he anywhere says just this, but I think it is a true characterization of his attitude. His discussion of a sound method for metaphysics in *Mind and the World-Order* begins by reminding us of what the method of ethics and logic must be, and proceeds to offer a conception of metaphysics which will bring it into line with them. His own description of the development of his philosophy[7] suggests to me that a fair way of expressing the most general question which set the stage for his conscious practice and advocacy of the reflective method might be: How can normative conclusions be

[5] Cf. C. I. Lewis, "Logic and Pragmatism," *Contemporary American Philosophy*, ed. G. P. Adams and W. P. Montague (New York: The Macmillan Co., 1930), Vol. II, pp. 31-51. See esp. pp. 32-44. Hereafter cited as "Log. Prag."

[6] MWO, p. 2.

[7] In "Log. Prag."

made out? All of his constructive work has been done in or for the normative disciplines.[8] And the supreme importance which he obviously ascribes to philosophy I would associate with his affirmation, "In all the world and in all of life there is nothing more important to determine than what is right."[9] For this pragmatist, then, philosophy is practical in the sense that its central concern is to define the various forms of the right, and the basic principles of appraisal which these require. Otherwise it would be practical only in some indirect sense.

A natural corollary of Lewis' appeal to practical responsibility is the belief that men as philosophers ought to occupy themselves only with issues which can be taken up in order and settled.[10] I think he usually holds this belief, but not invariably.[11] He constantly holds at least this—that though we may delight in logical constructions and in the play of ideas while we think, these are not what philosophizing is *for*. Further, this centering of philosophy in the normative and practical makes it inevitable that for Lewis epistemology (including some part of logic) must be the logically first philosophic discipline; for it is the normative study which lays down what settlement of questions requires, and by its standards we justly dismiss some beliefs and accept the guidance of others.

Although no philosopher should quarrel with the doctrine that reflection upon the criteria of the right is a direct responsibility of every sane human being, many would refuse to share Lewis' *tendency* —no stronger word would be accurate—to make the normative the chief and most distinctive subject-matter of philosophy, and to assign other serious topics first of all to the sciences. Although not (let us hope) without interest in the standards of validity for thought and action, they are more inclined to pursue man's natural interest in a world-view, or his interest in self-awareness, or to seek ideals higher than those which are commonly acknowledged and lie at hand for analysis. The dissatisfactions with Lewis' conception of philosophy which will appear in the course of this essay are largely traceable, I suppose, to the fact that these are my own inclinations. At this point I would merely observe

[8] The only possible exceptions are two papers, important but tentative: C. I. Lewis, "Some Logical Considerations Concerning the Mental," *Journal of Philosophy,* 38 (1941), 225-233, hereafter cited as "Mental," and C. I. Lewis, "Realism or Phenomenalism?" *The Philosophical Review,* 64 (April, 1955), 233-247, hereafter cited as "Real. Phen." In the second, philosophy is not presented as normatively centered.

[9] C. I. Lewis, *The Ground and Nature of the Right* (New York: Columbia University Press, 1955), p. 3. Hereafter cited as GNR.

[10] MWO, pp. 14 f.

[11] Particularly not in "Real. Phen." (See esp. pp. 233 f.) I find in Lewis' recent papers a tone far less confident than that of MWO.

the implication of the doctrine that everyone must be his own philosopher: either this is because philosophy *is* centered upon normative problems; or so far as that position is not taken, we must say (as I would) that the individual has some direct responsibility for his choice of a world-view, or for other nonnormative philosophic conclusions, and may not delegate them, like scientific matters, to other men.

That everyone *can* be his own philosopher, is an immediate consequence of the philosophic method which Lewis recommends. The philosopher is to investigate something already present in his experience, nothing that can be reached only by speculation or by technical knowledge. Thus philosophy is again distinguished from science; and speculative philosophy is rejected. Philosophers of many schools, it is true, like to say that they do but make clear what is already in everyone's possession. Lewis' conception is marked off in two ways. First: philosophy for him is strictly a conceptual activity—neither an evoking by metaphors of the quality of pure experience (Bergson, James) nor, except on the way, an elucidating of the use of words. Second (and this brings us once more to the factor of human responsibility): philosophy is to attend to that in experience which we have put there—our way of interpreting its data—and so can conceivably alter by taking more thought. This contrasts with Dewey's effort to describe 'experience-nature', and with the Whiteheadian project of conceptualizing the unvarying features of experience. Lewis' is the direct opposite of Whitehead's view that "Philosophy is the self-correction by consciousness of its own initial excess of subjectivity."[12]

## III. *Descriptive Analysis of Meaning*

"The distinctively philosophic enterprise," Lewis tells us, consists in "bringing to clear consciousness and expressing coherently the principles which are implicitly intended in our dealing with the familiar."[13] 'Reflection' is an appropriate name for this process, because of the double connotation of the word: a turning back of consciousness upon our mental habits; and an interest in improving them by providing sharp, coherent definition. Lewis insists that the procedure of philosophy be critical, not merely descriptive. The picture may be clearer to the reader, as it is to me, if the exposition is divided. The critical phase will be taken up in Section IV.[14]

12 PR, Part I, Chap. I, Sec. VI.

13 MWO, p. 3.

14 The practice of dividing philosophical analysis into 'descriptive' and 'revisionary' species—unfortunately, not phases—has recently become quite widespread, especial-

We face experience with a readiness to interpret, classify, evaluate, along certain lines and by certain standards rather than others. To have a particular readiness of this sort is to own a 'concept'; otherwise put, a concept is a criterion, or rule of discrimination, for some field of possible experience. But as we all know, we regularly make discriminations with something less than full awareness of the principles we have in mind. The first business of a conceptual analysis is literally 'explication': to make our conceptual meaning, i.e., intent—and so the concept which is being thought—wholly explicit, in words. Philosophy as the study of this element in experience, or "so to speak, the mind's own study of itself in action,"[15] concentrates on the analysis of those major concepts or clusters of concepts which are traditionally called 'categories'. The comparatively recent phrase, 'categorial analysis', provides the best short name I know for philosophy thus conceived.

In *Mind and the World-Order* Lewis used the notion of linguistic communication to define 'concept': "that meaning which must be common to two minds when they understand each other by the use of a substantive or its equivalent."[16] But he warned the reader that his choice of this sort of definition was partly an expository device (to prepare for his thesis that such understanding does not require qualitative identity of sense experience); strictly speaking, language is a usual but not a necessary condition for the presence of a concept.[17] Certainly a concept is not for Lewis, as it is for Körner,[18] a word in a certain use. And conceptual analysis is not, as in Oxford philosophy, a study of the use of a word through attention to its usage in this or that language. Of course a language has a life of its own; and as Lewis agrees,[19] we think largely in words. Inevitably, then, that sort of study must provide clues for the analysis of concepts in Lewis' sense. But the goal is not a fuller and more scrupulous awareness of the kinds of jobs words do. It is clear awareness and verbal formulation of our ways of interpreting experience and defining commitments for thought and action; of our ways of fronting the world.

ly among English writers. But Lewis' solid conception of the subject matter of philosophical analysis has not. Hence the proper division of a Lewisian analysis into descriptive and critical phases needs to be discussed.

[15] MWO, p. 18.

[16] MWO, p. 70; see also p. 89.

[17] MWO, pp. 87 f.

[18] Stephan Körner, *Conceptual Thinking* (London: Cambridge University Press, 1955), Chap. II.

[19] "Real. Phen.," p. 234.

And before this it is, and cannot help but be, self-knowledge. No one can analyze any concept which he does not himself conceive, and he can be directly acquainted only with his own conceptual intent. Furthermore, as Lewis indicated in *Mind and the World-Order*,[20] a published systematic analysis can do no more than appeal to its readers to reflect upon their own attitudes and modes of thought and perceive that they have been correctly portrayed. In an obvious sense, reflection upon meanings is for each of us a process which must begin and end at home.

It would be an error, though not an unusual one, to suppose that thereby everything is made a matter of introspecting states of consciousness. Some introspection there must be. But the concern of the analyzing mind is not with images; it is with its own intent. That is not an image, sense-datum, or feeling; nor is it at any time wholly manifested by these.[21] To begin with, one has a sense of his intended meaning, of some immediate distinctions and implications. There are others; no man can think a concept without committing himself to a whole conceptual network. But logical explication does not do itself. Some implications will be important, some not; some may be more easily expressed than others; and some may be unwelcome. In cases which are worth attending to, one must not only examine his sense of his meaning, but cast his mind about; try this verbal formulation, and that; observe the attitudes and unself-conscious practice of people who talk and act as if they were using the same concept; talk with others—both because they may have superior linguistic resources and because, left to himself, a man in setting forth his own thought, as in his understanding of written words or his delineation of anything, will favor some elements and neglect others. Observation, formulation, verification—these are needed to gain reliable knowledge of one's own conceptual meanings, as of anything else under the sun.

Before a conceptual meaning can be analyzed, it must be identified. It must be identified not as a particular but as a universal, thinkable on occasions other than the present occasion. This is usually done by

---

20 MWO, p. 23.

21 It must then be false that a concept is a sign—according to the terminology now customary, that it is a *symbol*. A symbol—more accurately, an instance of one—is necessarily something *before* the mind, as a presentation or image. A concept entertained is, in Lewis' phrase, a "criterion *in* mind." This is not the same thing as being a visual or auditory pattern instanced before the mind. Symbols are normally indispensable to thought; we think *with* them. But the identification of concepts and symbols is a plain confusion of categories. Lewis has taken care to avoid it (see *An Analysis of Knowledge and Valuation* (La Salle: Open Court Publishing Co., 1946). Chap. IV, Secs. 1, 2; hereafter cited as AKV; and "Some Suggestions Concerning Metaphysics of Logic," *American Philosophers at Work*, ed. Sidney Hook (New York: Criterion Books, 1956), pp. 94 ff. Hereafter cited as "Met. Log."

reference to language and to practice:—the concept I would analyze is the one which I (and, I trust, my hearers) express by a standard usage of a certain word or phrase, and the one which is manifested in application by certain modes of differential behavior with which we are familiar. Thus Lewis' paper, "Some Logical Considerations Concerning the Mental," is a partial explication of "what you and I mean by 'mind' ";[22] and he writes elsewhere that the analysis of physical concepts "looks to something implicit in the unself-conscious practice of physical science for those meanings which it is called upon to explicate."[23] We may note in passing that any way of reminding ourselves of any character, whether illustrated in our commerce with things or only imagined, may be used in identifying some concept for analysis.

The analysis of a meaning is to be checked not only for logical correctness, but by a more extended internal and external observation than was used in its identification—checked to see whether it faithfully conveys one's conceptual intent, and whether it covers our practice. Thus a categorial analysis of value must distinguish and spell out the initial and the implied intent of various modes of value-predication (each constituting a concept within this category), as the analyst is aware of them and as they are evidenced in behavior.

Recognition of the observational elements in identifying a conceptual meaning and evaluating an analysis does not in the least affect Lewis' claim that an analysis which contains no logical mistake states truths which are analytic, and, with respect to application of the concept to phenomena, a priori. However misdirected the observations may be, at least a partial analysis has been given of *some* meaning; relations of it to others have been stated, and these matters of conceptual fact hold independent of inward or outward observation. Lewis' claim is not about the correct identification of a meaning, but about its correct understanding;[24] not about the occurrent intentions by which meanings arise, but about the logical intensions which are determined once a meaning is 'fixed', however it may be fixed.

In sum, conceptual analysis seeks necessary, analytic truths within a context of experience which gives these truths whatever importance they have. It issues in a unique type of knowledge, in which analytic truths are united with the mind's empirical knowledge that its 'active attitudes' are thus and so. "As philosophers," Lewis writes, "we have

22 "Mental," pp. 225 f.
23 AKV, p. 468.
24 Cf. AKV, p. 24, and Chap. V, Secs. 2, 3, 6.

something we must be faithful to, even if that something be ourselves."[25] If, meaning to analyze a particular category of actual human thought, we spend our energies on some more manageable substitute,[26] or wrongly think we have fully covered our criterial practice, then we make material or philosophical, as opposed to logical, mistakes. They are the easiest ones to make, and the most pernicious. A group of philosophers may agree in some analysis of value, or of causality, which is far removed from the meanings which they use in action and in everyday thought. Reflection has then failed; a 'community of meaning' has been exhibited, but at the wrong level. Linguistic and psychological forces easily conspire to induce analytic philosophers to get their feet off the ground in this way. I believe that Lewis is a notable exception.

Although meaning is a personal activity, and I have so described it,[27] Lewis emphasizes interpersonal discussion and Socratic dialectic in his description of the reflective method. That is natural in a teacher. I think he overemphasizes it; philosophizing is a more lonely business than most of us like to admit. The meaning which the analyst would spell out must indeed be a common possession, so far as he hopes by analysis to give anything to anybody. That is: he assumes that his datum is in some nontrivial measure shared by many persons (and hence that agreement with his results is possible). The assumption is justified by antecedent observable similarities between him and them, and by the fact that his datum is always in part a product of social processes.[28] The relativity of thought to culture sets only an eventual problem. If the reflective philosopher can successfully analyze interpretive attitudes which are confined to his own culture, he will accomplish a good deal. The main difficulty, as I have suggested, is the one he and his readers will have in being faithful to themselves.

Categorial analysis is not for philosophers alone; it is for anyone who wants to be aware of the precise character and the logical implications of his recurrent conceptual acts, and those of the people he reads and talks with. I think that such knowledge is a good in itself, as well as an obvious instrumental good. Lewis does not emphasize this intrinsic

---

[25] MWO, p. 24. This is not the sort of goal for which statistical surveys are made and questionnaires distributed! The reflective philosopher does not (save incidentally) collect meanings as opinions and butterflies are collected. He already owns and uses his meanings; he speaks from them, striving to analyze his own thought, and that of any other person who thinks in the same manner.

[26] See Lewis' excellent description of this temptation, in the third paragraph of "Mental."

[27] As Lewis has said ("Real. Phen.," p. 233), "Meanings are something entertained by individuals in the privacy of their own minds."

[28] Cf. MWO, pp. 20 f.

value as much as it deserves; he cannot, consistently with his strong emphasis on the normative, practical function of philosophy. Instead he stops with a general statement which, like so many of his, is beyond dispute:

Self-consciousness may be an end in itself, but if it did not have eventual influence upon human action it would be a luxury which humanity could not afford. . . . So far as [philosophy] is to be of use, it must assume the function of sharpening and correcting an interpretation which has already entered into the fabric of that experience which is its datum.[29]

What can the reflective method provide as a standard of correction? That is our next question.

## IV. *Rectification of Meaning*

Criticism of meaning need not be a psychologically distinct step, waiting upon the completion of descriptive analysis. The difference is rather one of function. The theory of meaning must acknowledge it, because each act of meaning has just the conceptual content which was implicitly intended in that act and which, as thinkable on other occasions, we call our concept (or union of concepts in a proposition). Strictly speaking, only the articulation of that content should be called analysis of that concept (or proposition); for analysis is *of* an antecedent datum, and unlike 'reflection', 'analysis' does not necessarily imply criticism. (Probably it would be unwise to demand adherence to this strict terminology; 'analysis' has so often been used broadly, to include criticism, and I find that usage natural when a contrast with speculative philosophy is being drawn.) Another point to remember is that concepts as such do not change, any more than propositions do; to 'correct' one is to give it up and replace it by another.[30] The question to be discussed, then, is: what types of replacement does the reflective method authorize a philosopher to make?

Since concepts are essentially instruments, replacement is authorized if the new concepts promise to be substantially more useful than the old. So runs the general answer to be drawn from Lewis' conceptualistic pragmatism. But let us set aside, as the scientist's business rather than the philosopher's, replacements which are proposed solely in order to cover, or to cover more precisely, specific phenomena discovered by

---

29 MWO, pp. 18 f.

30 Lewis insists upon this point (MWO, pp. 69, 268), as required if there is to be any such thing as precise logical analysis. William James insisted upon it as central in the psychology of meaning (*The Principles of Psychology*, Vol. I, Chap. XII, first three sections).

observation; and likewise, replacements which may be needed to help resolve technical problems in science or everyday life. We are left with a broad notion of utility for other human purposes. When we then ask, as we must, for grounds for believing that a new concept will be more than momentarily useful, we must look to those features of it which directly serve our need to understand. Only there can we always expect to find such grounds if they exist: only in our concept's self-consistency, consistency with more authoritative concepts, consistency with other concepts which are to be applied to the same or to a related subject matter, coherence or intrinsic interconnection with such concepts, clarity, simplicity, intellectual economy and convenience, exactness of conceptual demarcations, and what Lewis calls "completeness of comprehension."[31] It is plainly more useful to us in the long run to respect such goals than to let concept-replacement serve merely personal or transitory purposes. If we interpret the last item in the above list not as bringing in what we have just assigned to the scientist but as demanding that no type of experience in our field be ignored, we may say that this is a list of the conceptual ideals which are important to the construction and formal evaluation of theory in all branches of philosophy. More: when we examine any instance of serious, cognitively oriented thinking, we find that these goals are implicitly desired. The general condition, then, under which reflection authorizes the replacement of a concept in use by a new one is, that the second comes closer than the first to meeting a general conceptual 'commitment' which the thinker has already made. (The test, in all the respects mentioned except comprehensiveness, calls only for examination of the concepts in question, not for comparison with observations.) Explicit statement of commitments made is an essential part of the descriptive phase of reflection on meaning. The critical phase consists in 'rectifying'[32] the meaning so as to live up to those commitments.

The point to remember is that we are false to the character of our own conceptual acts if we suppose that they contain no standards of their possible defectiveness. Many philosophers have made this supposition, in many ways. It is made anew today by those who identify a concept with a type of rule-governed verbal behavior. In itself that type can only be described; its correction must come from without. Thus Körner has developed the view that all "replacement analysis" is done

---

[31] MWO, p. 267. See his discussion of choice among conceptual systems, especially on pp. 266-273.

[32] I use this word without intending any reference to Dewey's use of it.

under "metaphysical directives."[33] Undoubtedly, much twentieth century 'analysis' was done under metaphysical inspiration; also, men often use their metaphysical preferences as directives in the building of theories. But these facts do not show that the use of concepts cannot be self-critical. Lewis has room for this because he takes not word-usage but the whole conceptual element in experience as the subject of his reflective method.

An immanent ground of rectification of meaning is shown in the following trifling example. When I read in the newspaper that a python has escaped from the zoo, the concept which I entertain is not the zoologist's concept of a python; but because it is intrinsically oriented toward cognition, my concept may be said to include the predicate, 'Something whose characteristics zoologists know better than I'. In thinking my concept I make a blanket commitment which authorizes its replacement by another, of unspecified content. And in holding mine for consistent, I repudiate in advance anything in it which should be inconsistent with the zoologist's concept. But when I read Kipling's *Jungle Book*, the concept of a python which I entertain, though (let us suppose) self-consistent, is not oriented toward cognition; it represents a different conceptual attitude; and its analysis will reveal nothing which commits me to accept this kind of concept-replacement. It is a different concept. Most analysts (including Lewis, I imagine) would not say so; they would talk of two ways of using one and the same concept. I think that the attempt to broaden our notion of what should count as content of a concept, so as to include all commitments which characterize that mode of thought, could contribute to the general theory of thought; but it is not easy, and this concept of a concept would be very awkward for logical theory. The point to be insisted upon at present is only that in every case of reflection on meaning, our general commitments must in one way or another be included within our datum.

My term, 'rectification of meaning', is not meant so literally as to exclude the invention of new concepts, perhaps never before entertained by anyone. Invention is often necessary. When we discover an inconsistency in a complex concept, we are not thereby presented with a self-consistent replacement. If, however, we cannot find one without broaching a major novelty in our principles of classification, then we ought not to say that we are only 'sharpening and correcting' a previously operative interpretation of experience; we should say that reflection

33 Cf. S. Körner, *op. cit.*, Chaps. II, XXXIII (esp. pp. 12, 292) ; also his essay, "Some Types of Philosophical Thinking," *British Philosophy in the Mid-Century*, ed. C. A. Mace (London: George Allen & Unwin, 1957) , esp. pp. 119-124; and his contribution to *The Philosophy of C. D. Broad*, ed. P. A. Schilpp (New York: Tudor Publishing Co., 1959. Now published by The Open Court Publishing Co., La Salle, Ill.) .

has led us into speculative thinking. This is of course a matter of degree.

We also depart from the distinctive orientation of Lewis' method whenever we look out at the experienceable world instead of at the principles by which we customarily categorize it. It is prima facie unlikely —and I shall argue in Section IX, untrue—that the metaphysical aim at a set of ideas comprehensive enough to accommodate all experiences, of whatever type, calls for the reflective method alone.

## V. *The Reflective Method in Normative Philosophy*

In each branch of normative philosophy our direct concern is with standards rather than with the world; there the reflective method faces a much more circumscribed situation, the manageability of which is shown by Lewis' analyses of knowledge, valuation, and the modes of rightness. The nonspeculative goal is here unclouded; it is, to arrive at satisfactory categorial criteria of the valid, the good, and the right, solely by careful analysis of those which you and I already have, and their rectification—by finding out the norms we acknowledge, and getting these acknowledgments straight. No new source of fundamental guidance, nor any redemptionist inspiration, old or new, is sought. In just that sense, this way of philosophy may be called naturalistic and humanistic.[34]

Many naturalists agree with this renunciation, but repudiate concern with conceptual meanings, branding them 'obscure mental entities', and assuming that they must be either Platonic Ideas or Berkeleyan ideas or denizens of some supernatural realm. Meanings are none of these things; they are simply the immediate products of our conceptual activity, which (as has often been said) is as natural as digesting and dreaming. Against them stands the dogma that only those 'entities' are natural which are externally observable. But no branch of philosophy is a behavioral science. That attempt to distinguish naturalistic from supernaturalistic philosophies is simply inapplicable.

However, a material issue arises on another point. A philosophy that is faithful to the reflective method can be *useful* in exact proportion to the power of consciousness—by clarification of ideals immanent in us and by persistent attention to the result—to affect what we do. Lewis' whole practical appeal is to this power. Anyone whose naturalism

---

[34] Lewis applies these terms only to his conception of intrinsic value: see AKV, pp. 398, 406, 414. The language he there uses in drawing the contrast with 'redemptionist norms', and his general description of the reflective method in MWO, suggest the appropriateness of also—in a related if different sense—calling the very method of his moral philosophy (that is, his ethics and theory of value) naturalistic and humanistic.

takes the form of maintaining that such consciousness is ineffective, cuts himself off from vital contact with Lewis'.

At the other extreme, anyone who believes that the effort after "clear and cogent self-consciousness"[35] can be effective, but tends to spoil rather than to improve human life, must reject his philosophy. I cannot myself take that counterdoctrine seriously. But I would say this: if some supreme good, for one who is capable of it, is to be got only by *letting go,* he ought so far to reject Lewis. To choose to let go is not necessarily to choose Cyrenaicism, as Lewis perhaps thinks; for some persons it might be the adoption of one kind of religious attitude.[36]

The essential limitation of the reflective method in moral philosophy is plain. The method is supreme in eliciting the *requirements* of the moral, in human civilization as we know it; but that is not enough to satisfy our imaginative sense of aspiration. The claim that it is the only method can be maintained only in a literal sense—by ruling out freer mental approaches to the ideal life as not *methodical.* If one insists, in the spirit of Lewis, that the business of philosophy is not to stir the soul but to settle questions, one may claim that there is no other philosophical method than the method which can demonstrate conclusions because it appeals to an existent sense of the difference between right and wrong. However, the overriding question is how to live. Mankind's handling of it will not be large enough without a further attitude of openness to moral insight, to the sort of thing that is to be found in the New Testament, and occasionally in Nietzsche and a few other philosophers. I am sure that Lewis is not blind to the larger moral aspirations.[37] My point is that you cannot nourish them if your moral meditation is entirely governed by the reflective method. If it were exclusively and universally adopted, the probable result would be an excessive emphasis on consistency, persistency, and integrity, hampering possible achievements of goodness by some kinds of people. Correlatively, I note that although Lewis never discusses conscience (its 'dictates' are much too specific to express the very general principles with which the reflective method is concerned), living out his methodical moral philosophy requires a concentration of attention upon general criteria (of goodness

35 MWO, p. 10.

36 His objection that a recommendation to let go is self-contradictory because it is made on principle, for a reason (see AKV, p. 481 f.; GNR, p. 86), although verbally correct, fails if the contradiction can be progressively eliminated by acting on the recommendation, until one lets go not on principle but by second nature. Psychologically this kind of process is not only possible but important.

37 Cf., for example, GNR, p. 84: ". . . the man of good will beyond the limit of obligation makes a gift, and it is to be appreciated as such and not construed as a requirement of the moral."

and rightness) already in one's possession, which is probably possible only for individuals who early acquired an overmastering conscience—and that is not an unmixed blessing.

## VI. *The Reflective Method in Metaphysics*

In the opening chapter of *Mind and the World-Order* Lewis, writing "about philosophy in general and metaphysics in particular," argued that "The problem of a correctly conceived metaphysics, like the problem of ethics and of logic, is one to be resolved by attaining to clear and cogent self-consciousness."[38] In claiming metaphysics for the reflective method, he turned to his advantage the association of the word 'reality' with this field of philosophy. As I see it, his distinctive formulation of the task of metaphysics is based on two points. The first is, that if the metaphysician would deal with a problem which is real and soluble, he should attend to "the mundane distinction of real and unreal *within* experience."[39] The second point is the 'systematic ambiguity' of 'real':

The ascription of reality to the content of any particular experience is always elliptical: some qualification—material reality, psychic reality, mathematical reality—is always understood. And whatever is real in one such sense will be unreal in others. Conversely, every given content of experience is a reality of some sort or other; so that the problem of distinguishing real from unreal, the principles of which metaphysics seeks to formulate, is always a problem of right understanding, of referring the given experience to its proper category.[40]

The main business of a sound metaphysics is, thus, . . . the formulation of the criteria of reality, in its various types.[41]

The ultimate goal is

to reveal just that set of major classifications of phenomena, and just those precise criteria of valid understanding, by which the whole array of given experience may be set in order and each item (ideally) assigned its intelligible and unambiguous place.[42]

It might occur to us that if everything in experience is 'real' in some sense, we can dispense with the word; 'phenomena' covers everything which is to be classified. We could then specify this reflective task of metaphysics as analysis and rectification of our *descriptive* categories—matter, mind, life, time, space, causality, relation, etc. (And, noting that the use of 'reality' to define metaphysics is in Western philosophy largely

[38] MWO, p. 10.
[39] MWO, p. 9; italics in text.
[40] MWO, p. 11.
[41] MWO, p. 14.
[42] MWO, p. 12.

a legacy of the nineteenth century, we might take a certain pleasure in dropping it.) But this would not be a good way of stating Lewis' conception. It fails to reflect the epistemological character of his approach to metaphysics. 'Real' and 'reality', when confined to mundane experience, are the words with which to do precisely that. They indicate that a cognitive test has been laid down and met. So it makes sense to say, with Lewis, that "reality is experience categorized," and "The 'unreal' is a temporary pigeon-hole for what requires to be sorted or analyzed in some further fashion,"[43] whereas it would be outrageous to speak in this way of 'existence' or 'being' and their negatives.

That Lewis' approach to metaphysics *is* epistemological, is quite evident. When he writes, "We can and must prescribe the nature of reality,"[44] it is his theory of knowledge, and nothing else, which assures us of this ability and necessity. Specifically, it is his pragmatic theory of the legislative, a priori function of concepts in human knowledge, which supplies the assurance. His conception of metaphysics as formulating "the criteria of the real, in its various types," is an application of his theory of the a priori.[45] His salutary difference from other philosophers who use 'reality' to identify metaphysics lies in this, that he does not find the clue for his discussions in a debatable metaphysical requirement—whether the requirement that the real be absolute and self-existing, or in any other—but in the single epistemological necessity that "whatever is denominated 'real' must be something discriminated in experience by criteria which are antecedently determined."[46]

Lewis takes the distinction of reality from appearance specifically and concretely; it is the distinction of what is verifiably an *x* from what merely seems to be so. This distinction arises in the ordinary process of empirical knowledge as part and parcel of the concept of *x* which we frame, and its application is prerequisite to any valid generalization about *x*'s. There is a familiar *general* meaning of 'real' which Lewis often uses and never forgets: that is real whose character is as it is regardless of whether and what anyone thinks about it. But as soon as we ask Lewis' constant question, how you would *find out* whether something sensed or imagined *is* thus real, we see that we can do so only by attributing to it *some* character, *x*, and addressing to experience a con-

---

43 MWO, pp. 365, 350.

44 "Log. Prag.," p. 47. Similar statements occur more than once in MWO.

45 See MWO, p. 14, for a reference to this theory in Lewis' exposition of metaphysical method, and pp. 45-48 of "Log. Prag." for a concise statement of the way in which it sets the stage for Lewis' conception of metaphysics.

46 MWO, p. x.

ceptual criterion of *x*-ness. The anticipation of these cognitive processes makes the adjective 'real' incurably epistemic.

Our momentary thought that the word could be dispensed with in
Lewis' conception of metaphysics was quite mistaken. The real, as
applied to given experience, is that experience when it is correctly
understood. Furthermore, the word meets the need for a term which also
applies beyond the given, to those realizable sequences of possible experience by which the given is understood as presenting a specific type of
reality. In all this Lewis has simply appropriated and consistently used
an ordinary meaning of 'real'—a meaning which I think must be called
epistemic. He is very far from the objective idealist doctrine that the
real is the content of an ideal knowledge which is somehow already
achieved. When he wrote, "every given content of experience is a reality
of some sort or other," he was not making a generalization from experience nor a claim about "the nature of things," but offering a plain
expression of our cognitive ideal.

When we look for limitations in Lewis' conception of metaphysics,
we may expect to find one source of them in this epistemological context
of it. Independently of that, we must remember that metaphysics according to the reflective method addresses itself to our thought-categories,
not to the external world—on the ground that we can analyze the former,
but, *qua* philosophers, can only speculate or dogmatize about the latter.
Yet the external world must at least be noticed in metaphysics! Lewis'
most explicit notice of it occurs in what I think is to some extent a
*supplement* to the reflective method. Let us next examine this
supplement.

## VII. *Lewis' Doctrine of Posits*

Lewis' writings contain quite a few passages in which the metaphysical
refers to some existence, being, or nature of things beyond or behind
observable phenomena. In some of these passages he uses 'metaphysics'
as a bad word, a name for the futile attempt to theorize about what is
thus transcendent, or to prove something about it. In others he insists
that philosophers, like other men, acknowledge a reality which they
cannot prove. I surmise that his hard common sense has always kept
him from following through to positivism instead. In Appendix C to
*Mind and the World-Order* he set down as an indispensable postulate
for ethics a belief which he then considered unverifiable—belief in other
minds. In the final paragraph of his Personal Statement in *Contemporary
American Philosophers* (1930), he contrasted "what have sometimes
been called the 'truths of description,'" (reached by "cognition of the

type of science") with " 'truths of appreciation,' " and suggested that "the foundation of these, not being found in knowledge alone, may rest upon some postulate." And he has recently asserted that all empirical knowledge requires metaphysical presuppositions:

> There are, in my opinion, metaphysical presuppositions which are essential to epistemology, for example, the nature of knowledge itself presupposes a reality to be known which transcends the content of any experience in which it may be known.[47]

In "Realism or Phenomenalism?"—a paper which is almost a model of clear, cautious reflection—Lewis calls this presupposition a 'posit'; that is the name I shall use.

In my understanding of Lewis this posit has another side, which should be called epistemological rather than metaphysical. There are two sides because we have two sorts of things in mind when we speak of knowing 'independent reality'.

> The content of [empirical] cognition is belief. What is so believed is some objective state of affairs; that some thing or things, or some kind of things, exist or do not exist. As implication of that, it is also believed that certain experiences will be realizable under specifiable conditions requisite for attesting this belief as to the objectively actual.[48]

The independent realities to which we are confined *within* epistemology are facts of actual experience and facts of possible experience. Lewis' pragmatism describes the latter as 'real connections' between possible actions and resulting experiences. We can know that there are such connections only if we assume the prima facie validity of memory, and "in some form or other, the Rule of Induction."[49] In sum, the epistemological half of our posit of knowable independent reality is the "assumption" that "one eventuation of experience can validly function as probability-index of another." Lewis in his theory of knowledge makes this assumption "without metaphysical trimmings, simply on the ground that, without what is so assumed, there could be for us no apprehension of a world of objective facts and things."[50]

The assumption itself says nothing about objects, and could be true if nothing existed behind the sequences of sense experience. That possibility is eliminated by the metaphysical half of our posit of independent reality: empirical knowledge "takes itself to be significant" of

---

47 "A Comment on 'The Verification Theory of Meaning' by Everett J. Nelson," *The Philosophical Review*, 63 (1954), 194.

48 "Real. Phen.," p. 236.

49 Cf. AKV, pp. 272 f., 362.

50 "Comment," p. 196.

"independently existent actualities."[51] These are not facts of possible experience, but sources of it. Lewis had kept this meaning of 'independent reality' in the background while he was analyzing knowledge, because all epistemological distinctions must be found within cognitive experience, not by appeal to transcendent objects.[52] I would distinguish the two meanings of 'independent reality' by the names 'independent factuality' and 'independently existent actuality', and take them for the intensional or implicative aspect, and the extensional aspect, respectively, of what to common sense is a single meaning.

As he brings the second aspect to the fore in "Realism or Phenomenalism?" Lewis identifies metaphysical problems as "those which concern the subject-object realation."[53] That is not how he had described them in *Mind and the World-Order*. He was then writing a book of epistemology; 'reality' meant "experience categorized"—by concepts which define various possibilities of 'real connection'. But the novelty is not a large item, and it fits perfectly onto the earlier conception. Lewis' interest in the subject-object relation is here limited to what the fact of empirical knowledge suggests about it.[54] Thus there is but one new 'metaphysical' question: whether a cognition, so far as it satisfies the criteria of "empirical veracity," is also "metaphysically veridical," i.e., is "a knowledge of existents as they are in themselves"[55]—as realism supposes. In Chapter VI of *Mind and the World-Order* Lewis had argued that the relativity of sense perception affords no valid argument for the rival suppositions of phenomenalism and idealism. He now advances realism as a suggestion, derived (if I read him aright) from analysis of that concept of 'an object', which we all use in pursuing empirical knowledge. This concept specifies the criteria by which, in that pursuit, we recognize something as an independently existent actuality. Our posit being granted, the concept cannot be empty.

The criteria we use are (in rough summary): being a spatio-temporal 'individual' (and so possessing an infinite number of properties), and having "some persistence of character" which is directly or indirectly manifestable to sense experience. The possibility of further modes or types of external reality is left open. Our epistemologist is content to conclude that empirical knowledge, and reflection on its

---

51 "Real. Phen.," p. 237.

52 Cf. "Real. Phen.," pp. 235 ff., and the contrast drawn in MWO, pp. 414, 425 f., between "the causal or 'cosmic' explanation, of science and common sense," and "epistemological investigation."

53 "Real. Phen.," p. 237.

54 "Real. Phen.," p. 240.

55 "Real. Phen.," p. 246 f.; cf. AKV. p. 15.

nature, cannot carry us beyond a realism of things knowable by their dispositional traits.[56]

Lewis has not followed the statement which I quoted, "There are, in my opinion, metaphysical presuppositions which are essential to epistemology, . . ." by mention anywhere of other presuppositions than the one just discussed. He implies that no further, distinctive posit concerning the thinking *subject* is needed; and that if some "being-in-itself" is to be attributed to the self, "at least it is inexpressible."[57] But since Lewis has given his doctrine of posits only the briefest exposition, and the doctrine is evidently fundamental, our understanding of it would be greatly helped if he were now to offer at least a list of the distinct unprovable assumptions (other than first principles of logic) which he considers that all men make.

Concerning man's other-than-cognitive interests, the only postulate he has ever mentioned is the one which ethics requires—that another person's observable behavior is a clue to his unobservable experience. But he added, "There are many motives—among them a powerful and perhaps central motive of religion—which move us to extend such postulation to reality as a whole."[58] Will he not say whether he accepts this extended postulate, and if he does, just what it asserts? I am asking about Lewis' philosophy of religion. That is a subject on which we rightly distrust those who talk readily, and those who have no feeling for the tragic side of human life. Lewis is neither of these. A clear mind can cast some light on a question—that of the relation of reality to the humanly ideal—which, as Lewis noted, "we inevitably raise."[59] His present position is unclear, because in his only published discussion of this subject, the extremely brief one in the Appendix to *Mind and the World-Order* entitled "Concepts and 'Ideas' "—does he still give some place to that distinction?—he grouped the philosophy of religion with ethics and aesthetics under "sciences of value" and, taking belief in other minds to be unverifiable, set these apart from empirical knowledge; but he has since written much more about value, and dropped this view of that belief—though without offering more than a 'may be' in its place.[60]

---

56 "Real. Phen.," pp. 246 f. Lewis sets forth the criteria of objecthood on pp. 240-245.

57 "Real. Phen.," p. 241.

58 MWO, p. 409.

59 MWO, p. 410. See also p. 55, below.

60 See "Mental," p. 233, where Lewis concludes: "In view of these facts (if these suggestions indicate fact), it may be that there is no fundamental difference, by reference to its verifiability, between the belief in other minds and the belief, for example, in ultra-violet rays or in electrons."

## VIII. *Categories and the General Features of Experience*

Further consideration of Lewis' doctrine that we posit independent reality will lead toward what I think is the main shortcoming, from the point of view of nonspeculative philosophy, in his reflective method.[61] In what follows I shall take this posit to mean, on the one side, positing an environment of individuals, and on the other, positing some Rule of Induction and the prima facie validity of memory.

Although we use this complex posit as an a priori principle, it does not admit of alternatives, and so does not fit Lewis' conception of the a priori. Nor does it fit his conception of an empirical generalization. As it contains an assertion of existence, Lewis may not present it as an analytic truth.[62] I suppose it is called a posit because we have no way of determining its truth. Yet we know a good deal about it, and know this by reflective analysis. Clearly it is the business of "the mind's own study of itself in action" to elicit not only its criteria of classification, which are not permanent and admit of alternatives, but also its unavoidable permanent assumptions, and to attempt envisagement of alternatives to these. So (and only so) do we discover what posits we make, how faithful to an intended posit various verbal formulations are, and that the posit is ingredient in our "sense of empirical reality," leaving us no choice.[63] As I would put this last: the only alternative to accepting an accurately stated posit which analysis has uncovered is the adoption (if one can *adopt* it) of an attitude which a sane man would classify as a

[61] I shall be developing some hints made in my short article, "Categorial Analysis, Metaphysics, and C. I. Lewis," published in *The Journal of Philosophy*, 55 (1958). Thanks are also due *The Journal of Philosophy* for permission to use passages from that article in Sections III, IV, VI, and IX (adopting a different position on one or two points) of the present essay.

[62] There is a little complication here. Prof. Paul Henle (*The Journal of Philosophy*, 45 (1948), 528) has interpreted Lewis as arguing in Chap. XI of MWO that the principle of induction is analytic, and retreating in AKV to the position that it is an indispensable postulate of empirical knowledge. I doubt that there is a substantial difference between the two discussions. Lewis seems to me to hold in AKV (pp. 356-362) that we acknowledge, and need not prove, the existence of independent 'empirical reality', and that to say this reality is knowable by inductive procedures, is to make an analytic statement. Will he not tell us whether he intended to take a different position in his later book from the one he took earlier?

Perhaps my exposition in the preceding Section diverges from Lewis' in AKV; or 'empirical reality' is ambiguous as between the two meanings of 'independent reality' which I distinguish. My account seems to me required by Lewis' permanent procedure in clearly separating epistemological from ontological matters. I also believe that the distinction (and union) of the two meanings is a fact of our human situation.

[63] AKV, p. 362.

form of insanity; thus we discover that the truth of the posit is not a subject of reasonable discussion.

I would argue that, beyond this Lewisian 'deduction', the positing of independent reality has another and prior ground. I find this implied in his own words: "*If* independent factuality *did not force itself upon us*, we should have to invent it in order to exist as beings who think and wish to do." It forces itself upon us as we confront "the facts of life." "We *find* ourselves in [its] presence." Our posit is not a postulate but, as Lewis says, "an original acknowledgment which all men make."[64] This raises doubts in my mind about a key element in his view of philosophy which I have not yet discussed—his concept of a 'category'.

In Lewis' usage, every category is a large pigeonhole (in some set of two or more pigeonholes) for sorting contents of experience. "Our categories are so divided that always we play a sort of game of 'animal, vegetable, or mineral' with the given."[65] So understood, "The categories differ in no wise from concepts in general except in degree of comprehensiveness and fundamental character."[66] Concepts in general are rubrics of classifications; they give rise to analytic a priori truths; those truths dictate nothing to experience—any concept might be found empty on some or conceivably on all occasions; for every conceptual distinction others are conceivable which we might instead address to experience, if they promise to serve our purposes better. These are basic, if roughly stated, truths about what I prefer to call *ordinary* or *sorting concepts,* i.e., all those, of whatever size, with which we propose alternatives like "animal, vegetable or mineral." Lewis' development of this view was an important event in the history of modern philosophy.

But does it fit our concepts of the most general features of experience? What about spatiality and temporality? We ask of what is presented whether 'physical' or 'nonphysical' applies, and if 'physical', whether 'living' or 'dead', and so on. We do not ask, 'spatial or nonspatial?' nor 'temporal or nontemporal?'. Rather we assume that every presentation has a spatial aspect and a temporal aspect, and then attend to the one which interests us most. I would also question whether character and thing ('the individual'), causality, potentiality, relation, and number are categories in Lewis' pigeonhole sense. We might call these—along

---

64 "Real. Phen.," p. 238; my italics. The context shows that Lewis' use here of 'factuality' in place of 'reality' has no significance for the present issue.

65 MWO, p. 349; see also p. 323.

66 "Log. Prag.," p. 48. This sentence there effects a transition from a discussion of the categories to discussion of concepts in general. It states a convertible proposition which I choose to read in the other direction, because I think that Lewis in fact assimilates all categories to 'concepts in general'.

with space, time and any other concepts with which we do *not* ask, 'animal, vegetable, or mineral?'—*Categories*, with a capital C.[67] Until each of them has been examined and found to conform to Lewis' concept of a category, we must have doubts about the adequacy of his view of categorial analysis. That examination would take a book which Lewis has not tried to write.[68]

Appearances are against him. It seems to me that when I have an experience, or remember or anticipate or imagine any occasion of experience, I never *refuse*[69] to ascribe to its content the categorial features I have mentioned. I don't say that I am dead sure of this counterthesis, but I do ask the reader not to suppose that a little phenomenology easily refutes it. And I am sure that the question is crucial for Lewis' pragmatic conception of the categories. His common-sense criterion for determining what the mind contributes to experience is: "I discover what I do solely by the difference in what ensues when I refuse to do, or do differently."[70] If I never refuse to apply Category C, I never discover that my mind imposed it on my experience. What is more, I doubt that I ever *can* refuse.

The freedom we obviously have, and which is easily evidenced in historical and cross-cultural comparisons, is only freedom *within* a Category—e.g., freedom to apply a Euclidean or a non-Euclidean concept of space, and to schematize temporal relations, if we have mastered Hopi thinking, in the Hopi way or in our way. When Lewis concedes, "Certain fundamental categories are doubtless very ancient and permanent,"[71] he counters only by pointing to such variations of detail. Our problem concerns the hard core in each Category. These are indefinable in the same way in which value as a mode of immediate experience is indefinable; they *are* recognizable and, like immediate value, demand acknowledgment in categorial analysis. They are given; and yet are categorial, because we consciously discriminate spatiality from temporality, and the

---

[67] After writing this I find a passage in Peirce which states a similar distinction, and is precisely right about what he calls "the universal categories"—they "belong to every phenomenon, one being perhaps more prominent in one aspect of that phenomenon than another but all of them belonging to every phenomenon." (*Collected Papers of Charles Sanders Peirce*, ed. Charles Hartshorne and Paul Weiss (Cambridge: Harvard University Press, 1934), hereafter cited as CP, 5.43.) Although philosophers differ in their identifications of the universal categories, Peirce claims general support for the idea that there are such.

[68] Cf. MWO, p. 239. Lewis has offered only general arguments (mainly in MWO, pp. 211-239) and these are almost entirely concerned with Kant's doctrine of the categories and forms of intuition.

[69] "Neglect" would be inaccurate.

[70] "Log. Prag.," p. 45.

[71] MWO p. 234.

causal production of a datum from its spatiality and temporality, in thought as well as in perception; and because these Category-names have meaning: 'spatiality' has a meaning (in all four of Lewis' modes of meaning)[72] which is constituent in the specific concept of Euclidean space with which I survey the night sky. The only conclusion I find credible is that, besides the mind-initiated categorizing of experience into real-unreal, physical-mental, animal-vegetable-mineral, which Lewis has so well described as essential to knowledge, there is a process concerning Categories—a process of conceptually registering them in consciousness as aspects of the texture of given experience, and incorporating them in variable forms into our active outlook.

This is most plausible in the case of spatiality and temporality. Let us briefly consider causality too. Lewis writes: "To think . . . seriously and to know . . . is to posit that which is and is other than the apprehension of it, and does not arise with or from the apprehension of it but bespeaks another ground."[73] Now what if 'bespeaking another ground' accurately describes a pervasive aspect of the given? Lewis himself, discussing the difference between predicating a property of an object and having a sheer awareness of the given such as might be expressed by the ejaculation, 'Sweet taste!', wrote, "The expressive ejaculation or cry is, so to speak, the salutation of the real or the acknowledgment of an existent."[74] Here acknowledgment of an existent could only be acknowledgment that something existent is *giving* the speaker the sweet taste.

Whitehead thought that causal experience was a distinct mode of perception. Another possibility is that it occurs as a universal characteristic of presentations themselves. One may doubt that even visual data—got awake or asleep—present themselves as pure apparitions, ungenerated; perhaps that is only how some epistemologists think they ought to occur.

Our dominant interest in specific information and in causal regularities explains the persistence of a mistake about causality. We hear a sound and ask whether we can know without inference that there exists an object *answering more or less closely* to what the sound suggests—e.g., a bell of some kind. From the obvious negative answer we rightly conclude that 'Bell!' represents an interpretation, but wrongly conclude that no causation has been experienced; so the very existence of a causal *environment* is assertible only by inference—or by a 'posit'. I do not

72 Cf. AKV, Chap. III, Sec. 3; Chap. IV, Sec. 4.
73 "Real. Phen.," p. 238.
74 MWO, p. 279.

impute this fallacy to Lewis,[75] for he has not discussed the question of causal experience. I think he ought to.

If one agrees that we enjoy an omnipresent sense that presentations are produced by agents, but insists that this, like any content of experience, may be illusory, there are two sufficient replies. First: Is this not a self-defeating attempt to apply the practical lesson, that what looks like an x may be a y—more fully, that the presentation, apparently *due to* an *x,* is actually *due to* a *y*—to the very context which this distinction assumes, and within which it arose? Second, there is the Whiteheadian answer, that if given experience includes no *objective* content, we have no empirical ground for any conclusion other than solipsism of the present moment.

To return to the Categories as a group. Lewis has never denied, he has more than once asserted, that our major modes of thought reflect the general nature of the independent given as well as human purposes. But after recognizing this commonsense truth, he has proceeded on the principle that "philosophy is particularly concerned with that part or aspect of experience which the mind contributes. . ."[76] His adoption of this limitation reflects his interest as a critic of Kant in the question, What *does* mind contribute by its "uncompelled initiative"? Lewis' answer—historically variable, pragmatically determined modes of conceptual interpretation—is an entirely convincing answer to that question; it does not settle my problem of the Categories. What the statement just quoted most reflects, however, is the practical character of Lewis' main concern with philosophy, which I sketched in Section II. Now in an obvious sense, practical interest in attending to modes of thought is limited to their alterable aspects. But I am also interested in becoming as aware as I can of my acts of thought in their entirety. If part of their content is forced upon me, I want to know all I can about that, as well as about the rest. In asserting the value of this interest of a self-conscious animal, I am perhaps merely exhibiting one of those differences from my subject-philosopher in general orientation, about which I warned the reader at the beginning. But naturally I think that I am proposing to free the reflective method in philosophy from a pragmatist's preoccupation with the humanly alterable. If we drop that limitation, we shall not have Lewis' clean doctrine (beautifully organized around an accurate theory of useful knowing) about the relation of

---

[75] It is committed, in a slightly different form, by C. D. Broad; see "Berkeley's Denial of Material Substance," *Philosophical Review*, 63 (1954), 178 f., where the phrase I have italicized occurs. This is a relatively clear example among many which can be found.

[76] MWO, p. 33.

thought to experience. We shall admit that the boundary region is dark. But we shall not need to supplement categorial analysis by positing that there is an independent reality, empirically knowable. No one, I think, makes that bare acknowledgment; everyone is forced by every experience to acknowledge the environmental existence of spatio-temporal, causal, propertied individuals, bearers of potentialities which it is the business of useful knowledge to distinguish. As reflected in our self-consciousness, this acknowledgment is our conviction that certain Categories always apply in some form.

If it is said that tomorrow's experience might be different, I am satisfied with the answer that I am unable to conceive of such experience, or to assign meanings to 'might be' and 'tomorrow' except by these Categories. For me, at least, it would be verbiage to say, "I might wake up tomorrow in a timeless world where nothing is caused." I do note that my imagination can *play* with the Categories, that is, make suppositions which I am unable to apply to any experience-event or in any self-consistent thought of one. There are several types of conceptual play, some valuable and some not.

Lewis' doctrine, "Laws which characterize all experience, of real and unreal both, are non-existent,"[77] is true of ordinary empirical laws, but not of Categorial ones, like 'All experience is temporal', or 'All presentations are produced, given by some donor or donors'. I suggest that these, and the quite different statement, 'Characters can recur, but individuals cannot', alike illustrate the fact that conceptualization of the hard cores of our Categories gives rise to analytic a priori truths. Understanding the unsophisticated meanings of such statements assures us of their truth; they are not synthetic, and only appear to be so if an attenuated form of a Category (with a correspondingly attenuated meaning of 'experience') is substituted for the original. Yet, since the Categorial relationships were forced upon us, it is misleading to say that an accurate statement of them is true *because of* our meanings. A priori principles dictate how things must be named and what may be called 'real', consistently with our intended meanings. Lewis' doctrine that this is all they dictate, is true when the a priori originates from ordinary concepts. Categorial statements, however, *also* dictate how thought must proceed, consistently with *the acknowledged texture of experience.*[78]

---

[77] MWO, p. 29.

[78] The salutary dictum that conceptual relationships contain no implication of *existence* likewise needs qualification when these relationships are not those of ordinary concepts—proposals with alternatives, to which experience will speak—but those expressed in Categorial acknowledgments. These say nothing about what would exist if there were no such thing as experience; they do say everything that Lewis says need not be proved because it is "forced upon us" by "facts of life."

Apart from neglect of the difference between categories and Categories, I think I see another basic omission in Lewis' view of the mind's meanings. It too originates in his epistemological and pragmatic orientations. It is illustrated by his analysis of beliefs about things and events.[79] He translates the entire sense meaning of a belief that there is a desk in the room next door into statements of the form, 'If a normal observer, A.B., should *put himself* in position to observe this room, A.B. would in all probability have the kind of experience meant by "seeing a desk"'. I have asked myself what I intend when I entertain that belief, and found that this is only half of my sense meaning. It expresses the anticipatory, verificatory element. There is another, obvious element, expressible in judgments of the form, 'If I *were now* observing the room next door, I should in all probability be getting the kind of experience meant by "seeing a desk"'. This judgment is imaginative but not anticipatory, nor referent to the action which must precede an actual observation; it is indirectly and partly verifiable but never verifying; it is there because of the natural fact that my conceiving mind is not tied down to action-sequences, and leaps outward across space as well as forward into time. Each of these components of meaningful belief in the absent plays an essential role; each serves the other, and neither can be reduced to the other. There are other points of comparison which I have made elsewhere,[80] and cannot even summarize here. The case is important because of what it shows about the activity of meaning, even when the belief entertained is easily verifiable. My criticism of Lewis is that he attends only to that part of this activity which aims at settling something for useful knowledge.

In sum, I do not think he does justice to the two realities of our conceptual life which lie, so to speak, one on each side of our planning and testing: our conceptual registration of acknowledged, unalterable Categorial features of given experience; and that part of our free imagi-

One might think that at least one mark of the Category of the individual—infinity of attributes—requires a posit. It seems to me that careful examination of the other Categories which are involved could reveal a ground of assurance that, no matter how many attributes we know of any thing that can be manifested to us as qualitied and in space-time, there are more to be known.

We must not suppose that what I have called (following Whitehead) the 'texture' of immediate experience is simply internal to single occasions of experience. It also joins this occasion to its neighbors. My concept of 'all possible experience' extends these connections without limit.

[79] See AKV, Chap. VI, Secs. 2, 3; Chap. VII; Chap. VIII, esp. Sec. 10.

[80] "Belief in Unobserved Contemporary Reality: A Realistic Experiential Analysis," *Journal of Philosophy,* 50 (1953), 541-556.

nation which operates outside the means-end continuum of realizable events.[81]

## IX. *Lewis' Rejection of Speculative Metaphysics*

Whether we adopt the reflective method as Lewis described it, or the modified form of it which I have suggested, in any case an important question remains. Is a method of this kind sufficient for metaphysics? As the goal there is a system of ideas capable of making every type of experience intelligible, I think that Lewis was right in mentioning only one alternative to reflection: speculation. The desired system is not progressively revealed to us by any rational, or mystical, power of intuition.

Lewis discussed (and rejected) but two forms of 'speculative' metaphysics.[82] One consists in making "guesses at what future observation or experiment may reveal." I cannot guess whether he had Spencer's Synthetic Philosophy or Whitehead's philosophy of organism in mind; but I agree that anything which the quoted phrase accurately describes is no model for philosophy. The other form of speculation tries "by sheer force of rational reflection to transcend experience altogether." Here Lewis referred to modern idealism. I imagine he was thinking primarily of Bradley and probably of Royce and Bosanquet. However that may be, I would not defend this endeavor. (I also doubt whether anything which is offered as logical demonstration should be called speculative philosophy.)

I believe that a third kind of speculative thought can be described—one which is profitable, and comparable to reflection in importance; and that these two, far from being enemies, correspond to two essential powers of our conceiving minds: clarity of self-consciousness, and imagination addressed to the world. I want to suggest that there is a proper place, not merely a historic one, for such speculation—in scientific theory and in metaphysics. Then we can see both the partiality and the strength of Lewis' conception of method.

Until we have tried to formulate the categories we habitually use, we cannot know that we need do more than use them faithfully; we cannot even raise that question with precision. Thus categorial analysis is the metaphysician's first task. It is in replacing defective concepts, if anywhere, that a need for speculation may arise.

---

[81] However, when Lewis discussed examples in "Experience and Meaning," *Philosophical Review*, **43** (1934), see 143 f.), the absence of hypotheses of action did not prevent him from defending the empirical meaningfulness of belief in immortality, belief that another person now suffers a toothache, and belief that "if all minds should disappear from the universe, the stars would still go on in their courses."

[82] MWO, pp. 4-10.

Four tasks of speculation may be distinguished, corresponding to four reasons for introducing conceptual novelty.[83] The first task arises when we are unable to clarify the definitive principles of a science without making substantial innovations.[84] The advocate of *critical* reflection cannot frown on this kind of speculation, though he may balk at the word.

When we reflect upon meanings, we face our own mental possessions; but (in the empirical sciences at least) *they* face outward, toward some aspect of the experienceable world which it is their business to make intelligible to us. Hence the philosophy of a science must not only clarify the principles which we are imposing, but ask whether they then enable us fully to understand its phenomena.[85] Of course Lewis has this in mind, and does not ask that the two concerns be permanently disjoined. I observe only that when, armed with a formally perfect theory, we face persistently baffling experiences which seem to be more the responsibility of this science than of another, speculation is necessary; the second of its four tasks appears. The difference from reflection is here not a matter of the degree of novelty that is required. Since the test of this kind of adequacy in a theory is external to our thought, every new idea that is offered in the hope of better meeting it is a speculative step. The only question of degree is the question whether the need for greater empirical adequacy is greater than the advantage of fidelity to recognized modes of thought. Probably what Lewis said about one pair of categories is true in general:

Nothing could *force* a redefinition of 'spirit' or of 'matter.' A sufficiently fundamental relation to human bent or to human interests would guarantee continuance unaltered even in the face of unintelligible and baffling experience.[86]

When we do seek new categories in the hope that with them we can cover the phenomena, we should not be charged with speculating about what future experiment may reveal. We are after new principles to function a priori, as the old ones did. Such proposals need not often

---

[83] The fact that imaginative speculation also occurs for no reason—sometimes to our gain—is important for a just conception of the human mind, but lies outside the present argument.

[84] See Sec. IV, above, especially the penultimate paragraph. 'Clarify' here means the same as 'rectify' there.

[85] We should note that whoever inquires about the adequacy of, e.g., current biological categories, must first explicate a definition of life in order to know what phenomena have to be accommodated. But we must not make too much of this fact. The definition is provisional, and does not solve the problem of framing categories which will be more adequate for understanding life; it may itself be modified in that process.

[86] MWO, pp. 264 f.

be made in the sciences. But they have played and do play a role in the development of sciences.

More often than not, the first and second tasks of speculation are undertaken as one, the structure and the empirical adequacy of prevailing principles being simultaneously attacked. Whitehead's *Enquiry Concerning the Principles of Natural Knowledge* and the other works of his middle period provide one example. He conceptualized and wove into a new theory features of perceptual experience which had been relatively unexploited in the physical theory of space-time. Lewis in 1951 emphasized the originality and value of this work, the radical nature of Whitehead's "revision of the categories of antecedent philosophies and prevailing common sense."[87] However, this 'revision' was accomplished not by cleaning up the earlier categories but by making a fresh start.[88]

The third task of speculation is the extension of the first and second to the ultimate goal proposed by Lewis for metaphysics. How he envisioned this goal in *Mind and the World-Order* is shown by the passage quoted on p. 38 above. I shall not dwell on the desirability of following reflective analysis with some new ventures as our distance from the goal becomes evident to philosophers. I wish to examine the all too brief description of metaphysics which appears in Lewis' later writings. This description differs from the earlier one by including the categories of the normative sciences as well as the categories of reality.[89] I doubt that the use of this larger definition of metaphysics represents a real alteration in Lewis' views. His mode of exposition in the opening chapter of *Mind and the World-Order* required the usual contrast between metaphysics and the normative areas of philosophy, but did not preclude recognition of a second meaning for 'metaphysics'. When it is used the wholly human perspective on metaphysics, which I think Lewis always adopts, becomes explicit.

The first of his later descriptions of the metaphysical goal appears to be this, written apropos of the field of logic:

[87] See Lewis' too little known essay, "The Categories of Natural Knowledge," *The Philosophy of Alfred North Whitehead*, ed. P. A. Schilpp (2nd ed.; New York: Tudor Publishing Co., 1951. Now published by The Open Court Publishing Co., La Salle, Ill.). My quotation is from p. 705. [Editor's note: The essay by Professor Lewis was written for the second edition of the Whitehead volume and does not appear in the first edition.]

[88] Since Whitehead worked with pervasive perceivable relations which we all know— e.g., spatial, and temporal, whole and part—he can *also* be said to have been studying categorial problems, as Lewis wrote in MWO (p. 15), in a "reflective or phenomenalistic or critical spirit."

[89] For their distinction in MWO, see Lewis' footnote on p. 11.

For any field of study, X, the theory of X attempts examination of the categories of the science of X—its fundamental classifications made, its base-relations, and its methods of utilizing these—and of the relationships between facts formulated in this science and facts in other fields. One goal of such theoretical investigation is an eventually comprehensive understanding, which would require a set of categories adequate to the formulation of facts in all fields, with complete consistency amongst them. This is likewise the goal of an adequate metaphysics.[90]

The theory of X is the distinctively philosophic element in the study of X. Although such theory is to some extent epistemological or at least methodological, the name 'metaphysics of X', which Lewis used in a talk given at Harvard and Johns Hopkins in 1954, is also natural. Metaphysics as a branch of philosophy, he said, would but for residual phenomena simply be "the genus 'theory-of.'" The suggestion that metaphysics should ideally have the structure of a classification of sciences, is chiefly important for procedure. It is not meant to exclude the categories of common sense and everyday life, so far as they are more than rough forms of current scientific categories. In his earlier exposition of the reflective method Lewis made frequent joint references to both, and there is no later suggestion to the contrary.

Lewis also describes metaphysics in his 1958 *Encyclopedia Americana* article, "Philosophy." It is worth discussing here, for his own conception of legitimate philosophical objectives appears to be stated in it, though perhaps not in as precise a way as he would wish the present reader to have. Lewis calls attention to our motives for pursuing metaphysics after a remark that theorists of physics and of jurisprudence may as such largely ignore each other.

Both the physicist and the student of law, however, live in one world which presents both physical and legal phenomena; and, as intelligent human beings in common both are called upon to frame some conception of the basic phases of reality and the main types of process which this world exhibits.[91]

It is not merely that, having a theory of X which is self-consistent and empirically adequate, we impose the formal requirement that it "be compatible with some likewise self-consistent and adequate theory of every other class of phenomena which reality exhibits and to which some other science may be addressed."

In addition to this, there is the fact of that curiosity which affects the human animal and can be satisfied with nothing short of some overall conception of

[90] Abstract of "Met. Log.," *Journal of Symbolic Logic*, 15 (1950), 76. Cf. AKV, Chap. XV, Sec. 4.

[91] *Encyclopedia Americana*, 1958 ed., Vol. XXI, pp. 771 f.

things which will cover all the diverse phenomena with which he is acquainted and serve his understanding of them.[92]

I do not know how Kantian Lewis' thought is here. Throughout the article only one philosophic method—'critical reflection'—is suggested; but the pursuit of an overall conception of things (in which valid norms are also to have a place) can scarcely be that nonspeculative investigation of "what we already know" which Lewis had recommended in 1929. And the whole history of philosophy contradicts any hope we may have of reaching our goal by simply assembling categorial analyses made in different fields of study.

Fidelity to the reflective method would require our metaphysical propositions to be analytic of meanings and to make no assertions of existence. In this connection I would offer two observations. (1) The objective is to harmonize "the meaning of aesthetic attributions," which the theory of aesthetics determines, with "what you and I mean by 'mind,'" and with what it means to call two physical events simultaneous, and with what it means to call an inference valid, a thing good, or an act right, etc., etc.[93] Of course these meanings ought to be compatible; but to make this the definitive task of metaphysics (instead of assigning some of it to the philosophy of man) is to adopt a wholly human perspective on metaphysics, and take as coordinate all departments of thought whose subjects are phenomena or norms that are characteristic of human life. Physics and jurisprudence were good examples. Religion too must be included, so long as there is any hope of discovering and conceptualizing a fairly common core of religious attitude among humans.

(2) Even without that, a humanistic metaphysics must (as Lewis insists) consider "the outstanding question of any philosophy of religion":—

Whether there is any ultimate factor in the nature of things which assures some essential relationship between reality and its processes, and what humans must observe as right and pursue as ideal. . . .[94]

Now the exclusion of existence propositions from metaphysics, here suspended, was in a way always tentative; a category must have applications or it is not worth analyzing. For many categories of reality the exclusion might be viewed as a division of labor between philosophers and scientific experts. Because there are no scientific experts on the question just stated, metaphysicians must tackle it; to set it aside would be a pitiful

92 *Ibid.*, p. 772.

93 Cf. AKV, Chap. XV, Sec. 4; "Mental," pp. 225 f.

94 *Encyclopedia Americana*, 1958, Vol. XXI, p. 773.

evasion. But it does lie outside the original bounds of the reflective
method. (And the affirmative answer to it, unlike the posit of independent reality, is not "an original acknowledgment which all men
make.") I know of no sound reason—in Lewis' thought, or in fact—why
the need for consistency of our rectified categories of the right and the
good with the categories of natural science should impose this problem
upon us. But it seems plain that a metaphysics of categories which are
merely consistent with each other cannot confer any overall intelligibility on human experience. Metaphysical construction involves some
stronger requirement. Phrases like "the synthetic perspective upon all
the sciences together"[95] suggest that Lewis has been thinking of something more than consistency. His requirement would not be a theoretical
one such as Whitehead's "coherence of fundamental notions," but a
pragmatic one, a human one; not the instrumentalism of Dewey (in
which, metaphysics being rejected, no requirement for it exists), and
nothing so crude as the satisfaction of James's "sentiment of rationality." Intelligibility for human beings, considered as active, self-conscious creatures who can acknowledge imperatives; that is all I am able
to suggest concerning Lewis' requirement. The theistic question is then
the question whether this intelligibility demands the addition of a
theistic postulate to the analytic propositions of metaphysics. As always,
a postulate is the only recourse of the metaphysician who will not
speculate. The price he pays in freedom of ideas is plain. For example,
we ought not to wish to limit by relation to ourselves as moral agents
the conceptions of God which may be attempted in metaphysics.

A practical argument against engaging in speculation seems to
accompany Lewis' doctrine of the social and historical character of
categorial attitudes. The advice is to concentrate on cleaning up and
reconciling the operative categories of the established disciplines and of
civilized common sense (including some nucleus of religion); after all,
these categories are what we've got, and we had better philosophize as
children of our time. In the modern world, the role of the metaphysician
who does this will be the important and sufficiently difficult one of "a
moderator among scientists." This phrase of Lewis'[96] well expresses his
view of what is feasible in metaphysics. A moderator promotes common
understanding between parties who are on the platform with him and
have their distinct ways of talking, productive but provincial—and sometimes productive of conflict. The metaphysical moderator waits upon
what they say; otherwise he might be charged with seeking to anticipate

95 *Ibid.*, p. 772.
96 It is from his talk of 1954.

the conceptual apparatus, if not the experimental results, of future science. Let him start with their "classifications *made*," be helpful in clarifying these, and be content in the end to move a little way toward "an *eventually* comprehensive understanding."[97] Unless, over-ambitious, he becomes preoccupied with that final speculative movement, he can say without a great deal of overconfidence what Lewis said in *Mind and the World-Order*: "the *main* business of a sound metaphysics" is with categorial problems which "by their nature must be capable of precise solution since they require only persistent regard for fact and self-conscious examination of our own grounds of judgment."[98]

In various ways Spinoza, Leibniz, Samuel Alexander, and Whitehead, among others, played a role which was not—or not only—that of a moderator. They offered to replace the prevailing, mixed metaphysics of common sense and established science *as a whole*. This is the fourth task of speculation. Before the twentieth century its work was usually misconceived, as logically demonstrative rather than speculative. I would note another limitation on its possibilities. If the speculative metaphysician seeks to escape from what in the last Section I called the hard cores of our Categories, he departs from that experience which is the datum of philosophy, and will hardly be intelligible even to himself. His business is to reclothe those cores in ways which experience suggests to his imagination, and ultimately to offer a new scheme for thinking together the spatial, temporal, thingish, causal, etc., aspects of the experienced world. In this largest possible task of metaphysical speculation the emphasis moves from clarification of meaning to imaginative search for meanings which might more adequately frame how things are: from analytic self-knowledge to a world hypothesis, an eventually verifiable general theory of existence.

There is a strong tendency in this century to assume that alterations in man's view of the world can be effectively suggested only in and by the slow, impersonal movement of science and culture, not by individual thinkers; that a Whitehead, or a Leibniz who might appear tomorrow, talks only to himself. Lewis' recommendation of the role of moderator among scientists falls in with this tendency.

The strength of a purely reflective method is that you can test its conclusions by appealing to the mind of any honest reader whose conceptual commitments are similar to yours. And *only* by formulating and mobilizing criteria which are already his, can you directly prove a philosophic thesis to him. I suggest that Lewis' recommendation of

---

[97] These phrases are from the passage quoted from Lewis on p. 54; my italics.
[98] MWO, pp. 14 f.; my italics.

reflection over speculation in metaphysics comes from the strong epistemological interest which he brings to this field. He wants a method for *determining* the nature of the real; speculation as such does not *determine* anything; it only makes proposals. By reflection we can settle philosophic questions currently at issue, so far as they can be settled in the terms in which they arose. By speculation we pass toward other perspectives. What is thus proposed need not transcend experience; it may be a conceptualization and synthesis of experiential elements not yet firmly and systematically conceptualized. All our concepts were once new.

The reflective philosopher should not take speculation for his enemy; the old notion that philosophy advances by interaction between these different orientations, is sound. The deadly enemy of both reflection and speculation is *talk*—'philosophy' which neither gets a firm grip on categories in use nor offers new ones, but engages in tame or wild edification, or in paper-games. The great value of Lewis' reflective method is that it offers the discipline of concreteness to those who want to be tough-minded thinkers, demonstrating their conclusions. I do not know who in the past century and a half has done more for the ideal of clarity in philosophic argument than he has.[99]

His basic reason for everywhere choosing the reflective method seems to be that for him the main purpose of philosophy is to clarify our minds for conduct. As I hinted earlier, in moral philosophy this method is a conserving force; it can define justice, and bring out the requirements of the moral; but there is value also in a continuing openness to further ideals. The fruit of that, when it first appears, may be a barely conceptualized attitude. In metaphysics categorial speculation is the activity which lies beyond reflection, and which must be cultivated if the goal of comprehensive understanding is to be progressively satisfied. (It would be best if the reflection were called 'categorial analysis of metaphysical concepts', and only the aim at a perspective of the world were called the *pursuit* of metaphysics. But it is vain to have hopes about what labels will be adopted.) Speculation and analytic reflection will to some extent be done by two different kinds of thinkers, each according to his gift. It would be foolish and ungracious to criticize Lewis for not attempting both. My disagreement is with his claim that the reflective method is "the proper method of philosophy." It is the humbler method; worthwhile speculation is so dependent on conceptual

99 A strong statement? It is meant as such. So far as twentieth century analytic philosophy is concerned, I suggest that Lewis is the analyst of whom one can most truthfully say that he had from the start a clear and not superficial conception of the base and touchstone of analysis.

imagination of a very high order, thoroughly disciplined, that most of us can apply to our own philosophical efforts—though not to our study of all philosophers—Lewis' statement that the reflective method is "the only method which holds promise." To say this of the present *age* (or perhaps of any) would imply unwarranted pessimism about the human imagination.

In arguing against speculation Lewis has been temperate, allowing it a historic place and title as 'philosophical'. That is not enough. Throughout its domain, and at all times, philosophy ought to encourage *stretching one's mind* as well as *nailing things down*.

VICTOR LOWE

DEPARTMENT OF PHILOSOPHY
THE JOHNS HOPKINS UNIVERSITY

2

## Paul Henle
# LEWIS ON MEANING AND VERIFICATION

THIS paper is divided into four sections. In the first, certain principles are presented which may be taken as basic to the theory of
meaning and verification given in Book II of the *Analysis of Knowledge
and Valuation*.[1] In the second, these principles will be shown to imply
the salient points of the theory. In the third, certain difficulties will be
indicated and in the fourth tentative suggestions for solution will be
made.

I

This section will indicate three basic doctrines in Lewis' position,
but first the sense in which they are basic must be made clear. They
are doctrines which Lewis does hold and which, I shall try to show,
entail the major aspects of his position. In this sense they may be taken
as fundamental. This is not to claim, however, that they are the only
statements of which this is true, and there presumably are other sets of
premises which Lewis would accept from which his position follows.
Neither is it to claim that the principles to be discussed have any sort
of priority in Lewis' own mind or that he would hold them as basic in
any sense other than that indicated. Nor is it to say that Lewis offers
these principles without proof; this is far from the case. In every case,
evidence is presented and all that is intended in calling them principles
is to mark them as major doctrines for the purpose of analysing Lewis'
position. Finally it is not claimed that the theory of knowledge is deducible in any strict sense, but merely that it follows from these principles
plus other noncontroversial statements.

Undoubtedly the most important principle of the system is what
may be called the *pragmatic principle*, the principle that the meaning
of a statement is its method of verification. As stated, the principle is
vague, since it is meant to represent not merely a tenet of Lewis'
philosophy but also an important aspect of the views of Peirce, James

---

[1] C. I. Lewis, *An Analysis of Knowledge and Valuation* (La Salle, Ill.: Open Court
Publishing Co., 1946). Hereafter cited as AKV.

and Dewey. It is meant to include such views as that the meaning of a statement is contained in the events which would verify it as well as those which would make the meaning consist in statements about the events. The events may be conceived either as physical happenings or as sensations; and furthermore the events may be thought of as occurring automatically or as ensuing conditionally, consequent on certain actions on the part of someone. In short, the principle is broad enough to include any view which has been part of the pragmatic movement. Its specification to fit Lewis' views will be given by its conjunction with other principles.

There is no doubt that Lewis subscribes to some form of the pragmatic principle. To quote one passage of many which would support the claim:

Categorical statements of matters of fact—of reality—are constituted out of hypothetical statements expressing our possible ways of acting and their believed in-consequences.[2]

And, indeed, the entire first chapter is devoted to advocacy of the principle.

A second principle to which Lewis equally clearly subscribes might be called the *principle of incomplete verification*. It states that no empirical statement about objective reality is ever completely verified. However strong or immediate the evidence for it may be there is still room for more and subsequent experience might render it highly improbable. This is not to deny, of course, that a statement may be overwhelmingly probable and may be a rational basis for action, but still there are possibilities that future experience might render it dubious. Summarizing a long discussion Lewis states:

Our general conclusion concerning objective beliefs and our possible knowledge of their truth will, therefore, be as follows. The theoretical as well as practical significance of such belief is to be found in what we should accept as confirmations of it; in those testable consequences taken as implied in the belief itself. No limited number of tests would completely exhaust this significant content of any empirical objective belief. And by the same token no complete and decisive verification of them is theoretically possible, bringing our conviction to such a pitch that no conceivable further evidence could possibly weigh against it. They are never better than probable, although the degree of probability which can be assured may, in favorable cases, amount to what is commonly called practical certainty.[3]

2 AKV, p. 21.
3 AKV, pp. 246 f.

Another aspect of the principle of incomplete verification is that no empirical statement about objective reality can be refuted conclusively. Since the conclusive refutation of any statement would amount to the complete verification of its contradictory, this version of the principle is clearly equivalent to the original statement. Thus according to the principle every empirical statement about physical objects will be something less than certainly true and something more than certainly false. Future experience will always be relevant.

A third aspect of Lewis' theory is what might be called the *inverse probability model for verification*. It is the belief that the increased credence which we give a statement after confirmation is an increase in probability of the sort elaborated in probability theory and that this increase may be described in terms of Bayes's theorem. The theorem may be stated in a number of forms, but all of them allow the computation of the probability of a statement after verification in terms of the probability of the statement before verification and of the probability of the verification if the statement is true and if it is false. Lewis presents a statement of the principle as follows:[4]

Let the antecedent probability of '$P$' $= W$
The antecedent probability of 'not-$P$' $= 1 - W$
Let the probability of '$E$' if '$P$' is true $= K$
Let the probability of 'not-$E$' if '$P$' is false $= N$
The probability of '$E$' if '$P$' is false $= 1 - N$

Then when '$E$' is found true by test, the probability of '$P$' is given by

$$\frac{WK}{WK + (1 - W)\ (1 - N)}$$

The way in which this formula functions in verification may be seen by representing the probability of $P$ after $E$ is found to be true by '$X$'. Then:

$$X = \frac{1}{1 + \frac{1 - W}{W} \cdot \frac{1 - N}{K}}$$

from which it is clear that the larger $W$ is or the smaller the ratio $\frac{1 - N}{K}$ the larger the value of $X$. This is to say that the larger the antecedent probability of $P$ or the smaller the odds on $E$ assuming $P$ to be false rather than true, the greater the probability of $P$ after $E$ is true.

4 AKV, p. 238 n.

If now there is a second confirmation of the type of $E$ say $E'$ for which values of $K$ and $N$ remain unchanged, the probability of $P$ after both $E$ and $E'$ are true will be given by the formula

$$\frac{1}{1 + \dfrac{1-X}{X} \cdot \dfrac{1-N}{K}} \qquad \text{or alternatively} \qquad \frac{1}{1 + \dfrac{1-W}{W} \cdot \left(\dfrac{1-N}{K}\right)^2}$$

so long as $\dfrac{1-N}{K}$ is less than unity this second confirmation will represent an increase in probability over the first and it is clear that if enough more statements of the type $E$ giving the same values to $N$ and $K$ are added, the value of the fraction can approach indefinitely close to unity. Even if the successive $E$'s do not give the same values to $N$ and $K$ but merely satisfy the condition that $K - (1 - N) > C$, where $C$ is some antecedently fixed constant, however small, the same result will occur. Thus the model shows how successive confirmations of a statement may increase its probability to a point of practical certainty though never to unity.

Thus far we have merely pointed out three principles inherent in the position of Lewis' AKV. I have referred to them as the pragmatic principle, the principle of incomplete verification, and the inverse probability model for verification. There is no doubt that Lewis holds all of them but it must be remembered that no claim has been made to show that Lewis regards these as in any sense basic or fundamental postulates of his view. I, not Lewis, have isolated them for the purpose of discussing the position. I shall try to show, nevertheless, that the chief features of Lewis' view of meaning and verification follow from these principles and also how difficulties arise due to the joint assertion of all of them.

## II

We may begin by noticing some corollaries of the three principles. First of all, the inverse probability model requires that verification proceed by discrete and definite steps. We have seen that a true statement $E$, stating the occurrence of some event relevant to the verification of an hypothesis $P$, changes the probability of $P$. The calculation, however, requires that $E$ be true and unless this truth can definitely be asserted, the whole calculation becomes impossible. The model contains no formula for a case in which $E$ is not definitely true but merely probably so and in the absence of a definite assertion of the truth of $E$ the whole calculation would be purely hypothetical—what the probability would be if $E$ were true—rather than anything relevant to an actual situation. Lewis himself emphasizes this difference between pertinent and irrelevant calculations of probability. He says:

There is thus the same distinction amongst probability conclusions as among ordinary deductive ones between those to be taken merely as valid and derivable from hypothetical or doubtful premises and those which are categorically asserted as also true *because the premises of them are asserted as true*.[5]

These considerations make it clear that no statement could increase in probability according to the inverse probability model unless some other statements could definitely be asserted as true. If now, we turn to the principle of incomplete verification we see that no synthetic physical-object statement can ever definitely be asserted to be true. Since, clearly, verifying statements must be synthetic, the corollary to be drawn from these principles is that the statements cannot be physical-object statements. The only other statements are statements about appearances. By a combination of these two principles, therefore, we reach the conclusion that physical-object statements are verified by statements about appearances. These for Lewis take the form of 'terminating judgments' and this conclusion, though not necessarily the route whereby it is reached, is completely consonant with everything he says.

If this latest conclusion be combined with the pragmatic principle which was first enunciated it results in a specification of that principle. As originally stated, the principle required merely that the meaning of an expression was given in terms of means of verification, leaving it open how such verification was to be construed. Since, now, however, we have seen that statements about objects are to be verified by reference to statements about appearances, it follows that their meaning is given by such statements about appearances.

Lewis develops special terminology to take care of the situation. A statement merely about present sensation, one which could not possibly be mistaken he calls an *expressive statement*.[6] A hypothetical whose antecedent and consequent are expressive statements, subject to one condition, Lewis calls a *terminating judgment*. The condition is that the antecedent must always express the appearance of an action, something which appears to be doing something, and the consequent is the ensuing sensation or appearance to be expected. Such judgments are called 'terminating' because their verification is immediate and complete. One may verify at once whether the antecedent has been satisfied, since it is concerned merely with an apparent action and then by verifying the

5 AKV, p. 269.
6 AKV, p. 183.

consequent, which does not go beyond immediate appearances either, be sure of the truth of the conditional as a whole. This is in contrast to ordinary statements about the physical world which Lewis calls *non-terminating*[7] since they can never be completely established or refuted in experience. The point is expressed in our principle of incomplete verification. The relation between terminating and nonterminating judgments is stated as follows:

> Third, there are non-terminating judgments which assert objective reality; some state of affairs as actual. These are so named because, while there is nothing in the import of such objective statements which is intrinsically unverifiable, and hence nothing included in them which is not expressible by some terminating judgment, nevertheless no limited set of particular predictions of empirical eventualities can completely exhaust the significance of such an objective statement.[8]

And again:

> The fact that both the meaning and the verification of empirical belief concern the predictions of further possible experience which the truth of it implies, makes the terminating judgments into which it is thus translatable centrally important for understanding the nature of empirical knowledge.[9]

So far the result of the combination of these three principles is that the meaning of every statement about the physical world—every nonterminating judgment—is given by the class of terminating judgments, which would ordinarily be said to be its consequences. The verification of the nonterminating judgment proceeds by adding to its probability, according to Bayes's rule, as the associated terminating judgments are decisively verified.

Another development of the view is now required by the principle of incomplete verification. If a terminating judgment is shown to be false, then by *modus tollens*, the nonterminating judgment must be falsified also. This decisive falsification, we have seen would run counter to the principle of incomplete verification. The only apparent solution, and certainly the one which Lewis takes, is to introduce a linkage between the two statements in terms of probability. Just how the linkage is to be introduced is a difficult question for Lewis and we shall consider it in more detail shortly, but for the moment it would be well to restrict attention to the conception of probability involved.

Empirical or frequency theories of probability make probability judgments matters of fact, matters to be verified by a future course of events.

7 AKV, p. 184.

8 AKV, p. 184.

9 AKV, p. 190.

A priori theories on the other hand make probability judgments incorrigible by any course of future experience, and in this respect like judgments of deductive validity. If, as we have seen, a nonterminating judgment is to be analysed into terminating judgments the connection between them must be a priori otherwise there would be no reduction but merely the empirical correlation. If the relation moreover is to be a probability relation rather than a relation of deducibility then the success of the reduction requires that it be an a priori view of probability. Thus the three principles attributed to Lewis require an a priori view of probability. It had best be made clear, however, that I am not arguing that Lewis holds the a priori view because he holds these principles, but rather that these principles would be sufficient to commit him. As a matter of fact, Lewis devotes most of Chapter X of AKV to an independent argument for the a priori theory.

Once it is clear that there must be a probability link—and a link involving a priori probabilities—in the relationship between terminating and nonterminating judgments, the next question is where. There are two possibilities. For one, we have seen that the nonterminating judgment is taken to be equivalent to a set of terminating judgments. Each one of the terminating judgments therefore is implied by the nonterminating judgment and this implication might be considered a probability implication. Thus, a given nonterminating statement $N$ might be defined as that statement which gives a very high probability to terminating judgment $T_1$, a slightly less high probability to $T_2$, a low probability to $T_3$, a middle probability to $T_4$, and so on through the entire infinite set of terminating judgments which make up the meaning of the given statement. As Lewis says,[10] it is not necessary that numerical values be assignable to the probability. This is one way in which the principle of incomplete verification might be saved. Even if the terminating judgment is refuted, *modus tollens* is not applicable and at most there is a reduction in the probability of the nonterminating judgment.

The alternative is to place the probability relation within the terminating judgment itself. Since the terminating judgment is a hypothetical the relation between its antecedent and consequent may be a probability relation and the relation between terminating and nonterminating judgments an implication of some nonprobability sort. This also would save the principle of incomplete verification since the terminating judgment could never be completely refuted. Even if the antecedent were true and consequent false, this would not definitively falsify the statement because of the probability relationship.

10 AKV, p. 237.

To decide which of these alternatives Lewis accepts is less easy than one might hope. In one passage he seems to lean strongly toward the first theory:

In consequence we shall be obliged to qualify our previous statement of the relation between the non-terminating judgment of objective belief and any terminating judgment which constitutes a test of it. If the terminating judgment be decisively found true, then the objective belief is thereby confirmed as probable. And if the terminating judgment is found false, then the objective statement is thereby proved improbable; is disconfirmed. It is the latter consideration which obliges the qualification; the former one has all along been explicitly recognized. We can no longer say that *if* the objective belief is true, then the terminating judgment will certainly be true; we can only say it will be probable—in most cases in some high degree, perhaps amounting to practical certainty.[11]

It is convenient to have some symbolism to represent the relationship and most of it has been provided by Lewis himself.[12] Largely following him we may let:

$P =$ a nonterminating judgment

$A =$ antecedent of terminating judgment

$C =$ consequent of terminating judgment

$X \rightarrow Y =$ If $X$ then as a consequence $Y$. Lewis does not describe this relation in detail but insists that it cannot be material implication.[13]

$X \, \exists \, Y = X$ has the analytic consequence $Y$

$(h) \, X =$ in all probability $X$

we may add also

$X \exists_p Y = Y$ has probability $p$ on hypothesis $X$, or $X$ implies $Y$ with probability $p$[14]

The passage quoted above would seem most properly translated by:

$$P \exists_p (A \rightarrow C) \tag{1}$$

When symbolizing, however,[15] Lewis used the form

$$P \, \exists \, [A \rightarrow (h) \, C] \tag{2}$$

and repudiates the form (1). His reason is stated as follows:

11 AKV, p. 233.

12 AKV, p. 248.

13 AKV, pp. 213 f.

14 This symbol is borrowed from Hans Reichenbach though it is not important for present purposes that it have the precise meaning he assigns. Cf. his *Theory of Probability* (2nd ed.; Berkeley and Los Angeles: University of California Press, 1949), p. 45. Hereafter cited as TP.

15 AKV, p. 248.

When we speak of a probability, *h*, that if *A* then *B*, what we intend to refer to is a probability, *h*, of *B* if or when *A* is the case. The analytic consequence of '*P*' which we wish here to express is not the probability of a relation '→' between '$S_1 A_1$' and '$E_1$' but a *relation of probability* between them.[16]

While it might seem that the probability of a relation is also a relation of probabilities there is at least a difference in the relata. In (1) the probability relation is between *P* and *A*→*C* while in (2) it is between *A* and *C* and this is what Lewis has in mind. He wishes to claim that the probability relation is within the terminating judgment rather than between it and the nonterminating.

This raises problems. As we have seen probability judgments are a priori for Lewis and the effect of this contention would seem to be to make every nonterminating judgment, which is supposed to be synthetic, equivalent to a set of analytic statements. This would vitiate the entire theory. Lewis notices this possibility and repudiates it in a passage immediately following the one quoted:

We have suggested for '(*h*) *X*' the idiomatic reading, "In all probability, *X*," instead of "It is highly probable that *X*," in order to obviate in some measure a difficulty which cannot be dealt with satisfactorily in advance of the discussion of probability and the logic of probable belief. One point involved may, however, be suggested here. If, for example, one looks at the sky and predicts rain, one does not intend to assert merely that there is a probability connection between the appearance of the sky and the later occurrence of rain: that assertion would remain equally true whether in fact rain follows or not. The prediction hazarded (as probable) is that *it will rain:* an assertion which the sequel will decisively prove true or prove false. The expression "In all probability it will rain" carries some sense at least of such decisively verifiable or falsifiable prediction.[17]

The point he makes here, Lewis expresses elsewhere as we have noticed by distinguishing between hypothetical and categorical judgments of probability.[18] Hypothetical judgments merely state that a given statement has a certain probability on a given hypothesis. The categorical asserts the truth of the hypothesis as well. The point of this distinction is to differentiate probability judgments which are relevant to a given situation from those which are not. If one holds four hearts in a game of draw poker it is correct and relevant to notice that the probability of completing the flush is 9/47. It is equally correct but irrelevant to notice that if one had held two pair the probability of

16 AKV, p. 250. In order to analyze more fully Lewis uses '$S_1A_1$' where I have used '*A*'; and '*E*' where I have used '*C*'.

17 AKV, pp. 250 f.

18 AKV, pp. 268 f.

drawing a full house would have been only 4/47. Irrelevant, because one did not have the two pair and so the probability computation could not influence one's play.

Now the distinction Lewis is getting at is of first rate importance. In a way what is wanted is an analogue in inductive logic for the deductive distinction between implication and inference. In any situation there may be many implications concerning some matter at issue but most of them are irrelevant because their antecedents are false. Thus, if it is raining, it is too damp for a walk; if it is snowing, it is too cold; if the thermometer says 90°, it is too hot; but if the temperature is moderate and there is a pleasant breeze, it is just right. All these are equally good implications. If, however, by some happy fortune, I can assert the last antecedent, it becomes relevant to the situation in which the others are not. I may assert that it is just right for a walk and set off. The truth of the antecedent allows one to assert the consequent by itself and so to use it in a way otherwise impossible.

All this is commonplace enough, but one would like to be able to say analogously that since one holds four hearts that therefore one may assert without hypothesis and qualification that the probability of drawing a flush is 9/47. This, of course, will not do because for someone watching the game and noticing that another player held two hearts, the probability would be different. Thus, no clear meaning can be assigned to a probability apart from the hypotheses on which it rests. Still some sort of indication is needed to mark the difference between a judgment relevant to action and one that is not. Lewis' distinction of categorical and hypothetical judgments does this and is thus far successful, but it is less successful for the purpose Lewis has at hand, the giving of empirical meaning to terminating judgments.

It is true that the categorical terminating judgment, since it consists both of a probability judgment and the assertion of the antecedent does have an empirical content—that of the antecedent. It would not do, however, to resolve the meaning of nonterminating judgments into statements of this sort since it would make the empirical meaning consist in the phenomenal antecedents of tests without requiring that the tests themselves be completed. It might even turn out that a statement and its contradictory had the same empirical content by this criterion. Clearly some sort of reference is required to the way in which the tests turn out and this, presumably is what Lewis has in mind when he speaks of a prediction hazarded. Still, the prediction cannot simply be asserted or even asserted by itself as probable, so just what the empirical content consists in remains unclear. This is not to deny that there is such content but merely that there seems no way of formulating it with sufficient clarity to make it useful in an exposition of a theory of knowledge.[19] One advantage of using concepts from probability theory is that they have been clarified and their formal properties worked out in considerable detail. To the extent that semantic and epistemological questions can be reduced to questions of probability, to that extent they gain in clarity and this I imagine is one of Lewis' motives in making use of probability theory and certainly one of his readers' motives in concurring. This advantage is lost, however, by the development Lewis has taken. There is no differentiation in probability theory between hypothetical and categorical probability judgments though the distinction could be added with no loss of clarity. When, however, one looks for an empirical content which is over and above the empirical content of the antecedent, there is a loss in going beyond the limits of probability theory. Much as one would like to agree that in some sense Lewis is correct, until the probability theory has been enlarged to include it, there has been no clarification of issues.

The whole problem could be avoided by taking the alternative view which we have seen Lewis suggests in at least some passages, namely that the probability relation holds between the nonterminating and terminating judgment. In this case the terminating judgment, not itself being a probability judgment, would have its ordinary empirical content and there is no objection to an a priori connection between the terminating and nonterminating judgments since Lewis holds that there was an analytic connection here anyway. There is, moreover, nothing contrary to the spirit of Lewis' view in this alternative. To assert a nonterminating judgment is to claim high probabilities for certain terminating judgments. If these highly probable judgments are found to be true then the nonterminating judgment itself is rendered highly probable; if they turn out to be false, it is rendered highly improbable. All this is in accord with the inverse probability model and involves no conceptions beyond those of classical probability theory.

It seems reasonable to conclude that within the framework of Lewis' theory the probability relation most properly belongs between nonterminating and terminating judgments. This also completes the development of some of the major outlines of his theory from the three principles, the pragmatic principle, the principle of incomplete verification and the inverse probability model for verification. They lead him to hold that statements about objects are verified by statements about

[19] The best analysis which I know of the problem is given in Reichenbach's notion of a 'posit'. (TP, p. 373.) Since posit is always interested, always made for the sake of an advantage, it does not seem relevant here.

appearances, that their meaning is given in such statements, that a priori probability relations are involved, and that this relation is, or at least should be, between the nonterminating and the terminating judgment. Having completed this development of the theory, we may notice some difficulties.

### III

Before entering into any extended criticism of the position just outlined, it might be well to consider a few examples of the relation between nonterminating and terminating judgments. From these examples it will be possible to elicit a basis for criticism of the general position. Perhaps as clear an example as any is given by Lewis himself.[20] Let the nonterminating judgment be 'There is really a doorknob in front of me and to the left' then it gives a very high probability to 'If I seem to see such a doorknob and if I seem to myself to be initiating a certain grasping motion, then the feeling of contacting the doorknob follows'. The consequent of the terminating judgment might perhaps better be stated without direct reference to the doorknob, perhaps in such terms as 'a feeling such as touching a doorknob follows' but the import is clear enough. Given the nonterminating judgment there is a high probability of the terminating and, since the terminating judgment is improbable on any other basis, the verification of the terminating judgment adds to the probability of the nonterminating and is part of its meaning.

Let us consider another example. Suppose I have discovered a small insectlike creature in the garden which, when I pick it up, shrinks up and plays possum. I may think 'This is a spider' and then not being sure, reflect that probably 'If I put it on the pavement and if it begins to move, I will be able to count eight legs'. As stated, this last is an objective judgment but it could easily be recast in the form of a terminating judgment 'If I seem to put it on a pavement and if it appears to move, I shall seem to count eight legs'. In this form we would have a terminating judgment rendered highly probable by the nonterminating judgment and improbable on any other basis, hence useful for verification and part of the meaning.

One more example. Suppose I wonder if a watch has been oiled recently. I may propose as a test to hold it to my ear to see if there is a sharp ping-like tick. This is not infallible. A watch which has not been oiled for a long time may have a good action and a recently oiled watch may have a poor one, but still this is a fair test and might be employed.

[20] AKV, p. 240.

The whole situation would be expressed in Lewis' terminology as follows. Let the nonterminating judgment be 'This watch has been oiled recently'. The terminating judgment would be 'If I seem to put this watch to my ear, I will appear to hear a sharp ping-like tick'. The terminating judgment would be rendered highly probable by the nonterminating and much less probable if the nonterminating judgment is false, hence it may serve to verify the nonterminating judgment and is part of its meaning.

In all of these examples, the terminating judgment serves to verify the nonterminating, and with this there can be no quarrel, but the relationship to the meaning of the statement seems different in the various examples. This is most evident in the last two, those of the spider and the watch. In the case of the spider, it is part of the definition of a spider that it shall have eight legs and thus makes it plausible to claim as part of the meaning the terminating judgment which specifies that under certain phenomenal conditions I shall appear to see eight legs. Of course, it may be that I would be unable to count the eight legs or that the spider would have lost a few in the course of whatever vicissitudes spiders undergo, but these contingencies are taken care of in the probability connection.

The case seems far different in the case of oiling the watch. Granted that the tick is a way of verifying that the watch has been oiled, it does not seem to be part of the meaning of saying that the watch had been oiled. One could know exactly what sort of oil to use in oiling a watch and be able to apply it to the right places and in the right quantities without realizing its effect on the tick of the watch. One might even know the purpose of oiling a watch—to reduce friction—without realizing that the reduction of friction manifested itself in a changed tick. One could know not merely how to oil the watch, but might be able to describe what is done and so know that oil is applied at the pivot holes, less on the teeth, etc. He would even know the function of oiling. I do not see how one could deny that the person knows the meaning of the statement 'This watch has been oiled', even though he does not believe that the terminating judgment about ticking is given any high probability by it. He might even have all the information suggested about oiling a watch and still believe that it has no effect on the tick. Such a belief might be erroneous or based on incomplete information, but I do not see how it could be denied that the person did know what it is to oil a watch.

It may be replied that the claim may be granted—the man does know the meaning of oiling the watch but he does not know the entire meaning. One is often said to know the meaning of a term even though he does not know its entire meaning. Thus one might properly be said to know the meaning of some statements involving seven even though he did not believe or even disbelieved that the cube of seven was one hundred greater than the fifth power of three. This fact might be doubted by some one who was otherwise perfectly competent to manipulate seven in the ordinary applications of the tables of addition and multiplication and, moreover, could explain what was being done. Understanding in this sense is compatible with a good deal of ignorance and even some misinformation.

What this rebuttal points out, of course, is that there are different senses of the term meaning. In the broadest sense, a term or statement means to a person anything which affects his understanding, expectations or feelings. This is what the statement signifies to him. This is the difference in his life which is made by the truth of the statement. This is, however, a very broad sense and apparently not the one which Lewis has in mind and that for two reasons: (1) In this sense the same statement will ordinarily mean different things to different people. Thus, 'The sun is shining today' will mean, to me, among other things, that I shall be uncomfortably warm and probably will feel obliged to cut the lawn. To a youngster it may mean the possibility of playing ball. This conception may be the starting-point of a theory of interpersonal meaning but it cannot be the end. (2) The difference between logical connections of statement, and factual connections is lost. Mowing the lawn is clearly part of what it means—to me—to have a sunny day today but one would not say that it is entailed by today's being sunny. Thus the distinction between what is logically implied and what is not cannot be made in terms of such a theory of meaning.

For these reasons some more restricted sense of meaning is required, some sense in which there may be interpersonal meanings and a sense in which a distinction can be made between what is meant by a statement and what may also be true if the statement is true. This seems to be the sense that Lewis is seeking and in this sense one might claim with some propriety that the terminating judgment about the spider's legs might be claimed to be part of the meaning of 'This is a spider' but the judgment about the tick of the watch is not so closely related to the watch being oiled. It is only in the sense that the shining of the sun means mowing the lawn that this is part of the meaning.

The objection may now be stated with more generality. Let $A$ be any predicate. Let it be believed that all or a great majority of $A$s are $B$s. Let $N$ be the nonterminating judgment 'This is an $A$' and let $T$ be a terminating judgment embodying a test for $B$ such as 'If I appear to act in manner $X$, I shall appear to discover an evidence of $B$'. Then $T$

is one of the terminating judgments to which $N$ may be reduced and part of the meaning of $N$. It is not required that the connection between $A$ and $B$ be analytic. One could see some excuse for the claim in this case, but the connection may be as contingent as one please and in fact need not exist—it need only be believed. This appears to me to be a mistake and a limitation required on what terminating judgments are to be included.

This is not merely an objection in itself but it introduces a still wider problem—how does one in general decide what terminating judgments are associated with a given nonterminating judgment. Since no nonterminating judgment can be conclusively verified, it is always subject to test by future experience. This is to say that additional terminating judgments are relevant to its verification and this, in turn, is to say that there is no limit to the number of terminating judgments which might verify a given nonterminating judgment. This, finally, implies that there is no limit to the number of terminating judgments constitutive of the meaning of a given nonterminating judgment.

If now we raise the question how shall one determine which terminating judgments are associated with a given nonterminating judgment, the answer cannot be by enumeration. The process would never end. The only alternative is to state some sort of rule which would pick out the required set. But how might such a rule be formulated and what might it say? It would have to be something like: select those terminating judgments which are given a high probability by the nonterminating judgment. This, however, seems to require that the meaning of the nonterminating judgment be known previously. In what sense then may it be said to be reduced to the terminating judgments?

The same point may be made in another way. We may consider the whole set of terminating judgments, not merely those which can be made at a given time, but those made at any time. Each terminating judgment would have its probability coefficient—its probability on the total evidence now at hand. We may then ask how these probabilities would compare if a given nonterminating judgment were taken to be true as against if it were false. In some cases the probability of the terminating judgments would remain unchanged—these terminating judgments would be irrelevant. In other cases there would be a shift—sometimes increasing sometimes decreasing. The meaning of the nonterminating judgment may now be expressed by saying that if it is true rather than false the probability of terminating judgment $T_1$ will be considerably increased, $T_2$ will remain unchanged, $T_3$ slightly decreased and so on. These shifts in probability constitute the meaning of the nonterminating judgment.

But though one can see, as indicated above, how, given the nonterminating judgment, the set of shifts in the probability of the terminating judgments might be worked out, it is difficult to see how the reverse process could be accomplished. How could one indicate a set of such shifts which would be equivalent to a nonterminating judgment? The difficulty exists not merely in practice but in principle as well. There seems to be no way of specifying and ordering the set of terminating judgments or of giving a formula for shifts in probability.

Whether in terms of the set of correlated terminating judgments or of the shifts of probability, the point remains the same. Given the meaning, one can decide, in principle at least, what to say about any terminating judgment, but not conversely. Even if one could describe the set of terminating judgments equivalent to a given nonterminating, a reference to the nonterminating would be required and the proposed analysis would be circular. The objection is similar to that of Socrates in objecting to Euthyphro's definition of piety as what is pleasing to all the gods. The gods are pleased by what is pious, so there has been no progress in analysis.

The criticisms thus far have assumed that, whatever difficulties there may be in deciding which terminating judgments are needed in the analysis of a nonterminating judgment, at least nothing more is required. There is no residue of other sorts of judgment. This assumption must now be brought into question and its correctness considered in particular with reference to the assignment of probabilities in connection with terminating judgments. We have noticed that there are difficulties in discovering just where the probability relations go whether between the terminating and nonterminating judgment or within the terminating judgment, but for the moment these differences are unimportant. The problem is how shall any probability be assigned. The initial answer very likely would be that it need not be assigned with any exactitude, there need not be a numerical coefficient. Though correct, this answer is insufficient for the problem is not how do we assign precise probabilities, but how do we assign any probabilities at all. To illustrate, let us recur to Lewis' illustration of the doorknob.[21] If there is really a doorknob before me and if I seem to see it and seem to initiate a certain grasping motion, then with a high probability the feeling of contacting the doorknob follows. Lewis assigns a probability of 0.99 though this exact value does not matter. Clearly, the probability would be influenced by a number of factors and influenced not merely in its numerical value but even in such loose assignments as large and small. Am I drunk or

21 AKV, p. 240.

sober, am I paralyzed or not and am I subject to hallucinations, these are questions whose answers will have major influences on the probabilities. Clearly if I am drunk my chances of grasping the knob and so getting the requisite sensation are less than if I am sober—how much less, depends on how drunk—and so with all the other cases. Before there can be even an approximate assignment of probabilities it would seem that the truth of certain nonterminating judgments taken to express the relevant facts must be established.

Before this conclusion may be insisted on, however, there is an alternative which must be considered: is it not possible that the probability can be established on the basis of expressive judgments rather than judgments about objective reality. Would it not be sufficient in the illustration, that I seem to be sober (to myself, that is) that I seem not to be paralyzed and not to suffer from hallucinations? The resultant probabilities might be less reliable than those based on the corresponding nonterminating judgments, but still could they not be used to avoid the objection? The reply is that it is hard to see how expressive statements taken by themselves and apart from any judgments about objective reality can be the basis of any probability judgments. Expressive judgments are defined[22] as being concerned only with appearances, and so make no claims about the future. They are verified or falsified once and for all by some present experience. In what way could any such judgment or any conjunction of them have any implication for the future, whether of probability or of some more definite kind? This is not to deny that expressive statements may have implications for the future in conjunction with statements of another sort. If the record shows that most of the time I say I feel drunk, I cannot pass a given test for sobriety, this together with the expressive statement that I feel drunk would have some relevance to my ability to grasp the knob, but, in the absence of some such objective fact, it is hard to see that the expressive statement could have any implications for experience. We are led then to the conclusion that the assignment of probabilities, integral to Lewis' view, requires belief in statements of objective reality.

The chief objections to Lewis' theory of statements involving physical objects may then be reduced to three: it counts too many terminating judgments as part of the meaning of a physical-object statement, it gives no way of determining the set of relevant terminating judgments, and it cannot complete the reduction to terminating judgments. It remains to consider the best way of obviating those difficulties.

22 AKV, p. 179.

## IV

It is by no means sure that Lewis will regard the problems which have been discussed in the last section as real difficulties and there may be ways of solving them which have not been considered. On the chance that no such means suggest themselves, there remains the problem of revising the general theory. Here the analysis of the second section may be of service. Since Lewis' view has been shown to rest on three principles, the question may be put by asking which of these may be modified so as to solve the difficulties with a minimum alteration in the general point of view.

One proposal would be to give up the doctrine that no statements about objective reality can be certain and to admit among them some so conclusively verified as to be incorrigible by future experience. Something of this sort has been suggested by G. E. Moore[23] and the positivist conception of a protocol[24] is at least related.

This proposal, however, neither solves Lewis' problem nor has any inherent plausibility. That it will not solve the problem may be seen as follows: no one would claim that all statements about objective reality are certain, to claim this would be to claim omniscience. Statements which are not certain are capable of verification and this process would remain much as Lewis described it with the exception that the statements about objective reality which were certain might be used in verification in addition to terminating judgments. Since they were used in verification they would be part of the meaning of these statements. The meaning of such statements would thus be a set of statements which included all of Lewis' terminating judgments and some other statements in addition. The problem of characterizing this set, far from being simplified, would be made more difficult. There would be all the old problems plus new ones in addition.

It might be argued that the intention is not to add the judgments about physical objects to the terminating judgments, but to substitute them. This is a proposal of considerable interest, but since it involves changes in the pragmatic principle, it will be considered later.

If the adoption of the view that some statements about objective reality are certain will not solve the systematic difficulties under consideration, neither is it to be recommended by any inherent plausibility. It seems to rest rather on a confusion between sureness, or psychological

23 G. E. Moore, *Philosophical Papers* (London: George Allen & Unwin, 1954), pp. 226 ff.

24 Cf. Rudolf Carnap, "Über Protokolsätze," *Erkenntnis* 3 (1933), 215 ff.

conviction, and certainty or impossibility of correction by future experience. Unquestionably, we feel sure of some statements. I am sure, for example, that I now have a pen in my hand and am prepared to act on the statement without hesitation. I am convinced, however, that I have been wrong, not often perhaps but still have been wrong about statements of which I was just as sure as the one in question. If it were possible to make an enumeration of all the statements of which I am sure, I would give odds that at least one of them is incorrect. Though I would be sure of each individual judgment, I would be reasonably sure that there was some mistake in the group. If there is a possibility of mistake, the judgments are not incorrigible and so not certain, at least in the sense indicated.

If Lewis' principle of incomplete verification is to be kept, we may turn next to the inverse probability model for verification. Again I believe it should be retained, though for reasons which are quite different. Briefly, what they come to is that I do not know any other model by which the process of verification may be explained. If there is to be any explanation at all, it must, so far as I can see, be of this type. It is not true, of course, that a poor model is better than none. Still, unless it is clear that the difficulty must fall at this point, I should rather retain it until the alternatives have been exhausted.

The two principles which it is proposed to retain roughly delimit Lewis' theory of verification, and the pragmatic principle serves to bring in the theory of meaning by prescribing, in effect, that any statement which serves to verify a statement about objective reality is part of its meaning. The objections raised in the last section were directed to the theory of meaning rather than to the account of verification, so there is special reason to be suspicious of the pragmatic principle. One objection said in effect that some statements might serve to verify a nonterminating judgment which did not properly belong to its meaning, another that there was no noncircular way of delimiting the class of terminating judgments which constituted the meaning. A third claimed that the meaning of nonterminating judgments could not fully be explained in terms of terminating. None of these raised any question with what was said about verification.

This suspicion is reinforced by the fact that the classic pragmatists do not seem to have held the pragmatic principle in the very inclusive form in which Lewis holds it. It may be interesting in this respect to notice how Peirce handles the question of meaning. His opinion as of about 1906 is summarized as follows:

A most pregnant principle quite undeniably will this kernel of pragmatism prove to be, that the whole meaning of an intellectual predicate is that certain kinds of events would happen, once in so often, in the course of experience under certain kinds of existential conditions—provided that it can be proved true.[25]

Peirce goes on to say, characteristically enough, that the principle can be proved but that the argument "requires just as close and laborious exertion of attention as any but the most difficult mathematical theorems." Without worrying about the argument which, fortunately or unfortunately, Peirce does not supply at this place, an illustration may be of use. One dictionary defines silver as:

A white metallic element, sonorous, ductile, very malleable and capable of a high degree of polish.[26]

If this definition be accepted, then, on Peirce's view, to say of something that it is silver is to say that if it is held in ordinary light, it looks white; if it is struck, it emits a musical tone; if it is pulled hard, it elongates instead of breaking; and so on. The illustration has taken a case where a term is defined by a conjunction of others, but this is purely a matter of convenience. The principle would be the same when a term is defined as a disjunction, a disjunction of conjunctions or any truth function of the sort.

There are a number of differences between Peirce's view and Lewis', for one, Peirce discusses meaning in terms of predicates, Lewis in terms of judgments. It is not difficult in principle at least, to make a connection. If, to work with the illustration above, we have the meaning of 'silver' we also have the meaning of the propositional function "$x$" is silver'. In giving the analysis of silver into hypotheticals, propositional functions were in effect used. From the propositional function, it is an easy transition to any of its substitution instances and from these, using the ordinary logical calculus or Lewis' modal calculus, one can go on to more complex statements. Thus Peirce's analysis provides a basis for discussing the meaning of statements in the manner Lewis proposes.

There is another surface difference between Peirce's statement and Lewis'. In the formulations we have been considering, Lewis equates the meaning of a statement about objective reality with a set of terminating judgments, keeping the entire analysis within the realm of language. Peirce equates meaning with certain expectations which, of course, are

25 C. S. Peirce, *Collected Papers* (Cambridge, Mass.: Harvard University Press, 1932-58), 5.468.

26 Webster's New International Dictionary (2nd ed.; Springfield, Mass.: G. & C. Merriam Co., 1945).

nonlinguistic and take meaning into the field of psychology. It must be remembered, however, that Lewis distinguishes two aspects of meaning, linguistic meaning and sense meaning. The linguistic meaning, which we have been considering, gives verbal equivalents of a given expression. Sense meaning which Lewis explains as "the criterion in mind by which what is meant is to be recognized"[27] is much closer to what Peirce suggests. Lewis further agrees with Peirce in giving priority to this sort of meaning. He says:

The question which of these two aspects or ways of construing intensional meaning is the more fundamental, and which is derivative, should find a partial answer at least from consideration of another question: Does language exist, in general, for the sake of signalizing characters found in things and for the sake of practice guided by sense-apprehension; or are classifying, naming and relating things activities which go on for the sake of supporting a language habit and exemplifying concretely our chosen forms of syntax?[28]

Peirce would also admit that the expectations he mentions can be given a verbal formulation comparable to Lewis' linguistic meaning so again it seems there is no substantial difference between the two views.

In spite of these similarities, certain differences remain. For one, even allowing that it can be translated into linguistic terms, Peirce's view is not phenomenalistic. We have noticed that the meanings of terms may be equated with certain conditional expectations formulable in certain conditional statements. Thus, if something is silver and if it is struck, it emits a musical tone. In form this is quite like the terminating judgments which Lewis employs, but there is an important difference: For Lewis both antecedents and consequents of the hypotheticals are expressive statements, concerned merely with how things appear. For Peirce, the antecedents at least are statements about physical reality. Thus in Lewis' illustration part of the meaning of saying that something is a doorknob is that if I appear to reach toward it, certain consequences will follow. For Peirce, if there were any parallel, it would be in terms of what might happen if one actually reached for it. In Lewis' terminology, Peirce would be understood to say that the meaning of a nonterminating judgment reduces to other nonterminating judgments, rather than to a set of terminating ones.

There is another important difference: meanings are general for Peirce in a way in which they do not appear to be for Lewis. Thus for Peirce to say, for example, that something is silver is to say that it stretches if pulled, but nothing is said as to who is to do the pulling or under what conditions. Even if one take a more limited case such as 'All dimes are made of silver' it would be part of the meaning to say that if any dime is pulled appropriately, it elongates instead of breaking. It would not, however, if I read Peirce correctly, be part of the meaning that if I pull a dime appropriately it elongates. This latter implies that I exist and the original statement does not. Generalizing from this example, if the expectation which constitutes part of a meaning may be expressed as a universally quantified statement, it does not follow that substitution instances are also part of the meaning. In this sense meanings of predicates and general statements are general and the meanings of singular statements involve no singular terms not directly involved in the statement itself.

Having noticed these differences between the views of Peirce and Lewis, I should like to suggest the possibility of modifying Lewis' view by bringing it into closer accord with what Peirce said. Suppose the phenomenalism be given up, so that the meaning of a statement about objective reality could be analyzed only into other statements about objective reality. Suppose, also, the meaning of propositional functions be taken as basic and the meaning of statements be analyzed through them. Suppose in doing this the meaning of the propositional functions be considered general in the way just indicated. How would the theory be altered? These changes might be summarized by saying that the meaning of a propositional function is the set of rules by which one anticipates (either invariably or probably) certain types of occurrence under certain types of conditions, if the function is exemplified. This statement since it is more specific than the general pragmatic principle discussed in Section I might be called the *limited pragmatic principle*. Our question now is how would Lewis' views be changed by the acceptance of the limited pragmatic principle?

In certain respects there would be very slight changes. We have seen that there is no important change involved in taking the meaning of propositional functions as the meanings in terms of which all others are to be described. In fact what Lewis has said about sense meanings being rules in mind[29] seems to be more applicable to predicates than to statements. It is hard to see what would be the rule for verifying a statement. Even if it is possible to find such a rule the whole treatment of propositions in the various modes of meaning[30] seems to make them adjectival in character. There seems to be no important change here.

More important is the fact that two of the objections raised to Lewis'

[29] E.g., AKV, p. 134.
[30] AKV, pp. 48 ff.

theory in Section III disappear. One objection was that there seem to be ways of verifying a statement which are not part of its meaning. This could be admitted on the limited pragmatic principle. Thus, to continue a previous illustration, it is a fact about silver that if it is exposed to the air under normal circumstances, it tarnishes, and this is a sufficiently constant characteristic that it might be used as a means of deciding whether or not something is silver. Though constant, this characteristic is not part of the definition of silver quoted above and so not part of its meaning. We are thus enabled to distinguish between the meaning of a term and usual properties of things to which the term applies.

From this point of view, none of the terminating judgments which Lewis mentions will be part of the meaning of any proposition about objective reality. Statements such as 'If I seem to strike this object it will appear to emit a sound' may be ways of deciding under ordinary circumstances that the object is silver, but it is not part of the meaning of saying so.

By the same token there would be no infinite class of judgments to be considered in an analysis of meaning. Meanings will be reducible to general rules rather than all the specifications which fall under them. Thus to say that something is silver is to say that if it is pulled it elongates, but it is not part of the meaning to say that if I appear to pull it at time $a$ and circumstances $x$ it appears to elongate or if I appear to pull it at time $b$ and circumstances $y$, it appears to elongate, etc. The whole problem of selecting which of the infinity of terminating judgments belong to the nonterminating judgment is solved by not allowing any of them as part of the meaning.

These two difficulties appear to be resolved by a return to something closer to a Peircean view of meaning. There remains the objection that the reduction of nonterminating to terminating judgments could not be carried out. Far from surmounting this difficulty, the revised theory does not even attempt to remove it and even denies that there is any need to. The problem arises at once then as to the sense in which the revised theory may be said to be an analysis of meaning. Lewis attempted to reduce the meaning of nonterminating judgments to terminating judgments and so might be said to explain one type of meaning in terms of another. According to the present proposal, one would never leave the realm of nonterminating judgments and there is the question how our understanding has been advanced. Though admittedly one does not go into another kind of judgment, at least one can claim this much gain, that all judgments about objective reality are explained in terms of one sort: hypotheticals in which the antecedent expresses perceptible actions and the consequent perceptible results. We have already noticed that both

Peirce and Lewis reduce the meanings of other terms to that of hypothetical statements, but whereas before we stressed the difference here we may notice the similarity: whether they be judgments about reality or about appearance, it is to hypotheticals about observable states that meanings are reducible. This is because in the one case as in the other, they are transcriptions of sense meanings. They state what may be expected under given conditions.

Even granted that all judgments about objective reality can be explained in this way, it may be argued that not enough has been accomplished. Lewis can perfectly well admit this analysis and in fact dictionaries do something of the sort. Granting the possibility of the analysis given in the revised view, Lewis might well question whether it is epistemologically interesting and whether, in order to have any interesting philosophical results, it is not necessary to reduce statements about objective reality to some other sort of statement. Admittedly the limited pragmatic principle will not do this and, admittedly again, it would be both interesting and important if the reduction could be carried out. Unless some way can be found of meeting the objections of Section III, however, the ideal seems impossible.

How much one insists on the ideal depends on how much rationality one expects to find by philosophical inquiries. The Cartesian ideal of course was that everything should be rational, that one should start with axioms so luminously self-evident that they and all their consequences would be seen clearly in the light they cast. A more modest claim is that one may clarify points by turning the spotlight of inquiry upon them, bringing them into light but leaving everything else in the dark. Although one would wish for the former situation, the part of wisdom is to accept the latter. In part Lewis recognizes this in pointing out that there are certain postulates of empirical knowledge.[31] They are not analytic nor can they be proved on the basis of experience; in fact, they are suspiciously like synthetic a priori judgments. Even granting this necessity, there is still a kind of rationality to Lewis' theory which is lost in the revision. The difference might be put in this way: suppose there were an intelligent being who knew the meanings of terms, but had no beliefs other than logic and Lewis' postulates of memory and induction. Lewis' theory might be taken as an account of how he acquired beliefs and the various probabilities he accorded them. The alternative view would not do this much, but would postulate beyond the original assumptions that there were some empirical beliefs and would content itself in trying to show how these beliefs were modified and other beliefs arose.

31 AKV, pp. 356 ff.

In explaining the workings of a clock, one explains how, when wound, it begins to run and continues; in the case of an internal combustion engine, however, one assumes it to be going and explains how it continues to go. A separate explanation of its starting is required. In this respect Lewis' original view of knowledge attempts to give an account more like the explanation of the clock, and its modification one more like the explanation of the internal combustion engine. Unquestionably there has been a loss of explanatory power, but I fear an inevitable one.

We have seen to what extent the revision of Lewis' views meets the objections to the original position, but it is not enough that an emendation gets rid of the objections it was designed to, the question remains whether it falls into greater difficulties of its own. In particular, one must ask, having separated the theories of meaning and verification, whether the reform of the theory of meaning does not lose the explanation of verification given by the original account. There is a difficulty since the process of verification depends on having some statements which are certain. The inverse probability model, as we noticed in Section II, requires that probability be computed relative to the truth of statements, which themselves are taken as certain not merely as probable. This is the value of terminating judgments in the process of verification, they are true once and for all, so that relative to their truth the probability of the nonterminating judgment must be computed. If now it is no longer claimed that terminating judgments are part of the meaning of non-terminating, how may they enter into verification or can something else take their place?

Peirce dealt with the question by taking a more psychological view of doubt. What was important was not what could be doubted, but what in fact was. This actual doubt, moreover, was not thought of as something which could be started by merely pronouncing the formula 'I doubt it'. It had to be brought on by some perplexity or baffling situation arising in experience. Doubt was thought of as a matter of behavior, of not being sure how to act, of a failure of belief rather than of merely noticing the absence of logical necessity. It is from such a standpoint that Peirce criticized Descartes, claiming that in his *Meditations* Descartes never doubted that he was sitting by his fire, that he had a body and the rest. From this point of view, there would be no problem of verification unless there were some reason to doubt. Some statements might be accepted at their face value without further consideration. If, however, verification were required it might be via other statements which were themselves undoubted. Thus to recur to the definition of silver discussed before, if there were doubt as to whether a spoon were silver, evidence might be sought by striking it against some hard object to see whether a tone was produced. There would be no further need, however, to verify that the spoon had been struck, because there would be no reason to doubt it. The process of verification would come to a natural rest.

This is not to say that one could not doubt that the spoon was struck. It could be doubted and even rejected as false if there were some reason for doing so. If, for example, I had gone through the motions of striking the spoon against a table and no sound were produced, I might doubt that the spoon had actually struck. Short of some such reason for doubt, however, the statement, though dubitable would remain undoubted.

It may be objected that this is not the sort of certainty required for a theory of knowledge. What is wanted is some logical rather than psychological sureness as the basis of the probabilities. For the present, it is worth indicating that the same general account of knowledge as before may be used and, in particular, the inverse probability model for verification. The solution lies in the fact noticed before and stressed by Lewis that while in general probability judgments are relative to premises and inseparable from them, there is a peculiar sense in which the fullest set of believed premises is relevant in which other sets of premises are not. We are prepared to act on them in a way in which we will not act on others. If these assumptions lead to an impasse or to a highly improbable situation one may revise his beliefs and take another set of premises as having peculiar relevance to action. Before attempting to make this view more precise, one or two illustrations may be useful.

Suppose I notice a game of dice in which I am acquainted with the players and none of them has a reputation for dishonesty. The dice look normal so, assuming that they are not loaded, I join the game. I am not of course certain that they are not loaded, but I am sure enough to act on the assumption and also sure enough to make it a relevant basis for probability judgments. Assuming this, it is clearly very unlikely that one of the players will throw an unbroken row of ten sevens. When this happens, I compare the probability of getting such a run using honest dice with the probability that the dice have been loaded. My faith in the integrity of the players may be such that I conclude that everything is proper and that there has been a freak run; on the other hand, I may conclude that there is something wrong with the dice.

In a similar fashion one assumes in scientific experiments that, with due care, no mistake has been made in the calibration of instruments or the observation of data. Theories are considered more or less probable on the basis of such observations. If, however, a theory has become highly probable, a discordant observation may be rejected on the grounds that it is more probable that the observation is wrong than that the theory is.

In either case assumptions are made, not groundlessly but on the basis of evidence. Once made, however, they are treated as certain for the purpose of making probability judgments. If, however, on this basis one encounters results of exceedingly low probability one may decide that a better explanation might lie in different assumptions. The better explanation is one which would give higher probabilities to the results. It must be noticed that this does not involve giving up an a priori theory of probability. It is not the correctness of a probability implication which is called into question, this remains unaffected by subsequent investigations. What changes is merely the relevance to the situation at hand claimed for a premise. It remains true after I have decided that I am being cheated in the dice game that if the dice are not loaded, the chances of throwing another seven after throwing ten is one-sixth. It is merely that this no longer seems a good basis of prediction and one predicts rather on the assumption that they are loaded.

What is said here about treating assumptions as certain in no way contradicts what was said earlier about not being certain about them when considered in a context of past mistakes. We venture to act as if they are certain without claiming certainty for them. Thus the requirements of probability theory are met, not as Lewis suggests by invoking a class of infallible judgments, but by a decision to treat as certain statements with less than theoretical certainty. This decision is not absolute and may be revised if necessary, in which case other theoretically uncertain statements will be treated in the same way. Descartes' dictum, that when forced to act on the basis of uncertainties one should treat them as if they were certainties, applies equally to the making of probability judgments.

I have been sketching a modification of Lewis' theory which deals both with problems of meaning and verification without requiring expressive statements. This is not to claim, however, that such statements cannot enter into the process of verification. In just the manner Lewis describes, they may be used to confirm a statement. We may, as Lewis suggests, use the procedure he describes about the doorknob or the one in the case of the spider to confirm a statement. It must be remembered, however, that since in many cases we are ready to assume the truth of a nonterminating judgment without further investigation, the whole process of verification is often omitted. This would probably happen in the case of the doorknob: one would simply take a look and that would be all. The opinion would be subject to verification only if there were later some reason to challenge it. Very likely there would be more doubt in the case of the spider and one might well go through the procedure of putting it on the sidewalk to see how many legs would show as it walked away. Even in this case, however, it is unlikely that one would distinguish between

'It has eight legs' and 'It appears to have eight legs'. Ordinarily there would be no reason to make the distinction, since either statement would be sufficiently certain and of sufficient evidential weight to take the place of the other. Under special circumstances, however, such as not getting a good look, it might be important to distinguish and in this case the expressive judgment might be used. It would be used, however, only in a context of nonterminating judgments. Only if they are assumed does the expressive judgment have any evidential force.

In the preceding discussion I have isolated three doctrines in Lewis' theory of meaning and verification which I have called the pragmatic principle, the principle of incomplete verification and the inverse probability model for verification. These principles determine the major outlines of Lewis' views. I have also raised three objections to Lewis' views, that it seems to include extraneous matter as part of the meaning of a statement, that there is no way of specifying the set of terminating judgments to be equated to a given nonterminating judgment, and that the assignment of probabilities in or to a terminating judgment presupposes nonterminating judgments. If these objections are well taken, one or another of the three principles must be given up. I have argued that it should be the pragmatic principle which should be modified along directions taken by Peirce, so as to use some judgments about objective reality to explain the meaning of others. This would require that some statements about objective reality be treated as if completely verified where they are not. It would not modify the principle of incomplete verification, however, since it would allow for further question of any such statement. This change, it will be noticed, does not disqualify any process of verification which Lewis allows; it does, however, also add some modes of verification which Lewis does not contemplate. It also involves a considerable change in the theory of meaning, bringing it closer to classic pragmatism. I have argued that the modified view meets the first two difficulties of the original theory and, with some regret, accepts the third. I have claimed that the modified theory is adequate to explain verification.

I have known Professor Lewis too long to believe that he has not considered the objections and modifications offered here. I have hoped, however, that a categorical statement of them might provoke a definitive reply.

PAUL HENLE

DEPARTMENT OF PHILOSOPHY
UNIVERSITY OF MICHIGAN

## 3

*Karl Dürr*

# LEWIS AND THE HISTORY OF SYMBOLIC LOGIC*

I AM well aware that it is a considerable presumption on my part for me to undertake to speak here on the subject "Lewis and the History of Symbolic Logic." I am not familiar with the world in which Clarence Irving Lewis lives and works; I can only speak on the subject with which we are here concerned on the basis of a knowledge of the writings in which Lewis expressed his ideas.

Among the works of Lewis there are two which are of primary importance in this connection and to which we will repeatedly refer in the following. The older of these is *A Survey of Symbolic Logic;*[1] the second is a part of a broader work, *Symbolic Logic* by Lewis and Langford.[2]

## I. *The Concept of Symbolic Logic*

In order to define the subject to be treated here, we will comment briefly on the concepts 'history of symbolic logic' and 'symbolic logic'.

If it is assumed that the concept of logic is sufficiently defined, it is easy to understand what is meant by 'history of logic'. We note that an historical consideration of the development of the separate sciences has proven itself of value. There exists today a brief history of logic by Heinrich Scholz,[3] many valuable contributions to the history of logic, especially to the history of ancient logic, and the recent work of J. M. Bocheński entitled *Formale Logik*, a history of the problems of logic and a comprehensive collection of texts which may be regarded as documents on the history of logic.[4]

---

* Translated from the original German by Norman M. Martin.

[1] C. I. Lewis, *A Survey of Symbolic Logic* (Berkeley: University of California Press, 1918) [215 9]. Hereafter cited as SSL. Here, and in succeeding references, the numbers in brackets correspond to the numbers in Alonzo Church's *Bibliography of Symbolic Logic* (Cf. *The Journal of Symbolic Logic*, 1, 121-216).

[2] C. I. Lewis and C. H. Langford, *Symbolic Logic* (New York: The Appleton-Century Co., 1932) [456 1]. Hereafter cited as SL.

[3] Heinrich Scholz, *Geschichte der Logik* (Berlin, 1931).

[4] J. M. Bocheński, *Formale Logik* (Freiburg/München, 1956).

We can thus say that once the concept 'symbolic logic' is explained, the concept 'history of symbolic logic' can easily be determined.

Lewis uses the expression 'symbolic logic' and speaks of the meaning of this expression in the introductory sections of both works cited above.

In the succeeding paragraphs we will follow Lewis' comments.

It is desirable that one have an expression to signify a certain form of contemporary logic which differs substantially from the older or traditional logic.

There are various expressions which seem suitable to indicate this form of logic and which are used by those who are concerned with the study and teaching of modern logic; three of these expressions will be considered: 'symbolic logic', 'algebra of logic' and 'logistic'. From the point of view represented by Lewis none of these expressions are completely satisfactory,[5] i.e., none of them completely achieve the purpose for which they are introduced.

The question of whether and to what extent the use of the expression 'symbolic logic' can be justified is of especial interest to us here.

Lewis notes that signs which can be regarded as symbols have been used in the field of logic from its beginning and is here thinking particularly of the fact that letters are used in Aristotelean syllogistics as variables which stand for terms.[6]

This remark of Lewis agrees completely with comments to be found in recent works on the interpretation of Aristotelean syllogistics. Jan Łukasiewicz explains that the introduction of variables into logic was one of Aristotle's greatest inventions[7] and notes in this connection that W. D. Ross, in his edition of Aristotle's *Prior and Posterior Analytics*, remarks that by his use of variables, Aristotle became the founder of formal logic.[8]

We also regard Lewis' remark that modern logic appropriately extended the system of symbols to be used and that it is distinguished from the older form of logic by this extension as particularly apt.[9]

I close this explanation of the concept 'symbolic logic' with the remark that the identification of the concepts 'symbolic logic' and 'modern formal logic' is incontestable.

[5] SL, p. 3.

[6] SL, p. 3.

[7] Jan Łukasiewicz, *Aristotle's Syllogistic from the Standpoint of Modern Formal Logic* (Oxford, 1951), p. 7.

[8] *Ibid.*, p. 8.

[9] SL, p. 3.

II. *Presentation of the History of Symbolic Logic*

In his review of *Symbolic Logic* by C. I. Lewis and C. H. Langford, R. Carnap remarked that this work replaces Lewis' *A Survey of Symbolic Logic* and that in the newer work historical considerations have yielded place to systematic ones to a considerable extent.[10] It is true that in the newer work less space is devoted to historical matters than in the older one; nevertheless one can find in both works illustrative remarks concerning important historical facts.

It is appropriate that we here insert some remarks concerning contributions to the history of symbolic logic which precede the presentation of this discipline to be found in the works of Lewis. One can find the works containing these contributions listed in the bibliography in *A Survey of Symbolic Logic*.

The treatises of A. Riehl[11] and Louis Liard[12] are among the oldest contributions to the history of symbolic logic. They describe the development of this new form of logic in Great Britain around the middle of the nineteenth century and examine in particular the work of George Boole and W. S. Jevons. This period of new development in logic will always be memorable and the treatises referred to have the value of historical documents for us today.

In the works of Ernst Schröder which present a systematic formulation of the algebra of logic, important remarks concerning the field of the history of symbolic logic can be found here and there. Central points in the history of symbolic logic are included. Schröder points out that Leibniz was the first to set up the ideal of a calculus of logic and that this ideal was realized in the works of George Boole.[13] In the beginning of the volume on the logic of relatives, Schröder remarks that indications for the development of this discipline are found in the works of Augustus De Morgan and named Charles S. Peirce the principal contributor to this part of logic.[14]

John Venn's *Symbolic Logic*[15] has an abundance of historical remarks and contains a bibliography listing the works in the field of symbolic logic known at that time. This work can in many respects

---

10 *Erkenntnis*, 4 (Leipzig, 1934), 65-66.

11 A. Riehl, "Die englische Logik der Gegenwart," *Vierteljahrsschrift für wissenschaftliche Philosophie*, 1 (1877), 50-80 [40 1]. Hereafter cited as "Engl. Log. Gegen."

12 L. Liard, *Les Logiciens anglais contemporains* (Paris, 1878) [41 3].

13 Ernst Schröder, *Der Operationskreis des Logikkalkuls* (Leipzig, 1887) [42 1], p. [iii].

14 Ernst Schröder, *Vorlesungen über die Algebra der Logik*, Vol. III, *Algebra und Logik der Relative* (Leipzig, 1895), p. 1 [42 12]. Hereafter cited as VAL, III.

15 John Venn, *Symbolic Logic* (London, 1881) [37 8].

be compared with Lewis' *A Survey of Symbolic Logic*. In this book, Boole's main work[16] is used as one of the points of reference with which older systems are compared.

It should also be noted that in the presentations of mathematical logic contained in the encyclopedic work of Giuseppe Peano, reference is frequently made to the fact that a certain proposition presented in the text of the article corresponds to a proposition in a work of Leibniz.[17]

In the well-known work of Louis Couturat, there is a chapter entitled "Le calcul logique."[18] This chapter can be termed a monograph in the field in the history of symbolic logic. Here for the first time the logic of Leibniz is presented on the basis of a comprehensive knowledge of the sources and is made readily understandable.

Following this historical review, we turn to the question to what extent one can say that Lewis has given us a new presentation of the history of symbolic logic.

In this connection, remarks of Lewis in the older of his two great works are significant. They are the following:

(1) A *history* of the subject will not be attempted, if by history is meant the report of facts for their own sake.

(2) Rather, we are interested in the cumulative process by which those results which most interest us today have come to be. Many researches of intrinsic value, but lying outside the main line of that development, will of necessity be neglected.[19]

One may say that the purpose of an historical investigation of a scientific discipline is expressed in these remarks with great clarity and that based on this statement of purpose we are fully justified in regarding the historical considerations in Lewis' works as a presentation of the history of symbolic logic.

III. *First Period of the History of Symbolic Logic*

The publication of the main work of George Boole[20] is a turning

---

16 George Boole, *An Investigation of the Laws of Thought* (London, 1854) [19 3]. Hereafter cited as ILT. [An exact reproduction of the original with the errata corrected but the pagination unchanged, was published by The Open Court Publishing Company in London, 1911, and reprinted in American Open Court editions in 1916 (Chicago) and 1952 (La Salle, Illinois).—the editors.]

17 Giuseppe Peano, *Formulaire de mathématiques*, 2, No. 3 (Turin, 1899), 9-10 [71 30], and *Formulaire de mathématiques*, 4 (Turin, 1903), 8-10 [71 40].

18 Louis Couturat, *La logique de Leibniz d'après des documents inédits* (Paris, 1901) [100 7].

19 SSL, p. 5.

20 ILT (cf. footnote 16 *supra*).

point in the history of symbolic logic. This was already recognized by John Venn and was clearly expressed in his book *Symbolic Logic;* however, our understanding of this fact is considerably improved by the historical considerations contained in Lewis' works.

In agreement with a remark of Lewis we can term Boole the second founder of symbolic logic[21] to which we may add the remark that Leibniz can be considered the first founder of symbolic logic.

It should also be noted that during the period preceding the second founding of symbolic logic research in the field of logic was continued by scholars who can be considered followers of Leibniz. Likewise, the first period in the development of symbolic logic may be defined as the period to which the attempts of Leibniz and his followers belong.

Nevertheless Leibniz occupies an exceptional position here. Lewis has indicated that the contributions of the successors of Leibniz as a whole are of less value than the logical works of Leibniz[22] and it is apparent that this is correct.

The investigation of the logic of Leibniz, begun and guided in the right direction by Couturat, was continued by Lewis.

In these historical considerations, Lewis distinguishes two closely related ideas of Leibniz, viz., the idea of a universal scientific language (characteristica universalis) and that of a calculus of reasoning (calculus ratiocinator).[23] These ideas are closely connected in Leibniz' plan for a reform of the sciences, since in his opinion the construction of a universal characteristic and a calculus of logic is indispensable for the reform of the sciences.

Lewis succeeded in lucidly demonstrating to what extent the ideas which lay at the basis of Leibniz' planned reform of the sciences have been realized in the later development of the sciences and to what extent they contain something of the nature of a Utopia, i.e., something that is not realizable.[24]

The universal characteristic was considered to be a system of science constructed on the following principles. Simple and complex expressions are to be distinguished. The simple expressions, when ordered, form the alphabet of human thought. Nonsimple expressions are of such a nature that one can recognize of which simple expressions they are composed.[25]

21 SL, p. 9.
22 SL, p. 7.
23 SSL, p. 6, and SL, p. 5.
24 SSL, p. 7, and SL, pp. 5-6.
25 SSL, pp. 6-7.

The universal calculus of logic was considered to be the science of mathematical or deductive form, i.e., a system of rules by which can be determined which transformations of given expressions are permissible.[26]

The idea of the universal characteristic is feasible for suitably limited domains and is thus shown to be quite valuable. The idea of an alphabet of human thought is utopian if one considers, not the symbolic system of individual scientific disciplines, but the whole of human thought. Furthermore, Leibniz' idea of a universal characteristic assumes that once the symbolic system is given, the conceptual system to be used in interpreting it is thereby also determined, while we today tend to the opinion that in general several possibilities exist in the interpretation of the fundamental concepts of a particular symbolic system.[27]

Essentially, Leibniz' idea of a universal calculus agrees with the idea of symbolic logic or the algebra of logic; furthermore, certain works of Leibniz may be considered to be valuable contributions to the realization of this idea. Lewis therefore rightly terms the universal calculus of Leibniz the predecessor of symbolic logic.[28]

Among the concepts essential to the universal calculus of Leibniz are the concepts of being contained in and of containing, which express relations of which each is the converse of the other and therefore only one—the relation of being contained in—will be analyzed in this connection. In his earlier work, Lewis explains the definition of being contained in presented in the document to which Leibniz originally gave the title "Non inelegans specimen demonstrandi in abstractis"; this document appears in English translation in the appendix of *A Survey of Symbolic Logic*.[29] The definition proposed there by Leibniz was: 'A is contained in L' is synonymous with 'A + B = L'.[30]

In explaining this definition, Lewis uses the two expressions 'extension' and 'intension'. He points out that Leibniz on one hand wishes to subsume the relation of a species to its genus and on the other also wishes to subsume the relation of a genus to its species under the concept of being contained in and notes that Leibniz had in mind in the first case the extension and in the second the intension.[31]

Lewis thereby proved that two applications of Leibniz' universal

26 SSL, p. 9.
27 SSL, p. 8, and SL, p. 6.
28 SSL, p. 9.
29 SSL, pp. 373-379 [1 6].
30 *Ibid.*, definition 3 and character 3.
31 SSL, p. 16.

calculus are possible. The first of these interpretations can be termed a logic of extension, the second a logic of intension.

The logic of extension may be considered a discipline which has been developed with great clarity in works of symbolic logic and with which we are well acquainted. Lewis discusses the question of whether and to what extent a logic of intension is possible in the chapter of *Symbolic Logic* entitled "The Logic of Terms." He points out that the logic of intension is a somewhat complicated matter and perhaps of no great importance;[32] nevertheless he regards it as possible. From an historical standpoint we must say that this form of logic was influential and that Leibniz had this application of the universal calculus primarily, though not exclusively, in mind.

Lewis commented on the work of several followers of Leibniz in a separate section of his earlier book.

Among the followers of Leibniz, Johann Heinrich Lambert deserves special mention. G. J. von Holland is therefore of special importance because of his correspondence with Lambert. A work of G. F. Castillon, which should also be mentioned in this connection, belongs to a later period.

Lewis shows that Lambert developed the calculus of logic from the standpoint of intension, that Lambert's calculus of logic should be interpreted as an intensional logic. Supplementing his exposition we will make the following points.

At the beginning of his treatise entitled "I. Versuch einer Zeichenkunst in der Vernunftlehre," Lambert gives the following equation:

(1) $a \gamma + a \delta = a.$[33]

This equation is typical of Lambert's calculus; it says that a concept is identical with the combination of its genus with its species and it is apparent that Lambert has the intension of the concept, and not the extension, in mind.

In the treatise entitled "IV. Versuch einer Zeichenkunst in der Vernunftlehre," Lambert undertook to develop a theory of the syllogism comparable to the syllogistic of Aristotelean and traditional logic and which can be regarded as a new foundation of syllogistic. We can assume from the fact alone that this treatise begins with an explanation of the expression 'logical analytics'[34] that a subject which was first treated in

---

32 SL, p. 66.

33 J. H. Lambert, "Sechs Versuche einer Zeichenkunst in der Vernunftlehre," *Johann Heinrich Lamberts logische und philosophische Abhandlungen*, Vol. I (Berlin: Johann Bernoulli, 1782), No. I-VI [8 8], p. 6. Hereafter cited as "Sechs Vers."

34 "Sechs Vers.," p. 79.

Aristotle's *Analytics* is to be discussed. This is confirmed by the fact that in the course of the treatise the problems of the determination of the moods of syllogisms of the first figure[35] and the determination of the particular formulae of syllogisms in all four figures are treated.[36]

According to Lambert's explanation, the universal affirmative proposition 'all A are B' has two different interpretations depending on whether its converse is also universal or not. In the first case, Lambert says, the subject is identical with the predicate and the proposition can be represented by the expression:

(2) $A = B$;

in the second case, the subject is broader or larger than the predicate and the proposition can be represented by the formula:

(3) $A > B$.[37]

The second expression can be read 'A contains B', it can also be read 'B is contained in A' and it can be replaced by an equation. Lambert remarks:

$A > B$ becomes $A = mB$[38]

and Lewis points out that in Lambert's system the expressions '$A > B$' and '$A = m$. B' are equivalent.[39]

With regard to this remark we may say that Lambert determines the concept of being included in in the same way in which it is determined by Leibniz in his essay "Non inelegans specimen demonstrandi in abstractis."

It is apparent that where Lambert speaks of the interpretations of the universal affirmative proposition 'all A are B', he has in mind the intensions and not the extensions of the concepts appearing in this proposition.

Lewis points out that in one of Lambert's essays an anticipation of the logic of relatives can be found.[40]

In his second and third "Versuche einer Zeichenkunst in der Vernunftlehre" Lambert constructs expressions that have a peculiar structure.

In these expressions a new elementary sign, which we will call the double colon, appears at various places.

An example of such an expression is the following sequence of signs:

(4) $i = a :: c$

35 "Sechs Vers.," p. 105.
36 "Sechs Vers.," p. 109.
37 "Sechs Vers.," p. 93.
38 "Sechs Vers.," p. 96.
39 SSL, p. 25.
40 SSL, p. 28.

Lambert interprets expression (4) by explaining that if ' $i$ ' is identified with 'fire', '$c$' with 'heat' and '$a$' with 'cause', then the equation (4) states: fire is the cause of heat.[41]

We are indeed justified in seeing in the construction of expressions of the above mentioned structure an anticipation of the logic of relatives.

The symbol that immediately precedes the double colon can be interpreted as a sign for a relation or, as Lambert himself says, a relationship, if it can be regarded as a constant, and it can otherwise be interpreted as a variable which may be replaced only by signs for relations.

The question of what interpretation the double colon has in Lambert's language cannot quite be determined with certainty; one can only say that this or that circumstance argues for or against a particular interpretation.

I know of three different interpretations of this sign which can be regarded as possible.

According to the standpoint represented by Lewis in *A Survey of Symbolic Logic*, expressions of the form

$$a::c$$

are to be regarded as relative products.[42] In this event it can be said that the double colon is synonymous with the sign of the relative product, whose interpretation is determined by definition 34.01 of *Principia Mathematica*.[43]

It seems to me that the following circumstance argues against this interpretation. On one hand we note that the relative product of two relations is itself a relation, while on the other it is clear that the expression 'the cause of heat' cannot be regarded as the sign of a relation.

I have suggested a second interpretation in the article "Die Logistik Johann Heinrich Lambert"[44]

If one adopts the second interpretation the expressions referred to would correspond in the language of *Principia Mathematica* to those expressions in which an inverted comma, which can be read as 'of', occurs and whose interpretation is determined by definition 30.01.[45]

The fact that Lambert states that the double colon is read 'as the article of the genitive' particularly supports this interpretation.[46] In

41 "Sechs Vers.," p. 19.

42 SSL, pp. 28-29.

43 A. N. Whitehead and B. Russell, *Principia Mathematica* (2nd ed., Vol. 1, Cambridge, England, 1925), p. 256 [194 1]. Hereafter cited as PM, I.

44 K. Dürr, "Die Logistik Johann Heinrich Lamberts," *Festschrift zum 60. Geburtstag von Prof. Dr. Andreas Speiser* (Zürich, 1945), p. 60.

45 PM, I, p. 235.

46 "Sechs Vers.," p. 40.

agreement with this remark of Lambert, we note that the expression
'the father of Socrates' can be regarded as an example of the structure
which has been described.

Alonzo Church gives a third interpretation in a review of the above
mentioned article in the *Journal of Symbolic Logic*.[47]

According to this third interpretation the expressions referred to
correspond to those expressions in the language of *Principia Mathematica* which are called 'plural descriptive functions'[48] and whose
interpretation is determined by definition 37.01.[49] The fact that Lambert expressly says that the letter that follows the double colon is to be
interpreted as a concept supports this view, while Lambert's remark,
which we have cited above, that the double colon is to be read as the
genitive of the article, tends to oppose it.

In a letter addressed to Lambert, G. J. von Holland set up principles
of a new calculus of logic;[50] according to Lewis' opinion, this calculus
is to be regarded as a logic of extension.[51]

It is naturally interesting to discover Lambert's opinion of this
attempt of Holland. In his answer, he remarks that the calculus of logic
whose rudiments Holland had set up in his letter relies on both the
subject and the predicate being taken not as properties, but as individuals.[52] From this one may conclude that Lambert also regarded Holland's calculus of logic as a logic of extension.

Lewis states that Holland's mode of representation could be made
a foundation for a successful calculus;[53] and it seems suitable to me to
further discuss the question that is here raised.

Holland makes an equation the starting point of the representation
of his logical calculus and obtains by specialization of his logical fundamental equation nine new equations. For each of these nine equations
the text contains an expression which can be regarded as a translation
of the equation in question into ordinary language. For example, for
the first of the nine equations, viz.:

(5) $\dfrac{S}{I} = \dfrac{P}{I}$

the text contains the expression:

[47] *The Journal of Symbolic Logic*, 12 (1947), 137-138.

[48] PM, I, p. 35.

[49] PM, I, p. 279.

[50] *Johann Heinrich Lamberts deutscher gelehrter Briefwechsel*, Vol. I (Berlin: Johann Bernoulli, 1781), pp. 16-20 [8 7]. Hereafter cited as LB, I.

[51] SSL, p. 29.

[52] LB, I, p. 37.

[53] SSL, p. 31.

(6) All S are all **P**

and it is clear that expression (6) is here to be regarded as the translation of equation (5) into ordinary language. Holland terms the nine equations and their translations forms of judgment and conjectures that every possible form of judgment is identical with one of these nine equations. Holland then notes that these nine forms of judgment may be reduced to four and characterizes these four types of judgment by means of four expressions taken from standard logical usage. By this means the new logical calculus is brought into correspondence with Aristotelean syllogistic and traditional logic.[54]

After having presented the principles of his logical calculus, Holland states: "It is then simple to represent a syllogism in this way"[55] and then gives three examples of syllogisms. In these syllogisms, certain nonlogical constants appear; among the nonlogical constants which appear in this connection are, for example, the expressions 'man', 'mortal' and 'European'. The corresponding rules of deduction can be constructed; this can be done if we interpret the letters which are considered to be abbreviations for nonlogical constants as variables in the equations which correspond to the premises and the conclusion; one may assume that such an interpretation agrees with Holland's intention. We will permit ourselves to use the expressions 'first, second and third figure' in the sense which they bear in Aristotle's *Prior Analytics*. One can then say: it is clear that in Holland's sketch the first of the three examples is intended to represent a syllogism of the first figure, the second example a syllogism of the third figure and the third example a syllogism of the second figure.[56]

One can also see what operations allow us, in Holland's opinion, to derive the conclusion from the premises.

The first and second example are of such a nature that one can indeed verify the calculus as successful; the third however seems to us to be essentially different. A difficulty is encountered there which seems to us to be unsurmountable. Lewis pointed out this difficulty himself when he indicated that Holland in the case in question transforms one of the equations in a manner that cannot be regarded as legitimate.[57] It is clear that Holland later became aware that the rule of deduction in question cannot be regarded as legitimate in his calculus; following his presentation of the three examples, he admits: "I am not satisfied

[54] LB, I, pp. 17-19.
[55] LB, I, p. 19.
[56] LB, I, pp. 19-20.
[57] SSL, p. 32.

with this mode of representation because if one applies operations which
are permissible in algebra to my formulae, results are often obtained
which have a mathematical but not a logical meaning."[58]

The fact that Holland in one of the three cases which he explains
did not succeed in showing that his calculus makes it possible to deduce
the conclusion from the premises through the use of legitimate operations seems to me to be of fundamental importance in deciding the question which here concerns us. Holland's attempt certainly deserves to be
mentioned and commented on in a history of symbolic logic; I would
however scruple at stating that it can be made the foundation of a
completely successful calculus.

Lewis calls our attention to the fact that in one of his letters to
Lambert, Holland discovered a difficulty to which Lambert's logical
calculus leads.[59]

In the letter to which Lewis refers, Holland shows that in Lambert's
calculus, from the two equations:

(7)  $A = mC$

and

(8)  $B = nC$

one can derive the equation:

(9)  $nA = mB$

and remarks that the calculus cannot decide whether the ideas $nA$ and
$mB$ consist of contradictory partial ideas or not and that the question
must be decided by material considerations.[60]

We will compare these remarks of Holland with a statement which
appears in the treatise of Lambert which was submitted to Holland
and which he had in mind while writing his letter.[61] Lambert points
out at the place in question that from the equations

(10)  $B = mA$

and

(11)  $C = \mu A$

one can obtain the equation

(12)  $\mu B = mC$

but adds the remark that no conclusion can be drawn in this case
because the middle has been taken as particular twice.[62]

58 LB, I, p. 20.

59 SSL, p. 35.

60 LB, I, pp. 262-263.

61 J. H. Lambert, "De universaliori calculi idea," *Nova acta eruditorum* (Leipzig,
1765), pp. 441-473 [8 4]. Hereafter cited as "Univ. Calc."

62 "Univ. Calc.," p. 467.

Lewis took a position on the problem in question and if I understand his remark correctly, it is his opinion that an inconsistency in Lambert's calculus has been discovered here.[63]

I must confess that I cannot agree with Lewis on this point. It seems to me that the only thing that can be established is that Holland was correct. The fact that by the laws of Lambert's calculus equation (9) can be derived from equations (7) and (8) and likewise equation (12) can be derived from equations (10) and (11) does by no means show that this calculus is inconsistent and thereby faulty.

The work of Castillon to which we have already referred, is entitled *Mémoire sur un nouvel algorithme logique*.[64] Lewis presents an analysis of this work which clearly indicates its typical properties.[65]

In agreement with a remark of Lewis, we note that Castillon's logic may be considered a logic of intension.

Lewis terms Castillon's theory the most successful attempt to construct a logical calculus based on the intension of concept but adds that this calculus is as unsound theoretically as that of Lambert.[66]

This can be confirmed by comparing the works of Lambert and Castillon. Actually, the only parts of Castillon's theory that are scientifically acceptable are those that are old, established by Leibniz and common to Lambert's calculus. Lewis' remark that Castillon's attempt was successful is justified in the sense that many of the propositions derived by Castillon agree with those of traditional logic and the added remark that the methods used by Castillon are scientifically unsound is justified since these methods are of such a nature that they can be used to derive false as well as true conclusions.

In order to justify this remark we call attention to the following. Castillon believes that he can show by means of his calculus that a particular negative proposition is convertible. In this case the methods used by Castillon lead to an incorrect conclusion. Castillon was, however, not aware of this since he states in the place in question: "tout jugement négatif particulier est convertible, ainsi qu'on l'enseigne ordinairement en logique."[67] Thus Castillon apparently assumes that one usually teaches that a particular negative proposition is convertible in logic. That this is not the case can be seen from the fact that in the first book

63 SSL, p. 35.

64 G. F. Castillon, *Mémoire sur un nouvel algorithme logique* (Berlin, 1805) [15 1]. Hereafter cited as AL.

65 SSL, pp. 32-34.

66 SSL, p. 34.

67 AL, p. 17.

of the *Prior Analytics* of Aristotle it is expressly stated that "if some B is not A, there is no necessity that some of the A should not be B."[68]

Lewis compares the development of symbolic logic on the continent of Europe with the progressive development of this discipline begun by the logical work of George Boole and Augustus De Morgan and points out that the first period resulted in failures while the second resulted in successes.[69] Such an interpretation may at first sight seem somewhat severe; it is, however, basically correct. Symbolic logic was not able to continue its development on the continent and when the scientific content of the logical works of Leibniz later came to be explicated, this was to occur under the influence of a school of thought which had its origin in Great Britain.

From an historical point of view the question may be raised why the efforts to found a new logic were not fully successful in the first period while those of the succeeding period were so rapidly crowned with success. In Lewis' works it is indicated that the reason for this lay in the fact that in the first period preference was given to the intensional standpoint, while in the second that of extension was preferred.[70]

Admitting this raises the question why it was not possible to systematically develop a logical calculus from the standpoint of intension. In his earlier work, Lewis states that consideration of the attempts of Leibniz, Lambert, and Castillon leads to the conclusion that a logically correct calculus based on the intension of concepts is either very difficult or, as Couturat says, impossible.[71] We have noted above, that Lewis in his later book remarks that the logic of intension is a somewhat complicated affair and possibly not of great importance. In this connection we regard the remark that the logic of intension is possibly not of great importance as significant. Castillon states at the beginning of his work *Mémoire sur un nouvel algorithme logique,* that he temporarily abandoned his attempts to develop a logical calculus because he got the idea that even the most complete logical calculus would never be of real use.[72] By a logical calculus, however, Castillon could mean nothing but a calculus based on the intensions of concepts. Castillon's remark points out that one could not ascribe great importance to the development of a logic of intension because of the impression that this logic

---

68 *Prior Analytics*, p. 25a.

69 SSL, p. 37.

70 SSL, pp. 35, 37.

71 SSL, p. 35.

72 AL, p. 3.

could not be applied to the construction of the other sciences and consequently had no real use.

## IV. *Second Period in the History of Symbolic Logic*

The second period of the history of symbolic logic, which begins with the second foundation of this discipline around the middle of the nineteenth century and continues to the present, is full of significant events; it is clear that in this respect the first period cannot be compared to the second.

The historical sections of Lewis' works give us for the first time a summary view of the wide expanse that we call the second period of the history of symbolic logic.

From the nature of things an historical commentary on the development of a science can only be successful when that development has come to a close. The development of symbolic logic reached a close with the appearance of *Principia Mathematica*. It is significant for the historical investigations carried out by Lewis that even in comparison with other more recent publications, *Principia Mathematica* can be considered a principal work and an embodiment of the idea of symbolic logic; in this it differs essentially from the publications that preceded it.

The principal features of the development of symbolic logic in the second period are clearly brought out in the historical considerations which Lewis devotes to this period; we will here attempt to present these principal features in summary form.

The first line of development lies entirely within the Anglo-American culture. It is worthy of notice that this development had its origin in Great Britain, then crossed to America and reached its culmination there with the logical investigations of C. S. Peirce. We consider it significant that for the first time in the history of symbolic logic one can speak of a development in the sense of a steady progress.

The succeeding development is not as unified as that of the preceding period. The area in which the study of the new form of logic was cultivated is broadened and is no longer restricted to the Anglo-American culture.

The various publications which belong to the second period of symbolic logic are treated exhaustively in Lewis' books; our commentary will follow his presentation.

One historical problem which occurs here is the question to what extent it can be said that the theory of the quantification of the predicate, represented in particular by Sir William Hamilton, was significant for the foundation of the new form of logic in Great Britain.

It was formerly assumed that Boole's system was based on the theory of the quantification of the predicate; this interpretation was already challenged in the works of John Venn. Lewis states that although Hamilton's theory is not directly important for the history of symbolic logic, this theory provoked discussions which awakened a lively interest in logical problems and thereby made the new foundation of logic possible.[73]

It seems to us that this is essentially correct; nevertheless, it should also be said that the theory of the quantifications of the predicate was based on a tenable idea, an idea important to logic, namely that it is possible that not only one, but also two of those expressions that modern logic terms quantifiers can occur in a proposition. Hamilton was not the first to have made an attempt in this direction and the eight new propositional forms of Hamilton referred to in historical presentations of English logic do not have the clarity which must be demanded in the field of logic. These propositional forms are, however, so constructed that one can see that within one and the same proposition quantificational expressions such as 'all', 'some', and 'any' can occur at more than one place.[74]

We wish to go into this matter more fully in order to clarify our point of view.

Lewis has pointed out that Leibniz knew and used the theory of the quantification of the predicate.[75]

In a work of Leibniz entitled "Mathesis rationis" which was first published by L. Couturat, four propositional forms are presented which, when translated into logistic language, were represented with the help of two quantifiers;[76] each of these four propositional forms correspond to one of the eight propositional forms of Hamilton which, also as we have already mentioned, are represented with the help of two quantifiers. Leibniz' presentation can help to clarify the meaning and significance of the propositional forms presented by Hamilton.

C. H. Langford points out in the ninth chapter of *Symbolic Logic* that an essential difference between the traditional formal logic of propositions and the modern version of this theory consists in the fact that while the older form allows only single generalizations, the newer allows also multiple generalizations.[77] We note that where multiple

---

[73] SSL, pp. 36-37 and SL, p. 7.

[74] Sir William Hamilton, *Lectures on Logic*, ed. H. L. Mansel and John Veitch (3rd ed.; Edinburgh and London), Vol. II, pp. 279-280.

[75] SSL, p. 36 and SL, p. 7.

[76] *Opuscules et Fragments Inédits de Leibniz*, ed. L. Couturat (Paris, 1903), p. 193.

[77] SL, p. 286.

quantifiers occur, multiple generalizations are represented and hence we come to the standpoint that the theory of the quantification of the predicate represented by Hamilton expresses a tendency which can be termed progressive.

It is of the highest importance for the history of symbolic logic that the characteristic features of the logistic systems presented in the two well-known works of George Boole be placed in proper perspective. Lewis described the main points of these systems in an exact manner in both his earlier and his later book and thereby brought out what can be regarded as the essential character of Boole's work; he calls those main points the fundamental ideas which determine the structure of Boole's system.[78]

In connection with the exposition to be found in the above mentioned works, we wish to call attention to the following points.

Boole does not distinguish between the operation of choosing elements of a class and the result of this operation; both are represented by one and the same variable, for example by the variable '$x$'.[79] Although one can say that the symbols in question are used equivocally, the scientific rigor of the calculus developed by Boole is not disturbed by this and the understanding of the formulae to be set up is facilitated by this equivocation.

Boole overcame the difficulties involved in the foundation of a logical calculus by bringing this calculus in close connection with a calculus which can be described as a special form of the algebra of numbers, namely an algebra with the peculiarity that the range of values of its variables is limited to the two numbers, 0 and 1.

Let us call that form of numerical algebra 'dyadic algebra'. One can then say: dyadic algebra differs from the other forms of the algebra of numbers in that the law expressed by the following formula holds:

$$x^2 = x;$$

this law is termed the index law by Boole.[80]

The index law can also be interpreted as a formula of the logical calculus and in that case says the following:

If one selects all of the elements of a class, the result of this operation is identical with the given class.[81]

These remarks lead to the question why Boole succeeded, while his predecessors failed, in giving a definite foundation for the calculus of

78 SSL, p. 52 and SL, p. 9.
79 SSL, p. 52.
80 SSL, p. 54.
81 SSL, p. 54 and SL, pp. 10, 13.

logic. Lewis mentions this question in reference to the problem of the meaning of the sign of addition in the logical calculus and remarks that the fact that Boole found a better solution than his predecessors is due more to his ingenuity than to greater logical acuteness.[82] We agree thoroughly with this remark and believe that it can be generalized; what distinguishes Boole from his predecessors is not so much logical insight as technical skill in the construction of a calculus.

Augustus De Morgan is associated with George Boole in the history of symbolic logic.

In his books, Lewis gives a summary of the logical theories which are presented in the works of De Morgan. The literature which must be taken into consideration here is quite extensive and it was a very valuable though extraordinarily difficult service to give a summary of these theories.

De Morgan attempts to present the system of simple propositional forms that are possible if two terms 'X' and 'Y' are given and introduces new symbols to represent these propositional forms.[83]

Lewis investigates the system of symbols introduced by De Morgan and shows that certain errors are connected with that symbolism. Lewis notes in particular that the simplest relation which can exist between sentences, a relation which we can briefly characterize by the term 'negation', is represented by De Morgan by a complex, rather than by a simple, operation.[84]

One can find in De Morgan's works important contributions to the development of a theory of relations.[85] De Morgan's theory of relations is comprehensively and intelligently presented in the earlier book of Lewis.

The logic of relations was not brought to full development by its founder despite his promising contributions. Lewis correctly attributes this to the fact that De Morgan was intent on providing a new foundation of the Aristotelean or traditional theory of the syllogism with the help of this new form of logic and therefore attempted to apply the logic of relations to an unfruitful field.[86]

W. S. Jevons can be considered a student of Boole and has as such his place in the history of symbolic logic.

[82] SL, p. 12.

[83] "On the Symbols of Logic," *Transactions of the Cambridge Philosophical Society,* **9**, Part I, 79-127 (1856), p. 91 [20 3]; cf. SSL, p. 38, note 63.

[84] SSL, p. 43.

[85] "On the Syllogism, No. IV, and on the Logic of Relations," *Transactions of the Cambridge Philosophical Society,* **10**, 331-358, esp. 341 ff. (1864) [20 6].

[86] SSL, p. 50.

In the historical treatises of A. Riehl and Louis Liard, Jevons is regarded as in a way comparable to Boole; Riehl holds that Jevons partly simplified and partly further developed Boole's logic.[87] In the above mentioned book,[88] John Venn refers often to the works of Jevons. John Venn's remarks and notes in connection with these references are valuable and reveal essential points of Jevons' system. Nevertheless a comprehensive and extensive presentation of Jevons' system can first be found in the earlier of Lewis' two books; the main points of this system are also explained in Lewis' later book.

Jevons constructed a new method for solving certain logical problems. Lewis compares this method with a method constructed by Boole in a highly instructive fashion. With regard to the results obtained by Lewis' investigations, the following may be stated.

(1) In certain respects, Jevons' method is simpler than that of Boole; for example, Jevons carries out his computation without making use of the converses of the operations of logical addition and logical multiplication.[89]

(2) Logical addition, or in other words the connective 'or', has a different meaning in Jevons' system than in Boole's. While in Boole's system, logical addition can only be carried out if the classes to be connected are disjoint, this operation can always be carried out in Jevons' system. As a result the duality principle holds in Jevons' system but not in that of Boole and it is undeniable that in this respect Jevons' system is preferable to Boole's.[90]

(3) If one attempts to solve particular logical problems by Jevons' method, one is obliged to follow a procedure which may be described as time consuming and tedious unless the problem in question falls under one of the simplest cases. Lewis shows for a particular case the number of individual steps that are necessary to solve a problem by Jevons' method,[91] and it is easy to generalize this remark by pointing out that if $m$ is the number of premises given and $n$ the number of terms which occur in these premises then the number of individual steps necessary to provide a solution by Jevons' method is $m \cdot 2^n$.

The point of view which is at the basis of the considerations presented under (3) above seemed to us to be of general interest. While we would not agree that a method must be unconditionally rejected if its

[87] "Engl. Log Gegen.," p. 61; cf. note 11 *supra*.

[88] Cf. note 15 *supra*.

[89] SSL, p. 73.

[90] SSL, p. 73.

[91] SSL, p. 78.

application results in time consuming labor; still, one would not contest that among all methods which yield the same results, that method is to be preferred which yields the results in the shortest time or with the least labor. This is simply a form of the general principle of economy.

The development and cultivation of symbolic logic expands with Charles Sanders Peirce, since it now spreads from Great Britain to the American cultural sphere.

Peirce's contributions to symbolic logic are extensive and the works in which they are contained are many and varied. Reference to some of these works can already be found in John Venn's book; and a list of Peirce's logical treatises, which can be regarded as complete, can be found in the first volume of E. Schröder's great book.

It should be noted also that Peirce's works have recently been reissued by Charles Hartshorne and Paul Weiss. The third volume of this edition which is entitled *Exact Logic* and was published in 1933, contains Peirce's contributions to symbolic logic. The publication of this volume facilitates the approach to the works with which we are concerned; this edition did not exist when Lewis undertook to explicate and interpret the logical works of Peirce.

At the beginning of his book devoted to the logic of relatives Ernst Schröder remarks that the study of this discipline is made appreciably more difficult by the variety of *'hieroglyphensysteme'* utilized by the founders of the discipline and adds that the principal proponent of this science, Charles S. Peirce, sometimes changes from system to system almost without warning.[92] Lewis himself points out that Peirce's works are difficult to read and that they therefore did not receive until then the attention which their content would call for.[93] Lewis' interpretation of Peirce's works from a modern standpoint and his interpretation of their place within the complex structure of the development of symbolic logic constitute an important contribution to the history of symbolic logic.

Lewis shows how Peirce systematically developed and then simplified Boole's calculus.

Peirce clarified the system of connective or two-place operations of the calculus of classes by comparing arithmetic and nonarithmetic or logical operations and was thereby enabled to add operations omitted by Boole. In Boole's system an operation can be found which can be termed arithmetic addition; Peirce adds logical addition. On the other hand in Boole's system an operation can be found which can be regarded

92 VAL, III, p. 1.
93 SSL, p. 106.

as logical multiplication, Peirce here adds arithmetic multiplication. By these additions, the system of connective operations is substantially clarified and Lewis' presentation of this theory facilitates a summary view of the new system of connective operations. Since the new system, which can be considered a systematic completion of Boole's older system, contains not only two but four connective operations, there are not only two but four inverse operations. In Lewis' book three of these four operations are exhaustively treated and their meaning explained with full clarity; with respect to the fourth of these operations it is pointed out that the corresponding relation of arithmetic is completely analogous.[94]

Lewis points out that in the work "Description of a Notation for the Logic of Relatives" which appeared in 1870 and may therefore be considered one of the early works, Peirce treated the system of four connective operations and the inverse operations with the exception of arithmetic division, while in the later works only two connective operations, logical addition and logical multiplication, are used and the use of inverse operations is discarded.[95]

In his later book Lewis expressly states that the discarding of two inverse operations, logical subtraction and logical division, cannot be regarded as a loss since everything that can be said by means of the operations in question can be expressed by means of the operations of logical addition and multiplication.[96] In this connection Lewis states that the inverse operations are only used in the construction of the negation function.[97] It seems to us that he thereby admits that the use of inverse operations in the calculus of logic is profitable and hence also justifiable.

Lewis also points out that Peirce in the work referred to above first introduced a sign to represent the relation of inclusion and remarks that the introduction of such a sign was justifiable since it is advantageous to represent this relation simply.[98]

In this connection it may be mentioned that in E. Schröder's system the sign of the relation of subsumption, which is identical with the relation of being contained in, is introduced as a primitive sign.[99]

Peirce treated the logic of relatives quite exhaustively. Lewis succeeded in demonstrating the true significance of this part of Peirce's

94 SSL, pp. 81-82.
95 SSL, p. 83.
96 SL, p. 15.
97 SL, p. 15.
98 SSL, p. 83, and SL, p. 15.
99 *Vorlesungen über die Algebra der Logik*, Vol. 1 (Leipzig, 1890), p. 159 [42 7].

system and in showing that Peirce here constructed a system of signs which was of fundamental importance for the further development of symbolic logic. Lewis points out that Peirce defines relatives by means of propositional functions and analyzes the definitions of relative product and relative sum constructed by Peirce. The analysis which is contained in Lewis' earlier book, demonstrates that, in the definitions of relative product and relative sum, Peirce makes use of signs that are now termed quantifiers.[100]

The development of symbolic logic from Peirce to the time of publication of Lewis' book *A Survey of Symbolic Logic* is covered in a separate chapter of that book; a mode of presentation is here chosen that is essentially different from the way earlier periods are treated. The works belonging to the new period are still of current interest and reference is therefore made in the historical consideration to the systematic development of theories, given in later sections of Lewis' book.

Lewis coined the expression 'the classical or Boole-Schröder algebra of logic', he often replaces this with the simpler expression 'the Boole-Schröder algebra'. These expressions are related to the expressions 'the algebra of logic' and 'Boolean algebras' which were previously used by other authors.[101] Lewis included Schröder's name in the designation of the discipline founded by Boole in order to indicate that Schröder gave it the form in which it is now presented to us. Lewis justifies the designation of the Boole-Schröder algebra of logic as classical by pointing out that this contains a prophesy; when this form of logic is designated as classical, the idea is expressed that Boole-Schröder algebra will be a source of further, highly important calculi.[102] We would like to add the remark that this designation also seems justified because the algebra of logic founded by Boole can be considered as that part of symbolic logic that was first constructed in a strictly scientific form.

In each of Lewis' two books, Boole-Schröder algebra is systematically presented in a chapter.

Lewis points out on one occasion that his presentation of certain parts of symbolic logic should not be considered as primarily historical, but as expository.[103] This holds for Lewis' presentation of the Boole-Schröder algebra. This presentation allows the reader to review the theory as a whole and to see how the individual theorems are established.

100 SSL, pp. 94-95.

101 Cf. H. M. Sheffer, "A Set of Five Independent Postulates for Boolean Algebras," *Trans. Amer. Math. Soc.*, 14 (1913) , 481-488 [196 2], esp. 481.

102 SSL, p. 118.

103 SSL, p. 279.

Lewis has indicated the respects in which his presentation of the classical algebra of logic differs from that of Schröder,[104] viz., that in Schröder's system the sign of subsumption appears as a primitive and in the presentations of this discipline given by Lewis, the sign of subsumption is defined.[105]

Schröder's propositional calculus corresponds to the discipline which is termed two-valued algebra in Lewis' books. The two presentations of this discipline in Lewis' books are largely in agreement; they do, however, also have differences which we do not wish to ignore here. In the earlier book, the formulae of two-valued algebra are presented by means of elementary signs which in general have already been used in the presentation of the formulae of Boole-Schröder algebra. In the later book, the elementary signs used in the presentation of the formulae of this discipline are almost without exception not previously used in the Boole-Schröder algebra but take the place of the elementary signs of this algebra and can be considered as synonymous with these signs. This new means of presentation makes it easier for the reader to regard two-valued algebra as a discipline not identical with Boole-Schröder algebra.

In both books the methods of two-valued algebra are subjected to a criticism of highly important nature.

Lewis shows:

(1) that two-valued algebra cannot be considered as a general or abstract system, but only as a propositional logic;[106]

(2) that when it is considered as a propositional logic, two-valued logic is revealed to be a discipline whose proofs are circular, since in the proofs of logical laws these laws are already assumed.[107]

In this connection it should be remembered that Schröder himself termed the discipline which Lewis calls two-valued algebra 'propositional calculus'.

Principal points of Schröder's algebra of the logic of relatives are treated in Lewis' systematic presentation of the logic of relations in *A Survey of Symbolic Logic*.

In this connection we note the following.

Schröder's presentation of the algebra of logic is based on a proposition which we will call the principle of duality. Lewis shows that the parallelism of logical formulae required by the principle of duality

[104] SSL, p. 111.
[105] SSL, p. 119, def. 1.9, and SL, p. 29, def. 1.03.
[106] SL, p. 116.
[107] SSL, p. 281, and SL, p. 117.

was already known to Peirce, but that Schröder emphasizes this principle more than Peirce does.[108] If the principle of duality is followed, the concept of the relative product will be related to the concept of the relative sum in the presentation of the logic of relations. These indeed occur in a work of Peirce in which the logic of relatives is treated.[109] One scarcely needs to point out that the concept of relative product and that of relative sum are treated dually in Schröder's *Algebra und Logik der Relative*.

Lewis' presentation of the logic of relations in the earlier of his two books resembles that of Schröder's *Algebra und Logik der Relative* in that the relative product and the relative sum are defined and thereby related to each other;[110] in the later work Lewis defines relative product, but neglects to introduce the concept of relative sum.[111]

In the earlier book, Lewis devotes a section to the explication of the logic of *Principia Mathematica*. We note that the sections in which two-valued algebra and the theory of one and many-place propositional functions are systematically presented precede this commentary.

In the section devoted to the explication of the logic of *Principia Mathematica*, points of agreement and disagreement between this logic and the theories presented earlier are indicated. This aids the reader in his understanding of the new logic and makes him aware of the close connection between the older and newer form of logistic. It should also be said that this mode of presentation makes clear the points in which the logic of *Principia Mathematica* significantly improved the earlier systems.

We will make the following remarks.

Lewis' commentary on the propositional logic contained in the first section of *Principia Mathematica* shows that, unlike earlier systems, the method followed does not, strictly speaking, lead to a circular proof; it is here no longer the case that logical laws are assumed in the proof of these laws.

In the logic of *Principia Mathematica* certain expressions containing signs for 'all' and 'some' are primitive concepts; in agreement with standard terminology we will call these expressions quantifiers. In the systematic development of the theory of propositional functions, Lewis represents universal quantifiers as products and existential quantifiers as

108 SSL, pp. 110-111.

109 "A Theory of Probable Inference," Note B, "The Logic of Relatives," *Studies in Logic by Members of the Johns Hopkins University* (Boston, Mass., 1883), pp. 187-203 [28 9].

110 SSL, p. 275, def. 17.02 and def. 17.03.

111 SL, p. 112.

sums. Such an interpretation of quantifiers appears to lead to difficulties if it is recalled that the number of values of the variables which occur in a propositional function need not be finite. Lewis points out these difficulties and shows that they can be avoided if certain assumptions are made; however, he states in a footnote that the method followed here, while not invalid, is neither ideal nor complete.[112] Lewis also shows that the methods used in *Principia Mathematica* in the development of the theory of apparent variables avoid all the difficulties which occur if quantifiers are regarded as products or sums of expressions;[113] it is thereby made clear that these methods are a substantial improvement over earlier methods.

The German mathematician Gottlob Frege is always given a special place in the history of symbolic logic. Lewis succeeded in describing the peculiar position occupied by Frege.

The following points are significant in this connection and are referred to in Lewis' works.

Frege's logical works remained almost unnoticed and in particular had no noticeable influence on the logistic presentation of the mathematical disciplines due to Peano and his colleagues.[114]

These works became historically important due to the influence which they had on Bertrand Russell.[115]

The logistic of *Principia Mathematica* may be regarded as a continuation of Frege's logistic.[116]

Among the logistic works which preceded *Principia Mathematica* and are closely related to it, the contributions of Giuseppe Peano and his colleagues, to which we have just referred, occupy a leading position.

Lewis compares the works of the Italian school collected in Peano's *Formulaire de Mathématiques* with *Principia Mathematica* in a highly instructive manner.

We wish to raise the following points in this connection.

Lewis points out that the two systems are concerned with the same objects,[117] or in other words that their aims can be regarded as identical;[118] this aim may be regarded as the presentation of mathematical disciplines in the form of deductive systems. On the other

---

112 SSL, p. 236.

113 SSL, p. 289.

114 SSL, pp. 114-115 and SL, p. 16.

115 SSL, p. 114.

116 C. I. Lewis, "La logique de la méthode mathématique," *Rev. Métaph. Mor.*, **29** (1922), 455-474 [215 12], esp. 460. Herafter cited as "Log. Méth. Math."

117 SSL, p. 116.

118 SL, p. 22.

hand, Lewis shows that there is an essential difference between the two systems in that *Principia Mathematica* allows as primitives only logical primitive concepts and logical postulates, while in the presentation of arithmetic and geometry contained in Peano's *Formulaire* arithmetic and geometric primitive concepts and postulates serve as primitives.[119]

## V. *Conclusion*

That the works of Lewis represent a considerable advance in the history of symbolic logic is undeniable.

Lewis succeeded in presenting a summary of the entire field by explicating the historical development of symbolic logic from its foundation by Leibniz to the present. In the presentation of the history of symbolic logic which he gave us can be seen the ways in which the development proceeded; an insight is given into the varied difficulties that were overcome. Through Lewis' interpretation of the logical theories handed down to us by historical documents from the standpoint of modern logic, he brought historical studies into a living and fruitful relationship with the study of modern logic.

KARL DÜRR

UNIVERSITY OF ZÜRICH
SWITZERLAND

[119] "Log. Méth. Math.," pp. 458-460.

# 4

## *William Tuthill Parry*

## THE LOGIC OF C. I. LEWIS

### I. *Lewis' Problems*

S YMBOLIC logic is one of Professor Lewis' oldest and strongest interests. His mastery of logic has provided a solid basis for his work
in other fields, as well as leading to important contributions to logic
itself.

Lewis tells us[1] that, from his first contact with *Principia Mathematica*
(PM) when he was Royce's assistant, he was troubled by the paradoxes
of material implication, such as 'A false proposition implies any proposition', 'A true proposition is implied by any'. This, he was convinced,
could not be the implication that forms the basis of logical deduction.
It could not be, for instance, that a theorem of PM follows from the
postulates only in the sense that both happen to be true; for then all
true theorems of any science would follow directly from the assumption
that Socrates was Greek.

The difficulty arose, it appeared, because the logic of propositions
formulated—as in practically all successful calculi of logic—was an *extensional* one, whereas deductive inference depends on the meaning of
the propositions involved, hence requires an *intensional* logic. He writes:

> Two sorts of problems were before me. First and most obviously: Is there
> an exact logic, comparable to this extensional calculus, which will exhibit the
> analogous relations in intension? And is the intensional analogue of material
> implication the relation upon which deductive inference is usually founded?
> Second, there were larger and vaguer questions: Could there be different exact
> logics? If I should find my calculus of intension, it and material implication would
> be incompatible, on some points, when applied to inference. In that case, in what
> sense would there be a question of validity or truth to be determined between
> them? And what criteria could determine the validity of logic, since logic itself
> provides the criteria of validity used elsewhere, and the application of these to
> logic itself would be *petitio principii*?[2]

[1] "Logic and Pragmatism," *Contemporary American Philosophy*, eds. G. P. Adams and
W. P. Montague (New York: Macmillan, 1930), vol. II, pp. 31-51. Hereafter cited as
"Log. Prag."

[2] "Log. Prag.," p. 35.

The problems of the first sort, technical logical problems, led to the development of the system of strict implication, which constitutes Lewis' best known and greatest contribution to symbolic logic. The second sort of problem led him to an interest in 'alternative logics', such as many-valued logics, and ultimately merged with other considerations leading to his conceptualistic pragmatism—an epistemological view into which we shall not inquire.

Of Lewis' other contributions to logic, perhaps the most notable are those to the history of symbolic logic, with which another writer will deal. This study will emphasize his system of strict implication, taking an historical approach, supplemented by critical considerations.

The system of strict implication was designed originally to deal with *implication* (as the converse of deducibility), and related notions such as consistency. It introduces the modal concepts of possibility, impossibility, and necessity, hence is often regarded as primarily a logic of *modalities*.

By surveying the history of theories of implication, we shall see that Lewis' system is a high point in a great (though relatively little known) tradition from which there is still much to learn.

## II. *Ancient Theories of the Conditional*

Discussion of the meaning of the conditional (i.e., the 'if-then' proposition) goes back to the Megarian logicians, Diodorus Cronus and his pupil Philo.[3] Philo gave a truth-functional definition, exactly the same as for Russell's material implication. Diodorus, however, held that a conditional is true "if it neither is nor ever was possible for the antecedent to be true and the consequent false."[4] Since for Diodorus "the possible is that which either is or will be,"[5] the conditional holds for him "if and only if it holds at all times in the Philonian sense." The Diodoran conditional cannot be defined as asserting that the Philonian conditional *is* necessary; but it may be defined as asserting that the Philonian conditional always was and is necessary (and hence will be).

The members of a Diodoran conditional are not propositions in the strict sense, but propositional functions (as they are usually called)[6] with an implicit time-variable.

---

[3] On Megaric and Stoic logic, I follow mainly Benson Mates, *Stoic Logic* (1953).

[4] *Ibid.*, p. 44.

[5] *Ibid.*, p. 37.

[6] The term 'propositional function' should perhaps be reserved for propositional expressions with an explicit variable.

Supposing it is day and I am conversing, Philo would assert 'If it is day, then I am conversing' to be true, while it is false for Diodorus, since it does not always hold. For Diodorus, it does not hold that a false proposition implies any, but a proposition which is always false implies any. 'If atomic elements of things do not exist, then atomic elements of things do exist', was said to hold, the antecedent being always false.

In concrete application, the Diodoran system does not agree with Lewis' strict implication (though some modern writers have identified them); for Lewis, a proposition may be possible though never true, and will not then imply every proposition. However, if we interpret Lewis' '$\diamond p$' ('$p$ is possible') as the Diodoran '$p$ was or is possible', i.e., '$p$ sometimes true', the formulas for strict implication[7] apparently hold for the Diodoran conditional. But an adequate formulation of the Diodoran system would require tense distinctions, omitted in Lewis' as in most logical systems.

Some Stoics (perhaps including Chrysippus) held a different view which seems closer to strict implication:

And those who introduce "connection" or "coherence" say that a conditional holds whenever the denial of its consequent is incompatible with its antecedent; so that . . . the above-mentioned conditionals ["If it is day, I am conversing"; "If atomic elements of things do not exist, then atomic elements of things exist"] do not hold, but the following is true: "If it is day, then it is day."[8]

This is the same as strict implication if the 'incompatibility' is Lewis' (logical) inconsistency. But there is little information about this view, and it may mean something else.

A fourth view, still more obscure, was held by some Stoics:

And those who judge by "suggestion" declare that a conditional is true if its consequent is in effect included in its antecedent. According to these, "If it is day, then it is day," and every repeated conditional, will probably be false, for it is impossible for a thing itself to be included in itself.[9]

The Stoics developed the Megaric logic of propositions; earlier, the Peripatetic Theophrastus had developed a logic of 'hypothetical syllogisms' which may also have paved the way for Stoic logic. But the fragments of these schools shed little further light on the meaning of the conditional.

---

[7] Including those for S5; for if $p$ is sometimes true ('possible'), then it is always true ('necessary') that it is sometimes true.

[8] Sextus Empiricus, quoted by Mates, p. 47 f.

[9] *Ibid.*, p. 48. Cf. B. Blanshard's view: note 118 below.

We notice, though, that Theophrastus overturned Aristotle's doctrine of modal syllogisms. Thus he adopted the principle that the conclusion of a modal syllogism follows the weaker premise (where Aristotle had drawn a necessary conclusion from one necessary and one assertoric premise). Underlying this and other changes one infers a basic difference in intuition of the structure of a modal proposition: Theophrastus consistently took modality as modifying the proposition as a whole rather than the terms.[10]

Both conceptions of modality were recognized in the middle ages. Thirteenth-century scholastics distinguished modal propositions *de re* (Aristotelian) and *de dicto* (Theophrastian).[11] But when propositional logic is taken as basic, as in the great fourteenth-century logicians—and Lewis—the conception of modality seems rather Theophrastian than Aristotelian.

Boëthius, a bridge between ancient and scholastic logic, has rules of propositional logic. Dürr tries to interpret them as strict as well as material implications, with indecisive results because of Boëthius's ambiguity.[12]

## III. *Scholastic Doctrine of Consequences*

In the middle ages, propositional logic appears as the theory of consequences, apparently reaching its high point in fourteenth-century schoolmen such as the Ockhamists Jean Buridan and Albert of Saxony.[13] The term *consequentia* is explained:

A consequence is a hypothetical proposition, since it is formed from several propositions by means of the connective 'if,' or by this word 'therefore,' or an

---

[10] I. M. Bocheński, *Ancient Formal Logic* (1951), §12C; *Formale Logik* (1956) —hereafter cited as FL—§17B.

[11] FL, §29 C.

[12] K. Dürr, *The Propositional Logic of Boethius* (1951). In Dürr's symbolic formulation, most formulas of *De syllogismo hypothetico* hold for both material and strict conditional; some (the second group of class 3) for material but not strict; some hold for neither. R. van den Driessche in *Methodos* (1949) notes that Boethius, to deny 'cum sit *a*, est *b*', writes 'cum sit *a*, non est *b*'. Taking the latter 'cum' as 'et . . . et', he turns all Boethius's rules into valid formulas of the two-valued calculus. I suggest another interpretation. In van den Driessche's 'complete list' of theses of *De syll. hyp.*, each designated as axiom holds in S2 if all conditionals and biconditionals are taken as strict. Only by auxiliary thesis A.2 — $(p \supset q) \equiv (p \cdot -q)$, inferred from the use of 'cum', do derived theses enter (as D. 22) not valid for strict conditionals. If we take 'non' as misplaced in 'cum sit *a*, non est *b*', and transcribe as '— $(pcq)$', don't we save Boethius's rules, taken for strict or Diodoran, as well as Philonian conditionals?

[13] On medieval logic, we follow E. A. Moody, *Truth and Consequences in Mediaeval Logic* (1953), hereafter cited as TCML; and FL.

equivalent. These words indicate that, of the propositions connected by them, one follows on the other.[14]

Consequences were analyzed with great subtlety and fine distinctions. Thus Paul of Venice (died 1429) lists 10 definitions of implication (i.e., 10 statements of the conditions under which a conditional is true), not including the Philonian nor probably the Stoic 'suggestion' view. To be sure, seven or more may be variant definitions of strict implication.[15] But until they are better understood, it would be rash to deny a distinction between any two of them.

We know, e.g., that Buridan objected to the formulation 'It is impossible that the antecedent be true and the consequent false', on the grounds that this would justify the fallacious inference: 'No sentences are negative, therefore some sentence is negative'. For if the antecedent were true, it would exist, and there would be a negative sentence. He holds that it is possible to have no sentence negative (i.e., it might be none is written or uttered), though impossible that 'No sentences are negative' be true. In effect, Moody concludes, Buridan defines implication as the impossibility of the conjunctive '$p.-q$', not the conjunctive '('$p$' is true and '$q$' is false.)'.[16]

While Buridan's definition seems equivalent to Lewis', we must consider, as Moody warns, whether the conceptions of impossibility are the same. First let us note the distinctions the scholastics made among consequences.

First, consequences—i.e., valid or true consequences—are either formal or material. A *formal* consequence, for Buridan and Albert, is one such that every sentence of the same form, if stated, is a valid consequence. (Ockham had used the term more broadly, FL 30.13.) A *material* consequence is one such that not every sentence of the same form holds. Buridan's examples of rules of formal consequence include: 'If $pq$ then $p$'; 'if $p$ then $p$ or $q$'; 'if $p.-p$ then $q$'; 'if $p$ then $q$ or $-q$'; also valid hypothetical and categorical syllogisms and immediate inferences.[17]

---

[14] Buridan, quoted in TCML, p. 66. Albert "gives the same description." Note that this, one of the 'more exact definitions' of 'consequence', lumps together the *proposition* 'if $p$ then $q$' and the *argument* '$p$ therefore $q$', which logicians today usually keep separate.

[15] FL 30.17. Six in some way require the *impossibility* of the antecedent without the consequent; one I take to require the *necessity* of the Philonian conditional; one, like the Stoic connective view, requires *repugnance* (incompatibility) of the contradictory of the consequent with the antecedent. The other two use epistemic concepts.

[16] TCML, pp. 67-69. Buridan's actual definition uses the semantic notion of signification, p. 67. "One proposition is antecedent to another, if it is so related . . . that, both propositions being stated, it is impossible that whatever the first signifies to be so, is so, and that whatever the second signifies to be so, is not so."

[17] TCML, pp. 70-73.

A material consequence is either a *simple* consequence, such that the antecedent without the consequent never could be true; or a consequence *as of now* (*ut nunc*), where it is impossible, given things as they are, though not absolutely impossible, for the antecedent to be true without the consequent. 'No animal is running, therefore no man is running', is a simple material consequence. (We know that men are animals from the meaning of the terms.) 'I see a certain man, therefore I see a deceitful man', when the certain man is in fact deceitful, is a consequence as of now.[18]

The formal consequence holds when $(p.-q)$ is *syntactically* impossible (by logical syntax); the simple material consequence holds when $(p.-q)$ is *semantically* but not syntactically impossible; and the consequence as of now—extended by Buridan to include the consequence "as of then" (FL 30.16)—holds when $(p.-q)$ is false, i.e., it is Philonian implication.

Buridan and Albert state many laws of consequences. Those which they state explicitly, and Moody formalizes in the "system of simple implication," are all contained in Lewis' S3 (the emended *Survey* system), but must be supplemented by principles Moody believes to be implicit. He believes also the C11 of SL is "probably implicit" in the system, which would reduce it to S5.[19] Buridan and Albert prove that an impossible proposition implies any, a necessary proposition is implied by any. Buridan also stated the paradoxical laws for implication as of now: a false proposition implies any, a true proposition is implied by any.[20]

Lewis' strict implication cannot be identified with the simple material consequence, since the asserted implication of his formulas holds as a formal consequence. It could be interpreted either as formal consequence or as simple consequence, where 'simple' means 'formal or simple material'. This distinction was made in my doctor's thesis[21] and its published summary (without benefit of medieval logic):

---

[18] TCML, pp. 73-77; cf. FL, §30 C. Moody compares the distinction of simple material from *ut nunc* consequences with the distinction of Diodoran from Philonian conditionals. But the simple material consequence of Buridan is narrower than Diodoran implication in two respects: it excludes formal consequences, and excludes cases where the Philonian conditional always holds factually but not semantically.

[19] C. I. Lewis and C. H. Langford, *Symbolic Logic* (New York and London: The Century Co., 1932), Appendix II. (See §VII below.) Hereafter cited as SL.

[20] TCML, §15. Buridan is the only scholastic known to have developed laws of *ut nunc* consequence (FL 31.41).

[21] W. T. Parry, *Implication* (1931, unpublished), on file in library at Harvard University.

A distinction is made between "structural" and "intensional" notions. Thus, a proposition is said to be "structurally necessary" (or impossible) if it can be known to be true (or false) by consideration of its logical structure alone. A proposition is "intensionally necessary" if it can be known to be true from a knowledge of the meaning of terms.

In terms of structural necessity . . . , a kind of implication is defined thus: "p structurally implies q" means "it is structurally necessary that p materially implies q." And analogously for "intensional implication." The system of strict implication may be interpreted in terms of these structural notions, or these intensional notions.[22]

Here intension ("the meaning of terms") includes logical intension (= logical structure), so every proposition structurally necessary is intensionally necessary, but not conversely. It is, e.g., intensionally but not structurally necessary that if something is red, something is colored. A structural implication is a formal consequence in Buridan's sense. Intensional implication is the medieval simple implication. (The medieval simple material consequence I would call 'content implication'.) The two definitions of necessity quoted use the epistemic term 'known' (better avoided, as by the Ockhamists); but the structural notions were held to be purely logical. The thesis pointed out that Lewis' example, " 'Today is Monday' implies 'Tomorrow is Tuesday,' " indicates he uses intensional notions, not purely structural. In scholastic terms, he intends simple consequence.

## IV. *A Modern Forerunner: MacColl*

The best medieval logic was ignored in the Dark Ages of logic, as Bocheński would say, that ensued. When the logic of propositions was revived by symbolic logicians, they used extensional functions, hence the Philonian conditional. Some pre-Boolean logicians, notably Leibniz, J. H. Lambert, and G. F. Castillon, developed intensional systems, but worked mostly with the logic of terms; and Lewis' careful study of these moderns in his *Survey of Symbolic Logic* did not reveal anything helpful for the concept of implication.[23] C. S. Peirce knew of the controversy between Philo and Diodorus, but chose to use the Philonian conditional.

Leibniz aside, the only clear forerunner of strict implication in modern times is Hugh MacColl. Bocheński characterizes his papers of

---

[22] Harvard University, *Summaries of Theses accepted . . . 1932* (1933), pp. 332-335.

[23] N. Rescher points out that Leibniz has one interpretation of his system of 1685-6, taking propositions as the 'terms', "which makes it the forerunner of C. I. Lewis' systems of strict implication" (*Journal of Symbolic Logic* 1954); cf. *Journal of Symbolic Logic* 17, 122. Hereafter cited as Jr. SL.

1877-78[24] developing propositional logic as forming in a sense "the high point of mathematical logic before Frege."[25] This is still truth-functional logic. But a paper of 1897[26] gives the essentials of his modal calculus.

His system is developed most fully in *Symbolic Logic and its Applications* (1906) (to which '§' in this section will refer). In addition to $+$, $.$, $'$, for (propositional) alternative, conjunction, negation, MacColl writes 'A$^\tau$B$^\iota$C$^\varepsilon$D$^\eta$E$^\theta$' to assert that A is true, B false, C certain, D impossible, and E variable (possible but uncertain); and 'A:B' for 'A implies B', defined '(AB')$^\eta$' or '(A'$+$B)$^\varepsilon$'.

The symbol A$^\tau$ only asserts that A is true in a particular case or instance. The symbol A$^\varepsilon$ asserts ... that A is *certain*, that A is *always* true (or true in *every case*) within the limits of our data and definitions, that its probability is 1. [§8]

He also uses $\varepsilon$, $\eta$, $\theta$ as propositional variables whose values are propositions of the corresponding modal value.

A proposition is called a *formal certainty* when it follows necessarily from our definitions, or our understood linguistic conventions, without further data; ... It is called a *material certainty* when it follows necessarily from some special data not necessarily contained in our definitions. [§109]

He uses '$\varepsilon$' (and '$\eta$') for either kind of certainty (and impossibility), depending on context.

Lewis does not compare this system with his own beyond saying that MacColl's "is a highly complex system, the fundamental ideas and procedures of which suggest somewhat the system of Strict Implication."[27]

We note, first, that the *proposition* of MacColl is broader than that of contemporary logic, which cannot change its truth-value; it is an 'intelligible arrangement of words' which may be a propositional function.

The *formal certainty* of MacColl is not the structural necessity of our section III, but rather the intensional necessity intended by Lewis. The *certainty* (material or formal) of MacColl is the certainty ($= 1$) of the calculus of probabilities. This, I think, is the *relative necessity* which Lewis distinguishes[28] from the absolute necessity of his system. "Relatively necessary," he says, "means 'implied by what is given or known.'"

24 "The Calculus of Equivalent Statements. . . ," *Proceedings of London Math. Society,* 9, 9-20, 177-186.

25 FL, §41B.

26 "Symbolical Reasoning (II) ," *Mind,* n.s. 6, 493-510.

27 C. I. Lewis, *A Survey of Symbolic Logic* (Berkeley: University of California Press, 1918) , p. 108. Hereafter cited as SSL.

28 SL, p. 161.

Formulas corresponding to those MacColl gives or uses (if I have missed none) all hold in the Lewis system S5.[29] Conversely, he states or uses formulas which give the system S5.[30]

Although MacColl gives, in fairly workable form, essentially the system S5, he is rightly regarded as a forerunner, not the founder, of the system of strict implication and contemporary modal logic. (1) The main reason is that, unlike Lewis, he has no proper deductive *system*. He does not give a set of axioms and rules from which all theorems are proved. He simply introduces formulas *ad libitum*, or uses them implicitly.

(2) Though his symbolism and procedures are very compact and flexible, they have peculiarities which led to the impression that his work was out of the main line of symbolic logic of his day; compare Russell's review of *Symbolic Logic* in *Mind* (1906). For example, the use of propositional variables restricted to certain modal values is convenient, but it was—and is—unusual. And use of the same letter for the restricted variable as for the corresponding modal function (as exponent in the latter case) may confuse some readers. Thus the formula $\eta{:}\epsilon$, any impossibility implies any certainty, seems paradoxical to some; probably, MacColl explains (§18), they confuse it with the absurdity that impossibility implies certainty, i.e., $Q^\eta{:}\ Q^\epsilon$.[31] Also, his doctrine of existential import is unusual in twentieth-century symbolic logic.

Lewis, on the other hand, started on the basis of PM, with symbolism and procedures modeled after that work as far as possible; thereby he made himself more readily intelligible and kept in the main stream.

(3) MacColl's terminology created difficulty, especially his use of

---

[29] An apparent exception are such formulas as: $(y{:}z)\ (y{:}x){:}(x{:}z')$ ' (corresponding to the syllogism Darapti) . But here $x$, $y$, $z$ are restricted to propositions possible but uncertain; hence it is not a real exception. (§§50, 51.) MacColl would regard the absence of a distinction between A and $A^\tau$, A' and $A^\iota$, as a deficiency in Lewis' system.

[30] In §19, he assumes $\theta^\eta{=}\eta$, which gives $A^\theta{:}\ (A^\eta)$ $^\eta$; we can prove $A^\iota{:}(A^\eta)$ $^\eta$; hence, since $A^{-\eta}{=}A^\iota{+}A^\theta$, we have $A^{-\eta}{:}\ A^{\eta\eta}$, which corresponds to C11, the characteristic principle of S5.

Doubt might be raised about substitution of equivalents; for he argues (§21) that the equivalence $(A{=}A^\tau)$ does not imply $A^\iota{=}\ (A^\tau)$ $^\iota$, failing in case "A denotes $\theta_\tau$, a variable that . . . happens to be true in the case considered." I think his supposing $(\theta_\tau)$ $^\tau$ a formal certainty is a fallacy. In any case, since $(A{:}B)\ {:}\ (A^\iota{:}B^\iota)$ "is easily seen to be a valid formula" (§13) , we can prove: $(A{=}B){:}(A^\iota{=}B^\iota)$. He constantly uses substitution of equivalents, which makes no known trouble in his system if not used with Greek-letter subscripts.

MacColl cannot symbolize directly the existence postulate 20.01 of the 1932 system (SL, p. 179), which distinguishes it from material implication. But he exposes as invalid for his system various formulas which hold for material implication; e.g. (§70) , $(AB{:}x)\ {:}\ (A{:}x)\ {+}\ (B{:}x)$ .

[31] Another puzzle: '$\eta^\eta{=}\epsilon$' is very compact; but does it correspond to

'proposition' to include what Russell called a propositional function. The difficulty went beyond terminology, because—unlike Lewis—he seemed not to recognize the distinction.[32]

(4) Lewis did a much better job of explaining the problem of implication in its theoretical and practical aspects than MacColl. Lewis used Russell's emphasis on material implication, and failure to grasp the problem, as a foil to set off his own conceptions. Further, Lewis' system is incorporated in his books, especially his two important works on symbolic logic, well organized and well rounded, in contrast to Mac-Coll's single limited book.

The second and third reasons given explain only why, in fact, Mac-Coll *was* not regarded as founder of Strict Implication; the first and fourth perhaps show also why he *should* not be so regarded. But he deserves high esteem as a forerunner, and is still worth reading.

### V. *Lewis' Early Studies*

Lewis' second publication—his first on implication—was "Implication and the Algebra of Logic."[33] He cites the paradoxes of "the algebra of logic"—a false proposition implies any, a true proposition is implied by any—as indicating that we must distinguish this sense of 'implies' from the ordinary one. Close analysis starts from the definition of '$p$ implies $q$' as 'either $p$ is false or $q$ is true', as in PM. Leaving aside exclusive disjunction:

Two meanings of disjunction remain. The implication of the algebra of logic bears the same relation to the one of these that the Aristotelian "implies" bears to the other. . . . Compare . . . the disjunctions: (1) Either Caesar died or the moon is made of green cheese, and (2) Either Matilda does not love me or I am beloved. . . . The second disjunction is such that at least one of the disjoined propositions is "necessarily" true. . . . If either lemma *were* false, the other would, by the same token, be true. None of these statements will hold for the first disjunction. . . . If 'Caesar died' *were* false, the moon would not neces-

---

'$-\Diamond p \, 3 - \Diamond - - \Diamond p$' or '$-\Diamond p \supset - \Diamond - - \Diamond p$'?

[32] Yet the difference is not as serious as it seems. In Lewis' formulations of 1913 ("A New Algebra of Implications . . .") and 1914 ("The Matrix Algebra for Implications"), he said that his variables symbolized "propositions or propositional functions"; whereas the mature systems of SSL and SL say that the variables stand for propositions. But whatever the values of the variables are said to be, one substitutes— as in PM—propositional functions or propositions indifferently; in fact, in the system itself, almost always propositional functions. MacColl, I think would not have needed to alter his formulas if he had acknowledged the distinction; only his way of explanation, and perhaps sometimes application.

His use of the word 'variable' for 'contingent' is also unfortunate.

[33] *Mind*, 21 (1912), 522-531.

sarily be made of green cheese,—if conditions contrary to fact have any meaning at all. It is this last which the algebra is, according to its meaning of disjunction and implication, bound to deny.[34]

Lewis holds that "the most significant distinction" between the two kinds of disjunction is that only the second, the intensional, is such that "its truth can be known, while it is still problematic which of its lemmas is the true one."

Lewis rightly held that contrary-to-fact conditionals are not explicable truth-functionally. But he has since found that some counterfactuals are not *simply* strict implications (in an absolute sense); e.g., the terminating judgment, 'If I turn my eyes right, this seen appearance will be displaced to the left', where the antecedent is false.[35]

But a surprise awaits us. We are told:

intensional disjunction is not restricted to the purely formal or *a priori* type of (2). Suppose a wholly reliable weather forecast [!] for the sixteenth of the month to be "Warm". This implies that (4) either today is not the sixteenth or the weather is warm. On the supposition made, this is an intensional disjunction. One might know its truth even if one could not find a calendar and were suffering from chills and fever. . . . We may say that extensional disjunction concerns actualities; intensional disjunction, possibilities. But one or more facts being given, the possibilities are thereby narrowed, and an intensional disjunction which is not *a priori* may be *implied*.[36]

Here "intensional disjunction" and the correlative implication, necessity, etc., are *relative* functions like those of MacColl (who is not mentioned). But this interpretation, so far as I know, was never given again, and was explicitly rejected in SL.

Strict implication is introduced: " 'Either Matilda does not love me or I am beloved' is equivalent to 'Matilda loves me implies that I am beloved.' " Using '3' for strict implication, 'V' for intensional disjunction,[37] this *could* be generalized to the equivalence:

(i)  $(p \ni q) = (-p \lor q)$.

[34] *Ibid.*, p. 523.

[35] *Analysis of Knowledge and Valuation* (La Salle, Ill.: Open Court Publishing Co., 1946), p. 212 ff. Hereafter cited as AKV.

[36] *Mind*, 21 (1912), 526.

[37] Lewis' symbols for a given strict or truth-functional constant vary. Disregarding this, we use the symbols of SL, except: (1) For negation, we use a dash —$p$ like the SSL, instead of a curl. (2) For impossibility, we use a curl ∼$p$ where Lewis uses a simple sign, as in the SSL. (Where he uses the compound sign, curl diamond, of SL, we use dash diamond —◇.) (3) For intensional disjunction (strict logical sum) we use 'V'. (Early articles use the wedge, SSL an inverted wedge, SL lacks a sign.) We sometimes alter Lewis' punctuation without notice.

Some indications are given of a calculus of intensional disjunction and strict implication. Lewis tells us (p. 530) that '$p \, 3 \, (pVq)$' is the only analogue of PM's postulates that does not hold for his system. Thus he has, with *modus ponens* for strict implication, also the principles:

(ii)      $(pVp) \, 3 \, p$,           (iii)      $(pVq) \, 3 \, (qVp)$,

(iv)      $[pV(qVr)] \, 3 \, [qV(pVr)](!)$,

(v)      $(q \, 3 \, r) \, 3 \, [(pVq) \, 3 \, (pVr)]$.

He also takes as undefined the conjunction or logical product $p \, q$, not definable in terms of $-p$ and $pVq$, and adds: (vi) $p \, q \, 3 \, p$. (Alternatively, he could "retain both extensional and intensional disjunction.") He lists no theorems or rules of procedure.

But (iv) is a big mistake, repeated in later articles and corrected in SSL,[38] which appeals to intuition

to confirm the fact that "Necessarily one of the three $p$, $q$, and $r$, is true" is equivalent to "Necessarily either $p$ is true or one of the two, $q$ and $r$, is true"—and this last is $pV \, (qvr)$.

This doesn't show that (iv) is wrong, but that it doesn't mean what it seems to. In fact, it *is* wrong. Substitute in (iv) $-p$ for $p$, $-q$ for $q$; then use equivalence (i) to obtain

(vii)      $[p \, 3 \, (q \, 3 \, r)] \, 3 \, [q \, 3 \, (p \, 3 \, r)]$    (!)

By (vii), the identity $(p \, 3 \, p) \, 3 \, (p \, 3 \, p)$ implies

(viii)      $p \, 3 \, [(p \, 3 \, p) \, 3 \, p]$    (!)

(viii) says that if any proposition $p$ (say, 'Some mammals fly') is true, then it is implied by the tautology $p \, 3 \, p$; that is, any true proposition follows logically from a corresponding analytic proposition, hence is itself presumably analytic. This is incompatible with the distinction between contingent and analytic (or necessary) truth.[39]

The first attempt at a complete postulate set for strict implication is in "A New Algebra of Implications and Some Consequences."[40] The variables $p, q, r$, etc., stand for "propositions or propositional functions":

38 SSL, p. 302.

39 These mistakes, long since corrected, show the fallibility of logical intuition. The greatest logicians from Aristotle onward have made serious errors. It is significant that Lewis, by more systematic work, contributed more to strict implication than MacColl, though the latter's logical intuition was less fallible.

40 *Journal of Philosophy*, **10** (1913), 428 ff; "read in brief" 1912. Hereafter cited as Jr. P.

"We reason in the same 'modes' about '$x$ is a man' and 'Socrates is a man.' " The primitive constants are negation, (strict) implication, and logical product. Of 19 postulates, two are equivalences (definitions of 'dilemmatic' [intensional] and 'nondilemmatic' disjunction), 13 implications—three 'optional', and four 'principles of operation' (formation and transformation rules). The rules and optional postulates hold for S2 ('the' system of SL), as do all but two postulates:

**P. 12**     $(q ⥽ r) ⥽ [(p ⥽ q) ⥽ (p ⥽ r)]$,

valid for S3 but not S2, and P. 11, the erroneous (iv). Substitution of equivalents is omitted as unnecessary; its effect can be obtained step by step. A dozen theorems are listed (not proved), including (i). But this system (with the optional postulates) reduces to material implication.[41]

This paper is the first of Lewis' to suggest that implication might be defined as the *impossibility* of the antecedent without the consequent, though the formal system lacks impossibility.[42] It has the first reference I find in Lewis to MacColl, cited as exception to the rule that algebras of logic have been based on material implication.[43]

The next paper, "The Calculus of Strict Implication,"[44] takes negation, intensional disjunction, and extensional disjunction as primitive ideas, returning to (i) as definition of strict implication. The system is equivalent to the previous one, including the fatal (iv). Lewis discusses the paradoxes of strict implication, "that absurdities imply anything, and that the necessarily true is implied by anything."[45] He thinks that if one objects to these, they may be eliminated by changing one postulate (but will later insist they are inescapable). He says: "Pragmatically, . . . material implication is an obviously false logic." SL, p. 238, expresses the point better: if material implication be taken as the converse of deduc-

[41] The reduction, never shown before, is sketched here. First (vii) is proved from (iv). Then
(ix)     $(p ⥽ q) ⥽ [(q ⥽ r) ⥽ (p ⥽ r)]$   (from P.12, vii),
(x)     $[p ⥽ (-q ∨ r)] ⥽ [q ⥽ (-p ∨ r)]$   (from P.19, i),
Transforming $p ⥽ {-}{-}(-q ⥽ p) ∨ p$ gives:
(xi)     $-q ⥽ [-(-p ∨ p) ⥽ p]$ (by x, P. 22, vii).
(xii)     $(p ⥽ {-}{-}p ∨ p) ⥽ (p ⥽ p)$   (from P.5, 18, etc.)
From (xi) (by P.22, x, xii, vii, P.22) we get:
(xiii)     $p ⥽ (-p ⥽ q)$ (!)
(ix), (xiii), and P.29 $(-p ⥽ p) ⥽ p$ correspond to the three principles which Łukasiewicz (1929) showed to be sufficient for the two-valued calculus.

[42] *Ibid.*, p. 432f.

[43] *Ibid.*, p. 430n.

[44] *Mind*, 23 (1914).

[45] *Ibid.*, p. 246.

ibility, we get such results as that each of any pair of true propositions can be deduced from the other, which "is quite surely an absurdity."

Next, "The Matrix Algebra for Implications,"[46] has almost the same system as SSL (cf. next section). The primitive ideas and definitions are the same, including Lewis' first formal definition of strict implication as the impossibility of $p$ and not $q$. The major difference is that this paper postulates as P5 the erroneous formula (vii), equipollent to (iv).[47] The erroneous equivalence 1.8 of SSL is also postulated. Theorems are proved for the first time. Consistency is introduced, defined: $(p \circ q) = - \sim(p\ q)$.[48] The system is called the **Matrix Algebra for Implications**. Consistency also occurs as primitive idea, with negation and equivalence, in a separate Calculus of Consistencies "which has never been developed," which postulates (iv). The system of "The Calculus of Strict Implication"[49] is reproduced as "the system of Strict Implication"; this and the Calculus of Consistencies are shown to be contained in the Matrix Algebra. Most important, it is shown that the system of Material Implication of PM is a subsystem of the Matrix Algebra. The key to this is that the conjunction of $p$ and $p \supset q$ *strictly* implies $q$; so the *modus ponens* of PM is valid. From now on, the system of Material Implication is regarded as a proper part of Lewis' system; but when mistakenly taken as the converse of deducibility, material implication remains a rival of strict implication.

## VI. *The Survey System*

In the *Survey of Symbolic Logic* (1918), Chapter V has the system of Strict Implication (almost the same as the Matrix Algebra above). The primitive ideas: propositions $p$, $q$, $r$, etc.; negation $-p$; impossibility $\sim p$; logical product $p\ q$; (strict) equivalence $p = q$, 'the defining relation'. The definitions:

1.01 *Consistency.* $p \circ q = - \sim(p\ q)$ . Df.

1.02 *Strict Implication.* $p \dashv q = \sim(p-q)$. Df.

1.03 *Material Implication.* $p \supset q = -(p-q)$. Df.[50]

---

[46] Jr. P, 11 (1914).

[47] The other differences, aside from symbolism, are that "Matrix Algebra" has (ix) of note 41 as postulate P6 for SSL's 1.6, and P7 $p = - (-p)$ for SSL's 1.5. But (ix) is a theorem of S3; and Lewis says P7 might be replaced by $p \dashv -(-p)$.

[48] This evidently corresponds to the compossibility of Ockham, TCML, p. 83.

[49] *Mind*, n.s., 23, No. 90, 240-247.

[50] Lewis uses here the subsumption sign '⊂' for material implication, an inverted

1.04  *Strict Logical Sum.* $p \vee q = \sim(-p-q)$ . Df.[50]

1.05  *Material Logical Sum.* $p \vee q = -(-p-q)$ . Df.[50]

1.06  *Strict Equivalence.* $(p = q) = (p \mathbin{3} q)(q \mathbin{3} p)$ . Df.

1.07  *Material Equivalence.* $(p \equiv q) = (p \supset q)(q \supset p)$ . Df.

We here define the defining relation itself [Lewis says], because by this procedure we establish the connection between strict equivalence and strict implication. Also, this definition makes it possible to *deduce* expressions of the type, $p = q \ldots$ But $p = q$ remains a primitive idea as the idea that one set of symbols may be replaced by another.[51]

The *postulates:*

| | | | |
|---|---|---|---|
| 1.1 | $pq \mathbin{3} qp$ | 1.5 | $p \mathbin{3} -(-p)$ |
| 1.2 | $qp \mathbin{3} p$ | 1.6 | $(p \mathbin{3} q)(q \mathbin{3} r) \mathbin{3} (p \mathbin{3} r)$ |
| 1.3 | $p \mathbin{3} pp$ | 1.7 | $\sim p \mathbin{3} -p$ |
| 1.4 | $p(q r) \mathbin{3} q(p r)$ | 1.8 | $p \mathbin{3} q = \sim q \mathbin{3} \sim p$   (!) |

*Operations* for deriving theorems (formation and transformation rules, in Carnap's terms) must be stated precisely, to follow what Lewis calls the logistic method.[52] The rule of *Substitution* has three parts: (i) (Formation rules:) "If $p$ is a proposition, $-p$ and $\sim p$ are propositions. If $p$ and $q$ are propositions, $p q$ is a proposition." (ii) "Any proposition may be substituted for $p$ or $q$ or $r$, etc." (iii) (Replacement of equivalents:) "of any pair of expressions related by $=$, either may be substituted for the other."

2. *Inference.*—If $p$ is asserted and $p \mathbin{3} q$ is asserted, then $q$ may be asserted. (. . . not assumed for material implication, $p \supset q$.)

3. *Production* ['Adjunction' in SL].—If $p$ and $q$ are separately asserted, $p q$ may be asserted.

The major change from "The Matrix Algebra" is correction of the mistake with regard to triadic strict relations made by (iv) and (vii) of section V. As triadic conjunction may be written $p q r$, defined as $p(q r)$

wedge for strict logical sum, and a plus sign for material logical sum. This is his first use of the hook for strict implication; hitherto he used the horseshoe for it.

51 SSL, p. 293. Also in SL, logical equivalence is defined, yet introduced as a 'primitive or undefined' idea of the system of Strict Implication. But how can it be both defined and undefined in the same system? If strict equivalence is the defining relation, why may it not be defined, yet serve as basis for an operation of replacement of equivalents, just as strict implication is defined, yet serves as basis for an operation of inference? On the other hand, if strict equivalence is undefined, the other strict concepts may be defined in terms of it and the truth-functions, as by Huntington (1937).

52 In chapter VI, §3, Lewis states with greater precision rules for the propositional calculus of PM, treated as if it were "simply a set of strings of marks," in accordance with his 'heterodox' view of logistic.

(3.01), so Lewis writes $p$ o $q$ o $r$ for '$p$, $q$, and $r$ are all consistent', defined as $p$ o $(q\ r)$ (3.02). He shows by an example that '$p$, $q$, and $r$ are all consistent' is not equivalent to $p$ o $(q$ o $r)$.[53] Likewise (p. 302), 'Necessarily one of the three, $p$, $q$, and $r$, is true' would be symbolized and defined: $p$ V $q$ V $r = p$ V $(q$ v $r)$. Neither (iv) nor (vii) is assumed.

But we still have the erroneous 1.8.[54] 1.8 is equivalent to the pair:

2.2   $(p\ 3\ q)\ 3\ (\sim q\ 3\ \sim p)$,          2.21   $(\sim q\ 3\ \sim p)\ 3\ (p\ 3\ q)$   (!)

2.21 is wrong: E. L. Post proved that it reduces the *Survey* system to Material Implication.[55] (In fact, it reduces S1, from postulates 1.1-1.7, to Material Implication.)

1.8 was replaced by 2.2 as postulate. The set of postulates 1.1-1.7, 2.2 (called A1-8 in SL), with the original definitions and operations, constitutes the amended SSL system, called S3. This was the first correct and reasonably complete postulate set for strict implication ever given.[56]

I exclude as not 'reasonably complete', though valid, the SSL "Calculus of Consistencies." This takes propositions, $-p$, $\sim p$, $p$ o $q$, and $p = q$ as primitive, and defines: $p\ 3\ q = -(p$ o $-q)$. The postulates: $p$ o $q\ 3$ $q$ o $p$, $q$ o $p\ 3 -\sim p$, $-\sim p\ 3\ p$ o $p$, and $p = -(-p)$. Substitution and Inference are assumed, and: If $P\ 3\ Q$ and $Q\ 3\ R$ are asserted, $P\ 3\ R$ may be. But the logical product is not definable, though Lewis says (p. 318) we need it "to create a workable calculus of deductive inference"; so 1.6 is not expressible.[57]

---

[53] "Let $p=$'Today is Tuesday'; $q=$'Today is Thursday'; $r=$'Tomorrow is Friday'. Then $q$ o $r$ is true. And it happens to be Tuesday, so $p$ is true. Since $p$ and $q$ o $r$ are both true in this case, they must be consistent: $p$ o $(q$ o $r)$ is true. But '$p$, $q$, and $r$ are all consistent' is false" (p. 300). Lewis has also shown (SL 156) that $p$ o $q$ o $r$ is not equivalent to $p$ o $q$ . $p$ o $r$ . $q$ o $r$.

[54] Lewis says of 1.8: "In developing the system, I had worked for a month to avoid this principle, which later turned out to be false. Then, finding no reason to think it false, I sacrificed economy and put it in." ("Log. Prag." 35 n.) No doubt the analogies that do hold between material and strict relations misled him here, as in the case of triadic relations.

[55] Lewis, "Strict Implication—an Emendation" (1920). We need not repeat Post's proof, but give a shorter one using SSL theorems, especially 4.54 $(\sim p \supset \sim q)\ 3\ (q \supset p)$ (!)

[3.42:$\sim p/p$;$\sim -p/q$]  $-\sim p\ 3\ (\sim p \supset \sim -p)$
[4.54:$-p/q$]          $3\ (-p \supset p)$
[3.46]               $3\ p$                                          (1)
[2.3:$\sim p/p$; $p/q$] (1) $=:\ -p\ 3 \sim p$                        (2)
[1.06]  (1.7) (2) $=:\ \sim p = -p$

[56] It is not an independent set; 1.5 is redundant. I would also call sets for S1 or S2 'reasonably complete'. The nearest thing to such a set in an earlier writer is the set (1) — (22) in MacColl, *op. cit.* §11, which might be taken as a postulate set. But no rules of inference are given, so it is no definite system. Even with substitution and replacement of equivalents, which MacColl uses freely, I cannot tell wether AB=BA is a theorem.

[57] Nor can we prove in this calculus all principles expressible in it and provable in S1.

The SSL sketches[58] the extension of strict implication to propositional functions. Notable is the view that, if $\phi x$ is a propositional function, $\sim\phi x$ is a *proposition*, not a propositional function (though $-\phi x$ is a propositional function). "For example, 'It is impossible that "$x$ is a man but not mortal"' is a proposition although it contains a variable." Similarly for $\phi x \mathbin{\prec} \psi x$.

Interpreting '$\Pi\phi x$' as '$\phi x$ is true of every $x$ which "exists,"' we have the law: $\sim\phi x \mathbin{\prec} \Pi-\phi x$; hence strict implication implies formal implication, i.e., $(\phi x \mathbin{\prec} \psi x) \mathbin{\prec} \Pi_x (\phi x \supset \psi x)$. But the converse of neither law holds—unless we take the universal quantifier as meaning 'For every *possible x*', as we might (328-31).

This account is superseded by "Notes on the Logic of Intension" in the Sheffer *Festschrift* (1951). Here Lewis develops a "calculus of predicates," to serve as "convenient basis for an intensional logic of terms." *Predicative functions* (of a single individual variable) $\phi\hat{x}$, $\psi\hat{x}$, etc., are taken as primitive, where "'$\phi\hat{x}$' stands for the *function itself*—for expressions such as 'that $x$ is a man,' ... —not for singular propositions which would be values of the functions." Negation, conjunction, self-consistency, and assertion are applied to the predicative functions; and definitions, postulates, and operations assumed exactly parallel to those of S2 (except that an assertion sign precedes the postulates).

Of functions such as $\Diamond \phi\hat{x}$, $\phi\hat{x} \mathbin{\prec} \psi\hat{x}$ (read as '$\phi\hat{x}$ entails $\psi\hat{x}$'), he writes:

any *intensional* function of functions is such that any value of it is *either analytic or else false*. . . . And, although we are unaccustomed to recognize the fact, any propositional function which is analytic is *for that reason* assertable, and is in fact a *true proposition*; although it still remains a function also, since it still has variable constituents and there are expressions which are values of it. [*Op. cit.,* p. 32; italics in text.]

On this view, 'that $x$ is red entails that $x$ is red' and '$\Diamond$ that $x$ is red' express analytically true propositions, but also functions.

Lewis also says (p. 33) that "the *assertion* of any intensional function, without quantification, is logically equivalent to assertion of the same function with the proper quantification." Thus he says that (1) $\vdash \cdot -\Diamond -\phi\hat{x}$ has the same logical force as $\vdash : (x) \cdot -\Diamond -\phi x$; and (3) $\vdash \cdot \Diamond \phi\hat{x}$ the same as $\vdash : (\exists x) \cdot \Diamond \phi x$.[59]

A model for it made from Group IV, SL, p. 493 f, shows that it does not contain 1.7.

SSL also has a "Calculus of Ordinary Inference," with $-p$, $p \mathbin{\prec} q$, $p\,q$, $p{=}q$ as primitive; but this postulates a false consequence of 2.21.

58 SSL, pp. 320-3.

59 These logical equivalences are disputable. Being a centaur is logically possible; does it follow that there is an actual $x$ such that it is logically possible that $x$ is a centaur?

The present writer holds a third view: that these intensional operators do not turn a propositional function into a proposition. What we mean by saying that it is impossible that $x$ be red and not red, may be expressed precisely by

(a)    $\sim\Sigma_x$ [Red $(x)$ . —Red $(x)$] or — $\Diamond\,(\exists x)$ : Red $(x)$ . —Red $(x)$.

No doubt this can also be expressed by literally predicating inconsistency of a predicate (i.e., predicative function or, better, functor), thus:

(b)    — $\Diamond_f$ [Red $(\hat{x})$ . —Red $(\hat{x})$],

Being red and not being red is not a self-consistent predicate.

But self-consistency for functors ( $\Diamond_f$ ) differs from self-consistency for propositions ( $\Diamond$ ) much as class conjunction differs from propositional conjunction. And (b), like (a), is a proposition, not a propositional function.

SSL (pp. 321-3) also applies the strict concepts to classes. Where $a = \hat{z}(\varphi z)$ and $\beta = \hat{z}(\psi z)$, we have the intensional relation "$(a \, \dashv \, \beta) = (\varphi x \, \dashv \, \psi x)$", distinguished from the extensional "$(a \subset \beta) = \Pi_x(\varphi x \supset \psi x)$". Intensional subsumption implies extensional, but not conversely. He also defines: "$1 = \hat{x}(\zeta x \, \dashv \, \zeta x)$", and "$0 = -1$". Then, says Lewis, since neither "$\varphi x \, \dashv \, (\zeta x \, \dashv \, \zeta x)$" nor "$-(\zeta x \, \dashv \, \zeta x) \, \dashv \, \varphi x$" holds, neither does "$a \, \dashv \, 1$" nor "$0 \, \dashv \, a$". These formulas do not hold for S3, but they do for S4 and S5. It would seem better to define '1' as $\hat{x}(\zeta x \supset \zeta x)$, and so have "$a \, \dashv \, 1$" and "$0 \, \dashv \, a$" in S1. It seems that a logically impossible concept (e.g., being red and not red) should strictly imply every concept, though a merely factually empty concept (e.g., being a centaur) should not.

The reduction of the original SSL system to Material Implication raises the question whether the emended system S3 is so reducible. A Polish logician, M. Wajsberg, answered the question by proving that "$p \, \dashv \, (q \, \dashv \, p)$" is independent of S3.[60]

Study of complex modalities in Lewis' system was initiated by O.

---

[60] In a communication to Lewis in 1927; see "Log. Prag." pp. 35 f; SL p. 492 n.

Such an independence proof is made by what Bernays (1926) called a "'group (in the wider sense of the word)'", i.e., a groupoid, called a matrix by Łukasiewicz and Tarski (1930). Wajsberg's proof used Groups II and III of SL, Appendix II. Groups I-III, found independently by the writer, were used in his thesis (1931) for this and other purposes.

Wajsberg also proposed taking material implication and impossibility as primitive, defining $-p$ as $p \supset \sim p$, and $p \dashv q$ as $\sim - (p \supset q)$ (Monatsch. f. Math. u. Physik (1933), see p. 125). He made a postulate set for S3 on this basis: $(-p \supset p) \, \dashv \, p, p \, \dashv \, (-p \supset q)$, $(p \supset q) \, \dashv \, [(q \supset r) \supset (p \supset r)]$, $-(-q \supset -p) \, \dashv \, -(p \supset q), (p \, \dashv \, q) \, \dashv \, (\sim q \, \dashv \, \sim p)$ (in an unpublished paper I saw in 1932). Of Lewis' operations, neither Adjunction nor replacement of equivalents—except for definitions—need be assumed.

Becker. For reduction of modalities, Becker proposed, *inter alia*, the principles: [61]

1.9 $-\sim p \, 3 \sim \sim p$        i.e., C11 $\Diamond p \, 3 - \Diamond - \Diamond p$

1.91 $p \, 3 \sim \sim p$        i.e., C12 $p \, 3 - \Diamond - \Diamond p$

1.92 $\sim - p \, 3 \sim - \sim - p$        i.e., C10 $- \Diamond - p \, 3 - \Diamond - - \Diamond - p$

Becker's main result was that, adding 1.9 to S3, 1.91 and 1.92 follow, and all modalities reduce to six, viz., $p$, $-p$, and the four first-degree modalities. This system, SL's S5, Becker called the six-modalities calculus. [62]

Becker's work led to Parry's study of modalities in S3. In 1931, he proved the theorems of S3: [63]

(P) 32.2 $- \Diamond - - \Diamond - p \, 3 - \Diamond - - \Diamond - - \Diamond - p$,

(P) 32.23 $\Diamond \Diamond p = \Diamond \Diamond \Diamond p$;

(P) 32.3 $\sim p \, 3 \sim \sim \sim p$.

In 1939, he added a key theorem:

(P) 32.5 $- \Diamond p \, 3 - \Diamond - \Diamond \Diamond - \Diamond \Diamond p$.

Then all modalities of S3 reduced to just 42 (including $p$ and $-p$).

The work (up to 1932) of Wajsberg, Becker, and Parry led to the next stage of development of strict implication, in *Symbolic Logic* (SL).

## VII. *Symbolic Logic*

Lewis, doubtful of certain theorems of the emended SSL system S3, and more doubtful of Becker's reduction-principles, retreated in *Symbolic Logic* (1932), written with C. H. Langford, to a weaker system S2 (with a stricter implication-relation). For more insurance against paradox, he began with an even weaker system S1—both in Chapter VI, by Lewis.

---

61 "Zur Logik der Modalitäten," *Jahrbuch f. Phil. u. phänomenol. Forschung* (1930), 497ff. The first form of each is given as by Becker; the second, as in SL, App. II, except the '—' for negation.

62 The degree of a modality is the number of times '$\Diamond$' occurs when it is expressed solely by '$\Diamond$', '—', and a variable.

Becker tried to form a 10-modalities calculus by adding 1.91 and 1.92 to S3, but they reduce S1 to S5; 1.91, the 'Brouwerian axiom', reduces S3 to S5: Parry, "Modalities in the *Survey* System . . . ," Jr. SL (1939), 137-154.

Becker, and H. B. Smith (1934), proposed the 'generalized Brouwerian axiom' C15 $p \, 3 - \Diamond_n - \Diamond p$ to effect a linear ordering of modalities without reduction. But C. W. Churchman showed that C15' $p \, 3 - \Diamond \Diamond - \Diamond p$ reduces S2 to S5. He rejected B6 (=1.6) rather than either C15 or the infinity of modal distinctions: Jr. SL (1938), 77-82.

63 Numbers preceded by '(P)' are those of Parry (1939), not necessarily indicating first proof; numbers in the 30's are theorems of S3.

The 'primitive or undefined ideas' of S1 and S2 are: propositions, negation,[64] logical product, and logical equivalence, as in S3, with possibility or self-consistency, $\Diamond p$, instead of impossibility. Logical (strict) equivalence (11.03) and the truth-functions $p \vee q$, $p \supset q$, $p \equiv q$ are defined as in SSL. Strict implication and consistency are defined:

11.02 $p \,3\, q \,.=.- \Diamond (p - q)$;        17.01 $p \,o\, q \,.=.-(p \,3 - q)$

Operations are as in S3: Substitution (a) of equivalents, (b) for variables; Adjunction; Inference; formation rules not stated.

S1 has the postulates B1-7 (or 11.1-.7):

     B1 $p \, q \,3\, q \, p$               B5 $p \,3 -(-p)$    (redundant)

     B2 $p \, q \,3\, p$                 B6 $p \,3\, q \,.\, q \,3\, r : 3 \,.\, p \,3\, r$

     B3 $p \,3\, p \, p$                 B7 $p \,.\, p \,3\, q : 3 \,.\, q$

     B4 $(p \, q) \, r \,.\, 3 \,.\, p(q \, r)$

This set is equipollent to SSL's first seven, given the operations and definitions, though there are three variations. J. C. C. McKinsey showed that B5 (1.5) is redundant in either set.[65]

Lewis proves in S1 theorems 12.1-18.92, 19.9-.92. A novelty is the introduction of 'T-principles'; e.g.,

16.1   $p \,3\, q \,.\, T : 3 : p \, r \,3\, q \, r$, where $T = : q \, r \,3\, q \, r$;

19.9   $\Diamond (p \, q) \,.\, T : 3 \, \Diamond \, p$, where $T = : p \, q \,3\, p$.

In general, $T$ is a formula always true by a previous principle, conjoined with another form in the antecedent of a strict implication. It can often be shown that a $T$-principle cannot be proved in a system without the $T$.[66] As principles of inference, the $T$-principles can be used just as if they did not have the $T$.

In Section 5, Lewis introduces the 'consistency postulate'

B8 (19.01) $\Diamond (p \, q) \,3\, \Diamond \, p$,

whose addition to S1 gives S2. In S2, $T$ can be dropped from all the $T$-theorems Lewis actually proved. (But $T$ cannot be dropped in S2 or S3 from the S1-principle $q \,.\, T : 3 \,.\, p \,3\, p$.) He concludes that

although there is no usable principle of inference in System 2 which is not also contained (in more complex form perhaps) in System 1, nevertheless we regard

---

[64] We use '—' for negation where SL has a curl or tilde.

[65] *Bull. Am. Math. Soc.* (1934), pp. 425-27. B5 follows from 11.02.03, B1, 2, 3, 6. Group IV (SL, pp. 493-95) shows that B7 is independent.

[66] Group V *loc. cit.* shows this for 16.1 and 19.9 in S1.

System 2 as superior on account of its slightly greater simplicity. It is this System 2 which we desire to indicate as the System of Strict Implication.[67]

To distinguish the system from Material Implication, Lewis adds an existence postulate in Section 6. For strict implication, unlike material, there must be cases where a proposition $q$ is independent of another $p$ (i.e., $p$ does not imply $q$), yet consistent with $p$ (i.e., $p$ does not imply $-q$). To express 'for some $p$', 'for some $p$ and $q$', etc., existential quantifiers are introduced, and the existence postulate is:

B9    $(\exists p, q) : - (p \mathbin{3} q) \cdot - (p \mathbin{3} -q).$

Universal quantifiers are defined, six rules for proving existence theorems given, and theorems proved. The system so enlarged I call 'S2e'. Existence of at least four distinct propositions is proved in S2e. One must be necessary, one true but unnecessary, one impossible, one false but possible. The postulates are satisfied by certain 4-element matrices (cf. Appendix II), so existence of more than four distinct propositions cannot be proved. Lewis holds that existence of "an infinite number of propositions which are consistent and independent" is "very likely," but "would be a very awkward assumption" (180-1 n).

A purist might object that logic cannot prove 'existence' of contingent propositions, which may presuppose existence of an actual world. On the other hand, if propositional 'existence' is a matter of possibility, it seems existence of an infinity of propositions could be known *a priori*.[68] An alternative is to distinguish Strict Implication from Material by the method of rejection of Łukasiewicz (*Aristotle's Syllogistic*, 1951).

Lewis (191 f.) adds three principles for moving quantifiers in relation to strict implication, e.g.,

21.01    $(p) \cdot \phi(p) \mathbin{3} K : = : \cdot (\exists p) \cdot \phi(p) : \mathbin{3} K,$

where $K$ is any proposition whatever. But $K$ *should* be restricted to propositions not containing a free occurrence of the quantified variable $p$.[68a] Lewis appeals to the reader's intuition of the truth of these principles.[69]

[67] *Ibid.*, pp. 178 f.

[68] Lewis says 'existence' here, like 'mathematical existence', "has to do with the possibility of intellectual construction, or of definite conception which is free from inconsistency" (*ibid.*, p. 182 n).

[68a] Otherwise 21.01 would give: $(p) \cdot p \mathbin{3} p : = : \cdot (\exists p) \cdot p : \mathbin{3} p$; the left member being true, Th. 20.1 $(\exists p) \cdot p$ strictly implies any proposition.

[69] But "If a technique sufficient for demonstrating logical principles which involve functions of the type in question were here available," they would be theorems, like

He then proves such theorems as

21.74    $-\lozenge-p = :\boldsymbol{\cdot}(q):q \mathbin{⥽} p\boldsymbol{\cdot}-q \mathbin{⥽} p.$

For interpretation and application, the choice of a specific form of system is important. Lewis explains in Appendix II why he takes S2 rather than S3 as *the* system of Strict Implication. As S3-theorem had been proven:

(P) 31.31    $p \mathbin{⥽} q\boldsymbol{\cdot}\mathbin{⥽}:q \mathbin{⥽} r\boldsymbol{\cdot}\mathbin{⥽}\boldsymbol{\cdot}p \mathbin{⥽} r.$

I doubt [says Lewis, p. 496] whether this proposition should be regarded as a valid principle of deduction: it would never lead to any inference $p \mathbin{⥽} r$ which would be questionable when $p \mathbin{⥽} q$ and $q \mathbin{⥽} r$ are given premises; but it gives the inference $q \mathbin{⥽} r\boldsymbol{\cdot}\mathbin{⥽}\boldsymbol{\cdot}p \mathbin{⥽} r$ whenever $p \mathbin{⥽} q$ is a premise. Except as an elliptical statement for "$p \mathbin{⥽} q\boldsymbol{\cdot}q \mathbin{⥽} r:\mathbin{⥽}\boldsymbol{\cdot}p \mathbin{⥽} r$ and $p \mathbin{⥽} q$ is true," this inference seems dubious.

Lewis believed, but could not prove, that 31.31 and A8, the distinctive postulate of S3, were independent of S2. Group V showed that these formulas were not provable in S1. So Lewis (p. 496) provided an escape clause:

If it should hereafter be discovered that the dubious principle [31.31] is deducible from the set B1-9, then at least it is not contained in the system [S1 with B9] . . . ; and I should then regard that system . . . as the one which coincides in its properties with the strict principles of deductive inference.

As Parry[70] subsequently proved by an 8-element matrix, 31.31 and A8 *are* independent of S2. This seems to remove any need for S1 except as a subsystem, and to establish on a sound basis Lewis' preference for S2 (reaffirmed in "Notes").

However, Lewis' argument against S3 cannot be accepted as an argument for S2. For, though S2 lacks 31.31, it has a Metatheorem—using as lemma an S2-theorem (P) 21.9 $p \mathbin{⥽} q\boldsymbol{\cdot}=\boldsymbol{\cdot}p = p\,q$:

METATHEOREM OF S2. If $p \mathbin{⥽} q$ is asserted, $q \mathbin{⥽} r\boldsymbol{\cdot}\mathbin{⥽}\boldsymbol{\cdot}p \mathbin{⥽} r$ may be asserted.

     By hypothesis, $p \mathbin{⥽} q$      (1)

     [21.9] $(1) = :p = p\,q$      (2)

     [19.52] $q \mathbin{⥽} r\boldsymbol{\cdot}\mathbin{⥽}\boldsymbol{\cdot}p\,q \mathbin{⥽} r$      (3)

     $[(2)]\ (3) = :q \mathbin{⥽} r\boldsymbol{\cdot}\mathbin{⥽}\boldsymbol{\cdot}p \mathbin{⥽} r$

If the hypothesis were, e.g., (of the form) $p\,q \mathbin{⥽} q$, (3) is implied by the Metatheorem. I see no objection to the Metatheorem as a principle of

---

analogous principles in the "extension of the two-valued algebra to propositional functions," chapter V. Restrictions preventing substitution for $p$ of an expression containing free the quantified variable $x$ should be imposed on theorems 8.3-.43 of Chap. V.

70 *Mind* (1934).

strict implication. But according to the intent of the system, if $Q$ is deducible from $P$, $P \prec Q$. Hence if the Metatheorem holds, 31.31 must be true. (Substituting in this $q - q$ for $r$,) A8 would follow, giving S3. So if S2 states correctly the properties of real implication (the converse of deducibility) as far as it goes, S3 does so more adequately.[71]

The Appendix considers reduction of modalities as suggested by O. Becker. There is a pair of contrary assumptions: C10 $-\lozenge -p \prec -\lozenge - -\lozenge -p$, and—first suggested here, I think—C13 $\lozenge \lozenge p$. Now, since in S2-3 "all necessary propositions are equivalent, it follows that if there is *any* proposition $p$ which *is* necessarily-necessary . . . then *every* proposition which is necessary is also necessarily-necessary; and the principle stated by C10 holds universally."[72] But though the systems require that there be a necessary proposition, there may be no proposition which is necessarily-necessary; i.e., it may be that, for every $p$, $-(-\lozenge - -\lozenge -p)$, or $\lozenge \lozenge -p$, which is equipollent to C13.

One alternative, then, is to add C10. Adding C10 to S1 gives S4, which contains S3. S4 has just 14 distinct modalities, viz.: $p$, $-p$; six affirmative proper modalities, $-\lozenge -p$, $-\lozenge -\lozenge -\lozenge -p$, $\lozenge -\lozenge -p$, $-\lozenge -\lozenge p$, $\lozenge -\lozenge -\lozenge p$, $\lozenge p$; and six negative proper modalities, each negating an affirmative (Parry, 1939).

The other alternative is to add C13 $\lozenge \lozenge p$ to S1, 2, or 3. Adding C13 to S2 gives what Alban called S6; adding C13 to S3 gives S7.[73] C13 is inconsistent with S4 and S5. The systems S6 and S7 have less intuitive appeal than S4. It seems more in accord with the intent of the system to hold that there *are* propositions which are necessarily-necessary.

Lewis writes: "Any two tautologies *are* deducible from one another; and the principles of logic and mathematics, strictly taken, are tautologies."[74] Then '$p \prec p$' is deducible from '$p \supset p$', and we should have:

41   $(p \supset p) \prec (p \prec p)$

(P)   $41.1 - \lozenge -(p \prec p)$ follows from 41 by S1-principles:

[71] Similarly, since $-\lozenge -p = -\lozenge -q$ can be inferred (in S1) from $p = q$, the S3-theorem (P) 31.12 $p = q \cdot \prec \cdot -\lozenge -p = -\lozenge -q$ must be true. Adding this to S2 gives S3 (Parry (1939) 138 n).

[72] SL, p. 499. The clause about C10 is misleading. It is true for S3: S3 has theorem (P) 32.1 $-\lozenge - -\lozenge -q \prec \cdot -\lozenge -p \prec -\lozenge - -\lozenge -p$, so adding a principle of the form $-\lozenge - -\lozenge -Q$ gives C10 as theorem. But S2 lacks 32.1, and adding principles of the form $-\lozenge - -\lozenge -Q$ does not give C10, as a matrix of McKinsey's shows, Jr. SL, (1940). S2 does have a meta-theorem: If a principle of the form $-\lozenge -p$ is asserted, $-\lozenge - -\lozenge -p$ may be asserted.

[73] M. J. Alban, Jr. SL (1943); S. Halldén, Jr. SL (1950). Halldén also makes a system S8 by adding $-\lozenge -\lozenge \lozenge p$ (called C14) to S3. A system could be made adding C13 to S1; Group V shows that B8 is not a theorem thereof.

[74] "Emch's calculus and strict implication," Jr. SL (1936), 77.

[18.7]   $(12.1) = . - \Diamond -(p \supset p)$    (1)

[18.53]   $(41) . (1) . 3 . (41.1)$

By 18.7, $41.1 = 41.11 - \Diamond - - \Diamond -(p \supset p)$. 41.1 is not a theorem of S3 (by Group I), but must be true by the argument above, and by intuition. Adding 41.1 or 41.11 to S3 gives C10 as theorem by 32.1 (note 72). So S4 is the most natural extension of S3.

The most natural extension of S4 is S5, got by adding C11 to S1. A8 (2.2) and B8 are theorems. All modal functions in S5 reduce to first-degree functions—i.e., those which (expressed in terms of '$\Diamond$', '$-$', '$.$') contain a diamond, but no diamond has another in its scope—by such theorems as: $\Diamond (- \Diamond p . q) = (- \Diamond p . \Diamond q)$.[75]

Professor Lewis concludes:

> Prevailing good use in logical inference . . . is not sufficiently precise and self-conscious to determine clearly which of these five systems expresses the acceptable principles of deduction. . . . Those interested in the merely mathematical properties of such systems of symbolic logic tend to prefer the more comprehensive and less 'strict' systems, such as S5 and Material Implication. The interests of logical study would probably be best served by an exactly opposite tendency.[76]

This section has argued that, if we assume S2 is true, and assume that when $Q$ is deducible from $P$, $P$ strictly implies $Q$, then we are forced to accept S3 and S4 as true. These assumptions seem clearly true in terms of either structural or intensional notions.[77] Starting with S1, similar reasoning would force us to S2 and hence S4. I also find C10 to have an intuitive appeal. Such intuitions are fallible, but must be respected till bad consequences appear.

I see no way in which the truth of S4 leads necessarily to that of S5. Plausible alternative interpretations lead to acceptance or rejection of C11, characteristic principle of S5. Thus, if it is intensionally possible that some book is in French (i.e., the meaning of the terms does not exclude a book's being in French), then it is intensionally necessary that it is possible (i.e., it may be known from the meaning of the terms that it is possible).[78]

---

[75] Wajsberg (1933). A modal function, unlike a modality, may contain binary functions.

[76] SL, pp. 501 f.

[77] McKinsey, Jr. SL (1945), 83, shows that every system of modal logic constructed on the basis of his syntactical definition of possibility is at least as strong as S4. The "intuitive basis" for his definition is: "to say a sentence is possible means that there exists a true sentence of the same form. Thus, . . . 'Lions are indigenous to Alaska,' is possible, because . . . 'Lions are indigenous to Africa,' has the same form and is true."

[78] R. Carnap, Jr. SL (1946), 33, interpreting 'necessary' as 'L-true', i.e., logically true, develops systems of modal propositional and functional logic. His interpretation leads clearly, he holds, to a modal calculus equivalent to S5. His method of defining L-con-

On the other hand, as Shen[79] argued, taking '$p$ is possible' as '$p$ cannot be finitely disproved', it may not always hold that, if $p$ cannot be finitely disproved, it can be finitely disproved that it can be finitely disproved. As a possible example, let $p$ be 'there are 50 successive 8's in the decimal fraction of $\pi$', in case no such sequence can be found.

Thus both S4 and S5 deserve attention. The relation of these systems to systems of different origin[80] reenforces this view. But as Lewis says, narrower systems—even narrower than S2 or S1—deserve attention too. Such, e.g., is S0.5, which postulates only principles of first or zero degree.[81] In Deontic Logic, A7 and B7 must be omitted. §X will consider systems which reject the definition of strict implication.

After Chapter VII, on truth-value systems (two-valued or multi-valued), Chapter VIII discusses implication and deducibility. How is a truth-implication $pIq$ related to the deducibility of $q$ from $p$? A truth-implication $pIq$ is a function in a truth-value system whose truth-value is determined by those of $p$ and $q$, with *modus ponens* satisfied non-vacuously.[82]

(1) The truth of $pIq$ does not guarantee that $q$ is deducible from $p$. (2) But from $p$ and $pIq$, $q$ may be deduced, because $(p$ and $pIq)\,I\;q$—or $p\,I\;:\;pIq\,.\,Iq$—is a tautology. (3) In general, $q$ can be deduced from $p$ when and only when $pIq$ is a tautology. (4) That '$p\;3\;q$' has the meaning of either clause of (3) is evidenced by the fact that it is equivalent to '$-\diamond-(p\supset q)$', which may be read '$p\supset q$ is a tautology'.

But tautologies are not limited to truth-functions; there is

the basic trichotomy of consistency, [Tri] "Either $p$ is consistent with $q$, or $p$ is consistent with '$q$ is false,' or $p$ is not consistent with itself," which represents the fundamental tautology of strict implication.[83]

cepts, suggested by ideas of Wittgenstein, includes a concept of 'state-descriptions' which represents Leibniz' possible worlds. Cf. Carnap, *Meaning and Necessity* (Chicago: Univ. of Chicago Press, 1947, 1956), §2.

[79] References to Shen are to very instructive talks with Professor Shen Yuting in 1930-31 and thereabouts, when we were graduate students at Harvard. The argument and example here are credited to Shen in my thesis.

[80] See §VIII F below.

[81] E. J. Lemmon, Jr. SL (1957). Substitution gives formulas of higher degree in S0.5. $T$-principles corresponding to all second-degree principles of S1 occur as instances of $A.(A\supset B)\,.\,3\,B$, where $A\supset B$ is a valid first-degree formula ($=T$). The necessity $L$ of S0.5 can be interpreted as 'It is tautologous by truth-table that'.

[82] Lewis' definition (SL, p. 237 n., less exactly on p. 233) is reworded to cover systems with more than one asserted (designated) value. This definition makes $p\supset q$, $p\equiv q$, $p\,q$, and $(pqv-pq)$ 'truth-implications' of two-valued PC. To exclude the last two, I would require also that $pIq$ may be true with $q$ false.

[83] SL., p. 260.

It is not explained *how* this tautology is fundamental.[84]

The concepts of tautology and strict implication in this chapter seem to be structural. But one passage in the book indicates that Lewis still has in mind intensional notions (which include the structural). In SSL,[85] Lewis had said that 'Socrates is a man' strictly implies 'Socrates is mortal'. He now says:

> The two premises "Socrates is a man" and "All men are mortal" together imply "Socrates is mortal." But does the single premise "Socrates is a man" imply "Socrates is mortal"? If the omitted premise "All men are mortal" is necessarily true (e.g., if 'immortal man' is a contradiction in terms), it does: but if this omitted premise is merely a contingent truth, it does not.[86]

Now 'Socrates is a man' clearly does not *structurally* imply 'Socrates is mortal', because the implication would depend on the meaning of the nonlogical terms; so the implication-relation in question (whether it holds here or not) [87] must be intensional.

## VIII. *Since* Symbolic Logic

In *Symbolic Logic* Lewis believed he had, in the main, solved his problem of developing an intensional logic whose implication is the usual basis of deduction. Without altering the system, he has since dealt with Strict Implication in discussion of Emch's calculus (§X) and of Alternative Logics (§XI), in the 1951 "Notes," and incidentally in AKV. On the many technical problems remaining, much has been done by other writers, as this section briefly indicates.

A. *Other Systems of Strict Implication.* Systems of Strict Implication other than the classic S1-7, and different postulate sets for the classic systems, have been proposed.

Notable is system T, "logique t" of R. Feys (1937). K. Gödel (1933) postulated, for a system equivalent to S4, Gödel's rule:

GöR. If $P$ is a logical law, then $-\Diamond-P$ is a logical law.

---

[84] Nor do I know how, though I have a letter from Professor Lewis (1931) explaining it. I take it he meant 'fundamental for S1'. $-\Diamond-$(Tri) is equivalent to:
$p \circ p . 3 : p \circ q . \mathbf{v} . p \circ -q$, i.e., 17.592 in S1. The converse of 17.592 holds in S2 but not S1 (except as *T*-principle). We might take (Tri$_3$) $p \circ -q . \mathbf{v} . q \circ -r . \mathbf{v} . -(p \circ -r)$ as basic trichotomy; $-\Diamond-$(Tri$_3$) is equivalent to B6. Substituting $-p$ for $r$ in Tri$_3$ gives Tri.

[85] SSL, pp. 332, 335.

[86] SL, p. 165.

[87] Presumably Lewis agrees with Langford's statement, chap. IX, 270, that 'Immortal men are not logically possible' is false, and hence rejects the alleged implication. Langford's examples here suggest *he* has intensional possibility in mind.

T assumed the 2-valued PC, *modus ponens* for material conditional, $p \supset \Diamond p$, $[-\Diamond -(p \supset q) . -\Diamond -p] \supset -\Diamond -q$, and GöR. A 'natural' system, it is equivalent to systems proposed independently: *V3* in Moh Shaw-Kwei (1950), *M* in von Wright (1951).[88] B. Sobociński (1953) showed T has infinitely many modalities—the broadest such system known. T contains S2 but not S3, is contained in S4 but not S3.

Other systems (some reducing to S1-5) are defined by Feys, Parry, Moh, von Wright, Lemmon, *et al.* Either von Wright's $M_1$, "the Logic of Pure First Order [=degree] Alethic Modalities," or his $M_1 + M_0$ ($= \Sigma M_1$), with just the valid formulas of first and zero degrees, is a good basic modal system.[89] A. Schmidt (1950) studies some systems for reducing modalities. He extends the *duality* of possibility and necessity (analogous to that of *or* and *and*) to *quarternality* (using also their negatives).

Huntington's (1937) formulation of a Boolean algebra interpreted as S2 is noteworthy. Its only undefined strict notion is $a \equiv b$, strict equivalence; *a* impossible is defined: $a \equiv Z$.

**B.** *Decision Problem.* Decision procedures in modal logic were given by Parry (1933) and Wajsberg (1933), by reduction to normal form. Parry gave a procedure for formulas of less than second degree; Wajsberg showed also how all formulas reduce to the first degree in a system equivalent to S5. Carnap (1946) has a decision procedure for S5. McKinsey (1941) gives decision procedures (nonpractical) for S2 and S4; extended to S6 by Halldén (1950). A. R. Anderson (1953, 1954, 1955) gives practical decision procedures for S4 and T. Curry (1952) claims to give in effect a decision procedure for S4 by Gentzen-type rules.

**C.** *Matrices.* Finite truth-tables (matrices) may give a simple decision procedure for *n*-valued logics (*n* finite). Contrary to a common belief, none of Lewis' systems is such a logic. As J. Dugundji shows (1940), there is *no finite characteristic matrix* for any of the systems S1-6, i.e., no finite matrix which satisfies just the theses of the system.

Matrices satisfying any of the systems must be Boolean algebras with respect to conjunction and negation (cf. Huntington). Matrices are *normal* if they satisfy conditions corresponding to Lewis' rules. McKinsey gives necessary and sufficient conditions that a matrix be a normal matrix satisfying S2 (likewise, S4) ; and shows how to construct an infinite normal characteristic matrix for S2 (likewise, S4). G. Bergmann (1949, 1956) characterizes the (finite and infinite) normal matrices for S5; one of the

---

88 System W of H. S. Leonard (1951), made by a special use of 2-valued truth-tables contains and may be equivalent to T.

89 Since the formation rules of S2-3 do not hold for $\Sigma M_1$, I would no longer put it in the S series (as 'S .1'); cf. Lemmon.

two types of finite matrices had been found by P. Henle (SL). Halldén (1949) has a 3-element characteristic matrix for a subclass of S5-theses.

D. *Number of Modalities and Functions.* S5 has six distinct modalities (Becker); S4 has 14 and S3 42 (Parry). A matrix of McKinsey's (1940) shows that S2 (also T), hence weaker systems, have infinitely many modalities, no two of different degree being equivalent. Distinct functions of one variable are infinite in S4 and weaker systems (McKinsey, 1941). S5 has 2 to the power (2 to the power $2^n + n - 1$) distinct functions of $n$ variables (Carnap, 1946).

E. *Functional Calculus.* An adequate language requires functional calculus. First steps in this direction for modal logic were taken by Langford,[90] with quantified individual and functional variables.

Ruth Barcan (later Marcus),[91] adds quantification for individual variables to S2. The implications of ordinary functional calculus hold as strict implications. The distinctive additional assumption is:[92]

11. $\Diamond(\exists\alpha)A \ni (\exists\alpha)\Diamond A$.

This system, S2¹, is extended to S4¹ by adding C10.1 $\Diamond\Diamond A \ni \Diamond A$. These systems are further extended (1947) to functional calculi of the second order.[93] Lewis (1951) expressed general agreement with this development.

Carnap (1946) starts with 'semantical systems' for ordinary propositional and functional logic, and corresponding modal systems with logical necessity N; he goes on to corresponding calculi, i.e., syntactical systems. His modal propositional calculus is equivalent to S5. His functional calculi are of first order with identity.

F. *Relation to Other Systems.* Lewis dealt extensively with Boolean algebra—'the Boole-Schröder Algebra'—in SSL and SL, and made it a 2-valued algebra of propositions by adding a postulate $a = (a=1)$, (or, for every $a$, $a=1$ or $a=0$). He did not remark that systems of Strict Implication are peculiar forms of Boolean algebra (adding a weaker postulate) till Wajsberg, Parry, and Henle pointed it out. This fact was exploited by Huntington and McKinsey; *Formal Logic* (1946) of A. A. Bennett and C. A. Baylis is the first book to use it systematically. Lewis still felt that "Boolean algebra is a rather unsatisfactory form for any

---

[90] SL, Chap. IX.

[91] Jr. SL (1946), 1.

[92] As in note 59, doubt arises: if it is possible that a centaur exists, must there be an actual thing which is possibly a centaur?

[93] A. N. Prior (1956) shows that, adding Łukasiewicz's rules for existential quantifier to a system equivalent to S5 (with Gödel's Rule), assumption 11 of S2¹ is a theorem.

calculus of logic and, in any case, is more usefully restricted to its usual extensional interpretation as a logic of classes" ("Notes," 1951). But he must have in mind the usual 'mathematical' form of Boolean algebra, not a logistic form.

McKinsey (1941) set up a correspondence between S4 and topology (suggested by Tang Tsao-Chen, 1938). A 'topological formula' is true for every topological space if and only if the corresponding sentence is provable in S4.

McKinsey and Tarski (1948), after relating S4 to closure algebras, give three methods of translating Heyting's propositional calculus into Strict Implication, such that a formula holds for Heyting if and only if the corresponding formula holds in S4. Thus one may replace a variable $p$ in Heyting by $-\Diamond-p$, and Heyting's disjunction, conjunction, implication, and negation, respectively, by v, •, ᧨, $-\Diamond$. Gödel (1933) had the other two methods as conjectures. These translations help us grasp Intuitionism; they do not work for S5. Not all formulas of S4 are thus translated.

G. *Non-Alethic Modalities.* Von Wright's *Essay in Modal Logic* (1951) calls necessity, possibility, and contingency 'alethic modes or modes of truth'. There are also *epistemic* modalities: verified (known to be true), falsified, and undecided; he finds a strict analogy between these and alethic modalities. And there are *deontic* modalities: obligatory, permitted, forbidden, applied to acts. These are analogous to alethic modalities, but lack a principle corresponding to A7: we cannot assert that if an act is forbidden, it is not performed. The quantifiers he calls 'existential modes', having a close analogy to modalities. Of the growing literature on non-alethic modes, I can list only two items: Prior's *Formal Logic* (1955), which also mentions studies of time-distinctions, imperatives, theological modes, etc.; and Lemmon (1957), who has two series of systems interpretable as epistemic and deontic, parallel to but weaker than corresponding Lewis modal systems. Thus Strict Implication and its modifications have a variety of useful interpretations.

## IX. *Criticism of Strict Implication*

Let us group the criticisms of Strict Implication into three main kinds: (A) Those which are rooted in objection to intensional logic in general (though some turn out to be really objections to a certain form of intensional logic) ; (B) objections which amount to charging incompleteness of some form of the system; and (C) objections to the paradoxes of Strict Implication: these lead to alternative systems, to be discussed in the next section.

**A.** *Objections to Intensional Logic.* Some eminent logicians like Russell, Leśniewski, and Quine resist or suspect nonextensional forms of logic. The fact that early successes in symbolic logic seem due to the extensional viewpoint may influence them. The objection may take the form of finding specific difficulties in use of intensional logic. An example is the following argument from Quine.[94] A logical truth is: (i) "9 is necessarily greater than 7." We also have a truth of astronomy: (ii) "The number of planets = 9." Then, interchanging equal terms, we get a false conclusion: (iii) "The number of planets is necessarily greater than 7." The solution is that, in a modal context, terms may not be interchanged on the basis of identity of denotation such as (ii) states, but only on the basis of identity or equivalence of connotation.[95]

Quine has an objection which applies also to the exposition and terminology of PM, but is more serious in Lewis' case. Implication, he holds,[96] is a semantic relation, properly expressed by putting 'implies' between the *names* of statements, not a statement connective like 'if-then' or '⊃'.

We may write:
(9) 'All men are mortal' implies 'all white men are mortal',
... but never:
(11) All men are mortal implies all white men are mortal
on the analogy of
(12) If all men are mortal then all white men are mortal,

(12) being a conditional, not an implication.

Iteration, as in ' $(p \supset q) \supset r$' or ' $(p \strictly q) \strictly r$', he says, shows that we have to do with a form of statement composition—a conditional (truth-functional or not), not a relation of implication. He has no objection to distinguishing *logical implication,* a semantic relation exemplified in (9), from the trivial semantic relation of material implication. But he is reluctant to admit a need for non-truth-functional *conditionals.*[97]

Lewis, like PM, ignores these distinctions in his verbal exposition. It would be more correct to read '$p \strictly q$' as 'If $p$ then necessarily $q$', or better, 'Necessarily, if $p$ then $q$', rather than as '$p$ (strictly) implies $q$'. But it is

[94] "Notes on Existence and Necessity," Jr. P. (1943), 113.

[95] Carnap handles such problems well in *Meaning and Necessity.* He calls the above an example of 'the antinomy of the name-relation'. See also A. Church, Jr. SL, 8, 45.

[96] *Mathematical Logic* (1940, 2nd ed. 1951), §5.

[97] Quine leaves a loophole for iteration of implication: "If we were willing to reconstrue statements as names of some sort of entities, we might take implication as a relation between these entities rather than between the statements themselves" and thus dissolve the distinction between implication and the conditional. He finds such entities too obscure. This concession is of no value to Lewis, who holds that all true propositions have the same denotation, viz., the actual world: AKV, pp. 50-2.

convenient to have a verbal form which, like the symbolic, puts the sign between the letters. ('*p* only if *q*' for the material conditional is correct but confusing.) Besides, can't we write 'John's being a man implies John's being mortal', or 'That John is a man implies that John is mortal', without quotes around antecedent and consequent?[98]

This part of the objection really concerns Lewis' verbal rendering rather than his system proper. As to the need for non-truth-functional conditionals: such functions are apparently not so necessary in mathematics, but in logic they are, if not necessary, at least very convenient for problems of the sort at hand.

Somewhat similar would be the justified objection that Lewis fails to distinguish the variables $p$, $q$, $r$, . . . of his object language from the syntactical variables he needs for rules of procedure. Thus he writes his rule of inference: 'If $p$ has been asserted and $p \exists q$ is asserted, then $q$ may be asserted', $p$, $q$ being propositional variables of the object language. This would justify use of *modus ponens* with concrete propositions, but does not justify directly the inferences actually made in his system. Logistic method requires a rule in terms of syntactical variables which take any well-formed formula of the system as value. He might write, e.g., 'If $P$ and $P \exists Q$ have been asserted, then $Q$ may be asserted', using capitals for syntactical variables. Some such change is often made by Lewis' successors, thus meeting the objection.

**B.** *Objections which Charge Incompleteness.* Of these technical objections, the most important is that charging failure to satisfy the deduction theorem. Articles by Ruth Barcan Marcus[99] and Moh Shaw-Kwei[100] throw light on this question.

We must distinguish the simple form of deduction theorem from generalized forms. The simple form states that, if B can be proved on the hypothesis A, using any principles of the logical system presupposed, then we may assert that A implies B—'implies' standing for some kind of conditional or implication. For 2-valued logic, the simple deduction theorem holds, in the form:

D1.   If A⊢B, then ⊢ (A⊃B)
i.e., if A yields B, then (A⊃B) may be asserted.

Generalized forms of deduction theorem hold for 2-valued logic. The usual form of generalized theorem is:

98 Cf. AKV, p. 49 f.

99 R. C. Barcan, "The Deduction Theorem . . . ," Jr. SL (1946), 115; R. B. Marcus, "Strict Implication, Deducibility, . . ." Jr. SL (1953), 234.

100 "The Deduction Theorems . . . ," *Methodos* (1950), 56.

D2. If $A_1, A_2, \ldots A_n \vdash B$, then $A_1, A_2, \ldots A_{n-1} \vdash A_n \supset B$,

where the antecedent abbreviates 'B is provable on the hypotheses $A_1, A_2, \ldots A_n$'. A generalized theorem may also take the conjunctive form:

D3. If $A_1, A_2, \ldots A_n \vdash B$ then $\vdash (A_1 \cdot A_2 \cdot \ldots A_n) \supset B$.

For a system of Strict Implication, there may also be forms with the consequent a strict implication. Thus corresponding to D1, D2, D3, would be D1′, D2′, D3′, respectively; e.g.,

D1′. If $A \vdash B$, then $\vdash (A \; 3 \; B)$.

A form weaker than D3, after Moh, p. 60, may be called the $T$-conjunctive form D3t—(similarly D3t′):

D3t. If $A_1, A_2, \ldots A_n \vdash B$, then $\vdash (A_1 \cdot A_2 \cdot \ldots \cdot A_n \cdot T) \supset B$, where $T$ is a conjunction of theorems of the system.

Which of these hold for Strict Implication? *None* of the forms holds for S1, S2, or system T; for in these systems $(\Diamond A = \Diamond B)$ is provable on the hypothesis $A = B$ (by replacement), but neither $(p = q) \supset (\Diamond p = \Diamond q)$ nor $(p = q) \; 3 \; (\Diamond p = \Diamond q)$ is a theorem.[101] So D1 and D1′ do not hold for these systems, hence none of the generalized forms.

The material forms D1, D2 (and the $T$-conjunctive form D3t′, hence D3 and D3t) hold for S3, 4, 5. (Results for S3 are in Moh.) But this is not enough. As Dr. Marcus says, at least *D1′ should hold* for Strict Implication; for if B follows from A, B must be deducible from A, and that is *what 'A 3 B' is supposed to mean.*

Our argument in §VII amounted to this: assuming the simple deduction theorem D1′ holds for Strict Implication—as it must, if strict implication is the converse of deducibility—we are led on from S1 to S2, hence to S3, hence to S4. (None of the systems S1, 2, 3 contains, e.g., the theorem $q \; 3 \cdot p \; 3 \; p$, though $p \; 3 \; p$ is provable from any hypothesis in these systems. So D1′—hence D2′ and D3′—fail for S1, 2, 3.)

For S4 and S5, D2, hence D3 and D1, hold; also the strict conjunctive form D3′, hence the strict D1′, hold. But the strict D2′ does not hold unconditionally for S4 or S5. "Although A, $A \supset B \vdash B$ can be shown in S4 and S5, $A \; 3 \; ((A \supset B) \; 3 \; B)$ does not always have a designated value" (by

[101] Their independence is shown for S1, 2 by Parry's 8-element matrix; for S1, S2, T by McKinsey's infinite matrix (1950), also by Moh's 8-element matrix (from Parry's), p. 73, ad *V3*.

Group III, SL) .[102] However, D2′ holds for S4, 5 if the following condition is satisfied:

CD.   $A_1 = -\Diamond -H_1, A_2 = -\Diamond -H_2, \ldots A_{n-1} = -\Diamond - H_{n-1}$

Dr. Marcus raises but does not answer the question, whether absence of D2′ "makes S4 or S5 inadequate for a systematization of the concept of deducibility, as Rosenbloom contends." This question is easy to answer. For $n = 2$, D2′ would destroy Lewis' system. A, B ⊢ A in any Lewis system; hence D2′ would give A ⊢ B ꓤ A (!), hence A ꓤ (B ꓤ A) (!), which reduces the system to Material Implication. Lewis' system aside, it is clear intuitively that A follows from the hypothesis of A and any proposition B; but it is not the case that, given A as hypothesis, it follows that A is deducible from B. We conclude (with Vredenduin Jr. SL 19, 294) that it is unreasonable to criticize Strict Implication for lacking D2′.

Our final conclusion on this topic is that the systems S1, S2, T may fairly be criticized for lacking any of the suggested forms of deduction theorem; and S3, for lacking the strict simple form D1′—the critical test; but S4 and S5 satisfy every form of deduction theorem that may reasonably be demanded.

An objection of 'semantic noncompleteness' is raised by Halldén[103] against S1-3 and generalized by McKinsey.[104] This criterion, like that of the deduction theorem, favors S4 and S5.

## X. *The Paradoxes and Rival Systems*

A. *The Paradoxes of Strict Implication.* We come to the major criticism raised against Strict Implication in all its forms: objection to the

---

[102] Marcus (1953), p. 235. All the results of this paper are said to hold for the corresponding functional extensions of the Lewis systems. Her 1946 paper considered only two systems, equivalent to the functional extensions of S2 and S4.
   The simple form D1′ was established for S5 by Carnap (1946).

[103] Jr. SL (1951), 127. There are formulas of the form $P \vee Q$, where $P$ and $Q$ have only one variable apiece, but no variable in common. If such a formula is true, at least one of its alternants must be always true, in any "normal interpretation,"—i.e., one in which truth-functions and variables are interpreted in the usual way, regardless of interpretation of the diamond. The formula
(H) $-[\Diamond (p \bullet -p) \ni p \bullet -p] \vee [\Diamond (q \bullet -q) \ni q \bullet -q]$
holds in S1, but neither alternant is a theorem of S3. (The second alternant would hold if D1′ were added as rule to S1; so this incompleteness implies incompleteness with respect to the deduction theorem.) Hence S1, S3, and intermediate calculi are not complete with respect to normal interpretations.

[104] Jr. SL (1953), 109. Dropping the restriction to one variable apiece, McKinsey calls a system 'unreasonable in the sense of Halldén' if a formula $P \vee Q$ is provable, where $P$ and $Q$ have no variable in common and neither $P$ nor $Q$ is provable. He proves that neither S4 nor S5 is unreasonable in this sense.

'paradoxes of strict implication' as principles of 'real' implication (the converse of deducibility). The two most important—call them 'the major paradoxes'—are: (1) An impossible proposition implies any; and (2) A necessary proposition is implied by any.[105] S2 and stronger systems have these in the strict forms: (SL) 19.74 $-\Diamond p \mathbin{3} . p \mathbin{3} q$, and 19.75 $-\Diamond -p \mathbin{3} . q \mathbin{3} p$. S1 and weaker systems have them only with the main relation material[106] or as $T$-principles, which makes little difference in their acceptability. Other formulas which seem to be paradoxes—as (3) Any two necessary propositions are strictly equivalent (19.84)—are generally corollaries of the major paradoxes.

No one, I think, has questioned the principle that if $p$ is impossible, then $(p . -q)$ is impossible. From this, by the definition of strict implication, the first paradox follows immediately.[107] This puts the onus for the paradox squarely on the definition; hence one who rejects the paradoxes must reject the definition. This would seem to entail an obligation to present an alternative system of implication—a task which the critics have undertaken to greater or less extent. The rival systems or fragments of systems range also from slight variations on Strict Implication to radically different conceptions.

Paradoxes (4) $p . -p . \mathbin{3} q$ and (5) $p \mathbin{3} . q \vee -q$ may be derived from the major ones, but may also be proved otherwise, as Lewis has shown. E.g., $p . -q . \mathbin{3} p$ gives (4) by the law of the Antilogism $(p \, q \mathbin{3} r . \mathbin{3} . p -r \mathbin{3} -q)$ and double negation. These paradoxes are not avoided by simply dropping the definition of strict implication. Systems of entailment may be divided into three types thus: those which retain '$pq$ implies $p$' (Simp) and Antilogism, like Lewis, hence have paradox (4); those which reject Simp to avoid the paradox (as Nelson); and those which reject Antilogism for this reason (Analytic Implication).

**B.** *Stricter Implication.* Systems of 'Stricter Implication' are ones which retain paradoxes (4) and (5) while rejecting (1) and (2). Such are the systems of Emch and Vredenduin.

A. F. Emch (Jr. SL [1936], 26ff., 58) defines a 'logical implication', said to be narrower than strict implication, in terms of a singulary 'logical consistency' $Op$, said to be wider than Lewis' possibility. But, as Lewis pointed out (*ibid.*, 77ff.), Emch's system contains analogues of every law of S2; e.g., an *inconsistent* proposition implies any. However, Emch's

---

[105] These two paradoxes are stated explicitly by Ockham, Buridan, Albert of Saxony, and Radulph Strodus (Ralph Strode): TCML, pp. 74, 87 f.; Bocheński, FL 31.14-.15.

[106] Cf. Halldén, Jr. SL (1948), 138.

[107] Albert of Saxony (following Buridan?) proves this paradox in precisely this way: Bocheński, *loc. cit.*

system is not as pointless as it seems: it makes sense if the wider $Op$ is interpreted as absolute possibility, and the narrower $\Diamond p$ as the relative possibility of the calculus of probabilities.[108]

P. G. J. Vredenduin[109] takes an implication relation as primitive. He accepts Lewis' arguments in favor of paradoxes (4) and (5), but rejects (1) and (2), since "it is not obvious that there are no other kinds of impossible propositions" than those from which a proposition of the form $p . -p$ can be derived. This may be so; but there are probably few who reject (1) and (2) who do not at least feel uneasy about (4) and (5).

C. *Nelson's Entailment.* A long line of logicians who studied at Harvard,[110] stimulated by Lewis, Sheffer, and others, has wrestled with the paradoxes of implication. E. J. Nelson's system is best known.[111] He defines *entailment* in terms of *consistency*, taking both as relations of meaning of propositions in relation to one another. His *primitive ideas*: Propositional functions, Conjunction $pq$ (not a "mere aggregate" but a unity which preserves the "joint force" of $p$ and $q$), Consistency $poq$, Contradiction $-p$, and Intensional equivalence $p = q$ (also defined). He *defines*: Inconsistency $p/q . = . -(poq)$, Entailment $pEq . = . p/-q$. His *postulates*: (1) $pEp$, (2) $p/q . E . q/p$, (3) $pE--p$, (4) $pEq . E . poq$, (5) $p \neq q \neq r . E\colon pEq . qEr . E . pEr$, (6) $pq . = . qp$, (7) $pqEr . E . p-rE-q$. Some *theorems*[112] listed (1930): (a) $p/-p$, (c) $pop$, (e) $pEq . = . -qE-p$, (j) $pqEr . = . p-rE-q . = . q-rE-p$, (k) $pqor . = . proq . = . qrop$. He also proved (1929): 2.8 $p = --p$, 5.4 $poq . = . qop$.

Theorems of this system proved in my thesis: (c′) $p-p \, o \, p-p$, 8.3 $po-p \, (p-p)$ [c′, k, 5.4], 8.5 $p-(p-q) . Eq$, 8.54 $po-p-(-p-p)$, 8.55 $po-p-(pp)$ [8.5 $(-p$ for $q)$, etc.], 8.6 $pqEr . = . pE-(q-r)$, 8.66 $pE-(-q-(p-q))$.

---

[108] Emch (Jr.SL 1937), found this interpretation acceptable after Lewis's analysis. But this system has a possibility relative to only one constant hypothesis, whereas a calculus of probabilities requires possibility relative to any consistent hypothesis.
As N. Yonemitsu (Jr.SL, 19, 66) points out, von Wright's (1953) system of relative possibility is incomplete. With SL p. 161, I interpret '$p$ is possible relative to $H$' as '$p \, o \, H$' or '$\Diamond (p . H)$'.

[109] Jr.SL (1939), 73.

[110] E.g., David Yule, *Theories of Abstract Implication* (unpublished thesis, 1921); later, Nelson, Parry, Bronstein, etc.

[111] "Intensional Relations," *Mind* (1930), 440; thesis, *An Intensional Logic of Propositions*, (1929; in Harvard library); *Monist* (1933), 268.

[112] Needed for *my* theorems. He mentions (1930) as rule of inference only *modus ponens* for E. His thesis lists substitution for variables, replacement of intensional equivalents, etc.

Our theorems suggest new criticisms of the system.[113] (i) The paradoxes of consistency are startling: $c'$, 8.3.54.55. They stem from post. 4 and (c). I fail to grasp Nelson's view that $p-p$ is consistent with itself.

He states (1933), 281f.:

> If at any place in a symbolic statement, an additional mark does not add to the logical significance, that mark should be dropped out. . . . We might formulate this as a principle of significance: pp. . . . [sic] must be given no significance, either in operations or in inference, beyond that possessed by p.

This seems to reduce 8.55 to $po-p$, contradicting theorem (a).[114]

(ii) Nelson (1930) rejects '$p$ entails $p$ or $q$', "because from an analysis of $p$ we cannot derive the propositional function '$p$ or $q$' where $q$ is a variable standing for just any other propositional function whatsoever." I agree. But if we define '$p \vee q$' as $-(-p-q)$, 8.66 becomes 8.66a $pE \cdot q \vee p-q$. This seems no better than '$p$ entails $q$ or $p$'.[115]

Suggestive of Nelson's ideas is Duncan-Jones's [116] '$p$ invokes $q$', $pNq$, defined: $pNq \cdot =_{Df} \cdot pEq \cdot - (\exists r,s) \cdot p = rs \cdot rEq$. He must reject '$pNp$', '$pN--p$', '$pqNqp$';[117] so 'invocation' is not likely to have much appeal as an alternative to strict implication.[118]

D. *Analytic Implication*. The present writer[119] has developed a

---

[113] Critics are: J. Bennett, *Mind* (1954), 451; D. Bronstein, *Mind* (1936), 157, *ibid.* (1937), 127; cf. Nelson's reply, *ibid.* (1936), 551.

[114] 8.3.54.55 may be avoided by certain restrictions on post. 7, hence on (k). But I find (k) less paradoxical than (c).

[115] Other criticisms: (iii) Nelson's definition of entailment is criticized in D below. (iv) Rejecting '$pqEp$', Nelson put a much-criticized condition in post. 5, so it cannot degenerate to instances of '$pqEp$'. But he still has theorems of this form: 8.5 gives by substitution $p-(p-p)Ep$. (v) He later (1933, '36) relented somewhat in his opposition to '$pqEp$'. He suggests restrictions on post. 7 to permit asserting '$pqEp$' without '$p-pE-q$'. Here he approaches Analytic Implication. But adding '$pqEp$' leads to contradiction in his system without 7. From $p-pEp$ follows $p-p/-p$ (by definition); but he would also have $p-pE-p$, hence $p-po-p$ (by 4).

[116] A. E. Duncan-Jones, "Is Strict Implication the same as Entailment?" *Analysis* (1935), 70. His entailment is discussed below.

[117] Any of these would give by substitution a formula of the form $p-pNQ$; but $p-pNQ \cdot = \cdot -p-QN-p$; the second equivalent never holds, by definition of N, so the first never holds.

[118] It might appeal to Brand Blanshard: *The Nature of Thought*, vol. II (1940), 395f. He finds '$p$ implies $pp$', '$pq$ implies $q$', paradoxical, also—like an unknown Stoic (§II)— '$p$ implies $p$'. Of the last, "it is hard to make sense," he says ;"if the two $p$'s stand for the same proposition, it is meaningless to say that one can be deduced from the other, for there are no 'one' and 'other' to be found." But if $p$ is asserted in a system (as postulate or theorem), then $p$ may be asserted in the system (e.g., as lemma for a later theorem). This seems to justify the deducibility of $p$ from $p$.

[119] Works cited, in notes 21, 22; and "Ein Axiomensystem . . . ," *Ergebnisse e. Math. Kolloq.* (1933), p. 5f.

radically different calculus, with none of the five paradoxes of Strict Implication, nor Nelson's paradoxes of consistency. The starting point is the view expressed in class by H. M. Sheffer: that the conjunction $pq$ really implies $p$, but that not always does $p$ imply $p$ or $q$. What is wrong with the latter? If a system contains the assertion that two points determine a straight line, does the theorem necessarily follow that either two points determine a straight line or the moon is made of green cheese? No, for the system may contain no terms from which 'moon', etc., can be defined. In general, for *analytic implication,* as I call it, a formula will not be valid if it permits the introduction of any term whatsoever in the consequent regardless of the antecedent; for in such case the terms appearing in a system would not be limited to those definable in terms of its primitive ideas. Hence the basic principle of analytic implication: *No formula with analytic implication as main relation holds universally if it has a free variable occurring in the consequent but not the antecedent.* I call this the *Proscriptive Principle* (cf. Sheffer's 'prescriptive principles', i.e., rules of procedure).

Besides formulas *directly* proscribed, others are indirectly ruled out as leading from accepted to nonaccepted formulas. Thus Transposition, 'if $p$ implies $q$, then $-q$ implies $-p$', derives a proscribed formula from any implication which eliminates a variable from its antecedent. Antilogism holds if and only if the terms of each proposition are definable by the terms of the other two; so it holds for categorical syllogisms, but not always for '$pq$ implies $p$'.

A definition of implication in terms of (in)consistency, like Nelson's, gives Transposition by the symmetry of (in)consistency. For if '$p$ implies $q$' is defined as $-(po-q)$ or $p/-q$, the tautology $-p/-q = -q/-p$ will yield: $(-p$ implies $q) = (-q$ implies $p)$. Likewise Lewis' definition of implication as $-\Diamond(p-q)$ leads to Transposition by commutivity of conjunction.

The primitive terms of Analytic Implication: propositional variables; negation $-p$; conjunction $p \cdot q$ or $pq$; analytic implication $p \to q$ (or $p$ im $q$); a variable functor $f(p)$, standing for any proposition constructed from $p$ and other propositions by means of the primitive terms, provided $p$ appears in the result. Substitution for variables, replacement of terms equal by definition, *modus ponens* for $p \to q$, and adjunction are assumed. Formation rules are as usual (permitting iterations). Truth-functions are defined as usual; analytic equivalence $p \rightleftarrows q$ (or $p$ mim $q$) as $p \to q \cdot q \to p$. We *could* define: $p \to q \cdot = \cdot p \rightleftarrows pq$.

A postulate set equivalent to the original one would be:

(1a) $pq \rightarrow qp$              (2b) $(p \rightarrow q)(p \rightarrow r) \rightarrow \cdot p \rightarrow qr$

(1b) $p \rightarrow --p$                (2c) $(p \rightarrow r)(q \rightarrow r) \rightarrow \cdot p \vee q \rightarrow r$

(1c) $p \cdot (q \vee r) \cdot \rightarrow pq \vee pr$     (3a) $p \rightarrow q \cdot \rightarrow \cdot p \supset q$

(1d) $p \vee (q \cdot -q) \rightarrow p$        (4a) $f(p) \rightarrow \cdot p \rightarrow p$

(2a) $p \rightarrow qr \cdot \rightarrow \cdot p \rightarrow q$      (4b) $(p \rightleftarrows q) \cdot f(p) \cdot \rightarrow f(q)$

Defining: $\lozenge p = -(p \rightarrow -p)$ Df, I would now add:
(2d) $-\lozenge -p \cdot (p \rightarrow q) \cdot \rightarrow -\lozenge -q$; and (3b) $-(p \supset q) \rightarrow -(p \rightarrow q)$,
independence unknown; but 3a is still independent.

Defining: $p \, 3 \, q \cdot = \cdot -\lozenge (p \cdot -q)$ Df, we can prove all formulas of S4,
so Strict Implication in this form is a subsystem of Analytic Implication
(with 2d).

For an alternative system containing S5, one may postulate:
(5) $-(p \rightarrow q) \rightarrow -\lozenge (p \rightarrow q)$, yielding C11A $\lozenge p \rightarrow -\lozenge -\lozenge p$.

A 4-element matrix shows that the Proscriptive Principle holds: no
formula A $\rightarrow$ B holds if B has a variable not occurring in A.[120]

Without reference to Analytic Implication, similar theories of 'entailment' were proposed by Duncan-Jones and Halldén. Duncan-Jones (*op.
cit.*) writes '*p*E*q*', meaning '*q* arises out of the meaning of *p*'. Not stating our
Proscriptive Principle, he always decides doubtful cases in line with it.[121]

Halldén,[122] adopting "the Duncan-Jones distinction between strict
implication and entailment," gives a postulate set for entailment formally the same as SL's for S1, except that entailment is taken as primitive, and
no equivalence corresponding to 11.02 appears. He shows that '*p* 3 *p* ∨ *q*'
and '*p* . −*p* : 3 *q*' are not theorems; he says they would be "highly paradoxical" for entailment. The 4-element matrix for Analytic Implication
shows that our Proscriptive Principle (not mentioned) holds here.
Nothing prevents completing this system in the direction of Analytic
Implication.[123]

---

[120] For completeness, Analytic Implication should satisfy the simple deduction theorem
D1A: If A⊢B, then ⊢ (A→B). I do not know if it does. Unlike S4, it does not and
should not satisfy D2; if $A_1$, $A_2$⊢B, it does not follow that $A_1$⊢$A_2$⊃B.

[121] He gives no postulate set, but asserts: $p$E$p$, $pq$E$p$, $pq$E$q$, $p$E$q \cdot q$E$r$:E$\cdot p$E$r$. He rejects
Lewis' definition for entailment, and rejects Antilogism since it turns $pq$E$p$ into a para-
dox. He decides '$-p$E$\cdot-(pq)$' is not valid though not an 'outrageous' paradox, hence
rejects Transposition. Analytic Implication agrees on all these points. The only clear
disagreement with Analytic Implication is that he does not think $p-p$ entails its own
denial; I assert (since $pq \rightarrow p \vee q$,) $p-p \rightarrow p \vee -p$, and $p \vee -p \rightarrow -(p-p)$. On consistency, he
agrees with Nelson (*contra* Lewis and me) that an impossible proposition may be con-
sistent with another proposition.

[122] *Theoria* (1948), p. 265.

[123] The definition of consistency as '$-(p \, 3 \, -q)$' will not do for this system, since the

Analytic implication, like strict, can be interpreted in the narrow sense of structurally analytic implication, or the broader sense of an intensional implication which may depend on the meaning of nonlogical terms in the antecedent. '(This is red) → (This is colored)' holds for intensionally analytic but not structurally analytic implication. Each form of Analytic Implication has a corresponding Strict Implication as subsystem, with its doctrine of modality and consistency. As Strict Implication puts into an object language certain laws of (in)dependence of the truth of propositions, Analytic Implication does something similar for (in)dependence of *meanings* (of terms and propositions). It needs to be extended to functional calculus, and related to metalogical study of the independence of primitive ideas.

## XI. *Alternative Systems of Logic*

Lewis returned to his second basic problem of logic.[124] If Strict Implication formulates the ordinary meaning of 'implies', there are alternative systems of logic—not merely equivalent systems. Material Implication remains, and multi-valued logics with many implication-relations; also various non-truth-value systems. Every law in each of these is "*absolutely true* (of the relations which figure in it)," being an analytic statement or tautology.[125] But basic categories and laws of these systems differ. For use as a canon of inference, we must choose among the systems, and "make use, at most, of two or three;" else we have "not a canon, but a chaos."[126] Since choice is not on grounds of truth, it must "turn on some pragmatic considerations such as *simplicity* or *comprehensiveness* or accord with our most frequent *purposes of inference*. On these grounds, there are perfectly definite and fairly obvious reasons for choosing the usual meaning of 'implies' " (my italics).[127] His choice is natural, but I find little theoretical discussion of these 'pragmatic considerations'.

---

symmetry of consistency then vanishes with Transposition. It may be defined as: $-[pq \ni -(pq)]$.

The system lacks '$--p \ni p$' and '$p \ni q . = . p = pq$' (not by choice, it seems). It should *not* be called S0; rejecting, e.g., the definition of strict implication, it is not of the S family.

Is it accidental that the postulates of S2 hold for analytic implication, or does it confirm the intuitions of Parry, Duncan-Jones, and Halldén?

124 "Alternative Systems of Logic," *Monist*, 42, No. 4 (1932), 481; "Reply to Mr. Ushenko," "Reply to Mr. Ushenko's Addendum," *ibid.* (1933), 292, 295; "Paul Weiss on Alternative Logics," *Philos. Review* (1934), 70. Cf. SL, chap. VII, VIII.

125 *Philos. Rev.*, 43 (1934), 71.

126 *Monist*, 42, No. 4 (1932) , 507.

127 *Philos. Rev.* (1934), 74.

First, on comparing systems: there may be equivocation in assuming that, where two systems use the same term or symbol, they are talking about the same thing (perhaps conflicting) ; likewise, where terms of two systems have the same or synonymous *names* ('Negation' = ?). There is good reason to suppose the 'negation' ('absurdity') of the intuitionists is not the same as PM's negation. Similarly, I think confusion has been caused by Łukasiewicz's use of '$Np$','$Cpq$' in both 2-valued calculus $L_2$ and his 3-valued calculus $L_3$. Though a generalized metalogical definition defines both $N$'s at once, they cannot be identified. One can, indeed, define in $L_3$ a pair of concepts: $N'p = CpNp$, $C'pq = C\ CN'pq\ q$, such that all laws of $L_2$ hold for $N'$, $C'$; these might be identified with the $N$, $C$ of $L_2$, making $L_2$ appear as a subsystem of $L_3$. In general, for complete systems, any $m$-valued calculus can be imbedded in an $(m+n)$-valued calculus by suitable definitions.[128] This suggests that the criterion of *comprehensiveness* favors multi-valued—ultimately infinite-valued—calculi, though the criterion of *simplicity* points in the opposite direction. Though the Łukasiewicz-Tarski infinite-valued calculus has not been *used*, the systems of Lewis and Heyting have, and they may be treated as infinite-valued calculi. We have the paradox that, in general, the more 'strict' and 'narrow' a system of implication is, the *richer* it is in definable concepts and subsystems. Comprehensiveness in the sense of richness should be supplemented by criteria of 'completeness' in its various senses. An advantage of S4 and S5 is that they incorporate Material Implication, and are complete in the sense of the simple deduction theorem; and of S4, that it incorporates Heyting's system also. Stricter systems may have further advantages. Simplicity is secondary for the pure logician, but he can supply simple systems for practical purposes.

On the other hand, there are senses in which Strict Implication is a superstructure on the basis of a 2-valued logic.[129] But this superstructure contains much that is not in the simple 2-valued calculus.

The decisive reason why Lewis favors Strict Implication, I think, is that he finds it in accord with "the usual meaning of 'implies.' " Here (as when the 'straight line' of Euclidean or non-Euclidean geometry is interpreted physically), a question of *truth* is involved; but one that is difficult to decide. Toward its ultimate decision Lewis has made a great contribution.

WILLIAM TUTHILL PARRY

DEPARTMENT OF PHILOSOPHY
UNIVERSITY OF BUFFALO

---

128 Prior, *op. cit.*, ch. II §1; Tzu-Hua Hoo, Jr. SL (1949). Note that $L_3$ is not functionally complete.

129 Cf. Prior, *Jr. of Computing Systems* (1954), p. 201; Leonard, *op. cit.*

# 5

## *Asher Moore*

## LEWIS' THEORY OF THE A PRIORI

THE traditional meaning of the term analytic is, Lewis has said, "determinable as true by reference to our meanings."[1] Whether or not this be a traditional meaning, there is another sense of the term which is at least equally traditional. In this other sense, a proposition[2] is analytic if it expresses the results of an analysis, a taking apart, a breaking down of a whole into its constituents, a making explicit of implicit components. Roughly, a proposition is analytic in this sense if what its predicate means is a part of what its subject means.[3] It is in this sense that Lewis himself uses the term analytic in MWO.[4] And in AKV he reverts to this usage in his discussion of analytic meaning, which is defined as the meaning of a complex expression insofar as this is constituted by the meanings of its constituent expressions[5] and is contrasted with holophrastic meaning, the meaning of an expression considered as a whole.[6]

Lewis probably believes that if a proposition is analytic in the former sense (certifiable by reference exclusively to its meaning), it is necessarily analytic also in the latter sense (certifiable by reference to its analytic meaning, that is, by reference to its meaning as analyzed into the component meanings which constitute it). Indeed, the theory of analytic meaning just is Lewis' explication of how and why proposi-

---

[1] C. I. Lewis, *An Analysis of Knowledge and Valuation* (La Salle, Ill.: Open Court Publishing Co., 1946), p. 35. Hereafter cited as AKV.

[2] While, like Lewis, I shall often use terms like proposition and statement, I believe, again like Lewis, that linguistic expressions derive their whole significance from the ideas and judgments which they express. (See AKV, Chap. V, esp. Sec. 8; Chap. VI, Secs. 5 and 7.) Nothing I say in this essay is concerned fundamentally with language as such.

[3] This is the meaning Kant gives to the term, as Lewis is aware. C. I. Lewis, *Mind and the World-Order* (New York: Charles Scribner's Sons, 1929), pp. 295-301. Hereafter cited as MWO.

[4] MWO, pp. 240, 245, 293-301, 433-434.

[5] AKV, p. 85. The extension of analytic meaning to elementary expressions is, he says, merely "convenient" and "hardly significant."

[6] AKV, p. 87.

tions are analytic in the former sense.[7] This is presumably why he uses
the term analytic in these two different senses. But even if it should be
true that a proposition is certifiable by reference to its meaning alone
only if it is certifiable by an analysis of its holophrastic meaning into
components, still, this truth would itself be the result of analysis. The
possibility of its being false, and the necessity of demonstrating its
truth, should not be obscured by using the same term for the original
notion and for its explicans.

I shall define 'analytic' as Lewis does—certifiable by reference exclusively to meanings. Correspondingly, a proposition is synthetic if it is
not so certifiable.[8] Thus it will not be self-contradictory to say that an
analytic proposition is certifiable only by noting a connection or synthesis of two distinct meanings or to say that a synthetic proposition
expresses the result of an analysis.[9] When a proposition is certifiable
only by noting a connection among distinct meanings,[10] I shall call it
a *copulative* proposition. When, on the contrary, a proposition is certifiable by discovering that the meaning of its predicate is a constituent
part of the meaning of its subject, I shall say that it is an *iterative*
proposition.[11] That is, it 'says again', in its predicate, at least a part
of what it has already said once in its subject. The terms are exclusive
and exhaustive.[12] The term analysis, however, I shall use in the sense
of a 'taking apart' or 'making explicit', following Lewis' usage in this
case also.

## I

One of the many admirable things about Lewis' treatment of the
a priori is the clear distinction he maintains between the question of
what a priori truths are about and the quite different question of how

[7] Lewis notes in passing a few exceptions to this, so the statement is not strictly true.
But he minimizes the importance of the exceptions to such an extent that I think the
statement does represent correctly the dominant tendency of his thought. See Section III.

[8] These definitions violate my own sense of both ordinary and philosophic usage.
But this is an essay on Lewis, and I want to inflict upon him as few departures as possible from his vocabulary.

[9] Or rather, if these are contradictions, that fact is not itself immediately obvious, but
must be elicited by analysis of the meaning of 'analytic'.

[10] Or even, in the case of nonanalytic propositions, among distinct existents.

[11] This corresponds exactly to Lewis' usage of 'analytic' in MWO and, more roughly,
to the sense given to 'analytic meaning' in AKV.

[12] Kant's problem of the 'synthetic a priori' would now be expressed as the question
whether any a priori propositions are copulative. And the 'paradox of analysis' would
be the paradox of profitable iteration.

we know they are true.[13] The former I call the problem of *content,* the latter the problem of *evidence.* In this section I shall discuss the problem of evidence.

Lewis' view is that the evidence for an a priori proposition consists in an inspection of its meaning. The relevant mode of meaning in this connection is intensional meaning.[14] And as between the two sorts of intensional meaning, linguistic and sense, the fundamental one is sense meaning.[15] The sense meaning of a proposition is the criteria-in-mind or the test-schema-in-mind by which we should determine whether the proposition in question was applicable to the world. A proposition is a priori if its test schema could not possibly fail, if it requires nothing which could conceivably be absent. Thus, the intension of an a priori proposition is zero, and its comprehension universal, which is to say that it is true of all possible worlds.[16] The evidence that a proposition does have zero intension consists in the same act of intuition or inspection by which we know what its intension is.[17]

Empiricism has, ever since Locke, tended to give one or the other of two accounts of the sort of evidence we have for a priori truths. Either it has been held, in the tradition of Hume and of Kant's theory of the iterative ('analytic') a priori, that this evidence consists in what we discover by introspection about the relations of our ideas. Or, in the manner of the positivists, the evidence is thought to consist in what we know about our language rules and their implications. Both views have been thought to stand in contrast to the rationalist notion that

13 In contrast to the all-too-common habit of *defining* either 'analytic' or 'a priori', or both, as 'vacuous', or 'empty', which serves only to conceal the question of whether, by an inspection of meanings, we can learn anything about reality. It is even worse, of course, to define a 'contingent' statement as one which describes reality and a 'necessary' statement as one which does not. To be sure, if reality consists wholly of contingent events, every necessary statement will be vacuous in content. But the chief point of contention in this whole matter is whether there are not also necessary realities.

14 While, as I shall note later, Lewis believes that comprehension, signification, and intension are correlative, the priority which he assigns to intension, in the order of evidence, is stated, implied, and assumed so generally throughout both of his books that any finite number of specific references would only weaken the reader's assurance on the point. The dubious might consult especially AKV, p. 37, Sec. (2), as well as the top of p. 36 where Lewis makes it plain that when he defined 'analytic' as 'certifiable by reference to meaning' he meant 'intensional meaning'.

15 E.g., AKV, pp. 37, 133.

16 E.g., AKV, p. 57.

17 E.g., AKV, p. 115, n. 3, pp. 118-19. In many cases we must 'analyze' the meaning into its components in order to see that the proposition as a whole has zero intension. But analysis is itself only a process of repeated intuition (see Section IV).

the evidence for an a priori proposition consists in what we can discover by thinking about reality itself—nonmental, nonlinguistic reality.[18]

I am not sure why so many empiricists have felt that only 'conceptualist' or 'nominalist' theories (if I may so name them) on this matter are compatible with empiricism and that a 'realist' approach necessarily commits one to rationalism.[19] I suspect it is because of the empiricist dogma that while sense-data and concepts and the logical connections of linguistic expressions, being phenomenal, may be 'directly' and 'immediately' known (known, that is, by acquaintance), the nonphenomenal objects of concepts are not so open to direct inspection. Since, obviously, the evidence for an a priori proposition, as for any proposition whatever, must be directly inspectable (if it were not inspectable, but had to be inferred, it would not be evident but would on the contrary need evidence); and since, by definition, propositions based upon acquaintance with sense-data are a posteriori, not a priori; then, if the above dogma were granted as a premise, it would follow by elimination that a priori propositions were based upon what is evident either about ideas or about the logical connections of expressions. In any case, Lewis' view that the evidence for an a priori proposition consists in what we can discover by introspection about the relations of our ideas[20] places him squarely in the Humian-Kantian, or conceptualist, branch of the empiricist tradition.

18 (a) In MWO, Lewis invariably thinks of rationalism as nineteenth-century rationalism and consequently interprets the rationalist theory of a priori truths as the belief that these truths reflect certain fixed and necessary ways of conceiving which are innate to the mind. But in AKV, he describes "rationalistic realism" in the way I have described it above, as the doctrine that *"a priori* truth describes some metaphysically significant character of reality, or that universals have some peculiar mode of being, obscure to sense but *directly disclosable to reason."* (p. ix—second italics mine.) And already in "A Pragmatic Conception of the *a Priori*" (*Readings in Philosophical Analysis* sel. and ed. by Herbert Feigl and Wilfrid Sellars [New York: Appleton-Century-Crofts, 1949], p. 286; hereafter cited as "Prag. Conc.") Lewis distinguished these two forms of rationalism, rejecting both of them.

(b) I shall not bother to repeat the 'nonmental, nonlinguistic'. It should be understood whenever, in this section, I speak of reality.

19 See again AKV, p. ix, where Lewis refers to the two positions opposed to his own as "rationalistic realism," or "Platonic realism," and "extreme nominalism." AKV, p. 134, indicates the same understanding of the possible alternatives.

20 There seems to me no reason to doubt that by "sense intension" Lewis does in the end mean an idea. The usage of both books supports this interpretation, for in AKV he calls sense-intensions "criteria-in-mind" while in MWO he calls them "concepts." He does, to be sure, explain that a concept is an "abstraction and an ideality" (MWO, p. 89); he explicitly distinguishes a concept from "the psychological state of mind when one uses a word or phrase" (MWO, p. 67); and he even goes so far as to call concepts "logical structures, Platonic ideas" (MWO, p. 269). But by such statements he seems to mean only that concepts are not identical with the full, concrete states of mind in which they are implicit. He does not seem to mean to deny that concepts, while being distin-

I, for one, do not wish to question Lewis' belief that the evidence for an a priori proposition consists always in an examination of its meaning, so that all a priori truths are analytic. I accept this assertion as established. One must be careful, however, not to think that this proves more than it does. In particular, one must guard against supposing that it refutes Kant or, indeed, has anything to do with Kant's problem of the copulative a priori. Lewis' handling of the a priori in MWO was an attempt to deal with Kant's problem, for there he used the term analytic in the sense I have given to iterative. Some of Lewis' readers have not noted the change in the definition of 'analytic' between his two books, and have supposed that when Lewis asserts, in AKV, that the a priori is analytic, this statement still means the same thing it meant in MWO.

In fact, it is only in a loose sense that one can speak of Lewis' having "established," in AKV, the view that the a priori is analytic, or even of his having attempted to establish it. Actually, until some specific meaning is attached to the term meaning in the assertion that the a priori can be certified by an examination of meaning, that statement is so obvious as to require no justification. How could one certify any proposition except by examining what it means, in some sense of

guishable from concrete psychological states are, after all, abstractions from them and to be explicated in terms of them. For he says that the concrete psychological state is the "bearer" of the meaning or concept (MWO, pp. 69-70).

That we are meant to interpret all of the above statements conceptualistically is made abundantly clear in MWO, pp. 70-72, where he explicitly rejects a realist handling of abstractions; also on p. 36, and again in Appendix D, where he insists that concepts and the a priori are "due to my mind." See also MWO, p. 89, where it is explained that while the concept is an abstraction or an ideality, this is "in no greater degree or different sense than are most of things which are commonly attributed to mind." Nor does it seem to me that the "ideal meanings" mentioned in MWO, pp. 287, 289, are meant to have any Platonic ontological status.

As will be brought out more fully in the last section of this essay, Lewis plays, in both books, with the idea that criteria-in-mind or concepts might be treated behavioristically. Thus, in AKV, p. 144, he says that, while he has himself been thinking of intensions as something "inwardly observable" (hence, presumably, inward, psychical), this aspect of his thought is dispensable, since "One may consider such criteria of application, as meanings entertained in advance, in terms of incipient behavior or behavior attitudes if one choose; and the observability of these will then be comparable to the observability of the use of language." But the last clause of this sentence brings out exactly the difficulty of making any such behavioristic notion of intensions compatible with Lewis' philosophy as a whole. For Lewis does not think that either behavior or the use of language is directly observable; whereas intensions must be directly observable. Except in a physicalist system, the use of language, and other forms of behavior, are not evident, but rather require evidence. Lewis appears to recognize this on the next page where he says that "our evidence of what another person means, in the mode of intensional meaning, can be inductive only .... Whether we have better assurance of our own meanings ... is perhaps a question just as well omitted."

'means'? Even if one were to specify that the meaning in question is not denotation, but a meaning which is fixed and determinable prior to any particular sense experience,[21] the statement that the a priori is analytic still seems to mean only that what is a priori (determinable by thought prior to particular sense experience) is indeed determinable by thought prior to particular sense experience (analytic). This, again, seems to require no justification. What Lewis tries, in AKV, to establish through argument is not that the a priori is certifiable by examination of meaning, but rather that the relevant sense of meaning is intension, and, more particularly, analytic meaning.

Nor would I quarrel with the further statement that at least one relevant sense of the term meaning as it occurs in the statement that the a priori is certifiable by reference to meaning is meaning in the mode of intension. Nor with the view that intensional meaning is something that we have, in some sense, in mind, as an 'idea'.[22] What I do wonder is whether the a priori is certifiable by an examination of the relations of ideas in any sense in which it would not be equivalent, and equally enlightening, to say that it is certified by an examination of the relations of objective realities. I wonder, that is, whether there is really any difference between Lewis' conceptualist handling of the problem of evidence and the realist handling which he rejects.[23]

Lewis repeatedly says that intension is correlative with signification and comprehension, that these three modes of meaning are necessarily dependent upon one another in such a way that, beginning with any one of them, we can ascertain, a priori, the other two.[24] In view of this, it would seem as if we should be equally faithful to Lewis' thought if, instead of saying that the a priori is certifiable by inspection of intensional meanings (ideas), we said that it was certifiable by inspection of significations or comprehensions.

Lewis has been loathe to adopt any particular view of the ontological status of significations and comprehensions.[25] But quite certainly he

---

[21] AKV, p. 144.

[22] Unless a thing were *in some sense* in mind, one would obviously be totally unacquainted with it.

[23] See nn. 18 and 19.

[24] AKV, p. 65. The exception there noted is not relevant to the present matter.

[25] The one statement I have been able to find is this: "They [meanings] are thus what they are, whether they live in Plato's heaven or whether their metaphysical status is merely that of the logical consequences of premises which no one will ever be interested to consider, or of commitments which we implicitly make by our decisions though no one ever will call them in question" (AKV, p. 110). The refusal in MWO (e.g., pp. 70-71) to grant Platonic status to meanings is concerned exclusively with concepts—i.e., with the mode of meaning Lewis later calls intensional meaning.

does not think they are linguistic expressions. Nor does he think of them as ideas.[26] Their ontological status is therefore at least this: it is nonlinguistic and nonmental.[27] Hence, whenever Lewis says that the evidence for an a priori truth consists in the inspection of intensions, could we not equally well say that it consists in the inspection of objective reality? And if we could, then what difference is there between the conceptualist theory, commonly supposed to be compatible with empiricism, and the realist theory, commonly assumed to be incompatible with it?[28] Is not Lewis' theory one with which anyone—bar only the linguists—could agree?

Lewis has been at pains, of course, to distinguish his view from that of anyone who believes that a priori truths can be based on our knowledge of denotative meanings.[29] The important distinction, he has insisted, is between denotation on the one hand and the other three, correlative modes of meaning on the other hand. But again, this seems to be a point upon which empiricism and "rationalistic realism" are agreed. I cannot think of anyone who has ever held that a priori truths are based upon an inspection of what propositions denote, in the sense in which Lewis uses 'denotes'.[30]

Lewis makes an important distinction between what is denoted by concrete terms and what is denoted by abstract terms.[31] What a concrete term denotes is a "concrete entity; a space-time slab of reality with all that it contains. . . ."[32] By the concrete, space-time world Lewis apparently means what Plato means by Becoming, Spinoza by the common order of nature,[33] and most contemporary philosophers by Existence as opposed to Essence. A concrete term, Lewis says, cannot be determined to be necessarily applicable (i.e., its intension cannot be determined to be zero, its comprehension universal) by an inspection of what it denotes. But I cannot think of any philosopher who ever held that we

---

26 The whole distinction between sense intension and signification is that signification consists of *properties* whereas intension consists of ideas of properties (e.g., AKV, p. 133, n. 3).

27 See n. 40.

28 See nn. 18 and 19.

29 E.g., AKV, pp. 66, 98.

30 An exception will be noted immediately below. But in those cases which are exceptional—cases in which a rationalist would indeed assert that a priori propositions can be evidenced by an examination of what they denote—Lewis himself agrees with the rationalist view.

31 AKV, pp. 41-42.

32 AKV, p. 53. See also p. 199.

33 Or "existence in relation to a fixed time and place."

could directly inspect Existence except through sense experience.[34] What rationalists have held, so far as I know, is that a priori truths are founded upon our inspection of a quite different sort of reality—a reality which has been variously called Being, Ideas, God or Nature, possibilities, essences, or eternal verities, a sort of reality which, since I am not concerned with metaphysical niceties, I may dub Platonic reality.[35] But Platonic reality, in this loose sense of the term, seems to be identical with what Lewis means to refer to by the terms signification and comprehension. In support of this statement one may note particularly the Leibnizian description of comprehensions as classifications of 'possible worlds'. And the statement that there are nonexistent entities which may be named.[36] Also the assertion, on the same page, that when one speaks of "actual or existent things," the 'actual or existent' is limiting. As I have previously indicated, Lewis seems to distinguish his view from any form of Platonism and to take it as an advantage of his conceptualist handling of a priori propositions that "it becomes unnecessary to suppose that *a priori* truth describes some metaphysically significant character of reality, or that universals have some peculiar mode of being, obscure to sense but directly disclosable to reason."[37] But if we take all of this literally, it becomes quite impossible to understand what a signification or a comprehension is. For surely these modes of meaning are not apprehended by sense, but by reason (in the sense of nonsensuous consciousness). And what could significations, anyway, be if not universals?[38]

[34] One must distinguish this question of evidence from a corresponding question about content: whether any a priori truths are about Existence.

[35] Not that all rationalists think that this sort of reality consists of universals, for they don't. But they do all think of it as the realm of objective necessities, as opposed to the world of contingencies. Many rationalists, to be sure, think that nothing whatever is contingent. But this does not undermine the definition of Platonic reality as the realm of objective necessities, since those rationalists who think that everything is necessary also think that, in the end, only Platonic reality is real, Existence being discriminable from it only negatively, or from some finite or self-contradictory point of view, or on the basis of inadequate ideas.

[36] AKV, p. 39.

[37] AKV, p. ix.

[38] Perhaps Lewis means us to put the accent on the "metaphysically significant" and to interpret this, in turn, in the light of the intimation, on the same page, that what he really objects to about Platonism is that it "may lead to the ancient fallacy of ascribing to essences some kind of cosmic efficacy." To whatever extent rationalists have attributed efficacy to universals—and I am not convinced that they typically have—then Lewis' conceptualism does indeed give us a desirable alternative. But then, so does realism itself, for no one is committed simply by his realism to the belief that universals are efficacious. One thinks here of Santayana.

In a previously quoted passage Lewis seems to deny that his theory of meaning has any Platonic implications, saying that his theory is neutral on the issue of whether meanings "live in Plato's heaven or whether their metaphysical status is merely that of the logical consequences of premises which no one will ever be interested to consider, or of commitments which we implicitly make by our decisions though no one will ever call them in question."[39] I do not know what Lewis means by 'Plato's heaven' when he offers it as one theory among many of the metaphysical status of meanings. But as *I* read Plato, the "logical consequences of premises which no one will ever be interested to consider," the "commitments which . . . no one will ever call . . . in question," the "meanings which *could* be thought of, [but] never *will* be thought of," and "the sum of two uncounted numbers" are exactly the sorts of entities that live in his heaven.

In "The Pragmatic Element in Knowledge," *University of California Publications in Philosophy*, VI (1926) Lewis seems to identify himself with those who analyze meanings conceptualistically, and he speaks a conceptualistic language throughout the article. Nevertheless, he indicates (pp. 223-24) that meanings may be treated *either* Platonically or conceptualistically. I might hazard the guess that, by the time of AKV, Lewis had reached the conclusion that meanings must be treated *both* Platonically and conceptualistically, and that 'intension' refers to meanings-as-concepts while the correlative terms signification and comprehension refer to meanings-as-Platonic. However, nothing in AKV explicitly confirms this guess, and p. 110 seems inconsistent with it.[40]

39 AKV, p. 110.

40 One of the most difficult points one confronts in trying to interpret Lewis faithfully is that of knowing whether or not he equates significations with "possible sense-data" or "qualia" (see MWO, p. 121). Intension consists of our idea-in-mind of signification; intension is our idea of possible sense-data (by the verifiability theory of meaning); from these two premises it would seem to follow that signification consists of possible sense-data. On the other hand, the predominant tone of AKV seems to indicate another view, according to which signification consists, not of qualia which are sometimes given in experience, but of properties which sometimes characterize objective realities. (AKV, p. 41, for example, indicates such a view at three different places.) The issue is this: is the signification of 'This ball is round' to be identified with the state of affairs 'being round' or is it to be identified (in part) with the state of affairs 'being an elliptical quale which can be given from such and such a perspective'? Lewis' adherence to the verifiability principle as regards *intension* tends towards the latter interpretation, whereas his realistic handling of the problem of the external world tends towards the former interpretation. Thus early works which are predominantly phenomenalist in tone lead naturally to a phenomenalist analysis of signification in terms of possible qualia (*Vide* Review of C. D. Broad's *Scientific Thought* in *Philosophical Review*, 34 (1925), esp. p. 409; "Experience and Meaning" (1934) in Feigl and Sellars, *op cit.*, pp. 132-37 and esp. p. 140; and, to some extent, MWO). Later works, more realist in tone, lead naturally to a distinction between properties and possible qualia (*Vide* "A Comment on 'The Verification Theory of Meaning' by Everett J. Nelson," *Philo-*

The seeming identity of the 'two' views becomes even more apparent if one considers the class of abstract terms. These, Lewis says, denote what they signify.[41] So here is a class of terms in the case of which we may say that the evidence of their applicability consists in an inspection of their denotations.[42] What accounts for the privileged position of

sophical Review, 63 (1954), 193-94. Hereafter cited as "Comment"; "Realism or Phenomenalism?" Philosophical Review, 64 (1955), 242-44. Hereafter cited as "Real. Phen.")
It is possible that there is a difference in this respect between the signification of non-propositional terms and of propositional terms, odd as that would be in view of the strict parallel Lewis finds between these two classes of terms. The signification of nonpropositional terms is consistently said to consist of a "property in things" (AKV, p. 39; see also p. 41) —or, more strictly, a property which, if it qualifies anything, qualifies things, not experience. It is only with regard to propositional terms that Lewis' verifiability theory tends to make signification consist of qualia. (See my article, "Verifiability and Phenomenalism," Journal of Philosophy, 47 (1950), 169-77.)

But it seems to me that in either case signification would be some sort of Platonic reality. For even if we interpret signification as consisting of possible sense-data, it consists of possible sense-data, not of actually given sense-data or of our ideas of possible sense-data (since these ideas are the intension). Indeed, Lewis himself indicates that a quale is probably a Santayanan essence (AKV, pp. 18, 188).

To be sure, the signification of a proposition is not 'objective' in the sense defined in MWO, pp. 120-121 and in AKV, pp. 214 ff. (unless the proposition is a 'concrete' one and happens to be true, which is a different matter). But Platonic reality has never, I think, been presumed to be objective in this sense. Platonic reality has been thought to be 'objective' only in this sense—that it is what it is regardless of what happens to be thought or said. (See William Earl, Objectivity (New York: Noonday Press, 1955), passim) And in this sense Lewis' significations are also objective.

Nor, of course, are significations and comprehensions the sort of reality which, Lewis thinks, the realist simply acknowledges as the field of action which confronts him ("Real. Phen.," p. 238). But then it has never been supposed that Platonic reality constitutes a field of action in the sense in which material bodies do. Platonic realities constitute a field of thought, or, better, a field of acquaintance, and perhaps also a field of aspiration. It is as such that the realist acknowledges them.

41 AKV, p. 42. In the light of this, the point made on p. 98, summed up in the assertion that "a definition cannot express . . . meaning in the sense of denotation" would have to be limited to concrete terms. Also the statement on the same page that: "Only acquaintance with the empirical can exercise that function [of making known the denotation of an expression]; and any variation of such existential and empirically cognizable fact would make a corresponding difference in the denotation of the expression in question."

42 Due to a curious twist in Lewis' philosophy, it is not possible to say with strict accuracy that abstract analytic truths denote what they signify and hence can be evidenced by an inspection of their denotation. For, in Lewis' usage, every true proposition (even a 'formal' one) denotes Existence as such, not some particular aspect of it. Thus the distinction he draws between abstract and concrete terms applies, strictly, only to nonpropositional terms. If one were to apply it to propositions as well, then all propositions would be concrete.

It is true that propositional functions may denote either particular segments of Existence or particular parts of Platonic reality, and hence may be distinguished as concrete and abstract (AKV, pp. 62-63). (When Lewis says on p. 63 that the denotation of a propositional function is a class of existents, the term existents must be taken as nonlimiting—otherwise the statement conflicts with what is said in lines 3-5 on the same page.) But abstract terms? Evidently, the fact that they denote properties not concrete things, Platonic reality not Existence, the necessary not the contingent. But does not this exactly correspond to the rationalist contention that, while Becoming must be discovered through the senses, Being may be explored through reason?[43]

If there is any difference between Lewis and "rationalistic realism" on this question, it would seem to consist in the fact that Lewis empha-

since propositional functions are treated as nonpropositional terms (pp. 62-63, p. 85) they are not *true* (p. 61).

But there are a number of considerations which indicate, I think, that this decision of Lewis' as to what shall constitute the denotation of a proposition is either ill-advised, or irrelevant to the point I am now trying to make, or both.

(a) Consider a proposition which is 'abstract', not exactly in Lewis' sense, but in the sense that all of the terms in it denote what they signify (i.e., a proposition obtained from an abstract propositional function by the substitution of a value for the variable (see AKV, p. 63). For example, 'Redness is a color property'. As Lewis has set up the matter, this proposition would have zero denotation, and hence be false, if in fact nothing exists, in the limiting sense of 'exists'. That Lewis' treatment of the denotation of propositions does have this consequence seems to me to cast doubt on the advisability of so treating it.

(b) If, in spite of this, we retain Lewis' usage, it is still the case that, in order to know that this proposition is true, all one needs to know, in addition to the fact that something exists, is the denotation of the *component terms*. In other words, one needs to know nothing whatever about the specific character of what the proposition as a whole denotes. The 'significant' part of the evidence consists of what one knows, by inspection, about what the component terms denote—and these are Platonic realities.

(c) In view of (a) and (b), it would seem that if one is going to say that every true proposition has the same denotation—the whole—then this whole should be 'reality', in some sense broad enough to include Platonic realities, and not just existence in the limiting sense.

(d) Lewis defines the "actual world" which every true proposition denotes as "that unique individual existent identified by the fact that all other existents are space-time parts of it" ("Notes on the Logic of Intension," in *Structure, Method and Meaning: Essays in Honor of Henry M. Sheffer*, ed. Paul Henle, Horace M. Kallen and Susanne K. Langer (New York: The Liberal Arts Press, 1951), pp. 27-28). I think it is tolerably obvious that this unique individual is not itself spatio-temporal. It is not, that is, the sort of thing that would usually be said to 'exist' in the same sense as chairs and tables exist. It is, rather, exactly that unique individual which Spinoza called God or Nature. It was because of this statement of Lewis' that I earlier capitalized the word Existence when I said that, in Lewis' view, all true propositions denote Existence as such. But *Existence* is not an *existent*. To be sure, it is not a universal either, but, as Lewis says, an individual. Still, in the loose sense in which I am using the expression Platonic reality, Existence is a Platonic reality.

(e) Finally, it is true in any case that all propositions *comprehend* a Platonic reality (a possible world). And 'comprehends' is Lewis' term for the ordinary sense of 'names' or 'applies'. So that, on the assumption only that something exists, an analytic truth can be evidenced by an examination of what it 'applies to'. In view of this, the fact that a priori truths cannot be based on an acquaintance with their denotation—in the very restricted sense Lewis gives to that word in the case of propositions—appears to distinguish his position from no one's.

[43] This does not mean, in the end, through reason*ing* or dialectic, but through the sort of immediate, nonsensuous apprehension (intuition) upon which dialectic rests for *its* evidence.

sizes, as I have said, intension, whereas the rationalists emphasize signification (which is, in the case of abstract terms, also the denotation).
But I think any rationalist would admit that, instead of saying that
we inspect significations and comprehensions, one could equally well
say that we inspect intensions, provided one realized that intensions
simply *are* ideas of significations. For all of this is simply a complicated
way of saying that we wouldn't know anything at all about significations, or indeed about anything, unless we did have an idea of it. And
I think Lewis, on his part, would agree that whenever we inspect an
intension we necessarily find out something about a signification, since
an intension just *is* the idea of a signification.

Or does Lewis think that our knowledge of intension is somehow
prior, in the order of evidence, to our knowledge of signification, so
that our knowledge of significations has to be inferred from our knowledge of intensions?[44] If so, in what might such priority consist?[45] Because of the infinite population of the Platonic world an idea of a
property could not fail to 'agree' with the property of which it is an
idea, because if it 'did not agree' it would not be an idea of that
property but of some other. To be sure, Lewis might not agree with
the way in which some realists (rationalists and empiricists alike)
explicate what an idea is—that it is nothing but the intensionality of
consciousness, nothing but acquaintance with an ideatum. He would
almost surely dissent from such an analysis of the ideas of physical
existents, and conceivably he might disagree with it also as an analysis
of ideas of properties. Without committing himself, Lewis is inclined
to use such terms as idea and concept more in the manner of the
idealists and the British empiricists than in the manner of Spinoza and

---

[44] Over and above the almost exclusive emphasis which Lewis places upon intension
as the foundation of the a priori (see n. 14), there is the following indication that he does
indeed ascribe to intension some kind of evidential priority: "Either it [an analytic state-
ment] affirms a relation of intensional meanings of constituents in it . . . ; or it asserts a
relation of constituents in some other mode of meaning such as denotation, but one which
can be assured—and can *only* be assured in advance of particular empirical occasions—
by assuring a corresponding relation of intensional meanings." This statement would be
irrelevant in the present connection if it simply ascribed to intension a priority over denotation. But the use of the phrase 'some other mode of meaning such as' does perhaps
indicate a priority of intension over signification and comprehension as well as denotation.

[45] One may remark the curious way in which Lewis, having on p. 65 of AKV noted the
equivalence of signification, comprehension, and intension, then proceeds, on pp. 66 ff., to
speak of intensional meaning as the one of these upon which analytic truth depends—
but with no defense of this procedure. I can only speculate that this undefended priority
he assigns to intension is the result of the kind of implicit reasoning described earlier—
that only concepts and sense-data may be immediately inspected. Cf. AKV, p. 145: "As
what we *intend* at the moment at least, a meaning seems to be as open to examination as
anything we are likely to discover."

of Moore's "Refutation of Idealism." He seems to think of an idea as a representation which may 'agree' with its object (either an 'external object' or a future experience), rather than as simply an openness upon its object. (The exception to this is, of course, the givenness of qualia—we do not have perceptions of qualia, but rather a perception is nothing but the givenness of a quale.) But that would be a disagreement about the nature of consciousness and, however important it may be, I cannot see what bearing it would have on the present issue. So long as my idea of birdness, for example, guarantees that birdness is indeed what I think it is, my knowledge of the idea of birdness does not seem to be prior, in any sense I can make out, to my knowledge of birdness. And in that case, it seems to make no difference whether I say that the evidence for my knowledge that birds are bipedal consists in what I know about my idea of birdness or to say that it consists in what I know about birdness.[46] It seems to me we should all agree that, if the term 'meaning' be allowed to include signification and comprehension on an equal footing with intension (and, in the case of abstract terms, denotation as well), then all a priori propositions are indeed determinable as true by reference exclusively to their meaning and are hence analytic. For in this case, the phrase 'certifiable by reference exclusively to meaning' says only 'certifiable without reference to any *contingent* thing'. And that an a priori proposition must indeed be so certifiable is immediately obvious from the meaning of 'a priori'.

None of this is intended to be critical of Lewis' views. It is a compliment to a man's views, I think, to say that they are in accord with the great weight of tradition, leaving only the linguists to consort with themselves. I have raised the matter because I hope that what Lewis may say about it will perhaps help us to become clearer about what realism and conceptualism are and about what rationalism and empiricism commit us to on that matter. For Lewis is not only a distinguished empiricist. He is also a philosopher who is generally identi-

---

[46] In other words birdness is a *datum* in the sense Lewis gives to that term in "Some Logical Considerations Concerning the Mental" (Feigl and Sellars, *op. cit.*, p. 388): "Such data, when given, are entities whose identity and character it is impossible to mistake—though admittedly any language used to name them may be inappropriate. . . . An appearance or datum is just what it seems to be, and is nothing more or other than what it appears to be." In view of Lewis' unwillingness to apply the term knowledge to apprehension of the sensuously given (on the ground that such apprehension is not subject to any possible error—AKV, p. 183), it is curious that he is willing to speak of knowledge of significations and comprehensions, which are also given, although nonsensuously. But this seems to me to cast doubt, not upon the fact that there is acquaintance with signification and comprehension, but upon the advisability of restricting the term knowledge to cases where error is possible.

fied with, and identifies himself with, the Berkeley-Kant-Absolute Ideal-ism-Pragmatism tradition in opposition to the "rationalistic realist" tradition of Plato, Spinoza, and the early Russell. Lewis frequently gives arguments against the sort of 19th century rationalism according to which a priori truths are founded upon certain ways of thinking which are compulsive to the human mind. His arguments, which seem to me sound ones, are mostly derived from the nature of logic—the multiplicity of consistent systems, the arbitrariness of what shall be premise, what theorem, etc. But it is perhaps instructive that he has never given any arguments against "rationalistic realism." He has sim-ply rejected it without stating his grounds. Thus, in "A Pragmatic Conception of the a Priori"[47] he dismisses the matter with the state-ment: "That the mind approaches the flux of immediacy with some god-like foreknowledge of principles which are legislative for experience, that there is any natural light . . . , it is no longer possible to believe." But what is the difference, except in the invidious names used, between "knowing what one means, in the modes of signification and comprehension" and, on the other hand, "natural light" and "godlike foreknowledge?"

## II

What is the content of an analytic proposition? There seem to be four types of answers to this question. The first three are similar to the sorts of answers distinguished in the previous section. There is the realist answer that analytic propositions are about realities, the conceptualist answer that they are about ideas, and the nominalist answer that they are about language. In addition, there is the answer that they are not about anything, possessing syntactic but not semantic meaning, or else not being really propositions at all.

In considering Lewis' answer to this problem it is necessary to dis-count a number of unfortunate statements which, taken at their face value, would associate him with the last of these positions. In his earlier writings Lewis sometimes indicates that a priori 'propositions' are stipu-lations, sometimes describes them as expressions of resolves, and, most frequently, suggests that they are performatory in character—fiats, com-mitments, promises that in the future one will not call a thing by a given name unless it possesses certain designated properties.[48] Such a noncog-

---

47 Op. cit., p. 286.

48 See MWO, pp. 13, 213, 228, 232. Remarks seeming to express such a noncognitivist view are especially numerous in MWO, pp. 246-47, which is itself reproduced from the earlier (1923) paper, "Prag. Conc." Thus he says that the laws of logic "formulate our decisions," "declare our purposes," are "legislative," are "principles of procedure, the parliamentary rules of intelligent thought and speech."

nitivist view of the a priori is of course incompatible with everything which Lewis was later to say on this question. Further, it seems clear that, even at the time of MWO, such noncognitivist statements did not correctly represent Lewis' thought,[49] but were, perhaps, anachronisms from a still earlier period. The view of MWO as a whole is identical with that which Lewis expressed more clearly in AKV—that while the decision to use a certain concept or mode of classification or to give such-and-such a meaning to a term is a stipulation, a commitment, this commitment gives rise to a priori statements which are genuinely cognitive, genuinely true *about* something.

But about what? AKV distinguishes between explicitly and implicitly analytic statements.[50] Explicitly analytic statements are about intensions (ideas, concepts).[51] Implicitly analytic statements are about the existents denoted by their component terms.[52] And, in accord with the predominantly realist treatment of the problem of the external world in AKV, these existents are supposed to be, in the usual case, nonlinguistic and nonmental.[53]

[49] See MWO, pp. 256, 273, pp. 298-99, 435-36.

[50] AKV, Chap. IV, Sec. 8.

[51] AKV, p. 93. This is not the *definition* of explicitly analytic statements, but it is universally true of such statements. The same qualification applies to the next sentence.

[52] For the most part, AKV is unambiguous in this view. Upon occasion, however, there is a tendency to revert, at least verbally, to the earlier suggestion that analytic propositions are not about anything. Thus on p. ix Lewis says that "analytic truth 'says nothing about' an independent reality." But I think the quotation marks around 'says nothing about' are intended to give to this phrase the sense of 'says nothing that could conceivably be false' or 'imposes no limitation upon'. The same interpretation should, I think, be put upon the 'existential' in the next sentence but one on the same page: "An analytic statement says something; and something whose factuality is independent even though it is not existential in significance." And also upon the 'vacuous' in "considered holophrastically only . . . all analytic statements have the same meaning and are thus vacuous" (p. 149).

[53] AKV itself is perhaps not entirely definite on this point. Lewis does indicate that terms may denote objective existents distinct from concepts and sense-data. But sometimes this seems to be only a half-way house on the path to the phenomenalistic position that 'objective existence' is itself to be defined in terms of the truth of contrary-to-fact conditional judgments about possible sense-data. At least, if someone were to interpret Lewis this way, I do not see how, on the basis of AKV alone, he could be proved wrong. But there are two things which should be said:

(a) Even if one did interpret AKV as holding that all terms and all propositions denote possible sense-data, it would still be a mistake to think of these sense-data as mental. For one thing, they are possible sense-data, not actual ones. And for another, they are, even when actual, Santayanan essences, not qualities of subjective experience.

(b) Two later papers, "Comment," and "Real. Phen." place it quite beyond doubt that, whatever may have been Lewis' view at the time of AKV, he now holds a realist, not a phenomenalist, theory of objective existence. Contrary-to-fact conditional judgments about possible sense-data explicate the *intension* of objective statements, but not their *denotation*.

MWO, with its more phenomenalistic tone, is not so clear. It often seems as if Lewis were there holding that analytic statements are, all of them, about concepts, or about such other mental states as attitudes or classification procedures.[54] Fortunately, the question whether or not Lewis ever really intended to say that all analytic statements are about such mentalistic entities is really irrelevant to the point I wish to make. For he *certainly* believes, and has always believed, that an implicitly analytic judgment is about something other than itself, that it is about existents which are distinct from and independent of the state of mind which is the judgment itself.[55] In saying that the content of an implicitly analytic judgment is, for Lewis, an *independent* existent I mean that it is not controlled by or guaranteed by that act of thought which is the judgment itself.[56] Explicitly analytic statements, on the other hand, since they state the evidence (i.e., what makes itself evident) for implicitly analytic statements, are presumably about concepts which are presently inspectable at the time the judgment is made and are, in fact, only the 'components' of that judgment. Since for the remainder of this section I shall be concerned only with implicitly analytic statements, I shall, for the sake of brevity, refer to them simply as 'analytic statements'. And I shall express their character of being about independent existents by saying they are about the 'world'.

[54] See MWO, p. 197, pp. 215-16, p. 231, 237. Even in MWO, of course, Lewis holds that such an analytic statement as 'Birds are two-legged' is about *birds*. But MWO often inclines to offer a Kantian-phenomenalist analysis of what birds are, reducing them to sense-data plus certain classifications of these data. The classifications are identified with concepts, and it then often seems to be said that analytic statements are about these concepts, not about the sense-data which they classify. This, in turn, seems to be one of the explanations offered for the fact that analytic statements place no limitations upon experience (i.e., sense-data).

On the other hand, MWO, p. 256 and pp. 435-36, say quite definitely that a priori statements may be about nonconceptual existents. On the basis of these passages, I think it safe to say, once again, that even in MWO Lewis was holding the realist position which he expresses more consistently in AKV and still more consistently in the two late papers already mentioned. In any case, as the text points out, my argument in this section can proceed independently of this point.

[55] Lewis has always insisted that knowledge is essentially self-transcendent in the sense of being about something which is not given as a part of the cognitive act itself. See e.g., "Realism and Subjectivism," *Journal of Philosophy, Psych. & Sci. Method*, 10 (1913), 43-49, and "Experience and Meaning" (1934), *op. cit*. This is true whether the knowledge be about a nonphenomenal external world, about future sense-data, or about concepts. Thus, even if analytic statements were held to be about concepts, they would not be about presently entertained concepts, but rather about future instances of these concepts. They would say something like: '*Whenever* I classify something as a bird, I shall do so only if it has two legs' or '*I shall *never* apply the concept bird to anything unless it has two legs'.

[56] See AKV, p. ix: "An analytic statement says something; and something whose factuality is independent...."

The first thing to be said about Lewis' view that analytic statements are about the world is that it certainly does seem to be true. Beside the simplicity and obviousness of this view of the matter, any other position —such as that analytic statements should never occur in the material mode of speech—seems far-fetched indeed. I, at least, have no doubts that Lewis is essentially right about the question of content.[57]

But is such a realist handling of the content of analytic statements compatible with the empiricist tenet that the character of the existent world cannot be known prior to observation? Lewis thinks it is, since, in his view, analytic propositions place no limitations upon reality. If the truth of an analytic proposition required that reality be one way rather than another, then its truth a priori would be incompatible with empiricism. But since the truth of an analytic proposition makes no such requirements, it does not contravene Kant's insight that an independent reality can be any way whatever, so that the only way of knowing which way it is is to look and see.[58]

What I have just said is a correct statement of the view of MWO, but it is not a wholly accurate description of the position of AKV. The arguments offered by the two books in support of the position that analytic statements place upon the world no requirements which are incompatible with empiricism are rather different, or at least appear to be rather different, so that I want to consider them separately. First, AKV:

AKV does not say that analytic statements require nothing of the world but only that they require nothing which could conceivably fail to be the case.[59] Lewis expresses this point in a variety of ways. Analytic propositions, he says, require nothing which could "possibly" fail, which could "consistently" fail, which "could" fail, which could "thinkably" fail. An analytic proposition is true of all "possible" worlds. A world in which what an analytic proposition requires would fail is not "thinkable," not "consistently thinkable," not "logically thinkable," not "possible." Logic is true of "whatever *could* be." Lewis takes all of these terms to be definable in terms of each other, so that all of them are simply different ways of saying the same thing.[60] And the clearest way of all of saying

---

[57] This does not, of course, imply that there are analytic truths about the *contingent aspects* of reality—what are often called "matters of fact"—if there be any such. *No one* ever held that view, as Lewis himself points out in MWO, p. 223.

[58] MWO, pp. 197, 213, 215-16, 251.

[59] E.g., AKV, pp. 57, 122. The 'conceivably' is not psychological but logical. (See e.g., MWO, pp. 196, 198; AKV, p. 115, n. 3.)

[60] The equivalence of these terms and the way in which Lewis does define them in terms of each other is apparent throughout AKV. Pp. 111, 122, 128, and pp. 57-58 may be especially noted. MWO, pp. 433-435, gives a number of these terms and says they are "equivalent."

that thing is simply this: an analytic proposition has zero intension and universal comprehension; its denial has universal intension and zero comprehension. That is, the most illuminating way of explicating all of these modal expressions is in terms of intension and comprehension.[61]

It is often said that an analytic proposition is one which is true by virtue of the principle of noncontradiction—that is, one the denial of which is self-contradictory. And for the purpose of this discussion I am going to accept contradictoriness as the fundamental idea in terms of which the other modal notions are defined. I am therefore going to call analytic propositions tautologies. I do this solely for reasons of expository simplicity. I do not offer the definition as a *clarification* of analyticity. As I have indicated, Lewis apparently thinks that contradictoriness should itself be clarified in terms of universal intension and zero comprehension, and it is not evident to me that he is wrong about this. But no error can be involved in taking contradictoriness as fundamental, since Lewis certainly agrees that contradictoriness and universal intension are *equivalent*.[62]

I can now phrase Lewis' view on the problem of content this way: tautologies require of the world nothing that could possibly fail to be the case. And since tautologies are all deducible from the principle of noncontradiction, the essence of his position is really this: that the world could not possibly fail to satisfy the principle of noncontradiction, it could not possibly be other than self-consistent.[63] This is why Lewis thinks that his realist theory of the content of analytic propositions is consistent with empiricism. If the world *could* be other than self-consistent, then the only way to determine *whether* it was self-consistent

---

[61] The practice is general throughout AKV, but one may refer particularly to AKV, pp. 50, 57-58, 137-38. See also "The Modes of Meaning," *Philos. and Phenomenol. Research*, 4 (1943), 243.

[62] And at least once, he seems, contrary to his usual procedure, to *clarify* the other modal ideas in terms of contradictoriness: "The *comprehension* of a term is, thus, the classification of all consistently thinkable things to which the term would correctly apply —where anything is consistently thinkable if the assertion of its existence would not, explicitly or implicitly, involve a contradiction." AKV, p. 40. See also "Notes on the Logic of Intension," *op. cit.,* p. 27.

[63] It should be evident that the issue I am now discussing is the traditional one of the 'laws of thought'. If I have phrased the matter in terms of the law of noncontradiction, this was, again, for the sake of simplicity. Actually, of course, an analytic proposition follows from the self-contradictoriness of its denial only if it be known that either the proposition must be true or its denial must be true. Only, that is, if we know also the law of excluded middle. The law of identity raises special problems, since it is at least doubtful whether it is a proposition at all, since its subject and predicate seem to be but two instances of one *symbol* (see AKV, p. 74; but, on the other hand, cf. p. 84). Having noted this possible exception, it will place us in the proper historical context if we state Lewis' position this way: the laws of thought could not possibly be false.

would be to look and see. But since it *could* not be other than self-consistent, this fact can be known a priori. To say that reality must be self-consistent places no real limitation upon it since it *could* not be otherwise.

I think I can understand the reasoning behind Lewis' view that the principle of noncontradiction places upon the world no limitations of a sort which are incompatible with the empirical tenet that the character of existence can be known only a posteriori. For consider: all such modal terms as must, could, could not, could possibly, etc., have been defined in terms of contradictoriness. What, then, does it mean to say that the world 'could' not be self-contradictory? Evidently, it means only that it would be self-contradictory for the world to be self-contradictory. And to say that the world must be self-consistent is simply to say that the world would be inconsistent if it weren't consistent. And so on. But all of these statements are themselves identical propositions and hence are themselves true by the principle of noncontradiction. That is, the laws of thought are self-guaranteed. The applicability of the laws of logic to the world is evidenced by the laws of logic themselves.

The reasoning I have described, while nowhere clearly put forward by Lewis, seems to me implicit in much of AKV, and it is at least strongly suggested in MWO, pp. 219-221, 246-47, pp. 368, 385. It is this reasoning, I think, which is behind Lewis' practice of 'justifying' the application to the world of one modal term by applying to it (the world) another modal term which has been previously defined in terms of the first. Thus he will say that the world *could not* make an analytic proposition false because this is not *consistently* thinkable because it could not *possibly* be the case in any *possible* world because such a world would be *self-contradictory*, etc. Either Lewis is, throughout AKV, simply revolving in circles; or else (and I think this is the correct alternative) he really believes that the principle of noncontradiction certifies its own applicability in the way indicated above.

So the situation is this. I asked the question: "Must the world satisfy the principle of noncontradiction?" And we thought, or at least I thought, that this was a question about a copulative proposition involving two distinct things—the principle of noncontradiction on the one hand and the world on the other hand. But now it turns out that all I was really asking was: "Would the world be self-contradictory if it failed to satisfy the principle of noncontradiction?" This, however, is a question about an iterative proposition involving just one thing, the principle of noncontradiction. For the term 'world' occurs vacuously and may be replaced by a variable. And the answer to this question is obviously, "Yes, it would be." Hence, since the requirement of self-consistency could not fail to be the case, it is not really a limitation. Furthermore, it now seems quite impossible to ask the question about the world which I originally thought I was asking, since *all* of the modal terms, at least one of which would have to be used in asking it, have been defined in terms of contradictoriness.

I might, to be sure, try to ask the question I wanted to ask by avoiding all modal terms and, instead of asking whether the world *could* be other than self-consistent, asking whether it *is* other than self-consistent. But to this Lewis would reply that from the explicitly analytic truth that something is necessary the implicitly analytic truth that it is in fact the case is deducible. And surely, in any ordinary sense of the term necessity, he would be right.[64]

So I complain: but see here, you are holding that the principle of noncontradiction can be known to be true simply by an inspection of those criteria-in-mind which constitute its intensional meaning. At the same time, you hold that it is about the world. Now those two assertions certainly imply that the structure of the world depends upon our intensions—upon the ideas we have of the world. And *that*, in turn, is just another way of saying that our thought does place limitations upon the world.

And I am answered, I imagine: you forget that when one says that the principle of noncontradiction is true about the world all one is saying is that if the principle of noncontradiction did not hold of something, the world or anything else, then that something would be self-contradictory. And that clearly does not 'forbid' the world to be as it will. It does not 'limit' reality to what is self-consistent.[65]

---

[64] This is why an a priori theory of the laws of thought is more difficult to deal with than an a priori interpretation of induction. As I have elsewhere argued ("The Principle of Induction," *Journal of Philosophy*, 49 (1952), 741-47; 750-58), an a priori theory of induction (like Lewis') is compatible with empiricism just because probability judgments do not commit one to any assertions about as-yet-unobserved facts. This is because 'A will most probably occur' does not imply 'A will occur'. Or, 'A will most probably occur' places no limitations whatever upon reality. But the laws of thought *do* seem to place a limitation upon reality, just because 'A must occur' does imply 'A will occur'. (Compare MWO, p. 320, with MWO, p. 435.)

[65] The whole matter is somewhat complicated, verbally at least, by Lewis' restriction of modal terms to occurrence in *explicitly* analytic statements. (This restriction constitutes the *definition* of 'explicitly analytic'—see AKV, pp. 89-90, also p. 91 n. 5.) I have tried to phrase the above argument independently of this view, since it seems to me not an essential part of Lewis' philosophy. I do not see that anything in his philosophy would be upset if he allowed modal terms to occur in implicitly analytic truths about the world, except that the word 'implicit', which indicates that the 'necessity' is implicit, would then be a misleading way of indicating the difference between propositions about necessary relations of presently inspectable meanings and propositions about necessary relations of independently existing things.

I see all of this. Yet I feel cheated. I feel that I really had a genuine question to ask, a question about two distinct things, the world and the law of noncontradiction. And somehow I feel I have been deprived, by some kind of legerdemain, of the vocabulary in which I might phrase my question.

Of course, it is not really a matter of not having the requisite vocabulary. If I had a clear question in mind, I could invent a vocabulary in which to phrase it. Yet I stubbornly persist in feeling that there is a question. I feel, that is, that there is some notion of possibility and impossibility which is not to be defined in terms of contradictoriness.[66] And that in that, wider, sense of possibility, it is not an identical proposition to say that the world must be self-consistent, and not a self-contradiction to say that it could possibly be self-contradictory.

In my paper on induction cited in note 64, I argued that there is no sense of 'probable' which is not definable in terms of observed data plus laws of logic. Accordingly, I concluded that it is silly to ask whether the world will 'probably' bring to pass that which has been determined, on the basis of past observation plus the a priori laws of logic, to be indeed probable. In other words, I said that there really isn't any 'problem of induction'. Those who have read that paper are apparently almost unanimously agreed that there is some other sense of 'probable' which is not to be defined in terms of observed data and the laws of logic, and that hence it is not a tautology to say that what is probable in one sense (as having been determined by valid inferences from past observations) is also probable in this other sense of 'probable'. And that my paper completely overlooked this other sense of 'probable'.

The point I am making here is that I have an equivalent conviction about the laws of thought—that there is some sense of 'could' which is not definable in terms of contradiction and in terms of which it is not a tautology to say that the world could not be contradictory. It seems to

---

If, for the moment, we accept Lewis' view that modal terms occur only in explicitly analytic truths, then it becomes much easier to see why it is impossible even to raise the question whether the world must be self-consistent in the sense in which I thought I was raising it. For the question contains a modal term and is hence a question about an explicitly analytic proposition, hence about my presently inspectable concepts. It asks whether my presently inspectable concept of the world involves the concept of self-consistency. So that whereas I meant to ask a question about the relation between the world and my concept of the world, it turns out that all I have really asked is a question about my concept of the world.

It is perhaps of some importance to notice that, in restricting modal terms to explicitly analytic statements, Lewis does *not* mean to restrict them to the metalanguage, but only to that part of the object language which is about concepts ("Notes on the Logic of Intension," *op. cit.*, pp. 25-26).

[66] And hence not in terms of universal intension and zero comprehension either.

me that Lewis is handling the laws of thought as I handled induction; and just as many think that I missed a legitimate sense of 'probable', I think Lewis has missed a genuine sense of 'could'.

While of course I wish I knew clearly what this sense of 'could' is, I feel perhaps less badly about this than I otherwise would because of the fact that no one has yet been able to explain to me clearly *what* sense of 'probable' it was that I overlooked in dealing with induction. I cannot say that anyone has made it clearer than Lewis himself, who says that the "sense of probable events" is as inexplicable as the "primordial sense of futurity" (AKV, p. 320). Possibly I might permit myself the same sort of explication of 'could' and say that the meaning of this term cannot be explained to anyone who lacks the "primordial sense of possibility."

That there is some wider sense of possibility seems to me indicated not alone by the stubbornness of my feeling that I had a real question to ask, but also by something very odd which happens in Lewis' reasoning. As already noted, Lewis believes that from the premise that the world must be self-consistent the conclusion can be deduced that it is self-consistent.[67] But, as I have indicated, it is apparently Lewis' view that the premise of this deduction is an identical proposition, asserting only that any entity which failed to be self-consistent would indeed fail to be self-consistent. From this, Lewis deduces a proposition which, since the term world occurs in it essentially, is surely copulative.[68] This is most peculiar.

MWO (along with those parts of "A Pragmatic Conception of the *a Priori*" which are reproduced in MWO) appears to sketch a rather different defense of the position that, while analytic and hence necessary propositions are about the world, this places upon the world no restrictions which are incompatible with empiricism.[69] According to this argument, analytic statements place no restriction *whatever*, possible or impossible, thinkable or unthinkable, upon the world—or, in the language of MWO, upon experience.[70] And this assertion is defended as follows.

There is no univocal sense of the term reality, everything being real in some sense and unreal in other senses.[71] A priori truths explicate

67 And this is merely a special case of his belief that every implicitly analytic statement can be deduced from an explicitly analytic one which states its evidence. See MWO, p. 435; AKV, pp. 92, 123.
68 In Kantian language, he deduces a synthetic proposition from an analytic one.
69 See, principally, pp. 213-229 and Chaps. VIII and IX.
70 MWO, pp. 246, 251, and the same passages in "Prag. Conc.," pp. 286, 288-89.
71 MWO, p. 263.

the defining characteristics of these various senses of 'reality'. That is, they define the categories of being. Thus the only limitation that an a priori truth places upon anything is a hypothetical one: that it must possess certain properties *if*, but only if, it belongs to the category defined by those properties.[72] It does not require that anything belong to a given category.[73]

And the argument continues: even if we did, contrary to the above, give to 'real' a univocal sense, the real would still not be the only category at our disposal for classifying our experiences. There would be also the category of the unreal. So that an a priori truth which expressed the defining characteristics of reality (now in a univocal sense) would limit experiences to the possession of those characteristics if, but only if, the experiences were 'real'.[74] Once again, it would limit experience to the possession of these characteristics only hypothetically.[75]

Now this does undeniably establish that many so-called categorial features of the world (or experience) are not really limitations of anything, since they hold only hypothetically. But Lewis apparently intends the same reasoning to apply also to the law of noncontradiction. And here, it seems to me, the argument fails. The law of noncontradiction applies to the world not hypothetically, but categorically.[76] Each category, however defined (and even the category of the 'unreal') either includes a certain item of experience or does not include it, *and not both*. We may agree with Lewis that an item of experience is not categorically required to belong to any special category of reality, or even to the category of the (univocally) real. But *whatever* category it belongs to, it must not at the same time fail to belong to it. Or in other words, no item of experience can both possess a certain character and fail to possess it. A thing may fail to be a bird. But the hypothetical statement that if something is a bird then it is two-legged applies categorically to each and every thing, bird or not bird, real or unreal.

In one curious passage which occurs with only slight modifications in both MWO and "A Pragmatic Conception of the *a Priori*" Lewis

---

72 MWO, p. 221.

73 MWO, p. 314.

74 MWO, pp. 197, 224, 227. Also "Prag. Conc.," pp. 290-91.

75 MWO, p. 222: "A priori principles of categorial interpretation are required to limit reality; they are not required to limit experience."

76 Sometimes, as on p. 237 and pp. 245-56, it seems as if Lewis intended his proof of the hypothetical character of the categories to apply only to categories other than those expressed by the laws of thought; that he recognized, even in MWO, that there is really no alternative to consistency. However, "Prag. Conc.," p. 293, says explicitly that the laws of logic differ from the other categories only in degree and that they do, like the other categories, have alternatives. And, on the whole, this seems to be the view of MWO as well.

seems to admit that the requirement of self-consistency is indeed categorical and then to argue that, notwithstanding, it "forbids nothing." I quote this passage in the form in which it is given in MWO:

Sometimes we are asked to tremble before the specter of the "alogical" in order that we may thereafter rejoice that we are saved from this by the dependence of reality upon mind. But the "alogical" is pure bogey, a word without a meaning. What kind of experience could defy the principle that . . . nothing can both be and not be . . .? If anything imaginable or unimaginable could violate such laws, then the ever-present fact of change would do it every day. The laws of logic are purely formal; they forbid nothing but what concerns the use of terms and the corresponding modes of classification and analysis. The law of contradiction tells us that nothing can be both white and not white, but it does not and can not tell us whether black is not white or soft or square is not white. To discover what contradicts what we must turn to more particular considerations.[77]

Now it is surely true, as Lewis says, that the law of noncontradiction does not, of itself, tell us what specific qualities contradict white. But it *does* tell us that if something is white then it cannot also possess any quality which contradicts white and the presence of which therefore implies the absence of white. In other words, it tells us just this: that if a thing is white it cannot at the same time fail to be white. And this *does* 'forbid' something. So that when Lewis says that the 'alogical' is a pure bogey, since no experience could contravene the principle that nothing can both be and not be, the reply must be made that any experience which both did and did not possess a certain quality would contravene that principle. And that if the idea of such an experience is a 'bogey', this can be only because what Lewis means in calling it a bogey is that such an experience would indeed be self-contradictory. Which returns us to the argument of AKV.

### III

Empiricism is often defined, not in terms of the problem of content ('there is no a priori knowledge of reality'), but in terms of the structure of a priori propositions ('all a priori propositions are iterative'). If any a priori propositions were copulative then it would be possible to get 'new' knowledge by purely rational means. And if such propositions were in addition supposed to be about the world, then we should have

---

[77] MWO, p. 246. Instead of "we must turn to more particular considerations," "Prag. Conc." reads "we must always consult experience" (p. 287). The change was indeed advisable. For according to Lewis' view of the matter, experience could never tell us "what contradicts what." Only an examination of the intension of 'black' can tell us that black contradicts white.

to hold, contrary to Hume, that there are necessary connections of matters of fact.

With this empiricist position, Lewis agrees. All a priori propositions assert a relationship of intensional meanings or a relationship of other entities which is cognitively derivable from such a relationship of intensional meanings.[78] This relationship of intensional meanings is the analytic meaning of the propositions as wholes, "their meaning as complex expressions whose intension is constituted by the intensional meaning of their constituents and the syntactic order of these."[79]

---

[78] AKV, p. 94. It will be simpler, in this section, to say that every proposition *asserts* such a relationship of meanings, remembering that this is strictly true only of explicitly analytic propositions (see AKV, Chap. IV, Secs. 8 and 9).

[79] AKV, p. 85. I have restricted the above description of analytic meaning to propositions. Actually, Lewis seems to apply it to expressions generally, nonpropositional as well as propositional (AKV, Chap. IV, Secs. 5, 6, 7), so that if any expression whatever has zero intension, this intension is a complex meaning built up from constituent meanings and their relationships. And this is, indeed, what he should hold, for he is actually trying to explicate zero intensionality in general and not just analyticity—'analytic' being nothing but the name we give to expressions of zero intenson when the expressions happen to be propositions or statements. But the extension of analytic meaning to nonpropositional expressions raises special problems which I may indicate but shall not consider in detail:

(a) Lewis' definition of analytic meaning seems to make that idea applicable only to complex expressions, since it requires that the meaning of the whole expression be built up out of the meanings of constituent *expressions*. ("It is hardly significant to speak of analytic meaning in the case of elementary expressions. Nevertheless it will be convenient to be able to extend this designation to them: let us say that the analytic meaning of an elementary expression is simply the intension of it," AKV, p. 85.) Now propositions are, by definition, verbally complex, so that they do have constituent expressions. But nonpropositional terms may be elementary. Since in the case of such expressions it is "hardly significant" to speak of their having analytic meaning, and since zero intensionality is explicated in terms of analytic meaning, the question arises whether any elementary expression could have zero intension. On this point Lewis appears to vacillate. He seems to recognize a very few elementary terms as having either zero or universal intension. He mentions 'being' and 'entity' as elementary expressions which are certainly of zero intension and 'thing' as a doubtful case. The only elementary expression of universal intension which he mentions is 'zero'. (AKV, p. 88. These are the exceptions referred to in note 7.) But then he goes on to say that there would be no "point" in using such expressions in isolation (AKV, p. 84), that "we should never have occasion to use terms like 'being' . . . if it were not that we convey something by *putting these in relation* to other expressions" (AKV, p. 89), and that "Obviously absolutely nothing can be said and no thought conveyed without using elementary expressions whose intension is neither zero nor universal" (AKV, p. 89; see also AKV, p. 152). The question is not, of course, whether elementary expressions of zero or universal intension say anything very interesting, but whether they say anything at all. ("The Modes of Meaning," *op. cit.*, p. 248, mentions this same matter, but does nothing to clarify the grounds of Lewis' objection to such expressions.) In the end, and in spite of all his attempts to minimize the number and importance of such expressions, it seems to be Lewis' view that there are meaningful elementary expressions of zero and universal intension. But if so, their zero intensionality cannot be explicated in terms of analytic meaning as Lewis has defined that, since these expressions have no constituent expressions. It seems to me, therefore, that analytic meaning ought to be defined as 'mean-

But it is not just any sort of a relationship of meanings which is asserted by an a priori proposition. It is the specific relationship which consists in the meaning of the explicans being included in the meaning of the explicandum.[80] An a priori proposition does not, that is, assert a connection of two externally related meanings, but simply iterates or makes explicit all or some part of one meaning.[81] If it iterates all of the

---

ing as constituted by constituent meanings', instead of as 'meaning as constituted by meanings of constituent expressions'. In this way, attention is focussed on complexity of meaning rather than complexity of expression. This would be more consonant with Lewis' general view that meanings are prior to their expression and need not be expressed at all (AKV p. 110; see also pp. 78, 131, 139, 148, 156; also "The Modes of Meaning," *op. cit.*, p. 236). And it would permit us to make a significant distinction between the holophrastic and the analytic meaning of elementary expressions. This is wholly desirable, since a typical explicative statement has an elementary expression as its explicandum (AKV, p. 98), and the best way of explaining what an explicative statement does is to say that it expresses the analytic meaning of its explicandum. I think the only reason that Lewis defines analytic meaning the way he does, so as to require that any expression which can 'significantly' be said to have analytic meaning be a complex *expression*, is because he is putting the notion of analytic meaning to two distinct uses. He is using it to explain why an expression may have zero or universal intension (AKV, Chap. IV, Secs. 7, 9). At the same time he is using it to explicate the fact that while any two expressions of zero or universal intension have the same meaning in all four modes of holophrastic meaning, they may still be said to have different analytic meanings (AKV, Chap. IV, Secs. 5, 6). The latter consideration leads him to emphasize the way in which the expression is constructed out of other *expressions*, an emphasis which is at best awkward when it is transferred to the former problem.

(b) But even if analytic meaning be redefined so as to eliminate the requirement of complexity of expression, our difficulties are not at an end. For one thing, Lewis' whole discussion of analytic meaning presupposes that analytic meaning is built up out of *elementary* components. This works well enough in connection with expressions, but when we apply it to meanings, it contradicts Lewis' view that there are no elementary meanings, all meanings being analyzable (MWO, pp. 81-83, p. 106). It would seem that we must either give up one of the very central theses of MWO, or else discard, as irrelevant to the analysis of meanings, a great deal of what Lewis says about 'analytic meaning' in AKV.

Furthermore, it is by no means evident that every meaning which can figure as an explicandum in an a priori judgment is complex. For example, the traditional idea has been that the meaning of such an expression as 'being' cannot be analyzed, but only grasped. Nor, traditionally, has this simplicity of meaning been thought to make this expression pointless or insignificant. If any part of Lewis' objection to such terms as 'being', 'entity', and 'zero' is based on supposing that these terms express simple meanings, then not only does this supposition contradict the view expressed in MWO, but nothing whatever is said to support the conclusion that this is objectionable.

But here again, if we restrict the discussion to propositions, we can avoid the difficulty, since a proposition has, by definition, a meaning which is complex (even such a proposition as ' "Being" has zero intension and is universally applicable').

80 For the sake of simplicity, I shall extend 'included in' so as to take in also 'identical with'.

81 This is another case in which the reader's conviction of the correctness of the proffered interpretation of Lewis would be only weakened by attempting to support with some finite number of specific references something which is obvious on nearly every page of both books. But one may note particularly MWO, pp. 37, 231, and esp. pp. 292-301, and the discussion of Kant in AKV, pp. 161-63.

meaning, then it is a definition and is called by Lewis an "explicative statement."[82] If it iterates only a part of the meaning, then it is still an explication and it follows from an explicative statement.[83]

"In a typical definitive statement, the expression to be defined is elementary, or at least verbally simpler, and the defining expression is more complex. Let us therefore take as our paradigm, 'A=BC Def.,' . . . ."[84] This is why a typical explicative statement accomplishes something more than just sheer repetition. It expresses constituents of the meaning of the explicandum which the explicandum itself left unexpressed.[85] But in any case, every a priori proposition, whether or not it

When MWO says (e.g., p. 5, pp. 81-83) that logical analysis does not dissect a concept into ultimate "constituents" but rather specifies its constant relations to other concepts, this is not really an exception to the view just stated. For these relations *are* exactly the constituents of the concept defined, they are what it is. In objecting to calling such relations constituents Lewis is simply warning that we must not suppose that by analysis we shall reach constituents which are simple and unanalyzable, since all definition is essentially circular.

MWO, pp. 68-69, is a genuine exception, for it states quite unambiguously that the explicandum and the explicans are "different meanings." I argue in n. 113 that this unique passage must be retracted, since, if left to stand, it shatters Lewis' whole treatment of the a priori.

[82] AKV, p. 99.

[83] E.g., 'Cats are feline animals' is an explicative statement. 'Cats are feline' is explicative, but not an explicative statement, since the meaning of the explicans is only a part of the meaning of the explicandum, so that no equivalence is asserted.

[84] AKV, p. 98.

[85] It would seem that there are, for Lewis, three different sorts of explicable statements, differing in the extent to which they have a 'point' and are 'significant'. There is also a class of pseudo-propositions which might be taken for explicative statements, but actually say nothing whatever.

(1) So-called 'identical' propositions (e.g., Tuesday is Tuesday) are pseudo-propositions which do not have even the significance of repetition, since their subject and predicate are merely two instances of the same *expression*. (AKV, pp. 74, 107. However, cf. p. 84.)

(2) When the explicandum and explicans of a proposition are different expressions, because symbolized by different symbols, but have the same analytic meaning, thus having the same meaning in *every* sense of meaning, then the proposition (e.g., circular is round) is a genuine explicative statement (AKV, pp. 85, 99) but a relatively unimportant, uninteresting, and atypical one. All explicative statements in which the explicandum and explicans both have elementary meanings (if, in contradiction to MWO, there be elementary meanings) fall into this class. Also all explicative statements the explicandum and explicans of which have complex meanings which are "analytically comparable." (AKV, pp. 85-86. However, one should eliminate from the definition of analytic comparability the prescription that none of the constituent meanings may be either zero or universal, since this prescription has to do with another matter. See n. 79.)

(3) When the explicandum and explicans have the same holophrastic meaning but differ in analytic meaning (i.e., are not analytically comparable), then the statement genuinely explicates in the sense that the explicans expresses components of the meaning of the explicandum which the explicandum itself did not express.

(4) If, in addition to being unexpressed, these constituent meanings were not even explicitly in mind, then the explicative statement genuinely explicates one's *meaning*. See Section IV.

be a "typical definitive statement," and whether or not it be even an "explicative statement" (i.e., a definition), is, in Lewis' view, explicative of its "subject" or explicandum. It is what I have called an iterative proposition. It is this 'problem of iteration' which I wish to examine in the present section.

Every a priori proposition is either such that its contradictory is "explicitly and by its form self-contradictory" or it is such that it is "so transformable that the contradictory of it will become explicitly and by its form self-contradictory,"[86] the transformation being effected by explicative statements. But an a priori proposition is also *necessarily* true. This means that its denial must be a necessary falsehood. It means, in other words, that what is self-contradictory (A and —A) must necessarily be false. A and —A must be incompatible, and not just in fact false for all values of 'A'.

The incompatibility of A and —A is of course exactly what is asserted by the principle of noncontradiction. So the net result of the last paragraph is that every a priori truth strictly entails some instance of the law of noncontradiction. But surely an iterative proposition cannot entail a copulative one. Hence, no proposition is iterative unless the law of noncontradiction is.

The same conclusion can perhaps be reached less rigorously by another route. For such a proposition as 'Birds have two legs', while it may be iterative, surely does not *seem* to be. It seems to assert a connection between two distinct things—birds and two-leggedness. 'A is incompatible with —A', on the other hand, does not even seem to be about anything except A. Surely if any proposition is iterative, this one is.

Consonantly with his general position, Lewis holds that logical laws in general, and the law of noncontradiction in particular, are themselves explicative. They do not, to be sure, explicate the meaning of such terms as 'birds', since, by definition of 'logic', such terms occur only vacuously in logical propositions. But they are explicative of the logical constants, such as 'all' and 'not', which occur in logical propositions essentially (AKV, Chap. V, Secs. 12 and 14).

But is it not the case, on the contrary, that the principle of noncontradiction asserts a connection of distinct meanings? The distinct meanings are simply those expressed by 'A' and '—A'. What the principle of noncontradiction asserts of these meanings is that they are incompatible.[87] Or, equivalently, one may say that the distinct meanings are —A and being incompatible with A, and that what the law of

86 AKV, p. 128.

87 The correct example is not, of course, white and black (cf. MWO, p. 246) but white and not-white.

noncontradiction says of these distinct meanings is that the former strictly entails the latter.

The alternative to this conclusion is, obviously, that 'incompatible with A' is itself nothing but an iterative explication of '—A'. If this were so, then to say that A and —A are incompatible would be only another way of saying that —A is indeed —A. That is, the law of noncontradiction would indeed be iterative, as Lewis holds.

Against such a construction of the situation I shall not raise the possibility that there are negative states of affairs, so that —A might be defined ostensively.[88] But even supposing that '—A' is defined intensionally in terms of 'A' and 'not', it is clear, at least to me, that '—A' means 'absence of A' and not 'incompatible with A'. And that what the principle of noncontradiction asserts is that the presence and absence of A, these being distinct things, are incompatible and cannot both be the case. I can say little by way of 'proof' of this. I have already reduced the issue to what seem to me its simplest elements. And on this level the only possible argument is a clear and distinct idea. The only sort of 'proof' I can think of is this. If to say that A and —A are incompatible were only another way of saying that —A is indeed —A, then the law of noncontradiction would be deducible from the law of identity. But this would be exceedingly odd, for all that the law of identity says (if, indeed, it says anything) is that A is A. The law of noncontradiction adds to this the information that if, as claimed by the law of identity, A is A, then A cannot also be —A—i.e., the information that A is incompatible with —A.

I do not offer this rephrasing of the principle of noncontradiction in terms of presence and absence as a clarification of the principle. 'Absent' is nothing but a synonym of 'not' itself; and 'presence of A' adds nothing to 'A'. But the point is that to say of —A that it is incompatible with A is to say *more* than to say of it simply that it is indeed —A. From the premise that something is a —A, it does not follow that it is not an A unless we assume that a thing cannot be both A and —A, unless, that is, we assume the incompatibility of A and —A, that is, the principle of noncontradiction.

If it be argued that Inc (A·—A) follows necessarily from the definition of '—', since —A just *is* the notness of A, then the answer to this is that it follows only if we assume that A cannot be both itself and not itself, both present and absent. This seems to me to be in accord with what Lewis says in MWO, p. 208, although incompatible with the position of AKV.

---

[88] If '—A' did have an ostensive definition, then of course it would immediately follow that '—A is incompatible with A' is copulative.

Or it might be argued that Inc (A•—A) is demonstrable solely from the truth-table rule that if we assign T to A then we must assign F to —A and vice versa, and that, since this rule constitutes a definition of 'not', Inc (A•—A) does follow just from the meaning of 'not'.[89] If this were urged, I should have to reply that Inc (A•—A) is *not* demonstrable solely by the above truth-table rule. It becomes demonstrable by truth tables only if we adopt the additional rule that if we put T under some element (including the main connective) we cannot also put F under it. But this rule is simply the principle of noncontradiction itself. And *it* does not simply explicate the sense of 'not', but the sense of 'incompatible with A'.[90]

Assuming, then, that tautologies are copulative, does this contradict the empiricist view that there are no necessary connections of distinct facts?

Well, it depends upon what you mean by 'distinct' (and the equivalent term copulative). If you mean 'distinguishable in any way whatever, in any sort of thought or experience, however confused', then obviously the existence of copulative a priori propositions does contradict the tenet that there are no necessary connections of distinct facts. Empiricism, in one generally accepted definition of it, is just false. But then it has been evident for a long while that Hume was wrong in thinking that there are no necessary connections among things which are in any way distinguishable. Insides and outsides, up and down, left and right—indeed, any relation and its converse—are obvious examples of things which are distinguishable but necessarily connected.

If, on the other hand, one means by the term distinct something like 'clearly and distinctly conceivable in isolation', then the conflict disappears. For in that case all of a thing's necessary connections are included in a 'totally clear and distinct idea' of what the thing is. Consequently all of the a priori truths about anything are iterative of its 'nature'.[91] What this alternative amounts to is defining the expres-

89 Lewis himself appears to argue in this way in "Alternative Systems of Logic," *Monist,* 42 (1932), esp. 485.

90 See MWO, pp. 206-10. There is of course also the rule to assign either T or F to each element. This rule does not, any more than the rule not to assign both values, explicate the sense of any of the logical constants in expressions testable by truth tables. Rather, it is just the law of excluded middle.

91 This is essentially the way in which Lewis proves, in AKV, pp. 158-63, that all analytic truths are iterative. For he there keeps urging that whatever is necessary to the application of a term is essential, and hence included in any adequate definition of that term. Or, alternatively, he urges that anything which is entailed by an event must be logically entailed by it, since whatever the event entails must be part of an adequate concept of it. Both of these are simply alternative ways of saying that if 'two' events should have

sion distinct (and hence also 'copulative') in terms of the absence of necessary connections.[92] But it now immediately follows, by definition, that propositions which state necessary connections cannot possibly be about distinct things, and hence that all necessary propositions are iterative.[93]

But is this not exactly the same alternative that many "rationalistic realists" have adopted? No rationalist, except possibly Parmenides, was so monistic as to deny that he could distinguish between his chair and his pipe. What many rationalists have urged is that a totally clear notion of the chair and of the pipe will disclose that these are not really distinct things, but rather, *just because they do have necessary connections,* 'abstractions' or 'moments' of a larger totality.

Now if the empiricist also adopts this alternative, it seems to me he will agree with the relevant part of what such rationalists have urged. He may not agree that there are necessary connections between the chair and the pipe, but he will agree that if there are such connections, then the things connected are not distinct things.

The disagreement which perhaps still remains, whether the pipe and the chair have necessary connections, seems to have nothing to do with the fact that one man is an 'empiricist' and the other a 'rationalist'. It is just a disagreement on the monism-pluralism issue. It is a disagreement about metaphysics—about whether the Hegelians are right that all things are necessarily connected so that the only distinct thing is the whole or whether the universe has looser joints than that. The question whether there are copulative a priori truths seems to have nothing to do with the matter except insofar as this question is just another way of asking what distinguishable things, if any, are necessarily connected.

Kant, to be sure, really did think there could be necessary connections among distinct things. But this was because he failed to realize that 'distinct' just means 'not necessarily connected'. Instead, he tried to distinguish two sorts of necessary connections, iterative and copulative, to define 'distinct' in terms of the absence of iterative connections

necessary connections, then they would be included in each other's definitions, and hence would not be 'two' but 'one'.

92 Since the 'conceivable' in 'clearly and distinctly conceivable in isolation' does not refer to what it is psychologically possible to conceive but to what could exist alone. And to say that a thing could exist alone is just to say that it has no necessary connections.

93 Given this meaning of 'distinct', the point I have been trying to make in this section about the principle of noncontradiction could no longer be described as the view that that principle is copulative. It would now have to be described as the view that while the principle of noncontradiction is iterative, being concerned with only one distinct meaning, it asserts a relation between two distinguishable meanings.

only, and then to raise the question whether two things which are distinct may nonetheless have necessary copulative connections. By an iterative connection he meant a whole-part relationship.[94] Not, however, a relation between an object and its parts, but rather between the concept of an object and *its* parts. What, then, are we to mean by 'the concept of an object'? A little reflection shows that this is exactly the same question we have already considered, viz., the question what we are to mean by 'distinct'. It therefore has the same two possible answers. 'The concept of an object' may mean any concept sufficient to distinguish its object. In that case there certainly are necessary connections among objects which are not included as parts in each others' concepts. On that point, Kant is right, Hume wrong.[95] Or, 'the concept of an object' may mean the whole or adequate concept of it—i.e., the concept which includes all that is essential to it, all that is posited when it is posited. But if we take 'the concept of an object' in this sense, then, as Lewis has shown, its 'parts' are exactly the necessary relations between 'this' object and 'other' objects.[96] And, as he has also shown, no concept of an object can be in this sense adequate or complete unless it contains as parts *all* of the necessary connections of its object.[97] On this point Lewis is right, Kant wrong. This is hardly surprising. Just as it is evident that Hume's principle that whatever is distinguishable is separable is, if asserted unrestrictedly, mistaken, so it is apparent that Kant's 'deductions' of the validity of copulative a priori truths are nothing but *analyses* of the *adequate* concepts of such things as 'object', 'nature', and 'experience'.

But as I have already indicated, this is a matter on which "rationalistic realism" would agree with Lewis. The rationalists are often accused of having failed to make a distinction between those of their self-evident axioms which were copulative and those which were iterative. Indeed, it was Kant himself who, as far as I know, first made this charge. But I think the reason they did not make Kant's distinction was that it never occurred to them to suppose that any self-evident truth could be other than iterative or that there could possibly be necessary connections among distinct things, i.e., substances. Every necessary proposition, with the

[94] Or, in the extreme case, an identity.

[95] At least, the Hume who said that whatever is distinguishable is separable is wrong. However, as soon as we throw the whole question into the language of ideas, as we have just done, it becomes obvious that even Hume himself did not apply the principle that whatever is distinguishable is separable to ideas. As he states this principle, he seems to intend it to have universal scope, but in practice he restricts it to impressions or 'matters of fact'.

[96] MWO, pp. 81-83, p. 106. See n. 79.

[97] AKV, pp. 158-63. See n. 91.

possible exception of the law of noncontradiction itself,[98] is iterative in the sense that a denial of it would contradict the adequate concept of its subject.[99]

I think the confusion in this whole matter can be laid at Kant's door and attributed ultimately to his failure to see that, of the two expressions 'necessary truth' and 'distinct thing', one must be defined in terms of the other. The monism-pluralism issue can be discussed by asking whether any, or perhaps all, distinguishable facts are distinct (i.e., without necessary connections), or whether, to take the opposite extreme, all distinguishable facts are necessarily connected parts of one Absolute Fact. Or it can equally well be discussed by asking whether any a priori propositions are copulative, in the sense of being about distinguishable facts. But these two sets of terms are equivalent. If you get both sets going at the same time, as Kant did, you are likely to overlook their equivalence. And because you overlook the equivalence, you are likely to suppose, as Kant did, that in addition to the question of whether there are any distinct facts short of the Absolute, there is also the question whether, supposing there are distinct facts, it is possible to have a priori knowledge of their connections.

## IV

An a priori statement may simply re-express a meaning.[100] More significantly, the explicans may express more or other constituents of a complex meaning than are expressed by the explicandum, it being supposed that these additional or other constituents were already in mind, but left unexpressed. But by far the most significant a priori statements are those which give voice to a judgment which is an actual analysis of the meaning expressed by the explicandum. Such analysis is not really analysis of an expression into constituent expressions, for the explicandum may well be an elementary expression, but an analysis of the meaning expressed by the explicandum.[101]

To analyze a meaning is to bring to explicit awareness implications

---

[98] See Section II.

[99] See MWO, pp. 320 ff.

[100] If, the meaning being 'elementary', the explicandum and explicans are synonymous; or if, the meaning being complex, they are analytically comparable (with the qualification previously observed).

[101] This sense of 'analysis', in which a meaning is said to be analyzed into its implicit constituents, is, I think, the sense of the term which is in question in 'the paradox of analysis'. It is also in this sense of the term, perhaps, that Lewis says that the peculiar business of philosophy is analysis (AKV, pp. 139, 142-43).

of it which were previously in mind only implicitly.[102] It is because a priori judgments may analyze a meaning in the sense of bringing explicitly to mind implications of it which were previously implicit that they can "convey something novel."[103] And such analysis is necessary because every meaning has an infinite number of implications, not all of which could be explicitly in mind at a given moment.

*That* a certain meaning is implicitly contained in another is presumably, in the end, a matter of intuition.[104] If the analysis is somewhat complex, we may call it 'deduction'. But deduction is just a series of intuitions.

What I want to do in this section is to point out what seems a critical difficulty in Lewis' handling of the notion that meanings may be *implicit*. There is an evident connection between this 'problem of implicitness' and the 'problem of iteration' with which I was concerned in the preceding section. For whether or not the principle of noncontradiction is in fact iterative, it does at least look as if it were iterative. But such an a priori statement as 'Cubes have twelve edges' doesn't even look iterative—and this is true either of the expression itself or of what we have explicitly in mind when we use the expression. The only hope of showing that, appearances notwithstanding, such a statement is iterative consists in showing that its iterative character is implicit. That is, it consists in showing that the meaning of 'having twelve edges' is implicit in the meaning of 'cube'.[105]

Which of the modes of meaning does Lewis have in mind when he speaks of meanings' being implicit in other meanings? Here, as in the question of evidence, Lewis places all of the emphasis upon intensional meanings, criteria-in-mind—or, as I have previously argued, ideas.[106]

---

[102] It will be well to keep this usage of 'implicit' and 'explicit' distinct from the sense Lewis gives these terms when he speaks of implicitly and explicitly analytic statements (see nn. 50-51). The two senses are of course related, since the 'implicitly' in 'implicitly analytic statement' indicates that the analytic character of the statement is not expressed —hence, in a sense, not explicit. But in that case the distinction is between what is and is not explicitly expressed. Here the distinction is between what is and is not explicitly in mind.

[103] AKV, p. 107. On the same page Lewis says: "That the intension of one expression is the same as that of another, may be a discovery of thought precisely because, and only where, there is some constituent of one intension, *as grasped,* which is not a constituent of the other, in the terms in which it is *antecedently grasped."* (Italics mine.)

[104] Note the use of terms like "direct insight," "simple and direct observation," and "grasp" in AKV, Chap. V, Sec. 8 and on p. 193, 242.

[105] In the broadest sense of 'meaning'—in which this term might receive a realist, a conceptualist or a nominalist interpretation.

I shall not in this section argue that such a statement is not iterative, but simply that Lewis has not provided any adequate explanation of how it could be iterative.

[106] See n. 20. Indeed, the present question is really one part of the problem of evidence. The evidence for a proposition the contradictory of which is "explicitly and by its form

Thus we can say that Lewis' view is this: certain ideas are implicitly implied in other ideas. It is because of this that a priori statements can genuinely explicate.[107] And it is because of this that we can say that many statements which do not seem to be tautologies really are.

I have already noted the way in which Lewis explicates all of the modal expressions in terms of the conceptualist notion of intension. This is representative of the manner of his attack upon all epistemological problems.[108] *All* notions such as axiom, theorem, implies, deducible, analytic, synonymous, equivalent, etc., he ultimately explicates in terms of concepts.[109] Accordingly, he explicates the 'implications' of an idea as consisting of constituent ideas, either explicit or implicit. To say that an idea implies such and such is simply, for Lewis, to say that the idea of such and such is a part of that idea.[110]

self-contradictory" is its zero intensionality; the evidence for a proposition which is only "so transformable that the contradictory of it will become explicitly and by its form self-contradictory" is its zero intensionality as this is explicitly disclosed by analysis.

[107] E.g., "all a priori truth is definitive, or explicative of concepts" (MWO, p. 37). "Such explication of what is implicit in the concept . . ." (MWO, p. 284).

[108] As he recognizes in AKV, p. 11. Cf. also AKV, pp. 50, 57, 129-30, 160, 195, plus the whole discussion of logic in Chap. V.

[109] It is interesting to note, however, that there is a certain discrepancy in this respect between what is said in AKV, Book I (on the a priori) and what is done in Book II (on empirical knowledge). If Book II practiced what is said in Book I, we should expect to find Lewis arguing that an infinite number of terminating judgments are relevant to the truth of a nonterminating judgment on the ground that he finds these terminating judgments implicitly included in the intension of a nonterminating judgment. What he actually argues, on the contrary, is that an infinite number of terminating judgments must be implicitly contained in the intension of a nonterminating judgment because they are relevant to the truth of the nonterminating judgment (see e.g., p. 194). This point has a certain importance in considering the worth of the argument Lewis gives for the verifiability theory of meaning. His argument seems to consist in pointing to the fact that an infinite number of possible experiences are relevant to the truth of a nonterminating statement. But whether that fact has any implications whatever for one's theory of meanings-in-mind (intensions) depends upon how one explicates relevance. If relevance were explicated realistically or nominalistically, then the fact that A is relevant to the truth of P would indicate nothing whatever about whether the idea of A must be a part of the intension of P. This consequence follows only if relevance be explicated conceptualistically. Only, that is, if it be maintained that to say that A is relevant to P is simply a confused way of saying that the idea of A is included in the intension of P. But in that case, the only argument which would show that an infinite number of possible experiences are relevant to the truth of a nonterminating judgment would consist in discovering the ideas of these experiences implicit in the meanings of nonterminating judgments. Which is, as I have pointed out, the opposite of Lewis' actual procedure.

[110] I am not supposing that Lewis makes the crude error of thinking that ideas are parts of one another in the same sense exactly in which a leg of a chair is a part of the chair. On the other hand, I am quite sure he does mean that, in whatever sense an idea may be said to have explicit parts, it may also be said to have implicit parts. There are times when he speaks as if all he meant was that one test-routine was a part of another test-routine. But such a view would be quite inconsistent with the exclusive emphasis he places upon in-

But now what can it mean to say that the constituents of an idea are 'implicit'?[111] *This* is my difficulty. I just cannot attach any sense to the notion of an implicit idea except this: that an implicit idea is an idea of which one is not conscious.

It will not do to say that by 'implicit' Lewis means only something like 'implied by', or 'logically deducible from' or 'part of the definition of'. For Lewis, as I have indicated, explicates *these* expressions in terms of the implicitness of ideas.[112]

Nor will it do to suggest, citing MWO, pp. 84, 87, that what Lewis means is not that there are unconscious ideas but simply that there are grades or degrees of consciousness. For again, the only explication Lewis gives of 'degrees' of consciousness is in terms of how much of an idea is conscious compared with how much of it is unconscious.[113]

tension, since test-routines are pieces of behavior, not criteria-in-mind. In the end, we must come back to the idea that what he means is that the idea of one test-routine is included in the idea of the other test-routine. Thus he says: "The question, 'Does your schematism for determining application of the term "square" include your schematism for applying "rectangle"?' is one determined in the same general fashion as is the answer to the question, 'Does your plan of a trip to Chicago to see the Field Museum include the plan of visiting Niagara to see the Falls?'" (AKV, p. 154). Furthermore, the use of such terms as component, constituent, includes and contains is completely general throughout both books, and such terms as implication, consequence, etc. are explained by reference to them and not vice versa.

[111] E.g., what can it mean to say that my plan to take the PRR from Boston to Chicago includes, but only implicitly, the plan of going around Horseshoe Curve?

[112] See, e.g., AKV, pp. 129-30. Very occasionally, Lewis seems to make the explication go in the opposite direction. The most serious example of this is in AKV, pp. 177-78, where Lewis is explaining how a meaning or belief could include an infinite number of consequences. He there explains that "included in" really means only "deducible from." But of course he has already explicated "deducible from" in terms of "included in." And while, at the time of MWO anyway, Lewis thought that philosophical analysis, like all analysis, necessarily goes in circles, I'm sure he did not intend it to go in such tight little circles as this. For as he says in AKV, p. 379, explicative statements must be "explications of one intension by another and more familiar or more lucid meaning. . . . Only if they have this character . . . can they contribute to the clarification of a serious matter. . . ."

[113] This is perhaps the best place to call attention also to a very curious passage in MWO, p. 68, where, in the course of discussing the way in which one may become clearer about a term's intension over the course of time, he says: "But if the meaning of a word or phrase undergo evolution, then, however normal or inevitable or commendable this process may be, we must, for the sake of clarity, recognize that this meaning is one unitary entity only in some generic and genetic sense, and that logically what we have is a succession of different meanings, related in ways which may be important." (This is the passage, referred to in n. 81, which unambiguously states that a priori truths are copulative, and which I there said has to be retracted, since it contradicts Lewis' whole treatment of the a priori.)

Lewis just *cannot* explicate clarification in terms of the logical relations among different meanings. For his whole handling of the problem of the a priori consists precisely in explicating logical relations in terms of clarification (see esp. MWO, pp. 292-95). Roughly speaking, it is Lewis' view that B is related to A by the logical relation

Now I would *like* to believe there can be unconscious ideas, and often it seems to me there must be. It does seem as if there were such a thing as 'clarifying one's ideas by eliciting into explicit consciousness constituents of them which were formerly implicit'. And such a thing as 'coming to know what one really believed'. And such a thing as "failing to observe what is involved in our own intentions and of mistaking our own meanings through inconsistency."[114] It does seem as if, when I count the edges of the cube which I am no longer seeing, or count the speckles on the hen after the hen has gone about her business, or remark that there were six people present at my seminar even though I hadn't noticed this fact at the time, I were noticing or bringing to consciousness parts of my ideas which had formerly gone unnoticed.

And it does seem as if, in analysis, we did more than just offer a linguistic reformulation of our original idea, spelling out in more detailed language the elements which we had in mind all the while. It seems as if we did something to the idea. And it seems as if what we did to the idea was not to substitute another, more complex, idea for it. Because in that case the connection of the two ideas would be copulative, whereas in fact the idea of a brother, for example, seems to be exactly the same idea as the idea of a male sibling. It seems, rather, as if what we did to the idea was to make it *clearer,* and as if there were no clearer way than this of saying what we did.

Furthermore, it does often seem to me, for example when I am reading Freud, that talk about the unconscious mind is meaningful in exactly the same direct sense as talk about the conscious mind.

Nor do the alternatives to Lewis' view—I can think of only two—seem to me to hold much promise. One alternative—which I may again call 'nominalism'—attempts to explain implicitness in terms of relations among symbols, and in particular in terms of the substitutability of symbols. In this view, to say that the ideas of being animal and feline are covertly contained in the idea of being a cat is just a less clear way of saying that the symbol feline animal is substitutable for, and more

---

of deducibility if clarification of A discloses B. And clarification, in turn, is explicated in terms of the making explicit of implicit constituents of an idea.

If we were to follow the above passage in supposing that a priori statements involve two meanings, then not only would a priori statements be copulative, but Lewis would then have to face the paradox of analysis: how can it be that of two distinct ideas one is only a clarification of the other? The whole point of Lewis' handling of analysis, or clarification, is that when an idea is clarified there are not two ideas at all, but only one idea in the case of which we are at first more or less unaware of its constituents but afterwards become increasingly aware of them.

114 AKV, p. 25.

'complex' (or, perhaps, more 'primitive') than the symbol cat.[115] And to say that there are two sorts of tautologies, those which are explicitly iterative and those which are only implicitly so, is, according to the nominalist, simply a way of saying that some tautologies are truths of logic as they stand whereas other tautologies have to be transformed into truths of logic by means of a dictionary of synonyms.[116]

In proof of the impossibility of any such view of the matter, it will be sufficient to refer to the arguments of Quine, and of Lewis himself.[117]

The realist, on the other hand, thinks of analysis as effecting a clarification, not of our ideas or language, but of our apprehension of Platonic reality. If we apprehend a Platonic reality with total clarity, we see all there is to be seen of it, including all of its inner detail, if it has any.[118] If, on the contrary, our apprehension is to some degree unclear, then we miss some of the detail.[119] In order to discover this

---

[115] And the term 'less clear' in this sentence is interpreted to mean 'less useful for some specified purpose'.

[116] Just as Lewis' general approach is to explicate all epistemological notions in terms of intensions or ideas-in-mind, so the nominalist approach is to explicate all of them in terms of characteristics of symbolic systems. What Lewis takes as primitive (notions like implicit, contains, same intensions, etc.) the nominalist tries to define in terms of such notions as substitutability-according-to-a-dictionary and deducibility-according-to-a-rule.

[117] W. V. Quine: "Two Dogmas of Empiricism," *Philosophical Review*, 60 (1951), 20-43. The relevant part of Quine's argument is this: if the dictionary in question be supposed to consist of stipulations then it will serve to explicate synonymy only within a given formal language where there truly are stipulated definitions—definitions which are "the explicitly conventional introduction of novel notations for purposes of sheer abbreviation" (p. 26). Further, even within the given formal language, only a small number of the definitions which occur in it can be explained as being stipulations since most of the definitions in it "are supposed to show how the primitive notation can accomplish all purposes, save brevity and convenience, of the redundant language" (p. 27). And this presupposes that the definiens have a meaning prior to the definition, a meaning which the definition must, within limits, preserve.

If, on the other hand, the dictionary be supposed to consist of reports of what symbols are interchangeable in ordinary usage, then the whole position becomes circular. For interchangeability guarantees synonymy only if it is interchangeability within necessary propositions. The argument therefore presupposes the distinction between necessary and contingent, whereas what the nominalist was trying to do was to define necessity and contingency in terms of interchangeability.

Lewis' argument against a purely nominalist handling of this or any other epistemological problem is centered in AKV, Chap. V, Secs. 7 and 8, and in Chap. VI, Secs. 5, 7, and (especially) 14.

[118] We then have what Plato, and "rationalistic realism" generally, called an 'intuition' or a 'clear and distinct idea'. I do not insist on the word 'inner' in the above sentence. It might be that what we apprehend is a connection between 'distinct' Platonic realities. Whether we do or not is exactly a realist formulation of the problem of iteration (see the preceding section).

[119] If the reality has no detail but is 'simple', like God or Nature in Spinoza's philosophy, then our apprehension of that reality cannot be other than adequate.

detail we resort to analysis, that is, to the "analytic clarification of existence."[120] An explicative statement gives us the results of this analysis, telling us that the whole we originally apprehended contains the detail we now apprehend.[121] This analysis may itself consist simply in an intuition or, if it is relatively complex, it may be called 'deduction',[122] that is, a remembered chain of intuitions.[123]

The critical difficulty of the realist view is that of explaining how any a priori judgment can be mistaken.[124] Typically, the realist attributes the fact that we can apprehend a reality vaguely and generally without apprehending it in all of its detail to something he calls inadequacy or unclarity. But to what is this unclarity due? Sometimes it is laid at the door of consciousness itself, as some sort of confusion or obscurity or distraction. But if this obscurity be thought of as a positive 'cloudiness' which somehow darkens the windows of the soul, then not only is it obvious that this is a visual metaphor which clarifies nothing whatever, but it is clearly incompatible with the view that consciousness just is transparency, presence, clarity. And *this* view is the very basis of the whole realist position. If, on the other hand, the obscurity be

120 W. Earle, "The Ontological Argument in Spinoza," *Philosophy and Phenomenological Research,* 11 (1951), 554.

121 E.g., in 'Cats are feline animals', the term cats expresses our initial, vague, preanalytic apprehension of the Idea of a cat and the term feline animals expresses our clearer, postanalytic apprehension of the same Idea.

122 As by Descartes. Or "dialectic," as by Plato, or the "second kind of knowledge," as by Spinoza.

123 Lewis will very occasionally suggest such a realist handling of implicitness, just as he will, when discussing more generally the nature of the evidence for an a priori proposition, occasionally suggest that this evidence consists in an inspection, not of the proposition's intension, but of its signification. For example, he says: "Such learning [of what properties are essential to the entities denoted by some term] . . . may occasionally represent simply our more accurate apprehension of what are the universal properties and relations of the familiar objects thus classified" (MWO, p. 68). And in AKV, p. 110, he says that meanings have whichever relations they have regardless of whether anyone has ever entertained the meanings in question, thus perhaps suggesting the realist view that implication is the containment, perhaps unapprehended, of one *signification* in another. But these suggestions are unique and surely do not correctly express what Lewis thinks.

124 This is of course merely one aspect of the general difficulty realism has with the problem of error. The problem in the present case is that of how we could be acquainted with a Platonic reality at all without being both perfectly and fully acquainted with it.

Incidentally, Lewis' conceptualism has the same difficulty, in addition to its peculiar difficulty with unconscious ideas. For not only may we fail to apprehend what is implicit in our ideas; we may also make a positive error as to what is implicit in them (AKV, p. 155). But I am willing to suppose that if one could make some sense of the notion of an unconscious idea in the first place, one could successfully explain how it is that we often make positive errors about what these unconscious ideas are.

thought of as simply a lack, an absence of clarity,[125] then it accounts for ignorance, but fails to account for positive error.[126] Furthermore, how could one fail to observe some detail of an essence, as if an essence had 'hidden' parts which are difficult to discern or a detailed structure which is too fine to be grasped on a cursory view. Such terms as these make sense when applied to physical substances, but they make no sense whatever when applied to a Platonic reality. An essence no more has hidden or concealed parts than it has an insides.

This is not because 'essence' is defined as 'appearance'. On the contrary, I am supposing that essences are independent of such a contingency as whether they are ever apprehended. What I am saying, rather, is that if an essence is apprehended at all, it is completely apprehended. This is due to the infinite number of essences. The Realm of Essence is exactly that sort of being in the case of which each thing is what it is, and not another thing, and *not anything more complex, and not anything more or additional. Everything* thinkable is a distinct essence. This means that if I think of a circumference but do not think of a center from which every point on it is equidistant, that circumference is a different essence from the essence of a circumference with a center.[127] And in general the essence which the realist says is an 'explicans' is more detailed than the essence it explicates, and is *therefore* a second distinct essence. If Santayana proved nothing else in *The Realm of Essence,* it seems to me he did prove this.

Both, therefore, because it *seems* to be true, and because I cannot see any promising alternative to it,[128] I should like to be able to accept Lewis' conceptualist explication of implicitness in terms of unconscious ideas. But in the end I just cannot swallow the notion that my ideas may have parts of which I am unconscious.

---

[125] As, e.g., by Spinoza. It is this notion which is behind such phrases as 'inattentiveness', 'failure to notice', and even, I suppose, behind Descartes' attribution of error to the over-hasty will.

[126] See MWO, pp. 176-80.

[127] I do not mean, of course, that this essence 'has no center' in the sense of positively excluding a center as contradictory to what the essence is. I mean that this essence neither includes nor excludes a center. The essence which has a center is a different essence from the one I am talking about, and so is the essence which positively excludes having a center.

[128] If the realist could make literal sense out of the highly figurative notion of 'mediate' consciousness, perhaps implicitness could be explicated in terms of this idea, so that analysis would be the process of making immediate what was formerly mediate. But, (a) I am not familiar with any analysis of 'mediacy' which does more than translate it into equally metaphorical terms; and (b) as soon as one admits mediacy into one's conception of consciousness, one's whole epistemology seems almost inevitably to take a conceptualist turn.

In AKV, pp. 194-95, Lewis says that,

> if it appears to constitute a difficulty that, as here conceived, what an objective
> statement means [consists of] . . . more detailed consequences, testable in
> possible confirming experience, than I could . . . explicitly remind myself of
> . . . . [then] The answer to the difficulty would appear to be that it is not a
> difficulty but a fact.

But this doesn't help me at all. It is true that Lewis has carried the analysis of the a priori a long, long way, so that a significant part of his richly deserved reputation rests upon the magnificent work he has done with this problem. It is also true that every philosophical analysis must somewhere come to rest in a not-further-defended fact. But the 'fact' that Lewis' analysis finally abuts upon is the 'fact' of unconscious ideas. And while I agree with Lewis that this does *seem* to be a fact, it also *seems* to be an obvious impossibility. If Locke proved nothing else in Book I of the *Essay*, it seems to me he did prove once and for all that there are no unconscious ideas.[129]

There are numerous indications that Lewis is aware of this difficulty and is less than totally happy about it.[130]

It is often suggested, particularly in MWO, that the unconscious implications of our meanings are not implicit in consciously entertained meanings (intensions) at all, but in something else—behavior, or attitudes. Thus Lewis says that while a priori truths are explications of concepts, concepts themselves are nothing but an explicit bringing to consciousness of what was already implicitly contained in forms of behavior ("our dealing with the familiar," "intelligent practice," "consistency of behavior"),[131] or in active attitudes,[132] or in "experience."[133] On the basis of such suggestions, one might suppose that what Lewis really means to say about the problem of implicitness, at least in MWO, is not primarily that a priori truths are explicative of what is implicitly 'in mind', but that they are, on a more thorough analysis, explications of what is implicitly contained or implied by behavior or active attitudes or 'experience'. One could then further suppose that Lewis means to equate 'analysis' with the 'reflective method' character-

---

129 Or rather, he repeats it so often in so many different terms that after a while it becomes self-evident.

130 He has certainly always been entirely aware of just what he is committed to: that I may mean something without being conscious, except perhaps in the most "vague and vestigial" way (AKV, p. 11), of what it is I mean. AKV, Chap. I, Sec. 3 is entirely candid about this.

131 MWO, pp. 3, 10, 85, respectively. See also pp. 85-89.

132 MWO, pp. 13, 14, 88.

133 MWO, pp. 19, 33.

istic of philosophy,[134] these being but two names for the process of bringing to consciousness what is implicitly implied in our active dealings with the world.

I think I need say no more about the suggestion that 'active attitudes' or 'experience' may have implicit constituents. Presumably attitudes and experience, like concepts, are a mode of consciousness, and it is no easier to see how there could be unconscious attitudes or experiences than it is to see how there could be unconscious concepts. This criticism could not, however, be brought against the notion that 'implicit implication' is explicable in terms of 'incipient behavior' or 'disposition to behave'— in particular, in terms of 'disposition to behave linguistically'.[135]

But two other comments would have to be made about any such behaviorist theory:

(1) It does indeed seem as if my present behavior did, in some sense, commit me to certain forms of behavior in the future, so that we might speak of these future forms of behavior as being implicit in the present behavior. And it does seem as if there were such a thing as becoming conscious of the implications of one's behavior. Just as there seems to be such a thing as becoming conscious of the implications of one's concepts. But it also seems as if these were two quite distinct things.

(2) More importantly, it seems quite impossible that there should be any necessary connections between my present behavior and my future behavior, between the incipience of an act and the overtness of the same act, between a disposition to perform an act under certain circumstances and the actual performance of it under those circumstances, between a 'commitment' to call certain things by a given name and actually calling them by it.[136] And it is therefore impossible to use such connections, which are clearly contingent, to explicate the necessary con-

---

[134] MWO, Chap. I.

[135] Actually, I think that such a behaviorist interpretation of what Lewis meant, in MWO, by implicitness cannot be borne out by a study of the complete text. While he undoubtedly believed that there is implicitness in the sense of the as-yet-unconscious implications of behavior, he *also* believed that concepts themselves contain unconscious implications. (See esp. pp. 86-87.) Nonetheless, the suggestion is repeatedly made. And it is revived in AKV, at least to the extent of saying that, while a behaviorist treatment of intensional meanings is not what Lewis has had in mind, such a treatment would be entirely compatible with the basic point he wishes to make about such meanings—that they are "entertained in advance of instances of application which are pertinent" (p. 144).

[136] Of course, one can so define 'disposition' and 'incipient' that a person cannot be said to have a disposition to an act, nor the act be said to be incipient, unless it would in fact be performed under the specified circumstances. This simply re-locates the problem. For now no presently inspectable fact is sufficient to guarantee with certainty that a person has such a disposition.

nection between the explicandum of a tautology and those implicit implications of it which are expressed by the explicans.[137]

Another suggestion Lewis often puts forward is that to say of one idea that it is implicit in another is simply a way of saying that the first idea, if it should in the future be explicitly entertained, *would* be acknowledged as a part of the original idea. What this amounts to is the suggestion that 'implicit ideas' can be explicated in terms of a disposition to be conscious of those ideas in the future.[138] But here, as in the case of behavioral dispositions, it seems clear that what I *would* have in mind at some future time, or what I *would* own up to as being a part of my original meaning, is a contingent matter, not at all fitted to explain how one idea may be a necessary implication of another idea in which it is not explicitly contained.[139]

Lewis seems, indeed, to recognize this fact. For while sometimes he seems to *explicate* 'implicit' in terms of a disposition to entertain an idea explicitly, he often adds the qualification that the idea which would

---

[137] It would thus appear that the "reflective method" of philosophy, the process of becoming aware of the implications of one's behavior, is an essentially empirical affair, standing in contrast to the a priori method of analysis.

[138] Thus:

(a) MWO, pp. 286-89, seems to say that when we do not have an intension explicitly in mind, we have it in mind "in a figurative sense." And the phrase 'in a figurative sense' is explained as meaning that, at some future time, we "could" say whether a given idea, should it be suggested to us, is or is not included in our original intension.

(b) "Even in the best and clearest cases of knowledge . . . our sense of what is meant . . . will be incomplete. We can go a little way in explication of these, but . . . . The utmost that can be demanded is that one who is truly said to know should be able to provide such explication when the need of it arises, and after reflection. . . ." (AKV, p. 10).

(c) AKV, p. 65, refers to an implicit meaning as "something which should be in mind and may be brought to mind by thinking."

(d) "epistemological procedure . . . might be said often to replace the actual content of the knowing state by something more explicit which would be accepted as the implied intent of it" (AKV, p. 11).

(e) AKV, p. 133, seeems to explain sense-meaning as the ability "to apply or refuse to apply an expression correctly under all imaginable circumstances . . . ."

(f) AKV, p. 174, says that something is included in a meaning only if "I were prepared to assent to it, in case my attention were drawn to the matter. . . ."

(g) See also AKV, Chap. XI, Secs. 3 and 5, where the related problem of how the grounds of our empirical knowledge may be only implicitly in mind is solved in terms of what I *would* cite as a ground of belief if belief were challenged.

(h) See also AKV, pp. 176, 328.

[139] It is interesting that, in connection with his discussion of how the grounds of empirical knowledge may be only implicitly in mind, Lewis imagines a critic to make the same objection as I have just been making: " 'Implicitly,' however, is here a weasel-word; what is really meant is that, by a process of reflection, a different state of mind, in which certain items are explicitly included, could occur at the later time, $t_2$" (AKV, p. 330). The reply Lewis makes to this is not relevant to the problem of a priori knowledge.

be entertained at a later time may not for that reason be said to have been implicit in the present idea unless it *was* genuinely a *part* of the present idea. The point seems to be that the implicitness of the idea of animal in the idea of cat can be explicated in terms of a disposition explicitly to entertain an idea under certain conditions in the future, but only if the idea which we have a disposition to entertain is not the idea of animal but the more complex idea that the idea of animal was indeed implicit in our earlier idea of cat, and only if, furthermore, this idea be true.[140] But this, if it be interpreted as an explication of implicitness, merely takes us in circles. The proper conclusion would seem to be that Lewis never intended it to be an explication of implicitness, but intended only to say that if one idea is indeed implicit in another, then it is a consequence of this that the second idea could be made explicit under certain conditions.[141]

So it seems to me there are, in the end, only two ways of interpreting Lewis on this point. Either he has not given us any explication at all of how a meaning may have implications of which the person entertaining the meaning is unaware, but has instead simply offered "dictionary definitions" of expressions like implicit, implication, deducible, etc., in terms of one another. Or, he has explicated all of these expressions in terms of the notion that ideas may contain constituent ideas which are unconscious.

### V

Solely for the sake of summary, and without presuming that Lewis will find all, or even any, of my queries worth discussing, I shall put what I have said in the form of four questions:

(1) In considering the problem of evidence, do you, Mr. Lewis, really mean to assign to intension a priority over the other modes of meaning —a priority of a sort which you think "rationalistic realism" would not assign it? If so, in what does this priority consist?

(2) Does not every a priori proposition "limit" the world to being self-consistent in a significant sense of the term 'limit', even though, to be sure, a world which was not so limited would be self-contradictory?

---

140 See MWO, p. 289, AKV, p. 195, and many of the passages cited in n. 138.

141 In MWO, Lewis clearly makes a distinction between a disposition to entertain an explicit idea, on the one hand, and having an implicit idea, on the other hand: "In such cases [cases in which the meaning is not explicitly in mind, but only implicit] the meaning is possessed by the mind both in the sense of this consistently determined attitude and in the further sense that *how* this meaning should become explicit and *what* would be recognized as essential, when the attitude became self-conscious, is already implicit in the attitude itself" (pp. 87-88).

(3) Would you not agree, along with "rationalistic realism" and against Hume, that at least some a priori propositions are copulative, in the sense of being about distinguishable, although not 'distinct', facts or meanings?

(4) Can you explain any more clearly than you have what you mean by implicitness?

ASHER MOORE

DEPARTMENT OF PHILOSOPHY
UNIVERSITY OF NEW HAMPSHIRE

# 6

## Charles A. Baylis

## LEWIS' THEORY OF FACTS

NO explicit statement of a theory of facts is to be found in Lewis'
published work. Indeed he seldom uses the word 'fact' except in
phrases like 'matter of fact' where it functions in a way that is not helpful for our purposes. It is possible however, by making use of the few
occasions in which the term does occur and of others in which some
closely related topic is discussed without use of the term, to attain at
least an approximation to the view that is inherent in his work. Such a
formulation, together with minor criticisms and suggestions, constitutes
part I of this essay. Major criticisms are offered in part II, and these are
followed in part III by an outline of a theory of facts which, in my
opinion, would cohere more satisfactorily with Lewis' philosophy as a
whole and would also be much more acceptable in itself.

### I

One of the few places in which Lewis discusses facts explicitly is in
his early article "Facts, Systems, and the Unity of the World." Here, after
remarking that the world may be regarded as constituted of objects or
individuals, Lewis continues:

It is equally true that the world is a system of facts, taking 'fact' to indicate that which a proposition (some actual or possible proposition) denotes
or asserts. That the world can be exhaustively construed as an array of such
facts follows from this; if there were any phase, part, or aspect of the real
not comprised in some fact, then the real would contain what could not be
stated or asserted, and hence could neither be known nor imagined, guessed at
nor inquired about. So far at least as the real is intelligible, it is constituted
of facts and their relations. In the array of all facts, objects and their relations
will be comprehended, just as all facts would be determined in the array of
objects. Hence either of these methods must lead to the same results in the
end. But the approach through facts may succeed where the other fails because
of the simpler relation of fact to knowledge. The *object* always transcends our
particular knowledge or judgment—as the whole transcends the part, or the
real transcends the apparent, or as the complex structure transcends its simpler
and more superficial elements. But the *fact* is by its very nature, the unit of
knowledge. It represents exactly that which thought can surely grasp in judgment and express in a proposition, that which our knowledge can completely
possess or surround. Moreover, the relations of facts are simpler to deal with

because they are at once the relations treated by the logic of propositions: facts may imply one another, as propositions imply one another, and facts are compatible or incompatible, as are the propositions which express them. Such relations are comparatively simple in type, and we possess the technique adequate to deal with them.[1]

This account suggests that Lewis (in 1923) regarded facts as being in some sense ingredient in the world. Every phase, part, and aspect of the real is comprised in some fact. Ordinary predicate terms, such as 'red' denote individual objects which are literally space-time parts of the space-time world, and (true) propositions denote aspects of the same world, construed in a different way, as members of an array of facts, which jointly constitute the world. There are many distinct facts and all are ingredient in the actual world.

But in the years since then Lewis' view has changed in a striking respect. He now writes:[2]

The only thing I would correct in the 'Facts' article is the use of the word 'denote' as their relation to 'states of affairs'. It should be 'signify'. Propositions 'apply to' or 'denote' the world; they do not, however, 'name' the world. Propositions are adjectival, comparable to attributives like 'red' as applied to objects rather than 'redness' which 'names' (denotes) the property it refers to. The state of affairs is the character (property) of the world.

This change which is incorporated in his account in *Analysis of Knowledge and Valuation*[3] leads to quite a different theory of facts. According to this revised version true propositions denote, not facts, but the whole space-time slab of reality which is the actual world. If we were to regard what is thus denoted as a fact, there would be only one fact, the universe itself. Lewis thus no longer describes facts as the extensional meaning of true propositions, but as something which is the content of a mode of their intensional meaning. Facts are properties of the world which true propositions *signify*.

Lewis first explains signification as a mode of intensional meaning for ordinary predicate terms, terms such as 'red' and 'round'.

A *verbal symbol* is a recognizable pattern of marks or of sounds used for purposes of expression and communiction. . . . Two marks, or two sounds, having the same recognizable pattern, are two *instances* of the same symbol, not two different symbols.

A *linguistic expression* is formed or determined by the association of a symbol with a fixed meaning.[3a]

---

[1] *Journal of Philosophy*, **20**, No. 6 (March 15, 1923), 141 f.

[2] In a personal letter dated July 1957.

[3] *An Analysis of Knowledge and Valuation* (La Salle, Illinois: The Open Court Publishing Co., 1946). Hereafter cited as AKV.

[3a] AKV, p. 73.

But a linguistic expression cannot be identified with either the symbol alone or the meaning alone.

"A *term* is a linguistic expression . . . capable of naming or applying to a thing or things, of some kind," actual or thought of.[4] Adjectival terms such as 'red' and 'round' *apply to* the particulars they denote. Attributive terms such as 'redness' and 'roundness' *name* the characters which they denote, the characters which are signified by 'red' and 'round'. Terms which thus name what some other term signifies, Lewis calls '*abstract*' terms. "Non-abstract terms are *concrete*."[5]

"The *signification* of a term is that property in things the presence of which indicates that the term correctly applies, and the absence of which indicates that it does not apply."[6] Signification is distinguished from connotation and intension as follows: "We should say that the term 'man' *signifies* animality (along with other properties) ; that animality is included in the *signification* of 'man'. And we shall wish to say that 'man' connotes the *term* 'animal' (along with other terms) ; that this term 'animal' is included in the connotation or intension of the term 'man'."[7]

Lewis sometimes describes the *intension* of a term as its connotation, in the linguistic sense of that term given above. But he sometimes speaks of the intension of a term as the sense meaning of that term, the criterion in mind—rule and imagined result—"by reference to which one is able to apply or refuse to apply the expression in question in the case of presented, or imagined, things or situations."[8]

As suggested by the derivation of the word, the intension of a term represents our intension in the use of it; the meaning it expresses in that simplest and most frequent sense which is the original meaning of 'meaning'; that sense in which what we mean by '*A*' is what we have in mind in using '*A*', and what is oftentimes spoken of as the *concept of A*. We shall wish to preserve this original sense of 'intension' and, specifically, to identify it with the *criterion in mind* by which it is determined whether the term in question applies or fails to apply in any particular instance. At a later point, the epistemological question, what precisely is the nature of such a criterion in mind, will be discussed; and we shall there speak of 'linguistic meaning' and 'sense meaning'. . . . The connotation or intension of '*A*'—all that it connotes—can be identified with the conjunction or logical product . . . of all the terms connoted by '*A*'.[9]

4 AKV, pp. 38-39.
5 AKV, p. 41.
6 AKV, p. 39.
7 AKV, p. 43.
8 AKV, p. 133.
9 AKV, pp. 43, 44.

Although he sometimes lists connotation (whether linguistic or sense meaning), signification and comprehension as all modes of intensional meaning, at other times Lewis distinguishes rather sharply between sense meaning and signification, sense meaning being described as mental, as "in mind," and signification being specified as an objective property. Thus:

As a criterion *in mind*, sense meaning is intensional meaning rather than signification: it is that in mind which *refers to* signification. Signification comprises essential properties; and these essential properties have their being when and where they are instanced, regardless of the association of them with any term or expression. Animality, for example, is a certain property objectively incorporated in animals, which would be just what it is regardless of any linguistic usage associating it with the symbol «animal». It was in order to dispel the subtle ambiguity of the traditional usage of 'intension'—ambiguity as between a meaning in mind and an objective character meant—that it seemed necessary to add signification to the list of fundamental modes of meaning.[10]

Turning now more specifically to the signification of propositional expressions, Lewis writes:

A proposition is a term capable of signifying a state of affairs. To define a proposition as an expression which is true or false, is correct enough but inauspicious, because it easily leads to identification of the proposition with the statement or assertion of it; whereas the element of assertion in a statement is extraneous to the proposition asserted. The proposition is something assert*able*: the *content* of the assertion: and this same content, signifying the same state of affairs, can also be questioned, denied, or merely supposed, and can be entertained in other moods as well.

For example the statement, "Mary is making pies," asserts the state of affairs, Mary making pies now as actual. "Is Mary making pies?" questions it; . . . and "Suppose that Mary is making pies," puts it forward as a postulate. . . .

If we wish to disengage this common content from any particular mood of its entertainment, we might do so . . . in the manner of indirect discourse, e.g., 'that Mary is making pies (now)', or by a participial phrase, 'Mary making pies (now)', which can be asserted, questioned, and entertained in all these different ways, and which signifies the state of affairs which they all concern.[11]

In AKV Lewis explicitly corrects what he now regards as his earlier mistaken use of 'denotation' to express the relation between a proposition and a state of affairs:

It will be noted that the state of affairs referred to is the *signification* of the proposition: not its denotation. "Mary is making pies" asserts that the state

10 AKV, p. 133, footnote.
11 AKV, pp. 48-49.

of affairs, Mary making pies now, has a certain status; namely that it is actual; that it is incorporated in the real world. And if this statement is true, then the denotation or extension of the propositional term, "Mary making pies now," is not the limited state of affairs which it indicates [signifies?] but is the actual world which incorporates that state of affairs and is characterized by it.[12]

Thus the extension of any proposition is the actual world, in case it is true. And since denotation or extension is in all cases confined to the existent or actual, the extension of any false proposition is null or zero; it applies to nothing actual.[13]

Lewis concludes his account of the intension and extension of propositions as follows:

> To sum up: Every statement asserts a proposition and attributes a state of affairs to the actual world. The proposition so asserted is a predicable term, which can apply to and denote what one or other of every pair of contradictory propositions can also apply to and denote. Every *true* proposition denotes, or has as its extension, the actual world. And every false proposition has, likewise, the same extension as every other which is false; namely, zero extension. Thus all true propositions are equivalent in extension, and all false propositions are equivalent in extension; and the important extensional property of any proposition is simply its truth-value.[14]

It should be remarked that Lewis is doing much more here, and in the preceding quotation, than merely summing up what he has said before. He starts out by noting that terms such as 'red' and 'round' signify characters, i.e., qualities or properties of individual things, whereas propositions signify states of affairs in the way in which 'that Mary is making pies (now)' signifies that Mary is making pies. But he now concludes that propositions also are predicable terms, terms that signify a property of the world as a whole, for example, the Mary-making-pies-(now) property which characterizes the actual world. His argument rests on an analogy between the ways in which ordinary predicate terms signify and denote and the ways in which propositions signify and denote, an analogy which we criticize in some detail later. For the present let it suffice here to remark a striking disanalogy, namely that it is appropriate to take an epistemic attitude, of belief, doubt, or disbelief, toward the state of affairs that a propositional term signifies but not toward the abstract character or universal which ordinary predicate terms signify.

In developing his general account, Lewis goes on to stress another point. What is signified by a proposition is not a concrete, particular,

12 AKV, pp. 51, 52.
13 AKV, p. 52.
14 AKV, p. 53.

object; it is not any part or slab of the space-time reality which we call the world, nor is it that world as a whole. It is rather an abstract entity, something which has implications and is implied by other abstract entities.

The fact that the *name* of any state of affairs is an abstract term, may serve to sharpen and clarify the meaning of this slightly vague expression 'state of affairs' (or the even vaguer and less appropriate expression, 'matter of fact', which we have sometimes used as a synonym). Such a state of affairs is *not* a concrete entity; a space-time slab of reality with all that it contains, but is a property or attribute. It includes nothing beyond what the *abstract* participial expression naming it entails or requires. It is confined to precisely what must be the case in order that the correlative predicable term, which is the proposition, should be applicable to reality.

For example, while Mary is making pies in the kitchen, either she burns her fingers or she does not. The space-time slab, or Whiteheadian event, which comprises Mary making pies now, either includes Mary burning her fingers or it definitely excludes this and is characterized throughout by Mary's fingers being unburned. But the state of affairs, Mary making pies now, which is asserted as actual by the statement "Mary is making pies," neither includes what is asserted by "Mary burns her fingers," nor what is asserted by "Mary does not burn her fingers." It includes only what Mary now making pies requires in order to be the fact.

One state of affairs or matter of fact may include another; as Mary now making pies includes pies being made, and includes Mary working. And one state of affairs may definitely exclude another; as Mary now making pies excludes Mary remaining motionless. But in the sense which is here requisite, what the state of affairs, Mary now making pies, includes is only what is deducible from "Mary is making pies." And what this state of affairs definitely excludes is only that whose non-factuality is deducible from "Mary is making pies."[15]

Lewis is quite consistent in emphasizing the abstract nature of what is signified by a proposition. He wants to insist that propositions signify something abstract, namely a state of affairs, and denote, if they are true, something concrete, namely the actual world as a whole. About the latter point we shall take issue with him, but on the abstract nature of what a proposition signifies he seems to be quite correct. He makes this point in a somewhat different way in connection with a brief discussion of the relevance of the concrete-abstract distinction to the absolute idealist doctrine of the internality of relations.

Thus a state of affairs is not the kind of entity for which the doctrine of internal relations would hold. That doctrine arises from confusing states of affairs with space-time slabs of reality (AKV 54).

The epistemological and metaphysical consequences which absolute idealism draws from the doctrine of internal relations rest on nothing more impressive

15 AKV, pp. 53-54.

than (1) the infinite specificity, logically, of any individual object—which is required by the Law of the Excluded Middle—and (2) the ambiguity of the verb 'to know'; which may refer to, as its object, an individual thing or may refer to an apprehended fact. An individual object is a space-time slab; and is something which we can no more know, in all its infinite specificity, than we can similarly know the whole of reality: on that point, the doctrine is on firm ground. But what we know in the sense of apprehending as fact or believing with assurance, is merely some limited state of affairs, which exhausts neither reality nor the object to which cognition is addressed, but comprises only those factualities about the object which our knowledge of it would enable us to state. It will be important, therefore, to observe the abstract and adjectival character of what is appropriately called a state of affairs, as something knowable and stateable: it includes all that the assertion of this state of affairs as actual implies, but it includes nothing which is not thus deducible from such statement. It is the signification of some formulated or formulatable proposition; not a 'chunk' of reality (AKV 54 f.).

We can perhaps sum up Lewis' concern here in this way: What a propositional expression signifies is not a particular, whether some space-time part of the actual world or that world as a whole, but always a limited state of affairs, an abstract entity. Thus 'that Mary is making pies' signifies all and only that which is expressed by propositions which are deducible from the proposition 'that Mary is making pies'. It does not indicate what color apron Mary is wearing, or indeed whether she is wearing an apron at all or not.

In his most recent article dealing with these topics,[16] Lewis follows in the main his account in AKV, but offers new emphases and some significant emendations. In particular he does his best to distinguish sharply three types of intensional meaning, first for ordinary terms and then for propositional expressions. The basic one of these is what he sometimes calls intension proper, namely the meaning or criterion in mind, usually referred to in AKV as sense meaning, in "Met. Log." as conceptual meaning. The second is linguistic meaning; the third is meaning in the mode of signification. Meanings of all of these types are abstract.

The meaning associated with a symbol and essential to its being a linguistic entity, must be a psychological or mental entity. . . . A meaning is something which is mind-dependent; no minds, no meanings. We speak of meanings as entertained, and the entertainment of a meaning is an occurrence; an event which is temporal if not spatial. But just as it is essential to a linguistic symbol that it be the same from page to page, and the pile of ink an instance of it only, so the meaning it conveys cannot be identified with the psychological occurrence called the entertainment of it: it must be the same meaning which is entertained when we read the same expression at different times, if the

---

[16] "Some Suggestions Concerning Metaphysics of Logic," *American Philosophers at Work*, ed. Sidney Hook (New York: Criterion Books, 1957), hereafter cited as "Met. Log."

pile of ink is to exercise the function of expressing the same meaning on different occasions. This meaning as characterizing different psychological events, and the same for any occasion of its entertainment, is the concept. And a meaning as relative to such entertainments, I shall speak of as a conceptual meaning.

Most meanings, and correlatively most linguistic expressions, have reference to external existents or states of affairs, spoken of as something meant. In relation to such an objective actuality, the meaning entertained or linguistically expressed constitutes the criterion which operates to determine which or what, amongst actualities which may present themselves, are those so meant. And it so operates by determining some recognizable *character* of actualities as essential to their being accepted as what is meant. This character, even if there be no more than one actual entity instancing it, never extends to the whole nature of any individual thing but is, again, an abstract or universal entity; a property or attribute.

Of these three abstract entities; first, the concept as psychologically instanced meaning, second, linguistic meaning as what patterns of sound or of marks convey, and as the meaning of such expressions in terms of other expressions, and third, the character or property of objective actualities which is essential to their satisfying the condition set by the concept and expressed in language; of these three, it is the first which is antecedent to the other two. We do not first have marks and sounds and then invent or try to discover concepts for them to convey, but devise language to convey what is conceptually entertained.[17]

At this point Lewis digresses a bit to explain his use of such expressions as 'has some manner of being' and 'exists'.

I have no intention of saying that concepts or that meanings exist. . . . Nevertheless I would suggest that they must be granted some manner of being and that if any logician were to say, "There are no such things as conceptual meanings," he would be using Occam's razor to cut his own throat. Existence—I take it—refers to a relation between a conceptual meaning entertained and an actuality, empirically found or evidenced, which satisfies the intention of that conceptual entertainment. But in this connection, it is of some importance to observe that no empirical presentment could determine that "So and so exists," if the conception of 'so and so' as a meaning entertained did not function as a condition to be satisfied or not satisfied by what may be empirically disclosed. . . . The basic relation of empirical knowledge is this relation between a character mentally entertained as the concept of 'so and so', and a perceptual finding of that which evidences this character essential to being 'so and so.'[18]

The subject of "So and so exists" is the conceptually delineated so and so, not the empirically discovered so and so. . . . What is *predicated* of this conceptually meant 'so and so' is a relation of correspondence of character between it and something empirically findable or evidenced by perception. And again incidentally, this shows that for the being of a *concept* or conceptual

---

17 "Met. Log.," pp. 94-96.
18 "Met. Log.," p. 96.

meaning, the ontological argument is perfectly good; whatever is mentionable must have this status as conceptual, whether it exists or not.[19]

Although Lewis is clearly right in distinguishing between our conceptually entertaining some character which serves as a criterion in mind and our finding that character exemplified by an object in our experience he seems to complicate his terminology unnecessarily by distinguishing the intensional or conceptual meaning of a predicate term from the signification of that term. For what is meant in both cases, as distinct from the mode of our becoming aware of it, is the same character. Thus we can conceive of the character which in Lewis' terminology is intensionally meant by 'red' or we can find that character exemplified in experience, in which case Lewis speaks of it as signified by 'red'. But it is precisely the same character which is in the one case conceived and in the other found exemplified. Why not have just one name for the relation between a predicate term and this character?

To be sure, in AKV Lewis described a criterion in mind as closely resembling what Kant had referred to as a mental schema, a rule or prescribed routine for testing the applicability of a term, and an *imagined* result.[20] However in "Met. Log." the criterion in mind is described as conceptual in nature, as a concept rather than an image. With this change in his account of the nature of 'a criterion in mind' we can say, as Lewis does in "Met. Log." that in empirical knowledge we find embodied 'in the world' the same character that we had conceived 'in mind'.[21]

"A character," Lewis writes,

is an entity which can be instanced, and is the same in all its instances. An instance of a character [of the lowest type] is an existent individual. Characters themselves do not exist [though they must be allowed some kind of being][22] but they are real or unreal. A character is real if an instance of it exists.[23]

He does not but might consistently have continued: A character which characterizes an individual we can, if we like, call 'a characteristic'. That same character may also be thought of and mentally entertained. As so conceived we can call it, as Lewis does, 'a concept', and say with him that "A concept is real if there is a psychological instance of its entertainment,"[24] i.e., if it is conceived.

19 "Met. Log.," p. 97.
20 AKV, p. 134.
21 "Met. Log.," p. 97.
22 "Met. Log.," p. 96.
23 "Met. Log.," p. 101.
24 "Met. Log.," p. 101.

These distinctions are both proper and useful to make. But since Lewis agrees that what is conceived or instanced is a character, and in the case of knowledge the very same character, there seems no need to have two different names for the relation between a predicate term and its associated character. We could say either that the term intensionally or conceptually means the character, or we could say that it signifies the character. 'Signifies' is the shorter term and its use seems to conform more closely to Lewis' own usage. Just as what a proposition signifies, according to some of Lewis' statements, does not vary with the truth of the proposition, so it seems reasonable that what a term signifies does not vary with the existence or nonexistence of what it purportedly applies to. The defining characteristics of a character are unaffected by its being or not being thought of or by its being or not being exemplified. The character signified by a predicate term may be conceived or exemplified or both or neither. The latter possibility may seem strange, but Lewis reminds us, albeit in a verbally contradictory way, "The notion of a concept never entertained may seem jejeune; but we should remind ourselves that this is the only kind of reality which any but an infinitesimal fraction of the natural numbers have. . . ."[25] How much simpler and more consistent it would be to say, "The notion of a character never entertained may seem jejeune; but we should remind ourselves that this is the only kind of being which any but an infinitesimal fraction of the natural numbers have . . ." A character which is neither conceived nor embodied we can refer to as 'a (pure) universal'. It is not in Lewis' terminology 'real', but it does have 'some manner of being'.

Even the slight thinning out of the Lewisian terminological jungle that is achieved by dropping the unnecessary 'intensionally or conceptually means' seems a step in the right direction. The question remains whether the simplifications proposed will also fit advantageously what Lewis has to say about propositions and their various modes of meaning in "Met. Log." His account follows:

A proposition turns out to be a kind of term. It expresses a meaning which, as conceptually entertained, stands as the condition to be satisfied if something is to be recognized as being the case; the condition to be met if this propositional term is to apply to the actual. The intension as *linguistic* is the 'and' relation of all propositions deducible from the one in question. And the signification of this propositional term is that state of affairs which must be found in what is actual if the proposition is to be accepted as true. For propositions, as for other terms, the conceptual meaning as entertained, the linguistic meaning as expressed, and the state of affairs signified, are all correlative; and none of these three is strictly correlative with the extension of it. The denotation or extension of a proposition—the existent to which it applies—is the actual world in case it is true; and is nothing in case it is false. Its extension is thus correlative with its truth-value.

> . . . the actual world is that unique individual existent identified by the fact that all other individual existents are space-time parts of it. Propositions are, thus, singular terms. But what a proposition signifies is some character or attribute of this individual, and *not* a part of it. The attempt to identify states of affairs with space-time parts of the world must fail—for several reasons, of which I shall mention only one. Whatever is true at some time and false at some other time, is not a proposition but a propositional function. Any proposition which has temporal reference requires, for the full expression of it, that this temporal reference be made explicit; and when that is done, it must be *always* true or else always false.[26]

> . . . there must be a conceptual meaning of the proposition, which is independent of its truth or falsity, because there must be a *criterion* of such truth or falsity—that is, a criterion of applicability of the proposition to what is actual—in order that such actual truth or falsity may be determined. This propositional concept is the same whether the assertion of the proposition—the statement—is true or false; only on that condition would any truth or falsity be discoverable. Correlatively, the intensional meaning of any expression of the propositional concept entertained, and the signification of it—the state of affairs *supposed*—must remain the same, whether the proposition is actually true or actually false.[27]

The suggestion made earlier in the case of ordinary predicate terms that we speak of one abstract entity, a character, which may be both thought of and exemplified or either or neither, seems to fit well also with Lewis' talk of propositions and their intensions and significations. On the basis of the analogy that Lewis urges throughout, a proposition signifies a state of affairs in a way analogous to that in which a term signifies a character. Moreover Lewis' last sentence quoted above implies that the state of affairs signified by a proposition need not be instanced by or in the world, but may be only 'supposed' to be so instanced. But this is to say that a state of affairs may be thought of even when it is not exemplified. And there seems to be no doubt that a state of affairs may be exemplified without having been conceived and hence without being known to be exemplified. Perhaps we do not speak as often of states of affairs that have neither been exemplified or thought of as we do of numbers that have this status, but we do occasionally reflect long enough to believe that there are no doubt a vast number of possible states of affairs that have neither been actualized nor conceived. 'State of affairs' thus seems a reasonable term to designate or name that complex entity which we may appropriately entertain, believe, disbelieve, or doubt, etc., when we understand a proposition. Thus again, we can dispense with

[26] "Met. Log.," pp. 99 f.
[27] "Met. Log.," p. 100.

C. A. BAYLIS

the term 'intensionally means' and use the one term 'signifies' to express the relation between a proposition and the state of affairs signified by it. 'Signifies' is correct whether the state of affairs is thought of or not or is actualized or not. If we wish to have names to mark the various possibilities we can call a state of affairs that is actualized 'an actual or a true state of affairs', a state of affairs that has been thought of 'a conceived state of affairs', and a consistent state of affairs which is neither conceived nor instanced 'a possible state of affairs'. Only if a state of affairs is conceived, can it be supposed or asserted, doubted or denied; and only if a state of affairs exists 'in the world' is a proposition that signifies it true.

Before attempting to summarize Lewis' views about facts we should note a certain ambivalence on his part as to how the term 'fact' should be used. In the 1923 article, "Facts, Systems, and the Unity of the World," he writes:

> Ordinarily the word 'fact' is restricted to that which a *true* proposition denotes. But in addition to the form of words which asserts or means, there is that which is asserted or meant, as much when the statement is false as when it is true. And lacking some word to indicate this objective or designatum of a proposition, without respect to its truth or falsity, there are certain problems which it is difficult to discuss at all. Let us, then, stretch the word 'fact' to this meaning, by omitting its usual connotation of truth, and intend by it simply what a proposition—some proposition asserts. When it is desirable to distinguish what is denoted by true propositions exclusively, we may speak of 'actual facts.' This is not to assign to 'unreal facts' any dubious metaphysical status; it is merely a convenience of language. . . . The logical relations of facts are unaltered by their actuality or non-actuality, just as the logical relations of propositions are unaffected by their truth or falsity.[28]

Though Lewis, cognizant of the misunderstandings that such a terminology would engender, has now abandoned it in his published writings, the fact that he is still tempted by it manifests itself occasionally in private statements, for example, the following which comes from a personal letter of July 1957.

> One thing I was never explicit about: whether speaking of 'fact' implies actuality. Frequently, of course, that is the common sense significance of 'statements of fact' and 'matters of fact.' I find the absence of any word for what *would be* a fact if it were actual, a linguistic bother. What a false statement *asserts* (is a fact?). It wouldn't be false if it did not *assert* one. What is it that ain't!

Actually, as indicated earlier, Lewis already has a term which will serve the double function he has in mind. It is the term 'state of affairs'.

28 *Op. cit.*, p. 142.

There seems no question but that it will do if he is willing to adopt my suggested emendation of his terminology so that we can speak of the same state of affairs as either conceived or embodied or both or neither. Propositions signify a state of affairs which we may (mentally) entertain. If a proposition is true the state of affairs which it signifies is also embodied in the actual world. This use of 'state of affairs' enables us to speak of a supposed state of affairs which may not be actual, or of an actual state of affairs which may not have been thought of, and even of a possible state of affairs which has neither been actualized nor conceived. Such merely possible states of affairs will not be 'real' in Lewis' sense of that term, but they will have 'some manner of being'.

Again, as in the case of predicate terms, I hesitate a little to urge using the same name for that which is conceptually meant and that which is signified by a proposition because of Lewis' earlier tendency to speak of a criterion in mind in terms of imagery. But he seems now in "Met. Log." to have given up this description of a criterion in mind in favor of an account in terms of a concept or a propositional concept, and hence we are justified, I believe, in adopting the language indicated in the preceding paragraph. I am happy to do so, in the case of both propositions and predicate terms, for I have long been troubled by Lewis' earlier vague references to schemata, and have been disturbed by the questions of some of his critics as to how we could ever know which of all the images available is the one to use as a criterion in a particular case of testing for the applicability of a predicate term or the truth of an empirical proposition.

But, as I see it now, these difficulties vanish if we think of predicate terms as signifying conceivable characters and propositions as signifying conceivable states of affairs. Once having conceived a character or state of affairs we can infer what sort of presentation in experience would justify us in applying the signifying term or asserting the signifying proposition. To be sure, in this process we should likely make use of imagery, but what imagery and what test procedures would be pertinent in various situations would be knowable through analysis of the conceptual meaning signified to us by the term or proposition, on the particular occasion of its use.

Using Lewis' terminology as modified by the suggestions made, I now summarize as best I can what I believe to be the essential features of his theory of facts:

There is a close analogy between predicate terms and propositions. Both signify abstract entities, and denote, unless their denotation is zero, concrete existents. Ordinary predicate terms signify characters, and denote, if they denote at all, particulars or individuals which instance the characters signified. These characters may also be conceived or thought of whether or not they characterize anything. Analogously, propositions signify states of affairs. Unless they are false and hence have zero denotation, they are true and denote that unique individual the world as a whole. In this case the state of affairs they signify is a characteristic of the world. Whether or not states of affairs are thus instanced they can be conceived or thought of.[29]

Now what in all this does Lewis call 'a fact'? To be sure he never says. But the whole trend of his developing theory seems to require his saying that when a state of affairs signified by a proposition characterizes the world, then that proposition is true. Presumably it is true in virtue of the fact that the world instances or exemplifies or embodies precisely that state of affairs, in virtue of the fact that the world has or exhibits or is characterized by the state of affairs signified. Either of these modes of expression suffice to describe the fact which justifies assertion of the proposition.

To illustrate this by Lewis' favorite example, we can say that the proposition 'that Mary is making pies now' is true if and only if the world is now characterized by the state of affairs, Mary-making-pies. The fact needed to make this proposition true consists of the world instancing precisely the state of affairs signified by the proposition or deducible from it, no more and no less.

Perhaps Lewis' theory of facts can be expressed briefly, yet without too much distortion in this way: When the world is characterized by a state of affairs, that state of affairs, perhaps identical in character with some conceived state of affairs, is instanced by the world. As so instanced it is in Lewis' terms, 'real'. It is an actual or factual state of affairs, in brief a fact. This omits reference to the space-time universe as the unique individual which instances the state of affairs. But since the whole world is the concrete embodiment of all first order facts, it distinguishes no one fact from any other whereas the instanced state of affairs does.

---

[29] Predicate terms which are self-inconsistent, e.g., 'round and square', and propositional terms which are similarly self-inconsistent, e.g., 'A=non-A', not only do not apply to anything but cannot. They have zero comprehension as well as zero denotation. The universal signification which they have cannot characterize anything because it is so broad as to be self-inconsistent. Contrariwise, predicate terms which would apply to any possible particular existent, and propositions which would apply to any possible world, have universal comprehension and zero signification.

## II

The outstanding difficulties with Lewis' theory of facts center on his treatment of propositions as predicate terms. Even his various ways of symbolizing a proposition, while they help him on his way toward maintaining that a proposition signifies a state of affairs which is a property of the actual world, lead him into difficulties that indicate he has taken the wrong path.

Thus he starts with a paradigm assertion, 'Mary is making pies'. To distill out the propositional content of this assertion, the proposition that may be questioned or affirmed, doubted or denied, etc., he suggests that we use the linguistic expression, 'that Mary is making pies now'. This seems not unreasonable for we can assert, deny, or doubt, etc. that Mary is making pies. But note just what it is that we thus assert, deny, or doubt, etc. We are talking about Mary and saying of her that she is making pies. We are using the predicate term of our clause, namely, 'is making pies now' to predicate something of the individual to whom the subject term 'Mary' refers. We are not explicitly saying anything about the universe and its properties, although doubtless something about it could be inferred from what we say. Similarly when we assert that Mary is making pies now we are not asserting that it is true that Mary is making pies now, although if what we assert, namely, that Mary is making pies now, is true, then indeed we would be justified in asserting also that it is true that Mary is making pies now. We are not predicating some property of the universe but of Mary. The proposition we asserted implies and is implied by a large number of others, but of all of these we have asserted only one.

But now Lewis suggests that 'Mary making pies now' will express for us what we have been expressing by 'that Mary is making pies'. But the substitution of the former for the latter won't even work satisfactorily at the grammatical level. Lewis writes:

It will be sufficient to assure the fact that expressions such as 'that Mary is making pies' are really terms if we observe that they can stand as subject in sentences or as predicate. E.g., "That Mary is making pies is what I doubt"; "That Mary is making pies calls for three cheers"; "The gratifying fact is that Mary is making pies"; "We believe that Mary is making pies." Also, with some violence to customary idiom, the participial phrase, 'Mary making pies (now)' is always substitutable for this other manner of indicating a state of affairs: e.g., "The gratifying fact is Mary making pies now"; "Mary now making pies is what I doubt"; and so on.[30]

30 AKV, pp. 50, 51.

There are several things wrong with this account. (1) To show that a propositional clause can function as a subject of a proposition does not at all show that it is a predicate term. It shows only that something we believe, doubt, or disbelieve, etc., which is just the sort of thing a proposition signifies, can be talked about, and can properly be said to be doubted or to call for cheers, and so on. (2) The examples given fail completely to show that a proposition can be a predicate term. In 'We believe that Mary is making pies' the predicate term is 'believe that Mary is making pies', not 'that Mary is making pies'. The latter is the object of 'believe' and indeed that Mary is making pies is quite an appropriate object of belief. In 'The gratifying fact is that Mary is making pies' we have an identity sentence rather than a subject-predicate sentence. (3) In the two examples offered which use the participial phrase 'Mary making pies (now)' there is more than "some violence to customary idiom." In both cases we feel a strong need to insert a 'that' before 'Mary'. With the 'that' understood we have in each case a propositional expression. With the 'that' explicitly omitted and 'Mary making pies (now)' explicitly characterized as a property term, both examples involve category mistakes. Whatever else a fact may be, it never, gratifying or not, is correctly identifiable with a property. It may be a fact that some specific property is exemplified but we would never say that the property itself is a fact. Similarly, in the example, 'Mary now making pies is what I doubt', it is quite incorrect to say that we ever doubt a property. We may doubt that a property is exemplified, but then we are doubting not a property but the believable or doubtable sort of entity that is signifiable by a proposition.

The basis of these linguistic criticisms is to be found in the fundamental difference between the kinds of entities which are signified by propositions and by predicate terms. Either clauses or sentences signify the sort of entity toward which it would be appropriate to have an epistemic attitude, that is, an attitude of belief, doubt, or disbelief, etc. Ordinary predicate terms signify qualities or properties or characters, as Lewis (and I) often generically call them. But such things are precisely the sort of things toward which any of these epistemic attitudes would be thoroughly inappropriate. A character, a universal if you like, e.g., roundness, is not the sort of thing that could reasonably be doubted, believed, or disbelieved. We might indeed reasonably believe or doubt, etc. that something is round, but not roundness itself. What we believe, doubt, etc., is always exactly the sort of entity that could be signified by a proposition but not by a term.

Lewis, as we have noted, speaks of what is signified by a proposition as 'a state of affairs'. But this locution invites equivocation in the same sort of way that 'Mary making pies now' does. If we take 'a state of affairs' to refer to a character that something might or might not have, then this character itself is precisely the sort of thing toward which an epistemic attitude would be categorially inappropriate. But if we take it to be a shorthand expression for an expression of the form 'that something, *a*, has a certain character, *c*' then indeed an epistemic attitude would be appropriate toward what such an expression would signify. Because it can easily be taken in either of these ways 'state of affairs' is hardly an ideal expression for referring to what is signified by a proposition.

If Lewis had used 'proposition' in its other common sense of that which is signified by a propositional expression, we could have used the latter term for the signifying expression whether a clause or an indicative sentence, or some other suitable symbol. But 'proposition' too has its disadvantages, just because it has been used in both these ways and is used by Lewis to refer to a linguistic expression. One suggestion that occurs to me is that we might use the term 'proposal' to refer to that which a proposition (in the Lewisian linguistic sense) signifies. To make this suggestion successful we should have to insist that we are using the term 'proposal' to stand for, not the act of proposing, but that which is proposed by a proposition, something thus put forward for consideration, belief, or doubt, etc., namely precisely the sort of entity which is signified by a proposition.

Professor David A. Keyt, in 1955, put his finger on much the same central difficulty that I have indicated in the preceding pages. He makes his point succinctly:

The roots of Lewis's error lie deep. The following passage, I believe, comes closest to exposing them: ". . . a state of affairs is *not* a concrete entity; a space-time slab of reality with all that it contains, but is a property or attribute. It includes nothing beyond what the *abstract* participial expression naming it entails or requires."[31] What is interesting about this passage is

[31] *C. I. Lewis' Theory of Meaning*, a doctoral thesis presented at Cornell University, June, 1955, p. 53.
Keyt has also gotten at some of the other difficulties that I have noted but by a different approach. He writes (*op. cit.* pp. 29-30) :
"Lewis distinguishes a proposition from a statement. Any statement, '*p*' can be expanded into the form from 'It is the case that *p*.' The clause "*that p*" is the proposition contained in or asserted by the statement 'It is the case that *p*.' This same proposition may be denied, supposed, questioned: . . .
" '. . . a state of affairs . . . is a property or attribute.' (A 53) I now argue that this statement is self-contradictory. I consider this statement rather than the statement that a state of affairs is a property of *the actual world* so that there can be

that Lewis considers only two alternatives: a state of affairs is either a concrete
entity or an abstract entity. The presupposition is thus that a state of
affairs is an entity. It is this supposition that is the root of the error. A state
of affairs is not an entity.[32]

One consideration that may have helped to lead Lewis to believe
that a proposal is simply a special kind of property is the point he
emphasizes that both are abstract entities capable of being conceived.
It is indeed true that both can be entertained conceptually, but the
only mode of entertainment possible for properties is to be conceived,
whereas some epistemic attitude toward proposals even if it be doubt,
rather than belief or disbelief, is demanded by their nature. Again,
properties characterize individuals or fail to, but are never true or false.
Proposals are necessarily true or false and never characterize any proper
individual. And even Lewis' suggestion that they can characterize a
Pickwickian individual, the space-time whole, has the further Pickwickian consequence of leading to the most bizarre terminology. We
never say such things as 'The universe is, or has, that Mary is making
pies'. Nor do we say that the universe instances or is characterized by
that Mary is making pies. Lewis' suggestion that we could say, "The
universe is characterized by Mary making pies now," begs the question
by assuming that 'Mary making pies now' has the same signification as
'that Mary is making pies now' but is nevertheless a predicate term.
If we came across 'Mary making pies now' chalked on a non-Lewisian
fence we would be at a loss to know what it signified. Is it a nickname?
an expletive? or what? On Lewis' fence, of course, we should take it to
signify what is usually signified by 'that Mary is making pies now' but
then we should realize that it would be appropriate to believe, doubt or
disbelieve this, and hence certainly inappropriate to regard it as a
property.

---

no doubt where Lewis's mistake lies. If the name of a state of affairs ("it being the
case that $p$") is the name of a property, then to assert the corresponding proposition
("that $p$") can only be to attribute this property to something. In short: if (1) a
state of affairs is a property, then (2) any statement '$p$' is an elliptical expression of
'$a$ is characterized by it being the case that $p$.' Now statement (2) is a universal statement. Thus if it is true, *every* statement is elliptical: '$p$' is elliptical, '$a$ is characterized by it being the case that $p$' is elliptical, '$b$ is characterized by $a$ being characterized by it being the case that $p$' is elliptical. Further, one statement is as elliptical
as another. No statement is any more complete than any other. But this is to deny
that one statement is an elliptical expression of another; it is to deny that statement
(2) is true. Therefore, statement (2) entails its own denial. Therefore, statement (2)
is self-contradictory. But statement (1) entails (2). Therefore, statement (1) is self-
contradictory."

[32] *Ibid.*, p. 30.

We can agree with Lewis that a proposal is abstract, but we should have to insist that it is abstract in a very different way from that in which blueness, say, is abstract. Blueness is multiply instanciable; the proposal that Mary is making pies now is not. Either 'Mary' or 'now' could of course be regarded as a variable with many arguments, but in that case, as Lewis notes, the expression 'that Mary is making pies now' would be not a proposition but a propositional function, and would be neither true nor false. The proposal that Mary is making pies now is abstract not in the sense of being capable of having instances but rather in the sense that it abstracts from all the things that could be considered about Mary's present activities and proposes for our epistemic consideration only one of these, namely that Mary is making pies. What 'that Mary is making pies' refers to is not any part of the space-time slab that is the whole universe, nor is it that universe itself. It isn't Mary with all her characteristics including the temporary one of making pies, for nothing is signified by 'that Mary is making pies' about whether she is wearing a red apron or not. Still less is it the whole universe with all its characteristics. It refers not to any space-time part of the universe but rather to what, in ordinary English we should refer to by 'the fact that Mary is making pies'.

Lewis goes astray again through thinking of a state of affairs as a property, by holding that when we conceive what a proposition intensionally means or signifies we are conceiving a property which is instanced in our mind. But whatever may be true about properties it seems a clear mistake to assert that proposals characterize our minds. What our minds do with proposals is to entertain them, believe them, or doubt them, etc. This means that a proposal can be the object or content of a mental act of believing, doubting, entertaining, etc., but this is a far cry from its being a characteristic of our mind or of its thoughts. When we believe that Mary is making pies that proposal is what we are believing but it is not a characteristic of our mental activity.

For all these reasons we should conclude, I suggest, that Lewis is mistaken in holding that what a proposition intensionally or conceptually means or signifies is a property. Unlike a property it can have no instances; unlike a property it can be believed, doubted, or disbelieved; unlike a property it is true or false; unlike a property, it normally requires for a symbol to express it, something like a clause or a sentence. Even to say that like a property a proposal is abstract is misleading, for it is abstract in the very different sense of being only a small selection, rather than exhaustive, of the truth about the subject of the proposition. There is indeed a considerable analogy between the modes of meaning of a term and of a proposition, but Lewis pushes the analogy much too far. As a consequence his theory that a fact is a property which characterizes the universe falls by the wayside.

## III

What kind of a theory of facts would fit well with Lewis' general position and yet be satisfactory on other grounds? Since this is not the place for a monograph on this complex and difficult topic, I limit myself to a few suggestions.

Let us begin with some examples of first order empirical facts. They are best referred to by means of clauses, indeed the same propositional clauses that *signify* first order proposals:

(1) 'That Mary is making pies now'
(2) 'That the quarter now in my pocket is dated 1959'
(3) 'That the Empire State building is taller than the Chrysler building'

The facts that these propositions *refer to* have constituents as follows:

(1) The individual, Mary, and the character of making pies on the date indicated by 'now'.
(2) The particular quarter now in my pocket, and the character of being dated 1959.
(3) The two particulars, the Empire State building and the Chrysler building, and the dyadic relation which holds between them in their listed order.

There are also facts which have three particulars as constituents and a triadic relation among them, and so on. But though these facts have particulars and characters or relations as constituents, they should not be identified with any array of such constituents. For an array of particulars and universals is not the sort of thing that could be a fact. That a certain particular is characterized by a certain universal may well be a fact, or that one particular is related to another particular in a certain way, and so on, but neither a particular nor a universal can be a fact.

At least one particular, though of course not the same one in every case, is a constituent of every first order fact; and at least one universal, though not the same one in every case, is also a constituent of every such fact. But even in the simplest case there is no fact unless the particular is characterized by the universal. This is why the normal way for referring to a simple fact is by means of a proposition the subject of which refers to a particular, and the predicate of which signifies a universal that characterizes that particular. The particular has a position in space or time or both. On one possible view the characterizing universal is nontemporal and nonspatial; on another the universal is instanced by the particular it characterizes and is embodied in that particular. But on either view the fact is neither a particular nor a universal. Even in the simplest case a fact is that limited and special sort of entity that can best be referred to by saying that the particular has a characteristic, or, if we are more careful, has a characteristic at time, $t$. The addition of the temporal reference, necessary in the case of first order empirical facts because they contain impermanent constituents with changing characters, guarantees that these facts are nontemporal. We like to think that facts are in some sense ingredient in the world, for it is to the world we turn to find out what the (empirical) facts are. And this desire of ours is realized to the extent that at least some of the constituents of a fact are literally located in the world. But the fact itself, e.g., that Mary is making pies at the time indicated by the utterance of 'now', is timeless.

Are facts observable? No, they are neither sensible nor perceivable, for they are timeless. But in many cases we can observe all that is necessary to know that there is a fact referred to by a given proposition and hence that this proposition is true. We can observe this blotter before me, for instance, and we can notice that it is blue, and we can take account of the fact that the time is, say, $t_2$. Thus we can know it to be a fact that this blotter is blue at $t_2$.

All self-consistent propositions signify proposals. The true first order empirical propositions among them refer to facts. Referring is a mode of extensional meaning very similar to what Lewis calls 'denoting' except that he seems to limit denoting to particulars, and a fact is not a particular. It resembles a particular, however, in being actual or factual, and thus can be referred to. The proposal that is signified by a proposition, true or false, is, however, something quite different. A proposal is conceptual in nature, and may be entertained or conceived. A proposal we can say, making use of Lewis' terminology, has 'some manner of being', and if conceived is 'real', but it does not exist, as a fact does, and hence is not actual or factual. A proposition, and the proposal it signifies, are true, if and only if there is a fact to which that proposition refers.

A second order empirical assertion states that two (or more) first order characters are related by some empirical relation, for example, by the 'real connection' that Lewis discusses.[33] The fact in virtue of which such an assertion is true would be a second order empirical fact.

Whether or not we want to say that a statement asserting that two universals or two proposals or two facts are necessarily related, say by

[33] AKV, pp. 226 ff.

entailment, is true in virtue of an a priori fact that one does entail the other, seems to be, at least to some extent, a matter of terminological choice. On a realistic view of universals it seems to be the case that some timeless entities do entail others, and it thus seems reasonable to hold that statements asserting this are true in virtue of such facts.

CHARLES A. BAYLIS

DEPARTMENT OF PHILOSOPHY
DUKE UNIVERSITY

## 7

*Roderick M. Chisholm*

# LEWIS' ETHICS OF BELIEF

ANY belief which "explicitly or implicitly has the character of inferred conclusion"—any belief which is such that the test of its
correctness will "involve test of some inference implicit in it"—is either
"justified, warranted and *right*" or "unjustified and *wrong*."[1] This ethical statement expresses one of the fundamental principles of C. I. Lewis'
theory of knowledge. In the present paper, following the suggestion of
the quoted statement, I shall consider Lewis' theory as an ethics of belief, as a type of moral philosophy. In this way, I believe, it will be possible to throw light upon one of the most important of twentieth century
contributions to epistemology and to formulate some of the questions
with which it leaves us.

## I

We must ask, first of all, whether it makes any sense to speak of an
"ethics of belief." Can a belief be called *wrong* in the sense in which a
criminal act can be called wrong? 'Belief' sometimes refers to the proposition a man accepts, to the doctrine or set of theses he subscribes to.
And we cannot say, of course, that a proposition, doctrine, or set of theses
is wrong in the same sense in which we can say that a criminal act is
wrong. But 'belief' may also refer to a psychological *act*—to the
fact that a man *accepts* a proposition, or *takes* it to be true. In this active
sense of 'belief', a belief—a believing—*may* be called wrong and in
much the same sense as that in which a criminal act may be called
wrong.

Perhaps it is not in accord with ordinary use to describe a belief or
assumption—a believing or an assuming—as an 'act'. We do not say that
a man is active merely because he is opinionated. An *act*, in the ordinary
sense of the word, must involve some physical change, such as the
motion of limbs. But even in this sense of 'act', the motion of limbs or

---

[1] C. I. Lewis, *The Ground and Nature of the Right* (New York: Columbia University
Press, 1955), pp. 27 f. My italics. Hereafter cited as GNR.

similar physical change is not *sufficient* to constitute an act. If a man's body is submitted to electric charges, with the result that it is put into violent motion, these motions may not be acts of his, nor need they be in any way involved in what can be called his acts. For they may be nothing that *he* does himself. They may be entirely the result of the electric charge, given his general physiological condition, and entirely beyond his control. In this case they are not anything for which he is himself responsible. No bodily motion can be called an act, or can be said to be a part of an act, unless it is something the man could avoid, something under his control and for which, therefore, he is responsible. It is true that the habits of a malicious man may become so ingrained that we are tempted to say, of some of his misdeeds, that he could not have avoided them. But these habits are, as Lewis puts it, "subject to critical review and to self-discipline."[2] It is still appropriate for us to say, of the man for whom malice has become second nature, "He should never have let himself get in that state." And even he, in defending or accusing himself, will assume that he could have done otherwise.

If self-control is what is essential to activity, some of our beliefs, our believings, would seem to be acts. When a man deliberates and comes finally to a conclusion, his decision is as much within his control as is any other deed we attribute to him. If his conclusion was unreasonable, a conclusion he should not have accepted, we may plead with him: "But you needn't have supposed that so-and-so was true. Why didn't you take account of these other facts?" We assume that his decision is one he could have avoided and that, had he only chosen to do so, he could have made a more reasonable inference. Or, if his conclusion is not the result of deliberate inference, we may say, "But if you had only stopped to think," implying that, had he chosen, he could have stopped to think. We suppose, as we do whenever we apply our ethical or moral predicates, that there was something else the agent could have done instead.

To be sure, we may be mistaken in supposing that our thinker could have reasoned otherwise or that, had he chosen to do so, he could have arrived at a different conclusion. And, similarly, we may be mistaken in supposing that the criminal could have behaved in any other way or in supposing that, had he chosen to do so, he could have avoided his criminal act. It is extraordinarily difficult to decide which of our actions are really our own—which, of what would seem to be our actions, are in fact our actions. And I think it must be conceded that, not only is it difficult for us to apply the concept of an *act*, but it is also difficult for us even to understand the concept, or at least

2 GNR, p. 27.

to understand how it is related to the concepts of cause, and necessary and sufficient condition. But it is "this distinction of active passage from passive enduring"—this distinction "of what is attributable to us as our own activity from that which happens to our case by reason of what is alien and other"—which, according to Lewis, "lies at the bottom of any sense of self in contrast to the non-ego of the external world."[3] And it lies at the bottom of any distinction between right and wrong, or moral and immoral. If there is any reason to suppose that we ever act at all, then there is reason to suppose that what Lewis calls our "believing and concluding" are to be counted among our acts.

Leibniz proposed a reason for saying that our believings are *not* acts: "As all belief consists in remembering previous proofs or reasons, it is not within our power nor within our free choice to believe or not to believe, since memory is not a thing that depends upon our will."[4] But even if it were true that all of our beliefs are memories—which is hardly plausible—there are respects in which our memory *is* a thing depending on our will. If a memory judgment cannot be avoided, it may yet be altered. One can be persuaded that he mistakenly thought he remembered something. One may say: "I thought I remembered once having visited him, but I realize now that I couldn't have been there." Or one can be persuaded that some perceptual judgment upon which an (ostensible) memory depends was false. After saying "I remember seeing him there," one may be led to concede, "I certainly thought it was he at the time, but I realize now it couldn't have been," and hence to withdraw the original memory statement.

Peirce once said of our reasoning, our believing and concluding, that "we have here all the main elements of moral conduct; the general standard mentally conceived beforehand, the efficient agency in the inward nature, the act, the subsequent comparison of the act with the standard."[5] This is a statement to which Lewis might well subscribe. Our ethical judgments, even those that apply to particular actions, always presuppose some universal ethical principle or standard which holds for everyone. I may say, for example, that the lawyer acted wrongly in betraying the confidence of his client. I may be condemning only this particular person and it may be that I have given no thought to anyone else who might find himself in a similar position. But if I am allowed to defend, or to justify, my moral judgment, I will try to show,

---

3 GNR, p. 23.

4 G. W. Leibniz, *New Essays Concerning Human Understanding,* trans. Alfred Gideon Langley (La Salle, Ill.: Open Court Publishing Company, 1949), Book IV, Chap. 1, Sec. 8.

5 C. S. Peirce, *Collected Papers* (Cambridge, Mass., 1931), 1.607. Hereafter cited as CP.

first, that the lawyer was in a position such that *anyone* finding himself in that position would have certain obligations to another man
and, secondly, that in betraying the confidence of his client the lawyer
did not fulfill these obligations. Whatever I may have had in mind in
making the moral judgment, my defense of it may be formulated in
such a 'practical syllogism', one premise of which is a universal ethical
principle which holds for everyone. We defend our believing and concluding in a similar way. If you ask me to defend some conclusion of
mine which you may think unreasonable, I will present evidence which
I take to be such that, for anyone having that evidence (and no additional relevant evidence), the conclusion is a reasonable one to accept.
Here, too, my justification may be formulated in a 'practical syllogism';
the major premise will say that anyone having just the evidence in question is warranted in accepting the conclusion; the minor premise will
say that I am in the position of having just that evidence; and these
premises will imply that I am justified in accepting the conclusion.

Lewis has often said that perception involves *interpretation*. The
word 'interpretation' may be misleading, particularly if it is taken to
imply conscious or deliberate inference. "To say that the cognitive element in cognition is always inferential would hardly be precise; but it
will be fully correct to say that cognition is always such that any test of
its correctness will involve test of some inference implicit in it."[6] I may
see, or perceive, that the river is frozen, without having *inferred* that it
is frozen. And since I am acquainted with the river and with the way
it looks when it is frozen, it sounds strange to say I *interpreted* certain
visual clues as a sign that the river is frozen. My perception is not like
the thought-process that occurs when one diplomat interprets certain
words as a sign that another diplomat is now willing to negotiate. But if
you challenge my perceptual judgment, saying "What makes you
*think* you see that the river is frozen?" or "Why do you *take* it to be
frozen?" and if I make a reasonable reply, I will, once again, appeal
to premises which are such that, for anyone having adequate evidence
for those premises and having no additional relevant evidence, the conclusion is one which would be reasonable for him to accept. I may indicate some features characteristic of the way the river appears and
note that, as we have learned from previous experience, these features
are a reliable sign of the fact that the river is frozen. In thus defending my perceptual judgment, I will be formulating what Lewis calls
the inference implicit in it, or the interpretation which it involves.

6 GNR, p. 26.

We punish people for doing what they hadn't ought to do, but we seldom consider punishing anyone for believing what he hadn't ought to believe. We do not pass *laws* saying that people should not have unreasonable beliefs. Should we say, then, that when one speaks of the 'ethics of belief', or of what people 'ought to believe' or 'ought not to believe', we are using the words 'ethics', 'ought', and 'ought not' in a Pickwickian sense, in a sense they do not have when applied to those activities which involve bodily motion and which are subject to legislation and punishment.

Lewis says, in one place, that "rightness in concluding and believing is, perhaps, principally important to ourselves and suggests that our other activities—those involving bodily motion—are more likely to be of concern to others."[7] If this were true, it might provide an explanation for the fact that our believing and concluding seem to be immune from legislation and punishment. But surely it isn't true; what we believe and conclude is, or should be, of considerable concern to others. If our overt activities depend upon what we believe and conclude (Lewis, as much as any contemporary philosopher, has stressed the relevance of belief to action) and if our overt activities are important to others, then what we believe and conclude is also important to others. What we fear most, in the present age, are those activities which may arise because of some other person's unreasonable beliefs about our own intentions. It is not the unimportance of our believing and concluding that explains our failure to pass laws against, and to punish, unreasonable believing and concluding. One reason for not punishing a man who believes what he hadn't ought to believe may well be this: We do not punish a man for those ostensible actions that occur when 'he is not in his right mind' or when he is not behaving as a rational human being. But when a man fails to conform to the ethics of belief he is, *ipso facto*, behaving irrationally. On any occasion those beliefs we ought not to have and those conclusions we ought not to reach are precisely those beliefs and conclusions which would be *unreasonable* on that occasion. And another reason for not punishing those who fail to fulfill their epistemic obligations lies in the fact that such punishment would not be compatible with our right to freedom of thought— a right which, although it allows one to believe what one hadn't ought to believe, has compensating advantages in our present society.[8]

7 GNR, p. 39.

8 I think, incidentally, that one of the best philosophical discussions of this right is to be found in Lewis' "The Meaning of Liberty," *Revue Internationale de Philosophie*, 6 (1948), 14-22.

## II

In Chapter One of *Mind and the World-Order*, Lewis describes one of the principal tasks of philosophy as that of formulating "the logical essence of goodness, the canons of validity, the criteria of the beautiful, and likewise, the principles of the distinction of real from unreal."[9] The formulation of the canons of validity presents problems very much like those involved in determining the essence of goodness. The former problems—that is to say, the problems of epistemology, or of what, in *The Ground and Nature of the Right*, Lewis calls the "critique of cogency"—can be clarified, I believe, by much the same methods which Lewis and other philosophers have recently applied to the concept of goodness and to the other concepts of moral philosophy.

Logic may be thought of as a part of the 'critique of cogency' but it is only a part. When logic is considered in this light, one could say, with Lewis, that it has to do with relations of consistency and entailment. It can tell us what propositions, or sentences, are consistent with each other and it can tell us when one proposition, or sentence, entails another. But by itself, logic does not tell us what we have a right to believe or what we ought to refrain from believing. Even the logic of probability and induction is not sufficient to serve as the 'critique of cogency'. Inductive logic will not tell us what propositions we have a right to believe unless we apply it to *premises* which we have a right to believe. Indeed, when we apply the logic of probability and induction, in order to evaluate an hypothesis, we must do so in accordance with two epistemological principles—two prior principles of the 'critique of cogency'. First, the premises to which we apply this logic must be evident; they must be premises we ought to believe, or, at least, premises whose denials we ought *not* to believe. And, secondly, they must include all the relevant evidence available; of the propositions which we ought to believe (or of those whose contradictories we ought *not* to believe), we should consider all that we know to bear on the probability of our hypothesis. "No inductive conclusion is well taken and justly credible unless the obligation to muster all the given and available evidence which is relevant to this conclusion has been met."[10] Lewis illustrates this second principle—*the requirement of total evidence*[11]—by means of the following example. If I know that the coin looks exactly like a half-

[9] *Mind and the World-Order* (New York: Chas. Scribner's Sons, 1929), p. 17. Hereafter cited as MWO.

[10] GNR, p. 32.

[11] Rudolf Carnap uses this term in the *Logical Foundations of Probability* (Chicago: University of Chicago Press, 1950), p. 211. Hereafter cited as LFP.

dollar, I may say that, in relation to this information and to what I know about half-dollars, the probability is that, if the coin is repeatedly thrown, it will land heads just one half the time. Although this probability conclusion may be validly derived from propositions which I have a right to believe, it may yet be that I have *no* right to accept it. For I may have *other* evidence which, when added to my original premises, will change the conclusion. I may happen to know that the ostensible coin is a false one, manufactured so that it will land heads all of the time.

To see what is involved in the 'critique of cogency', let us first see how all of ethics, on Lewis' view, might be said to presuppose the ethics of belief. I shall turn, then, to certain of Lewis' views about the right and the good.

## III

The following four statements, each of which may seem true when considered independently of the others, are mutually inconsistent.

(1) No act is right unless its consequences are at least as good as are those which any of its alternates would have. (2) It is right for us to do what we ought to do and we never ought to do what isn't right. (3) It sometimes is possible for us to know what we ought to do and what we ought not to do. (4) But it is never possible for us to know what all the consequences of any act, or of any possible act, will be.

If all four of these statements are true, as each of them may seem to be, then some of the terms occurring in them are being used equivocally; they do not mean in one statement what they mean in another. This equivocation may be attributed either to the use of 'right' or to the use of 'ought'.

We may say that the word 'right' in statement (1) —'No act is right unless its consequences are at least as good as those which any of its alternatives would have'—has its *absolute* use. Right, in this sense, is a function solely of good; one can never know, with respect to any act at all, whether the act is right, in this sense of 'right', for one can never know what all of its consequences will be. When we say we *know* that some act is, or isn't, right and think of the act as being worthy of praise or blame, we are using 'right' in another sense.

Lewis mentions two further uses of 'right'—its *objective* and *subjective* uses. I think we may say that an act is 'objectively right', in Lewis' sense of this expression, if the agent has adequate evidence for believing that it is absolutely right, in our sense of the latter expression. "An act, then is objectively right to do just in case, on the evidence available to the doer, it is that alternative of action which affords the (correctly judged) highest probability of good results."[12] And an act is 'subjectively right' if the agent believes—whether truly or falsely, whether reasonably or unreasonably—that it is objectively right. I think that these two definitions of 'right', when taken with the definition above of the absolute sense of 'right', serve to clarify all but one of the important uses of this term. We may make an analogous set of distinctions for the use of 'ought'.

With such distinctions, we can interpret statements (1) through (4), above, in such a way that they are true and therefore consistent with each other. We could say, for example, that 'right' should be taken in its absolute sense in (1) and (2), and that 'ought' should be taken in its absolute sense in (2) and its objective sense in (3). Or we could reformulate (1) through (4) in such a way that 'right', and not 'ought', is the equivocal term. But in either case we must appeal to the concept for which Lewis uses 'objectively right'—the concept of an act which, on the *evidence available* to the agent, is the one which is, in all probability, absolutely right. And in either case, therefore, we must appeal to the concept of right believing and concluding.

To have adequate evidence for a proposition is to have sufficient reason for accepting it. "To have a sufficient reason for believing or for doing is to be justified in so deciding, and to have no reason is to be unjustified . . . "[13] A man acts rightly in believing a proposition if he has adequate evidence for it; he acts wrongly in believing a proposition if he has adequate evidence for its contradictory.

Thus we see how all of ethics, on Lewis' view, presupposes the ethics of belief. No act is objectively right unless the agent is *justified* in believing—unless it is *right* that he believe—that that act will have good results. And no act is subjectively right unless he believes it is right for him to believe that the act will have good results. This epistemic sense of 'right' is presupposed by Lewis' definitions of *objectively* and *subjectively right*.

## IV

In the spirit of what has just been suggested, we may say that a man has *adequate evidence* for a proposition or hypothesis provided only he is *not* justified in believing—has *no* right to believe—its contradictory. We could say that it would be *unreasonable* for him to accept a proposi-

12 GNR, p. 56.
13 GNR, p. 88.

tion or hypothesis if it were one such that he had adequate evidence for its contradiction. We could say that a proposition is *acceptable* if it is not unreasonable, and that a proposition is *dubitable* ('expendable') if it is not evident. If I do not have adequate evidence for a certain proposition, then the proposition is one which, for me, is dubitable and its contradictory is acceptable.

Our four terms thus form a logical square. *Evident* and *unreasonable* are contraries; no one can have adequate evidence for a proposition which it would be unreasonable for him to believe. But there are some propositions which are neither evident nor unreasonable; such propositions could be called *indifferent*. *Acceptable* and *dubitable*, on the other hand, are *subcontraries*. Many propositions—namely those that are indifferent—are both acceptable and dubitable, but no proposition is neither. *Evident* and *dubitable*, like *unreasonable* and *acceptable*, are contradictories.

There are passages in *The Ground and Nature of the Right* which suggest a more rigid ethics of belief. In the quotation cited at the beginning of this paper, Lewis says that every belief—or every belief which is in the subject's control—is either "justified, warranted and right or unjustified, and wrong."[14] And after saying that to have a sufficient reason for believing is to be justified in believing, Lewis adds that "to have no reason to be unjustified and non-rational or irrational."[15] I have just said, however, that we are unreasonable only if we believe a proposition whose contradictory is evident; a proposition is acceptable provided only it is one whose contradictory is not evident; and thus, according to what I have said, if there are any indifferent propositions, propositions such that neither they nor their contradictories are evident, such propositions are acceptable. But if Lewis intends the passage quoted as I have interpreted it, then, according to him, we are justified in believing *only* when we have adequate evidence. This difference illustrates the kind of ethical dispute that arises when we consider the ethics of belief, but it does not affect any of the issues to be treated here.

Kant said, categorically, "There is no obligation to believe anything."[16] We could agree with this and still retain what we have said above. For we needn't say that a man ought to believe anything, not

[14] GNR, p. 27.

[15] GNR, pp. 88-89.

[16] Immanuel Kant, *The Metaphysics of Morals*, conclusion of Part *I* ("Jurisprudence"). Included in the Abbott translation of *Kant's Theory of Ethics* (6th ed., London: Longman's Green, and Co., Ltd., 1927).

even that he ought to believe what is evident. We need say only that he ought *not* to believe—that he ought to *refrain* from believing— what is unreasonable. There may be no obligation to believe anything, but there are obligations to withhold belief.

The 'critique of cogency' has to do, then, with the *rules* of right believing—in part with the rules of logic, deductive and inductive, and, as we have noted, with additional rules as well. It is the additional rules which concern us here.

The 'rules of cogency' which Lewis adduces give us the characteristic features of his theory of knowledge. These are controversial and I would not myself subscribe to everything that Lewis says about them. But what Lewis says about the *nature* of his inquiry, about the nature of the 'critique of cogency', seems to me to be true and to go more deeply than do the writings of any other philosopher on this subject. I shall say something about the 'critique of cogency', as Lewis conceives it, and then try to show that a philosopher may perform this task and yet arrive at an epistemology rather different from that of Lewis.

## V

In formulating the rules of right believing and concluding, the philosopher is making explicit those rules which he and others pre- suppose in appraising and criticizing particular instances of believing and concluding. As in moral philosophy and logic, he is "bringing to clear consciousness and expressing coherently the principles which are implicitly intended in our dealing with the familiar."[17] The principles of right believing are like the principles of ethics—or, rather, like the *other* principles of ethics. We may ask puzzling questions about 'the ground of their validity' and we may even wonder whether the state- ments expressing them are true or false, or whether they are informative in the way in which statements expressing the results of science are in- formative. I think that whatever may be said, in this connection, about the status of the other principles of ethics may also be said about the principles of right believing and concluding. But fortunately we may say a number of things about the 'critique of cogency' without attempt- ing to answer such questions.

It would not be accurate to say that, in eliciting the principles of right believing and concluding, the philosopher is trying to *find out* which instances of believing and concluding are right and which are not. For he cannot formulate these principles unless he *already knows* which

[17] MWO, p. 3.

instances of believing and concluding are right and which are not. The following remarks, which Lewis makes about ethics and certain other philosophic enterprises, also hold for the 'critique of cogency'.

The nature of the good can be learned from experience only if the content of experience be first classified into good and bad, or grades of better and worse. Such classification or grading already involves the legislative and application of the same principle which is sought. In logic, principles can be elicited by generalization from examples only if cases of valid reasoning have first been segregated by some criterion. It is this criterion which the generalization is required to disclose. In esthetics, the laws of the beautiful may be derived from experience only if the criteria of beauty have first been correctly applied.[18]

The 'preanalytic data' for any epistemology are just those propositions we think we know. Any epistemology, or 'critique of cogency', implying that we don't know what we think we know is, to that extent, inadequate. Here, then, we have one way of evaluating any epistemology —including that of Lewis.

There is a second test of adequacy, a second way of evaluating an epistemology. I shall quote a very important passage from Lewis' article, "Realism or Phenomenalism?," in which this second test is clearly formulated. The epistemological problem, Lewis says, is

that of the critique of cognition as valid or invalid, justified or unwarranted, correct or mistaken. The problem of such criticism is already implicit in the fact that cognition is called knowledge only on the presumption of its correctness. These questions of critique concern what is determinable by application of those criteria satisfaction of which is required by, and will be sufficient for, warranted validity of empirical belief and by reference to which any disclosure of experience is to be taken as confirming or as disconfirming a belief in point. Questions of that kind call for answers which can be formulated in terms of experience itself and criteria applicable to experience, for the simple reason that there is nothing beyond experience which can be adduced for our inspection and to which such criteria can be applied, nor anything other than disclosed or disclosable characters of experience upon which the decision they may afford can turn.[19]

Another way of formulating this test of adequacy is to say that the epistemological principles elucidated by the philosopher must be principles which one is clearly able to apply. It will not do to say, "One has adequate evidence for a certain proposition $p$, provided only that so-and-so occurs," if one has no way of telling whether so-and-so occurs. An adequate epistemology will not be content merely to say: "We have adequate evidence for just those of our beliefs which are shared by the

---

18 MWO, p. 29.
19 *Philosophical Review*, 64 (1955), 235. Hereafter cited as "Real. Phen."

scientists of our culture circle." This principle, or criterion, merely transfers the problem, for we must now have a way of deciding which, if any, of our beliefs are the ones we share with the scientists of our culture circle. Our epistemological principles must be principles we can directly, or immediately, apply; their application must not presuppose still further principles.

On the other hand, it would not be informative merely to say: 'We have adequate evidence for just those propositions which we know— or perceive or remember—to be true'. We are looking for criteria by means of which we can apply 'adequate evidence'. But the words 'know', 'perceive', and 'remember', as they are used above, presuppose these criteria. We cannot identify any instance of believing or concluding as an instance of knowing, remembering, or perceiving, unless we are able to say that the proposition which is thus accepted is one for which the believer has adequate evidence.

Now, I think, we can understand the importance of 'the given' in Lewis' epistemology. If we can know anything about the world, if there is any proposition or hypothesis for which we have adequate evidence, then something is given to us by means of which we can test the proposition or hypothesis. 'Experience' is another name for what is thus given. Any critical judgment as to the justification of a belief "can be made only by reference to some content disclosed or to be disclosed in experiences which will test it."[20]

It is very easy to misinterpret what Lewis has said about 'experience' and 'the given'. One may point out that there are senses of the words 'experience' and 'given'—possibly the most usual senses of these words—which are such that Lewis' remarks about the given, when taken in those senses, are false. But this is to miss the point of what Lewis has to say.

A more serious criticism would be this: that, as Lewis interprets such terms as 'given', 'data', and 'experience', these terms can be defined only by reference to knowledge or evidence. The word 'disclose', in the quotation above, might suggest this criticism. In such a case, Lewis' views about the relation of our knowledge to the given might be said to be uninformative and his reasoning said to be circular. But I believe we can define 'given', as Lewis uses this term, in such a way that this criticism does not apply.

We could say that a state of affairs is given to a believer at a certain time, provided only that, at that time, no matter what else he should believe, it would be impossible for him to believe that the state of

---

[20] "Real. Phen.," p. 236.

affairs is *not* taking place. (We might then say that one of the 'pre-suppositions' of knowing is, that if a state of affairs is thus given, then it is one which is in fact taking place. Or we might add another phrase to our definition, stipulating that a state of affairs is not given unless it is one which is taking place; in this case, we might say that one of the 'presuppositions' of knowing is that, whenever it is thus impossible for a believer—a man having some beliefs—to believe that a certain state of affairs is taking place, then that state of affairs is taking place.)

In the present sense of 'given' we may say, informatively, that ap-pearances—or ways of being appeared to—are included in what is given. (Feelings, as well as the image-content of dreams, imagination, and hal-lucination are also included; but we need not here discuss these 'sub-jective experiences'.) Whether or not we use the words 'given', 'experi-ence', or 'data', to refer to ways of being appeared to, the important thing is this: we may say of the ways in which we are appeared to (or, at least, of *some* of them) that, whenever anyone is thus appeared to, then, no matter what else he may then believe, it would be impossible for him to believe that he is *not* being thus appeared to.

One of the several senses of 'looks' and 'appear' is such that, if, in that sense, something now looks white to me, if I am now 'appeared white to', then I cannot believe that nothing looks white to me, or that I am not now being 'appeared white to'. The statement 'Something now looks white', or 'I am now appeared white to', Lewis would say, expresses "the direct and indubitable content of my experience," something concerning which "I can have no possible doubt"; the "ap-prehensions of the given" which such statements formulate "are not judgments" and they are not to be "classed as knowledge," for "they are not subject to any possible error."[21] But such statements are true and —here is what is characteristic of Lewis' theory and what to me seems doubtful—they constitute our ultimate evidence for what we believe about the world. They constitute the 'bases of empirical knowledge'.

We can agree in general, I think, with what Lewis has to say about the 'bases' of our knowledge:

Our empirical knowledge rises as a structure of enormous complexity, most parts of which are stabilized in measure by their mutual support, but all of which rest, at bottom, on direct findings of sense. Unless there should be some statements, or rather something apprehensible and statable, whose truth is determined by given experience and is not determinable in any other way,

21 C. I. Lewis, *An Analysis of Knowledge and Valuation* (La Salle, Ill.: Open Court Publishing Co., 1946), pp. 174, 179, 183. Hereafter cited as AKV.

there would be no nonanalytic affirmation whose truth could be determined at all, and no such thing as empirical knowledge.[22]

If we know anything at all, if there are any hypotheses or propositions for which we have adequate evidence, then there are some 'basic statements' constituting our ultimate evidence for these hypotheses or propositions. There are some statements, that is to say, which (1) express a kind of belief in judgment that is incapable of error and which (2) are such that, in relation to them, our claims to knowledge are made probable—more probable than not. But, I think, Lewis overemphasizes the role of appearances.

## VI

Lewis' emphasis on the basic role of appearances in our knowledge of the world has led him to what I believe to be a questionable form of empiricism. The *meaning* of any ordinary statement about a physical thing, Lewis has said, may be explicated solely in terms of appearances, where 'appearance' designates not only the ways in which we are appeared to, but the 'subjective experiences' referred to above. Such statements as 'That thing is red', 'There is rain on the roof', and 'That is a door' have as analytic consequences, according to Lewis, certain other statements referring solely to appearances, or ways of being appeared to. And Lewis would say that there is a sense in which the entire meaning of any thing-statement is exhausted in those appear-statements which are its consequences.[23]

Lewis concedes that there is a practical difficulty in showing, with respect to any particular thing-statement, just how to express all of its meaning in terms of actual and possible appearances. No one has ever made an 'empirical translation' of even the simplest of thing-statements. I believe, moreover, that the difficulty is not merely a practical one. There are theoretical objections to the thesis that thing-statements, like those above, have consequences referring solely to appearances. To draw any such consequence from 'This thing is red', for example, it would seem necessary to take 'This thing is red' in conjunction with still another thing-statement—some statement referring to the physical conditions under which the thing might be observed and referring also to the nature of the observer. And, what is more serious,

22 AKV, p. 171.

23 See AKV, pp. 181, 246; "Professor Chisholm and Empiricism," *Journal of Philosophy*, 45 (1948), 517-24, esp. p. 517. Hereafter cited as "Chis. Emp." The latter paper was written in reply to "The Problem of Empiricism," by myself, which appeared in the same issue of the *Journal of Philosophy*, pp. 512-517.

for any appear-statement *T*, which our thing-statement *P* might seem to entail, we can think of some other thing-statement *Q* (one describing certain abnormal observation conditions) which is such that the conjunction of P and Q does *not* entail *T*. But if the conjunction of *P* and *Q* does not entail *T*, then *P* does not entail *T*.

Lewis has said, in reply to the foregoing criticism, that his view requires only that appear-statements be 'probability-consequences' of thing-statements. No thing-statement *P* entails any simple or categorical appear-statement *T*; but *P* may well entail 'in all probability *T*' or some compound appear-statement in which a probability-qualification occurs. Lewis writes that, in his account, "objective statements of fact are said to *entail* such probability-consequences because it is consequences of this sort which are *contained in what it means*—in one sense of meaning —to assert the objective-statements from which they are derivative."[24] If a man knows there is a doorknob in front of him, he also knows that if he has certain bodily feelings (those which, as it happens, he usually has when he moves his arm) then, in all probability, he will experience certain tactual appearances. This appeal to probability meets the difficulty, Lewis believes, because the

familiar rule, "If 'P' entails 'T', then for any 'Q', 'P and Q' entails 'T'," can not be applied, in the manner one is likely to attempt, where 'T' is any kind of probability-statement. Probabilities are relative to the premises (factual or hypothetical) from which they are determined. And in consequence of this fact it can be—and frequently is—true that on the premise 'P' alone something, 'R', is highly probable, but on the premise 'P and Q,' 'R' is highly *im*probable and something else, 'S', which is incompatible with 'R' is highly probable. In such a case, what must be noted is that, although 'R' and 'S' are incompatible as unqualified statements of fact, the two statements, "On the premise 'P' alone, 'R' is highly probable" and "On the premise 'P and Q,' 'S' is highly probable," *can not be incompatible since both are true* and no true statement can ever be incompatible with any other which is also true. (It must also be noted that the probability-consequences themselves, " 'R' is highly probable" and " 'S' is highly probable," are not incompatible because, in this form, they are incompletely stated and require the preface "Relative to 'P' " or "Relative to 'P and Q' " in order to be accurate statements of fact.)[25]

But this implies, if I am not mistaken, that the probability-consequences are no longer statements referring merely to appearances or to the kind of experiences Lewis has discussed. For if P is a thing-statement, the preface 'Relative to "*P*" (as Lewis would interpret it) is also a thing-statement; hence these probability consequences, when made ex-

24 "Chis. Emp.," p. 524.
25 "Chis. Emp.," pp. 522-3.

plicit, contain thing-statements in their prefaces and thus do not refer to appearances alone.[26]

The issues involved in this question are extraordinarily complex. They concern not only the nature of our knowledge, but also the nature of meaning and of probability—not to mention that of physical things and appearances. I am certain that we cannot settle these issues unless we are prepared to undertake the kind of inquiry Lewis has made in *An Analysis of Knowledge and Valuation*. But I do wish to suggest that Lewis' view is controversial and, going back to the epistemological principles which are the foundation of his view, to propose an alternative—one which lays less emphasis upon appearances.[27]

## VII

Lewis has defended his empirical view by suggesting that, if his view is not true, then we do not know what we think we know about the world. If the criticism we have just been discussing can be made good, then, he says, "there will be nothing left for us but skepticism."[28] This, of course, is a proper point to make; we have seen that one requirement of any 'critique of cogency' is that the critique enable us to say that we know pretty much what we think we know. But I believe that Lewis is mistaken in suggesting that the only alternative to his view is a skeptical one.

When Lewis considers memory, his 'critique of cogency' takes a form rather different from that we have just considered. Let us recall briefly what Lewis says about remembering and then apply what he says to the rest of our empirical knowledge.

---

[26] Although, in one of their uses, such statements as 'A is highly probable' are elliptical and require, in their full statement, a reference to their premises, these statements have another use in which they are not thus elliptical. In this second use, such statements as 'A is highly probable' mean something very much like 'It is evident that A', in the sense of 'evident' discussed in Section 4 above. If the probability-consequences we have been discussing were taken in this second sense, they could no longer be said to have prefaces containing thing-statements. But in such a case, the logical rule, 'If "P" entails "T", then for any "Q", "P and Q" entails "T"', could not be circumvented in the way Lewis describes above. And I believe, if we found any such categorical probability statement T (describing appearances and other experiences) which we believed to be an analytic consequence of some thing-statement P, we could find some other thing-statement Q (describing abnormal observation conditions) which is such that the conjunction of P and Q does not entail T. Compare Roderick Firth's discussion of this issue in "Radical Empiricism and Perceptual Relativity," *Philosophical Review*, 59, 1950, esp. 178-82.

[27] My own views on these questions are formulated in somewhat more detail, in *Perceiving: A Philosophical Study* (Ithaca, N. Y., 1957).

[28] "Chis. Emp.," p. 519.

We sometimes think we remember events which, in fact, did not occur at all; that is to say, we are sometimes mistaken with respect to what we think we remember. Given the fact that what we take to be our memory is thus fallible, we may ask what ground we have for accepting any ostensible memory as genuine. In asking this, we are looking "for some other and supporting ground beyond the immediate item which presents itself with the quality of recollection."[29] Any 'supporting ground' for memory must itself be something which, in a broad sense of the term, is 'given'; this follows from what has been said about the nature of the 'critique of cogency'. If a man thinks he remembers being in the mountains yesterday, and if this ostensible memory has the kind of supporting ground we are looking for, then this ground must be something which is 'given' to him. In other words, if there is something G that provides a man with supporting ground for a particular memory, a particular instance of thinking-that-he-remembers, then the presence of G must be something concerning which he can make no mistake. What could G be?

An extreme empiricist might insist that G could only be the appearance-like content that is, so to speak, before the mind when one thinks that one remembers. He might insist that when our subject thinks he remembers having been in the mountains, the supporting ground of this ostensible memory—if there is any supporting ground—must be those vague memory-images, resembling the appearances of the mountains, which may be called up in the subject's experience. What else is there, the empiricist might ask, for the supporting ground to be?

Lewis summarizes his own answer this way:

First; whatever is remembered, whether as explicit recollection or merely in the form of our sense of the past, is *prima facie* credible because so remembered. And second; when the whole range of empirical beliefs is taken into account, all of them more or less dependent upon memorial knowledge, we find that those which are most credible can be assured by their mutual support, or as we shall put it, by their *congruence*.[30]

(Perhaps we should note, what has misled some of Lewis' critics, that the word 'remember' is here to be taken in such a way that no contradiction is involved in saying that a man remembers something falsely. The intent of the passage might have been clearer had Lewis used words such as 'ostensible memory' instead of 'memory', and

29 AKV, p. 334.

30 "A set of statements, or a set of supposed facts asserted, will be said to be congruent if and only if they are so related that the antecedent probability of any of them will be increased if the remainder of the set can be assumed as given premises." AKV, p. 338. [Original is italicized.]

'think-that-one remembers' instead of 'remembers'.) For our purposes the more important part of Lewis' answer is the first.

Using the terms of an older psychology, we might say that, according to Lewis, the supporting ground for any particular memory is not the *content* or imagery that is before the mind when one thinks one remembers; it is, rather, the *act* of thinking that one remembers.

The 'act' of thinking that one remembers is something that is *given* to the one who thinks he remembers. Our subject may be mistaken in thinking that he was in the mountains yesterday. But he cannot possibly be mistaken in thinking that he thinks he remembers he was in the mountains yesterday. No one ever believes falsely that he thinks he remembers that so-and-so occurred. Thus Lewis tells us, in effect, in the first part of his theory of memory, that whenever a man thinks he remembers that a certain event occurred, he is, *ipso facto*, justified in believing that that event occurred. Perhaps Lewis could have said, more strongly, that under such conditions, the man has adequate evidence for the hypothesis that the event occurred.

Hence we seem to find a supporting ground for memory, or ostensible memory, without falling back upon the imagery to which the extreme empiricist might lead us. This ground of memory-judgments may not be sufficient by itself; Lewis' theory of memory, as the above quotation indicates, makes use of still another principle. But the availability of this type of ground suggests that we might look for its analogue in the case of our other empirical knowledge—our ostensible perceptions.

## VIII

Lewis has said that one 'supporting ground' for our ostensible perceptions is constituted by those appearances which are before the mind when we think we perceive. And I believe it is correct to say that, according to Lewis, the *only* 'supporting ground' of our empirical knowledge are these appearances taken together with the type of memory judgment we have just considered. If my criticism of Lewis' form of empiricism is accurate, it may be that these two types of ground are not sufficient to support that 'enormous edifice' which is our empirical knowledge. In such a case, Lewis' 'critique of cogency' would not meet the first test of adequacy which he has set down for any such critique; it would not conform to our 'preanalytic data' concerning what we know about the world. It may be well, therefore, to look for an additional type of support for our empirical knowledge—another ground we can fall back upon if need be.

. Taking our cue from Lewis' theory of memory, we may find this ground in the 'act' of (ostensibly) perceiving. Should we say that, whenever a man thinks he perceives that a certain condition obtains, he is, *ipso facto,* justified in believing—or he has adequate evidence for believing—that that condition obtains? Thinking-that-one-perceives is like thinking-that-one-remembers. If I think that I see snow on the mountain then, although I may be mistaken in this, I cannot possibly be mistaken in believing that I think I see snow on the mountain. According to the present suggestion, if I think I see snow on the mountain, then, whether or not I really do see it, I have adequate evidence for believing I do; I have adequate evidence for the proposition or 'hypothesis' that there is snow there. (It may be well to note that, whenever we *think* we perceive a certain state of affairs, in the present sense of 'think we perceive', we are likely to say, more strongly, that we *perceive* it. But if anyone challenges our claim to perceive, then, whether or not he thinks we really do perceive it, he will ask, 'What makes you *think* you do?') The present suggestion could also be expressed by using the word 'take': If I *take* something to be snow on the mountain, I have adequate evidence at that time, for the proposition that there is snow on the mountain.[31]

It may be that this suggestion gives us more than we want. Possibly the present suggestion would count as evident many of those beliefs which, preanalytically, we don't want to count as evident, or which we want to count as unreasonable. But this defect, I think, may be remedied in one of two ways. (1) We might enunciate *two* principles, similar to those of Lewis' theory of memory. Using his concept of *congruence,* we might say: first, that we are *justified* in believing, at any time, what we *take* to be true at that time; and secondly, that of such takings the *evident* ones are those which are congruent with the rest of our justified beliefs. Modifying Lewis' definition of *congruence* slightly, we might say, that a set of hypotheses is congruent if and only if the hypotheses are such that any one of them is, in relation to the conjunction of all the others, more probable than not. The second of these principles, it must be conceded, would be difficult to apply.

(2) Another way of modifying our suggestion would be this: instead of saying, simply, that all of our 'takings' are evident (at the time they occur) , we might specify some subclass of takings and say only that they are evident. For example, we might list a set of characteristics —what Aristotle called 'the proper objects of sense' and 'the common

<hr/>

[31] H. H. Price suggests a modification of this view in his *Perception* (London: Methuen, 1933), pp. 139 ff.

sensibles'[32]—and say that, whenever anyone takes anything to have such a characteristic (thinks he perceives that it has such a characteristic), he then has adequate evidence for the hypothesis that the thing does have that characteristic.

It may well be—but this remains to be shown—that, by following one or the other of these suggestions, we can say that we know pretty much what, preanalytically, we think we know. I think, therefore, that if Lewis' form of empiricism is subject to the difficulties I have mentioned above, we need not be left with skepticism. For there may be alternative epistemologies—other ways of satisfying the requirements of the 'critique of cogency'.

RODERICK M. CHISHOLM

DEPARTMENT OF PHILOSOPHY
BROWN UNIVERSITY

[32] See *De Anima*, 425a-427b.

## 8

## Bernard Peach

# LEWIS' THEORY OF ANALYTIC STATEMENTS [1]

IN the Preface to *The Analysis of Knowledge and Valuation* Lewis tells us that he considers the doctrine of analyticity fundamental to theory of meaning, this in turn to theory of empirical knowledge and this to valuation and ethics. In each field there are basic statements which are designed to explicate the properties that are the peculiar interest of that field. Such statements can, he believes, be only definitive and a priori. If they are interpreted as expressing nothing but stipulated relations of linguistic forms or procedural rules for manipulating symbolism he anticipates that the results may well be disastrous. Thus his discussion of analytic statements is no mere exercise in analysis. He considers a correct understanding of them necessary if we are to avoid skepticism in knowledge, cynicism in valuation and, most importantly, relativism in standards of conduct. His theory of meaning and the analytic consequently represents an attempt to delineate the fundamental sense of 'meaning' in which meanings can neither be manipulated nor altered, while at the same time acknowledging the scope and importance of choice as to classification and linguistic symbolism.

The discussion of analytic statements, then, is central to his entire philosophy; but it is apparent that any discussion of them in an article must be limited. I have consequently confined my attention primarily to questions regarding their status as statements and to some of the problems that arise from such an approach.

The frequent occurrence of such phrases as 'Lewis seems to hold' are ingenuous. I have frequently been in doubt as to the correct inter-

[1] Discussion of analytic statements in the literature is so extensive that I may have incorporated material that is originally due to someone else. If so, they should claim it. I should like to acknowledge aid from the reviews of *An Analysis of Knowledge and Valuation* by Hempel, *Journal of Symbolic Logic,* March, 1948; Ducasse, *Philosophical Review,* May, 1948; Stace, *Mind,* January, 1948; Henle, *Journal of Philosophy,* September 9, 1948; and Baylis, *Philosophy and Phenomenological Research,* September, 1947. I have also profited from reading the dissertations of D. A. Keyt, "C. I. Lewis' Theory of Meaning," Cornell, 1955 and C. D. McGee, "C. I. Lewis' Theory of Sense Meaning," Harvard, 1956. Especially I am indebted to discussion with my colleagues at Duke and with P. F. Strawson at Oxford.

pretation. If I have nevertheless misunderstood, my misunderstandings are perhaps common, and it will serve one of the main purposes of this series if they should be dissipated.

I propose to examine what Lewis means by the term 'statement', in the hope that this will make it possible to say what kind of statement an analytic statement is. I shall show that Lewis' general doctrine that a statement is the assertion of a proposition admits several interpretations due to the ambiguity of the term 'assertion' and to complications arising from his definition of 'proposition'. The general doctrine that a statement is the assertion of a proposition compresses these ambiguities but does not remove them, and in any event does not include statements that result from substituting into statement functions or closing them quantificationally. I argue that it is consequently not clear how the modes of meaning appropriate to propositions considered as terms can belong to statements which assert those propositions. In addition the way in which Lewis expresses his views regarding naming, applying-to, denoting, comprehending, and signifying permits alternative interpretations of certain aspects of his doctrines about the modes of meaning of analytic statements.

His subsequent introduction of the holophrastic-analytic distinction either gives up or shifts attention from the doctrine that an analytic statement is the assertion of an analytic propositional term. In answering what he regards as the important epistemological questions, What is the nature of analytic truth and how do we know it? he holds that an analytic statement is the assertion of a relation between fixed meanings. This tack encounters difficulties of its own. Sense meanings cannot fill the bill of fixed meanings regarded as 'meanings in themselves', which must apparently be unitary entities independent of language and antecedent to particular applications of terms. They either lack the required sharp edges or must be made sharp by decision. Concepts are better candidates but must ultimately be rejected, as must also things meant when considered as independent of being so meant. Actual or possible classifications come closest to fulfilling the requirements laid down, but do not seem adequate to Lewis' purpose.

I shall finally argue that if fixed meanings are understood as specified meanings this meets the difficulties previously encountered but sacrifices the claim of independence from decision and language. Fixed meanings in this independent sense seem unnecessary anyway. The result secured by such independence would seem to be guaranteed by the simple fact that terms cannot both be used as they are used in making a statement and not used in that way. Appeal to meanings as independent in a way that resists attempts at further analysis tends to shift attention away from the pragmatic circumstances of statement-making.

While Lewis apparently wants a theory of analytic statements free from a consideration of such factors it seems doubtful that such a general theory can be formulated that would be adequate to analytic statements generally or to the pragmatic foundations of his own philosophy.

# I

Lewis never actually defines 'statement' although he comes close to it several times. For example, he says that defining a proposition as true or false is inauspicious because it easily leads to identification of the proposition with the statement or assertion of it.[2] This suggests that a statement is the assertion of a proposition. He says that the statement 'Mary is making pies' asserts the state of affairs, Mary making pies now, as actual. This suggests that a statement is what asserts a state of affairs as actual. This is also suggested, although with a variation, when he says[3] that a statement attributes a state of affairs to the actual.

In discussing negative statements Lewis cautions about their interpretation because '$A$ not being $B$' would often fail to correspond exactly to the asserted content of 'It is false that $A$ is $B$'.[4] This suggests that a statement is an asserted proposition. A variation of this view occurs when Lewis indicates that the truth or falsity of a statement depend upon context.[5] Here 'context' refers to the sentence in which the term is used. It has a wider application, although Lewis does not use the term with its suggestion of 'contextualism'. In this broader sense 'context' can refer to other factors as well, such as those that might be part of the content of assertion. Lewis seems to have such factors in mind when he speaks of doing "patient justice to intended meaning on each occasion,"[6] and of our decisions to adopt or neglect certain meanings.[7] It is particularly evident in his doctrine that the Cyrenaic contradicts himself pragmatically by seriously uttering the injunction, "Have no concern for the future."[8] These inclusive factors sug-

---

[2] C. I. Lewis, *An Analysis of Knowledge and Valuation* (La Salle, Ill.: Open Court Publishing Co., 1946. Hereafter cited as AKV. A more descriptive title of the essay would be "Lewis' Theory of Analytic Statements in AKV."

[3] AKV, p. 52.

[4] AKV, p. 51.

[5] AKV, pp. 73-78.

[6] AKV, p. 77.

[7] AKV, pp. 95, 110, 124.

[8] AKV, p. 481.

gest the view that a statement is a proposition as asserted by someone in certain circumstances.

Another doctrine of statements emerges from Lewis' discussion of functions. A statement results from substituting certain constant (non-variable) value expressions for each variable expression in a statement function. Thus, '$x$ is a man' is a statement function and by substituting the expression 'Socrates' we get the statement 'Socrates is a man'.[9] This is a different version of a statement because substituting is a different process from asserting or attributing. But it creates a difficulty about the distinction between statements and propositions.

Lewis, of course, denies that the statement function, '$x$ is a man', is the assertion of the propositional function, '$x$ being a man'.[10] Since the same substitution should affect the two functions in the same way, however, it would appear that 'Socrates is a man' ought not to be considered the assertion of 'Socrates being a man'. This would not agree with the view that a statement is the assertion of the corresponding proposition. It would seem, therefore, although there are of course many difficulties with the notion itself, that Lewis needs something like the notion of a sentence. 'Socrates is a man', then, regarded as the result of substituting into '$x$ is a man' could be regarded as a sentence that could be used by someone to make a statement. This would add another version of a statement as the assertion of a sentence.

I leave aside formal statements, although it should be noted in passing that there is in Lewis' definition of a formal statement an additional version of a statement, as the result of binding all the free variables in a statement function.[11]

Lewis might object that I have neglected the distinction between propositions as pronomial and predicable expressions. According to that doctrine 'Socrates being a man' may have two senses. In its predicative sense it denotes the world in the way in which 'hot' denotes hot things. It is in this sense that it is equivalent to 'that Socrates is a man' and is predicable of the world. In its pronomial sense it names the property that is essential to the world if the propositional term in its predicable sense is to denote it. If this distinction indicates that the participial form is assertible only in the sense in which it is equivalent to the clause of indirect discourse it constitutes a qualification of the general thesis

9 AKV, pp. 58 f.
10 AKV, pp. 59, 113-114.
11 AKV, p. 114.

that the participial form is the assertible content of statements and can always be substituted for the clause of indirect discourse.[12]

Even granting that the only assertible term is the clause of indirect discourse, it is not clear that this would clarify the relationship of proposition to statement nor reduce the number of different interpretations of 'statement'. Consider, in particular the status of 'that'. Is it part of the proposition or not? If it is, then there is no way to distinguish the proposition from the statement in the phrases 'the proposition that Socrates is a man' and 'the statement that Socrates is a man'. And if one asks what is literally asserted in asserting that Socrates is a man, the answer apparently must be: 'Socrates is a man'. Lewis might reply that this is niggling over a purely verbal matter that dissolves as soon as it is recognized that the use of 'that' makes quotes unnecessary.[13]

This, however, does not meet the difficulty. It might indicate another version of a statement, namely, that asserting a proposition is represented linguistically by removing the 'that'. The statement would be what remains. It might also indicate that what Lewis offers as a proposition is the name of the statement or is the statement as mentioned rather than used.

These views about what is literally asserted receive support from Lewis' discussion of the literal meaning of expressions.[14] 'Crito asserted, "Socrates is a man"' would read in indirect discourse, 'Crito asserted that Socrates is a man'. This seems to support Lewis' description of a statement as the assertion of a proposition. The proposition, however, appears in figurative language. Literally it means, 'Crito asserted (or uttered) the expression signifying that Socrates is a man and symbolized by «Socrates is a man»'. It would not do to put «that Socrates is a man» or «Socrates being a man» where we now have «Socrates is a man».

This, however, returns us to the suggestion, although from a different approach, that the distinction between statement and proposition is the difference between the use of a sentence on a given occasion and the sentence that is used in making that statement. If this is correct then it does not appear to be possible to distinguish between the proposition and the statement on purely terminological grounds. While the distinction which Lewis wants to draw between assertion and non-

---

[12] AKV, pp. 50 f.

[13] "Some Suggestions Concerning Metaphysics of Logic," *American Philosophers at Work*, ed. S. Hook (New York: Criterion, 1957), p. 99. Hereafter cited as "Met. Log."

[14] AKV, pp. 101-104.

assertion is important, if the preceding discussion is well taken he has
not provided a way to make it.

It would be convenient—it would, for instance, be much less complex—to be able to say that one of these versions correctly represents
Lewis' view of statements. It might then be possible to say directly what
further characteristics a statement has that make it analytic. Unfortunately, this is not possible. One or another of these doctrines is dominant
at different places in Lewis' discussion depending on what aspect of
analytic statements is in question. I shall most frequently speak as if it
is his view that a statement is the assertion of a proposition. It should
be remembered, however, that this compresses the different versions
into a more compact one offering an omnibus version of several distinguishable doctrines.

## II

Consider next the expansion of this version of a statement in terms
of the definition of a proposition and its elements. A statement is the
assertion of a proposition. A proposition is a term capable of signifying
a state of affairs.[15] A term is an expression capable of naming or applying to a thing or things of some kind.[16] An expression is formed or
determined by the association of a symbol with a fixed meaning.[17]
A symbol is a recognizable pattern of marks or of sounds used for purposes of expression and communication.[18]

One may think that the difficulties with assertion that we have so
far examined only begin to bring out the complexities contained in
Lewis' version of a statement. Attention will be directed here to 'capability', 'state of affairs', and 'naming or applying-to', particularly the
last, since it raises problems about Lewis' description of analytic statements as those having universal comprehension. The topic of fixed
meaning will be central to later discussion of his epistemology of analytic
statements. We should note in passing that Lewis does not distinguish

[15] The modes of meaning of terms are as follows: The *denotation* of a term is the
class of all actual things to which the term applies. Each such thing is denoted by the
term. The *comprehension* of a term is the classification of possible or consistently
thinkable things to which the term would apply. The *signification* of a term is the
property in the thing that is essential if the term is to apply correctly to it. The
*linguistic intension* of a term (connotation) is the infinite conjunction of terms connoted by it. A term, 'B' is connoted by another, 'A', if in relation to the criterion in
mind for applying the term 'A', 'A' applies only if 'B' also applies. The criterion in
mind is the *nonlinguistic intension* (sense meaning) of 'A'.

[16] AKV, p. 39.

[17] AKV, p. 73.

[18] AKV, p. 73.

precisely or consistently between a symbol as a recognizable pattern of marks and as an expression; but the sense can usually be ascertained from the context.

The notion of capability enters the expanded version of a statement in two connections; once in ascribing to a propositional term an ability to signify a state of affairs, and once in ascribing to a term an ability to name or apply to a thing or things of some kind.

Two questions arise, Do terms have abilities? What is the relation between the ability to signify and the ability to name or apply-to? In the first case it seems advisable to distinguish between what Locke would have called active and passive powers. A term has the passive capability of being used to name, apply-to, or signify, but only a person has the active capability of using terms to name. This reflects an emphasis on the version of a statement in which someone uses a sentence to make an assertion. And it provides an interpretation of the versions in which Lewis apparently holds that statements assert states of affairs as actual or attribute states of affairs to the actual.

Lewis' general emphasis on intensional meaning would indicate that he regards the ability of a term to be used to signify as a necessary condition of its being used to name or apply-to. This is not entirely clear, however, since he uses 'name' in a very broad sense to include denotation, comprehension and even signification, in the case of abstract terms. Things that do not exist, can be named. So naming is basically comprehending. Naming is denoting only when the named things are actual.[19] Also an abstract term can name, in the sense of denote, what it signifies.[20]

When combined with the modes of meaning of propositions these doctrines lead to certain results that seem unnatural and difficult to accept. Briefly, a proposition in case it is true, denotes the actual world; as a predicable term (analogous to 'hot' or 'sweet') it signifies the property that the world must have if the proposition denotes it; as a pronomial term (analogous to 'hotness' or 'sweetness') it denotes (and in this sense names) this property, and also signifies it, this property being a state of affairs.[21] It comprehends any world which would incorporate the state of affairs it signifies; and it connotes all propositions that it entails.

An abstract term, and therefore presumably an abstract propositional term, denotes (names) what it signifies.[22] It follows, since a term denotes

19 AKV, pp. 38-39.
20 AKV, p. 42.
21 AKV, pp. 42, 53-54.
22 AKV, pp. 42, 52-53.

the entities that have the property signified by it, that the state of affairs has the same property that it is. Thus the state of affairs signified by 'Socrates being a man' has the property of Socrates being a man. A variant of this difficulty arises when we ask what it means to say that a statement is true. It means, according to Lewis, that the world is characterized by the property that the statement attributes to it. In fact the world is the only particular of which any property can be predicated by a statement. Thus,

(1) 'Socrates is a man' is true

is equivalent to

(2) The world is characterized by the property, Socrates being a man. Now if we ask what it means for (2) to be true the answer must be that it attributes a property to the world and (2) is equivalent to

(3) The world is characterized by the property, the world being characterized by the property Socrates being a man.

The series may not be vicious and there may be ways in which Lewis could adjust his theory to meet this and the former difficulty.[23] Nevertheless it indicates a difficulty with the notion of a state of affairs as a property and therefore with his theory of statements as the assertion of propositions. In any case every proposition must denote the same thing, namely, the world.

When we say 'Diamonds are harder than glass' we would think we were attributing the property of being harder than glass to diamonds. According to Lewis, however, we are attributing the property of diamonds being harder than glass to the actual world. Perhaps Lewis intends to distinguish between empirical and analytic statements in this connection. He says, however, that "Every statement asserts a proposition and attributes a state of affairs to the actual world."[24]

In a simple paradigm case, e.g., 'All cats are animals' we are, according to Lewis, attributing the property of cats being animals to all possible worlds and *a fortiori* to the actual world. It seems all right to say that the actual world has the property of being, say, unbounded; even to say that the realm of possible worlds has the property of being infinite, though this is more suspicious. But what is it to say that all possible worlds have the property of cats being animals? And this becomes even more difficult when one considers examples of analytic state-

23 Cf. C. A. Baylis, "Facts, Propositions, Exemplification and Truth," *Mind*, October, 1948.

24 AKV, p. 53.

ments that are not paradigms, for example, "Mnemic present-as-pastness is constitutive of the only reality which as humans we can envisage."[25] or "In all the world and in all of life there is nothing more important to determine than what is right."[26]

### III

The questions that have been encountered in the examination of Lewis' general theory of statements bring us to questions about the modes of meaning of analytic statements. Lewis asserts sufficiently often that analytic statements have zero intension and universal comprehension that there can be little doubt of his holding that view.[27] He does not, however, explain how the modes of meaning of propositions are related to the modes of meaning of statements.

His discussion of functions does not explain it. He does say that it is appropriate to consider the intension of statement functions to be statement functions. But, as previously indicated, this is not entirely consistent with his other views about statements unless asserting is to be considered quantifying or substituting into a statement function. We seem, rather, to have an open sentence, a sentence and the use of a sentence to make a statement. On this interpretation there is no need to appeal to the proposition at all if the meaning of the sentence can be otherwise explained, say, as a sequence of symbols or marks whose meanings are known by the functions they serve. Lewis makes a suggestion along these lines. "Language is not brought down from heaven but is a product of human devising[28] . . . for the sake of signalizing characters found in things and for the sake of practice guided by sense-apprehension . . ."[29] This, however, is vague and any development of a theory of analytic statements in terms of the use of sentences would be a very dubious interpretation of Lewis in any case. Although his discussion of functions has other merits it does not explain how modes of meaning of propositions attach unchanged to statements.

Consider the propositions and statements themselves. A proposition comprehends any consistently thinkable world which would incorporate the state of affairs it signifies. The classification of such possible worlds constitutes the comprehension of that proposition. An analytic proposi-

25 AKV, pp. 357-58.
26 *The Ground and Nature of the Right* (New York: Columbia Univ. Press., 1955), p. 3. Hereafter cited as GNR.
27 AKV, pp. 71, 83, 89, 111, 128, 137.
28 AKV, p. 168.
29 AKV, p. 146.

tion, e.g., 'All cats being animals', has universal comprehension. It is a term that would apply to or hold of every possible world. This is plausible but unclear. We might try other ways of understanding comprehension that seem clearer, for example, by considering the parallel between propositions and terms.

Any such attempt, however, encounters difficulties in the phrase 'name or apply to'. The notion of 'applying-to' is not itself clear nor does Lewis clarify it despite its crucial role. In particular, it reflects a lack of clarity between reference and characterization.

In addition to the different modes of meaning that Lewis suggests are to be understood as naming there is the scope and vagueness of his suggestion that to avoid question-begging restriction on the verb 'to name' we must recognize that anything that can be thought of can be spoken of.[30] It does not, then, seem possible to explain comprehending by appealing to naming as a clearer notion.

There is, furthermore, the question of the relation between naming and applying-to. In some passages he seems to use them as if they were interchangeable; for example, "Traditionally any attribute required for application of a term is said to be of the essence of the thing named."[31] The possibility that 'name or apply-to' means 'name, i.e., apply-to' has the following significance. Lewis says that a term names or correctly applies to anything it comprehends.[32] If the parallel holds between terms and propositions then it follows that a proposition with universal comprehension names all possible worlds. And the assertion of it, that is, the analytic statement, is the assertion of the name of all possible worlds. This would result in the anomalous doctrine that 'All cats are animals', 'All squares are rectangles', and so on through the infinity of analytic statements, are, each one of them, the assertion of the name of all possible worlds. It is doubtful that Lewis would admit to such a doctrine. Still many passages in AKV support this interpretation.[33]

On the other hand, if naming is distinct from applying-to then this result need not follow; and there are at least three passages which support such an interpretation. They deal with the abstract and concrete senses of terms and propositions and with attributives.[34] This interpreta-

---

[30] AKV, p. 38.

[31] AKV, p. 41.

[32] AKV, p. 67.

[33] I take it that Hempel, op. cit., p. 40 ("Each of the elements of the comprehension is said to be named by the term.") and Ducasse, op. cit., p. 266 (". . . one could not say that the real world is called Mary and making pies.") find this a plausible interpretation.

[34] AKV, pp. 42, 52-53, 80.

tion can be made evident by conflating the passages, using AKV, pp. 52-53 as basic, borrowing from AKV, p. 42 and AKV, p. 80 and making appropriate substitutions to indicate how they are relevant to the doctrine that analytic statements have universal comprehension.

> . . . any participial phrase like ['All cats being animals'] can have either of two senses. In one of these it is a predicable expression, like the adjective 'hot' or 'sweet': in the other it is abstract and pronomial, like 'hotness' or 'sweetness'. It is the former of these in which it is equivalent to ['that all cats are animals'] and is to be identified with the proposition. It is in this sense that it is predicable of [all possible worlds]. In the other—the abstract sense—it *names* the attribute predicated; that is *names* the state of affairs attributed to [all possible worlds] by asserting ['All cats are animals.'][35] . . . and has no other application.[36]
> It is only in their concrete sense that such attributives are predicables. In their abstract sense they name what they signify and are substantives.[37]

This interpretation avoids the result that analytic statements are the assertions of the names of all possible worlds. Yet it is not entirely clear. It does not seem unequivocally to leave intact the doctrine that a term names or correctly applies to anything it comprehends. What we apparently have are two expressions, not one. The concrete expression denotes the actual world which has the property the expression signifies. In this sense it applies-to, but does not name, the existent member of its comprehension. It also comprehends all possible worlds and in this sense applies to them. 'Applying-to' in the two cases seems different, however; in the second case it is just comprehending over again. The abstract expression names the property that the world has and also names the property that the possible worlds must have, or would have if they were actual. Again the 'naming' seems different. Having a name ready that would name a thing if it were actual is different from naming. The naming of a hoped-for child is different from a christening. And, incidentally, one is tempted to think of 'name' and 'apply-to' as similar rather than different in the latter cases.

It is the property signified by the propositional phrase as a concrete expression that is named by that same phrase as a different, abstract, expression. It is not a possible world that is named. Applying-to, in turn, must be understood, when it is not just comprehending over again, as the denoting (but not the naming) of the existent member of the comprehension, that is, the one actual world. In short, if we attempt to transfer to the mode of the comprehension of propositions the doctrines

35 AKV, pp. 52-53.
36 AKV, p. 42.
37 AKV, p. 80.

that enable us to avoid the conclusion that propositions name actual or possible worlds we find ouselves no longer in the mode of comprehension but in the mode of signification or denotation.

Lewis himself does not adopt, in the case of participial phrases, the device he suggests for distinguishing, linguistically, between the concrete and abstract senses of terms. "For every concrete term 'C' there is a cognate abstract term—let us call it 'C-ness'—which denotes the signification of 'C'."[38] Had he made use of this device for propositional phrases, some of his difficulties might have been avoided. However, other difficulties would remain.

In the mode of signification any abstract phrase such as the analytic one 'All cats being animals', would signify the property, all cats being animals, and in the mode of denotation would name that property. But since all analytic properties are equivalent, it will name equally any analytic property. But this is a consequence almost as unfortunate as those which Lewis has escaped by denying that abstract terms apply to what they denote. 'All cats being animals' names not only the property it signifies but all other analytic properties, including, for example, three being greater than two, all amoeba being protozoa, too much being more than enough, and so on. This indicates that the interpretation[39] which makes it possible to avoid the conclusion that propositions name actual or possible worlds and that analytic statements are the assertions of such names, leads to this other result that any analytic propositional term names all analytic propositional properties.

Again, it is a consequence of Lewis' view that the property named by an abstract term has the property that it is. This follows from the fact that the naming in point is denoting and that a term denotes whatever has the property it signifies. Consequently the property of (all cats being animals)-ness must have the property of (all cats being animals)-ness. This seems very strange indeed. It is even worse if it follows, as it appears to, that since all analytic properties are equivalent, the property of (all cats being animals)-ness has all analytic properties.

There is perhaps no need to consider separately the zero-intensional mode of meaning of analytic statements. It presents, in similar variants, the difficulties we have encountered in considering comprehen-

---

[38] AKV, p. 42.

[39] C. A. Baylis has called my attention to a letter to him from Lewis in which Lewis says that propositions do not name the world and do not name the states of affairs which characterize what they (propositions) denote. Thus the latter of the two suggested interpretations would seem to be correct. Nevertheless it seems to me that on the basis of what Lewis has written in AKV they must both be considered possible interpretations.

sion and signification. Lewis himself points out one of them: Statements with zero intension all seem to say the same thing and to say nothing.[40] This he suggests would not accord with common sense and would impose serious difficulties for our understanding of analytic truth.[41] He consequently proposes a distinction between the holophrastic and analytic meanings of statements.

This distinction is important not only in meeting the difficulties that arise from considering statements as single units but also in providing a foundation for the development of his answer to the epistemological questions: What is the nature of analytic truth and how do we know it? The development, however, seems not to meet the difficulties we have encountered in our consideration of statements, propositions as terms, and the modes of meaning of analytic statements. It leaves unanswered the questions of how the modes of meaning of analytic propositions attach unchanged to analytic statements, of how properties can be characterized by the properties they are, of how abstract analytic participial terms are each one the name of every analytic property, and of how such terms are not, if indeed they are not, asserted in analytic statements.

It seems to me not to meet these difficulties because the holophrastic-analytic distinction in effect turns away from a consideration of the issue that gives rise to them; that is, the assimilation of propositions to terms and the difficulties that arise from the attempt to deal with statements as the assertions of such terms. There are many respects in which propositions are unlike terms. Some of them have been indicated here. Other writers have pointed out others.[42] This may account, in part for the difficulties of attempting to base a theory of the meaning of analytic statements on the respects in which they are alike. If the difficulties which have appeared in the examination of the modes of meaning of analytic statements seem to lie somewhat near the surface and to require only relatively minor readjustments, difficulties in his explanation of our knowledge of them may lie deeper.

## IV

The meaning of an analytic proposition as a whole is the result of the modification of the meaning of each constituent by the others. It is when regarded in this way that it has zero intension and universal compre-

40 AKV, pp. 70 f.

41 AKV, p. 70.

42 Cf. Ducasse, *op. cit.*, pp. 265-268; also E. W. Hall, *What is Value?* (London: Kegan Paul, 1952), pp. 29-34.

hension. Lewis maintains that it is also possible to regard analytic propositions according to the meaning of their constituents. There is a sense, for example, in which 'This is the day following Monday' and 'This is the day preceding Wednesday' mean the same thing. This is their holophrastic meaning. In the same sense 'The day following Monday is the day preceding Wednesday' means the same as 'Tuesday is Tuesday'. There is also a sense in which the former of these last two statements means something different from the latter of them. This is their analytic meaning. Furthermore, there could be a point in saying the former when there is not in saying the latter. Lewis denies that this point is limited to giving linguistic information or instruction in the use of language.

Analytic statements, considered analytically, say something, according to Lewis, that is significantly factual[43] and is different from what other non-synonymous analytic statements say.[44] Statements that are explicitly analytic assert a relationship of fixed meanings.[45] Lewis says they assert a relationship of intensional meaning and later specifies this as sense meaning. He also uses the term 'fixed meaning', however, throughout this discussion and since 'fixed meaning' is the more inclusive term it is the appropriate one to use in stating his doctrine. Particularly because, as I shall suggest, sense meanings are just one of several possible candidates for the title of fixed meanings.

"An explicitly analytic statement . . . asserts the logical necessity of something. An implicitly analytic statement is one which asserts something which is logically necessary . . . but does not assert that it is logically necessary."[46] The vague term 'something' in these definitions indicates difficulties arising from his theory of statements. One expects the term 'proposition' in the definitions where 'something' is used. Such a definition of analytic statements, whether explicit or implicit, would be difficult to reconcile, however, with his denial that the significance of analytic statements is linguistic in nature. There is tension in another direction, too, since we have statements that are not the assertion of propositional terms but the assertion of some relationship.

There was some difficulty earlier when this interpretation of a statement was proposed, however, due to the way in which it compressed

---

[43] AKV, p. 87.

[44] The term 'factual' as introduced here is perhaps innocent enough, but there are places in his appeal to fixed meanings where it seems to get out of hand. For a discussion of Lewis on facts, see the essay by C. A. Baylis.

[45] AKV, p. 89.

[46] AKV, pp. 89-90.

a number of distinguishable versions of statements. The holophrastic-analytic distinction effectively changes the earlier doctrine of statement and proposition. A statement is now to be regarded as a combination of individually significant constituents. Assertion would seem to be essentially involved in such combining, as relating the constituents in such a way that they constitute a statement. While ambiguities still remain, the holophrastic-analytic distinction pretty well rules out any consideration of a statement as the assertion of a propositional term, no matter how complex that term may be considered to be.

This distinction, then, not only raises further doubts about Lewis' version of a statement as the assertion of a proposition but also casts doubt on the acceptability of his version of a proposition as a term from which the assertive element is entirely divorced. I am not saying this could not be worked out, but that Lewis has not shown how it is to be done nor developed his doctrines in accordance with it.

If Lewis' denial of an assertive element in analytic statements was intended to rule out as irrelevant the pragmatic circumstances of statement-making it seems that he has not accomplished that purpose. In fact, the holophrastic-analytic distinction itself is essentially based on a reference to attitudes or interpretations. The meaning of a statement is either holophrastic or analytic only as regarded so by somebody in some context, in relation to some purpose.

## V

When the holophrastic-analytic distinction is augmented by the doctrine of fixed meanings and the distinction between linguistic and sense meanings, the latter when precise and explicit constituting a schema for the application of a term, Lewis is able to offer an answer to the epistemological questions which 'conventionalism' in his opinion answers incompletely, and therefore incorrectly.

Conventionalism as portrayed by Lewis (he is careful to say it could not be attributed to a particular logician or school in this way without qualification) is the doctrine that analytic truths are those that can be certified by definitions together with logic.[47] There are three reasons why conventionalism fails to answer these questions. First, because the definitions appealed to must themselves be analytic. It is only definitions correctly connecting expressions in accordance with the relations that in fact hold between antecedent fixed meanings that qualify as such definitions. Second, the principles of logic are also analytic

---

[47] AKV, pp. 96, 129.

statements and can be distinguished from other analytic statements only on pragmatic, not epistemological grounds. Third, the question why a principle of logic is valid asks for a demonstration that it is analytic.[48]

The attempt to answer the epistemological questions in conventionalist terms then must finally be circular. To avoid such circularity in answering those questions Lewis considers the most powerful and comprehensive ally of the holophrastic-analytic distinction to be the doctrine that there are fixed meanings, independent of language and convention. He maintains that such meanings are sense meanings but it is not clear that they are the only candidates.

Briefly, Lewis describes sense meanings by distinguishing them from linguistic meanings. Linguistic meaning is intensional meaning in the linguistic mode. Linguistically, expressions mean other expressions. We could know all the linguistic entries in an Arabic dictionary in the sense of knowing their relations to one another without, in another sense, knowing what they mean. This other sense is sense meaning. When we know the sense meaning of a term, we know the meaning of it in a sense that would enable us to apply the term or refuse to apply it to any item that could be presented to sense experience. Sense meaning, therefore, involves imagery but imagery in the sense in which we can know in advance of any particular empirical presentation whether, for example, a presented figure will be a chiliagon because we can imagine what it would be like to count the sides and come to the last one as we said 'one thousand'.

A sense meaning when precise and explicit, is a schema, in the sense indicated by Kant: "a rule or prescribed routine and an imagined result of it which will determine applicability of the expression in question."[49] Lewis says that the sense meaning is "in mind" in the sense of "entertained in advance of instances which are pertinent." There is no need to make the contrast between sense meaning and linguistic meaning a matter of contrast between 'inner' and 'outer'. "The real point is the distinction between meaning as indicative of and indicated by application on the one hand, and on the other, meaning as relation not to objects and objective occasions but to other linguistic expressions."[50] In either case, Lewis says, a meaning must, in order to be precise enough to serve the interests of logic and like problems, "be something deter-

48 AKV, pp. 129-130.
49 AKV, p. 133 n.
50 AKV, pp. 144-145.

minate beyond what any number of observed occasions of the use of expressions will assure with theoretical certainty."[51]

At the beginning of his discussion of empirical knowledge Lewis indicates that the sense meaning of an objective statement (a statement that an object has a property) must be considered to be "a criterion of possible *confirmations* of the objective statement and would be exhibited *in extenso* by the totality of terminating judgments implied or included in objective attribution of the property or character to be tested."[52] An objective statement would be, e.g., That thing in front of me is square. A terminating judgment would be, e.g., If something that looks square is given, then if I look at the (apparent) corners they will appear to be right angled and four in number. In some places Lewis says that an unlimited number of such terminating judgments are analytically implied by the objective statement,[53] but in other places that the relation is one of probability.[54] An exchange with R. M. Chisholm[55] has indicated that the latter is the correct version.

Sense meanings nevertheless provide the basis for our knowledge of analytic truth. According to Lewis we can determine that if a thing is square then it is rectangular, even though we cannot determine with theoretical certainty that a thing is absolutely square or rectangular: From "inspection of the criteria of possible confirmations" we can see that whatever confirms squareness must *ipso facto* confirm rectangularity in like degree.[56]

His earlier version reads: "We know that 'All squares are rectangles' because in envisaging the test which a thing must satisfy if 'square' is to apply to it, we observe that the test it must satisfy if 'rectangle' is to apply to it is already included."[57] It is possible to know that one schematism for applying a term includes another in the same general way that it is possible to know whether one plan includes another, e.g., whether the plan to go to Chicago includes a plan to go to Niagara Falls.[58]

This answer to the question how we know analytical truth suggests that relations of sense meanings also answer the other epistemological question as to the nature of analytic truth. He says that this kind

51 AKV, p. 145.
52 AKV, p. 193.
53 AKV, pp. 248-253.
54 AKV, Chap. X.
55 *Journal of Philosophy* (Sept. 9, 1948), 517-524.
56 AKV, p. 193.
57 AKV, p. 152.
58 AKV, p. 154.

of fact, discovered by performing the experiment in imagination and finding one test schema included in another, is a logically necessary fact, independent of language altogether. "Taking these sense meanings apart from any question of their verbal expression, a relation of them is as much a brute fact, unalterable to our wish and will and obdurate to any decision or convention of ours, as is the fact that trees have leaves and rocks are hard."[59]

One is struck by the versatility of sense meanings as imaginative schema. Without sense meanings which enable us to apply or refuse to apply an expression there would be, he maintains, no such thing as apprehensible empirical fact or empirical truth or falsity.[60] Sense meanings, then, enable us to ascertain not only analytic truth but empirical truth as well. In addition they are the constituents which, considered analytically rather than holophrastically, stand in the relations which Lewis says are asserted by analytic statements. It would seem possible that Lewis demands more from sense meanings than they can supply, and that their ubiquitous nature adds to the danger, contained in the language he uses, of confounding empirical with logical factuality.

In recapitulating his view[61] Lewis displays a tendency to reduce these demands when he speaks of relations of 'fixed meanings' as the content of analytic statements. Also his discussion of explicative statements, when he introduces the concept of a meaning as an independent entity (AKV, pp. 105-111) suggests that the category of fixed meaning is broader than the category of sense meaning.

Lewis does not define a fixed meaning. He speaks of "penetrating the circle of independent meanings and making genuine contact with them by our modes of expression."[62] Meanings in this sense are also spoken of as "antecedent to and independent of any conventions affecting the linguistic manner in which they are to be conveyed."[63] A further facet of their independence is brought out by his doctrine that they are assigned to symbols to give expressions.

Incidentally, it would be more accurate of Lewis to use 'mark' or 'pattern of marks' where he uses 'symbol' in discussing the assignment of meanings to symbols, since he uses 'symbol' in the sense of a mark that had no meaning until assigned a fixed meaning. He also suggests the notion of a sentence as a string of marks, although he does not dis-

---

59 AKV, p. 153.
60 AKV, p. 135.
61 AKV, p. 155 f.
62 AKV, p. 131.
63 AKV, p. 148.

cuss it beyond asserting that "literally nothing is said" by such a string of marks "until the conventions affecting expression are fixed and hence the meanings in question are fixed."[64] This suggests the view that anything being said by a string of symbols (marks) depends upon conventions about how it will be expressed. (I take it that 'expression' is not being used here in the sense of a symbol associated with a fixed meaning. This would of course undercut his whole doctrine of independent fixed meanings.)

Fixed meanings furthermore must apparently be understood if anything true or false is to be conveyed by a statement: ". . . nothing in the nature of a truth to be told (or a falsehood) puts in its appearance until the linguistic symbolisms used have a fixed and understood meaning assigned to them, or until the syntactic structure of the kind of verbalism called a statement conveys an equally fixed and understood relationship of meanings symbolized . . ."[65]

The requirment indicated by 'understood' seems, on one reading, to be too strong since it would conflict with independence and antecedence. It might mean that truth or falsity are impossible unless someone understands the terms and their relation. It might, on the other hand, simply mean that in order to tell whether a statement is true the sense in which the terms are used must be, or be made, evident. If this amounts to the doctrine that we must know what the terms in a statement mean before we can know whether a statement is true or false, or analytic, then it seems as acceptable as the former interpretation seems unacceptable. In this sense, however, fixed meanings would simply be specified, or announced, meanings.

Lewis says also that "until symbols have fixed and specific meanings, a relation of them conveys no relation of meanings; and as soon as the meanings attaching to symbols are fixed, the question whether a relation of symbols expresses truth depends on the relation of meanings so expressed."[66] This passage gives us another characteristic of a fixed meaning, specificity. It also suggests that the meanings attaching to symbols are fixed not only in the sense of being affixed or assigned but also that they are fixated, made fixed as contrasted with being left changing or variable. The one suggests that in themselves they are fixed, definite, or precise; the other that they become fixed by being affixed to a symbol. Lewis' language indicates that he intends the former. The

64 AKV, p. 148.
65 AKV, p. 148.
66 AKV, p. 156.

latter is also a possible interpretation, though it too would undercut the position he seems to be arguing for.

A final characteristic of a fixed meaning is contained in the statement that "language is not language until it possesses fixed meaning determining what expressions signify and require as essential for their application."[67] This would seem to rule out extensive ranges of language as it is ordinarily conceived. But for present purposes the passage indicates that fixed meanings are characterized by an absence of plurality. It could not of course be considered the absence of ambiguity since this is a characteristic of the expression that results from attaching the meaning to the symbol. Yet it is difficult to see how assigning a meaning to a symbol could give an unambiguous expression, granted the initial independence of the symbol and the meaning, unless the meaning itself were something unitary. An ambiguous expression would be a symbol to which more than one fixed meaning has been assigned. But since, by definition, these would be two expressions, there can be no ambiguous expressions. A fixed meaning attached to a symbol establishes what property a thing must have if the expression is to apply to it.

The characteristics of fixed meanings then are these: they are independent of and antecedent to language or its conventions, determinate, and unitary. When they are assigned to symbols the result is an unambiguous expression with sharp boundaries as to what it applies to and does not apply to, signifies and does not signify. The antecedence referred to is not entirely clear. Sometimes it seems to be antecedence to particular applications of a term, sometimes absolute antecedence to language altogether. I shall call the first relative antecedence, the second absolute antecedence. The latter may be the same as independence.

## VI

It seems immediately apparent that although sense meanings have some of the characteristics of fixed meanings they do not have them all. While they may be, as Lewis describes them, independent of language and relatively antecedent, they do not seem to be determinate or unitary. They often are unnecessary in the application of terms, particularly familiar terms that are part of our working vocabulary. The criterion of the applicability of these terms is often nothing more specific than our ability to use the words of a language. In these circumstances the significance of any appeal to sense meanings would seem to be an

67 AKV, p. 168.

appeal to such abilities, presumably acquired through the various and complex processes by which we learn a language. This, in fact, might be one way to interpret the relative antecedence of sense meaning, that is, as our learned linguistic habits and acquired linguistic abilities.

There are also many cases in which the eventual experience fails to conform to the anticipatory imagery and we nevertheless apply the term. The number of ways, for example, in which we could anticipate 'the speaker for tonight' is infinitely various, as Lewis points out. And we would still apply the term even though the experience was quite different from what we explicitly anticipated. It is, in fact, quite evident that if sense meanings are to be the criterion for the application of terms to items of experience or possible experience they must be various and open-textured.

There also seem to be enormous numbers of terms for which there are no sense meanings at all, for example, many that would be called 'abstract' in common language, but which might better be considered second or higher order terms, such as 'theory', 'necessary', 'generalization', 'analytic', 'a priori', 'synthetic' and the like. How would we tell, by comparing criteria in terms of sense for applying the terms, that the statement 'All a priori statements are analytic' is analytic?

Difficulties with sense meanings become even more evident in cases that are more difficult to determine than Lewis' paradigms, say, the examples at the end of section II. What are the sense meanings of 'mnemic-present-as-pastness', 'constitutive of the only reality we as humans can envisage', 'what is right', or '. . . nothing more important . . . than'?

The remarks Lewis makes at the opening of his discussion of empirical knowledge, especially AKV, p. 192-194, stress the variability of sense meanings to the point of maintaining that a sense meaning can be exhibited fully only by the totality of terminating judgments implied or included in the attribution of the property or character. When this complexity is put alongside his statement that for purposes of logic (and presumably for purposes of detailing analytic truth) a criterion in mind must be identified with something that exhibits it,[68] one wonders how the comparison of sense meanings can be the way in which we know analytic truth or how the relations of such meanings could constitute the nature of analytic truth.

It would seem that for sense meanings to fit the role of fixed meanings they must be more restricted than Lewis indicates. It might seem that this restriction is provided by Lewis' introduction of the test

[68] AKV, p. 44.

schema. Apparently what makes the test schema precise and explicit is the fact that it is "that in mind which refers to signification."[69] But as Lewis points out, signification comprises essential properties, and as he also points out, it is meaningless to speak of the essence of a thing except in relation to its being named by a particular term.[70]

Also there are analytic statements which involve obviously sensory terms, yet explaining their analyticity or necessary truth in terms of a comparison of sense schemata is quite impossible. For example, "Between any two shades of color there is another."[71]

There is a more serious difficulty. Suppose the term in question is 'man'. Then the schema for the application of 'man' to any presented entity is the test routine for, and imaginative anticipation of, the essential property. Not to raise too many issues at once, suppose the essential property is humanity. How is one to identify the essential property in terms of an envisaged test routine and imagined result? It would seem that the recognition of the essential property in terms of sense, if possible at all, is possible in as many and various ways as the recognition of the man himself. In fact, one might be inclined to say that in this case at least it would be easier to construct a schematism for the recognition of a man than of man's essential property.

If we make the schema more precise and less essential then we have the difficulty of justifying it as a criterion for example, 'If, when I speak to it, it answers in a way that is intelligible to me then I will apply the term "man"'. But any such particular schematism will be one out of a possible infinity of them. Thus there is, despite Lewis' disclaimer, nothing in the theory to rule out subjectivism in the decision to accept a specific schema. The more crucial difficulty is, however, that there is no criterion provided either by the infinite set of all possible schemata nor by the schematism itself for judging that this particular schematism is the sense meaning that guarantees correct applicability.

These difficulties are augmented rather than relieved in case we want to compare the sense meaning of 'man' with the sense meaning of 'rational animal'. Practically, of course, there may be no difficulty in this particular case. The sample of the set nearly anyone would use to determine the applicability of 'man' would probably include the sample of the set he would use for 'rational animal'. But this leaves the theoretical problem untouched, particularly when the applicability of the term

69 AKV, p. 133 n.

70 AKV, p. 41.

71 *Mind and the World-Order* (New York: Charles Scribner's Sons, 1929), p. 431. Hereafter cited as MWO.

is regarded as probable, to some degree or other, in case the imagined result of the test schema is found to be fulfilled. So it is not correct to say that whatever confirms the applicability of the subject term *ipso facto* determines applicability of the predicate term.

If, as I should be prepared to conclude, sense meanings cannot meet the requirements of fixed meanings and so cannot provide the foundation of an adequate general theory of analytic statements, there may nevertheless be other candidates, universals or concepts, for example.

It might be argued that the independence, antecedence, unity and determinateness of universals makes them the best candidates, that their relations constitute the relations expressed in analytic statements and that our knowledge of analytic truth is a knowledge of these relations. In "Some Suggestions Concerning Metaphysics of Logic" Lewis apparently holds that there is a quality or characteristic common to the three elements that are crucial to analytic knowledge: (1) to the concept as a 'psychologically instanced meaning' and criterion or rule in mind for applying the term; (2) to the thing to which the term correctly applies, the essential property or signification, and (3) to the linguistic intension when it correctly relates the concept or rule of discrimination to objective entities which satisfy it.[72]

I shall not discuss the details of this interpretation. (Mr. Baylis discusses it in his paper although from a different standpoint.) I shall only say briefly, and therefore inadequately, that in addition to other difficulties it seems to suffer from some of the difficulties found in sense meanings, for example, how do you know which universal exemplified in the thing is the one to which the criterion in mind refers? Further, it runs the risk of reifying meanings as another kind of objects than the sense presented, existing in a realm of nonlinguistic, 'logically necessary facts', a view which Lewis warns against in the Preface to AKV[73] but seems to fall subject to in his discussion of fixed meanings.

Instead I want to consider, though briefly and therefore again perhaps inadequately, concepts as they appear in *Mind and the World Order*. I should say as they appear in certain passages, for it would be impossible in brief compass to deal with the details of that complex theory. I shall confine attention to concepts as they might qualify or fail to qualify as fixed meanings.

Lewis defines the pure concept as the "meaning which must be common to two minds when they understand each other by the use

[72] "Met. Log.," pp. 95, 98.
[73] AKV, p. ix.

of a substantive or its equivalent."[74] He later redefines it more accurately to take account of its ideal and abstract nature: "a definitive structure of meanings, which is what *would verify* completely the coincidence of two minds when they understand each other by the use of language."[75] He holds that while individual differences of perception and imagery preclude common sharing of experiences of those kinds, common definitions, common applications of substantive and adjectives to the same objects can be shared. These are the only practical and applicable criteria of common knowledge. Assurance of common meanings at the level of sense or imagery must always remain incomplete, since the correlation of concept with specific sense quality is inevitably individual and in any case intrinsically unverifiable. In fact there is always a correlation of concept with imagery but the concept as independent of imagery is the abstraction which it is necessary to make if we are to discover the basis of our common understanding.[76]

The point of present relevance is that the concept, when explicit, is not only definitive in nature, but must be in order to provide anything explicit enough to serve as a criterion of 'what we mean'. This is so no matter where the stress of this ambiguous phrase falls. It could fall on what we *mean* in the sense of what we intend to refer to, or the sense in which we intend our words to be taken. It could fall on what *we* mean in the sense of what we have decided to refer to or the way in which we have decided to use our terms. It could fall on *what* we mean in the sense of the things that are referred to, independently of whether we intend to refer to them.

The concept, therefore, is an abstraction and an ideality in relation to the imagery with which it may be associated; although as Lewis points out[77] no more so than most things commonly attributed to mind. No explicit conceptual meaning directly matches anything that might be psychologically 'in mind' although Lewis suggests that it would be legitimate to say that the concept is figuratively 'in mind'.

In MWO Lewis asserts that the necessity of statements that can be known a priori to be true is due to the element of fiat or legislation that they involve.[78] Their necessity might be interpreted, in part, as a result of the process of making precise and explicit concepts that were 'in mind' only vaguely and implicitly. This would be analogous to deciding

74 MWO, p. 70.
75 MWO, p. 89.
76 MWO, pp. 70-80.
77 MWO, p. 89.
78 E.g., MWO, p. 197.

to accept a particular sense schema as a criterion for application of a term from among the infinitely many possible candidates. It provides a sense in which concepts would be relatively antecedent. The choice or decision would provide the element of fiat and the basis for further applications of the term. There is no such appeal to sense meanings, however, in MWO. The concept when it comes to be 'literally in mind' rather than 'figuratively in mind'[79] when it becomes a 'pure' concept, is a 'definitive structure of meanings'.

Do concepts so conceived qualify as fixed meanings? Lewis maintains that truths *about* such concepts and their relations to other such concepts are absolute and eternal.[80] This seems entirely acceptable but beside the present point, since it does not distinguish concepts from anything else that can stand in relations and of whose relations true statements can be made. The difficulty is to distinguish a definitive structure of meanings from a universal or pattern of universals on the one hand and from a definition or pattern of definitions on the other. Both the basis on which concepts become pure concepts and the difficulty of distinguishing them from definitions seem to rule them out, although in respect to their specificity and their necessary connections with other definitive structures of meaning they seem to provide a basis for explaining the necessity of one type of analytic statement.[81]

Finally, we might try to find fixed meanings in the area of the modes of meaning. Lewis speaks of the meaning of a term as what it denotes, signifies, comprehends or connotes.[82] None of these would qualify because they are what they are only in relation to a term. In other places, in which he stresses the independence of meanings from language[83] he speaks of independent meanings in a sense which indicates that they are what we intend to refer to by using a term, but independent of that intended reference. In this latter sense a meaning will be anything that could be denoted, signified, comprehended, or connoted, but

---

[79] MWO, p. 286.

[80] MWO, p. 272.

[81] ". . . where our empirically acquired, *a posteriori* criterion-in-mind is too vague or scanty to enable us to decide in a given case whether a term applies or not, *we then sharpen our criterion by decisions ad hoc.*" Ducasse, *op. cit.*, p. 273. ". . . it is questionable whether the meanings of all terms are so completely fixed as to render the requisite decisions unequivocally possible. Rather, it seems, that the exact meaning even of familiar terms, and thus the analyticity of certain explicative statements, will in part have to be determined by conventions." Hempel, *op. cit.*, p. 42. It should be added of course, and Lewis' writing in MWO makes it evident, that the "decisions *ad hoc*" and the "conventions" need not be, and usually will not be, capricious, but will in many cases be based on pragmatic grounds.

[82] AKV, p. 77.

[83] E.g., AKV, p. 165.

independent of being so denoted, signified, comprehended or connoted.

I take it that expressions that might be connoted are what they are regardless of being so connoted but are not possible candidates, since they are not independent of language. Properties regarded as being what they are whether they are signified or not are of course just properties. Granting that properties and things that could be denoted are independent, absolutely antecedent and unitary they hardly provide the fixed meanings we are looking for. It is odd to consider them meanings at all; and if analytic truth is to be explained in terms of their relations there can be no distinction between analytic and synthetic truth.

The case of classes and classifications is more doubtful. Actual classes and classifications are ruled out because of their necessary reference to the application of a term.[84] But possible classes and classifications would seem to qualify in the sense that they are what they are, namely, possible groupings of actual or possible things, and have the relations they have to other possible groupings of actual or possible things whether a symbol is assigned to them or not. This is an untoward denouement, however, of the holophrastic-analytic distinction that was introduced because the doctrine that all analytic statements mean the same thing would not agree with common sense and would make it difficult to understand analytic truth.

It seems doubtful that this is any more in accord with common sense. For it suggests that the reason one analytic statement says something different from another is that one possible classification of actual or possible things is different from another. Nor does it seem to contribute to an understanding of analytic truth. It is undoubtedly true that possible classifications are what they are and have the relations they have to other possible classifications and that nothing we can do or say or decide can affect this. But there is nothing here that is distinctive to possible classifications. As we know from the Cambridge Platonists, Joseph Butler, and others, in this sense everything is what it is and stands in the relations it stands in "not by will but by the nature of the thing." There is no explanation of why any particular relation should be a necessary one.

We might, then return to the suggestion made earlier, that fixed meanings are specified meanings. Such a move gives up the attempt to discover what a fixed meaning is independently of language. This seems plausible, however, in view of previous results.

We are no longer looking for something which is a meaning independently and in its own right. We are no longer looking for something

84 AKV, p. 39.

that is one terminus of a relation signified by 'attached to', 'affixed to', 'assigned to', or 'associated with', and the other terminus a symbol (more accurately, a mark). An example in the mood of his doctrine is in fact offered by Lewis.

If the expression 'rats' (more accurately, the symbol «rats») was used as in fact 'cats' is used, and 'some', 'triangle' and 'bite', as in fact 'all', 'animal', and 'are' are used, and if the conventions of syntactic order were those of statements in German, then "Some rats triangles bite" *would be* analytically true.[85]

This suggests that symbols acquire a meaning from the way in which they are used, can be given a meaning by being given a use, and have that meaning whether so used or not. Less hypostatically, it suggests that symbols are significant if they have a use, can be made significant by being given a use, and are significant whether so used or not. And since, as Lewis sometimes stresses, language was not in fact brought down from heaven but is a product of human devising it also suggests that the circumstances in which it might be advisable to specify the usage of symbols might be as various, and the means of doing this as various, as there are uses to which expressions could be put.

If so, one of the most important factors to take into account in attempting to formulate a theory of analytic statements will surely be the pragmatic factors involved in the circumstances in which they are asserted. The details of such a theory are another matter, but in working them out much can be learned from looking at the analytic statements Lewis makes, not the examples he mentions in illustrating analytic statements. The examples cannot really be considered statements at all. They are not asserted. They are sentences put forward for consideration, strings of symbols that would seldom, if ever, be used to make a statement, but he does assert that empirical reality is knowable; that our memory of the past, felt as significant in the present, is a necessary part of being human and having human experiences; that success is the desideratum of all action; that to act, to live, in human terms, is necessarily to be subject to imperatives; that in all the world and in all of life there is nothing more important to determine than what is right. And unless I very badly misread the significance of these statements any analysis in terms of a comparison of sense meanings or the assertion of a relation between antecedent, independent, unitary fixed meanings would not even come close to the depth and scope of the arguments with which Lewis supports the contention that they are analytic.                                      BERNARD PEACH

DEPARTMENT OF PHILOSOPHY
DUKE UNIVERSITY

85 AKV, p. 150.

## 9

*Lewis White Beck*

## THE KANTIANISM OF LEWIS [1]

TWO diametrically opposed criticisms of Kant's theory of knowledge are distinguished by their divergent attitudes towards the
Copernican Revolution. The first is the objection that Kant, through
this Revolution, and facing the question of how there can be a priori
synthetic knowledge, gave an answer which destroyed the objectivity of
cognitive judgments generally. The argument of those who put forth
this criticism is that Kant makes 'knowing' a kind of 'making', so that
the essence of knowledge as the grasp of the antecedent fact and independent factuality is misrepresented. Critics who make this objection
assert the possibility of a priori synthetic judgments. But since they hold
that knowing is not a manufacture of objects out of the data of sense,
they do not limit the scope of these judgments, as Kant did, to things
in experience. True judgments, they say, are about an independent and
metaphysically real object, and it is only an accident whether these objects are sensuously given or not. About how such judgments are possible, these critics differ among themselves, according to whether they are
phenomenologists or scholastic, American, or British realists; but they
are at one in opposing the subjectivism they find inherent in Kant's
apriorism. These who make this kind of attack on Kant I shall classify, in
spite of their diversity, as the 'realist critics' of Kant.

The second objection comes from those philosophers who see in
Kant's work an unsuccessful attempt to give knowledge an objective
and perhaps metaphysical ground that it does not in fact possess. In
their opinion, the Copernican Revolution is not radical enough. In

[1] This essay is based in part upon, and includes a few paraphrases and quotations
from, three earlier studies of mine: "Die Kantkritik von C. I. Lewis und der analytischen
Schule," Kant-Studien, 45 (1954), 3-20; "Can Kant's Synthetic Judgments be Made
Analytic?" *ibid.*, 47 (1956), 168-81; "Kant's Theory of Definition," *Philosophical Review*, 65 (1956), 179-91. I am grateful to the editors of these journals for permission
to use some material that first appeared in their pages. In this article I have not dealt
with the relation between Lewis' and Kant's theories of value, but would call attention
to Mary Mothersill, "C. I. Lewis, Hedonistic Ethics on a Kantian Model," *Philosophical
Studies*, 5 (1954), 81-88.

Kant's work, this Revolution ends with a series of allegedly necessary synthetic principles which are presupposed in all possible knowledge. But while Kant denied to such principles the transcendently metaphysical status that realists say they have, he did assert their unique-
ness, certainty, and necessity. This 'universal and necessary' character
is what the other critics of Kant deny. They wish to push the Copernican
Revolution still further, and in doing so they welcome, as a first step,
Kant's denial of what would universally be regarded, for good or ill,
as transcendent metaphysics. But they see in his own 'immanent metaphysics' ('metaphysics as science') still too much metaphysical dogmatism in the form of a single, uniquely necessary set of eternal presuppositions. They deny the validity of Kant's claim to give a transcendental deduction of categories necessary to all possible knowledge of phenomena, just as the realist critics deny its validity with respect to the repudiation of knowledge of noumena. While claiming that
Kant was correct in insisting upon the subject's activity in the construction of phenomenal objects, they deny that his rules for such construction are necessary and unique. They find pragmatic variables entering into a situation which Kant believed was logically—in some sense
of the word 'logically'—fixed.

Philosophers who criticize Kant in this way are indebted to him and
to Hume for the key to their own epistemological edifices. But in-
debtedness of this kind often contributes to bitterness of criticism. Though
Hume's psychologism has usually been merely rapped on its knuckles,
some of the most thorough-going censures of the Kantian philosophy
have come from positivists, pragmatists, conventionalists, language analysts, and sociologists of knowledge all of whom join Kant in regarding physical objects as some sort of construction. In spite of their divergences among themselves, for our present purposes I shall call them
all by the same name, viz., the 'analyst critics' of Kant.

It is noteworthy that the realist and the analyst critics of Kant are
closer to him than they are to each other. Each has learned something
important from Kant, and but little or nothing from each other. This
is all the more remarkable when elements of each type of criticism are
found in the writings of one man.

## II

Clarence Irving Lewis has seemed to many to be a leader of the latter movement of anti-Kantianism—a leader in part because of the
originality and cogency of his own constructive work, and in part because unlike most analyst critics he has come to his critical position

with a sympathy for and a detailed knowledge of Kant's philosophy that many of his fellow analyst critics seem never to have had. He speaks, in his autobiographical essay, of his youthful admiration for Kant and of the unmistakable "evidence of Kant in [his] thinking."[2] Yet a critic he is; and an apocryphal story points up this ambivalent position that Lewis occupies vis-à-vis Kant. "I am a Kantian, " he is reported unreliably to have said, "who disagrees with every sentence of the *Critique of Pure Reason*."

But ambivalent or not, *Mind and the World-Order*[3] can be seen as a *locus classicus* for analytical criticism of Kant. The conceptual pragmatism espoused in that book emphasizes the freely creative act by which complexes found in experience are supplemented by expectations and interpreted as objects. These complexes, spread out in time and attended with anticipations, are the real things of experience, because they meet our freely chosen but pragmatically justified criteria for the ascription of the status of reality. The concepts are, as it were, the constitutional law for a world we create from the flux of experience. They are a priori because they are not given in experience or dictated by experience, while they regulate the admission of experience to the status of evidence for or against some object. In Kantian language, they are like categories which inform raw experience and make it experience in the sense of knowledge of objects. At most, experience may suggest them to a pragmatically interested being or advise him to modify them; but experience cannot refute the principles employing them.

While Kant sharply distinguishes between forms of intuition, which govern our experience, and the categories which govern experience in the sense in which he identifies experience with "knowledge of objects," Lewis denies the "transcendental machinery" by which categories seem to be brought to bear upon the data of intuition; and he rejects out of hand the notion of any a priori regulation of experience in the former sense. For the transcendental machinery, often (though not by Lewis) misinterpreted as psychological, Lewis substitutes a pragmatic machinery that gives the categories the "character of fiat" and of "deliberate choice." The principle of substance, for instance, is not an existential statement that there is a permanent in perception, as in Kant's first Analogy of Experience. It is rather a freely chosen decision not to ascribe substantiality except to those chains of experience which

[2] "Logic and Pragmatism," *Contemporary American Philosophy*, ed. G. P. Adams and W. P. Montague (New York: The Macmillan Co., 1930), Vol. II, pp. 31-51, esp. pp. 31-32. Hereafter cited as "Log. Prag."

[3] (New York: Chas. Scribner's Sons, 1929). Hereafter cited as MWO.

exhibit the analytical consequences of our freely chosen definition of substance as that which is permanent amidst change. Such definition is not a command to experience; it is a claim which experience may or may not honor, but which it cannot abrogate. Such a principle of the permanence of substance is true "no matter what." All that my experience might *force* me to do is to admit sadly and with disappointment that I never seem to come across any substances; but it might *suggest* to me that my system of concepts might be a little less of an "unearthly ballet of bloodless categories" if I modified my definition of substance. Only categories that do find continuous and repeated application can render knowledge effective in the control of our future passages of experience.

*Mind and the World-Order* ends with a kind of challenge to experience. In the last chapter, Lewis, having surrendered any governance of experience by a priori factors, says to the flux of experience: be as chaotic as you will, I shall still be able to interpret you with some categories that will make intelligent anticipation possible. But he cannot venture to say what categories will serve.

### III

It is easy to see why *Mind and the World-Order* made Lewis a representative thinker among the analyst critics of Kant. Yet the book was not quite typical of the analytical movement as a whole. What was most distinctive in that book was the pragmatic origin and variability of the categories. But there were elements of realism, in various senses of the word, which hardly conformed to the typical positivistic model of a relativistic theory of categories which did not also contain a perhaps metaphysical acknowledgment of the hard coerciveness of independent factuality.

*An Analysis of Knowledge and Valuation* brings these divergences from the typical analysts' position to light, and shows Lewis to be in many respects closer to the camp of the realist critics. If we think of orthodox Kantians (if there are any today) involved in a two-front war with, say, Ayer to the left and the ghost of Prichard to the right, we must think of Lewis as fighting against both the left wing and Kant, using some of the weapons of the realist critics against both, and yet so cautious and meager in his commitments to realism that the realists hardly can claim him as an ally. The tactical picture is therefore very complicated. But Lewis' main effort is clearly directed against the other analysts, for he regards the battle against Kant, on the central point, to have already ended with victory by those who deny that there is any a priori synthetic knowledge.[4]

Yet it was a Pyrrhic victory, for in it the conventionalism of the linguistic a priori made it incapable of doing the job assigned to the a priori elements of knowledge. A view that the analytic is equivalent to the a priori but is dependent upon linguistic conventions cannot, Lewis maintains, justify the epistemic function of the a priori, which is characteristic of knowledge independent of sense experiences. It explains the analytic by divesting it of that object-relatedness which alone can make cognitions true.[5] Yet Lewis believes that the results of recent developments have clearly shown that all a priori knowledge is analytic, and that the Kantian question is a "dead issue" in philosophy.[6] It was incumbent upon him, therefore, to develop a realistic theory of the analytic in which the analytic is equivalent to the a priori and in which a priori knowledge really is knowledge and not just a decision to talk in a certain way, no matter what.

Such a theory presents, however, only a minimum concession to the realists. I pointed out that armed with a realistic theory of the a priori, these critics of Kant had extended the scope of knowledge into speculative metaphysics. Because of Lewis' theory of meaning, however, in which the meaning of a proposition resides in its verifiable consequences in future passages of experience, nothing in the way of knowledge of objects absolutely transcending experience is gained by Lewis' rejection of the typical analytical doctrine concerning a priori knowledge. It is for this reason that Lewis is hardly a bona fide member of the realist school of critics of Kant.

## IV

Lewis' criticism of the analyst critics is that they are not able to give a plausible account of the epistemic function of analytic judgments. They make linguistic meaning basic, with the result that 'analytic' means 'determined by language rules'; but 'determined by language rules' does not mean 'known independently of experience', and it is the latter which is characteristic of a priori knowledge.

Against Kant, on the other hand, Lewis argues that the necessary connections between intensions are not synthetic but analytic connections. What can be known independently of experience is what follows

[4] An Analysis of Knowledge and Valuation (La Salle: Open Court Publishing Co., 1946), pp. 35, 158. Hereafter cited as AKV.

[5] AKV, pp. 36, 147.

[6] AKV, p. 158.

by analysis of the meanings involved in our interpretation of the given, though not necessarily by analysis of the meanings actually entertained in consciousness. Sense meaning is the criterion in mind by which decision on the applicability of a term to a part of experience is to be determined, and this criterion may not be found merely by a cursory inspection of what is included in the sense meaning as actually entertained. The applicability of a complex concept to a part of experience requires a step-wise process. If the decision to apply the term 'square' presupposes the decision to apply the term 'rectangle' then 'every square is a rectangle' is an analytic proposition.

While 'every square is a rectangle' would certainly have been regarded by Kant as analytic, there are judgments that Kant held to be synthetic yet necessary; and this is what Lewis denies. Lewis joins with Kant in denying that there is an intellectual intuition of necessary but not analytic relations between concepts or meanings. But Lewis affirms what Kant denies, to wit, that all epistemically necessary connections are logical connections; even if not formally logical, they are still connections between meanings. Kant's theory on this point, of course, is that pure concepts refer to necessary schemata in time; that there is an intuitional or sensible element in even pure schemata which is necessary, determined not by the concept but by the structure of time itself as a given; hence that meanings can be got from schemata that were not put into the schemata by the concept. To the extent that the schema has its own a priori structure, what follows from it by a kind of phenomenological analysis is not restricted to what follows from the concept itself by a logical analysis.

Lewis suggests that his sense meanings are schemata in the Kantian sense. The Kantian schema is the condition of the application of an intellectual concept to a sensuous material; but given the concept itself, the schema is not in any sense a logical part of it. One can think with the concept without knowing or using its schema; what the absence of the schema limits is not logical analysis, but application to experience, and hence knowledge. Lewis' schemata are very different from Kant's; but on the basis of *his* conception of the schemata which he does not sufficiently distinguish from Kant's, Lewis brings a devastating criticism against the Kantian theory.

The criticism is this. The schema must be included logically in the concept itself as a criterion of its application. It is not, as Kant believed, a 'third thing', neither wholly conceptual nor wholly sensuous, which bridges the gap between concept and data. Accordingly, if the schema as the sense meaning is not included in the concept and stated in its real definition, it appears that a judgment using the unschematized concept is synthetic; on the other hand, the judgment expressed in the same sentence but using the schematized concept is a priori. This is the error with which Lewis charges Kant, and he says that Kant's error is based upon a "failure of analysis."[7]

I shall examine this alleged failure of analysis by reference to Lewis' criticism of the second Analogy of Experience. Lewis argues as follows. The notion of a necessary but nonanalytic proposition such as 'every event has a cause' is based on an equivocation. 'Event' as a concept which does not contain 'having a cause' as a part of its intension is not the same as 'event' of which it is said to be necessarily true that it does have a cause. 'Event' in the second case means 'phenomenal event in one objective space and time', while in the former case it is not so restricted, and denotes, *inter alia*, perceptual or conscious events as well as perceived events. The judgment that every event has a cause is synthetic only when 'event' has the thinner meaning; but it is a priori only when 'event' has the richer meaning. It appears to be a priori synthetic only because it is erroneously believed that 'event' means the same thing in both sentences.

A term needs to be fixed before one can pronounce a judgment in which it figures to be analytic or synthetic. In defining its meaning, Lewis says, we must include in its meaning everything needed in order to determine its applicability to experience; if we do not do so, the definition is faulty, and arguments based upon the definition are fallacious.[8]

None of the elaborate and almost infinite variety of criticisms of the Analogy offered during the past century and a half approach in elegant simplicity this attack by Lewis. Yet its full evaluation requires a detailed consideration of matters in the philosophies of both Kant and Lewis which do not have the straightforward character of this perspicuous refutation, and which have been left in considerable obscurity by both philosophers. To these more obscure matters it is necessary to turn now.

## V

It would perhaps have been more appropriate for Lewis to have accused Kant of a "failure of synthesis." For the essential question is not: what can be got from a concept or meaning by analysis? but: how are meanings constituted, so that analysis can get at the necessary

7 AKV, p. 163.
8 AKV, pp. 161 f.

truths employing them? In Kantian language, analysis presupposes synthesis; and if we are to replace allegedly a priori synthetic judgments with analytic judgments, we must *pari passu* replace thinner concepts with richer ones—we must, as it were, provide a priori synthetic concepts to take the place of a priori synthetic judgments.

Kant says that the *Critique* exists for the study of the synthesis of knowledge, not for the analysis of concepts. Let us forget for the moment that Kant is concerned with establishing the possibility of a priori synthetic judgments. Let us grant for the moment the validity of the Lewis criticism of the Second Analogy. But if we do so, only the locus of the problem is changed; to speak the classical language, we could say that we now have to do with a problem in the logic of concepts instead of in the logic of judgments. So long as both philosophers believe that there is a rule by which later events are determined by earlier ones—as they do—the problem itself remains essentially unchanged. And Kant's answer to it is fairly clear. The relation of a concept to an experience which falls under it is not a logical relation found by the analysis of the concept. It is not our conception of the conditions of its application which is essential in the constitution of actual knowledge, but it is the actual conditions of application themselves. This condition is the givenness of data in a variety of fixed temporal patterns, which Kant has argued from the beginning are not adequately defined except ostensively.

To take a simpler example than that of cause, we do not know how to apply the concept 'red' by knowing its 'analysis' (if it has one). Stating in the 'analysis' of the concept that " 'Red' applies to red things" does not in the least help us to find out whether there are any red things or not. Similarly, " 'Cause' applies to that without which an event would not occur" is a conceptual analysis (a poor one) of cause; but " 'Cause' applies to an event in one objective time if there is another event which regularly follows it" does not help us in the application of 'cause' unless we are given some directions for deciding what is meant by 'follows'. And in Kant's view, the meaning of 'follows', like the ostensive meaning of 'red', cannot be found just by analyzing the connotation of a concept.

It is for this reason that so much of the Kantian philosophy stands or falls with the success or failure of what is often regarded as its weakest part, the Transcendental Aesthetic. But unless there is an a priori content of experience (e.g., necessary spread-outness in space and time) to which some concepts have an intuitively necessary application, a controlling factor in the constitution of a priori synthetic concepts is missing. Without intuition, the concepts are empty no matter how many *concepts* of intuitions are included in them. Of this Kant is firmly convinced, so much so that he even suggests that concepts and forms of intuition may have a common root.

While Lewis has written of the social origin and the pragmatic determinants in the constitution of concepts, throughout his work there is a Platonizing assumption of the directly given and privately inspectable ready-made meanings,[9] and in his later book he "take[s] reality as we find it already disclosed and conveyed in our common-sense meanings."[10] The concepts we analyze arise through neither induction or definition nor stipulation. Not through induction, because without them experience can neither be classified nor queried. Not through real definition, because real definition is an analysis of them and presupposes them.[11] Not through stipulation or nominal definition, because meanings so established are merely linguistic. Sometimes definitions seem to be reports on what *we* mean or expect or intend; sometimes they seem to be reports on what the things themselves mean in terms of eventual experiences. But in any case they are fixed, and from the fixing of them there follows a hard and fast dichotomy of analytical consequences and accidental accompaniments of their application. Expressions for the meanings may be changed, and it is worthwhile to establish a language in which what does follow from them analytically will be linguistically necessary; but we must recognize in advance what connections of meaning, however expressed, are in fact necessary before it is worthwhile developing a language in which the sentences reporting on these connections are linguistically necessary.

Lewis' expressed purpose in *Analysis of Knowledge and Valuation* was not to give a phenomenological, transcendental, or genetic account of the structure and growth of knowledge, but to discover by analysis the criteria of the validity of knowledge we already have.[12] It is not fair to criticize a man for writing the book he did write and not another one. But it is fair to point out that one may fairly inquire concerning what must have gone on before to provide us with these wonderful meanings which make a priori synthetic judgments otiose, inasmuch as they can be replaced with analytic judgments which say the same thing because they contain more complex concepts.

9 MWO, pp. 70-88.
10 AKV, p. 22, cf. p. 353 n.
11 AKV, pp. 112, 130.
12 AKV p. 22.

## VI

We are now ready to return to the criticism of the Second Analogy. There are two passages in Kant relevant to this criticism, written nearly thirty years apart and having quite different implications.

The first, an early fragment,[13] suggests that the distinction between the analytic and the synthetic is arbitrary, depending solely upon the amount of knowledge we have of the analysis of the concepts. The implications of this modern-sounding suggestion seem never to have been explored by Kant. Had they been worked out, many of the examples of so-called a priori synthetic judgments in Kant's major works would never have been given, and the essential points which they are meant to illustrate would not have been hidden by Kant's poor examples. I sometimes wonder, however, if Kant himself would have discovered what I shall try to show is his essential point, had he held to this early and all-too-easy belief. Be that as it may, when Kant was challenged late in life by Eberhard, who held precisely this gradualistic view of the analytic-synthetic distinction, the essential doctrine of the *Critique* had been established in Kant's mind, and he was then prepared to give an answer to Eberhard which provides us with a key to the answer that I think he would have made to Lewis' attack on the Second Analogy.

Eberhard, like Lewis, believed that there were no synthetic a priori judgments, and that redefinition of the terms would show this to be the case. Kant replied[14] by inviting his opponent to add any attributes he wishes to a concept, so that whatever he wishes to prove can be proved analytically. But then Kant asks him: How did you come to include in the concept precisely those attributes needed in order to render analytic what was previously said in a synthetic judgment? He cannot reply that he is giving a definition of the concept, unless he can show that in doing so he is obeying the rules of proper definition. That is, he must be able to show both that the newly added attribute is independent of those already included, and invariably present in the entities denoted by the original definiendum, so that the conjunction of the old and the new attributes has the same denotation as the original definiendum. A narrower denotation will not do, for that means that a new concept (with the same name) has been introduced by definition. In order to know the identity of denotations, he must know the connection of the independent attributes before stating them in the new definition; and he must know this not by analysis, else the rule is infringed that the attri-

13 Reflexion 3928, *Gesammelte Schriften*, Akademie Ausgabe, **17**, 350.
14 *Ibid.*, **20**, 408 f.

butes stated in the definition must be independent. Hence definitions devised for the purpose of rendering synthetic judgments analytic are not real definitions, or in making them we must already know with certainty the synthetic judgment they were designed to translate into an analytic judgment. If they are nominal definitions, they do not do the job; if they are real definitions, they are (or include) the synthetic truths in question. In fact, Kant elsewhere states that real definitions— definitions which refer to the sensuous conditions of their applications —when possible at all are synthetic a priori propositions.[15]

When possible at all—but Kant argues repeatedly that definitions are not possible of the basic philosophical concepts or categories. By a definition is meant a complete listing of essential and independent attributes; yet we are able to make analytic judgments without first possessing a definition.[16] By a real definition, he means a definition that refers to a real predicate, a *Bestimmung*, which when found will show that the definition does have application. The *Bestimmung*, however, is not a predicate contained in the definition; it is not even the concept of a condition of application; it is the condition of application itself. A real definition is a true synthetic judgment, having objective validity. When dealing with categories, Kant gives nominal definitions of them; but these nominal definitions (e.g., "Substance is that which is subject but not predicate") do not guide us in finding substances within experience. To show the objective validity of the categories, we must cite the necessary condition of their application, and this is always some mode of sensibility, e.g., a schema.

The categories with which Kant was concerned could not be given objective validity (application to experience of objects) by definition; this is known to every empiricist since Hume. However, many conditions of application are formulated as predicates and put into definitions, a more extended Humean criticism of the enriched concept would again show that the semantic bridge between conception and object had not been erected. Assuming a broader definition, a proof that the concept is objectively valid because the objective condition is included in the definition would still fall before the Humean criticism. By enrichment of the concept, we could make more judgments analytic, without giving any one of them a claim to objective validity. Apriority is not dependent upon such factitious analyticity; there must be recognition of some special dignity of function which makes it worthwhile

15 Reflexionen 2955, 2994; *ibid.*, 16, 586, 606 f.
16 *Ibid.*, 2, 61, 282; *ibid.*, 4, 273.

to formulate it in an explicitly analytic manner.[17] This special dignity of function for Kant is that it makes *experience of objects* possible.

Now Kant, apparently unlike Lewis, did not tacitly assume the necessary temporal features of experience, nor did he assume the direct givenness of the causal relation. He tried to show that causality was inherent in the order of objective time, and in doing so he found that he had to add to the concept of sufficient reason not further predicates, but quite other conditions that neither Hume nor the rationalists had suspected. He found that he had to refer to 'possible experience' as the enabling ground of its application to any actual experience. To have suppressed this interpretation for the sake of a merely conceptual enrichment of the concept, so that the Second Analogy could be made analytic, would have distorted the whole procedure of the critical philosophy, and would have only deferred the Humean question: How can *this* causal judgment, with a definitionally enriched set of terms, be valid of all possible experience of objects? To answer this question, it does not suffice to construct or inspect concepts; it is necessary to construct an object in series under the condition of sensible givenness of the data, when the order of the data may not correspond to the order of events.

While Lewis calls sense meaning a schema, a part of the intension of the concept which must be included in the definition of it, I do not believe that his theory meets the Humean question even where Lewis believes that there is such necessary objective validity.

In order to show this, I shall first examine the way in which Lewis would handle a concept that admittedly does not have necessary objective validity. Let us take the concept of red. If 'red' is to be applied to some experience, we can state conceptually some of the conditions of its application; we can state the conditions under which we would normally expect to produce a red sensation; we might even say that we should not apply the term 'red' except to things which look red. (The latter is, of course, an oversimplification; but the overly simple element in this illustration does not have any bearing upon the point at issue here.) That the concept does have objective application depends upon the fact or is equivalent to the fact that some things do look red; and this is of course not entailed or included in our 'definition' of red. For this reason, no one has ever said that the concept of red has necessary objective validity; red is not a category. A statement about red is a claim upon experience that may or may not be honored; it is not a fiat that experience must obey. Most of the concepts

[17] Cf. AKV, p. 167.

that Lewis deals with are of this kind, and are not categories in the Kantian sense of being necessarily applicable to every experience. Lewis' categories are high-level abstract concepts such as 'physical object' or 'Euclidean triangle', which experience may or may not provide examples for. With respect to these concepts, therefore, neither Lewis nor Kant would wish to meet the Humean attack; Lewis joins in it.[18] Only one monitory note must be added: it is sometimes thought that the Kantian categories are like the concept of red in our example, and that all principles therefore are, in Hume's sense, 'relations of ideas' and all applications of them hypothetical.

But implicit in the process of testing concepts for application to experience there are hidden other categories which, if Lewis' philosophy is to work, do have a necessary objective validity, do involve a real antici-pation of experience. This validity and anticipatory function cannot be got at analytically merely by including a concept of the ex-periential condition of application in the definition of the cate-gory. You cannot build the condition of application into such a category by logical synthesis, without falling into an ontological argument. As Kant says,[19] it is the *sensuous condition* itself, a necessary given, which provides the categories with validity for experience. The *concept* of the sensuous condition will not serve. Such categories are necessarily associated with a sensuous schema, and therefore they cannot fail to have objective reference.

The categories I have just described formally and epistemically re-semble the Kantian categories. I make no defense of the specific list of categories Kant gave; but his list does have the virtue of not being rhapsodic and episodic. Lewis has correctly remarked that "the easily rec-ognized categories do not cover the easily recognized distinctions,"[20] and we do not find anywhere in Lewis' writings a list of the concepts of which he ought to have said that their application to experience is not contingent upon the content of experience.

I will suggest four such categories or principles which function in Lewis in much the same way the categories function in Kant. The *if* . . . *then* of terminating judgments and the serial character of the verif-icatory experience and procedures are categorial in the sense of being illustrated in every possible experience. They are not categorial by virtue of any *definition* of time or of the relation of real connection,

18 AKV, p. 353, 353 n.
19 *Critique of Pure Reason*, A, 244-5; omitted from B.
20 "Log. Prag.," p. 47.

which experience might or might not illustrate. Then there are two principles, the Principle of Induction and the principle that

mnemic presentation constitutes a *prima facie* probability of past actuality, [which are] ingredient in and, together with the certainties of given experience, are constitutive of our sense of that reality which we cannot fail to acknowledge, unless we would repudiate all thought and action and every significance of living. That we cannot do.[21]

Neither of these principles is an analytic proposition. Yet they are both a priori in the two senses attached to this word by Kant, and not merely in the one sense in which the a priori is characterized by Lewis. That which is a priori for Lewis is irrefutable by experience because any experience which would refute it is ruled irrelevant by the classification of experiences into evidence and nonevidence by the meaning itself. This is characteristic of the analytic a priori. But the principles that I am considering at the moment are a priori in the Kantian sense, a sense neglected or denied but still used by Lewis. This is the characteristic that the concepts or principles are necessary in application to experience, and therefore universally applicable to experience, be its content what it may. The justification or deduction of the a priori that has both of these characteristics cannot be that of the analytic a priori. The justification of the principles by Lewis is precisely of the kind that Kant gave of his principles, to wit, in conjunction with the given they make experience as knowledge of objects possible, whatever be the generic traits of the objects. It is easy to see that defining 'mnemic presentation' in such a way that it would logically imply any probable propositions about the past would accomplish nothing. But to speak of these principles as having a pragmatic vindication rather than a logically analytic justification should not obscure the fact that the mode of justification employed is of the kind that Kant called a transcendental deduction.

Lewis is almost alone among analytical philosophers in the importance he attaches to these uniquely fundamental principles. To say that there are principles or concepts which must be applicable to every experience is to say something the pragmatic analysts are not in the habit of saying. Such a priori presuppositions cannot be relativized by linguistic analysis, for they do not arise by analysis of given conceptual meanings or by conventional stipulation of what we shall decide to mean by 'induction' or 'hypothetical connection' or 'mnemic presentation'. Their application is not to just those parts of experience selected by us because of harmony with them. They are principles for the inter-

---

21 AKV, p. 362.

pretation and anticipation of experience itself; Kantian apriority and not analytic apriority is their mark. The *if . . . then* of terminating judgments and the seriality of verificatory procedures are constitutive of experience somewhat like the Kantian categories and forms of intuition respectively; the principle of induction and the principle by which memory is justified are regulative very much like the dynamical principles of the *Critique*.[22]

For the elaboration and defence of these a priori presuppositions, the *Critique*—though every sentence in it should prove wrong—has given Lewis a model for the justification of principles as conditions of possible experience and knowledge of a common objective world. It is these presuppositions that are the mark of Kant, albeit faded, that is still discernible in Lewis' epistemology.

LEWIS WHITE BECK

DEPARTMENT OF PHILOSOPHY
THE UNIVERSITY OF ROCHESTER

[22] Not to be confused with the regulative Ideas, cf. *Critique of Pure Reason,* A 178=B 220–1; A 180=B 223.

## 10

*Roy Wood Sellars*

# IN DEFENSE OF "METAPHYSICAL VERACITY"

THIS paper may be of some historical interest since Lewis and I belong to much the same period of American philosophy. Pragmatism had attacked idealism only to find itself confronted with various forms of realism. It was not surprising that pragmatism, in its turn, had some variations. Lewis' variation is often called conceptual pragmatism and showed some Kantian influence. As I recall it, one of the queries of the time was where his concepts came from. Dewey, as I shall try to show rather incidentally, met the realistic challenge in terms of a non-cognitive presentationalism of "things are as they are experienced as." Cognition is a special affair pointing towards the future. As Woodbridge and others have pointed out, Dewey met the common belief in 'antecedent reality' in a rather dialectical fashion, making knowledge concern itself with results and consequences. In any case, pragmatism stressed prediction and the future and tended to shrug off the past and the co-existent. This perspective went with a negative attitude towards the category of substance and the correspondence approach to truth. All this, as I see it, stands—or falls—together. Suppose we call this perspective *experientialism*. I am not certain that I want to call it phenomenalism.

Expressions like observability, verifiability, if-then, seem native to this outlook. But, if the more realistically inclined seek a framework in which to locate these 'abilities', he is assured they are basic. Any such search is motivated by ideas of transcendence, correspondence, and what Lewis calls 'metaphysical veracity'. As we shall see, he argues that this line of thought is self-defeating. Is he right? I shall try to introduce some novelty which is meaningful to me. If he makes the necessary effort, I think it will be meaningful to him. At least, I want him to try. The alternative would seem to be a supplementation of the 'given' in a conceptual and predictive way. Thus is attained that *thick experience* of the world of things which is the *datum* for philosophical reflection. And "thing-hood means a stability or uniformity of appearances which can be re-covered by certain actions of our own." Now I do think that things appear and give evidence of themselves in our sensory experiences and are, in that sense, observable. I do not see how one could be an empiricist otherwise. But *appearance* seems to me an elliptical expression for the *function*, the way a thing appears to an observer, which involves a complex mechanism, a mechanism which I shall later examine. If appearance is thus taken, it presupposes a thing which appears to an observer and the thing cannot be reduced to its appearances. But this gambit points to the kind of epistemology which Lewis thinks is self-defeating. It is well to have a debate on it. I expect something solid and not an affair of arbitrary definitions and stipulations, such as the logical positivists indulged in. After all, Lewis is a trained philosopher and not a specialist in logic or physics who, in his pride, has gone amuck. As I pointed out, Lewis belonged to the same historical period in American philosophy that I did. And I think he had respect for the work done in it. Like Dewey and myself, he is naturalistic and humanistic in his outlook. The divergence is, accordingly, a technical matter.

In my book, *The Philosophy of Physical Realism,* I wrestled with Lewis' type of experientialism and I am now returning to the encounter after these many years during which I have sought to clarify my own analyses and during which Lewis has had the opportunity and incentive to expand his position. I think we have much in common. I imagine he is as tired as I am of deontological intuitionism and the 'naturalistic fallacy'. But to work. It is, then, a question of alternatives. It may not be amiss for me to devote considerable space to the exposition of the epistemological position which I offer as an alternative to Lewis' experientialism. I have reason to doubt that he has ever quite understood what I was driving at. The fault was, undoubtedly, partly mine. *But a basic difference in frameworks easily holds up communication.* It constitutes a barrier not readily broken down. And I do want Professor Lewis to understand my form of realism, the more so that I find myself sympathetic to his stress on concepts and on rationalism in ethics.

I am, of course, an empiricist. I would call myself a *realistic empiricist* in that I think that knowing of the world rests on the evidence of the senses, worked over and used in an inductive and deductive way. When I speak of the *evidence* of the senses, I mean that our sensations are information-carrying, not themselves terminal in perceiving, as the tradition in British empiricism held. From the standpoint of realistic empiricism, much of modern empiricism can be called *phenomenalistic empiricism.* But a point to be kept in mind in this terminology is that the phenomenalistic empiricist is usually convinced that there is no realistic alternative to his analysis. Therefore, he does not consider himself to be a phenomenalist in this contrasting mode. Or, to put it in another fashion, appearances *are* the thing, a position close to naïve realism.

Critical realism, as I sought to develop it, was a form of realistic empiricism. It explored the possibility of a *direct realism* of a new type. Its aim was to overcome the Lockean gambit which made ideas terminal and resulted in a tantalizing kind of untestable representationalism. The thing to do was to reanalyze perceiving and to bring out its response and referential base. For this approach, sensations would be guiding and evidential and direct perceiving as a complex operation. Existentially, they might well turn out to be intracortical. But the operation of perceiving itself would be tied in with response and concern itself with the objects to which the organism was adjusting itself. The unit would, accordingly, be of the sensori-motor type. At the human level, perceiving would rise to the stage of concern with, reference to, and descriptive characterization of the things man had to deal with and talk about. This was a direct realism of a referential type which recognized the mediating role of sensations and concepts. The point was that these were not terminal cognitively but played a role in the achievement of knowledge. We know through and by means of them. The interplay of sensations and concepts in this operation needs careful study. Concepts, it would seem, take up and develop the information carried by sensations with their eye, so to speak, on the object. One speaks of conceiving the object or of applying concepts to it. Here again, we have direct realism. But it is not of the intuitional kind. Yet the directness of concern and the dominance of the attitude, reference, or intention involved encourages the belief in a sort of giveness, or intuition, of the object perceived. This is not surprising since the complex mechanism operates more or less automatically.

Historically, the traditional, causal approach to perceiving expressed an incomplete analysis of its mechanism. It got as far as the arousal of sensations and made these terminal. Theorists were handicapped by lack of biological knowledge and by the prevalent mind-body dualism. The lack of biological knowledge led them to ignore response and adjustment and prevented them from seeing the operation as a whole. The mind-body dualism induced a stress on introspection and states of mind. Thus the historical setting gave support to traditional empiricism with its view that sensations are terminal for perceiving. As we are beginning to see it today, the brain is an organ of adjustment and its elementary unit is sensori-motor. Sensations are *factors* within perceiving as a complex and directed operation. Their location *in* the brain does not mean that we are perceiving brainstates. Russell seems to have gotten himself into this impasse. The escape is to realize that sensations in the brain guide response and play a role in outwardly-directed perceiving of the referential type. One must emphasize the fact that the unit of the mechanism of perceiving is sensori-motor. As we shall see, it is upon this unit that the human mind develops, adding cortical and conceptual complications.

Now I am inclined to hold that this framework will throw light upon the import and reach of human knowing. If sensations are information-carrying, the job of the brain-mind is to elicit this information and to use it in deciphering *facts about* external things. Later I shall connect up this approach with a new formulation of the so-called correspondence theory of truth, giving human knowledge a correspondence-foundation in the mechanism of its attainment. I shall, also, have some remarks to make on the status of so-called universals, connecting them with the operative use of evidence in knowledge-claims. As I see it, they are not entities, *ante, in* or *post,* but terms involved in the import of knowing as an achievement. I am sure that I should not have readily grasped this view of the status of universals as tied in with cognitive acts and their conditions had it not been for Professor Wilfrid Sellars treatment of the topic in his study of "Aristotelian Philosophies of Mind" in the book *Philosophy for the Future.*[1] If one concentrates on sensations and images as entities and ignores the use made of them in perceiv*ing* and conceiv*ing* as cognitive acts, then their information-carrying role is ignored. To conceive an object or to apply a concept to it is not just to *have* a concept, just as perceiving is not just to have a supposed psychological entity called a percept. The fault in much of psychology is to disregard *knowing* as an operative claim and achievement. Traditional empirical epistemology must take part of the blame for this.

Now I was never persuaded that Professor Lewis grasped what I was driving at in critical realism as a form of direct, referential realism connected with an analysis of the mechanism of perceiving. It had elements of novelty and its clarification took time. But I still think he was a little impatient with Pratt and myself. If one has a well-worked-out framework, it is hard to grasp an alternative. That requires a complete reorientation. The debates between idealists, pragmatists and logical positivists illustrate this fact. They go on within different sets of assumptions. To my way of thinking, these assumptions are inadequate and are all tied in with the initial mistakes of Descartes and Locke, which tended to make *ideas* terminal in human knowing. I have found myself

---

[1] *Philosophy for the Future* (New York: The Macmillan Co., 1949). Hereafter cited as PF.

more sympathetic to the framework of neo-Aristotelianism, though I have not discovered it in the sort of analysis of the mechanism of perceiving to which I was led by my study of modern biology and neurology. Moreover, my schematism fits in with ontological materialism and the movement from molar things to all sorts of particles. The information-carrying capacity of sensations seems to me to connect up more with the reproduction of pattern than with the transfer of an entity called 'form'. Aristotelian teleology seems to me outmoded. I prefer to work along evolutionary lines and to stress levels of causality with emphasis on immanent causality and the development of guidance and direction. It will be remembered that I speak of sensations as guiding perceiving.

But to return to Professor Lewis. Let us take the idea of transcendence and the revised notion of the correspondence-foundation of knowledge and truth as typical of the framework I am asking him to understand as an alternative to his experientialism. I have been re-reading Professor Pratt's *Personal Realism* and find that I agree largely with his principles but that his mind-body dualism gave a slant somewhat divergent from mine. While I sought to explore the mechanism of perceiving to give a basis for external reference, Pratt was more inclined to appeal to mind and the self as the source of transcendent reference. Suppose I put it this way. If perceiving, as founded on a sensori-motor mechanism, displays itself as a guided reference to the things around us, we have the base for denoting, symbolizing and characterizing. All that is needed is the operative insertion of conceptual intelligence. The assistance given by language is, of course, immense. But I take the sensori-motor framework to be foundational. Denotative and descriptive meanings develop within it. At the human level, the percipient points, means, relates, compares and describes. He confronts the world actively.

What, then, about transcendence? It seems to me that there is nothing mysterious implied. All that is involved is the tested use of the information carried by the senses. This is developed and applied in terms of concepts. Guided reference is half the battle; the use of the controlled information, given by the evidence of the senses, is the other half. Transcendent reference is thus an achievement rooted in organic life and its concern for its environment. Starting from guided responses, it is lifted to the level of conscious reference and the symbolic application of concepts drawing on the resources of sensory evidence under the responsible control of patterned stimuli. I shall have something more to say about this perfectly natural situation later. It will have bearing upon Lewis's rejection of 'metaphysical veracity'.

Traditional empiricism, I have argued, tended to make sensory appearances terminal. As I see it, Professor Lewis continues this tradition. In contrast, I am arguing for a view of perceiving which connects with response and lends itself to the employment, by the organism, of the evidence furnished by the senses. As we pass from the lower animals to man, this framework is increasingly exploited because of the addition of emergent abilities. Man finds himself *looking at things out there* and describing them without much idea of how he is able to do it and just how the ability is achieved. The result is what philosophers call naive realism. Puzzling at it, epistemologists got lost, as Locke did, by concentrating on the causal approach to sensations without grasping *the whole sensori-motor circuit.* This approach also made it difficult to understand the nature and import of concepts and conceiving. Surely, conceiving is an operation which has, so to speak, one eye on sensory appearances but the other on interrogating the object. That is the evidence of the senses is made use of in the interest of asking questions about the object being perceived and conceived.

Now I see nothing mysterious in these directed operations. What I am trying to do is to rob the notion of 'transcendence' of the mysteries read into it inevitably by those who start with sensations as terminal, as Locke did, and do not appreciate the relevance of the response and the *circuit* it makes possible. When I look at this chair before me, I am looking at it *through* my visual field. The 'looking at' is of the nature of a guided response involving the interplay of stimulus and attitude towards. 'Feedbacks' are, undoubtedly, operating. That is why I call it a circuit. But it is a circuit dominated by a basic concern with the object. This concern operates in delayed responses when we take time to size up the object. It is, perhaps, well to begin with the idea of reference and note how it is supported by the mechanism of perceiving. *Transcendence* calls additional attention to the cognitive claim as saying something about an object other than the act with its propositional content. Here, I take it, we need to appreciate the information-carrying function of sensations and their evidential use in the building up of concepts regarded as having objective import in conceiving things. As cognitive acts, perceiving and conceiving are quite complicated affairs. It is, as I see it, quite necessary to get an adequate framework; and I do not think that Berkeley and Hume had it. Biology and neurology and psychology were not sufficiently advanced. But that is no good reason why philosophers should refuse to grasp the import of this new knowledge and the reorientation it makes possible.

Thus far, I have largely concerned myself with what could be called an operational clarification of 'transcendence' with the intent to show

how cognitive acts are built up and directed at external things. It is *this chair* which I am looking at and pointing to that I am talking about. Speech clearly moves within the framework set by guided response. It is in this context of perceiving and speech that we can take external things to be terminal for cognitive acts. They are what we mean, refer to, identify and describe. Of course, this outlook breaks completely with Lockeanism. How significant the break is one can realize when one recognizes that Russell and the logical positivists made sensations terminal and sought to construct things out of them and their possibility. To the critical realist, this endeavor largely displayed misused ingenuity. Logic is a powerful instrument, if you will, but it cannot replace sound epistemological analysis. Recently, Stace has formulated the axiom of this traditional empiricism to make statements terminate on sensory factors, *not as their evidence but as their meaning.* I shall say nothing here of that explosion called German romantic idealism. Great ability was exhibited but the foundations were weak. If Kant had realized that his sense-manifold was information-carrying, he would not have fallen back on things-in-themselves. But this would have meant the enlargement of the causal view of perceiving I have desiderated.

I suppose that philosophy is a difficult subject just because it is mixed up with foundations and orientations. Because of this fact, I shall not hesitate to repeat myself. What I want to do is to get Professor Lewis to understand the alternative I am offering. Since I began working in the subject in the first decade of this century I have noted many fashions and winds of doctrine. What I have sought to do is to carry through an integration of epistemology and ontology in an adequate framework.

Let me turn now, in a preliminary sort of way, to the revision of the correspondence theory of truth which goes with obejctive reference and the kind of transcendence I have outlined. It must be disconnected from the Lockean impasse which implied that, while we only know our ideas, we believe in 'unperceived things' outside the mind and would like to make a comparison between them and our ideas, a comparison which, by the very nature of the supposed situation, is impossible. The gist of the matter is that, if external things are the objects of tested and evidenced cognitive acts, such a comparison no longer has point. Cognitive ideas are of the nature of propositions, or statements, used in the referential act and, in cognition, we are asserting that things are as we so conceive them. It is testing them evidentially and logically before we assert them that is required. Of course, if our sensations are not information-carrying they are not evidential.

But why hold this thesis when we note that our knowledge-claims, so based, do work and enable us to dominate the world and build up a comprehensive view of it by the use of scientific method?

As I see it, then, *true* is just a term expressing a favorable verdict on, or endorsement of, a statement used in a cognitive claim, affirming that knowledge has been achieved. And knowledge as an epistemological category *implies* the cognitive value of the statement which carries it and, hence, its agreement, or correspondence with the object. *True* affirms knowledge and points back to the testing of ideas, that is, to verification. It is, accordingly, a two-directional term. As affirming the achievement of knowledge, it *implies* correspondence of the sort needed. As the culmination of a process of verification, it guarantees the foundation in sensory evidence and logical consistency. If one did not have this feeding in of evidence, correspondence would have no operative foundation. Of course, this means that sensations are not terminal, as they are for Bradley, Whitehead and Lewis, but indicative and information-carrying. We come back, accordingly, to our circuit, from things to directed acts of perceiving concerned with them and following their indications.

I have quite a long memory in these matters and I recall my conviction that pragmatism gave up the epistemological battle before really engaging in it seriously. Idealism had already largely turned its back on epistemological questions, citing Locke and Kant's things-in-themselves. Dewey was confronted by the realistic movement after he came to Columbia and tried to make his adjustment to it. As I have indicated, I shall consider what Sidney Hook regards as his best effort. Peirce and James had fallen back on 'immediate perception' that is, the *givenness* of the object in perception. James's radical empiricism and Russell's neutral monism are but expressions of this gambit. I have a strong suspicion that Lewis' version is a deepening of 'immediate perception' by means of a conceptual 'If-then' thickening. And, if there were no viable alternative, it might well stand.

The alternative I am trying to clarify is a referentially *direct realism* which puts the act of perceiving in the context of stimulus and response, stresses a feedback circuit, assigns a guiding and evidential role to sensations, stresses the building up of concepts within the cognitive act—with one eye, as it were, on sensations and the other on the referent to be known. The emphasis here should be on preceiv*ing* and on conceiv*ing*. We don't perceive percepts and we don't conceive concepts. We perceive and conceive what we are concerned with. This context gives, I take it, a better account of the rise and cognitive import of concepts than is traditional. I have even hinted that it does away with the need for universals as entities. Concepts, of course, function linguistically as universals. But what they cognitively grasp are *facts about the referents* to which they are cognitively applied. This thing is three feet long. That is a fact reached by measurement. But this other thing is, also, three feet long. Another fact. But why project a universal into them? It is better to have some notion of the mechanism of human knowing. Universals are not entities but functions in cognitive acts. They are not to be located in things nor in sensations nor in images. They are functionally connected with the cognitive use of sensations and images as information-carrying and the rise and role of concepts in conceiving with the employment of symbols. At the human level of perceiving, we both indicate indexically—to use Peirce's terminology —and describe by employing descriptive symbols. I do not see how human knowing could have avoided developing this *equipment*.

What I have tried to do is to show that referential direct realism can give empirical meaning to transcendence and to correspondence by working out the mechanisms involved. The brain is an organ of adjustment into which patterned stimuli feed and which, thereupon, directs a guided response. It is within this setting that acts of perceiving emerge. The information carried by sensory factors under control of patterned stimuli, themselves under the control of the external thing, is, as it were, read off and developed by cortical equipment into concepts which can be cognitively applied to the stimulating thing in a circuit-like fashion. I have no doubt that neurologists will soon be exploring these mechanisms and equipment. In point of fact, they are. What philosophy can do, in aid, is a clarification of the nature of human knowing in an up-to-date fashion and not linger in the cultural era of Locke, Berkeley, Hume, and Kant. These were great thinkers but limited by the knowledge of their time.

The import of all this is that it is the very function and task of human knowing to have 'metaphysical veracity', *Anglice,* import for the world around us of which we are a gifted and distinctive part. The alternative, for me, would be agnosticism which hardly has point in these days of mounting scientific knowledge of our world. Besides, the word was used by its coiner to express a theological stalemate. My dispute with Lewis turns on the contrast between 'immediate perception', however thickened, and direct perceiving. In a way, I am not defending what he is attacking, Lockean representationalism and Kantian things-in-themselves. I am just indicating a somewhat novel alternative. My point is that British empiricsm made sensations terminal in perceiving and that they are *not* terminal. I have intellectual respect for Bradley's sentiency and centers of experience and for Whitehead's version of it. My colleague, DeWitt Parker, even tried to acclimate sub-stance to this climate. But I think that this gambit was mistaken and outmoded. I must confess that the King Canute role of philosophy does not awaken my enthusiasm. Professor Montague told me that it was my radicalism which prevented me from getting any lectureships, for com-mittees are conventional. That may be. But it is quite likely that I had not sufficiently clarified my position.

One other point. An attempted solution of the mind-body problem was involved in this view of perceiving. The role of sensations as guid-ing and as *between* stimulus and response indicated that they were, in some sense, *in* the brain. Thus arose my double-knowledge approach and my view of consciousness as a 'natural isolate' in the functioning brain-mind. I note that Professor Donald Williams in a recent number of the *Review of Metaphysics*[2] associates me with Russell. As a matter of fact, I have priority on this thesis since I defended it in 1907 against Baldwin to whose lectures I listened at a Summer Session at Chicago in 1906. He was then the editor of the *Psychological Review* and was good enough to publish my paper. With Watson's advent, as editor, such philosophical nonsense was excluded. Recently I have found biologists and neurologists more friendly. Coming back to Rus-sell, as I see it, his motivation was in line with the traditional causal theory of perception. He got into the brain but could not get out. It will be noted that I take perceiv*ing* as dominated by response and the unit as sensorimotor.

I do hope that Professor Lewis will now understand the alternative framework which I am offering. Later I shall give my understanding of his outlook which strikes me as a logical expansion of the tradition of 'immediate peception', of *givenness,* as an alternative to the impasse of Lockean representationalism. What we critical realists were seeking was a *via media.* We wanted directness with mediation. As I increasingly saw it, this required a mechanism involving information-carrying on the part of sensory factors and objective import on the part of perceiving as an operation. It was as though Kant's sense-manifold dis-closed facts about his things-in-themselves. In our biological and nat-uralistic era such a role would seem to be a natural one. In intention, then, I have sought to naturalize human knowing as an achievement made possible by the directed operations of the brain-mind, operations in which we consciously participate the more complex they become. The circuit is there as a foundation; and the conceptual level emerges as capacities and problems require it. The result is a responsible inter-

2 "Mind as a Matter of Fact," *Review of Metaphysics,* 13, No. 2 (Dec. 1959).

course with the things around us. This is the level of common-sense realism. And it is from this that scientific method took its rise, as culture made it possible. I shall have something to say about this in connection with what I call the *epistemology of atomism*. Atoms and their constituent particles are, in my opinion, not scientific constructs but physical realities, though our concepts of them are efforts at conceiving them.

I suppose that I have always regarded pragmatism as a half-way house between idealism—subjective or objective—and physical realism. It was not that I did not see merits in its emphasis upon meaning and verification and the use of knowledge. But I was persuaded that it had not faced up to epistemology imaginatively enough. The antagonist pragmatism had in mind was idealism. The rise of realism was unexpected by both James and Dewey. Woodbridge is an interesting figure in this connection. I was, at the time, somewhat irritated by his attacks on epistemology but I have come to realize that, like Dewey, he had in mind the tradition of Lockean representationalism, just as Lewis has. Woodbridge sought to return to presentational or naive realism. Curiously enough, Dewey finally did the same, things are as they are *experienced* as. This is the gambit of 'immediate perception', of the given. The alternative I have been developing is to grasp the role of the given as disclosing and the use made of it in perceiving as a directed operation. Woodbridge—quite rightly, I think—criticized Dewey's resort to dialectic when rejecting the notion of an 'antecedent reality' and stressing knowledge as terminating on results of inquiry as such. For what is inquiry about? Its own results? There is ambiguity here. On his part, Woodbridge falls back on *sensing* external things (naive realism), while arguing that sensations are a myth.[3] Dewey took much the same gambit. Both these able thinkers were afraid of a subcutaneous mind and the subjective. *Make sensations terminal for perceiving* and in the brain-mind and one cannot get back into the outer world. What both these able thinkers did was to ignore sensations and the subjective and jump into the external world by sensing or experienceing. They did not work out the difference between *having* sensations and perceiving. I cannot see that Russell did either.

Well, what I have sought to do is to analyze more carefully the mechanism of perceiving and to show the role of sensations within it

3 F. J. E. Woodbridge, "The Promise of Pragmatism," "Experience and Dialectic," "Deception of the Senses," *Nature and Mind* (New York: Columbia University Press, 1940).

as not terminal but as guiding and evidential. Surely, this fits in with the function of the sense organs.

Of course, we all know what the new realists did in reformulating Berkeley and Hume along lines suggested by William James. This was a tour de force of 'immediate perception'. It was the strategy of pan-objectivism and the searchlight view of knowing. It was linked with extreme behaviorism. Perry appealed to Bergson's doctrine that the 'percept'—strange entity—is *dans les choses* and that consciousness could not be *in* the brain. But neurology is not so certain of this denial these days and *extreme* behaviorism has had its best period. But, if perceiving is a more complicated operation than having sensations, Berkeley's and Hume's revision of Locke is not the right one. Having sensations is *not* equivalent to perceiving. The biological mechanism is more complicated than that.

Now I have the impression that Lewis is prepared to accept Santayana's essences as synonyms for the 'given'. But, in my form of critical realism,—and I had some priority here which the Atlantic seaboard largely ignored—essences were rejected in favor of sensations and concepts. It may be recalled that, following the suggestion of Professor Wilfrid Sellars, I have connected *universals* with cognitive activity in which information is used and developed and applied. In the strict sense, they are not entities. On the whole, I think that Pratt and I had most in common but he worked within a dualistic framework. He appreciated what he was pleased to call the subtlety of my double-knowledge approach but did not think it did justice to the 'self'. Now I think that the *self* develops around the act of perceiving and the attitudes involved, drives, desires and the need of direction and choice. Here I bring in agential causality as a high level of emergent causality. But this would take me into the metaphysics of ethics. I am persuaded that 'directedness' is a characteristic of immanent causality. I was very pleased when my friend, Herrick, took this idea over to replace teleology.

It is obvious from all this that I suspect that Lewis took the path of presentationalism and is as much a naïve realist as a phenomenalist. Things are *experienced*. Thinghood means a stability of uniformity of appearances which can be recovered by certain actions of our own. Thickening comes from non-terminating increments. There is always more to *experience*. In contrast, I shall argue that things, *made objects*, are referred to and *known, not experienced*. And they are known through and by means of sensory factors and concepts developed in the exploratory acts of perceiving and conceiving. Both perceiving and conceiving involve the use of indications, discriminations, constructions, the solving of problems, and not a mere work of abstraction from the given. Appearances furnish evidence. But things are clearly other than their appearances. It is in perceiving and conceiving that we work out such categories as thing-hood, space, time, causality and dispositional properties. Such categories are cognitive achievements and are capable of improvement and clarification. They are neither innate in the Kantean sense nor subjective, as for Hume. They have cognitive import and are of the nature of decipherments of the constitution of the world.

That Professor Lewis' position is a logical development of the tradition of 'immediate perception' is evident. The choice, as he sees it, is between immediate perception in which the appearance *is* the thing and a Lockean sort of representative realism which starts with a qualitative datum as terminal in the first step of perceiving and then *somehow* moves to an object other than itself which it *somehow* signifies. That is, he has in mind the traditional difficulties of this approach. By what right do we *infer* an external object from the given? And what guarantee can we have that the datum can mediate ascriptive knowledge of the inferred and nongiven object? The contrast is put succinctly on pages 14 to 16 of his book, *An Analysis of Knowledge and Valuation*[4]. As he puts it, theory of knowledge "has puzzled itself for centuries and still continues to do so as to the authenticity or nonauthenticity of this mediating function."

I am not going to attack the details of Lewis' construction though I shall point out now and then to the tenets to which it leads him. The result hovers between phenomenalism and naïve realism. Judgments terminating on the given are supplemented by judgments of a nonterminating sort which thicken the former. For expository purposes I shall indicate how Dewey and Woodbridge tried to meet the problem of perception along lines of naïve realism. My own conviction is that the only way of escape is the one I have outlined which brings in the whole circuit of referential perceiving, makes sensations information-carrying, and considers the act of perceiving direct in import. This approach brings me out into the company of Aristotelian and dialectical materialists but, I think, with advances in technical equipment linked with developments in modern biology and linguistics. It is, if you will, a return to perennial philosophy with a difference. I do not here attempt to assess the contribution of idealism and objective rationalism. They, undoubtedly, loosened the texture of thought and brought the

4 C. I. Lewis, *An Analysis of Knowledge and Valuation* (La Salle, Ill.: Open Court Publishing Co., 1946). Hereafter cited as AKV.

human self into the picture. But they built on insecure foundations and usually nourished a suspicion of science. Neo-Thomism, of course, had similar motivations for escape from naturalism and materialism and rested its case on the soul and on 'active reason'. In connection with a brief discussion of the epistemology of atomism I shall pay my respects to 'dialectical materialism'. As I understand it, it builds on the 'reflective' import of sensations for the material world. In its controversy with positivism, it saw that, without some such reflective import, sensations would be epistemologically terminal as idealists and postivists held. My own ontological materialism rests on a reanalysis of the mechanism of perceiving to bring out the dominance of response, attitude and adjustment. It is in this framework that language develops. I suspect that Lewis' subordination of language to the *primacy of appearance* goes with his epistemology.

To my way of thinking, many of the traditional problems of philosophy, such as solipsism, the external world, the status of other minds, vanish in this new kind of objective framework. Simplification and unity are usually signs of advance. There is nothing mysterious in *having* sensations as events. Their assignment to the brain is indicated and is held back by epistemological confusions which I have tried to meet by my double-knowledge approach. I really think that psychology and neurology would be the better for an adequate epistemology. I must confess that I do not think that Ayer and Ryle quite came up to their opportunity in their handling of the questions raised by the galaxy of brilliant neurologists in the book, *The Physical Basis of Mind*. As I see it, the proper cues were missing. Brilliance is not enough.

Since I am trying to see Lewis in his setting, I am now going to turn to Dewey's reactions to the rise of realism in American thought. He was too able a thinker just to say, as I have heard some smart young philosophers quip, that the new realists could not account for error and that critical realists could not account for truth. It will be recalled that I have completely restated the correspondence theeory of truth, making true an endorsement of a knowledge-claim and showing how knowledge is achieved through sensory information explored conceptually. If sensations are regarded as terminal and having no information function, then knowledge must become an intraexperiential affair. Such is the strategy of both Lewis and Dewey. Hence the denial of the 'metaphysical veracity' of cognitive claims. Hence Dewey's shift to warranted reconstruction and prediction. It is all quite logical. It is, if you will, a bypass, a detour. Ontological materialism was escaped and atoms became 'scientific constructs'. As is well known, Mach took the same stand. If one makes sensations terminal, one must. Whitehead's rejection of 'vacuous actuality' is similarly motivated. Like Bradley, he was immersed in sentiency.

I suppose I should apologize for handling Dewey as brusquely as I do. But it must be remembered that I began thinking in a realistic way in the first decade of this century and was always confronted by Dewey's detours. His cultists, or epigoners, followed his bypassing with loud acclaim. I do not put men like Sidney Hook and Ernest Nagel in this class for both are outstanding thinkers. And these are difficult problems involving orientation.

There are three steps in any systematic understanding of Dewey's pragmatism (1) his fear of subjectivism and a subcutaneous mind; (2) his attack on epistemology and 'antecedent reality' as tied in with false assumptions of the representational sort; and (3) his effort to work out a substitute for realism which would give him data within which knowing could work relationally and predictively. It was a sort of *experiential presentationalism* which would avoid the kind of cognition the new realists had in mind and give a context for knowing as problem-solving. Dewey came to grips with critical realism in an essay entitled "A Naturalistic Theory of Perception" now incorporated in his book, *Philosophy and Civilization*. Professor Hook recently called my attention to it.

The motivation here is, clearly, to avoid a terminal subjectivism of the mind-in-the-brain or 'subcutaneous mind' variety. The proper gambit is to reject it and start with the outer world as given. The quagmires of subjectivism and representationalism are thus avoided and bypassed. In this fashion, Dewey moved from objective idealism to experiential presentationalism linked with behaviorism. And, by this device, the mind-body problem was robbed of its complexity. I fear that Ryle tried much the same gambit. I admit the temptation but it simply won't do. Nevertheless, to use a Dickensian phrase, it had been all 'gas-and-gaiters' for ardent disciples. I fear that it has brought with it a certain philosophical obtuseness. When the bands of pragmatists and logical positivists play, disciples march along shouting their slogans. It is not altogether a pleasant spectacle.

Now I think that Lewis has been a little more *rusé* than Dewey. But Dewey's *things are as they are experienced as* is similar to Lewis' identification of things with appearances. And both regard *traditional* representationalism as the only alternative. In this I think they were both mistaken. A more adequate analysis of perceiving was required. Sensations are *in* the brain but they are not terminal for perceiving.

Both Dewey and Woodbridge now swung to forms of naïve, or presentational, realism. Woodbridge dropped sensations and set up consciousness as a relation between things somewhat analogous to space and time. Of the nature of cognition, it was something added. The eye is the organ of seeing things as they are. But how about illusions, like the stick bent in water or the converging railroad tracks? Well, these have their natural conditions. Light is bent in passing from a denser medium to one less dense. The eye should see it that way. But what is the status of what the eye sees? The critical realist holds that the sensory pattern which guides perceiving is in the brain and is the result of natural conditions. But that we learn to take account of these conditions in locating the external thing, as in spearing a fish, for instance. Must we fill the world with illusions and contradictions as the new realists tended to do? Or should we recognize that perceiving is a complex operation involving learning and adjustment?

Dewey makes much of a linguistic caution. When the adjectives, 'sense' and 'sensory' are prefixed to the *qualities perceived* as well as to the act of perception, the usage is metaphorical. The qualities perceived are not sensory. Sensory applies to the conditions of their occurrence but not to their nature. It is by a similar usage that we speak of a house as a building because it is the outcome of an operation of building. Things are as they are perceived, or experienced, as. But such a perceiving is not a knowing. That is a special affair of solving problems by reconstructing experience. Thus, while Woodbridge is dominated by realistic beliefs, Dewey moves dialectically *within experience* as an affair of learning, locating, reconstructing. The mistake of the new realists was to start with an omnipresent cognition of the searchlight sort. Perceiving, for Dewey, is not that kind of thing. It simply gives the raw material or data. It is a point of departure. But, cautions Woodbridge, the realist, is that not too anthropomorphic? Can we identify physical reality, the material world that science concerns itself with, with the ideas we work out? Forget about any antecedent reality we are supposedly seeking to know about? Replies Dewey. That way lies the false puzzles of 'copying', the 'passive spectator', 'dualism', 'transcendence'. Now, in essentials, Lewis makes the same choice though he develops it differently. And the only answer to both is the actual working out of a theory of perceiving which makes it direct and referential and separates appearance from things. Things undoubtedly appear but they are not summations of appearances.

Like the new realists, Dewey did not so much master the subjective and see its role in perceiving an external world as seek to eliminate it. I know what Professor Hook's query will be. Do I not rob the world of sensory qualities? Let us recall Dewey's linguistic strategy. Quali-

ties are not in themselves sensory. I would put it differently. The role
of a red sensation is to evidence the application of a concept to the
object. Knowledge is always conceptual. Red, as a color concept symbolized in language, applies in a guided and evidenced way, to things.
Here we are using what I would call our natural, biological technique.
It is the level of perceptual knowing. But scientific technique works
with measurement and instruments. And it arrives at light frequencies
and dispositional properties. One must not confuse these two sets of
concepts. They can be correlated. The second supplements the first. But
I see no reason to project our sensations into the world. They are information-carrying and aid discrimination.

I think that it is one of the weaknesses of the 'natural language'
theory that it stresses words developed at the level of perceptual
knowing. This thing is soft, has a sweet odor, etc. It should have a
place for technical terms in the context of scientific technique. When I
come to consider the status of atoms and other particles I shall come back
to this point. Since Berkeley's day, philosophy has moved in the context
of sensations and could not do justice to material things and their constituents. These, of course, went with techniques of weighing, measuring, dividing, inventing new instruments for probing. What Galileo
began and Huyghens and Newton continued was a process of interrogating nature, material things, and their constitution and behavior. It
has taken a long time to arrive at the state of naturalizing man and
his mind.

I have called pragmatism a halfway house between idealism and
realism. I agree, accordingly, with Professor Murphy's contention that
the first stage of Dewey's thought was to escape from objective idealism
with its stress on logical coherence and timelessness. But Cartesian dualism, rationalistic intuitionism, and Lockean *ideaism* were already out
of bounds, as they had been for objective idealism. And he saw no good
reason to return, with Russell, to Hume and traditional British empiricism. By this time he was confronted with the realistic movement and
made his adjustments to it in the fashion I have indicated. An expe-
rientialistic kind of naïve realism feeding into experimental logic was
the result.

Since I am, in this paper, sketching my own outlook by way of contrast with others, I may as well note that I do not think that Professor
Blanshard's revision of objective rationalism quite meets the issues. His
attacks on pragmatism and on logical positivism were well carried
out. But he seems to have given up any hope of revising the correspondence theory of truth in a non-Lockean way and to have fallen
back on the coherence theory. But can this do justice to reference and

aboutness? As I see it, his principle is that the world is as we think it. But what is the relation between thought and things?

Now I welcome his acceptance of the metaphysical veracity of tested thought. But I seem to myself to be more of an empiricist and concerned with the feeding in of information and the tested building up of concepts. Knowledge seems to me the primary epistemological category, *true* the endorsement of a knowledge-claim which has been tested evidentially and logically. Under these conditions, correspondence strikes me as an implication of trueness. This analysis fits in with the sensory feeding in of information. Logic seems concerned largely with the need for identification of what we are talking about and the avoidance of inconsistency. These demands are well founded on the needs of perceiving, conceiving and communication. In this fashion, logic seems to me to have an ontological foundation. But this is a large question into which I cannot here go. If concepts mediate knowledge, I should think that what the concept entails has factual involvements. But such concepts should be empirical ones.

With all this as a background, I shall now interrogate Lewis on certain pivotal points. I have great respect for his analytic competence. It is a question of divergence of frameworks.

Some twelve years ago in a chapter I contributed to the book, *Philosophy for the Future*, I pointed out how realistic Lewis could sound.[5] He affirms that we knew *through and by means of presentations* some objective thing or event. Is he, like Dewey, a naïve realist with pragmatic intent or a phenomenalist? But I have the conviction that he regards these presentations as constituents of the object known. This fits in with 'immediate perception' and the rejection of critical realism. Sense-meanings are thus part of the object. In other words, appearances have an objective status and are inseparable from the thing. I quoted his definition of thinghood on this point. For me, appearances operate in sense-perceiving as information-giving. Like Dewey, Lewis wants an experiential participation in the external world as an alternative to traditional representative theories. Objective knowledge is a kind of thickening of experience in a predictive way.

Now all those who accept a causal foundation for perceiving—from Aristotle to the present—must hold to what Feigl calls a nomological account of sensations. The sense-organs have an adjustmental function. At the animal level, they guide. At the human level the data they contribute can be used as evidence and serve in building up concepts. If so, they are not terminal but of objective import. In other

---

[5] PF, see the chapter, "Materialism and Human Knowing," p. 96.

words, perceiving is quite a complicated achievement. Much is made these days of the reproduction of pattern.

The pivotal question comes to be this. What is the import of objective statements? It is asserted by Lewis on page 189 of AKV that it must be *translatable* into predictive statements of terminating judgments. This thesis fits in with his conception of sense-meanings. For him, as I understand it, sense-meaning is the most important element of significance, epistemologically, in intention or connotation. Sense-meaning constitutes the criterion by which what is meant is recognized. Linguistic expressions of what is meant and what is apprehended are dependent and derivative phenomena. Now I do not deny that we perceive *through* sensations and images and so decipher objects. I am an empiricist.

To make a long story short, we are back to the question of the meaning of empirical statements about things. When I say that there is a piece of white paper before me, am I talking about the operation of perceiving it and what this operation would involve? I cannot see that I am. Of course, I can shift my attention to the seen appearance and what would happen if I turn my eyes to the right. Surely, the meaning of an objective statement is not identical with the method of its verification. Even the logical positivists—now largely scientific empiricists—have gotten over this stance. A cognitive claim is normative and statable in facts about, that is, items of knowledge. Though Lewis criticized logical positivism and emphasized a certain autonomy in concepts, he still wants to connect them up with sense-meaning in a terminal way. Now I want empirical concepts to be responsible to sensory factors but to go beyond them in import. When I say this valise is heavy I am not saying that I am having certain kinds of muscular sensations. I am assigning a property to the valise and I am not surprised when the technique is adopted of weighing on the scales with numbers coming up. I have already indicated how biological technique is supplemented by scientific technique. But, peace to Eddington, it is the same table I am dealing with. I just know more about it.

Now I have been very impressed in recent reading on Lewis' appeal to a sort of conceptual apprehension. I do think we know through concepts. But that means metaphysical veracity, as I see it. Perhaps, Lewis is fighting an outworn battle.

Recently, Chisholm has been moving towards physical realism under the guidance of Brentano. He wants to make appearances mediate knowledge and yet not be constituents of it, as Lewis holds. In a review of Chisholm's book in the *Journal of Philosophy*, Baylis hovers uncertainly between the two positions. I think he is quite right in holding that appearance is a complex term involving the role of sensations in perceiving as in the *appearance* of this table from this angle and distance. Cognitional reference is already at work. If this is all that Chisholm has in mind, then I would agree with him so far. But there is no need to eliminate sensations in noting how they function in perceiving. Perceiving is a more complex level.

I suppose one difficulty in handling perceiving came from the mixture in it of two levels, the sensory and the referential cognitive. The traditional causal approach stressed sensations and took them as terminal. The term appearance may well be taken as symbolic of the cognitive, referential supplement which goes with response and brings in the circuit. As we have noted, Russell gets sensations into the brain but has no clear idea of perceiving. In the famous note on page 187 of AKV, Lewis speaks of presentations as ingredients in objects, the bent stick in water is an ingredient of the really straight stick, the term ingredient here showing Whitehead's terminological influence. Woodbridge met the same difficulty, as did the new realists. The correct answer, as I see it, is to recognize the internal complexity of the act of perceiving. This is the line taken by critical realism.

I pointed out how Dewey's jump to external presentationalism simplified for him the mind-body problem into behaviorism. I have never been able to get clearly in my mind Lewis' solution of the psychophysical problem. He certainly seems very vague about it. My attention was called to it by the fact that Professor Kuiper appealed to it to avoid my location of consciousness *in the brain*.[6]

As a sort of epilogue, I want now to say a few words about the *epistemology of atomism* within materialism.

When Aristotelian physics and cosmology broke down, it was replaced by the experimental interrogation of nature wedded to applied mathematics. As I have indicated, the biological technique of perceiving, which had led to commonsense belief in external, material things, was now supplemented by instrumental techniques of measurement. Quantities and laws were discovered. The ancient Democritean and Lucretian theory of atoms was entertained but empirical evidence for chemical atoms and molecules had to wait until Dalton and the principle of combining units. Chemical technique improved until we have now the ability to synthesize such complex molecules as that of chlorophyll. I refer to Woodward's achievement. Here we have a terrifically complex pattern built up bit by bit with one magnesium atom surrounded by four nitrogen atoms with carbon, hydrogen and oxygen atoms added.

6 See the Symposium on my philosophy in *Philosophy and Phenomenological Research*, 13 (Sept. 1954).

Looking back at the development of modern science I find myself agreeing with Conant that new concepts developed in intimate relations with problems and techniques. And I take these concepts to have cognitive significance. Today, atom smashers are classified as belonging to the genus of microscopes. And, as Bridgman puts it, scientific knowledge is tied in with the use of instruments.

As a physical realist, I take the concepts, thus evolved, as having denotative import. I do not say they are adequate or final. But they are continuous with the fact of divisibility which the ancients had already noted. In other words, I take the particles already in some measure reached by photographical technique as literally existing. Of course, I recognize fields, relations, patterns as supplementary.

What I am calling in question is the tradition in philosophy from Mach to Dewey and Whitehead to speak of such particles as essentially 'scientific constructs' within experience. Of course, all concepts are, as such, constructs. When I say there are lions, I am saying that the concept lion has application in the world of animals. I presuppose the existence of things. To say that things exist is a tautology. Russell could—and, of course, would—ignore this primary ontological meaning. The point I am making is that the tradition in empirical philosophy was to make ideas terminal. Bradley and Whitehead are immersed in sentiency and so material things are vacuous. Dewey moves within 'experience' and makes logical constructs therein. The logical positivists want to translate material-thing statements into statements about actual and possible sensations, etc. Lewis wants to stress appearances and sense-meanings. Now I do not think ideas are terminal in either perceiving or conceiving. We identify, refer to, and characterize, material things; and by means of techniques, supplementing our biological equipment get information about them. So far as I can see, accordingly, the epistemology of even ultramicroscopic particles is but an extension of the epistemology of perceiving chairs and tables. We must be careful in the use of language of course. After Ryle's warning against muddle-headedness, even philosophers can learn to speak the language of science.

The upshot of all this is that philosophy should come back to the old tradition that its job is to do for human knowing and valuing a work of theoretical explanation which enables us to naturalize it. Now I believe that Professor Lewis, as a naturalist and humanist, has been concerned to do such a job which might well put the capstone on science. As Professor Waismann recognizes this involves more than analysis. It involves creative imagination. It is of the same texture as science and should fuse with it. But I do think it will need its own careful terminology.

It is a pleasure and an opportunity to interrogate a thinker of the stature of Professor Lewis. What I have tried to do is set one framework of thought over against another. Some new insight may come out of this. That is the value of debate in philosophy when kept at a high level.

ROY WOOD SELLARS

DEPARTMENT OF PHILOSOPHY
UNIVERSITY OF MICHIGAN

## 11

### William H. Hay
## LEWIS' RELATION TO LOGICAL EMPIRICISM

WHEN I was invited to discuss the relation of the philosophy of C. I. Lewis to logical empiricism, I saw at once that it would not be an easy matter to make a thorough study of such a topic. There is too much diversity of opinion on certain issues among philosophers who might be willing to accept such a label.[1] Nor would I be altogether happy to be identified as a logical empiricist, for their treatment of ethical and political philosophy seems to me grossly defective. On the other hand, their manner of treatment of logic, of theory of knowledge, and of metaphysics seems to me to be on the right track. I have thought, therefore, that I could best define the relation between Lewis and the movement of logical empiricism by trying to state briefly what I understood to be Lewis' views on these topics, and by stating in contrast the criticisms which I would make. I shall not claim to speak for anyone else.

In his account of knowledge Lewis takes his starting point from Common Sense like G. E. Moore. This is like Edmund Husserl's beginning from the natural standpoint. It is also like Jacob Loewenberg, who begins with pre-analytic data. All of these admit that we know many things. "In philosophy we investigate what we already know."[2] He does not claim to offer a psychological or genetic account of how we acquired our present beliefs. Rather he attempts to analyze our beliefs and to offer a reconstructed version which will make more clear what our beliefs are beliefs about. "Just this business of bringing to clear consciousness and expressing coherently . . . is the distinctive philosophic enterprise."[3]

---

[1] Compare the expositions given in such brief statements as Herbert Feigl, "Logical Empiricism," *Twentieth Century Philosophy*, ed. D. D. Runes (New York: Philosophical Library, 1943), pp. 371-416; Rudolf Carnap, "Scientific Empiricism," *Dictionary of Philosophy*, ed. D. D. Runes (New York: Philosophical Library, 1942), pp. 285-86; Gustav Bergmann, "Logical Positivism," *History of Philosophical Systems*, ed. Vergilius Ferm (New York: Philosophical Library, 1950), pp. 471-482; Julius R. Weinberg, "Logical Positivism," *American Philosophy*, ed. Ralph B. Winn (New York: Philosophical Library, 1955), pp. 183-192.

[2] Clarence Irving Lewis, *Mind and the World-Order*, 2nd ed. (New York: Dover Publications, 1956), p. 2. Hereafter cited as MWO.

[3] MWO, p. 3.

This is like the program of rational reconstruction, proposed by Bertrand Russell, elaborated by Rudolf Carnap, Hans Reichenbach, and Moritz Schlick, and most recently defended by Gustav Bergmann.

Lewis gives an account of knowledge of analytic truths which I shall not discuss here. Aside from this, all knowledge depends, Lewis holds, on knowledge gained through perception, and he devotes his main discussion to that topic. In a number of passages Lewis takes as an example of knowledge what is expressed in the statement that this is a white piece of paper. According to Lewis what occurs when I know such a truth by perception is that there is a "given stimulus or presentation" or "content of awareness,"[4] and to this there is attached what Lewis calls a meaning, so that the given signifies a certain kind of "future possible experience, contingent upon action."[5] On this account the claim of knowledge exceeds (Lewis says "transcends") the given. This enables him to account for truth or falsehood. "Veracity in the sign-function . . ., which attaches to the given content in perception and marks it as cognitive, depends simply on the question whether or not the empirical eventualities which are signalized actually ensue when the mode of action is adopted."[6]

When this analysis is given its full-length treatment Lewis introduces the technical phrases of 'judgment of objective fact' and 'terminating judgment'. 'There is a piece of white paper now before me'[7] is taken as an example of a 'judgment of objective fact'. Lewis indicates his awareness of the emphasis of logical empiricists on verifiability by explaining how such a judgment "implies nothing which is not theoretically verifiable."[8] Verification can give evidence relevant to veracity as just described "only by something disclosed in *some* passage of experience."[9] The meaning of an objective statement is identified with its verifiable claims, and "such an objective and non-terminating judgment must be translatable into judgments" about experience.[10] These latter are called 'terminating judgment'.

Terminating judgments are not judgments of what my experience is or will be, but rather judgments of what experience is possible, for

4 Clarence Irving Lewis, *An Analysis of Knowledge and Valuation* (La Salle, Ill.: Open Court Publishing Co., 1946), p. 14. Hereafter cited as AKV.

5 AKV, p. 14.

6 AKV, p. 14.

7 AKV, p. 174.

8 AKV, p. 181.

9 AKV, p. 181.

10 AKV, p. 181.

"what *is* realized is experience; what *could be* realized is objective fact of reality."[11] Hence any terminating judgment is a claim about an objective reality. It will take many terminating judgments, Lewis thinks an inexhaustible number, to unfold the meaning of one of our usual judgments of objective fact, such as that there is a white piece of paper before me.

The form of relevant terminating judgments will be 'If *A* then *E*', or '*S* being given, if *A* then *E*'.[12] All three of these letters are to stand for possible experiences. '*S*' stands for a possible sensation, while '*A*' represents some mode of action. (We must take note that Lewis has watered pragmatism down by explicitly stating that by 'action' is meant only a feeling of will, not "an objective state of affairs" such as "a condition of my musculature in relation to the environment.")[13] '*E*' represents "an eventuality of *experience*, directly and certainly recognizable"[14] in case it occurs. Terminating judgments so defined enable us to satisfy a meaning criterion that will give us statements with a definite extralinguistic meaning. By means of terminating judgments we locate the meaning of judgments of objective fact.

In his earlier book, *Mind and the World-Order*, Lewis played with every sense of 'meaning'. There facts, gestures, experiences, and feelings are said to have meaning, import, and significance. The philosopher familiar with nineteenth century idealism is not surprised by this, but anyone who is mainly familiar with logical empiricism is quite dazed by the many meanings of 'meaning'. In *Analysis of Knowledge and Valuation*, Lewis shows himself sobered by his encounters with logical empiricism and tries to give an account of the meaning of words and sentences.[15] He identifies two main kinds of meaning. In the first place when we ask the meaning of words we may be offered other words. So far as these words are taken as the meaning of the first, we have only what Lewis calls linguistic meaning.[16] Lewis proposes an escape from the circle of dictionary entries through what he calls sense meaning. Sense mean-

11 AKV, p. 23.

12 AKV, p. 184.

13 AKV, p. 184.

14 AKV, p. 184.

15 Those familiar with Lewis' book will note that I suppress any discussion of intension. Since intension is defined as "the conjunction of all other terms each of which must be applicable to anything to which the given term would be correctly applied" (AKV, p. 38), we have to ask for the *meaning* of the intension of a word to get sense meaning. I have thought we might as well go directly to the kinds of intensional meaning.

16 AKV, p. 37.

ing is "constituted by the criterion in mind by which what is meant is to be recognized."[17]

Lewis claims that at least most words we use have such a sense meaning, since "there must be some criterion in mind, in grasping their meaning, which would determine applicability or truth by way of sense-presented characters."[18] This criterion involves imagery but more than imagery. "The valid answer was indicated by Kant. A sense meaning, when precise and explicit, is a schema: a rule or prescribed routine and an imagined result of it which will determine applicability of the expression in question."[19] The routine is what appears as the if-clause of Lewis' terminating judgments. As we shall see later, Lewis argues that not only most but all terms and statements, including "terms of universal applicability and analytic statements whose falsity is not logically possible, have such sense meaning."[20]

So much one is eager to agree with. Existing language requires examination of just what it means. In a half-hearted way Lewis is ready to subscribe to the use of an ideal language (to use Russell's phrase) which will record the results of such examination by reconstructing my ordinary statements in terms whose meanings are found within my experience.[21] This appears to be the familiar verifiability-in-principle thesis of the logical empiricists. Indeed in replying to the criticisms of logical empiricism (it was called logical positivism then) in Lewis' Presidential Address to the Eastern Division of the American Philosophical Association, "Experience and Meaning,"[22] Moritz Schlick expressed surprise at Lewis' belief that the thesis of meaning and verification limited meaning to what was in fact verified. On the contrary Schlick maintained that he agreed with Lewis that the test of meaning is "what would be seen or touched by a person."[23] Lewis aligned himself in his later book with the logical empiricists' rejection, as meaningless, of any statement "having no conceivable consequence of its truth or falsity which would be testable or bear upon any rational interest."[24]

17 AKV, p. 37.

18 AKV, p. 135.

19 AKV, p. 134.

20 AKV, p. 135.

21 I have contrasted several versions of this thesis in my review of three articles by Hans Reichenbach, Carl G. Hempel, and Gustav Bergmann in *Journal of Symbolic Logic*, 17, 134-136.

22 *Philosophical Review* 43, 125-146.

23 "Meaning and Verification," *Philosophical Review*, 45, 354.

24 AKV, p. 177.

Let me underline the turn Lewis has given his meaning criterion. The meaning (that is, sense meaning) of a statement is not merely something which experience has informed us of. The meaning is quite baldly certain experiences. "The cognitive significance may *attach to* the data of sense but cannot simply *coincide with* such given data. To know is to find what is presented significant of what is not, just now, presented."[25] "Berkeley was an idealist because he *did* intend what may be suggested by saying, 'There is a tree out there' refers to the same event or chunk of reality as does the statement 'I have a percept of a tree.' "[26] Lewis follows Berkeley's advice of "laying aside all use of words in their meditations, and contemplating their bare ideas."[27] Lewis sees that if the statements about the paper mean his experiences, the paper is a set of ideas. To avoid this he supposes that the statement about the paper means something about certain *possible* experiences, what he *would* hear and *would* see.[28]

At this point I feel compelled to stop and protest my astonishment and bewilderment on being told that when I say "There is a white piece of paper in front of me" I'm talking about an inexhaustible set of possible experiences, only a few of which will ever be actual experiences. I am astonished because I thought that I was talking about something which was not an experience at all, though indeed something which may at times be within my experience. Instead I am told even more outrageous things such as: "That a sheet of white paper is now before me, means that in no possible way can I now proceed directly to presentation of something green and circular here in front of me."[29] I am not merely astonished. I am also bewildered for I am not at all sure that I understand what these possible experiences are.

It is also a little puzzling to me how, if what I mean is always my possible experiences, there can be any meaning to such statements as "what any mind like ours *would* experience if contrary to hypothesis any

25 MWO, p. 44.

26 AKV, p. 201.

27 George Berkeley, *Principles of Human Knowledge* (La Salle, Ill.: Open Court Publishing Company, 1957), Section 23 of the Introduction.

28 Lewis fails to remember that Berkeley also included what he might perceive in his famous statement: "The table I write on, I say, exists, that is, I see and feel it; and if I were out of my study I should say it existed, meaning thereby that if I was in my study I might perceive it, or that some other spirit actually does perceive it." (*Principles of Human Knowledge*, Part I, Section 3.) See my "Berkeley's Argument from Nominalism," *Revue Internationale de Philosophie*, 7, 19-27.

29 AKV, p. 210.

mind should be there."[30] What sense meaning can I give on Lewis' terms except what *I* would experience? If part of the meaning of a statement is someone else's experiences, I should like to be told how I am to know them. Indeed in *Mind and the World-Order* Lewis seems to claim that no sense meaning (as he would later say) can be given to statements about some other person's experiences and that only the structure at most of another person's experience can be known, which amounts to what in his later book he calls "linguistic meaning." There are places even in his later book where he seems to take this view, as for example:

Use of the same expressions in the presence of the same objective facts does not necessarily imply the same sense-criteria of application. . . . What may be thus in another's mind, we can only argue to from the observed similarity of his behavior, including his use of language, and from his observable similarity to us in other respects.[31]

I do not see how this constitutes a solution, since my hypothesis ought to be classed by Lewis as having as its sense meaning only certain possible experiences. Or am I to suppose that the qualities found in a presentation may be found in a presentation which is not presented to me? If so, why may I not suppose that they belong to something which is not itself a mind?

Now it may indeed be possible to make clear what these possible experiences are. I have not been able to do so from what Lewis has written. Nevertheless these objections lead me to ask why he should be contented with speaking of possible experiences. I shall proceed to suggest what beliefs of his we might displace that would enable us to offer an explanation of what he could be talking about. So my complaint is not that he does not show in detail how to carry through the translation from objective judgments to an inexhaustible set of terminating judgments, but that he does not give us a clear idea of these building stones called 'possible experiences'. In dealing with the writings of another philosopher one should always explore every interpretation one can think of that will assign a tenable view to him. When difficulties seem to appear one should search for some interpretation that would resolve them. Afterwards the text of the author can be re-examined to be sure that it supports the interpretation. Otherwise there is every danger of attacking a straw man, built up out of misunderstandings. Can I suggest an interpretation of 'possible experience' that will make clear what Lewis is talking about?

[30] Clarence Irving Lewis, "Experience and Meaning," *Philosophical Review*, **43**, 142-43.

[31] AKV, p. 143.

It was noticed some years ago that there was a striking resemblance between certain features of the pragmatic tradition, which Lewis claims to continue, and logical positivism (the softer phrase, 'logical empiricism' had not yet been proposed) as it appeared in some of the writings of Rudolf Carnap, Hans Reichenbach, and Moritz Schlick. In his lectures published as *Philosophy and Logical Syntax* Carnap stated his meaning criterion in terms of propositions "about a present perception, e.g., 'Now I see a red square on a blue ground' which can be tested directly by my present perception."[32] Indeed Carnap makes the unqualified generalization that "every assertion $P$ in the wide field of science has this character, that it either asserts something about present perceptions or other experiences, and therefore is verifiable by them, or that propositions about future perceptions are deducible from $P$ together with some other already verified propositions."[33] We know that Carnap writes this way for a popular audience, but that he actually uses the strategy of reconstructing science within a formally constructed artificial language when he gives a full exposition of his views.[34] Can the same be done for Lewis? Can we explicate Lewis' use of 'possible experience' by the use of a formally constructed artificial language to give a completely linguistic turn to his doctrine?

In formally constructing such a language we would be wise to follow the injunction of Bertrand Russell in his *Problems of Philosophy:* "Every proposition which we can understand must be composed wholly of constituents with which we are acquainted."[35] This makes the linguistic turn, for it takes the meaning to be a complex of parts each of which is known to me. The important difference from Lewis lies in substituting for statements about experiences statements composed of words each of which refers to something with which I have had experience. In this way we avoid the paradox of apparently referring to something which exists, since we think of it, but does not actually exist. The linguistic turn and the requirement that the components of the statement refer to entities with which I am acquainted enable us to avoid the difficulty of how a statement can mean something and yet

[32] Rudolf Carnap, *Philosophy and Logical Syntax* (London: Kegan Paul, Trench, Trubner & Co., 1935), p. 10. Hereafter cited as PLS.

[33] PLS, p. 11.

[34] See his *Logical Syntax of Language* (London: Kegan Paul, Trench, Trubner & Co., 1937), hereafter cited as LSL; *Meaning and Necessity* (Chicago: University of Chicago Press, 1947), and *Logical Foundations of Probability* (Chicago: University of Chicago Press, 1950).

[35] Bertrand Russell, *The Problems of Philosophy* (London and New York: Henry Holt & Co., 1912), p. 91 (edition of 1946, p. 58).

be false,[36] and so how I can talk about an experience that is possible but never occurs. To speak of $P$ which states a possible experience may be interpreted as speaking of a statement $P$ which is composed of parts each part of which refers to something with which I am acquainted. So to talk of a possible experience is to talk of a sentence describing a situation in terms of what I have experienced. There is then no suggestion that I myself would be able to experience what is described. It might be an event that occurred at a time or in a place which I could not possibly occupy.

Indeed if we explore Lewis' book with this in mind we find that he pronounces that "sense meaning . . . is in no wise dependent upon the existence of what is meant."[37] What he calls the analytic meaning of a statement is recognizable as just what I have described. "Expressions which have the same intension may still be significantly different in this further sense which will be called *analytic meaning*."[38] This is disclosed by considering "the manner in which . . . a linguistic expression can be analyzed into constituents each having its own meaning.[39] "Analytic meanings . . . have reference not merely to resultant intensional meaning but to the manner in which this is determined from their constituents and syntax."[40] Unfortunately Lewis does not feel any paradox in talking about possible experiences. He makes use of his doctrine on analytic meaning only to explain how he would account for an obvious difference in meaning between "two analytic statements such as 'Iron is a heavy metal' and '2 + 2 = 4' "[41] and for the difference between such statements as 'Yesterday was Monday' and 'Tomorrow will be Wednesday', which he thinks can be deduced from each other and hence have the same intensional meaning. By and large Lewis does not analyze statements into their constituents, but deals with what a statement implies, in an unanalyzed sense of 'implies'. It is only seldom that he uses the logic of predicates and relations with quantifiers. We shall see how he interprets this logic.

The mere fact that Lewis does not himself use the classification of analytic meaning to make this explication of 'possible experience', does not exclude it as a tenable explication. Let us test it out in the light of

---

[36] It was this difficulty that led Plato to formulate the doctrine of *Sophist* 261-263 that every judgment has two parts in that it is about something and says something about that thing.

[37] AKV, p. 137.

[38] AKV, p. 71.

[39] AKV, p. 71.

[40] AKV, p. 85.

[41] AKV, p. 84.

other discussions in his book. We have suggested that his statements about possible experiences be taken to be statements whose meaning is a complex composed of parts found in different experiences. This does not commit us to supposing that the meanings of the component words form a composite meaning, quite apart from the words. To do so would be to follow Berkeley's conviction that words are not only dispensable, but that thought is clearer without them.

The meaning criterion of the logical positivist allows us to talk of what exists but is not experienced. It does not require us to talk of them as possible experiences. There are passages even in Lewis which seem to allow us to distinguish existence of objects from the possibility of experience. These are places in which facts instead of words are said by him to mean something. The unwary then might read such a distinction into such passages as "existence of an object through a time empirically *means* the continued possibility of verifying it if appropriate routines of action be followed. . ."[42] Similarly one might be misled by: ". . . if we render the significance of that fact in terms of the experiences which will give evidence of it. . ."[43] In the context of Lewis' book the possibility of such a distinction is repudiated.

The logical empiricist can make the distinction between existence and the possibility of experience because of the distinction in his candidate for the ideal language between logical and descriptive terms. Such logical (nondescriptive) terms as 'all', 'none', 'some', 'if', 'and', 'not', and 'or' are needed to form any but the simplest sentence. Their function is to combine descriptive terms into a sentence. Hence later forms of the meaning criterion explicitly distinguish the classes of signs and lay down the principle that it is the 'undefined descriptive signs of the ideal language' which 'refer to the entities with which we are directly acquainted'.

When I have the experience of seeing something red on a blue ground, I can make a statement describing what I experience without using any logical terms. For example, I can say: "This is red. This is surrounded by that. That is blue." The statement is understood because 'this' and the 'that' name things with which I am acquainted. To say: "There is an $x$ and there is a $y$ such that $x$ is red and $x$ is surrounded by $y$ and $y$ is blue" may be true without my ever having had just such an experience. In Lewis' way of talking the latter would be said to describe a possible experience. The logical empiricist would not however be committed to supposing that the words mean possible experiences, only that they

42 AKV, p. 20.
43 AKV, p. 209.

mean what might be experienced. The difference between the two statements consists in the use of individual constants or proper names ('this' and 'that') as opposed to the use of an existential quantifier ('there is a') and individual variables ('$x$' and '$y$'). It is by means of the quantifier that I am able to talk of what is not in my experience. My statement is meaningful because the predicates ('red' and 'blue') and the relation word ('is surrounded by') refer to what I am acquainted with. If this is what Lewis is after by talking of the meaning of the intension of a word being possible experiences, the paradoxes can be removed from talking of possible experiences which it is not possible for me to have.

How far Lewis is from this we can see from his treatment of quantifiers. In fact Lewis' account of quantifiers rules out the distinction between descriptive and nondescriptive words, and so removes the chance of talking of anything but my experiences. Lewis allows that the variable constituents (the '$x$'s and '$y$'s in the above) have "no meaning save the syntactic meaning which is conferred by their context. They are in fact merely a notational device by which the syntax of the predication may be preserved."[44] (The logical empiricist would reject the statement that the syntactical meaning 'is conferred by their context'. In any formally constructed language a set of marks is assigned to a syntactical category of a form-class, and the rules of syntax identifying the admissible expressions (or well formed formulas) are stated by reference to the lists of form-classes.) [45] Lewis does not, however, allow that quantifiers have merely syntactical meaning. 'Nothing' is said by him to be among "one-word expressions of universal intension."[46] " 'Anything' or . . . 'nothing' . . . always apply or never apply."[47] Hence they have on the one hand zero intension and on the other universal intension. In another passage he speaks of there being a "relation" (or relations) expressed by "All — — — — is."[48]

We must admit that there are passages which do not insist on sense meaning and might allow a merely syntactical meaning, as when Lewis remarks that "we should never have occasion to use terms like 'being,' 'everything,' and 'nothing,' if it were not that we convey something by *putting these in relation* to other expressions."[49] Elsewhere, however, he makes it plain that they are not exceptions to the general principle that

44 AKV, p. 62.

45 See, for example, the treatment in LSL, Eng. trans. (London and New York: Harcourt, Brace & Co., 1937).

46 AKV, p. 88.

47 AKV, p. 88.

48 AKV, p. 118.

49 AKV, p. 88.

"if a criterion of the application of a linguistic expression lacked sense-significance, we should be unable to determine in any given case whether the factually presented conformed to it or not."[50] He clearly says that "terms which have zero intension and are applicable to everything must have such meaning."[51] (He has just been speaking of sense meaning.) The same is true of the truth-functional logical constants. He lists 'and' and 'not' as having constituent meanings which are part of the meaning of a sentence in contrast to the syntactical relation of the signs for those meanings.[52] The question does not, however, arise very sharply for Lewis. Perhaps this is so in part, because he follows Russell in interpreting 'not $p$' as the same as 'it is false that $p$', which can be taken to be my disbelief in $p$ rather than a statement which has no more reference to belief or disbelief than $p$.[53]

Lewis has some half-expressed views about what are the sense meanings of the quantifiers in favor of which they are dispensable. They stand for items, actual or possible, whose names could be substituted for the variables. This is the same contrast of the actual and the possible which we have run into before. Lewis seems to suppose that there are not only proper names which name items, but also proper names which name nonexistent but 'consistently thinkable' and hence possible items. He has not defended at any length how a name can name what does not exist. He simply says that it does.[54] All we can find is a passing remark that to be a possible entity is to be a consistently thinkable entity. We are not told whether he proposes to make use of Russell's Theory of Descriptions to construct a term with the iota-notation which will function like a proper name. The logical empiricists would like some answers to this question. Since there are no arguments presented, I can only try to show what Lewis' view is and why it is mistaken.

We find that Lewis claims that in some statements "for all $x$" means "for all existents denoted by values of '$x$'."[55] He claims, for example, that "the physicist who writes '$v = gt$', meaning 'For all values of "$v$" and "$t$" the measure of the terminal velocity, $v$, of a freely falling body near the earth is equal to the measure of the time of fall, $t$, multiplied by the gravitational constant, $g$,' ... is speaking of *actual* velocities and

50 AKV, pp. 154-55.
51 AKV, p. 137.
52 AKV, pp. 120-21, 151.
53 AKV, p. 120.
54 AKV, pp. 38-39.
55 AKV, p. 116.

*actual* times of fall only, and otherwise his statement would be false."[56] In contrast to this it seems to Lewis that in what he calls a "statement of *logic*, 'For all values of "$x$", $x$ is red or $x$ is not red,' such a restriction of what is asserted to the actual existent is unnecessary; the statement holds for any *meaningful* substitution of values for the variable and for all thinkable things named by expressions which are such values."[57]

What is Lewis driving at by his contrast of actual values with any possible value? We find a clue to this when he remarks that "All men have noses" subsumes "particulars of fact" such as

Socrates had a nose, and Plato had a nose, and this man has a nose, and that man has a nose—and I can't tell you how many other men have lived or are alive or will live, but each of them severally has a nose. . . . When I say "All men have noses," I *mean* something about each and every particular man; and I know that now, and know what I mean about each. That I can't tell it to you, naming each, should not be thought a difficulty.[58]

Now I will not here go into this doctrine of supposition, as it was called by medieval logicians, nor how it is treated by John Stuart Mill. Let me point out that it would be quite indefensible to say that from 'All men have noses' we can deduce 'Socrates has a nose'. All we are entitled to infer is 'If Socrates is a man, then Socrates has a nose'. Modern notation and rules of inference makes this quite unambiguous.

When Lewis is faced with statements in modern logical notation (the example just discussed would appear as 'For all $x$, if $x$ is a man, then $x$ has a nose'), he seems to suggest that the only intended values of '$x$' are the names of men. He ignores and doesn't discuss the substitution of names which are syntactically appropriate, but which are in fact not the names of men. Thus he states that he interprets "For every $x$, if phi $x$, then psi $x$" as "every *existent* having the property, phi (or of which phi is truly predicable) has also the property, psi."[59] This is to interpret it in such a way that no value can be substituted for '$x$' except those of which phi is truly predicable. Such is not only at variance with the rules of modern logic; it makes an indefensible restriction.

In another example, Lewis talks in such a way as to make the same commitment. He is discussing 'For all $x$ if $x$ weighs 150 pounds and falls 25 feet then $x$ acquires a momentum sufficient to injure a human body upon impact'.

[56] AKV, p. 115.
[57] AKV, p. 115.
[58] AKV, p. 195.
[59] AKV, p. 218.

What it says is only that the class of *actual* cases of 150-pound weights falling 25 feet is included in the class of actual cases in which momentum is acquired sufficient to injure a human body. . . . What *would* happen *if* such a weight fell such a distance, in any instance in which the weight does not in fact fall, it does not tell us.[60]

This is plainly wrong, for the reasons I have stated. We can deduce "If William Hay weighs 150 pounds and falls 25 feet, then William Hay acquires a momentum sufficient to injure a human body upon impact." We are not prevented from deducing this by the falsehood of the antecedent clause.

Lewis confuses matters by discussing explicitly only contrary-to-fact statements. We do indeed agree with him that "For any $x$, if $x$ laughs, then $x$ is human" is true and that "If War Admiral should laugh, he would be human" is false.[61] Consequently the second could not be validly deduced from the first. This does not in any way discredit the validity of deducing 'If War Admiral laughs, then War Admiral is human'. This latter is very useful for giving reasons why I think that War Admiral will not laugh. Of course, 'War Admiral is human' is false, but the fact that it is false is different from knowing or believing that it is false. These are again different from saying that I believe it is false. Consequently I am not required to put the statement in the conditional form nor does the falsehood of the statement prevent me from considering the statement.

Bertrand Russell long ago called attention to this point. "Any $a$ is a $b$" does not mean the same as "For any $x$, if $x$ is an $a$, then $x$ is a $b$" inasmuch as "any $a$ is a concept denoting only $a$'s, whereas in the formal implication $x$ need not be an $a$."[62] In the modern notation "The notion of a restricted variable can be avoided by the introduction of . . . the hypothesis expressing the restriction."[63] This enables us to allow 'for any $x$' to cover "any meaningful substitution." Examining Lewis we find surprisingly that he agrees that "intended restriction . . . could always be expressed in the function-part."[64] Lewis queers his statement, however, by qualifying the word, 'restriction', as "restriction to the existential." This is evidence that he is committed to claiming the quantifier has a sense meaning.

60 AKV, p. 222.
61 AKV, p. 223.
62 Bertrand Russell, *Principles of Mathematics* (Cambridge: Cambridge University Press, 1903), p. 91.
63 *Ibid.*
64 AKV, p. 116.

The point at issue is whether meaningful statements can be composed of words which got their meaning from what I have experienced but are so combined as to make a claim beyond experience. The logical empiricist uses a set of classes of logical terms in his candidate for the ideal language which do not receive any interpretation in terms of what is experienced, along with descriptive terms which do. Lewis' doctrine on the quantifier wipes out the distinction of logical and descriptive, and with that the only way I know to explicate his phrase, 'possible experience'.

If we turn to Lewis' account of actual experience we find that he thinks it is never possible merely to *describe* the content of an experience. As previous quotations have shown, it is his official and repeatedly stated conviction that any judgment such as 'This is white' or 'That is middle C' exceeds the given. In *Mind and the World-Order* we were for the most part forbidden even to express the given, which was alleged to be ineffable. Later in *Analysis of Knowledge and Valuation* he makes available for this purpose the expressive use of language. Notice how he describes it. "Our sense certainties can only be formulated by the expressive use of language, in which what is signified is a content of experience and what is asserted is the givenness of this content."[65] Expressive language is said to assert the givenness of the content. To be given is for someone to be conscious of something. Thus Lewis gives evidence that he holds a half-expressed view that there is a flow of consciousness which contains objects only when meanings are added. To express the stream merely reports the qualities of which there is consciousness. Hence these reports are awarded only the title of statements, just as John Dewey awarded them only the title of propositions. 'Judgment' is the title reserved for knowledge. The same contrast appears in other passages in which "statements of what is directly given" are contrasted with "empirical judgments."[66] When I go beyond expressing to naming or describing he takes the same position as in *Mind and the World-Order* that "even that minimum of cognition which consists in naming is an interpretation which implicitly asserts certain relations between the given and further experiences."[67] The claim is stated many, many times, as in another passage, he says that "in whatever terms I describe this item of my experience, I shall not convey it *merely* as given, but shall supplement this by a meaning which has to do with relations, and particularly with relation to other experi-

65 AKV, p. 186.
66 AKV, p. 254.
67 MWO, p. 132.

ences which I regard as possible but which are not just now actual."[68]

The given is subjective for Lewis. It is only judgment that brings us to the objective. "Expressive language *neither asserts any objective reality of what appears nor denies any.*"[69] Everywhere Lewis takes the given as an item or as an array of items. The clearest statement of this in *Mind and the World-Order:* "In any presentation, this content is either a specific quale (such as the immediacy of redness or loudness) or something analyzable into a complex of such."[70] These qualia are experienced. The presentation is the experiencing of them. Hence, "the presentation as an event is, of course, unique, but the qualia which make it up are not."[71]

By now I hope the reader has begun to recognize that this is the same theory of judgment as is found in James's pragmatism and Dewey's instrumentalism. Judgment consists in imposing an idea on experience. An idea consists of "What conceivable effects of a practical kind the object may involve—what sensations we are to expect from it, and what reactions we must prepare."[72] Such judgments are true when they give "human satisfacton in marrying previous parts of experience with newer parts."[73] We can cite similar statements from Dewey's *Logic.* "Judgment . . . is a continuous process of resolving an indeterminate, unsettled situation into a determinately unified one."[74] In this the existential conditions "are indeterminate in significance."[75] "Ideas are of that which is not present in given existence."[76] "They are, however, proposals and plans for acting upon existing conditions to organize all the selected facts into a coherent whole."[77] It is such a coherent whole which is "the settled outcome of inquiry."[78]

There are deeper sources than pragmatism for this theory of judgment, as will be recognized by the reader whose education has included that study of the past so useful in helping us avoid repeating its mis-

[68] MWO, p. 50.

[69] AKV, p. 179.

[70] MWO, p. 60.

[71] MWO, p. 60.

[72] William James, *Pragmatism* (New York: Longmans, Green and Co., 1940) , pp. 46-47. Hereafter cited as P.

[73] P, p. 64.

[74] John Dewey, *Logic: The Theory of Inquiry* (New York: Henry Holt & Co., 1938) , p. 283. Hereafter cited as LTI.

[75] LTI, p. 107.

[76] LTI, p. 110.

[77] LTI, pp. 112-113.

[78] LTI, p. 120.

takes. Leafing through two works of another teacher of Lewis, Josiah
Royce, I found myself struck at once by the occurrence of many of the
common phrases of both of Lewis' books. I have already spoken of
the ubiquitousness of 'meaning'.[79] 'The World-Order' is another easy
one to spot. So too is 'possible experience' as a generic term and 'possible experiences' in the plural. Royce openly identifies these last, as
Lewis does not, as translations of Kant's *Moegliche Erfahrung*. These
pre-echoes are not merely verbal. We find the same theory of judgment
in Royce's discussion of what he calls the Third Conception of Being,
Critical Rationalism, which is presented as having been Kant's view.
Royce describes making an objective judgment as "trying to find
out, in all our search for Being, precisely what experience we may hope
to get under given conditions, and what we may not expect to get."[80]
As he says in another place, "sometimes it is a definite group of
sense-experiences that we mean in advance; then we are said to be
observant of the physical world."[81] Exactly Lewis' view of the objective fact is found in still a different passage: "There are countless possible experiences that you never test, and that you still view as belonging to the realm of physical and social validity."[82] Lewis' theory of
judgment as an activity of a mind adding ideas to the given is unmistakably expressed in the pronouncement that "of course, my
private will, when viewed as a mere force in nature, does not create
the rest of nature. But my conscious will as expressed in my ideas does
logically determine what objects are my objects."[83]

This theory of judgment has a plausibility as applied to perception of objects in the world about me. In Lewis' examples of seeing
the granite steps and of seeing the piece of paper, it does seem as though
more is seen than is there given. It is not given that this is paper.
Something (Lewis would say a meaning) has been added to what is
given. In calling it 'paper' I use a word whose complex meaning is
not articulate for me. It may have a sense-meaning without my being
able to say what it is. And when it is said the saying of it may be intoler-

[79] I owe the suggestion of considering the affinity of Lewis' views to those of his
teacher, Josiah Royce, to Professor Eliseo Vivas, who remarked on it to me in a
conversation in Bloomington, Indiana, just after Lewis had read his Mahlon Powell
lectures.

[80] Josiah Royce, *The World and the Individual* (New York: The Macmillan Co.,
1899), I, p. 203. Hereafter cited as TWI.

[81] TWI, I p. 334.

[82] TWI, I, p. 258.

[83] For other parallels see TWI, I, esp. pp. 248, 250, 257, 259, and II, 62, together
with Josiah Royce, *Spirit of Modern Philosophy* (Boston: Houghton Mifflin Co., 1892),
pp. 387-88.

ably complex. As Lewis says, "a sense meaning must have a kind of complexity not previously noted."[84] Instead of saying that possible experiences are meant, we can say that something which could be experienced, because it is stated by a sentence all of whose constituents which refer stand for items, qualities, or relations with which I have been acquainted. Consider looking at a billiard-ball. I see a spherically shaped surface. What is given is less than the whole surface of a sphere and yet if I discover a red spot on the other side, I feel that I have to revise a belief. Somehow I perceived that there was a spherical and uniformly colored surface. That perception is now seen to be erroneous. Perception gives more than sensation. The more which it gives is in part beliefs which quantifiers are required to render articulate, because there is a belief in items not seen though of a kind which I know.

If Lewis insists on his theory of quantifiers, words will say no more than can be directly contemplated without the medium of words. This can only be done at the cost of limiting what I can say. The proposal to increase the range of statements by including possible experiences is an empty proposal without some definition of the term, 'possible experience'. Lewis has proposed none for himself. We have argued that he can not accept certain definitions without giving up his theory of judgment.

Lewis' logical theory depends on recognizing logically true statements as being analytic of meaning and so necessarily true. If my criticism of Lewis' refusal to recognize a class of nondescriptive, logical signs is sound, this theory of logic collapses, since words like 'all' and 'not' play an indispensable role in an analytic statement, as Lewis himself has seen. If the distinction is made, the contemplation of sense meanings would be limited then to the meanings of the descriptive terms, which would not form any complex unit of meaning, since those sense meanings are related to each other on my proposal not by other sense meanings, but by the syntactical meaning of the logical words. We have had since 1934 Rudolf Carnap's criticism of Lewis' proposal for an intensional logic and Carnap's translation of intensional sentences into extensional, syntactical sentences.[85] This seems to me to be a far more satisfactory way of handling logical truth, implication, and the modalities than is Lewis' system.

While I have been perhaps severe in my condemnation of Lewis' account of possible experiences, I can find a justification for his ad-

---

[84] AKV, p. 192.

[85] LSL, Secs. 69, 70, and 71. Rudolf Carnap. Logische Syntax der Sprache (Vienna: Julius Springer Verlag, 1934).

326    W. H. HAY

herence to this position so close to idealism. Lewis did not cling to his theory of judgment out of ignorance of any alternative. We have shown ample evidence in his writings that he read carefully certain of these logical empiricists (or logical positivists, as they then called themselves). Indeed, his 1934 Presidential Address was one of the first widely noticed discussions in English. In this he quotes Rudolf Carnap, Moritz Schlick, and Ludwig Wittgenstein. These along with Hans Reichenbach are also quoted in his *Analysis of Knowledge and Valuation*. There are many passages in the latter which echo or reply to views expressed by logical positivists. Given all this it is plausible to suppose that the linguistic turn which Lewis gives to his arguments in the later book but which was missing from *Mind and the World-Order* resulted from his study of these adversaries. I suggest that Lewis may have stuck by his theory of Judgment because the alternative view, which I have advanced, had led with its Thesis of Extensionality[86] to physicalism, which is for all purposes a materialism. There is at least one passage in which Lewis flirts with a behavioristic physicalism and allows that "one may consider such criteria of application, as meanings entertained in advance, in terms of incipient behavior or behavior attitudes."[87] For the most part, however, he is faithful to the Cartesian goal of reconstructing the beliefs commonly expressed in ordinary language in terms which he himself has scrutinized and found the meaning of.

Bertrand Russell and Ludwig Wittgenstein are among the more famous who ended up in behaviorism. Indeed it is not at all easy (but I do not say impossible) to see how modern logic can include the act of experiencing. While G. E. Moore and Bertrand Russell in their early days spoke of mental acts by which physical facts were known, it is rare to find any one in that tradition today who does not openly accept behaviorism. Aside from the fears of the charge of dualism and the association of private mental events with grosser forms of religious doctrines of immortal souls, the greatest block is to make out how one event (a knowing) can include another event (the physical happening). In ordinary language sentences occur that have that form. One sentence contains another sentence within itself, as for example, does "I was aware that I had made a mistake." The only translation of this in conformity with the Thesis of Extensionality will be in terms of aptitudes and readinesses of the body. That lets escape the distinctive

[86] LSL, see Sec. 67.
[87] AKV, p. 144.

difference between what I know about my own experience and what I know about someone else's.

Among those who have discussed this difficulty is Gustav Bergmann, and he is the only one, so far as I know, to come forward with any definite proposal of how to modify the ideal language to give more than a behavioristic version of experience.[88] This is not the place to expound and discuss Bergmann's proposals, but I think they illuminate the kind of difficulty Lewis faced. They seem to me to do justice to the relation between the act of experiencing and the content of experience. It is only when an adequate account is available that we could expect Lewis to be ready to relinquish this theory of judgment. Without it, his allegiance to Royce, James, and Dewey is preferable.

In conclusion, let me try to summarize the relation of the philosophy of C. I. Lewis to logical empiricism. We have found that in his second work, *Analysis of Knowledge and Valuation,* in contrast to his earlier *Mind and the World-Order,* Lewis shows the influence of his study of the work of such logical empiricists as Rudolf Carnap, Hans Reichenbach, and Moritz Schlick. I have argued that he has not, however, altered his position on knowledge set forth in the earlier volume. He has merely given a linguistic turn to his doctrine that knowledge of any sort is knowledge of possible experiences. I have claimed that his resistance to logical empiricism has centered in his theory of judgment, which like that of Josiah Royce, William James, and John Dewey is one which assigns to language a role purely of communication. It denies that language is indispensable to articulate thought. Thus it is impossible to say anything except about my experiences, actual or possible. The alternative account of meaning found in the logical empiricists depends on a distinction between logical and descriptive words. This distinction is rejected by Lewis. It is conjectured that his rejection is linked to the apparent commitment of such an account of meaning to some form of materialism or behaviorism. Lewis' avoidance of materialism has kept him tied to a form of pragmatic idealism.

WILLIAM H. HAY

DEPARTMENT OF PHILOSOPHY
UNIVERSITY OF WISCONSIN

[88] See Gustav Bergmann, "Bodies, Minds and Acts," *Metaphysics of Logical Positivism* (New York: Longmans, Green, 1954), pp. 132-152. Gustav Bergmann, "Intentionality," *Archivio di Filosofia: Semantica* (Roma, 1955), pp. 178-216. Gustav Bergmann and Herbert Hochberg, "Concepts," *Philosophical Studies,* 8, 19-27. (These latter two are reprinted in Gustav Bergmann, *Meaning and Existence* [Madison: The University of Wisconsin Press, 1960] pp. 3-38, 106-114.)

## 12

*Roderick Firth*

# LEWIS ON THE GIVEN

THERE is probably no philosophical doctrine more closely associated with the name of C. I. Lewis than the doctrine that our knowledge of the external world can be justified, in the last analysis, only by indubitable apprehensions of the immediate data of sense. The central features of this doctrine are summarized by Lewis in a brief passage of *An Analysis of Knowledge and Valuation*. "Perceptual knowledge," he says, "has two aspects or phases; the givenness of something given, and the interpretation which, in the light of past experience, we put upon it." When we see a piece of white paper, for example, we apprehend something given, and "what is given is a certain complex of sensa or qualia . . . describable in expressive language by the use of adjectives of color, shape, size, and so on. . . . Such apprehensions of the given are characterized by certainty, . . . and without such sense certainties, there could be no perceptual knowledge, nor any empirical knowledge at all."[1]

Three of the most common objections to this doctrine concerning the given can be labeled (1) the ontological objection, (2) the phenomenological objection, and (3) the epistemological objection. I shall devote most of this essay to the last of these three objections. But the other two, although much less important for understanding and evaluating Lewis' theory of knowledge as a whole, deserve at least a brief comment here if only to show that they can safely be bypassed without prejudice to the more fundamental question.

There are many philosophers who have objected to speaking as Lewis does about the given, on the ground that it represents a dangerous form of ontological overindulgence. The idioms that Lewis customarily employs when speaking about sense experience are idioms containing a *noun* which purportedly designates a particular nonmaterial *entity*. In *Mind and the World-Order* Lewis occasionally uses such nouns as 'sense-datum' and 'datum of sense', but he prefers the term 'presentation'. A presentation is a particular event, he says, "historically

[1] C. I. Lewis, *An Analysis of Knowledge and Valuation* (La Salle, Ill.: Open Court Publishing Co., 1946), p. 188. Hereafter cited as AKV.

unique," the qualitative content of which is "either a specific quale (such as the immediacy of redness or loudness) or something analyzable into a complex of such."[2] The term 'presentation' is used again in *An Analysis of Knowledge and Valuation,* especially in Chapter VII, together with a variety of other nouns. In speaking thus of presentations, data of sense, etc., Lewis is employing what is sometimes called a 'sense-datum terminology', and thus conforming to a tradition which has dominated the philosophy of perception in modern times: a noun such as 'phantasm', 'sensible idea', 'impression', 'appearance', 'sensation', 'sense-datum', or 'sensum' is used to refer to what is sensibly given in perception, and the principal task of the philosophy of perception is construed as the task of explaining how the things or events so designated are related, epistemically, to certain other kinds of things or events such as material objects, shadows, mirror images, and mirages.

It has been argued, in opposition to this tradition, that we are committed to a less extravagant ontology, and one less likely to lead us into pseudo-problems, if we abandon the sense-datum terminology in favor of locutions which represent a relational, rather than a substantival, analysis of sense experience. Instead of saying that the paper presents a white appearance to me (or that I apprehend a white presentation when I look at the paper), thus suggesting that there is a 'third entity' which somehow serves as mediator between me and the paper, I might simply say, in a colloquial idiom, that the paper *looks white* to me. And for cases of complete hallucination, cases in which we cannot say that there is any particular material thing which looks or appears in such and such a way, there are other familiar idioms which enable us to describe our sense experience without using the sense-datum terminology. Perhaps we might say, for example, that the drunkard *seems to see* a pink rat, or that *it looks* to Macbeth *as if* he is seeing a dagger.

This is not the place to discuss the merits and defects of the sense-datum terminology, for the methodological issues at stake are broader and more fundamental than most philosophers seem to recognize. The notions of 'ontological simplicity' and 'ontological commitment' are far from clear, and so also are the criteria for deciding whether certain problems about sense-data (e.g., whether they ever exist unsensed as 'views' or 'sensibilia') are to be classified as pseudo-problems. It is only important, however, for present purposes, to see that Lewis' theory of knowledge—as opposed, we might concede, to his ontology—seems to be entirely independent of the use of any one particular terminology

2 C. I. Lewis, *Mind and the World-Order* (New York: Chas. Scribner's Sons, 1929), p. 60. Hereafter cited as MWO.

for the description of sense experience. Lewis never makes the mistake that Thomas Reid so eloquently charged to Descartes and the British Empiricists—the mistake of treating sense experience as though it were the *object* of perception and not just a necessary condition of perception.[3] And Lewis' use of the sense-datum terminology is governed by explicit restrictions which would allow his statements about sense experience to be paired one to one with statements in the most reputable of the alternative terminologies. It is said, for example, that pseudo-problems about the existence of unsensed sensa and the unsensed parts of sensa, can be raised only in a sense-datum terminology; but Lewis himself rules out these problems by denying, on pragmatic grounds, that statements about unsensed sensa are meaningful. "A sensum which is not sensed," he says, ". . . is merely a new kind of *ding an sich*."[4]

Finally, and even more important, Lewis is apparently quite willing to treat his statements about 'presentations' as synonymous with statements which do not employ a sense-datum terminology. He offers us, in Chapter VI of *An Analysis of Knowledge and Valuation,* a variety of examples and alternative locutions to explain what he means by the term 'presentation of sense'. Sometimes he uses nouns in the manner characteristic of a sense-datum terminology: he speaks of a visual pattern, a feeling of pressure, muscle-sensations, the appearance of paper, and so on. But he also uses, and even stresses, a number of colloquial idioms which enable us to avoid nouns of this kind. He suggests, for example, that we may describe the visual presentation of a flight of granite steps by saying "I see what looks like a flight of granite steps."[5] And later[6] he uses the locution 'I seem to see' to formulate two constituent propositions of a terminating judgment: 'I seem to see a doorknob' and 'I seem to myself to be initiating a certain grasping motion'. It is possible, of course, to raise difficult questions about the proper interpretation of these idioms and to argue that in everyday speech they are not ordinarily used to characterize our sense experience. But we are at least justified in inferring that Lewis does not intend his theory of knowledge to be bound inseparably to the sense-datum terminlogy. We may infer, to put the point hypothetically, that if there is *any* terminology in which we can characterize our sense experience without at the same time making statements about 'objective reality', this ter-

[3] In this connection see MWO, pp. 57 f.
[4] MWO, p. 64.
[5] AKV, p. 179.
[6] AKV, p. 240.

minology would enable Lewis to formulate the central doctrines of his theory of knowledge.

A similar point can be made with respect to what I have called 'the phenomenological objection' to Lewis' doctrine of the given. In Chapter V of *Mind and the World-Order*, Lewis describes sense experience in much the same way that it was described by the British Empiricists, and, more recently, by Wundt, Titchener, and the 'structuralist' or 'introspectionist' school of psychology. He seems to think, for example, that if we examine our sense experience when we see a penny that is held obliquely to the line of vision, we shall discover that we are ordinarily aware of an elliptical sensum, and he seems to hold that a visual presentation of an apple can only be characterized by adjectives of shape and color—adjectives such as 'round' and 'ruddy'. (An adjective of taste, like 'sweet', would only be applicable to a gustatory sensation—or, in its objective sense, to something like the apple itself, which transcends the given.) These views about sense experience are characteristic of the 'sensory core' theory of perception which has been criticized by James, Royce, Husserl, the Gestalt psychologists, and others, on the ground that it is based on the fallacy of reading into ordinary perceptual experience (in Royce's words) "a more sophisticated state of mind which the psychologist, by his devices for analysis, has substituted for the original and naive consciousness."[7] These philosophers and psychologists have argued, in effect, that we do not *discover* the elliptical appearance of the penny by analysis of ordinary perception, but rather *create* it by adopting a special attitude—an aesthetic attitude, a skeptical attitude, a psychologist's attitude, or whatever we may wish to call it. What is actually *given* in ordinary sense experience has a considerable 'constancy' under varying conditions of observation and is not just a color patch or a sound or an odor but something more aptly described as a 'whole object' with characteristics not restricted to those that we ordinarily associate with any one sense modality. And this argument, when fully developed, leads finally to the conclusion that no limitations can be placed on the adjectives which may correctly be applied to a sense experience: an apple may look sweet, and juicy, and heavy, and perhaps even dangerous or forbidden, in exactly the same phenomenological (noninterpretive) sense in which it may look ruddy.

Interesting and important as this phenomenological issue may be, however, it has very little bearing on the central doctrines of Lewis'

---

7 Josiah Royce, *Outlines of Psychology* (New York: The Macmillan Co., 1903), pp. 109-110.

theory of knowledge. Even if this Gestalt theory is correct, it should not be allowed to obscure the distinction between sensing and perceiving. And this distinction is all that Lewis requires in order to identify the given in the way which is essential for his theory of knowledge. However we may describe the look of an apple, to assert that an apple *looks* sweet to me (in a phenomenological, 'noninterpretive', sense of 'looks') is still not to assert or imply either that it *is* sweet or that I take it to be sweet. If we choose to say, therefore, with some of the Gestalt psychologists, that what is given in visual perception is a 'whole apple', characterized by sweetness as well as ruddiness, we shall have to introduce some special terminology in order to preserve the distinction between sensing and perceiving. We shall have to say, for example, that this 'whole apple' is a 'phenomenal' or 'sensible' or 'ostensible' object, and not to be confused with the 'real' object—this latter being something which may be sour although the ostensible apple is sweet, which may have worms in it although the ostensible apple does not, and which, assuming that Berkeley is mistaken, is not dependent on consciousness for its existence. In this special terminology the ostensible apple would be the given, and the judgments we make about the real apple (e.g., that despite its ostensible sweetness and perfection it is quite possibly sour and wormy) would be part of what Lewis calls our 'interpretation' of the given.

The issue at stake here, to speak in more general terms, is an issue concerning the internal character of sense experience, and thus has no direct bearing on epistemological questions about the relationship between sense experience and other things. The Gestalt phenomenology of sense experience is compatible with causal realism, subjectivism, phenomenalism, and with every other theory about the epistemic relationship between sense experience and the external world.[8] And the role of the sensory core theory in Lewis' writings is so limited that he could adapt his philosophy to the Gestalt phenomenology, if he wished, by changing only a very few passages. He would have to alter or delete the few sentences in *Mind and the World-Order* in which he attempts to characterize what is given when we look at a penny, an apple, etc. He could no longer maintain, furthermore, that the character of the given is unaffected by changes in interests and attitudes, and that the infant, the savage, and the philosopher will therefore all have the same sense experience when they look at a fountain pen.[9] But there is

8 For a more complete discussion of the philosophical implications of the Gestalt phenomenology, see Part II of my "Sense-data and the Percept Theory," *Mind* (January, 1950), 35-56.

9 MWO, p. 50.

nothing in Lewis' epistemology which implies that our knowledge of a 'common world' depends on the existence of such a common sensory core in our perceptual experience; in fact Lewis argues at length, in connection with a related issue, that for knowledge of a common world it is sufficient that there be a common *pattern* or *structure* of sense experience among human beings.[10]

It should not be overlooked, finally, that in his later book, *An Analysis of Knowledge and Valuation,* Lewis tends to characterize the given in a much more abstract and noncommittal way; and the colloquial idioms which he approves for reporting the qualitative content of sense experience (e.g., "I seem to see a doorknob") are in themselves entirely neutral with respect to the phenomenological issue.

Let us now turn to the third, or 'epistemological' objection to Lewis' doctrine of the given. What has been said about the ontological and phenomenological objections is sufficient, I think, to show that these objections, even if valid, would not affect the essential structure of Lewis' philosophy. But the case is very different when we come to evaluate Lewis' assertion, in the passage quoted at the beginning of this essay, that "apprehensions of the given are characterized by certainty." For without such sense certainties, Lewis adds, "there could be no perceptual knowledge, nor any empirical knowledge at all"; and this conviction is basic not only to Lewis' theory of probability and his theory of terminating judgments, but also to his conception of the purpose and methodology of a theory of empirical knowledge.

The epistemological objection to Lewis' doctrine of the given, as construed here, is actually a combination of several separable objections which can be raised to Lewis' views about certainty. One might variously argue 1) that *no* apprehensions of empirical fact are certain, or 2) that apprehensions of the given are not *uniquely* certain because, contrary to Lewis' theory, some judgments about objective reality are equally certain, or 3) that Lewis fails to define the relevant senses of 'apprehension' and 'certain' precisely enough to provide us with a clear-cut issue, or 4) that even if apprehensions of the given are certain, this certainty is not so important that without it "there could be no perceptual knowledge, nor any empirical knowledge at all." To deal satisfactorily with the fourth of these objections we should have to exceed the proper limits of this essay in order to evaluate Lewis' theory of knowledge as a whole. But none of the other three objections will be excluded if we attempt to answer the following question: Does Lewis

10 MWO, Chap. IV (summarized pp. 115 f).

succeed in showing that there is some sense of 'certain' in which apprehensions of the given are certain and judgments about the external world are not? The answer to this question will depend on what Lewis means by 'apprehension' and 'certain'. Let us first consider the term 'apprehension'.

When a policeman apprehends a criminal he seizes or lays hold of the criminal by physical means; and there is an analogous psychological sense of the word in which to apprehend a sensory presentation is simply to lay hold of it with the mind, i.e., to become conscious of it, or, in a word, to *experience* it. But this cannot be the sense in which Lewis uses the word 'apprehension', for it would be meaningless to say that the mere *experiencing* of sensory qualities is either certain or uncertain. The terms 'certain' and 'uncertain', in the sense in which they are relevant to epistemology, are applicable only to beliefs or judgments, or else, derivatively, to the statements in which beliefs or judgments are expressed. What is certain or uncertain is never my experiencing of (say) a loud noise, but something 'judgmental' or 'propositional', e.g., *that* I am experiencing a loud noise. When Lewis says, therefore, that apprehensions of the given are certain, we may assume that 'apprehension' is to be understood in a judgmental sense, so that what is said to be certain is my apprehension *that* such and such is the case (e.g., *that* I seem to see a doorknob).

This conclusion, I hasten to admit, seems to stand in direct contradiction to Lewis' categorical statement that "apprehensions of the given . . . are not judgments."[11] We may infer from the context, however, that this statement is a corollary of the statement which immediately follows it in the text, namely, that apprehensions of the given "are not here classed as knowledge, because they are not subject to any possible error." This latter statement, as Lewis carefully explains, represents a terminological distinction which he introduces in order to emphasize the fact that apprehensions of the given differ in two respects from what we ordinarily think of as knowledge: 1) They do not refer beyond the given experience, and 2) they do not stand in contrast with some possible kind of error.[12] And it seems clear that Lewis' distinction between apprehensions and judgments must be interpreted in the same innocuous way; for unless those apprehensions of the given which Lewis calls certain are judgmental—in the sense that they are apprehensions *that*, as opposed to mere apprehensions *of*—they could not play the justifying role which Lewis assigns to them in his theory of knowledge. Probable

[11] AKV, p. 183.
[12] AKV, p. 188. See also AKV, p. 375, and MWO, p. 124.

knowledge can be justified, Lewis maintains, only by an argument that starts from empirical premises which are absolutely certain; and the premises of an argument, of course, must be either judgments or statements capable of expressing judgments. In saying that these premises are formulated in 'expressive language', Lewis may intend to suggest that they express the given; but we could just as well think of them as expressing *judgments about* the given. What, we may now ask, does Lewis mean when he says that these judgments are certain?

It is quite possible, of course, to use expressive language, either intentionally or unintentionally, in such a way that we produce in other people a false belief about the character of our sense experience; and at some future time we may even be misled ourselves by the words in which we now record our own present sense experience. But errors resulting from such uses or misuses of language are irrelevant to the issue of certainty, as Lewis conceives it, except to the extent that someone might conceivably argue that they reflect errors or confusions in the judgment itself. Consequently, although it is convenient to employ Lewis' terminology and to discuss the issue of certainty as an issue concerning expressive *statements*, it should always be kept in mind that we are concerned ultimately with certainty as a property of psychological states of one particular kind, namely judgments.

There is nothing in Lewis' writings, so far as I can determine, which is obviously intended to be a formal definition of the term 'certain'. In arguing for the certainty of expressive statements, however, Lewis says a good deal about the *differences* between expressive statements and statements of objective fact; and Lewis would no doubt consider some of these differences to be definitive of the distinction between certainty and uncertainty. Let us examine them, therefore, one by one.

When Lewis wishes to contrast the certainty of expressive statements with the uncertainty of objective statements, he sometimes says that our direct judgments about sense experience *cannot be mistaken.* "One cannot be mistaken," he asserts, "about the content of an immediate awareness."[13] And again: "Apprehension of the presented quale, being immediate, stands in no need of verification; it is impossible to be mistaken about it."[14] This fact, indeed, will even provide us with a criterion for identifying the given element in perception. "Subtract," Lewis says, "in what we say that we see, or hear, or otherwise learn from direct experience, *all that conceivably could be mistaken*; the remainder is the

13 MWO, p. 131.
14 MWO, p. 125. See also AKV, p. 188.

given content of the experience inducing this belief."[15] Statements of this kind suggest what may seem to be a relatively simple answer to our question: they suggest that to say that our judgments about sense experience are certain, is simply to say that in making these judgments we cannot be mistaken.

This proposal will not help us at all, however, unless we can find a clear explanation of what it means to say that judgments about sense experience 'cannot be mistaken'. If these judgments are to serve as premises for the justification of our empirical beliefs, Lewis must construe them as synthetic. If they were not judgments at all, but ostensive definitions of sensory terms, we might say that they are exempt from error in the trivial sense in which a definition is necessarily exempt from error. If they were analytic judgments we might be able to argue along familiar lines that they are at least exempt from *empirical* error. Since they are synthetic judgments, however, it is necessary to show by other means that it is absurd or self-contradictory to make assertions of the form: "I think I am experiencing such and such a taste (odor, sound, etc.) but I may be mistaken." And prima facie such an assertion is not absurd. Lewis would not deny, I think, that it is possible to make expressive statements *with varying degrees of doubt and conviction*. But how is it possible to be doubtful about the truth of our expressive statements unless we believe, in one familiar use of the words, that we *can* be mistaken? How could we doubt if we thought that error were impossible?

It is surely conceivable, for example, that I should sip an unfamiliar fruit punch and be genuinely in doubt whether it has a slight vinegary taste to me at that moment. Let us suppose, next, that I try a second sip— in the hope, perhaps, that this will provide further evidence on which to base an objective judgment about the recipe followed in making the punch. It is surely conceivable that this time I should still be somewhat doubtful, but strongly inclined, nevertheless, to think that it now does have a slight vinegary taste to me. And finally, after a third sip, I may say: "Yes, this time it definitely does have a slight vinegary taste to me." Each time, of course, I am passing judgment on the content of a different sensory presentation: for present purposes the example is not intended to suggest that it is possible for the later judgments to confirm or disconfirm the earlier judgments. The point is simply that it would be quite appropriate, while savoring the second sip, to assert: "I *think* it now has a slight vinegary taste to me, but I may be mistaken." For at this stage I am no longer so doubtful that I refuse to commit myself at all; but neither am I sufficiently confident so that I can

15 AKV, pp. 182 f.

conscientiously refrain from adding the clause 'but I may be mistaken'. This shows that there is one familiar sense of the words in which we all believe that our expressive statements 'can be mistaken'.

It is possible to maintain, in opposition to this argument, that any doubts we may have when making an expressive statement are doubts resulting from a lack of clarity in our concepts—in the concept, for example, of a vinegary taste. But this position can be defended only by adducing independent evidence to show that we ought not to trust the observations which we make of our own states of conviction; and it is hard to imagine what this evidence might be. There are times when we surely *seem* to have no doubts about the meaning of a phenomenological adjective (say 'vinegary') but seem, nevertheless, to be doubtful whether the characteristic that it designates is actually present in our experience. For present purposes, moreover, I think we are justified in bypassing this issue on the ground that Lewis may be quite willing to concede that judgments about the given may be mistaken in the sense we have been considering. He says, in *Mind and the World-Order*:

All those difficulties which the psychologist encounters in dealing with reports of introspection may be sources of error in any report of the given. It may require careful self-questioning, or questioning by another, to elicit the full and correct account of the given.[16]

There are various ways of interpreting this statement, but it seems to indicate that Lewis does not intend to maintain flatly that judgments about the given are necessarily exempt from error: his point seems to be a more subtle one which can be understood only by considering the context in which he makes the assertion that expressive statements cannot be mistaken.

When we examine the context of this assertion, we find that he makes the assertion in order to emphasize his doctrine that in some important sense, which we have so far not discussed, we cannot confirm or disconfirm our own expressive statements in the way we confirm and disconfirm objective statements. It is clear, for example, that even if Lewis were willing to concede that expressive statements can, in theory, be *false*, he would insist, nevertheless, that in some important sense they are not *falsifiable*. This doctrine seems to be the heart of the matter, and if we come to understand it fully, we shall no doubt understand Lewis' use of the term 'certain'. There are, as we shall now see, several different ways in which we might be inclined to interpret it.

16 MWO, p. 62.

Every statement of objective fact, Lewis maintains, is "further test-able and less than theoretically certain." No matter how fully we may have investigated a statement of objective fact (e.g., "A piece of white paper is now before me")

there will be further consequences which must be thus and so if the judgment is true, and not all of these will have been determined. The possibility that such further tests, if made, might have a negative result, cannot be altogether precluded; and this possibility marks the judgment as, at the time in question, not fully verified and less than absolutely certain.[17]

This passage suggests that certainty is to be understood as implying the *impossibility of further tests which might yield negative results*. But it is very difficult to develop this suggestion in a way which is compatible with Lewis' theory of knowledge in general.

The force of the quoted passage depends, in the first place, on our interpretation of the initial proposition. What does it mean to say that the future consequences of an objective judgment "*must* be thus and so if the judgment is true"?[18] One might be inclined to suppose that Lewis intends this to be a *logical* 'must', for he soon proceeds to argue[19] that any objective statement which we can now make, even a statement about the remote past, will logically entail statements about the future. (Each of these statements about the future, as Lewis puts it, will express part of the 'intensional meaning' of statements about the past and the present.)[20] But this pragmatic doctrine is one that most philosophers (including, I should think, most phenomenalists) would deny; and it is hard to believe, in the absence of an explicit declaration to that effect, that Lewis intends to base his theory of the given on his con-troversial pragmatic analysis of the meaning of objective statements. Elsewhere[21] Lewis has made no mention of this pragmatic analysis in defending his view that apprehensions of the given are certain; and the order in which he develops his epistemological position as a whole, sug-gests that he conceives his views on the given to be more fundamental than his pragmatic analysis of objective statements.

However this may be, it is at least quite clear that the argument under consideration becomes relatively uninteresting if we assume that one of its essential premises is Lewis' pragmatic analysis of objective state-

[17] AKV, p. 180.
[18] Italics mine.
[19] AKV, pp. 189 ff.
[20] AKV, pp. 197 ff.
[21] "The Given Element in Empirical Knowledge," *The Philosophical Review*, 61, No. 2 (April, 1952), 168-175. Hereafter cited as "Giv. Elem. Emp. Knowl."

ments. For if by 'certain statement' we mean 'statement which does not logically entail statements about the future', then it follows analytically that any philosopher who admits that there are statements about sense experience which do not entail statements about the future, is ipso facto admitting that these statements are certain. And—a point which is perhaps even more startling—any philosopher who maintains that there are some statements about the past which do not logically entail statements about the future, is ipso facto maintaining that *these* statements, however inadequate the evidence for them may be, are necessarily certain. Surely these consequences are sufficient proof that to interpret the term 'certain' in this way can only frustrate a serious attempt to deal with the issues which philosophers have traditionally associated with that term.

The alternative, and a very reasonable one, is to assume that the 'future consequences' of a judgment may be understood to include all consequences of the judgment which are evidentially relevant to the judgment. In any particular case some of these consequences might be logical consequences (deducible from the judgment itself) but others might be 'natural' or 'causal' consequences (deducible from the judgment only in conjunction with laws of nature). And to say that the future consequences "must be thus and so if the judgment is true" would be to use the word 'must' noncommittally as synonymous with the disjunction 'logically must or naturally must'. This interpretation of the argument strengthens it tremendously in one respect, for unless we accept a radical form of indeterminism it is hard to deny that every objective judgment, even a judgment about the remote past, has future causal consequences which would in theory constitute evidence for it.

Unfortunately, however, we are now faced with a dilemma; for if we interpret Lewis' argument in this way, it clearly fails to show that there is some sense of 'certain' in which expressive statements are certain and objective statements are not. Every sensory presentation is an event belonging to the causal nexus of the natural world; and as such, like any other event, it has future natural consequences which would in theory constitute evidence for its occurrence. Indeed, if this were not so— if sensory presentations were not lawfully related to one another, to their physical stimuli, and, ultimately, to physical and psychological events in general—the given could not possibly perform its epistemic function as clue, evidence, and justification for judgments about objective reality. If, for example, my memory tomorrow should be hazy in certain respects, and I were in doubt at that time whether I have today had the sensory experience of seeming to taste pineapple juice, I could surely think of tests and consequences which would be relevant to a rational decision. An empty can of pineapple juice, reports from my associates about what I said yesterday, memories recaptured by retracing yesterday's activities, all of these could be evidentially relevant and hence could qualify as future natural consequences of my seeming to taste pineapple juice today.

There are, of course, some familiar logical issues which arise from the fact that the expressive statement 'I seem to taste pineapple juice now' contains two egocentric terms, 'I' and 'now'. It might be maintained, for example, that the statement that I am able to test tomorrow is some different statement such as 'I seemed to taste pineapple juice about 10 A.M. yesterday'—different, notably, because it contains terms like 'yesterday' and '10 A.M.' which refer to physical time. For present purposes, however, since we are looking for features that serve to distinguish expressive statements from objective statements, it is unnecessary to discuss the logic of egocentric terms. It is enough to observe that some of the statements which Lewis would classify as objective —statements such as 'I am (actually) tasting pineapple juice now' and 'I am drinking pineapple juice now'—also contain the same two egocentric terms. If these objective statements are testable in the future, despite their egocentric terms, so also is the expressive statement. Normally, indeed, since it is usually the case that I *am* tasting (or even drinking) pineapple juice whenever I *seem* to taste pineapple juice, the testable natural consequences of the expressive statement would include the testable consequences of these corresponding objective statements.

We are forced to conclude, therefore, that Lewis is mistaken if he intends to say that the certainty of expressive statements consists in, or is a result of, the fact that they have no consequences testable in the future. There is no logical contradiction, indeed, in admitting to ourselves, at the very moment of uttering an expressive statement, and even of judging it to be certain, that at some future time, on the basis of the evidence then available to us, we may be fully justified in denying that statement. In this respect we seem to understand by 'certainty', as we do by 'probability', a characteristic which is relative to the available evidence. All of this is compatible with Lewis' theory of probability and is suggested by his doctrine that all knowledge has its ground in a continually changing 'epistemological present'.[22]

I am inclined to think, however, that the passage which we have been considering does not give an entirely accurate picture of Lewis' position. There are other ways of interpreting his use of the term 'certain', and some of these are suggested by a statement that immediately precedes this passage. Any test of an objective judgment, Lewis asserts, "constitutes a partial verification of the judgment only; never one which is absolutely decisive and theoretically complete."[23] This suggests the possibility that the certainty of an expressive statement consists in the fact that its verification, unlike that of an objective statement, may be *decisive* and *complete*. Let us consider these two adjectives separately, beginning with 'complete'. I shall save the other for discussion at the very end of this essay.

In one sense of the word 'complete', to say that the verification of a statement is complete is to imply that new evidence for the statement will never become available because the existing evidence is exhaustive. In this sense, as we have just seen, the verification of an expressive statement is *not* complete: if every objective statement has an inexhaustible crop of future consequences which are evidentially relevant, so does every expressive statement. In another sense of the word, however, to say that the verification of a statement is complete would imply, perhaps more conservatively, that the *weight* of the favorable evidence (or, perhaps better, the *degree* to which the statement is justified) cannot be increased by obtaining new evidence. In this sense, it might be argued, the verification of an expressive statement is complete at the moment the statement is made, whereas the verification of an objective statement is never complete. *After* the expressive statement has been made, as we have seen, new evidence can be accumulated for it, as for an objective statement, by observing its 'natural consequences'; and such new evidence, it may be said, together with memory and induction, can never justify the expressive statement with more than high probability. But the fact remains, it can be argued, that the verification of an expressive statement is complete at least for the moment when it is made; and perhaps this is just what is meant by saying that the expressive statement is *certain* at that moment.

I think that the most obvious objection to this proposal, as an interpretation of Lewis' position, is the fact that there are some objective statements which one might also declare to be certain in this sense. Consider, for example, a simple statement like 'This is a spoon'. If I hold a spoon in my hands, twist and turn it in every conceivable way, place it in my mouth, tap it on a table, and repeat these and other experiments for five minutes (or five hours, if this makes the case stronger) it is not unreasonable to maintain that at some point the weight of the evidence for the statement will reach an upper limit and thus be complete in the sense under consideration, i.e., the degree to which the

23 AKV, p. 180.

statement is justified could not be increased by obtaining new evidence. After this critical point has been reached, it might be argued, further experimentation can yield new evidence only at the expense of a compensating loss in the reliability of my memory of the earlier experiments. This argument is very persuasive, and there is no possible way, so far as I can see, to refute it. We have no assurance, therefore, that completeness of verification, in the sense under consideration, provides an adequate criterion for distinguishing expressive statements from objective statements. And unless we were assured of this, we could scarcely be content to use it as the basis of a theory of knowledge.

There is still a third sense in which we might want to say that the verification of an expressive statement can be complete but the verification of an objective statement cannot. Without making any reference to the possibility of acquiring additional evidence, or to the effect of such additional evidence, we might mean simply that our warrant or justification for an expressive statement, at the moment we make it, is *as great* as the justification for any statement ever can be, and *greater* than the justification for an objective statement ever can be. This proposal, however, is as dubious as the previous one and thus equally unacceptable as a premise for the theory of knowledge. Once we have admitted that expressive statements, like objective statements, may be mistaken, it is by no means clear that *every* expressive statement (when we make it) is better justified than *any* objective statement ever can be. How convinced do we feel, for example, that our justification for an expressive statement about the taste of punch ('I experience a vinegary taste') is greater at the time we make it than our justification for the statement 'This is a spoon' would be, under the conditions described above, at some other time?

It should be observed, furthermore, that certainty, if defined in these quantitative terms, cannot be distinguished from a practical limit of *probability*. Someone who held that expressive statements are as probable as human limitations permit any statement to be, and that objective statements never quite reach this level, could also say that only expressive statements are completely verified in the sense we are now considering. And this fact alone would be a sufficient reason for denying that a certain statement, as Lewis conceives it, is simply a statement which is completely verified in this sense. It is a basic doctrine of Lewis' philosophy that unless some empirical statements are certain, no other statements can be probable. For it is a mistake, he says, to suppose "that if enough probabilities can be got to lean against one another they can all be made to stand up."[24] And this implies that there is, so to speak, a qualitative epistemic difference between a statement that is certain and one that is highly probable. It does not mean merely that some empirical statements must be as probable as possible in order for other empirical statements to be less probable. Perhaps Lewis might agree to the proposition that a statement which is certain is, in a quantitative sense, more justified than any statement which is merely probable (although this proposition, as we have just seen, is a very dubious one if our statement 'This is a spoon' is an example of the 'merely probable'.) But his arguments suggest that there is some other, more fundamental, characteristic which distinguishes the certain from the merely probable—some characteristic which might *explain* the fact (if it is a fact) that objective statements are never as well warranted or justified as expressive statements— some characteristic, at least, which explains why no statement can be probable unless other statements are certain. It is this characteristic which we must try to identify if we are to uncover the heart of Lewis' doctrine.

One characteristic of expressive statements that might seem to meet this requirement is suggested by a passage in Lewis' paper entitled "The Given Element in Empirical Knowledge."[25] Lewis contends in this passage that it would be wrong to deny an expressive statement (in this case called 'protocol statement') because we find difficulty in reconciling it with statements made at a later time. The examples he uses, and the fact that he denies variously that we should 'alter', 'correct', or 'eliminate' expressive statements, suggests that he is here conceiving the problem of ordering knowledge on analogy with a game of cards: we are provided with cards representing past and present expressive statements, and cards representing objective statements, and we are required to order them, in accordance with the rules of evidence, but without casting out any of the expressive cards.

Lewis would be the first to grant, of course, in view of his doctrine that knowledge has its ground in a continually changing 'epistemological present', that this is an idealized and oversimplified way of representing the problem. In the game of knowledge, as we play it in real life, our task is complicated by the fact that it is always an open question whether we have dealt ourselves the right expressive cards—i.e., whether in the past we did in fact make all the expressive statements which we seem to remember making. In real life we are sometimes justified in altering, correcting or eliminating an expressive card because it is probable, in

24 "Giv. Elem. Emp. Knowl.," p. 173.
25 "Giv. Elem. Emp. Knowl.," pp. 173-74

the light of the total evidence, that we have been mistaken in thinking that we made a particular expressive statement.

Despite the fact that this card game analogy oversimplifies the epistemological issues, however, it does show that there are two ways of interpreting a philosopher who asserts that we shall never be justified in denying an expressive statement on the basis of future evidence. For the verb 'to deny', and other verbs closely related to it, are ambiguous in a subtle way. To deny an expressive statement, in one sense of the words, is simply to accept another statement which contradicts it; in this sense, as we have seen, there can be no doubt that we are sometimes justified in denying an expressive statement which we have previously made. In another sense of the word, however—a sense better rendered, perhaps, by words like 'retract' and 'recant'—to deny one of my past statements is to contradict it *knowing that I have previously affirmed it.* Similarly, when we speak of 'correcting' or 'eliminating' a past error, we may also intend to imply a self-conscious retraction of some past judgment. Taking these facts into account, it is possible to formulate a counterfactual analysis of certainty which Lewis might be inclined to accept.

An expressive statement, we might say, is certain in this sense: if at any future time I were justified in believing that in the past I did in fact make the expressive statement, I should at that future time be justified in accepting the statement no matter what the contrary evidence might be. This analysis, it should be emphasized, does not imply that there cannot *be* any future evidence which will count against an expressive statement if that statement is certain. For future evidence against my expressive statement can always be construed as evidence that I did not make the statement; and if I am not justified in believing that I made the statement, there is nothing in the analysis to imply that I am obliged to believe that the statement is true. But the analysis does imply that if expressive statements are certain, I can never be justified in believing both (1) that I have made a particular expressive statement, and (2) that this expressive statement is false. It also follows that there are in theory two ways in which an expressive statement can be justified if it is conceived as a statement which might have been made by a particular person $A$ at a past time $t$. Without making any reference to what $A$ actually believed or said about his sense experience at $t$, we might be able to show by inductive arguments that the statement is probably a correct description of $A$'s experience at $t$. Or we might simply show, perhaps more easily, that in fact $A$ made the judgment or statement at time $t$. This would be enough, if expressive judgments are certain in the sense under consideration, to insure that the judgment is warranted—i.e., that we are justified in accepting it as true.

This analysis, I believe, does allow us to say that expressive statements are certain and that objective statements are not. For it seems clear, on the one hand, that any grounds we may have for denying a past expressive statement are also grounds, and equally good grounds, for denying that we made that particular expressive statement. And it also seems clear, on the other hand, that the same cannot be said with respect to objective statements: we may know that we have made a particular objective statement and yet be fully justified in deciding that the statement is false. Lewis seems to be right, therefore, if he intends to say that expressive statements, but not objective statements, are certain in this sense. There is, to be sure, no way to *prove* that expressive statements are certain in this sense. We are dealing here with an ultimate principle of justification which cannot be justified without circularity. But if we reflect we shall find, I believe, that the principle of justification embodied in this definition of certainty is a principle that we do in fact accept.

It seems doubtful, however, that certainty, when defined in this way, can have the epistemic implications that make the concept of certainty important in Lewis' theory of knowledge. To get to the bottom of this matter would require us, as I have previously observed, to exceed the proper limits of this essay; but it may be useful to comment on the nature of the difficulty that confronts us. Certainty, as Lewis conceives it, has these two features among others: (1) it is a characteristic of those judgments which we make about sense experience in what Lewis calls the 'epistemological present', and (2) it qualifies those judgments to serve as ultimate premises from which probable knowledge about the objects of perception can be inferred. The analysis we are considering can reasonably be said to take account of the first of these two features, for this analysis, formulated as it is in a counterfactual statement, allows us to attribute certainty as a dispositional property to our present judgments about sense experience: to say that these judgments are certain in the present, at this very moment, is to say that in the future, after we have made them, it would be irrational to believe that we have made them and yet they are false. But there is no reason to think that this analysis could possibly take account of the second of these two features. For the mere fact that a judgment about present sense experience has this dispositional property called 'certainty', seems to have no bearing at all on the fitness of this judgment to serve right now, in the present, as an ultimate premise for epistemic purposes. And later, of course, if we should want to use or refer to this judgment in the course of an epistemic argument, it will always be an open question, subject to decision by appealing to memory and induction, whether in fact we ever made this judgment: our ultimate premises in the future 'epistemological present' will not include this judgment itself but other judgments from which this one might turn out to be derivable in one way or another. It is possible, to be sure, that this concept of certainty has important epistemic implications which do not meet the eye; but until someone shows us what they are, it is reasonable to assume that we must look elsewhere for a concept that will make Lewis' position defensible.

I shall now propose, by way of conclusion, an analysis of certainty which is suggested by Lewis' remark, previously quoted, that objective statements are "less than absolutely decisive." This analysis is compatible, I think, with Lewis' basic doctrine concerning the given, and might be acceptable to him.

If a philosopher says that the verification of an expressive statement is *decisive,* he might mean merely that the evidence for the statement is sufficient to justify the decision that the statement is true. In this sense, of course, the verification of an objective statement can also be decisive. But to say that the verification of an expressive statement is *absolutely* decisive, suggests a much stronger thesis: it might mean that the statement is justified in such a way that no amount of new negative evidence can count against it to the slightest degree.

Now this thesis, without qualification, is obviously too strong, for there can be no doubt, as we have seen, that new evidence in the future *can* count against an expressive statement *in the future,* i.e., after the experience characterized by the statement no longer exists. To make it plausible, therefore, it must be interpreted to mean that no future evidence can count against an expressive statement at the moment the statement is made. But this, of course, could be construed as a tautology on the ground that the future evidence, being future, does not even exist at the time the expressive statement is made. It is necessary, therefore, to formulate the thesis as a proposition about what would be the case if, perhaps contrary to fact, we knew about the future evidence at the moment of making the expressive statement. Thus we might maintain that the verification of an expressive statement, at the moment we make it, is absolutely decisive (and the statement *certain*) in this sense: even if we were justified at that moment in believing that new evidence in the future would tend to disconfirm it, we should nevertheless not be justified, for that reason and at that moment, in having less confidence in it than otherwise (i.e., less confidence than we should be justified in having if we did *not* know about the future disconfirming evidence).

This relatively complex definition of the term 'certain' allows us to say, I think, that expressive statements are certain at the moment we make them, but objective statements are not. In this case, as in the previous one, a basic principle of justification is embodied in the analysis of certainty, and there is consequently no way to *prove* that expressive statements are certain in the sense defined. But if we reflect we shall find once again, I believe, that we do in fact accept the principle of justification embodied in the analysis. Consider, for example, the objective statement 'This is a spoon', made under the hypothetical circumstances already envisaged. No matter how thoroughly the spoon has been examined, and no matter how completely the statement is justified, it is nevertheless true that we can always think of some possible future events which, if they occur, would *then* count as evidence against our statement. (We might suppose, for example, that the ostensible spoon will seem to turn into a butterfly.) Furthermore—and this is the important point—if we were justified at the moment of making the objective statement, in believing that such an event would occur, we should be justified, for that reason and at that moment, in having less confidence in the statement than otherwise. With respect to the expressive statement 'I seem to taste pineapple juice now', on the contrary, only half of this can be said. It must be admitted, as our earlier discussion has shown, that we can think of possible future events which, if they occur, would *then* count as evidence against this statement. If, for example, I am later told by a reliable witness that I did not drink fruit juice at the time in question, this would be *some* evidence against the statement. But the difference is this: if, at the moment of making the expressive statement, I knew that such negative evidence would be forthcoming, this would not give me the slightest justification, at that moment, for having less confidence in my judgment about the character of my present sense experience. If the truth of an expressive statement seems to be causally incompatible with events that I expect to occur in the future, it is always the future events or the causal laws that must yield, so to speak, to the higher authority of my present judgment about my sense experience. In this sense the expressive statement, unlike the objective statement, is certain.

There are several important observations to be made about the meaning of certainty when interpreted in this way. As it stands, first of all, there is nothing in the analysis to insure that a statement which is certain is a statement that we are justified in believing: the analysis merely stipulates that the credibility of a statement which is certain would not be less because of any knowledge that we might conceivably have about the future. It will bring the analysis closer to ordinary usage if we add a clause to rectify this omission: a statement is certain, we may say, if and only if (1) we are justified in believing it, and (2) its credibility would not be less because of any knowledge which we might conceivably have about the future. We can even say, if we wish, that for a statement to be certain we must be *completely* justified in believing it—in the third and last sense of 'completely' discussed above. This qualification would insure that no statement which is merely probable can be better justified than a statement which is certain; but it also implies that all statements which are certain are equally well justified. If there is any reasonable doubt, therefore, that all expressive statements, at the moment we make them, are equally well justified, it would obviously be best, for purposes like those of Lewis, to omit this qualification. Otherwise, so far as I can see, our decision on this point will make no significant difference.

It should be observed, in the second place, that there is no inconsistency in asserting that expressive statements, although certain in the sense we have defined, may nevertheless be mistaken. The essential point in this connection, is that the doubts which we may have at a given moment about the character of our present sense experience—about the presence of the vinegary taste, for example—cannot at that moment be resolved in a rational way by appealing to anything that we might conceivably know about the future. It is possible to make a mistake in judging the character of our sense experience; but in the "epistemological present," as Lewis calls it, there simply is no further knowledge which, if we had it, could help to prevent us from making a mistake. Another way to express this fact is to say that such mistakes are incorrigible, even in theory, at the time they are made. But the proposition that we may be incorrigibly mistaken is entirely compatible with the proposition that our judgments are completely justified: a false statement, of course, if we do not know that it is false, may be eminently credible.

It should be observed, in the third place, that there is also no inconsistency in asserting that objective statements, although they can never be certain in this sense, are sometimes so well verified at a given moment that no additional knowledge of future events could justify their denial at that moment. It would not be unreasonable, indeed, to maintain that the objective statement 'This is a spoon', when 'completely' verified in the manner already envisioned, is so thoroughly justified that even the foreknowledge that it will soon seem to turn into a butterfly would not be sufficient reason for denying that it is now a real spoon. For there are, of course, many consistent ways of explaining such an apparent metamorphosis without giving up the original 'hypothesis'. But foreknowledge of such an impending experience is at least some reason for having *less confidence* in the original hypothesis: it helps to support alternative hypotheses by increasing the probability, at least to a slight degree, that I have been deluded in taking the object in my hand to be a spoon. This is the fact which obliges us to say that an objective statement is not certain in the sense we are now considering.

It should be observed, finally, that this proposed definition of the term 'certain' could be generalized in two ways without altering the denotation of the term. Instead of referring only to new future evidence, it could be generalized to refer to all additional evidence which would count against the statement at any other time. And it could be further generalized by removing the restriction imposed by the word 'against' to allow for positive as well as negative evidence. Combining these two changes, we could say that an expressive statement, at the moment we make it, is certain in this sense: (1) we are justified (or completely justified) in believing it; and (2) even if we were justified at that moment in believing that there is, has been, or will be additional evidence which would count for or against it at some other time, we should nevertheless not be justified, for that reason and at that moment, in having either more or less confidence in it than otherwise.

This analysis of certainty, or the less generalized version of it, would allow Lewis to say that expressive statements are certain although objective statements are not; and even though Lewis himself does not explicitly formulate such an analysis, it nevertheless does embody a number of distinctions that he makes in the course of the arguments we have considered. If this is what Lewis means by certainty, he is right at least in his contention that expressive statements are certain and objective statements are not. And if there is some important respect in which expressive statements are evidentially ultimate—or, at least, more fundamental than objective statements—then Lewis is also justified in maintaining that empirical knowledge is, in that respect, ultimately based on what he calls 'sense certainties'. It is a much larger issue, however, whether it is true, as Lewis asserts, that "without such sense certainties there could be no perceptual knowledge, nor any empirical knowledge at all." This is an issue that can only be treated, as Lewis himself treats it, in the context of a general discussion of the nature of evidence and probability.

RODERICK FIRTH

DEPARTMENT OF PHILOSOPHY
HARVARD UNIVERSITY

## 13

*Arthur Pap*

# LEWIS ON CONTRARY-TO-FACT CONDITIONALS

L EWIS began to be concerned about the meaning of 'implication', of 'if—then', when as a young man he studied *Principia Mathematica* and found it a philosophically unsatisfactory system of logic. He found it philosophically unsatisfactory because the only kind of implication that is symbolically represented in that system is material implication, and material implication is obviously not the relation one asserts to hold between $p$ and $q$ when one says that $q$ is a logical consequence of $p$. Accordingly Lewis constructed a system of 'strict implication' in which the relation of logical consequence is directly represented by a special symbol, the hook ($\dashv$). In order, for example, to assert in PMese (to borrow Wilfrid Sellars' abbreviation for "the language of *Principia Mathematica*") that $q$ is a logical consequence of the conjunction $p \cdot (p \supset q)$,[1] one must ascend to the metalanguage and there declare $(p \cdot (p \supset q)) \supset q$ a theorem (a brief symbolic expression of such an assertion is the assertion sign $\vdash$, prefixed to the theorems). In Lewis' system one can express this idea directly in the object language, by means of the formula: $(p \cdot (p \supset q)) \dashv q$. When we say that $q$ is a logical consequence of $p$, Lewis pointed out correctly, we mean to say that it is *impossible* for $p$ to be true while $q$ is false; but all that is expressed by a material implication is that *it is not the case* that the antecedent is true while the consequent is false.

Partly due to the influence of Lewis' own pioneer work in modal logic, the use of modal operators to supplement the truth-functional connectives of *Principia Mathematica* and other extensional systems of logic has become perfectly respectable among most formal logicians—in spite of the misgivings of such staunch extensionalists as Quine, Nelson Goodman, and Gustav Bergmann. But it had to be recognized sooner or later that even with the help of the logic of strict implication there is no satisfactory way of analyzing the meaning of 'if—then' in

[1] Lest those of my readers who are pedantical semanticists accuse me of a sloppy confusion of *use* and *mention* of symbols, I hasten to announce that I frequently use symbols autonymously, as names of themselves, just in order to avoid a clumsy and untidy looking proliferation of quotes.

*causal* implications, such as 'if you swallow arsenic, you will be poisoned'. A particularly clear and convincing statement of this limitation of logical theory is contained in Chapter VIII ("Terminating Judgments and Objective Beliefs") of Lewis' *An Analysis of Knowledge and Valuation*. "If I should jump from a second story window, I should hurt myself." Clearly this is not a material implication. For I assert it as true—indeed, my belief in its truth is responsible for my *making* it 'contrary to fact'; yet, the material implication 'I jump from a second story window at $t \supset$ I feel better at $t+dt$' is equally true if the antecedent is false. In short, *every* contrary-to-fact conditional whatsoever would be true just by virtue of being contrary-to-fact, if such statements were construed as material implications. For equally obvious reasons, such conditionals about causal connections cannot be interpreted as strict implications, for strict implications can be established a priori by "reflection on meanings," whereas the statements in question are *factual*. Lewis considers a third possibility: perhaps such conditionals can be construed as what Russell calls *formal implications?*

A formal implication, unlike a material implication, relates propositional functions, not propositions: $(x)(Fx \supset Gx)$. As Russell expressly noted, a formal implication is a generalized material implication. It is really an indefinite conjunction of material implications: $(Fa \supset Ga) \cdot (Fb \supset Gb) \ldots (Fn \supset Gn)$, where $a,b \ldots n$ are the values of the variable $x$. Now, a philosopher who holds that the extensional language structure of *Principia Mathematica* is ideal for purposes of analysis of scientific language will, indeed, have to attempt an analysis of contrary-to-fact conditionals (henceforth abbreviated: CF-conditionals) by means of formal implications. He will be led to such an analysis especially if he follows the precept of early logical positivism: discover the meaning of a factual statement by reflecting on the method of its verification! Well, what are one's grounds for asserting a CF-conditional like 'If I were to jump from a second story window, I should get hurt'? Clearly the fact that other people who did jump from second story windows got hurt, or, if one does not know of any people having jumped from second story windows, that people who fell to the ground from great heights got hurt. This suggests the following first approximation to an extensional analysis of 'if $a$ were $F$ (which it is not), then $a$ would be $G$':

$$\sim Fa \cdot (\exists x)(Fx) \cdot (x)(Fx \supset Gx) \qquad A_1$$

But 'if $a$ were $F$, then $a$ would be $G$' really makes the same positive assertion of a causal connection whether or not the antecedent be presupposed to be false. Therefore the first conjunct may as well be dropped:

$$(\exists x) Fx \cdot (x)(Fx \supset Gx) \qquad A_2$$

For convenience, and following Lewis' own notation, let us introduce the arrow to represent the sort of natural, or causal connection between events which is asserted by a CF-conditional. Then our present problem is whether $A_2$ is acceptable as an analysis of $Fa{\rightarrow}Ga$. What speaks for $A_2$ is that it satisfies the following important adequacy condition: $Fx{\rightarrow}Gx$ should be so analyzed that it is incompatible with $Fx{\rightarrow}Hx$ if $Hx$ is incompatible with $Gx$ (at least provided $Fx$ is self-consistent). Let us interpret '$Fx$' as '$x$ jumps from a second story window at $t$' (where $t$ is an arbitrary but specific time), and '$Gx$' as '$x$ gets hurt at $t+dt$', and '$Hx$' as '$x$ feels better at $t+dt$'. Allowing ourselves, for the sake of the argument, to ignore those numerous cases where people jumped from second story windows to safety, landing in a net held out by firemen, we may suppose that $(x)(Fx \supset Gx)$ has been confirmed and has not been disconfirmed. But any instance which confirms this formal implication in the sense that it has both properties $F$ and $G$, disconfirms $(x)(Fx \supset Hx)$ if $H$ is incompatible with $G$. In other words, if $G$ is incompatible with $H$, then the two formal implications in question cannot both be true *unless* $F$ is an empty property; and if $F$ is empty, then according to $A_2$ both of the intuitively incompatible CF-conditionals are false, not true.

Yet, $A_2$ is not an acceptable analysis. To see this, just suppose that during the entire history of mankind nobody ever jumped from any second story window. Would we not say that even so $Fa{\rightarrow}Ga$ is true, or at any rate the more qualified conditional 'if I jumped from a second story window and landed on the hard pavement, then I should get hurt', whereas 'if I jumped from a second story window and landed on the hard pavement, I would feel better and instantly recover from all my ailments' is false? But according to $A_2$ one of these conditionals is as false as the other on the assumption made. The mistake that must be corrected is obviously this: the formal implication which according to the lover of PMese is implicitly asserted when one asserts a singular CF-conditional need not contain the same antecedent and consequent predicates $F$ and $G$. This was recognized above, when it was stated that possibly the ground on which one affirms $Fa{\rightarrow}Ga$ is just that people who fell from great heights, not necessarily from second story windows, got hurt. The antecedent predicate of the formal implication that has been instantially confirmed may be one of greater extension than $F$. To add an illustration: the antecedent of 'if this piece of sugar were dropped into the tea, it would dissolve' contains redundant information, in the sense that the effect, dissolving, does not depend on those specific traits of sugar that distinguish it from other substances that likewise dissolve in tea. Therefore one could have grounds for asserting this CF-conditional even if no sugar were ever dropped into tea or indeed into any liquid. Fortified by this reflection, the extensionalist may try once more, coming out with a somewhat more complicated analysis:

$$(\exists f) \, ((x) \, (Fx \supset fx) \cdot (\exists x)fx \cdot (x) \, (fx \supset Gx)) \qquad\qquad A_3$$

The obvious fault of $A_3$, however, is that it presupposes that $F$, the antecedent predicate in the singular CF-conditional, expresses a causally *sufficient* condition, though possibly one containing redundant elements, for $G$. Whereas it happens just as often that the antecedent of a confidently asserted CF-conditional expresses only a *necessary* condition. 'If you had arrived at the station five minutes earlier, you would not have missed the train': clearly that statement presupposes that the train did not leave before a specified time, which is an equally necessary condition for catching it than arriving at the station platform not later than that specified time. If one concentrates on this aspect of singular CF-conditionals, one may be tempted by an entirely different analysis in terms of formal implication:

$$(\exists f) \, ((\exists x) \, (Fx \cdot fx) \cdot (x) \, (Fx \cdot fx \supset Gx)) \qquad\qquad A_4$$

$A_4$ allows for the special case that $F$ is by itself sufficient for $G$, since $F$ is a value of the predicate variable $f$. But now the existential clause makes trouble. For, as we have already seen, one may have grounds for asserting a singular CF-conditional though its antecedent predicate $F$ is entirely empty; and if $F$ is empty, then $F \cdot f$ is empty. There is, on the other hand, no way of producing a satisfactory extensional analysans devoid of existential clause, because one must counteract the 'paradoxical' feature of formal implications that they are true, regardless of the meaning of the consequent predicate, provided the antecedent predicate is empty.[2]

No doubt, $A_1 - A_4$ do not exhaust the possibilities that are open to an ingenious extensionalist. But let us turn now to Lewis' fundamental reasons for denying that 'real connections', such as are asserted by practically important CF-conditionals, can be expressed by formal implications. Lewis points out correctly that a synthetic formal implication refers only to actual cases. And to say that there is, in actuality, no case of $F$ which is not a case of $G$ is not to say anything about what *would* happen if such and such *were* the case. From 'all freely falling bodies fall with constant acceleration', interpreted as a formal implication, one cannot deduce that this body would fall with constant accel-

---

[2] A further difficulty besetting $A_3$ and $A_4$ is that the predicate variable must be so restricted that trivial satisfaction of CF-conditionals is precluded. But this matter has received sufficient attention in the voluminous literature on CF-conditionals.

eration if it were now engaged in a free fall; all that follows is that it is not the case *both* that this body is now falling freely and is not falling with constant acceleration. But while this point will presumably be granted by any extensionalist, Lewis has not shown that it is impossible to construct a, more or less complicated, analysans for CF-conditionals in an extensional language, which is adequate in the sense that the conditions under which one would be justified in asserting a CF-conditional as true, or as probably true, are the same as the conditions under which one would be justified in asserting the corresponding analysans as true, or probably true. Lewis is aware that an extensionalist might defend the adequacy of PMese as a language structure within which causal conditionals are analyzed, by reference to the grounds on which CF-conditionals are actually asserted. He replies[3]—in my transcription —that though one's grounds for asserting $Fa{\rightarrow}Ga$ may consist in numerous instantial confirmations of the formal implication "$(x)$ ($x$ weighs 150 lbs and falls 25 ft $\supset$ $x$ acquires a momentum sufficient to injure a human body upon impact)," the latter "still says nothing as to what would happen if I (weighing 150 pounds) should jump from a second story window (25 feet above the ground)."

Lewis is certainly right in denying that $Fa{\rightarrow}Ga$ is deducible from $(x)(Fx \supset Gx)$; only $Fa \supset Ga$ is deducible. But this is not a conclusive refutation of extensionalism. That it is not, can be clearly shown in connection with the following citation:

At least the objector will admit that on *this* occasion no weight of 150 pounds— whether my body or anything else—drops 25 feet. That being so, the formal implication, "If $x$, weighing 150 pounds, drops 25 feet, it acquires sufficient force to injure a human body" could *still* be true even if it were *false* that if I should now jump out this window I should hurt myself.[4]

More explicitly, what Lewis means to say is that there might be no known counterinstances to the formal implication $(x)(Fx \supset Gx)$ while there might be positive grounds for disbelieving $Fa{\rightarrow}Ga$; and that therefore the grounds for accepting a given formal implication need not be grounds for accepting a corresponding singular CF-conditional, even if the grounds for accepting the formal implication are positive confirmations, not just vacuous confirmations, i.e., failure to find instances of the antecedent predicate. This is perfectly true, and it is easy to show it concretely in terms of the very example Lewis uses: if it is known that the firemen at this moment are holding out a well

3 *An Analysis of Knowledge and Valuation* (La Salle, Ill.: Open Court Publishing Co., 1946), p. 222. Hereafter cited as AKV.
4 AKV, p. 223.

checked net under the window, this is a positive reason for denying the CF-conditional $Fa \rightarrow Ga$. But just because that conditional is *CF*, the supposed fact is no refutation of the corresponding formal implication; the latter can be refuted only by an *actual* case of *F* which is not a case of *G*. Yet, this is no argument against a more sophisticated extensional analysis, say, one that avails itself of a predicate variable: to say that *G* would happen if *F* happened is to say that *there are conditions C* which are now fulfilled and which are such that *F* never happens when *C* is present without being followed by *G* (*C* may be positive or negative conditions). Suppose that we have extensively confirmed the formal implication $(x)(Fx \cdot Cx \supset Gx)$ and also disconfirmed the simpler formal implication $(x)(Fx \supset Gx)$. And suppose that we found the disconfirming cases to be characterized by the absence of *C*. Then, if in a given situation *S* we know *C* to be absent, we have reasons for denying the CF-conditional 'if *F* should happen in *S*, then *G* would follow'.

What I think is strongly suggested by this analysis is that Lewis is right in denying that the *meaning* of a CF-conditional can be expressed in terms of formal implication, though one's *actual grounds* for asserting or denying a CF-conditional can be formulated in extensional language. In order to see that Lewis is right in his denial, though his argument is insufficient, it is important to get convinced that even a more sophisticated extensional analysis in terms of predicate variables will not do. 'If the match were struck, it would light'. Undoubtedly an assertor of such a CF-conditional presupposes that certain other conditions that are causally necessary for the effect, besides the one mentioned by the antecedent, are in fact fulfilled in the situation to which his statement refers: the match is dry, so is the matchbox, enough oxygen is present, etc. It may not seem farfetched, therefore, to propose the following analysis: there are conditions which are fulfilled in the present situation and which are such that whenever a match is struck while they are fulfilled, it lights. The 'conditions' that are mentioned indefinitely by way of existential quantification may be clearly in the speaker's mind or he may have only a confused knowledge of them. The clearer his knowledge of them, the clearer is the proposition he intends to assert and the better his position to support it by empirical evidence. Now, it must be admitted that the *evidence* in terms of which the CF-conditional is to be supported consists in specification of conditions $C_1, C_2 \ldots C_n$ which are (a) fulfilled in the situation referred to by the speaker, (b) such that the formal implication 'any situation in which $C_1, C_2 \ldots C_n$ are fulfilled and in which a change *A* occurs, is a situation in which a change *B* follows' has actually been confirmed and rarely, if ever, disconfirmed. But if the law, whether strictly causal or statistical, whose past confirmations support the belief expressed by the CF-conditional were a Russellian formal implication, then its truth would be entailed by the emptiness of the antecedent predicate. Suppose, then, that the kind of antecedent change which is mentioned by the CF-conditional never occurred at all. It is surely conceivable that no match should ever be struck. Or, with reference to the CF-conditional 'if this object were heated up to $x$ degrees $F$, it would melt', it is conceivable that no object whatever reached the specified temperature at any time. On those suppositions, therefore, both the CF-conditional to be analyzed and a CF-conditional that is intuitively incompatible with it would be true if the law were a formal implication. The desire to satisfy the all important adequacy condition already mentioned,[5] therefore, forces the extensionalist to add as part of his analysans the requirement that the corresponding formal implication be *nonvacuous*. That is the reason why all the four sample analyses, above, contain an existential clause.

It is at this point that the extensionalist's subtle confusion of *meaning* and *evidence* shows up. On any view which is Humean in that it analyzes the concept of 'real connection' of one event with another in terms of the concept of 'constant conjunction', it is a contradiction to assert a CF-conditional $A \rightarrow E$ while denying that there is a law $L$ and conditions $C$ such that the conjunction $A \cdot C \cdot L$ implies $E$ with a high probability. But it is not a contradiction to suppose that $A \rightarrow E$ though $L$ has not been *confirmed* and perhaps never will be confirmed. If no relevant law has been confirmed, one has no ground for asserting a singular CF-conditional, but that is different from saying that one has a reason for denying such a proposition. Yet, inclusion in the analysans of an existential clause, expressing actual instantial confirmation of a relevant law, commits one to just that untenable claim.[6]

On the controversial question of what exactly is the correct analysis of the concept 'law of nature', Lewis has little if anything to say. He does maintain, as we have seen, that a law of nature cannot be expressed by a formal implication; his reason being that laws of nature entail CF-conditionals whereas formal implications do not. He is also clear that laws of nature, being contingent generalizations, cannot be ex-

---

5 AKV, p. 223.

6 I have elaborated this point, in connection with a discussion of disposition concepts, in more detail in the following publications: *Analytische Erkenntnistheorie* (Vienna: Springer Verlag, 1955); "Reduction Sentences and Disposition Concepts," in *The Philosophy of Rudolf Carnap,* ed. Paul Arthur Schilpp (La Salle, Ill.: Open Court Publishing Co., 1963), p. 559, and "Extensional Logic and Disposition Concepts," in *Minnesota Studies in Philosophy of Science* (Minneapolis: University of Minnesota Press, 1957), Vol. II.

pressed by strict implications. Yet I did not find in Lewis' writing a positive analysis of the meaning of 'real connections'—unless the very statement that real connections are expressed by practically important CF-conditionals be accepted as a positive analysis. Of course, one can say that $A$ is really connected with $B$ if a case of $A$ without $B$ is *impossible*. This would be illuminating if the relevant sense of 'possible' were sufficiently clear. Hopefully one turns to Lewis' discussion of 'possibility' in the context of a differentiation of 'modes of meaning' (*op.cit.*, Ch. III), but is disappointed to find a curious lack of connection between his distinction of 'modes of meaning' and his later discusssion of the possible meanings of universal statements. According to Lewis, 'all objects which are $A$, are $B$' admits of two interpretations. It may mean that all *actual* (existing) objects which are $A$ are $B$, or it may mean that all *logically possible* ('consistently thinkable') objects which are $A$, are $B$. This distinction corresponds to his distinction between the *denotation* and the *comprehension* of a term: the denotation of '$A$' is the class of all existent objects to which '$A$' applies, the comprehension of '$A$' is the class of all consistently thinkable $A$'s. The denotation— comprehension distinction is, of course, correlated with the synthetic— analytic distinction: if 'all ravens are black' is intended as synthetic, then, according to Lewis, it asserts that every actual raven is black— where an 'actual' raven is any raven that exists at some time or other. But 'all ravens are birds', being analytic, asserts that every consistently thinkable raven is a bird. Putting the same distinction in terms of 'denotation' and 'comprehension': 'all ravens are black' asserts that the denotation of 'raven' is included in the denotation of 'black', whereas 'all ravens are birds', intended as an analytic statement, asserts that the comprehension of 'raven' is included in the comprehension of 'bird'.

But whatever one may think of this way of speaking—we shall presently find reasons for condemning it—, it surely does not help Lewis to throw light on the analysis of synthetic universal statements that express (supposed) laws of nature. How would Lewis analyze the difference between 'all ravens are black' and 'all inhabitants of New York whose surname begins with $A$ have a telephone'? Since both statements are synthetic, both deny only the *actual* existence of certain kinds of objects, not the *logical possibility* of there existing such objects. Nevertheless Lewis would contest, I suppose, that 'all ravens are black' is synonymous with '$(x)(x$ is a raven $\supset x$ is black$)$', whereas he would, rightly, be satisfied with a transcription of the second statement as a formal implication.

It means one thing to say "Every *existent* having the property $\varphi$ (or of which $\varphi$ is truly predicable) has also the property $\psi$." And it means a different thing to say, "Every *thinkable* thing which should have the property $\varphi$ must also have the property $\psi$."[7]

Yet, obviously neither of these interpretations fits 'every object which weighs at least 150 lbs and falls from a height of at least 25 ft acquires sufficient momentum to injure a human body' if this statement asserts more than the corresponding formal implication, i.e., is capable of supporting CF-conditionals. The trouble is that Lewis uses the notion of *logical* possibility to bring out an alleged ambiguity of the universal quantifier but says nothing about *empirical* possibility. Let us define an empirically possible state of affairs as a state of affairs which is logically compatible with all the laws of nature. One would then expect Lewis to say that a universal conditional 'for every $x$, if $\varphi\,x$, then $\psi\,x$' which expresses a law of nature asserts neither 'for every *existent* $x$, if $\varphi\,x$, then $\psi\,x$', nor 'for every *consistently thinkable* $x$, if $\varphi\,x$, then $\psi\,x$', but 'for every *empirically possible* $x$, if $\varphi\,x$, then $\psi\,x$'. A merely accidental universal statement denies the existence of instances of a certain conjunction of properties; an analytic universal statement denies the logical possiblity of such existence; a lawlike[8] generalization denies the empirical possibility of such existence.

While the criticism just made refers to a mere sin of omission, the following criticism concerns a sin of commission. I contend that it is inappropriate and even meaningless to use 'existent' and 'possible' as predicates. Russell and logical positivists have commendably warned philosophers to beware of grammatical analogies. One such misleading grammatical analogy is that between 'all American ravens are birds' and 'all existing ravens are birds'. It looks as though each were an understatement: it is not just all American ravens that are birds, but all ravens whatever; and it is not just all existing ravens that are birds but even all possible ravens. It is thus suggested that existing ravens constitute a proper subclass of possible ravens (some possible ravens—a pity on them—are *merely* possible) . This is no doubt a travesty of Lewis' philosophizing, but unfortunately he uses just such misleading language when he introduces comprehensions of terms as classes of existing and merely possible entities and says that the denotation of a term is a proper subclass of the term's comprehension. Consider the comprehension of 'raven', i.e., the class of all consistently thinkable ravens. What entities are excluded from

7 AKV, pp. 217 f.
8 A lawlike statement is a statement which, if true, expresses a law of nature. The term is Nelson Goodman's.

it? The obvious answer may seem to be: any entity that is described by a predicate whose signification is incompatible with the signification of 'raven'. Presumably, then, a man is not a consistently thinkable raven. Yet, in order to construct a description that uniquely applies to a given man it is not necessary to use any predicates whose significations are incompatible with the signification of 'raven'. I might describe a given man as the animal which occupies space-time region $R$, and the statement that the animal which occupies $R$ is a raven is not self-contradictory, false though it may be.

If for a constant expression '$a$', "$a$ exists" is not self-contradictory, and '$\varphi\, a$' is not self-contradictory, then '$\varphi x$' or '$x$' characterized by $\varphi$ comprehends $a$.[8a]

But no matter what self-consistent function '$\varphi\, x$' we take, and no matter what entity $a$ we take, we can find a suitable definite description '$a$' such that neither '$a$ exists' nor '$\varphi\, a$' is self-contradictory. Therefore all self-consistent functions whatever have a universal comprehension; which is to say that the concept 'comprehension' as defined by Lewis serves no purpose at all. But it is worse than useless, it even gives rise to contradiction. For, let the predicates '$\varphi$' and '$\psi$' have incompatible significations. As we have seen, if only we pick suitable descriptions, we can prove that the same entity $a$ belongs to both the comprehension of '$\varphi$' and the comprehension of '$\psi$'. And since '$a$ belongs to the comprehension of "$\varphi$"' entails '$a$ has the attribute $\varphi$', this obviously entails that $a$ has incompatible attributes.

Lewis' mistake, it seems to me, is to talk as though the difference in the meaning of 'if-then' in the contexts 'if $x$ is a raven, then $x$ is black' and 'if $x$ is a raven, then $x$ is a bird' entailed a difference in the range of the variable. That he does talk that way I have already documented by the quotation on p. 359, where he claims the universal quantifier 'for every $x$' to be ambiguous as between 'for every *existent* $x$' and 'for every *thinkable* $x$'. That '$x$ is a raven' strictly implies '$x$ is a bird' means, according to this way of speaking: pick any (logically) possible particular $x$ at all; if $x$ is a raven, then $x$ is a bird. But what could be meant by a 'possible particular', and what could be meant by saying of a possible particular that it is, or is not a raven? Perhaps 'possible particular $x$ is a raven' means '$x$ is possibly a raven'? Yet, on this interpretation the statement that every possible particular which is a raven, is a bird, means that whatever is possibly a raven is possibly a bird. In the symbolic language of modal logic: $(x)(\Diamond \text{raven}(x) \supset \Diamond \text{bird}\ (x))$. But this is clearly weaker than the originally intended statement: $\Box[(x)(\text{raven}(x) \supset \text{bird}$

8a AKV, p. 63.

$(x))]$, since the latter entails: $(x)(\text{raven}(x) \supset \text{bird}(x))$, which cannot be deduced from the former statement.[9]

Note that one does not ordinarily make a statement of the form '$x$ is possibly $\varphi$' unless $x$ is explicitly or tacitly qualified as having some property $\psi$. The 'possibly' then refers to the compatibility of $\varphi$ with $\psi$. When I say 'John is possibly a musician', what I mean is that the properties which I know John to have are both logically and causally compatible with being a musician (or, in a stronger sense of 'possible', that those properties make it to some degree probable that he is a musician). If $x$ is not characterized in any way, it is meaningless to say that $x$ is possibly $\varphi$, unless it just means that $\varphi$ is not a self-contradictory attribute. And if it means the latter, then '$x$' occurs vacuously in the modal statement, i.e., any other individual constant could be substituted and the statment would remain true. Hence a statement of the form '$x$ is possibly $\varphi$' either says nothing specifically about $x$ or else is elliptical for '$\psi$, which is a property of $x$, is compatible with $\varphi$'. There is, however, another use of 'possible' in which what is referred to is an *incompatibility* (by one of those illogical oddities of ordinary language), not a *compatibility*. Suppose a Democrat said 'all Republican congressmen represent special interests, not the people'. A still more ardent Democrat might well reinforce that deprecation by adding 'indeed, all *possible* (conceivable) Republican congressmen represent special interests, not the people'. He means to say that this unworthy feature characterizes not only the Republican congressmen that happen to be in the saddle at the moment, but that it would be quite impossible for a politician to be a Republican congressman without having that undesirable quality. Returning to the dry plane of abstract logical analysis: 'all possible $\varphi$ are $\psi$' does not mean '$(x)(\Diamond \varphi x \supset \psi x)$' nor 'for every possible $x$: $\varphi x \supset \psi x$', but: '$\sim \Diamond (\exists x)(\varphi x \cdot \sim \psi x)$'. Idiomatically: 'no $\varphi$ can fail to be $\psi$'. And this holds no matter whether the possibility in question is logical or empirical.

The distinctions between material implication, strict implication and nomological (lawlike) implication, correlated with the distinctions between factual falsehood, logical impossibility, and empirical impossibility, are located in the meanings of 'if-then', not in the range of the variables of quantification nor in the meanings of the predicates.[10] Let us, accord-

---

[9] In general, $\Diamond p \supset \Diamond q$ is compatible with $p \cdot \sim q$. From $p$ we can move to $\Diamond p$, and from there together with $\Diamond p \supset \Diamond q$ to $\Diamond q$, but $\Diamond q$ is compatible with $\sim q$.

[10] An attempt to analyze the lawlike-accidental distinction on the basis of an alleged ambiguity of class terms (extensional vs. intensional interpretation) has been made by Karl Popper, in "A Note on Natural Laws and So-Called 'Contrary-to-Fact Conditionals'." *Mind*, Jan. 1949. In my opinion, however, Popper's analysis is inadequate. See my article "Extensional Logic and Disposition Concepts," *loc. cit.*

ingly, avoid such quantifiers as 'for every logically possible $x$' 'for every empirically possible $x$', as well as modal predicates 'is possibly $\varphi$', 'is necessarily $\varphi$'. Taking as the range of our variables uniformly the class of things that exist at some time or other, or the class of events (depending on the nature of the predicates used) , we can express the difference in the kind of connection between antecedent and consequent by means of different implication symbols: '$\varphi x \supset \psi x; \varphi x \to \psi x; \varphi x \, 3 \, \psi x$'. The problem I wish to investigate now is whether the second kind of implication, *nomological* implication, must be accepted as a primitive concept because, as we have seen, it does not seem to be analyzable in PMese; or whether a Humean analysis in terms of contingent regularity may nonetheless be feasible. Modal statements are nonextensional with respect to their component statements, in the sense that replacement of a component statement with a materially equivalent one may change the truth-value of the modal statement. Thus, let $p$ and $q$ have the same truth-value, and suppose that $p$ is contingent and $q$ necessary. Then substitution of '$p$' for '$q$' in the modal context 'it is necessary that $q$' leads from a truth to a falsehood. Nevertheless, an extensional interpretation of the logical modalities, i.e., an interpretation by means of the quantifiers, 'some' and 'all', is to some extent[11] feasible. Such an interpretation of logical necessity was, though sketchily and incidentally only, suggested by Russell[11a] long ago. Take a statement of the form 'it is logically necessary that $P(a)$ or not-$P(a)$ ', where '$P$' represents a definite predicate and '$a$' a definite name. According to the analysis suggested by Russell, this means the same as: for all values of $f$ and $x$: $fx$ or not-$fx$, where '$f$' is a predicate variable of lowest type and '$x$' an individual variable. In general terms: let $p\,(a,b,c \ldots n)$ be any proposition involving the nonlogical constants $a,b,c \ldots n$ and besides only logical constants (possibly including bound variables) . And let $p(x_1,x_2 \ldots x_n)$ be the propositional function which results when the nonlogical constants are replaced by appropriate variables, the same constant being replaced by the same variable throughout. Then 'it is logically necessary that $p(a,b,c \ldots n)$' means: $p(x_1,x_2 \ldots x_n)$ is true for all values of $x_1,x_2 \ldots x_n$. Analogously, logical possibility is interpreted in terms of existential quantification. For example, 'it is logically possible that there are immortal men' becomes: $(\exists x)(\varphi x \cdot \psi x)$ is true for some values of the predicate variables $\varphi$ and $\psi$. But note that this interpretation of the logical modalities rests on the assumption that all necessary truths

---

[11] The reason for my qualification is that this interpretation breaks down for modal propositions of the form '$\square\ p$' or '$\lozenge\ p$' where '$p$' contains only *logical* constants.

[11a] In "On the Notion of Cause" (reprinted from *Mysticism and Logic* and *Our Knowledge of the External World*) in *Readings in the Philosophy of Science*, eds. H. Feigl and M. Brodbeck (New York: Appleton-Century-Crofts, 1953) .

are *formal* truths, i.e., truths that are independent of the meanings of nonlogical constants. It entails that once a necessary statement is translated into primitive vocabulary, it shows itself as true by virtue of its form. And this is by no means self-evident, as demonstrated by the famous examples 'whatever is red, is colored', 'nothing is both red and blue all over at the same time'.[12]

Now, a somewhat analogous extensional interpretation of causal necessity is the very core of the Humean 'regularity theory' of causation. According to the above analysis of logical necessity, all nonlogical constants whatever occur vacuously—in Quine's phrase—in logically necessary statements (at least if no defined descriptive constants are used). Causal implications differ, of course, from the strict implications of modal logic in that descriptive predicates occur essentially in them, but according to the Humean conception individual constants occur vacuously in them. If a specific event $a$ caused another specific event $b$, then, by the very meaning of 'cause', *any* event like $a$ is followed by an event like $b$. Let us formalize this conception. Suppose that '$a$' and '$b$' are coordinate descriptions of small space-time regions, and $R$ the relation of contiguity. Let $F(a) \rightarrow G(b)$ represent a causal implication asserting, in tenseless space-time language, that if $a$ has $F$ and $aRb$, then $b$ has $G$. Then '$a$' and '$b$' occur vacuously in the singular causal implication in the sense that the latter entails: for any $x$ and $y$, if $Fx$ and $xRy$, then $Gy$.

The usual objection to such an extensionalization of causal necessity is that it fails to distinguish accidental 100% correlations from genuine causal connections. It is conceivable that all Frenchmen who sat on a green park bench on their 50th birthday suffered a heart attack shortly thereafter and that in future (perhaps scared by a superstitious belief in a causal connection!) no Frenchman will ever sit on a green park bench on his 50th birthday again. But such a 'constant conjunction' would be a sheer coincidence. This is an example of what in recent discussions of 'law-likeness' has been called an accidentally true universal statement. Let us ask ourselves, however, why we would dismiss this as a coincidence, why we would say that it is nevertheless *causally possible* for a Frenchman to sit on a green park bench on his 50th birthday without suffering a heart attack shortly thereafter. Clearly it is because of such known facts as that other Frenchmen sat on brown park benches on their 50th birthday without subsequent heart attack, or that Englishmen sat on park benches on their 50th birthday without detriment to their heart, etc. In short, statistics tell us that there is no high correlation between reaching an

---

[12] For a full discussion of this and related problems, see my book *Semantics and Necessary Truth* (New Haven: Yale University Press, 1957).

age of fifty and suffering a heart attack, nor between sitting on a park bench and suffering a heart attack, nor between membership of a specific nationality and suffering a heart attack at a specific age, etc. Furthermore, suppose that, in the sense of formal implication, all Frenchmen who sit on a green park bench on their 50th birthday suffer a heart attack whereas some Frenchmen who sit on a brown park bench on their 50th birthday do not. If we assumed that the complex characteristic of being a Frenchman who sits on a green park bench on his 50th birthday *causes* a person to acquire the characteristic of suffering a heart attack, we would implicitly assume that the greenness of the bench is a determining condition of the observed effect. But this assumption conflicts with our experience that there is no correlation at all between the color of a bench or chair or any kind of seat and accidents or illnesses that may befall a person after sitting on it. A priori, of course, we cannot make such a judgment of causal irrelevance. There is no contradiction in supposing that, under varied circumstances, people suffer a heart attack after bodily contact with a green object, or that, under varied circumstances, people suffer a heart attack when they enter a public park at the age of fifty. And if the world were such, we would not dismiss the fact that all Frenchmen who sat on a green park bench on their 50th birthday suffered a heart attack shortly thereafter as a mere *accident;* for we could *explain* it deductively in terms of extensively confirmed generalizations.

Undoubtedly the deducibility of an observed correlation from extensively confirmed generalizations is a criterion of its causal, nonaccidental character. If there are, in the entire history of the world, very few instances of attribute $\varphi$, and these are all instances of $\psi$, then $(x)(\varphi x \supset \psi x)$ is true, but will be accepted as expression of a 'real connection' only if it is deducible from a generalization that is inductively well established.[13] If, on the other hand, the generalization which would 'explain' the observed correlation if it were true is known to have many exceptions, then the correlation is dismissed as mere 'coincidence'. The logic behind this criterion of distinction is that if $\varphi$ is a reliable predictor of $\psi$, then instances which resemble the observed $\varphi$'s in relevant respects should also be instances of $\psi$. We may have excellent reasons for believing that never again will a Frenchman sit on a green park bench on his 50th birthday, and hence for believing that there are no exceptions to the confirmed generalization 'whenever a Frenchman sits on a green park

---

[13] This is, roughly, the criterion of lawlikeness offered by R. B. Braithwaite, in *Scientific Explanation* (Cambridge, 1953), Chap. 9. But for the reasons stated below I cannot accept it as an *analysis* of lawlikeness in terms of formal implication plus deducibility. (A criticism of Braithwaite is contained in my paper "Extensional Logic and Disposition Concepts," *loc. cit.*).

bench on his 50th birthday, he suffers a heart attack'. Still, we would not regard it as expressing a causal connection because we know of many instances that closely resemble the instances of its antecedent predicate but are not instances of the consequent predicate, and the respects in which they differ from the instances of the antecedent predicate are unrelated to the kind of effect in question. In accepting $(x)(\varphi x \supset \psi x)$ as expression of a causal connection we manifest the disposition to expect that instances which resemble the known confirming instances in being $\varphi$ also resemble them in being $\psi$. The perception or thought of one resemblance thus associates the thought of another resemblance. But if we already know instances that are closely similar to the known instances of $\varphi$ yet lack $\psi$ (in other words, if we already know counterinstances to a more comprehensive generalization from which $(x)(\varphi x \supset \psi x)$ follows as a special case), the tendency of associating $\varphi$ with $\psi$ is weakened.

But what about the ultimate, extensively confirmed generalizations by reference to which we distinguish accidental from causal sequences of events? Can they be formulated without using the subjunctive? Suppose that a divine statistician who recorded all the 'constant conjunctions' that occur in the universe inspected his immense protocol after the extinction of human life, and found there the following entry: whenever a pipe-smoking college professor sneezed while reading a German novel, the lights in the room went out. In saying that this is not a law, no matter how many confirming instances there may be for it, we are saying that even though the lights did go out whenever the specified event occurred they *might not* have gone out. And of course we mean more by this than that it is *logically* possible that they might not have gone out. We mean that $A$, the antecedent event, was invariably followed by $B$, the effect in question, only because $A$ was invariably accompanied by a condition $C$ such that, had $C$ been absent, $B$ would not have followed. An obvious choice of '$C$' fitting the fantastic example is that the light bulbs got burned through just when the professor sneezed. In the language of John Stuart Mill: even though $A$ may be an invariable antecedent of $B$, it is not the cause of $B$ unless it is an *unconditionally* invariable antecedent of $B$. As we have just seen, however, we need the subjunctive in order to formulate this idea. The idea of unconditionally invariable sequence is the idea of an event $A$ being followed by an event $B$ *under all conceivable* circumstances. This means that for any condition $C$ which is logically compatible with $B$, $B$ will occur if $A$ occurs, no matter whether $C$ is present or absent.[14] Clearly, this is a way of saying that $A$ by itself

14 The qualification that $C$ be logically compatible with $B$ is required because the assertion of unconditionally invariable sequence (or coexistence) is a causal implication and the principle of 'exportation' is not valid for causal implication. Suppose that

is a sufficient condition for $B$. If the law in question is a law of coexistence of properties in objects, we obtain: for any property $P$ (logically compatible with $B$) and for any object $x$, if $Ax$ and $Px$, then $Bx$. But now it should be evident that the proposition we have in mind cannot be expressed by a formal implication. For, $(x)(Ax \supset Bx)$ entails $(P)(x)$ $(Px \cdot Ax \supset Bx)$, by the principle that if $p$ implies $q$, then the conjunction of $p$ with any arbitrary proposition also implies $q$; hence the latter proposition is not stronger than what may be a merely accidental conjunction. Therefore, the intended distinction between an accidental conjunction and a causal connection is entirely lost in this extensional formulation.

We thus come to the following conclusion: causal necessity can indeed be extensionalized, in partial analogy to the explained extensionalization of logical necessity, in the sense that a causally necessary sequence is analyzable into a sequence which is *invariant* with respect to changes of conditions. This invariance can be expressed by means of universal quantification over a predicate variable. To say that a nail will *necessarily* be driven into the wood if it is hammered with at least a specified force, is to say that such an operation will lead to such a result *no matter what else may be the case*. But this idea of unconditional invariability can be expressed only by a subjunctive conditional: $A$ would again and again be followed by $B$ even if any of the conditions that happened to be present in the observed cases of $A$ were lacking or if any of the conditions that were absent in the observed cases of $A$ were present. The evidence for such a subjunctive conditional is, of course, that $A$ has been found to be followed by $B$ under widely different conditions, and this evidence can be expressed in extensional language. But the proposition it is evidence for, cannot be expressed in extensional language.

The point is sufficiently important to be clarified in still another way. Suppose that $a,b \ldots n$ are all the instances of $\varphi$ there happen to be, and that they all happen to be also instances of $\psi$. Our best positive ground for denying the status of law to the true statement 'all instances of $\varphi$ are instances of $\psi$' is surely that we know $a,b \ldots n$ to have a common property $X$, other than $\varphi$ and $\psi$, which we have reason to believe to be

---

$C = \sim B$. Then, using material implication, we would get $A \cdot \sim B \supset B$, hence $A \supset (\sim B \supset B)$, hence, since $(\sim B \supset B) \supset B$, $A \supset B$. And since $A \supset B$ entails $A \cdot \sim B \supset B$, $A \cdot \sim B \supset B$ is simply equivalent to $A \supset B$. But from $A \cdot \sim B \to B$ we cannot deduce $A \to (\sim B \to B)$ on the strength of a general principle of exportation. Therefore $A \cdot \sim B \to B$ is not equivalent to $A \to B$. A system of causal implication that contains 'paradoxes' of causal implication would allow us to assert $A \cdot \sim B \to B$ in case $B$ is causally necessary. But I am here considering causal implication as a relation between *causally contingent* events, i.e., events whose occurrence or nonoccurrence is not deducible from a causal law alone (without assumptions of 'initial conditions').

a necessary condition for $\psi$. The property $\varphi$, in that case, is not a reliable predictor of $\psi$, because we have reason to believe that if an instance of $\varphi$ did not have $X$, it would not have $\psi$. But this notion of a causally necessary condition cannot be defined in terms of formal implication, even if we assume that all the properties whose necessary conditions we investigate have instances (so that the 'paradoxical' feature of formal implication, its vacuous satisfiability, is not directly responsible). For, we have frequently occasion to speak of disjunctively complex necessary conditions: $A$ is not necessary for $B$, and $C$ is not necessary for $B$, but $A$ or $C$ is necessary. In other words, in order for $B$ to occur, either $A$ or $C$ must obtain, though $B$ can occur without $A$ and can also occur without $C$. If this state of affairs, however, is described by means of material implications, it turns out to be self-contradictory. Take the following typical example: $b$ will not get married unless he either falls in love or needs money; but $b$ need not fall in love in order to get married, and he might get married even if he does not need money. Using '$Mb$', '$Lb$' and '$Nb$' for the three propositions involved, we obtain: $Mb \supset (Lb$ v $Nb) \cdot \sim(Mb \supset Lb) \cdot \sim(Mb \supset Nb)$, which is a contradiction because $\sim(p \supset q)$ is equivalent to $(p \cdot \sim q)$. This impasse is due to the fact that the denial of a material implication involves affirmation of the antecedent, while the denial of a causal implication amounts to affirmation of the *possibility* of the antecedent being true without the consequent being true (not 'he *will* get married though he won't need money', but 'he *might* get married without being in need of money').

Now, it is true that we do not fall into such contradiction if we define 'necessary condition' as a relation between attributes, not individual events, in terms of formal implication: ($A$ is a necessary condition for $B$) $= (x)(Bx \supset Ax)$. For, from $\sim(x)(Bx \supset Ax) \cdot \sim(x)(Bx \supset Cx)$ we can only deduce $(\exists x)(Bx \cdot \sim Ax) \cdot (\exists x)(Bx \cdot \sim Cx)$, not $(\exists x)(Bx \cdot \sim Ax \cdot \sim Cx)$. Nevertheless, we cannot express the idea that some property common to the instances $a, b \ldots n$, other than $\varphi$, *might* be a necessary condition for $\psi$—so that 'all $\varphi$ are $\psi$' *might* not be a law even if it is true—in terms of formal implication. For, let $a, b \ldots n$ be all the instances of $\varphi$, and let them be instances of $\psi$ without exception, and let $\psi$ have no other instances than $a, b \ldots n$, and suppose that $X$ is another, logically independent common property of them. Then $(x)(\psi x \supset Xx)$ is also true, which would mean, on the criticized definition of 'necessary condition', that $X$ is a necessary condition for $\psi$. But we want to be able to say that $X$ may not be a necessary condition for $\psi$ though it accidentally accompanied $\psi$ in every instance; and also that an instance of $\varphi$ *might* not be an instance of $\psi$ if it did not have $X$, though in fact all the $\varphi$'s that are $\psi$'s are also $X$'s. Further, according to the ordinary use of the terms 'necessary condition' and 'sufficient condition', the proposition that X, a property which is logically independent of $\varphi$, is a necessary condition for $\psi$, entails that $\varphi$ is not a sufficient condition for $\psi$. If $\varphi$ were a sufficient condition for $\psi$, then instances of $\varphi$ would be instances of $\psi$ no matter whether they were instances of X or not; which is precisely denied by the proposition that X is a necessary condition for $\psi$. Yet, if the actual extensions of $\varphi$, $\psi$, and X happen to coincide, then, *in the extensional sense*, X is a necessary condition for $\psi$ although $\varphi$ is a sufficient condition for $\psi$! Thus, we can conceive the world to be such that all and only bald American composers drink invariably prune juice for breakfast, and that these individuals, and only they, are married to women who are sisters of twin brothers. Yet, it would sound queer to say that if the world were such, then being a bald American composer would be a sufficient condition for the habit of drinking prune juice for breakfast (even if there were medical evidence that such a breakfast habit is conducive to a long and healthy life, Americans who hate prune juice could hardly be expected to overcome this unhealthy disinclination by becoming composers and taking measures to lose their hair) and *also* marriage to a woman who is a sister of twin brothers a necessary condition for such a breakfast habit (the latter statement would suggest to the prune-juice-hating Americans that losing their hair and becoming composers will not lead to that healthy habit unless they also get married to a woman of the described sort).

All these reflections confirm Lewis' contention that 'real connections' cannot be expressed in an extensional language, a language without subjunctive modes of speech. I do not see, however, that this result in any way invalidates the Humean analysis of causal connection in terms of 'constant conjunction'.[15] For a natural formulation of an assertion of 'constant conjunction', bringing out the predictive content of causal generalizations, is just "if at any time an event of kind $\varphi$ should occur, it would be followed by an event of kind $\psi$." Lewis tells us that "such connections are what Hume referred to as 'necessary connections of matters of fact'."[16] That is, Hume is alleged by him to have meant by a necessary connection between two events x and y, characterized as instances of $\varphi$ and $\psi$, the relation which is expressed by the universal (synthetic) subjunctive conditional: if an event of kind $\varphi$ *should* occur, it *would* be followed by an event of kind $\psi$. If so, then in denying that we have any knowledge of

[15] I do not agree with A. W. Burks's suggestion that Humean analysis of causality entails the possibility of expressing causal propositions in PMese ("The Logic of Causal Propositions," *Mind* [1951], 364). On the same point I disagree with R. B. Braithwaite's statements, in *Scientific Explanation*, p. 296.
[16] AKV, p. 228.

necessary connections between matters of fact, Hume was denying that we know any such propositions to be true or even probably true. If Lewis is right in his interpretation of Hume, then Hume's skepticism with regard to knowledge of causal connections results from his analysis of causal propositions as *subjunctive* assertions of regular sequence. It is not entirely clear to me how Lewis proposes to overcome Hume's skepticism, for surely an eloquent endorsement of just that analysis of causal propositions which is alleged to be the source of that skepticism cannot undermine Hume's skeptical arguments. But be this as it may, a case can be made for the correctness of Lewis' interpretation of Hume on this point, as follows.

In denying that we have any knowledge of necessary connections between matters of fact—though we have a strong propensity to *believe* in them—Hume was denying (a) that a priori knowledge of such connections is possible, (b) that they can be established by *induction*. He denied (b) on the ground that no synthetic universal proposition is (i) entailed by a conjunction of observed facts, nor (ii) even rendered probable by such a conjunction, since the proof that it is rendered probable would presuppose a principle of the uniformity of nature which is itself a synthetic universal proposition. If we argue "the unobserved instances of $\varphi$ *probably* resemble the observed instances of $\varphi$ in being $\psi$ because in the past predictions based on the assumption that the unobserved instances of a natural kind resemble the observed instances have *usually* been successful," we beg the question, according to Hume; for we infer from the premise that the inductive policy has been successful in the past, in the sense that predictions in accordance with it *usually* turned out to be true, that the same policy will continue to be successful, which is just the type of inductive inference to be justified. But without entering here the debate as to whether Hume's skepticism is invincible (parenthetically, I don't think it is), I wish to show that it *presupposes* the subjunctive interpretation of synthetic generalizations. My argument is simply that a formal implication is merely an abbreviation of a finite conjunction of statements of the form $\sim(\varphi x \cdot \sim \psi x)$, which are entailed by statements of the form $\varphi x \cdot \psi x$, which are descriptions of observable facts if $\varphi$ and $\psi$ are observable properties of observable objects. In that case synthetic generalizations, interpreted as formal implications, clearly *could* be entailed by finite conjunctions of observed facts. That is, this is at least logically possible, since no matter how large a finite set of observable facts you take, it is logically possible that all members of it be *observed* facts at some time. It may be replied that Hume's denial (bi) could be supported by an interpretation of synthetic generalizations as *infinite* conjunctions of the form: $\sim(\varphi a \cdot \sim \psi a) \cdot \sim(\varphi b \cdot \sim \psi b) \ldots \ldots$

But it seems to me that such infinite conjunctions make sense only in mathematics, where the variables range over numbers, not in empirical discourse. The reason why a synthetic generalization of lawlike character is not entailed by any finite conjunction of singular statements is not that it makes an assertion about infinitely many objects. The reason is that no matter how many confirming instances we have observed, it never follows deductively that *if there were* a further instance to which it applies, it *would* also confirm it.

Lewis is to be commended for emphasizing that "real connections," belief in which is presupposed by all intelligent action, need not be "100% correlations" but may be only probability implications. An extensional formulation of practically important probability hypotheses appears to be as inadequate as an extensional formulation of practically important universal hypotheses. If the inference of "*x* will be hurt" from "*x* jumps from the roof of a house of a height of 30 ft" can be warranted —in the sense that there is good evidence supporting the corresponding CF-conditional—even if nobody ever jumps from the roof of a house of that height, then likewise an inference of the form '*x* is $\varphi$, therefore *x* is *probably* $\psi$' may be warranted although the class determined by the antecedent predicate be empty. This suggests that an extensional interpretation of a probability implication of the form 'on the evidence that *x* is $\varphi$, it is probable to degree m/n that *x* is $\psi$' is inadequate. Extensionally interpreted, such a statement asserts that m/n is the relative frequency of $\psi$'s in the class of $\varphi$'s. But if the reference class determined by $\varphi$ is empty, then it is meaningless to speak of a relative frequency with which an attribute occurs in it. Yet, it is perfectly meaningful to make a statement like 'if *x* were known to be $\varphi$, it would be rational to believe *x* to be $\psi$ with a high degree of certainty, though not with complete certainty', regardless of whether or not anything is $\varphi$. And if most $\varphi$'s are $\psi$'s just accidentally, in the sense that there is no well confirmed statistical law[17] from which this follows with high probability, then the probabilistic CF-conditional 'if *x* were $\varphi$, then *x* would probably be $\psi$' is unjustified. Accordingly, it would not be a useless proliferation of symbols if one introduced '$\Rightarrow\rightarrow$' (with or without numerical subscript, depending on whether the probability statement is vague or precise) as the logical connective in a *nomological* probability implication, i.e., in a statistical

---

[17] The concept of 'confirmation' of a statistical law has, of course, its notorious difficulties. Specifically, probability enters into its very definition, since a confirming sample frequency is not deducible from the statistical law it confirms. Lewis has a clarifying discussion of this issue in Chap. X. For an especially close, and mathematically precise, treatment of the problem, see R. B. Braithwaite, *op. cit.*, Chap. VI.

law. This symbol[18] suggests that causal laws are limiting cases of statistical laws, just the way Reichenbach's symbol '∋' for probability implication was intended by him to suggest that formal implications are limiting cases of extensional probability implications.[19]

One is inevitably led, I believe, to a subjunctive interpretation of statistical laws by consideration of the required nature of a so-called reference class, i.e., a class within which a specified attribute is said to occur with a specified relative frequency. Those who advocate the definition of statistical probability[20] as a *limit* of relative frequencies require the reference class to be infinite. Indeed, if there is any cogent reason for defining 'the probability that a $\varphi$ is a $\psi$' as the limit approached by the relative frequencies of $\psi$'s in larger and larger sequences of $\varphi$'s, it is that it is meaningless to speak simply of the *ratio* of the numbers of two classes at least one of which is infinite. The 'proportion' of heads in an infinite sequence of penny tosses does not make sense, hence the probability of heads must be defined as the limit approached by the proportions of heads as the 'runs' grow larger and larger. The question I wish to raise is just what could be meant by saying that an empirical reference class, like the class of penny tosses, is infinite. My answer is that it can only mean that no matter how many penny tosses have occurred it remains *conceivable* that yet more will occur. The essential use of a statistical law, like that of a causal law, is *prediction*. Lewis reflects this predictive use of probability implications in their very formulation: "the probability that an unobserved or undetermined instance of $\varphi$ will be an instance of $\psi$ equals $r$." It may be helpful to invoke here again our divine statistician. Suppose that after the last penny toss in the history of the universe has occurred he looks at his complete statistical protocol and finds that the relative frequency of heads was .51. Would there be any reason for him to say "the *probability* of a penny toss yielding heads is .51" instead of "the relative frequency of heads in the class of *actual* penny tosses is .51"? If he used the word 'probability' as it is actually used in human life, then he would make the former, the probability statement in order to predict the relative frequency to be expected in any future

[18] I first introduced it in my book *Analytische Erkenntnistheorie*, Chap. II.

[19] Consistently with this conception, Reichenbach has an axiom in his *Wahrscheinlichkeitslehre* (Eng. trans. with new additions, *The Theory of Probability*, Berkeley, 1949) to the effect that if the reference class is empty, then the antecedent implies any arbitrary consequent with any arbitrary probability. This, I suppose, amounts to the same as excluding probability implications with empty reference classes as meaningless, since a numerical probability relation between two attributes, or classes, is characterized by a *unique* number.

[20] 'Statistical probability' is here used in contrast to 'logical probability' in the sense of some form of range theory (e.g., Carnap's).

runs of penny tosses if such should occur. The reference class of penny tosses is *open* in the sense that, for any finite number $n$, if $n$ is the number of observed penny tosses, it is still logically possible that the number of penny tosses, observed or unobserved, be larger than $n$. And this is logically possible simply because it cannot be deduced from the meaning of the predicate determining the reference class how many members the latter has; any finite number of members is compatible with its (intensional) definition.

Let us, then, define an open class as a class which, though finite, is such that *any* finite number of members is compatible with its definition. As we have seen—and as Lewis argues convincingly (p. 279 ff.)—, it follows from the essentially predictive function of statistical probability statements that their reference classes must be open. This openness, however, calls for a subjunctive, not an extensional, formulation. For, it follows from the very meaning of 'statistical law' that it is impossible to know that a statement purporting to express a statistical law is true; one can only *estimate* the relative frequency of a specified attribute in what statisticians call a 'population'. But if the statement asserted that the relative frequency of $\psi$'s in the class of *actual* $\varphi$'s equals $r$, then it would be logically possible that it should be known to be true. The point is that even the divine statistician would speak of a *probability* only if he considered the possibility of there being still more $\varphi$'s; in other words, if he regarded the class of $\varphi$'s as open. It may be objected that statisticians estimate probabilities from observed sample frequencies, not because it is logically impossible to discover the relative frequency in the entire population but because it is just practically impossible to make a complete survey. But I contend that if such knowledge is only *practically* impossible, then the probability statement is not *lawlike*, and the use of 'probability' is then improper. Consider the following example. A statistician estimates, on the basis of a nationwide census, that the relative frequency of families owning a TV set within the class of American families with an annual income of at least $4000 equals ¾. Would it be logically possible for him to have conclusive evidence for this statistical hypothesis? The answer depends on what exactly is intended as the reference class. If the latter is restricted to American families with the specified minimal income within a definite period of time, say 1950-1960, the answer is affirmative; if it is not so restricted, the answer is negative, since the possibility of there coming into existence still more American families always remains. But if a statistician obtained conclusive evidence for the temporally restricted hypothesis by examining absolutely every family of the specified kind during the specified period, he would not have established a statistical *law*, and it would be improper for him to express the proposition in terms of 'probability'. It is not that the reference class must *actually* have as yet unobserved members in order for probability language to be appropriate. What is required is only that it be *conceivable* (i.e., compatible with the definition of the reference class) that it have as yet unobserved members. Such conceivability, or openness of the reference class, is expressed by the subjunctive probability statement: for any $x$, if $x$ should be $\varphi$, then it would be probable to degree $r$ that $x$ is $\psi$. Insofar as 'the probability of an American family with an annual income of at least \$4000 owning a TV set equals $\frac{3}{4}$' is a *lawlike* statement, it means, not that every *actual* sample, but that every *possible* sample of the reference class is likely[21] to contain approximately the specified proportion of families owning a TV set. And the word 'possible' here simply reflects the openness of the reference class, in the same sense in which 'possible' in 'all possible samples of iron conduct electricity' reflects the openness of the class of samples of iron.

Unfortunately, ordinary English does not provide an accurate formulation of subjunctive probability implications. 'For any $x$, if $x$ were $\varphi$, then it would be probable to degree $r$ that $x$ is $\psi$' is misleading in the same way in which 'for any $x$, if $x$ is square, then $x$ is necessarily equilateral' is misleading. Take a substitution instance of the latter: if $a$ is square, then $a$ is necessarily equilateral. It has the form: if $p$, then $\square\ q$. But what is intended is rather: $\square$ (if $p$, then $q$). I think that this inaccuracy of ordinary language is partly responsible for the frequent confusion, even among professional philosophers, of the necessity of a conse*quence* with the necessity of a conse*quent*. Usually the conse*quent* of a necessary conse*quence* is contingent, but this is disguised by the displacement of the modal operator to the consequent. It is unfortunate that Lewis does not overcome this defect of the ordinary idiom in his symbolic formulation of subjunctive, or lawlike, probability implications. He writes: $\varphi x \rightarrow (h)\psi x$, where the arrow expresses a 'real connection' and $(h)$ $\psi x$ means: it is probable that $x$ is $\psi$. But what a lawlike probability implication asserts is not that the antecedent causally implies that the consequent is probable, but that the antecedent probability-implies the consequent. It is for this reason that I recommend my nomological variant of Reichenbach's symbol for extensional probability implication: $(x)(\varphi\ x \underset{r}{\Rightarrow} \psi x)$.

This is not by any means a trivial question of choice of symbols. Lewis' formulation invites one to apply *modus ponens* to probability

---

21 The word 'likely' here is used as in Bernouilli's theorem, the "law of large numbers," according to which the likelihood that a random sample of the reference class contain the attribute in question in approximately the same proportion as the reference class itself is an increasing function of the size of the sample.

implications: $(x)(\varphi x \to (h)\psi x)$; $\varphi a$; therefore $(h)\psi a$. Now, this mode of deduction is clearly invalid since it leads to contradiction.[22] There may be other relevant evidence, $Xa$ (it may or may not be a conjunction containing $\varphi a$), which has been verified and is such that relative to it the same proposition, $\psi a$, is improbable, hence the same proposition (or event) could be argued to be both probable and improbable, or, in case numerical probability is involved, to have different degrees of probability. In order to avoid such contradiction, an inductive logician may rule that 'probable' and 'probable to degree $r$' are never to be used as monadic predicates but always, like 'implies', as relational terms. Indeed, from $(x)(\varphi x \overset{\to}{\ni}_r \psi x)$ and $\varphi a$ nothing can be deduced at all, for '$\overset{\to}{\ni}_r \psi a$' is no more a sentence than '$\supset q$' or '$\to q$'. Lewis, however, rightly retorts that we do make *categorical* probability statements all the time which seem perfectly meaningful. If $h$ is probable relative to evidence $e$ and $e$ has been assured to be true (which assurance is normally conveyed by the very use of the word 'evidence'), then we say that $h$ *is* probable. Fortunately, there is a simple way of reconciling Lewis' distinction between hypothetical and categorical probability statements—'$h$ is probable relative to $e$' vs. '*since $e$, $h$ is probable*'—with the inapplicability of *modus ponens* to probability implications. The reason why the attempt to 'detach the consequent' of a probability implication leads to contradiction is that probability implication differs from total implication (i.e., implication of maximum degree, whether material, causal or strict) in the following way: if $p$ totally implies $q$, then, for any arbitrary $r$, $p \cdot r$ totally implies $q$; but the probability of $q$ relative to $p \cdot r$ may be widely different from the probability of $q$ relative to $p$. This consideration suggests that *modus ponens* in inductive logic is a safe operation provided the evidence which is asserted to be a fact is the *total relevant evidence*. For, on any interpretation of probability, whether statistical or logical, the probability of a proposition relative to the total relevant

---

22 Lewis seems to impute advocacy of just this self-contradictory rule of deduction to a priori theories of probability. Having emphasized the relational character of probability statements and the distinction between valid and true conclusions (well known in deductive logic), he writes (p. 269): "But bearing in mind this distinction as well as the relativity which every probability determination has to the ground of judgment, we can still formulate the distinctive thesis of an *a priori* theory of probability quite simply: *A probability determination which follows from its premised data according to correct rules of probability inference is valid; and a valid determination is true when the premises of it are true.*" The second part of this 'distinctive thesis' gives rise to contradiction, but I don't know whether Lewis was aware of it, nor what the justification for his imputation is. Carnap, the master proponent of what Lewis calls "a priori theories of probability" sounds a clear warning against applying *modus ponens* to probability implications, in Sec. 10 of his *Logical Foundations of Probability* (Chicago: University of Chicago Press, 1950).

evidence is unique. Thus the following deduction schema is unobjectionable: $e \Rightarrow_r h$; $e$; $e$ is the total evidence relevant to $h$; therefore *the probability of $h$ equals $r$*. What I call '*the probability of $h$*' corresponds to the truth-value of the conclusion of an argument in two-valued deductive logic. Notice that, regardless of whether the probability implication is analytic or factual, one can never be certain of the truth of a categorical probability statement which is deduced in accordance with the above rule. For one cannot be certain that one knows all the relevant evidence, and therefore must be resigned to modest conclusions of the form: it is fairly probable that *the* probability of $h$ equals $r$.

Let us summarize: Lewis is right in his claim that the very belief in an objective reality that exists even when unobserved, as well as the belief in 'real connections' between natural events, can be expressed in empirically testable form by means of CF-conditionals only; and that the latter cannot be adequately analyzed within the framework of an extensional language (i.e., a language containing only *truth-functional* connectives) , even if the latter is supplemented with logical modalities. There is no escape from the admission of a kind of *nomological* implication which is stronger than material implication and weaker than strict implication. Even statistical laws must be construed as nomological implications if they have a predictive use and can, therefore, be properly stated in probability language. On the other hand, the empirical evidence which anyone could ever conceivably have for asserting a nomological implication can be described in extensional language. Suppose we call, following Carnap, 'observation language' the language used for describing the observations that confirm or disconfirm scientific hypotheses. Then we may say that CF-conditionals cannot occur in the observation language even if the predicates in them are observation predicates. But since the evidence for or against them can be expressed in the observation language, this limitation of the observation language need not in the least disturb an empiricist who has abandoned the old preconception that a genuine factual proposition must be expressible in observation language. Lewis, who is not only an empiricist (in epistemology, at any rate) but also a sophisticated phenomenalist, insists that the factual meaning of any statement about objective reality must be expressible in nomological implications relating sense-experiences. It should be noted, however, that if phenomenalistic empiricism requires the *translatability* of factually meaningful statements into a phenomenalistic observation language, then Lewis' very insight which I have supported in this essay makes it impossible for him to endorse phenomenalistic empiricism. For, let $S_1$ denote a sense-experience which, in the light of past experience, is a reliable indicator of another sense-experience $S_2$. Then the 'terminating judgments' which according to Lewis are analytically entailed by physical propositions have the form: $S_1 \Rightarrow_r S_2$. And clearly no finite conjunction of statements describing actual sense-experiences entails a nomological probability-implication, as we have seen.

Whether there remains a genuine issue between phenomenalists and realists once the former admit that the *confirmability* of factual propositions in sense-experience does not entail their *translatability* into an extensional language of sense-experience, I very much doubt. But this is a different question, one that is dealt with elsewhere in this volume.

ARTHUR PAP

DEPARTMENT OF PHILOSOPHY
YALE UNIVERSITY

## 14

*E. M. Adams*

# C. I. LEWIS AND THE INCONSISTENT TRIAD
# OF MODERN EMPIRICISM

## I

MODERN epistemologists have been plagued by what most have considered to be an inconsistent triad, which may be formulated in the following manner:

(1) The principle of subjectivism, which states that all possible knowledge of matters of fact, without the aid of self-evident truths known by the natural light of reason, to speak in the Cartesian fashion, consists of, or is exclusively grounded in, truths known by the immediate apprehension of all that is asserted by them; and, furthermore, all statements knowable in this manner simply assert the existence of certain appearances, the immediate contents of one's consciousness, the presentations of sensation and introspection, variously called 'sense-impressions', 'sensa', 'sense-data', 'qualia', and so on, which are conceived to be subjective and private.

(2) The empirical verifiability theory of meaning, which first appeared in Locke's idea-empiricism and was further developed by Berkeley and Hume. A more sophisticated formulation of the same principle is that the meaning of a sentence consists entirely and exclusively of the experiences, conceived as appearances or sense-data, required to verify it completely; or, as it is sometimes stated, especially by pragmatists, the meaning of a sentence consists of the way in which all possible experience (sense-data) would be different if the sentence were true from the way in which it would be if the sentence were false; in short, the meaning of a sentence is its experiential truth-conditions.

(3) The principle of realism, which holds that objective statements, statements about things and the way they are independently of being experienced, are meaningful and can be known.

Empiricists, without the aid of self-evident truths known by the natural light of reason, thought that (1) committed us to skepticism concerning (3) until Berkeley and Hume introduced (2), and thereupon skepticism yielded to phenomenalism. There have been various attempts to carry out the translation of prima facie objective statements into sets of sense-datum statements, or to treat 'objective statements' as not really *statements* at all but sense-datum prediction licenses or formulae for coordinating sense-data and directing action.

Professor C. I. Lewis is somewhat unique among those who have attempted to solve this Cartesian-Humean problem from within in that he, while clearly and unequivocally accepting subjectivism and the empirical verifiability theory of meaning, espouses realism also. In a recent article[1] he states his realism in this way:

There are stars in the heavens, but constellations only for our seeing. Perhaps likewise there are molar masses only for our senses, directed upon the quanta or wavicles which inhabit the ocean of energy. But at least the potentiality of so appearing to us, instead of otherwise, and of being discriminable as just these molar masses, in just these relations to one another, is in the ocean itself, as constituted independently of us.[2]

or again:

The suggestion is that we know objects only as we know certain objective properties of them, which are potentialities or reliable dispositional traits resident in the nature of them as they objectively exist, and whose manifestations are variously observable; directly in the presentational content of human experience to which they give rise, and indirectly through the observable interactions of objects with one another. We never know or can know all the properties of any individual thing, but what we do or may know is metaphysically veridical; these properties are in the things themselves as in our knowledge of them—provided we do not fall into confusions about the nature of our knowledge.[3]

Descartes was able to get from knowledge of subjective appearances to objective reality by the device of rationally proving the existence of a nondeceiving God; Santayana on the basis of animal faith. Lewis' position is similar to Santayana's, but perhaps it would be more enlightening to say that it is a matter of categorial commitment. He puts it this way: "Independent reality is not something to be proved but an original acknowledgement which all men make confronting the facts of life."[4]

Even though the principle of realism needs no proof or is not susceptible of any, Lewis is encumbered with the obligation of showing that it is at least compatible with subjectivism and the empirical verifiability

---

1 "Realism or Phenomenalism?," *The Philosophical Review*, 64, No. 2 (April, 1955), 233-47. Hereafter cited as "Real. Phen."

2 "Real. Phen.," p. 246.

3 "Real. Phen.," pp. 245 f.

4 "Real. Phen.," p. 238.

theory of meaning. This he attempts to do in *An Analysis of Knowledge and Valuation*[4a] by (1) analyzing meaning so that an objective statement is intensionally equivalent to a set of sense-datum statements, and yet the objective statement, in the sense of denotative analytic meaning, refers to physical objects and the sense-datum statements refer, in the same sense, to only sense-data; and (2) by construing the terminating sense-datum statements to which the objective statement is intensionally equivalent to be contrary-to-fact conditionals.

It is our purpose in this paper to examine his case for the consistency of the triad.

## II

In this part, we shall state the two arguments in some detail, and defer criticism to Part III.

The first argument is the case for the intensional equivalence of a physical-object statement and a conjunction of sense-datum statements,[5] while the terms within the physical-object statement refer to, in the sense of denote, physical objects in a nonreduced sense, and the terms in the sense-datum statements refer to only sense-data. If this contention can be made out while maintaining the principle of subjectivism and the empirical verifiability theory of meaning, Lewis will have shown, at least, that the so-called 'inconsistent' triad is a misnomer, and that he, in subscribing to all three principles, is consistent.

First of all, I shall state the salient points of his theory of meaning in terms of which these distinctions are made, although they are probably well known to the reader already. He holds that terms have four modes of meaning: (1) *denotation*, defined as "the class of all actual things to which the term applies";[6] (2) *comprehension*, defined as "the classification of all possible or consistently thinkable things to which the term would be correctly applicable";[7] (3) *signification*, which means "that property in things the presence of which indicates that the term correctly applies, and the absence of which indicates that it does not

---

[4a] La Salle, Illinois: The Open Court Publishing Company, 1946. Hereafter cited as AKV.

[5] Lewis does not make any distinction between statements like 'I seem to see a piece of paper,' 'I see what appears to be a piece of paper,' 'I see what looks like a piece of paper,' 'I see the appearance of a piece of paper,' 'I see a paperish expanse of white,' and so on. For some purposes, distinctions should be made, but since Lewis does not make such distinctions and none are required for our purposes, we shall call them indifferently by the same name.

[6] AKV, p. 39.

[7] AKV, p. 39.

apply";[8] and (4) *intension,* which he subdivides[9] into (a) linguistic intension or *connotation,* the conjunction of all other terms that must be applicable to anything to which the given term would be correctly applicable;[10] and (b) *sense meaning,* the criterion in mind, in terms of sense, "by reference to which one is able to apply or refuse to apply the expression in question in the case of presented, or imagined, things or situations";[11] "It is that in mind which *refers* to signification."[12]

Lewis considers statements, or at least statements with the assertional factor extracted, which he calls 'propositions', to be terms and thus to have all of the above modes of meaning. But we may speak of the meaning of a statement in two ways: holophrastically and analytically. The former is its meaning as a whole; the latter is its meaning in terms of its elements.

It is obvious that if two statements, $P$ and $Q$, are intensionally equivalent in the sense of "consequences implied" so that $P$ "is a sufficient premise for exactly the same inferences as" $Q$ and vice versa, then whatever is confirmatory of either is confirmatory of the other. Now if $P$ is a physical-object statement and $Q$ is a conjunction of sense-datum statements, and $P$ and $Q$ are intensionally equivalent, then $P$ can be confirmed by truths such as "I seem to see a red object," "I seem to see a pen," and so on.

Usually it has been thought that this kind of an analysis of a physical-object statement in terms of the principle of subjectivism and the empirical verifiability theory of meaning reduces physical objects to logical constructions out of sense-data and thereby denies the principle of realism. But Lewis attempts to save realism by contending that "such equivalence of intension, and hence coincidence of what may verify or confirm one statement with what will verify or confirm another, argues no identity whatever between items mentioned in the one and in the other affirmation."[13] The two statements 'yesterday was Sunday' and 'tomorrow will be Tuesday' are intensionally equivalent, but it does not say that the day referred to by 'yesterday' in the first statement is the same day as the one referred to by 'tomorrow' in the second and neither does it say that Sundays are Tuesdays. Thus two statements may be intensionally equivalent and yet be about quite different things.

8 AKV, p. 39.
9 Cf. AKV, p. 131.
10 AKV, p. 39.
11 AKV, p. 133.
12 AKV, p. 133, note 3.
13 AKV, p. 201.

In the case of a physical-object statement, according to Lewis, although its intensional meaning may be said to be 'reduced to' or to be identical with that of its equivalent conjunctive sense-datum statement, its analytic denotative meaning, the denotative meaning of its terms, is not in any sense reduced to or shown to be identical with that of its subjective correlative.[14] Physical-object statements mention physical objects and say something about them, but no sense-datum statement does. So physical objects as distinct from bundles of sense-data, actual or potential, are not denied but clearly affirmed.

It might seem from the above statement of the case that Lewis makes a case for realism only at the analytic denotative level and yields to reductionistic subjectivism at the holophrastic intensional level. But this is not so. His second argument applies at the higher level.

We have so far spoken of the sense-datum statement intensionally equivalent to a physical-object statement simply as a conjunction of sense-datum statements, and of the sense-datum conjuncts as though they were of the form 'I seem to see a table'. However, Lewis' account of the matter is much more complex. Falling in between objective statements and statements of the form 'I seem to see a table', which are statements in expressive language, are what he calls 'terminating judgments'. They are like objective and unlike expressive statements in that they are corrigible. One can go wrong in believing them; that is, one can be in error about them. This is not possible, he claims, in the case of expressive statements. Of course one may be in error or in doubt about the correctness of the language one uses to express the presentational content of consciousness, but not, according to Lewis, in regard to the presentational content itself. Yet he does not choose to call this 'knowledge' because of the impossibility of error. Nevertheless, this kind of apprehension, about which there is complete certainty, in accordance with the classical Cartesian principle of subjectivism, is taken to constitute the foundation of all knowledge of matters of fact. Terminating statements, however, are unlike objective statements precisely in that they are terminating while objective statements are not; that is, they are completely and decisively verifiable in terms of expressive statements. As Lewis puts it:

They are phrased in terms of direct experience, not of the objective facts which such experience may signalize or confirm; and for this reason they are statable only in expressive language, the terms of which denote appearances as such.[15]

They are of the form 'S being given, if A then E', where, as Lewis says:

14 AKV, p. 201.
15 AKV, p. 203.

'A' represents some mode of action taken to be possible, 'E' some expected consequent in experience, and 'S' the sensory cue . . . Both antecedent and consequent of this judgment, "If A then E," require to be formulated in expressive language; though we shall not call it an expressive statement, reserving that phrase for formulations of the given. Also, unlike statements of the given, what such terminating judgments express is to be classed as knowledge; the prediction in question calls for verification, and is subject to possible error.[16]

The importance of terminating statements in his analysis is evident in the following statement of his fundamental thesis:

The sense meaning of any verifiable statement of objective fact, is exhibitable in some set of terminating judgments each of which is hypothetical in form; it is a judgment that a certain empirical eventuation will ensue if a certain mode of action be adopted. Such judgments may be decisively verified or found false by adopting the mode of action in question and putting them to the test. And it is by such conclusive verification of terminating judgments, constituent in the meaning of it, that the objective belief—the non-terminating judgment— receives its confirmation as more or less highly probable.[17]

It is in his account of the 'if . . . then' of the terminating statement that he makes a case for realism. As he says:

It is this question of the *kind of connection* between the mode of action A and the expected experience E which is believed to hold in believing "If A then E," which will turn out upon examination to have a bearing on those issues which lie between subjectivism or phenomenalism and realism, as well as between skepticism and belief in the possibility of knowing an independently real world.[18]

It is argued that the 'if . . . then . . .' of the terminating statement is not one of entailment, nor is it either formal or material implication. It is said to be a 'contrary-to-fact conditional' and is characterized as follows:

(1) the consequent of this hypothetical statement is not logically deducible from the antecedent. (2) Nevertheless the truth of the hypothetical statement itself—like that of one which states a relation of logical entailment or deducibility—is independent of the truth or falsity of the antecedent or hypothesis: for the if-then relation which such a hypothetical statement asserts as holding, the hypothesis has the same consequences whether it is true or false. (3) Hence this hypothetical statement may be significantly asserted when the hypothesis of it is contrary to fact and is known to be so.[19]

16 AKV, p. 184.
17 AKV, p. 211.
18 AKV, p. 211.
19 AKV, p. 223.

How the contrary-to-fact character of the 'if-then' of the terminating statement argues for realism is stated summarily in this manner:

> As long ago as Hume, it was suggested that there is no difference between the common-sense supposition of a real world (when the significance of this supposition is validly interpreted) and the summary statement that at certain times we have certain specific sense impressions . . . the common-sense man regards this Humean suggestion as equivalent to the supposition that objective reality may 'go out' when unobserved but always 'come back' when observed; . . . the difference between such fantastic subjectivism and our belief in a world which is knowable and verifiable but exists independently of being observed, is the difference between supposing on the one hand that empirical generalizations which are justified have no valid significance beyond that of formal implication, and supposing on the other hand that the verifiability of such empirical generalizations includes reference to hypothetical statements about possible experience and that these hypothetical statements have the characteristics summarized [above].[20]

Again he says:

> This belief in a real world is belief in innumerable specific consequences of innumerable possible ways of acting which, at any given moment, we find no reason to adopt. This belief in objective reality is only as strong as the correlative belief that although certain hypotheses are now false, they have certain consequences (which *would* be found true if the tests *were* made) and not others.[21]

### III

Such are Lewis' two arguments to show the possibility of realism, if not to prove it, within the limits of his subjectivism and the empirical verifiability theory of meaning. Let us now take a critical look at them.

In regard to the claim that the terms of a physical-object statement denote physical objects while the statement as a whole is intensionally equivalent to a set of terminating statements the components of which are formulated in expressive language and denote only appearances or sense-data: clearly the terms that denote physical objects must signify objective properties, for a term signifies properties that an object must possess in order for it to be denoted by the term and, of course, a physical object, in a realistic sense, can possess only objective properties; and, holophrastically, the statement must signify an objective state of affairs, since it describes physical objects in terms of objective properties or relations. And if a conjunction of terminating statements is intensionally equivalent, in the sense of identical entailments, to a given physical-object statement, it must also have the same significa-

20 AKV, pp. 223 f.
21 AKV, p. 215.

tion as the physical-object statement.[22] But the terms of a terminating statement, formulated in expressive language, signify only qualia, subjective and private sense-data, and the statement as a whole signifies only a subjective state of affairs, involving only appearances of individuals, qualia and their relationships. And certainly the signification of a conjunction, although infinite, of terminating statements, which is truthfunctional, cannot involve something other than, to say nothing of something different in kind, that involved in its conjuncts. Therefore, the signification of the conjunction of terminating statements offered as intensionally equivalent to a physical-object statement is different from that of the physical-object statement. As we have seen, according to Lewis' own statement,[23] any two expressions having the same intension, in the linguistic sense, must have the same signification. If we hold on to this, and it seems obvious, we cannot accept the intensional equivalence of a physical-object statement and a conjunction of terminating statements.

Perhaps the 'intensional' equivalence here is to be taken only in the sense of sense meaning. He does speak of the sense meaning of a physical-object statement being exhibitable in a set of terminating statements.[24] And, as he puts it, "a sense meaning is a criterion of possible *confirmations,* and would be exhibited *in extenso* by the totality of terminating judgments implied or included in objective attribution of the property or character to be tested."[25] Again, he says: "the sense meaning of . . . [ a statement of objective empirical fact] coincides with what it would mean, in terms of experience, to determine fully that it is true."[26] These statements suggest that there is no significant distinction between the signification and sense meaning of terminating statements, or at least that the two coincide. If so, perhaps what is meant by an objective statement's being intensionally equivalent to a conjunction of terminating statements is that they have the same sense meaning, but yet different significations, since the sense meaning of the conjunction of terminating statements coincides with its signification but not in the case of the objective statement. On this account it might appear, on first thought, that the analytic denotative meaning of the objective statement could, as he claims, be in terms of physical objects and that of the terminating statements in terms of appearances. But he precludes this by

22 AKV, pp. 65, 199.
23 AKV, p. 65.
24 AKV, p. 211.
25 AKV, p. 193.
26 AKV, p. 193.

explicitly stating that what is meant by 'equivalence of intension' is identity of consequences implied or entailed.[27] And even if he did not explicitly say it, a little reflection would show that any two terms that have identical sense meaning must have identical linguistic intensions, since the application of a term is determined by its sense meaning. And, if two statements have the same linguistic intensional meaning, they must have, as we have already observed, the same signification. But this cannot be, as we have seen above, if, in terms of analytic meaning, one denotes physical objects and the other only appearances.

Lewis attempts to show by example that two statements can have the same signification and yet different denotative analytic meaning. But he has chosen for his paradigm 'Yesterday was Sunday' and 'Tomorrow will be Tuesday'. Both of these are objective statements and quite peculiar ones at that. He has defined 'signification' so that for a statement it means all the facts that *must* be the case in order for the statement to be true. Clearly exactly the same set of facts are required for the truth of the two statements cited. Hence they have the same signification. Yet, as he claims, 'yesterday' in the first statement refers to one day and 'tomorrow' in the second refers to another. Also what the first says of the one day is different from what the second says about the other.

I think that Lewis has brought in, under the ambiguity of 'must' in his definition of 'signification', and also of 'intension', several kinds of requirements, all of which are not equally relevant to meaning analysis. The obvious requirement for the truth of 'yesterday was Sunday' is precisely for the day denoted by 'yesterday' to be a Sunday. Lewis seems to agree with this in his latest article when he says: "Truth concerns the subject-object relation: 'Snow is white' is true just in case snow is white."[28] The requirement that tomorrow will be Tuesday for the truth of 'yesterday was Sunday' is a different kind of *must* and should not be confused with it. As Lewis says, the first is a subject-object relation. If the subject has the specified relation to the object, it is true. And that is the end of the matter. The relation of this fact to some other fact is something else. The two relations, the subject-object and the fact-fact, should not be spoken of in the same way with regard to what *must* be in order for the given statement to be true. Within Lewis' terms, there is no way of saying that the fact *yesterday was Sunday* is meant any more so by 'yesterday was Sunday' than the fact *tomorrow will be Tuesday*.

27 AKV, pp. 197, 201.
28 "Real. Phen.," p. 238.

There is clearly a difference here that our terminology needs to mark. Failing to note this difference is the trick by which Lewis has been able to maintain that all necessary truths are analytic, since the same confusion is carried over into intension. Clearly in determining the signification and intension of a term or sentence, on Lewis' account, one would have to rely upon one's insight or direct apprehension of necessary property-to-property and fact-to-fact connections beyond those set-up by linguistic rules, and even if these connections should come to be built into linguistic rules, this would in no way abrogate the necessity for having to have first apprehended them without such aids.

Of course there is a sense in which I could not fully know that yesterday was Sunday without knowing that yesterday was separated from Tuesday only by today. But take the example 'this is a right angled solid'. I could know perfectly well what this meant with respect to what is necessary for it to be true in the sense that 'snow is white' is true just in case snow is white without knowing that it entails 'this has twelve edges'.

But to go further and to talk of equivalences in all modes of meaning, except analytic denotative, among statements of different categories of being is far more serious. We have seen that the terms of terminating statements, according to Lewis' own statement, denote only appearances, and, therefore, can signify only qualia, for if they signified objective properties they would denote physical objects. This being so, certainly the terminating statement can signify only subjective states of affairs in the realm of appearances. Furthermore, a truth-functional conjunction of such terminating statements can signify only subjective states of affairs. Yet Lewis claims that such a statement, a conjunction of terminating statements, is equivalent in all modes of meaning, except denotative analytic, to a physical-object statement. This means, of course, that an objective state of affairs *must obtain* in order for the conjunctive terminating statement to be true. Certainly this 'must', this requirement, is quite different from the requirement of the subjective state of affairs. Also it is quite different from the requirement by 'yesterday was Sunday' that *tomorrow will be Tuesday;* and the requirement by 'this is a cube' that *this has twelve edges.*

On Lewis' account, apparently the requirement of the objective state of affairs by the subjective state of affairs, and, therefore, the requirement of the objective state of affairs for the truth of the subjective statement, is of an explanatory nature. We assume the objective state of affairs in order to interpret and 'account for' the subjective state of affairs. This is borne out in some of his statements: "It is the interpretation put upon this presentation which constitutes belief in or assertion of some objective fact. This interpretation is imposed in the light of past experience."[29] Again he speaks of "this significance ascribed to the fact of the presentation and expressed by statement of the belief aroused . . ."[30] In other places, he speaks of sense presentation or appearances *signalizing* objective properties or states of affairs:

. . . real objects exist having certain properties signalized by certain visual and other clues.[31]

They [terminating judgments] are phrased in terms of direct experience, not of the objective facts which such experience may signalize or confirm;[32]

It *is* essential, if the purposes for which language exists are to be met, that they should signalize the same objective realities by the same language. But it is not clear that the presence of the same objects is, or must necessarily be, signalized to different individuals by qualitative identical presentations in their experience.[33]

or again: "As criterion *in mind*, sense meaning is intensional meaning rather than signification: it is that in mind which *refers* to signification."[34]

Here it is obvious that the sense presentation, the quale or the subjective state of affairs, is taken as a *sign,* and indeed a *natural sign,* of the objective property or state of affairs. But something comes to function as a natural sign of something else by the observation of causal connections or uniform association, and no such connection or association can be observed between an objective property and a quale or between objective and subjective states of affairs. As Berkeley maintained, a sense idea can be a sign of only other sense ideas. Lewis clearly recognizes this fact. He says:

To construe this interpretation of the given experience—this belief in objective fact which it arouses—as verifiable and as something whose significance can be envisaged in terms of possible confirmations of it, is what dictates that the statement of this objective belief . . . must be translatable into the predictive statements of terminating judgments.[35]

What this amounts to is that we interpret a subjective state of affairs as signalizing an objective state of affairs on the basis of a posited or assumed realism, but then interpret the objective state of affairs in

29 AKV, pp. 188 f.
30 AKV, p. 189.
31 AKV, p. 236.
32 AKV, p. 203.
33 AKV, p. 143.
34 AKV, p. 133, note 3.
35 AKV, p. 189.

terms of subjective states of affairs. This, of course, reflects the difficulties that subjectivism and the empirical verifiability theory of meaning impose upon realism. I wonder if this 'play' with realism gets us any further than a *direct* interpretation of a given subjective state in terms of its complex relations with other subjective states, which could, of course, include contrary-to-fact conditionals. Such a direct interpretation would be phenomenalism. It is difficult to see how the indirect interpretation is not also phenomenalism.

Lewis attempts to give more substance to his realism in his recent article. He says:

> . . . we know objects only as we know certain objective properties of them, which are potentialities or reliable dispositional traits resident in the nature of them as they objectively exist, and whose manifestations are variously observable; directly in the presentational content of human experience to which they give rise, and indirectly through the observable interactions of objects with one another.

Again, he speaks of

> . . . the quanta or wavicles which inhabit the ocean of energy

and says

> the potentiality of so appearing to us, instead of otherwise, and of being discriminable as just these molar masses, in just these relations to one another, is in the ocean itself, as constituted independently of us.[36]

Here his realism is clear precisely because he gives the interpretation of subjective states in terms of objective conditions without going on, as his empirical verifiability theory requires, to interpret the objective conditions in terms of subjective conditions. In short, he lets his realism show by temporarily abandoning the empirical verifiability principle.

Let us return to the main point. Lewis, I think, claims equivalence of linguistic intension and signification of a conjunction of terminating statements and a physical-object statement, but not analytic denotative equivalence, by a confusion that amounts to this. The conjunction of terminating statements *signify* a complex subjective state of affairs, and the complex subjective state of affairs is taken to *signalize* the objective state of affairs *signified* by the physical-object statement. This, I submit, does not yield equivalence of *signification* of the two statements, and thus also not equivalence of linguistic intension. This is so apart from any of the difficulties involved in holding, within the limits of subjectivism and empirical verifiability, that the subjective state of affairs signalizes objective conditions.

---

36 "Real. Phen.," p. 245 f.

Thus we cannot have two statements equivalent in intension and signification and yet the terms of one denote physical objects and the terms of the other denote only subjective appearances. And this pulls one of the pillars out from under Lewis' case for the consistency of the triad of subjectivism, empirical verifiability theory, and realism.

His second argument, it will be recalled, concerns the contrary-to-fact character of the 'if . . . then' in terminating statements. The point of this is to show that there are 'real' connections between appearances of certain kinds that are not restricted to actual past, present, and future appearances. In a statement already quoted above, he says: "this belief in a real world is belief in innumerable specific consequences of innumerable possible ways of acting which, at any given moment, we find no reason to adopt."[37] These 'possible ways of acting' and 'specific consequences' are, of course, to be taken as formulatable in expressive language and, therefore, are only appearances.

Here it would seem that his argument is that belief in a real world is nothing more than belief in such contrary-to-fact or 'real' connections between appearances. Apparently he thinks that the assumption of realism is necessarily involved in considering contrary-to-fact conditional terminating statements meaningful and some of them true in that he thinks that when the antecedent sense-datum statement of the terminating statement is false, there must be some statement that is true or might be true, namely, an objective statement, that makes meaningful, and in some cases true, the assertion of a connection between the two nonexistent, in all tenses, subjective conditions. But is his kind of realism necessarily involved in this? It seems that the 'real' connections between appearances that are not restricted to actual past, present, and future subjective states could be interpreted as connections between *kinds* of appearances that hold because of the *kinds* involved. Then one could meaningfully say: "If an appearance of kind *A* on occasion *O*, then an appearance of kind *E* on occasion *O*." This, it seems, need not involve the assumption of metaphysical realism. Perhaps he would reject this possibility on the alleged ground that such a relation between *kinds* of appearances based on the *kinds* involved would make the 'if . . . then' an entailment relation. However, this need not be. It could be a generalization based upon experience. On his account of things, it is certainly just as reasonable to think that we can discover by experience such relations between kinds of appearances as between *kinds* of physical objects. In fact, he speaks of the so-called 'real' connection of appearances as "an inductively established correlation by virtue of which one observable item in experience is a probability-index of another."[38]

If we should interpret him to mean that the belief in a real world is *just* this belief in contrary-to-fact conditional terminating statements and that they are to be interpreted to assert connections between *kinds* of appearances, such a 'realism' would be, however, a Humean realism of appearances and their connections, and, of course, the point in speaking of 'appearances' would be lost. Indeed the principle of subjectivism would be robbed of any significance and, on most points, if not all, such a position would not be distinguishable from naive realism. This is obviously not his meaning. He says: "Coincidence of these qualia with properties resident in objects is precluded in the metaphysical nature of the case, and by facts of life which should be obvious."[39]

The only argument, it seems, that can be made for his kind of metaphysical realism from the contrary-to-fact character of terminating statements is that the assumption of an objective, independent, real world, which, as we have seen, cannot be stated within the limits of subjectivism and the empirical verifiability theory of meaning, is necessary in order to account for the 'real' connections between kinds of appearances asserted in terminating statements. It would seem that a similar argument could be made if the 'if . . . then' of the terminating statement were interpreted to be either formal or material implication, since the connections between actual appearances would need 'accounting for' or 'being grounded' just as much as those between kinds of appearances as such. So it seems that the contrary-to-fact feature of terminating statements does not constitute a special or peculiar case for realism.

Furthermore, there are some serious difficulties involved in interpreting terminating statements to be contrary-to-fact conditionals.

Lewis gives two basic formulations of the terminating statement:

(1) $S_1A_1 \rightarrow E_1$ [40]

. . . terminating judgments are, in general, of the form, "If *A* then *E*," or "*S* being given, if *A* then *E*," where '*A*' represents some mode of action taken to be possible, '*E*' some expected consequent in experience, and '*S*' the sensory cue . . . Both antecedent and consequent of this judgment, "If *A* then *E*," require to be formulated in expressive language . . .[41]

[38] AKV, p. 250.
[39] "Real. Phen.," p. 246.
[40] AKV, pp. 184, 205.
[41] AKV, p. 184.

(2) $S_1 A_1 \rightarrow (h) E_1$ [42]

Lewis says, because of

. . . finding a predictable consequence of an objective statement to be false will disconfirm it but will not prove it certainly false . . . we can no longer regard any terminating judgment, "When $S$ is given, if $A$ then $E$," as strictly implied by an objective statement, '$P$', which is believed. We can only say, "If $P$, then when presentation $S$ is given and act $A$ is performed, it is more or less highly probable that $E$ will be observed to follow."[43]

In the statement just cited, Lewis now says that objective statements do not entail terminating judgments of form (1), but only those of form (2). Obviously (2) is not a terminating statement. Whatever follows or fails to follow in experience upon $S_1$ and $A_1$ cannot conclusively verify or falsify the statement '$S_1 A_1 \rightarrow (h) E_1$' because of the probability factor. But the whole point in analyzing objective statements into an equivalent set of terminating statements was to have statements that could be decisively verified or falsified.

Lewis recognizes this difficulty and tries to save the situation by claiming decisive verification for (2). He says:

We have suggested for '$(h) X$' the idiomatic reading, "In all probability, $X$," instead of "It is highly probable that $X$," in order to obviate in some measure a difficulty. . . . If, for example, one looks at the sky and predicts rain, one does not intend to assert merely that there is a probability connection between the appearance of the sky and the later occurrence of rain: that assertion would remain equally true whether in fact rain follows or not. The prediction hazarded (as probable) is that *it will rain*: an assertion which the sequel will decisively prove true or false.[44]

The point in regard to (2), however, is not the decisive verification of '$E_1$'. That is granted. What needs decisive verification or falsification is the whole terminating statement '$S_1 A_1 \rightarrow (h) E_1$'. To verify '$E_1$' does not do it. If '$S_1$', '$A_1$', and '$E_1$' being verified would decisively verify '$S_1 A_1 \rightarrow (h) E_1$', this terminating statement would have to be truth-functional. But Lewis has argued strongly against any such interpretation even of '$S_1 A_1 \rightarrow E_1$'.

He seems to recognize that something is wrong somewhere. Just following the above cited attempt to maintain decisive verification, he says:

42 AKV, pp. 237 f.
43 AKV, p. 237.
44 AKV, p. 250-51.

Considerations of this sort further emphasize the necessity of remarking that the terminating judgment $[S_1A_1 \to E_1]$, which expresses a prediction, does not itself occur as an unqualified constituent in the belief to be confirmed.[45]

This admission would seem to undermine all that he has done. The whole thesis is that objective statements *entail* a set of terminating statements that are decisively verifiable or falsifiable and that thereby objective statements can be confirmed or disconfirmed. If such terminating statements are not *entailed* by objective statements, all is lost.

Although he does not, perhaps Lewis might attempt to save the situation by holding that a statement like (2), '$S_1A_1 \to (h) E_1$', could be confirmed by statements like (1), '$S_1A_1 \to E_1$'. But for this to be so either (a) (2) would have to entail a set of statements like (1), or (b) (2) would have to entail that some given percent or most of a specifiable set of statements like (1) were true. (a) is precluded on the grounds that if an objective statement, $P$, entailed (2), and (2) entailed a set like (1), then $P$ would entail the set like (1), and Lewis has shown that objective statements cannot entail statements like (1). As far as the problems so far considered, (b) would be a possibility, but there are further difficulties that preclude it also.

A difficulty that Lewis has not even hinted at lies embedded in the so-called 'terminating' statements of the form of (1), $S_1A_1 \to E_1$, because of its contrary-to-fact character. As previously quoted, Lewis says: "The relation here represented by '$\to$' depends on what we have spoken of as a 'real connection'; an inductively established correlation by virtue of which one observable item in experience is a probability-index of another."[46] Certainly no such statement can be conclusively verified by the verification of the expressive component statements '$S_1$', '$A_1$', and '$E_1$'. In fact, any conditional, genuinely terminating statement, on Lewis' account, would have to be truth-functional; that is, its 'if . . . then' would have to be material implication, and Lewis, by arguing that the 'if . . . then' of the so-called 'terminating' statements expresses a contrary-to-fact conditional, has robbed them of their terminating character and thereby undermined his whole position.

In regard to his argument for realism from the fact that his terminating statements were contrary-to-fact conditionals, we have concluded that even if they were contrary-to-fact conditionals, this fact would not support even the possibility of realism in the manner claimed; and that by interpreting them as contrary-to-fact conditionals in order to show his realism, he undermined his case for the empirical verifi-

45 AKV, p. 251; also, cf. p. 250.

46 AKV, p. 250.

ability account of the meaning of objective statements within the limits of subjectivism.

This conclusion, coupled with the negative results concerning his first argument for realism, which attempted to show that objective statements were intensionally equivalent to a conjunction of terminating statements but that their terms denoted physical objects and the terms of the terminating statements denoted only appearances, shows, I think, that unless I have completely misconstrued his meaning, Lewis has not made his case for the consistency of the triad of subjectivism, empirical verifiability theory of meaning, and realism. It still seems to be an inconsistent triad. Within the limits of subjectivism and the empirical verifiability theory of meaning, one may, perhaps, be a realist, but one cannot consistently state his realism.

E. M. ADAMS

DEPARTMENT OF PHILOSOPHY
UNIVERSITY OF NORTH CAROLINA AT CHAPEL HILL

## 15

## Charles Hartshorne
# LEWIS' TREATMENT OF MEMORY

### I. *Memory Proper*

CONCERNING what is commonly called memory, Professor Lewis and I differ on but a single point.[1] This one matter of disagreement, however, has such interconnections with other topics in epistemology that to break with Lewis here tends to transform the entire theoretical structure. I shall therefore explain some of these interconnections as I see them, although this may seem to carry us, at times, rather far from the assigned subject. (Any reader who objects to this detouring has only to skip section II and perhaps also III.) My excuse is that except for the one difference and its ramifications I should have nothing to do except paraphrase an author who expresses himself with great clarity and economy. Besides, if I were to keep narrowly to my topic, I should be open to the chief methodological criticism I could make of Lewis, namely, the adherence to a piecemeal method, the relative isolation of epistemological from ontological problems, and even of epistemological problems from one another.

My task is the more difficult in that many readers may be expected to side with Lewis just where I feel forced to deviate from his position. If a few such persons are led to pause and reconsider, I shall not have wasted my efforts. And if Lewis himself can be induced to comment on certain ideas so remote from his own point of view that he has hitherto for the most part avoided discussing them, this too will be a rich reward.

For the validity of memory, Professor Lewis appears to make but one claim: it normally establishes a significant probability that something like what is remembered was really experienced. (Similarly with perception: it establishes a probability that what is perceived is real, which for Lewis means that further perceptions will or would conform to the indicated pattern.) These are minimal claims which no one can

---

[1] I shall base my account largely on Chapter XI, "Probable Knowledge and the Validity of Memory," in *An Analysis of Knowledge and Valuation* (La Salle, Ill.: Open Court Publishing Co., 1946). Hereafter cited as AKV.

avoid making, and which indeed every higher animal makes merely by living. The only question is whether we should not go further. Could memory disclose even a probability, if (*per impossibile*—for I hold this to be not genuinely conceivable) it accomplished no more than that? Can we understand the functioning of memory except by seeing that it discloses, not simply probable truth about the past, but the past itself?

Lewis is one of those who hold that not merely is something given as probable, but something is given—period. It is meaningless to ask, how probable is the given? Were there such a probability, then that which disclosed it to us must itself be given, and not with probability, but with certainty. I agree with Lewis so far, but I also think that his critics have had some justification. For I do not find that he has furnished us with a satisfactory account of the given.

Is the given temporally present, or is it past, or is it sometimes one and sometimes the other? If it is always present, then in this respect perception and memory are not distinguishable, and the pastness of the thing remembered is wholly due to interpretation, although in some mysterious way there is a probability-assurance governing this inter- pretation. Is this Lewis' view? It appears to be, unless one reads another conception into his deliberately somewhat noncommittal term 'epistemological present'.[2] If such be his doctrine, then he is accepting a widespread theory, as old as Aristotle, according to which memory consists entirely in something *merely* present being taken as a sign of something past—a theory which prejudges half the issues in epistemology and ontology. Is it a sound theory?

It does appear to have a certain congruence with some other features of Lewis' general view of knowledge. Thus, were he to hold that hearing, or vision, for instance, is the givenness of events occurring outside our bodies, he would in effect be admitting that past occurrences can be direct data. For example, the physical explosion I hear took place a short time before my hearing it. But Lewis does not say that such things are given; what he seems to hold is that the given is neither event nor actual physical object, but just—the given, a ghostly entity, having no other status than that it is given, a bare 'sense-datum' or quale.

There are difficulties with this attenuated view of givenness. Indirect knowledge of nature seems to imply direct awareness of nature at some point. By 'nature' we mean (or ought to mean) an orderly system of events or processes which are not, save incidentally, human experi- ences. Once we have direct awareness of some portions of the natural system, the rest can be inferred by scientific method; but we are

2 See AKV, pp. 330-32, 334, 338.

scarcely advanced in analyzing this process by the assumption of non-natural entities called 'data', which are nowhere, save in our experiences, and in being aware of which we bring into being (mysteriously aided, perhaps, by nature) the very things we are aware of (though not the 'objects' whose probability is thereby somehow established). I still think G. E. Moore's old argument against what he called 'idealism' applies validly to this view. Awareness accepts, it does not make, its data, not even with the help of an object itself not given.

From these, and other considerations, some of which will appear presently, I conclude: unless something past is given, nothing identifiable is given. Even my seeming to perceive steps before me, to take one of our author's examples, cannot be proved to be given as merely present, since there is a good case, not so far as I know rejected by Lewis, for the view that introspection is really retrospection. Must we not find some escape from the theory of memory so central to skeptical philosophies from Hume to Santayana which denies that the past is ever literally given? This denial seems to drive us to the desperate position that nothing is given, not even the seeming givenness of various entities. (In Santayana, essences are given, but *that* they are given is apparently a mere inference or belief.)

Why, after all, must memory be thought to have as datum something wholly in the present? Lewis seems not to employ here the a priori argument: what is past is gone, nonexistent, hence it cannot be given. This reasoning seems to me almost silly, for if there is no such thing as a past event, how can there be historical truths? Or are these truths true of nonentities? Lewis says that all truth refers to the future, but he must surely admit that historical truth (and historical knowledge) refers to the past also, and not merely to the future. Indeed, he says propositions refer to the whole of space-time.[3]

There seems but one further argument, that from the illusions and mistakes of memory. How could we be mistaken about the absolutely given? The reasoning is the same as Lewis' about perception: some seen objects turn out not to have been there, hence the seeing was not literal givenness of the objects, but only of the sense data. Similarly, since the remembered often turns out not to have taken place, the remembering cannot have been literal givenness of the past, but only of an 'image' or (Lewis' word) 'surrogate', in the present. This is the argument which Lewis employs. Let us grant that the reasoning proves something. Does it prove the total nongivenness of past events? I think not. In

3 See "Some Suggestions Concerning Metaphysics of Logic," *American Philosophers at Work*, ed. Sidney Hook (New York: Criterion Books, 1957), pp. 99-100. Hereafter cited as "Met. Log."

many instances, a particular event which we took ourselves to be remembering was not, indeed, literally given, for no such event had occurred. But Lewis himself is fond of pointing out how inevitably the given is everywhere mixed with thought; indeed, he suggests that unless the given is thought about, interpreted, it probably cannot become a permanently available item of recollection. Thus probably all memory, *so far as consciously reported upon,* involves interpreting the given, and such interpretation is fallible. However, this does not prove that the very pastness of the remembered is supplied by the interpreting process, or that the given in memory is not a part of the past. The theory I propose is rather this: in conscious memory, e.g., verbally reported memory or recollection, certain real past happenings, now given (no, this is not a contradiction!) , are interpreted as signs affording more or less reliable information about still other, usually more remote, past happenings which are no longer given, at least not with the same degree of distinctness and vividness. I am convinced that this theory (to be further elucidated presently) explains everything that the other can explain, and infinitely more besides. And I am inviting Professor Lewis to state, if he so please, his attitude to this theory, which he has neither asserted nor, perhaps, quite unequivocally rejected.

The objects of memory are aspects of past psychical events. I remember, let us say, C. I. Lewis as my teacher; but really what I remember is how it was for me, in a certain stage of my development, to listen to him and talk with him. I remember him as object of certain experiences which I had of him. It would, of course, be hazardous to impute accuracy to any report which I might make upon the basis of these memories. Conscious inspection and verbal report upon data introduce many possibilities of error. Obviously the having of past experiences as given is itself nonverbal, except so far as past verbal experience is itself mnemonically had. Consequently, to *say* what we remember involves all of the risks which verbalization always involves, not only of failing to communicate to another, but of self-confusion. Suppose I say that I remember a sentence uttered by Professor Lewis in 1919, and suppose it could be proved that what he actually said was somewhat different; would this mean that I am now merely imagining the incorrect words, and imputing them to the past? Not at all. If I have (inwardly or outwardly) repeated the sentence to myself at various times since hearing it, I may now be remembering, quite correctly, one of these earlier 'repetitions'. And when I thought up the false rendering, I may well have been trying, even consciously trying, to guess, from fragments of memory, what some forgotten words would likely have been. (I speak for myself: this is how *my* mind at least operates, of this I am sure.) Sometimes I am quite aware of this element of guessing in my recollecting; perhaps never am I aware, with absolute clarity and certainty, where the memory stops and the guessing begins. Thus, when I now recall, not so much an original experience of days or years past as subsequent recollections of that experience, I am partly guessing, with respect to aspects not now noticeably given, the import of a blend of past experiences of various dates, only one of which, at most, corresponds to the date of the original experience that I am trying to recall. So, in two or many steps, usually many, the first experience becomes confused with other factors of imagining and inference, all of them past in relation to the case of memory under consideration. Thus the facts fit the supposition that what recollection utilizes as 'sign' of things past is itself always something past.

As Whitehead says, and there is every justification in the literature for the charge, philosophers rarely consider memory in its primary form, that of the awareness of the *immediate* past—less than a second ago, say. All more remote memory is probably a mass of memories referring to the same still earlier experience, re-remembered many times over, mostly not very consciously. No wonder unambiguous knowledge fails to result! On the other hand, extremely short-run memory, where no intermediate case with the same past datum intervenes, scarcely leaves room for verbalization. Thus nature bars the door to any easy, obvious treatment of memory. Philosophers are mystified, and most of them seem not to suspect the trick, so to speak, that has been played upon them. They hypothetically ask nature to furnish verbalized instances of 'certain knowledge' of the past, and then, finding no unambiguous case, they deny altogether any immediate possession of the past. Yet what errors have really been proved against very short-run memory, apart from reports upon it? I begin a brief phrase, or long word, and as I finish it, do I not realize that I also began it? Yet the 'specious present' (which Lewis refuses to relate to the 'epistemological present') probably does not include this beginning; hence the latter is remembered. (By the flicker tests, for instance, the literal present is shown to be less than a tenth or fifteenth of a second.) I, for one, am sure of no case of error in this sort of thing. It is so little fallible that theorists have scarcely noticed it as a case of mnemonic awareness (I do not say, 'knowledge') at all. Operations which never go astray are taken for granted.

How indeed can anything, any sort of givenness, be more certain than memory in its most immediate aspect? Mathematics is meaningless apart from memory of what one just began to say or think about or write down or look at on a page of symbols. To have any sort of datum is useless unless one can be aware that one has just been having it. Lewis seems to see this vividly—yet not quite vividly enough! His 'epistemological present' blurs the issue. The 'fallibility of memory' is either the fallibility of all cognitive functions whatever, and then there are no 'data', or it is really the fallibility of some types of memory, or more strictly, memory reports, mnemonic interpretations, most of which, largely without knowing it, are trying to deal simultaneously with many cases of memory, vague or faint enough to blend into an apparently single case.

If it be asked why or how direct possession of data can involve vagueness, faintness, and hence the possibility of erroneous report, I shall give a short reply: the notion of absolutely clear, direct intuition is the classic idea of deity, in one formulation; and we are not divine. The contrary assumption (that we are, in this respect, divine) is implicit in the argument from the mistakes of memory to the conventional theory that its data are merely present, not past, realities. But the divine memory would involve no mistakes; so the argument is self-inconsistent. I do not wish to accuse Lewis of this inconsistency; but his argument is at least lacking in explicitness.

What follows from the foregoing reasoning, if, for the business in hand, we accept it as sound? One thing which follows is something Lewis himself asserts: to remember consciously that $X$ occurred (that one experienced $X$) is to establish some probability that it occurred. This is bound to be so, if our theory of memory is correct. For at each step of mnemonic interpretation there is possession (not just imputation) of previous experience, perhaps even of the most remote past experiences, as more or less faintly, unclearly, or unconsciously re-remembered. This possession of the past imposes limits on the deviation of conscious or verbalized reports from the events reported upon; and the probability of memory reports simply expresses these limits. Let us inspect this more closely. Though the mnemonic interpretation is wholly in the present, its datum, or what is interpreted, is a portion of the past. Thus the unity of present awareness includes the past. That this is not a contradiction, I have repeatedly argued (following Whitehead, Bergson, Montague, and others) ; but I do find definite contradiction in the idea that there is *not* an inclusive (retrospective) unity in process. For temporal relations of succession must be in some realities or other, and where if not in events as realities? (Or are they in a metaphysical vacuum 'between' events?) And if relation to predecessors is in events, then so are predecessors; for we are not speaking of *relation to*, but of relation to predecessors, $p$, $p'$, etc. (From what I know of Lewis on relations he *might* accept the argument at this point.) Very good, past events are constituent of present events of experience as remembering; further, an experience is one, and this unity colors all its subjective functions, including the interpretive function we are interested in. Hence it is impossible that this function should proceed as though the past events had not occurred, or had been otherwise. Their past occurrence, just as they were, must make some difference (for relation to them is constitutive), and the probability of the rightness of a retrospective report expresses the general direction of the range of possible differences. Because of faintness or vagueness, and the complexity of the data of memory (all but the just previous experience being re-remembered) interpretation can deviate from the truth more or less widely. But it cannot proceed simply as though the given events were not given; and they could not have been given had they not occurred. For givenness (no matter how interpretive) does not create its data, it merely accepts and uses them. (I regard this as an analytic truth.) Thus we have *explained* (in some degree) and not merely postulated the validity of memory.

There is another of Lewis' assumptions which we can, to some extent, explain, that of 'real connections' in events, causal limitations upon possibility, converting merely logical into 'real' possibility—possibility here and now, in a given context.[4] For, as we argued above, it is not possible (meaning, not really conceivable) that a phase of experience should fail to contain relations to previous phases; hence each phase must make a difference to the next one. Insofar, we have causal necessity, the very thing Hume looked for and failed to find. We do not indeed have complete deterministic necessity with respect to the next event (nor, according to Lewis, does science require this).[5] For it is one thing to say that the given data make a difference to the total experience, and quite another to say that the total present experience was uniquely prescribed by the data which its past offered for it. Experiences, to be sure, accept their data, they do not make them; but neither do the data dictate their own reception. Were there but one logically possible way to receive the given, it must already be or contain the responses to itself; and this is the converse absurdity to the notion that the response creates its stimulus, or the subject its object. Thus I conclude: the same consideration which explains the probability of the truth of memory reports also explains how there can be probable predictions, at least in one type of case. Because the past is literally had, judgments about it cannot deviate without limit, and with equal prob-

4 See AKV, pp. 226 ff.
5 AKV, pp. 228-29.

ability, in every direction; also, because future experiences must contain their own unity with their predecessors (to some extent, remember them), and in this fashion literally possess them, there are limits upon what the future, so far as it consists of experiences, can be. (The generalization of this principle beyond anthropomorphic limitations will be touched on later.) Present experience requires its particular past; here there is necessity in the actual structure of the world. Present experience does not require a particular succeeding event, but only some one or other of a class of events, any one of which would fit the requirements; here there is only probability, whether in our knowledge or in the world. I believe this fits the statistical concept of laws which is now—however much some dislike it—the operative one in science. And even the real necessity of the particular past is reduced to mere probability for our conscious knowledge of each particular case, since introspection and verbalization, as pointed out above, are fallible, limited procedures, and involve elements of guessing, conscious and unconscious, the effect of which is often multiplied over and over—as we remember, and re-remember, the same incident. Even so, if we make our memory reports unspecific enough, they can approximate in reliability to the intuitive certainty upon which they rest. Thus "I remember experiences of some sort or other" can scarcely go wrong.

## II. *The Generalization of Memory*

I wish now to suggest a generalization of memory as we have interpreted it. Assuming some theories of 'substance', both one's present and one's past experiences are merely attributes or 'accidents' inhering in an identical concrete reality, the individual person. Accordingly, memory, even though it grasp the past itself, cannot furnish an illustration of epistemic 'transcendence', it cannot exhibit an actuality experiencing another actuality. On the contrary, for such theories, memory at most exhibits an actuality experiencing 'itself' (as in the past). If, however, one breaks cleanly with such forms of substantialism by taking as the concrete specimen of reality the event, unit-process, or 'experient-occasion', rather than the thing or person, then one may find in memory, interpreted as direct possession of past experiences, a clear case of one actuality experiencing, not itself, but another quite independent actuality—for surely, my previous experience owed nothing of its nature to the way I *now* remember it!

The edge of this issue, unfortunately, has been blunted for our author, since, as he explained orally at a philosophical meeting some years ago, he thinks of the individual as merely a determinate long-span unit-process, or sequence of events, from birth to death. (Here Leibniz was an actual influence, I believe.) The doctrine implies that I should have been another than myself had I just now done or experienced something other than what I did do or experience. Lewis is here looking for the concrete determinate actuality, that which finally 'has' properties, in contrast to properties (as universals). But the momentary states, experiences, or unit-events, meet the requirement; unless one insists (as Lewis, I fear, does) that the truth about all time must be timelessly real, so that a thing must be related, in its own definiteness, to later as well as earlier events.[6] This is a case of what I shall later charge is a failure to do justice to the primacy of asymmetrical, as compared to symmetrical relations. For this and other reasons I hold that the identity of an individual personality through time is not that of a sequence of experiences defined extensionally, by its members, but must be defined in part intensionally, and with a certain indeterminacy, so that alternative possible states, after some initial state, taken as given, would equally serve to continue the sequence constituting the life of that individual.

The question I wish now to ask is, may not something like memory connect us also with past events not belonging to our personal sequence? No doubt there are limitations on such a possibility. If I could be as vividly aware of your past feelings, or a frog's, as of my own past feelings, I should probably have a very confused sense of my own identity. Thus it is not surprising that telepathy, if real, is rare and scanty. It would be psychologically destructive otherwise. But does it follow that I can have no direct experience of concrete events other than my own past states? Any states belonging to a 'foreign' sequence must be adequately subordinated, in any awareness I have of them; but to suppose them necessarily excluded altogether is illogical, since even one's own past experiences are (a) numerically other than, and (b) only relatively akin and congenial to, one's present experiences. So the way is logically open to admit that there may be direct possession of actualities other than one's own past experiences.

Where shall we look for such direct possession of 'foreign' actualities? Apart from telepathy, and from claims to experience the divine, there are but two plausible candidates for the status we have outlined: physical processes outside the body, and physical processes inside the body. To accept the first (the position of naïve realism) would involve us in paradoxes, because of the elements of illusion and distortion from which there is no good reason to think the perception of extra-

6 AKV, pp. 54 ff. See also above, fn. 3.

bodily things is ever wholly free. And Lewis is certainly not a naïve realist in the sense in question. Actualities directly possessed are, by definition, necessary to the experience, so that the latter *could not* occur without them; but the evidence is that you can have any sort of visual or other sensory experiences you please, no matter what is out there beyond your skin, provided only that certain nerve cells can be suitably stimulated, perhaps by electrodes applied to them. But is the neural process itself not indispensable, can we for example, have the experience of red unless the optical system is acting in the as yet unknown way in which (presumably) it ordinarily does act when we have this experience? For all we know, at least, the neural process is invariably present when the experience is present. It is a good working hypothesis for science that this is so; but philosophically or epistemologically, I suspect that it is more than a working hypothesis. For the only apparent alternative is the admission that when I experience red (say, in an after-image) there is nothing identifiable which must be there besides my experience itself. This, however, would mean that I experience red merely as a quality of my experience—my experience of what? (For a 'sense-datum'—as many current writers argue—is a merely verbal entity, which does not furnish an actuality, other than my experience, to which the red can be attributed.) 'Red' is an adjective; but what corresponds to the noun, the entity given as red in its quality? Is it my experience alone, or (in addition) physical processes outside the body, or a physical process within the body, which has the given *quale*? The first would make experience its own object, which I find unintelligible; the second is contradicted by the pervasive elements of partial 'subjectivity' in perception; the third is contradicted by no presently-known fact.[7]

Would Lewis perhaps urge, against this neural datum theory, that inspection of direct experience fails to make neurologists of us (the familiar argument)? Such inspection certainly does not give us all the facts of neurology, or of any other science (those who suppose that we directly experience stones must admit that we cannot read off molecular theory from mere sense perception). Nevertheless, to say that direct experience reveals none of the facts of neurology is quite simply to beg the question here at issue. Of course, we do not know the meaning of 'neural system' by direct experience alone, any more than of 'molecule'. Nevertheless, what physiologists speak of as 'neural process' may be found, when more fully known, to include the given

[7] Not even, I think, by such facts as are cited by W. R. Brain, in *Mind, Perception and Science* (Oxford and Toronto: Oxford University Press, 1951), pp. 8, 70 f.

sensory pattern in those structural aspects which, as Lewis is fond of saying, are all that science is able to measure and ascertain. We have no reason to think, and strong reason to deny, that the objects we see in front of us will be found to possess exactly this pattern; for the optical system, like all recording or receiving instruments, is imperfect and more or less distorts what it registers. (Only direct experience, apart from inference, does not distort: it merely simplifies, in the sense that much detail is introspectively unavailable.) If we cannot know cell-theory (though we can know certain properties of Something which in fact, unknown to us, may be a mass of cells) without the indirect knowledge of the physiologists, still less can we know atomic theory; though in normal cases we can safely infer some rough truths about Something which in fact is a system of atoms, without the indirect knowledge of the physicists. No one, whatever his philosophy, denies that the natural and quasi-instinctive claim of sense perception is to relate or adapt us to the extra-bodily environment; but this claim is logically quite compatible with the view that the direct possession is of the inner-bodily process. We have been learning since birth (or longer) that the practical import of sense experience is chiefly in its power to give information about (not necessarily 'acquaintance' with) the extra-bodily sources of stimuli. But perhaps still more exact information concerning the neural reactions could, if we learned how, be extracted from sensation.

How is all this connected with memory? If memory is the givenness of certain past personal experiences, and perception is the givenness of certain neural events, then we confront the following possibilities: (1) the two modes of givenness are alike in that in both the data are temporally prior to the experience having them as data; (2) the givenness of neural events expresses a radically different principle from memory, in that in the former the data are simultaneous with the experience. Such a dualism of principles is never to be adopted unnecessarily. In this respect, the notion, which is apparently Lewis', that the given is always merely present is preferable to the notion that it is sometimes past and sometimes not. But this unity of principle can also be achieved by holding that to be given means, in all cases, to be past in and for some present. This view has the following additional advantages: (1) Symmetrical relations (Lewis the logician knows this better than I, whether or not Lewis the epistemologist does) are derivative from asymmetrical ones; consequently, to say that data are symmetrically co-present with the experience and with one another, a mere array of relations in space but not in time, is to assert that experience in principle gives us only what could be inferred, and is insofar superfluous, while withholding the information from which alone both temporal and spatial relations follow, namely information as to temporal-causal relations of before and after! (2) If, and only if, the datum is past, can we construe the realistic postulate which seems essential to the meaning of knowledge, the postulate that knowledge conforms to the known, not vice versa. This is an asymmetrical relation, which cannot be made intelligible in terms of the notion that the two are contemporary, a symmetrical relation. That only a few neglected metaphysicians have recognized these elementary considerations may show that our treatment of basic epistemological questions, in spite of the subtleties of recent semantics, remains still a long way from adequacy.

In accordance with the foregoing reasoning, we now ask, may it not be that in sensation we 'remember' (or possess as given—the word is not important) what has just occurred in the nervous system as it received certain stimuli? Somewhat as many thinkers, including apparently Lewis, have tended to overleap the primary personal memory, the sense of what is past by less than a second or two, which is in itself quite certain, being possession of its datum, but is not at all obvious *as* a case of memory (there being insufficient time to reflect on or verbalize it as such), and have turned rather to the obvious, but not so certain, secondary form of memory, recollection of the more remote past, so similarly have many philosophers tended to pass over the unobtrusive but certain possession of just-elapsed inner-bodily process, the primary sensory givenness, in order to meditate upon the teasingly manifest, but for the most part, at least, only apparently direct givenness (really 'instinctive' judgment) of extra-bodily objects. In both cases, the oversight has the same source, the lack of ready introspective availability of the immediate. Some superhuman being may be able to know in all cases that he experiences (feels, enjoys, intuits, possesses, senses) what he does experience, down to the last subtle detail, but should we credit ourselves with such an absolute self-observing power?

Some readers may think that Lewis should have 'brain traces' in mind when he speaks of 'surrogates for the past' in memory. There are, I presume, necessary cortical conditions for our remembering, and by my own argument they must be data; but (a) I should regard them as immediately past, not merely present, and (b) they are data, not instead of, but along with the personal experiences remembered, and (c) their function is to give memory its selectiveness by their congruity (emotional, aesthetic, intellectual) with certain items in the past, and still more, by their incongruity with all the other items; for as Bergson reminds us—and it probably took genius to see something so simple—we have incomparably more 'forgetting' than recollecting to explain.

The generalization of memory to include sensation is by no means the end of the story. The further questions arise: are human, or verte- brate, animals the only remembering creatures, and if not, where is the lower limit of this function? The question may seem to belong merely to empirical science; but this is doubtful. For we have seen that memory, as direct possession of the past, furnishes a clue to the possibility of real connections among events such that probabilities may be objective char- acters of the world, in knowing which we really do know something other than just our knowledge itself. Now a clue to causality is rele- vant, not to this or that science, but to all science, and indeed to meta- science, to ontology as such. Hume did a good job in showing that there is no other clue to causality. Lewis comes closer than Hume to seeing that there is at least this clue. I am trying to urge him closer still.

There are definite reasons why our philosopher has not taken the path we wish him to take. I shall never forget (my 'memory' may, however, somewhat deceive me, since I am in part guessing where I do not exactly recall) his telling me, long ago, how strongly he felt that inanimate physical objects lack any inner life, feeling, or value of their own; they exist, he said, simply to be experienced and used. This anthropocentric position (as I feel it to be) is exactly what prevents Lewis (and so many others with him) from making any really intelli- gible and more than verbal distinction between phenomenalism and realism.[8] For is not the sense of reality social through and through? What is it to recognize a process, other than one's own actual experience, as also actual, if it is not to attribute to that process some sort of inner life, value, feeling, and memory (here the causal nexus comes in) of its own? Is there any other way of extracting any real juice, so to speak, from the realist-phenomenalist issue?

It happens that Lewis has, quite explicitly, discussed some such view as the one just expressed.[9] His verdict: If (but only if) we suppose knowledge to require an 'analogy of quality', as well as of structure, be- tween our experience and what we know, then the social view of 'real- ity' properly follows; moreover, for other than cognitive purposes, for instance in ethics, we do need to suppose such an analogy—though only in limited application, that is, so far as other conscious beings are concerned. But (a) even in this limited sense, the social principle tran-

---

[8] For his latest attempt, see his fine article, "Realism or Phenomenalism?" *The Philosophical Review*, 64 (1955), 223-247.

[9] *Mind and the World-Order* (New York: Charles Scribner's Sons, 1929), Appendix C.

scends all verifiable knowledge and is simply a 'postulate'; and (b) insofar as inanimate nature is concerned, it may not even be meaningful to try to deal with it in terms of 'empathy' (the attribution of qualitative analogy to ourselves). Presumably, Lewis is afraid here of the 'pathetic fallacy', and one understands his fear. But there is another fallacy, more insidious among trained minds, which one may call 'the prosaic fallacy', the error of supposing that what is not, for our casual inspection, obviously endowed with a life of its own is thereby shown to be mere lifeless stuff, or bare structure without inner 'quality'. But surely the world is not obvious. Think of the history of science, of the microstructure or megalostructure of things, both different even in principle from what direct perception for ages led people to think.

Please note, too, that we cannot even postulate something as a contingent truth unless we are able to form a conception of an alternative which could be true. But what is the alternative in this case? It is not enough that we have reason to say, "this thing does not feel" (hence does not remember). For a crowd of persons in an elevator does not feel or remember either, though each person does so. Also, a finger does not feel, though it can be a normal finger only as part of a being who does feel. Moreover, its cells may feel. Thus, to be known as a reality whose nature does not in any way include sentience, a thing must be known both not to consist of constituents which feel *and* not to be essentially a part of a larger whole, perhaps the universe, which feels. Now I at least cannot conceive how all this could be known by any mind whatever. I incline therefore to suspect that there is nothing here to know, but rather a pseudo-conception. Wittgenstein wittily says that a teapot is too 'smooth' to have feeling attributed to it. But is not this smoothness the teapot's lack of dynamic singularity? The teapot does not 'do' things, as a single agent, in response to the environment. However, individual response is in this case masked for our perception, as modern science shows—such response being on the micro-level. And it needs no science to tell us that the only way to experience an object as objectively one, in the causal system of things, is to experience it as an active, responsive, agent in the world. I therefore suggest that the notion of a duality of sentient and insentient portions of nature could not be anything but an attempt to get knowledge out of ignorance, out of a blurred view in which aggregates appear as quasi-singulars, and/or arbitrarily discriminated parts appear as wholes.

If then there is no alternative, other than verbal, to the notion that dynamic singulars feel—and such wit as I have suggests none—then the empathic principle itself is not a postulate, nor does it need verification. The function of postulation, as of verification, is to rule out possible alternatives; where no alternative can be defined, there is nothing either to postulate or to verify. We are then dealing either with something self-evident, a metaphysical necessity, or else with a mere absurdity. But Lewis agrees that the empathic principle, in some instances, is not an absurdity. If, moreover, no alternative can in any instance be offered, the principle must universally apply. The task for empirical knowledge or, in lieu of this, for postulation, is only to specialize the general 'analogy of feeling' to fit particular cases. Here verification is more or less possible. Not only does feeling express itself in behavior, but, as recent British authors have stressed, and sometimes overstressed and overstated, feeling gets its character from its expression to such an extent that there are logical limits to the possibility of deception or mistake as to how another feels. To imagine that any sort of behavior could accompany any sort of feeling, or lack of feeling, is an anarchic mode of thinking which deprives the conceptions of diverse modes of experience or feeling of any clear meanings. As we have suggested in the case of sensation, human experience and bodily process are not merely thrown together, but (like all constantly associated things in nature) have intrinsic connections, direct or indirect.[10]

## III. *Epistemology and Ontology*

Our philosopher might say that I have been discussing science, ontology, or metaphysics, whereas he has dealt with epistemology. If, indeed, the theory of knowledge is to be sharply separated from the theory of nature, then Lewis' way of doing this is my choice. But how much isolation of theory of knowledge is worthwhile? Perhaps a good deal, if the aim is merely defensive, to ward off skepticism and dogmatism. However, the following considerations suggest (they may not prove) that epistemology is essentially an aspect of ontology, not a separate and prior study.

If we know some actual cases of knowledge, then we know certain samples of actuality, in something of their true nature. Our cognitive experiences are real, and if we can theorize effectively about them, then we know at least these instances of reality. And just possibly these are the most accessible and illuminating of the samples available to us.

10 That Lewis holds the anarchic view of merely factual correlations between behavior and feeling seems to follow from what he asserts in *Our Social Inheritance* (Bloomington, Ind.: Indiana University Press, 1957), pp. 80 ff. about the possibility of a world in which "felt pain automatically induced" creatures "to persevere in the act which caused it" so that life would become "progressively less satisfying and more grievous for creatures which survived." I do not find that I can conceive such a world.

Furthermore, if we know instances of knowing, then we must know some reality which is known in these instances. For otherwise, what we would have is not instances of knowledge, but (for all we would know) of illusion. Lewis gives us something of a theory of reality: a real object is at least a concrete law or pattern, a matrix of conditionally predictable human experiences. But why are we concerned to predict human experiences? Because of our social sense! We tend to sympathize with and care about future experiences, imagined or expected, for our-selves or for others. This is one aspect of the social sense of reality, which, as I believe, is the only sense of reality there is. And is not the separation of ethical interests and cognitive ones at this point almost meaningless? Whether or not we call it knowledge—and it might be better to speak of understanding, or self-understanding—surely we wish to grasp or comprehend what knowledge is, and what it is doing in the world. If this comprehension is not 'knowledge', it is still capable of truth and falsity, or at least, of clarity and confusion, or of adequacy and inadequacy. Perhaps 'wisdom' is a better word here, the wisdom which philosophy is in search of.

It is a paradox, well illustrated in Lewis' work, that in an age which makes 'intersubjectivity' an object of devoted and at times almost frantic seeking, the kind of ontology or metaphysics which views inter-subjectivity (sociality) as the basic principle of existence is scarcely dis-cussed. The concept of the physical object is supreme in science—why? Because it is intersubjectively utilizable. But who does not see—certainly Lewis sees—that the concept of 'subject' is itself put beyond question and made primary in this approach? We need to transcend the subject not in order to deal with a mere object, but in order to deal with another subject—or at least with other experience, perhaps one's own future experience. There are really but two doctrines to choose between: (1) there are subjects, or sequences of experiences, and there are also, or at least may be, concrete singular things which are not subjects or experiences; (2) concrete singulars are always instances or sequences of experiences or subjects, these being of many kinds (imbeciles and infants, frogs and amoebae, philosophers and statesmen, indicating only a small part of the total array of kinds). It happens not to be fashion-able to discuss seriously the issue between these two positions. But this seems to mean that, for some cultural reason, the center has been dis-placed toward the periphery, the center being the status of the social concept of existence. It does seem that a theory of knowledge should throw some light on this matter.

A final argument against the attempt to purify epistemology from ontological commitments is the general principle of intellectual method according to which an ultimate test of ideas is unexpected applicability, so-called fruitfulness. This is shown when ideas designed to explain one region of facts or one aspect of experience illuminate also quite other regions or aspects. Our theory of memory does this; for it exhibits certain epistemic relations as making not only the possibility of knowing but the structure of reality in general more intelligible.

Lewis urges that no special contingent fact needs to be assumed to explain probable knowledge, beyond those facts already involved in the mere existence and continuance of experience and thought themselves. Let us grant this. Let us grant too that in no possible world or state of affairs would there not be probabilities to discover. Such probabilities are already included in any meaningful concept of 'world' or 'state of affairs'. But two questions may be distinguished: (a) do past events impose limitations on possibilities for the future? (b) *how*, or by virtue of what real connections, do they do so? The first question answers itself; for even animals 'know' that the past discloses information about the future. The second question we are not indeed forced to answer. It is not defensively required. But why be defensive here? Curiosity has done a lot for man. Perhaps we might indulge it here. Memory may be (Bergson, Whitehead, Peirce, and others think it is) our best key to temporal structure in general. That the present is potentially past is, they hold, that it is potentially remembered. In any case epistemic relations, such as those of memory, are also facts in nature, and having been carried across these bridges to certain parts of nature, we should not forget that the bridges also are parts of nature. Moreover, if the very concept of reality involves probability as objective, as a system of limitations actually obtaining with respect to possible modes of succession, and if such limitations are intelligible only in terms of the mnemonic structure of experience, fully generalized, then this suggests that the notion of a state of affairs not constituted by forms of experiences, or again the notion of experiences whose data are all confined to the temporal present, are alike devoid of coherent meanings.

Need it be said that to speak of 'memory' is not to speak of something necessarily human? Amoebae have been shown to learn; and there is no good reason why all the forms of memory must be detectable by us in the foreseeable scientific future. Memory might operate in millionths of a second, or over millions of years, to mention only the most obvious dimension of variability.

## IV. *Summary of Questions*

Now that my point of view has been stated, some of its differences from, and agreements with, that of Lewis, can be summarized and documented as follows. Lewis holds that there are 'indubitable', 'entirely certain' data;[11] I agree. But he seems to think no such data are temporally past; and that all cases of 'present-as-past' are, as such, probable only,[12] the sheerly given being 'surrogates' of the past in the 'epistemological present'.[13] I hold, on the contrary, that the given is never something temporally present, but always consists of antecedent events literally 'present' epistemically, though past temporally. I deny that this presentness of the past involves contradiction. Lewis does not explicitly discuss the contradiction argument, either way; instead, he seems to reason to the surrogate theory from the errors of memory.[14] But this, on his own showing, looks like a nonsequitur; for in the case of the sensorily given, he admits that it is always difficult to put the given into words or judgments without error, that the data are more or less 'inexpressible'.[15] It is also clear that the errors of memory he has in mind are not taken from instances of immediate or short-run memory, concerning which there has been no time for verbal or other interpretation, but rather, they are recollections of relatively remote past occurrences, such as we have in mind when we judge the future on the basis of conjunctions observed in the past.[16] Such recollections are needed in induction; but they do not suffice to show us what memory in principle is. That they can err no more shows that nothing past is intuitively possessed than do the errors of sense-perception show that nothing is possessed in sensation. Lewis rejects the argument against indubitable sense data which reasons from the difficulty of putting this indubitability into explicit formulation. Why should he so readily accept the similar argument against the indubitable givenness of something past? And indeed, how can he prove that even the data of sensation are anything more or less than aspects of just-occurrent (neural) process, that is, factors temporarily past? Thus my challenge to Lewis is: how can you show that anything merely present is ever given (is not even 'introspection' really retrospection?) —and how can you show that the data of memory are mere surrogates? Do you show it by pointing to the 'mistakes of memory', neglecting the difference between indirect memory (re-remembering) and direct or immediate memory, also the difference between having and interpreting of data; and if this is your

11 AKV, pp. 182 f., 321, 333, 335.

12 AKV, pp. 332, 334, 338.

13 AKV, p. 331.

14 AKV, pp. 331, 334.

15 AKV, p. 321.

16 AKV, pp. 326, 328.

reasoning, does it leave intact your defense of indubitable sense data? Or is your argument that of those who see a contradiction between 'past' and 'given in the present'? In that case, are you assuming that no relation of an event $B$ to an event $A$ can ever be intrinsic to term $B$? (The doctrine of direct memory is that it is a relation of the remembering event $B$ to an earlier event $A$, this relation being internal to $B$.) And will you tell me where relations of succession can be if not in the succeeding events? Finally, does not a relation to $A$ include $A$?

Lewis has a long discussion of how memory judgments, none of them certain, can, without vicious regress, by their congruence achieve substantial probability greater than that possessed by any of the judgments taken separately.[17] Congruence is held to be weaker than the 'coherence' (everything internally related to everything) of absolute idealists, and stronger than mere 'consistency'. This discussion I find admirable and for all I know entirely correct. I am only concerned about the questions, Does not the probability of nonimmediate and interpretive memory rest on a sheer givenness of the immediate past in immediate memory (and as element therein, of the more remote past), just as the probability of sense perception rests on the sheer givenness of something not simply my present awareness?

Lewis is eloquent and cogent on the subject of those who would claim to know (or even to conceive) that the past is unknowable; is it much better to claim to know or conceive that the past is present exclusively as probable? We may say to him: If certainty is 'only an ideal' with regard to the past, is it not an ideal in any reference, and are you not then left with the vicious regress of 'probability of probability' which you seek to avoid? (For that we have memories at all is itself known by retrospection.) Why should not that 'epistemological present' you speak of include the past itself, and your 'surrogates', giving only probability, be a mixture of the given past with fallible interpretive processes? How could you possibly know that this is not true? And since it helps to make the probability we must take for granted intelligible, while leaving the errors of memory also intelligible, can we not reasonably know it *is* true? Does not admitting this strengthen, rather than weaken, your basic scheme?

I do hope my former teacher—and very fascinating and stimulating he was—sees fit to satisfy just a little my considerable curiosity as to how the foregoing seems to him to deviate from good sense. For deviate

17 AKV, pp. 338-362.

somehow I presume it must seem to him to do. Such is the fate of philosophers, no matter how highly they may think of one another.

CHARLES HARTSHORNE

DEPARTMENT OF PHILOSOPHY
UNIVERSITY OF TEXAS

## 16

### Arthur W. Burks

## THE PRAGMATIC-HUMEAN THEORY OF PROBABILITY AND LEWIS' THEORY*

### I. Introduction

FROM the very beginning probability theory has been used to guide action. At first it was applied mainly to a limited kind of life situation, namely games of chance, though Pascal in his famous 'wager' applied it to what for him was the most important decision in life. This tendency to treat life itself as a 'gamble and a game' has become more and more pronounced as probability theory has developed. One recent type of theory is based entirely on the use of probability to guide choices made when the outcomes are uncertain.

Frank Ramsey outlined such a theory about thirty years ago in his "Truth and Probability."[1] Later, but independently, Bruno de Finetti published his subjective theory of probability.[2] Since then economists and psychologists have applied probability and utility theory to individual and managerial choices made under conditions of uncertainty.[3] Recently the theory has been developed and refined by L. J. Savage,[4] who calls his version "a personal theory of probability."

The theories of probability developed by this movement are closely related to pragmatic theories of belief and meaning, and for this reason

*Added in proof: This paper was written a long time ago, and I would treat some of the points in it differently now. The most important changes would concern indeterminate probabilities. None of the changes would, however, affect what I say about Lewis. My present views on probability are expounded in my forthcoming book, *Cause, Chance, and Reason*, to be published by the University of Michigan Press.

1 Written in 1926, published in 1931, in F. P. Ramsey, *The Foundations of Mathematics and Other Logical Essays* (New York: Harcourt Brace, 1931), pp. 156-198. Cf. also 199-211, 256 f.

2 "La prévision: ses lois logiques, ses sources subjectives," *Annales de l'Institut Henri Poincaré*, 7 (1937), 1-68.

3 John von Neumann and Oskar Morgenstern, *Theory of Games and Economic Behavior*, 1947.

*Decision Processes*, ed. R. M. Thrall, C. H. Coombs, and R. L. Davis (New York: John Wiley & Sons, 1954).

4 *The Foundations of Statistics* (New York: John Wiley & Sons, 1954). Hereafter cited as FS.

I have called them *pragmatic theories of probability*.[5] This name is used by neither the advocates of pragmatic theories nor traditional pragmatic epistemologists, because for the most part the connections between these two movements have not been recognized. Though Ramsey was stimulated by C. S. Peirce's pragmatism, most of the architects of pragmatic probability theories have been mathematicians, economists, and psychologists. They were not aware that their work was closely related to something in philosophy; indeed, most of them did not even know of Ramsey's work in this area. Likewise, pragmatic philosophers are generally unaware of pragmatic theories of probability. Thus Professor Lewis mentions neither Ramsey nor de Finetti when discussing probability in his *An Analysis of Knowledge and Valuation*.[6]

In Section II ("Pragmatic Theories of Meaning and Probability") I will develop the similarities between pragmatic theories of probability and pragmatic theories of belief and meaning. I am not, of course, asserting that either logically implies the other. Lewis' theory of meaning is similar to Peirce's, and each is logically compatible with either Lewis' a priori theory of probability or Peirce's frequency theory.[7] All I wish to claim is that a pragmatic theory of probability coheres well with a pragmatic epistemology, of either the Peirce or the Lewis variety.

The comparison of pragmatic epistemologies and pragmatic theories of probability will lead to a criticism of the latter in Section III ("Probability and Investigation") and then to some positive claims about partial belief in Section IV ("Indeterminate Probabilities"). In Section V these positive claims will be combined with a pragmatic theory of probability and a Humean philosophy of induction to give a new theory of probability which we will call a Pragmatic-Humean theory of probability. Finally, in Section VI we will consider this new theory in relation to the theory of probability Professor Lewis presents in *An Analysis of Knowledge and Valuation*.

## II. *Pragmatic Theories of Meaning and Probability*

1. To show the relation between pragmatic theories of probability

---

[5] "The Presupposition Theory of Induction," *Philosophy of Science*, 20 (July, 1953), 177-197. See p. 185. Hereafter cited as "Presup. Theo. Ind." See also my "On the Significance of Carnap's System of Inductive Logic for the Philosophy of Induction," in *The Philosophy of Rudolf Carnap* (La Salle, Ill.: Open Court Publishing Co., 1963), pp. 742 f. Hereafter cited as "Signif. Carnap Syst."

[6] La Salle, Ill.: Open Court Publishing Co., 1946. Hereafter cited as AKV.

[7] *Collected Papers of Charles Sanders Peirce*, vols. 1-6 ed. Charles Hartshorne and Paul Weiss, vols. 7-8 edited by Arthur Burks (Cambridge: Harvard University Press, 1931-35, 1958). Hereafter cited as CP and references will be made by volume and paragraph number; e.g., CP 5.403 refers to par. 403 of vol. 5.

and of meaning we need to distinguish *partial beliefs* from *total beliefs*. A man examines a coin carefully, tosses it a few times and then concludes that the probability of a head on the next toss is one-half. He tosses it, and observes that it does fall heads. His belief that the probability of it falling heads is one-half is a partial belief, while his belief that it did fall heads is a total belief.

Traditional pragmatic theories of belief and meaning give analyses of total beliefs. Such, for example, is Peirce's thesis that a belief is a habit of action. According to this thesis, a sentence of the form '*A* believes that *p*' implies that *A* has dispositions to act in various ways under given conditions and to expect results of various kinds depending on the circumstances. Peirce's theory of meaning leads to two patterns of analysis for '*p*', the proposition believed, which tell us how to spell out the actions, conditions, and expectations involved in a total belief.[8] According to the first pattern 'This diamond is hard' is to be analyzed into *practical consequences* such as 'If it is rubbed with the point of a knife it will not be scratched'.[9] The 'practical consequences' in this pattern of analysis are hypotheticals of the form 'If I act in a manner $\phi$, I will have experience $\psi$'.

The antecedent and consequent of a Peircean practical consequence are physical object propositions. By making both antecedent and consequent sense data propositions instead we get Lewis' version of pragmatism. Thus Lewis says that the meaning of 'A piece of white paper is now before me' consists of an infinite conjunction of judgments of the form of 'If I act in manner *A*, the empirical eventuation will include *E*', and then goes on to say "the presentation, the envisaged action, and the expected consequence—must be described in language which will denote immediately presented or directly presentable contents of experience."[10]

Peirce suggests a second pattern of analysis for beliefs.

... the intellectual purport of a concept consists in the truth of certain conditional propositions asserting that if the concept be applicable, and the utterer of the proposition or his fellow have a certain purpose in view, he would act in a certain way.[11]

---

[8] Peirce's analysis is of the content of the belief rather than of the belief itself, but since this analysis makes reference to an agent it can easily be converted into a description of a belief, and we will often do this. Nevertheless, it should be remembered that the pragmatist is here abstracting those public elements common to the beliefs of all people understanding the sentence being analyzed, and is not interested in the purely subjective aspects of a person's beliefs.

[9] CP, 4.45, 4.435n1, 5.9, 5.403, 5.411-412, 5.467.

[10] AKV, pp. 178-180; cf. p. 16.

[11] CP, 5.528. See also 5.438, 5.212, 5.402, 5.428, 5.548.

Here the analysis is in terms of the actions taken to realize desires under specified circumstances. Thus Peirce is suggesting that '$B$ believes $p$' can be analyzed into practical consequences of the form "If $B$ wants $\phi$ and should be in circumstances $\psi$, then he would act in manner $\theta$."[12]

Peirce applied this analysis almost exclusively to total beliefs;[13] e.g., '$B$ believes it is raining' has the practical consequence 'If $B$ wants to avoid getting wet and should have to go out, then he would put on his raincoat'. But it may be extended to cover partial beliefs, and when it is the result is approximately the analysis pattern offered by pragmatic theories of probability, as we shall now see.

2. Whereas belief in 'It will rain tomorrow' would usually lead to our calling off a planned picnic, belief in 'It will probably rain tomorrow' will only lead to this action in more restricted circumstances. Hence the latter proposition will imply the practical consequence 'If he should very much want a successful picnic, and it's not hard to postpone it, then he would call it off', but will not imply the practical consequence 'Even if he doesn't care much about a successful picnic, and it's hard to postpone it, he would call it off'. Thus it is evident that in formulating the practical consequences of partial beliefs we must take into account the value of the goal and the cost of attaining it, as well as the magnitude of the probability involved. But these first two factors really should enter into the analysis of total beliefs. For example, 'It is raining', does not entail that if my aversion to getting wet is mild that I should nevertheless put on a raincoat at any cost (e.g., by stealing it or buying it at an exorbitant price).

Therefore a pragmatic analysis of any belief should take into account the amount of value associated with an action. A practical consequence will then be something like 'If $B$ wants $\phi$ to degree $x$, and should be in circumstance $\psi$, and thinks action $\theta$ will cost $y$, then he would act in manner $\theta$'. Now a detailed formulation of the conditions of action is extremely complicated for total beliefs, and of course more so for partial beliefs, where the additional concept of probability enters in. For this

[12] In his later period Peirce believed that material implication is inadequate here and that the 'would' is essential; CP, 4.546, 4.579-584, 5.467, 5.528, 8.380. Likewise Lewis holds that material implication is inadequate for the terminating judgments of his pragmatic analyses; AKV, pp. 226-230.

[13] At one place Peirce briefly suggests a pragmatic analysis of partial beliefs. "Doubt has degrees and may approximate indefinitely to belief, but when I doubt, the effect of the mental judgment will not be seen in my conduct as invariably or to the full extent that it will when I believe. Thus, if I am perfectly confident that an insurance company will fulfill their engagements I will pay them a certain sum for a policy, but if I think there is a risk of their breaking, I shall not pay them so much." CP, 7.314n4. It is interesting that this occurs in Peirce's first work on pragmatism, the hitherto unpublished Logic of 1873.

PRAGMATIC-HUMEAN PROBABILITY THEORY    419

reason the developers of pragmatic theories of probability do not attempt
to give analyses of probabilistic propositions or partial beliefs, in the
sense of alternative statements with the 'same meaning'. Instead, they
describe how the concept of probability is and should be used, and how
a person with a partial belief does and should behave.

There is an extensive literature on pragmatic theories of probability[14]
and we do not have space to give a complete description of them here,
so we will confine ourselves to the main points of the analysis and to
some evaluative remarks.

Partial beliefs are of various strengths, which according to the pragmatic theory of probability, may be measured (see Section III,2). The
strength of a belief is called the *degree* of that belief and according to
the pragmatic theory is identical with a probability. Let $c$ and $d$ be
propositions or statements, let '$P(c) = x$' symbolize 'the probability of
$c$ is $x$', and let '$P(c, d) = x$' symbolize 'the probability of $c$ on evidence $d$
is $x$'; these probabilities are called 'nonrelative' and 'relative' respectively. A pragmatist in probability theory identifies a partial belief in
$c$ of degree $x$ with a total belief in $P(c) = x$, that is, on his theory
degree of partial belief and nonrelative probability are the same thing.
He gives a similar account of relative probabilities.

The pragmatic theory explains partial belief in terms of choices
made in situations where the possible outcomes are uncertain. Since the
simple gambling situation has been historically influential on probability
theory generally and pragmatic theories in particular, we will begin with
it, confining our attention mostly to nonrelative probabilities. The
pragmatic theory of probability holds, as a first approximation, that $B$
has a partial belief in $p$ of degree $x$ whenever $B$ is willing to bet on $p$
with odds $x$ to $1-x$. This simple formula must be elaborated in two basic
respects. The relation between probability and value must be described
in more detail, and the descriptive aspects of probability must be separated from the normative elements. We will take these topics up in turn
in the next two subsections.

3. It is characteristic of pragmatic epistemologies in general, and of
pragmatic theories of probability in particular, that they assert a close
and essential connection between these three: (1) belief and knowledge,
(2) value, and (3) choosing from alternative courses of action. A basic
principle which connects all these is 'maximize expected utility'.

---

[14] We have already cited several references. Two additional ones are: Kenneth J.
Arrow, "Alternative Approaches to the Theory of Choice in Risk-taking Situations,"
*Econometrics*, 19 (1951), 404-437; D. Davidson and P. Suppes, *Decision Making, An
Experimental Approach* (Stanford, Calif.: Stanford University Press, 1957).

420  A. W. BURKS

*Expected utility* is an amalgam of probability and value, of the 'probably true' and the good. Expected utility can be defined in terms of probability and value (utility), or it may be taken as primitive and the concepts of probability and value defined by means of it. Since a pragmatic theory makes expected utility basic, the latter is the best approach for it. For our purpose, however, it is more convenient to define expected utility in terms of probability and pure utility (value).

Suppose a man has his choice of actions $A$ and $A'$. Suppose further that action $A$ will have one of two consequences, $C_1$ and $C_2$, that $C_1$ occurs with a probability of $x$ and $C_2$ with probability $1 - x$, and that the utilities of $C_1$ and $C_2$ are $u_1$ and $u_2$ respectively. Action $A'$ is analyzed in a similar way. The expected utility is calculated by summing over the products of the probabilities and the utilities of the individual consequences. Thus the expected utility of $A$ is $xu_1 + (1 - x) u_2$. According to the pragmatic theory a rational person should, and often does, choose the action which seems to him to have the largest expected utility.

The formula $xu_1 + (1 - x) u_2$ is acceptable as a first approximation, but various criticisms may be made of it. One may object that not all alternatives are comparable and reducible to a common measure; this criticism will be presented in Sections III and IV. The formula is also inadequate because it does not take into account the value of gambling per se or of certainty.[15] An example will illustrate this. I would prefer

(A) $2,000,000 with a probability of 0.20, nothing otherwise

to

(A') $500,000 with a probability of 0.21, nothing otherwise

on the ground that success in both cases is unlikely and the prize of $A$ is much larger. But I would prefer

(B') $500,000 with certainty

to

(B) $2,000,000 with probability 0.20, $500,000 with probability 0.79, nothing otherwise,[16]

because B' gives me a small fortune with certainty. Now when

(C) $500,000 with probability 0.79

is added to $A$ the result is logically equivalent to $B$, and when this same 'prize' is added to $A'$ the result is $B'$. This being so, by the principle of maximizing expected utility I should prefer $B$ to $B'$. But I originally

[15] Peirce pointed out that an element of security motivates our choices: "Mere certainty is worth a great deal. We wish to know our fate. How much it is worth is a question of political economy." CP, 7.6, cf. 7.186.

[16] It is intended here that these probabilities concern mutually exclusive options; thus one cannot get both the $2,000,000 and the $500,000 prize in $B$. A similar remark applies to the results of combining $C$ with $A$ and $C$ with $A'$.

preferred $B'$ to $B$ and still do, since there is no element of chance in $B'$ while there is in $B$.[17]

To a large extent the principle of maximizing expected utility turns out on interpretation to be an a priori regulative principle. This brings us to the normative aspect of pragmatic theories of probability.

4. Analyses of meaning are usually partly descriptive (telling us what we actually mean) and partly normative (telling us what we ought to mean). This was true of Peirce's original pragmatic analysis, which he presented as a maxim for making our ideas clear. It would be interesting to hear from Professor Lewis the extent to which he intended his analyses of nonterminating judgments and of probability to be normative.[18] Certainly pragmatic theories of probability contain normative as well as descriptive elements; it is for this reason that we sometimes used such locutions as 'one should, and usually does, choose' in presenting the pragmatic theory. These normative aspects are best presented by considering a person's total system of partial beliefs rather than a single such belief. The normative elements in pragmatic theories appear on at least two levels: first, in the attempt of a rational individual to make his partial beliefs fit a norm, and second, in that a pragmatic theory may itself be put forward as (partly) a recommended norm.

At the first level, then, one's system of partial beliefs is based on a set of norms. Most people will try to make their partial beliefs satisfy certain probability principles, such as $P(c, d) = 1 - P(\sim c, d)$, and other principles of the calculus of probability. This norm may function only dispositionally—e.g., the person may be ignorant of probability theory but is nevertheless willing to abide by its principles when they are explained to him. Or the norm may function more explicitly, in that the person may claim or believe that his partial beliefs are in accord with general probability principles. These principles may be arranged in a hierarchy, so that there are levels within this first level. Thus students often accept the calculus of probability and also the principle that after a run of heads on a fair coin fairly tossed a tail is more likely than not, and then give up the latter principle when they see that it (together with their belief that the tosses are independent) contradicts the calculus of probability.

Some if not all pragmatic theories of probability are normative themselves, making recommendations as well as giving descriptions closely related to these recommendations. Thus the maxim 'maximize expected

---

17 This example is due to M. Allais. See FS, pp. 101-103 for a different analysis of it.

18 Of course an analysis can be normative in many ways, so Lewis might answer this question in the affirmative without making the practical claims for his theory of meaning that Peirce made for his.

utility' is both descriptive and normative. Unfortunately, it is not usually made clear how much of the theory is descriptive and how much normative, and until this is done it is difficult to evaluate these theories. Often pragmatic theories are used to guide experimental work on how humans behave in conditions of uncertainty, and this of course tells us about people's actual partial beliefs. But while these empirical studies are valuable and are a great step forward, they have been restricted to gambling type situations with small stakes. Insofar as the pragmatist is offering a general theory of probability he must cover cases where the stakes are large, the alternatives are not clear cut, and the probabilities are not measurable. For example, it is sometimes said that utility is bounded; what does this mean? Just that life is finite (i.e., man is mortal), or something more? An objection I have to most pragmatic theories is that they do not make their scope clear—they do not tell us how much of life they are urging us to construe as a gamble and a game. Of course the pragmatist can say that he only intends his theory to cover the kinds of cases he is investigating empirically, or that he leaves it open to cover what it will, but if so he is not really offering a theory to compete with the traditional theories of probability.

## III. *Probability and Investigation*

1. The last section was devoted to a pragmatic analysis of belief in terms of action and values. We will next discuss the relation between belief, or rather the lack of it, and investigation. Peirce, you will recall, held that a false belief ultimately gives rise to surprise and doubt, which in turn lead to investigation and finally to a revised belief. Without agreeing with Peirce that all investigation starts this way, we can agree that there is a connection between lack of belief and investigation: when a person is undecided about a proposition, but for some reason needs to know its truth status, he will often make investigations until he passes into a state of belief in that proposition or its negation. How, now, is this process of inquiry related to partial belief and probability?

Consider a belief whose object is a nonprobabilistic proposition. Suppose a detective starts a case with no prior opinion concerning Watson's guilt, becomes more and more confident as the investigation proceeds that Watson did commit the crime, and ends by being fully convinced that he did. Let us say that initially he is in a state of *unbelief*. His terminal state is clearly a case of total belief as we defined that term. Now is it the case that in the intermediate stages the detective has partial beliefs of various strengths in the proposition under investigation? It seems to me that he does, on the following ground. At any of these intermediate stages he might be forced to act on the proposition, and since he has left the state of unbelief but not yet reached the state of total belief, these actions must be manifestations of a partial belief. It is clear from what we have said before and from the material to be presented in the next subsection that the advocate of a pragmatic theory of probability would agree with the thesis that in the intermediate stages of inquiry the investigator would have partial beliefs of various strengths. But though this thesis is unobjectionable by itself, the result of combining it with another doctrine of the pragmatist leads, I think, to difficulties.

2. The doctrine in question is that all preferences are comparable and transitive. Savage has expressed this very well in his postulate that a person's preferences are simply ordered. He introduces the relation 'is not preferred to', symbolized by '$\leq$', which relates the actions or choices of an individual (see Section II,3 above). He then postulates that this relation is a simple ordering among the acts of a person. That is, for any alternative acts $A_1$, $A_2$, $A_3$ of the same person

(S 1) Either $A_1 \leq A_2$ or $A_2 \leq A_1$.

(S 2) If $A_1 \leq A_2$ and $A_2 \leq A_3$, then $A_1 \leq A_3$.

He interprets this postulate both empirically and normatively, but emphasizes the latter interpretation.[19]

Before we can discuss the justification of the postulate of simple ordering we must give it empirical content. This is usually done in some such manner as the following. A person is placed in a controlled experimental situation and made to choose between acts that involve uncertainty (in general) and value (e.g., money, merchandise). If he selects $A_2$ over $A_1$ we interpret this to mean that $A_1$ is not preferred to $A_2$, i.e., that $A_1 \leq A_2$. It does not follow, of course, that because $A_1 \leq A_2$ is true that $A_2 \leq A_1$ is false. For $A_1$ and $A_2$ might actually be equally preferable for the person, so that he might well sometimes choose $A_1$ over $A_2$ and sometimes choose $A_2$ over $A_1$, in which case we should conclude both that $A_2 \leq A_1$ and $A_1 \leq A_2$, and hence that $A_1 = A_2$. Of course he might also choose $A_1$ over $A_2$ at one moment and $A_2$ over $A_1$ at the next moment because he had changed his mind, first preferring $A_1$ and then $A_2$, and we have not yet provided any mechanism for distinguishing this case (fickleness) from the preceding case (equal preference). Indeed, assuming that the subject is cooperative and always does make a choice, we have not yet provided enough interpretation of '$\leq$' to enable one to establish $\sim (A_1 \leq A_2)$.

One can provide for the falsification of $X \leq Y$ by introducing an act of positive value, that is, an act which is definitely preferred to the null

19 FS, pp. 17-21; see also pp. 27-33, 59.

alternative (which neither pays anything nor costs anything). Suppose
$B$ = receive one dollar if it rains tomorrow
is such an act. Let

$A_1$ = receive a certain Hi-Fi record if a coin falls heads
$A_2$ = receive a specified book if a die falls six.

We can supply the interpretation needed for falsifying $A_1 \leqq A_2$ by considering combinations of acts. Thus suppose the experimental subject
not only chooses $A_1$ over $A_2$ but also chooses $A_1$ over the combination
of $A_2$ and $B$, that is, he chooses to try for the record rather than receiving
the book if the die falls six *and* receiving a dollar if it rains. This empirically establishes that he prefers $A_1$ to $A_2$, and hence that $\sim (A_1 \leqq A_2)$.

We have now given sufficient empirical content to '$X \leqq Y$' so that
the simple ordering postulate becomes an empirical proposition. As one
would expect, many of an intelligent and stable person's choices at a
given time will correspond to it, but not all. Thus we may get for the
same subject $A_1 \leqq A_2$, $A_2 \leqq A_3$, but $\sim (A_1 \leqq A_3)$, so transitivity
breaks down. At this point the normative aspect of probability enters.
The pragmatist will argue that we ought to make our choices transitive.
He will allow, of course, that we may change our mind, but will maintain
that once we have reflected on matters carefully we should impose a
simple order on our possible acts.

Why we should is never made clear. Generally a vague appeal is
made to consistency, but since inductive consistency is defined by postulates (this one and others) such an appeal is circular. All of the putative
justifications given for this and other probabilistic 'ought' statements
by pragmatists are unsatisfactory because they do not make clear the
type of justification claimed and the alternatives considered. In particular, the justifications for the simple ordering postulate with which
I am acquainted do not rebut the objection to be brought against it in
the balance of this section.

3. In the extreme case when the 'payoffs' of acts $A_1$, $A_2$, and $A_3$
are identical (i.e., the same prize is given in each) the simple order
postulate imposes a simple order on probabilities. For if the payoffs are
the same, the utilities are equal, the acts differ only in their probabilities
$P_1$, $P_2$, and $P_3$, and for this case the postulate reduces to

(S' 1)   Either $P_1 \leqq P_2$ or $P_2 \leqq P_1$.
(S' 2)   If $P_1 \leqq P_2$ and $P_2 \leqq P_3$ then $P_1 \leqq P_3$.

Hence the postulate implies that probabilities are simply ordered. Thus
both acts and probabilities are simply ordered. To the simple order
postulate the pragmatist adds other postulates which yield the result
that numbers may be assigned (though not uniquely) to expected

utilities and probabilities so that they can be manipulated in various ways, e.g., by the calculus of probability.[20]

Now many have objected to this use of numbers in dealing with expected utilities and probabilities. Keynes, for example, held that probabilities are not simply ordered, only partially ordered.[21] This means that he accepted the transitivity principle (S'2) but rejected the comparability principle (S'1). B. O. Koopman has given an axiomatic set in which probabilities are partially ordered but not simply ordered.[22] But these men and many others who had similar views wrote without acquaintance with the pragmatic theory of probability, so the question needs reevaluation.

Consider a person who knows nothing about the Detroit Red Wings except that it is a professional hockey team. Presented with three alternatives pairwise suppose he chooses

($D_1$) $1 if a penny falls heads

over

($D_2$) $1 if the Red Wings win their next game

and the latter over

($D_3$) $1 if of five pennies exactly one or two fall heads.

Let us suppose further that the person is convinced that the coin is fair and knows that the probabilities associated with ($D_1$) and ($D_3$) are $\frac{1}{2}$ and $\frac{15}{32}$ respectively. Now doesn't the fact that he placed ($D_2$) between ($D_1$) and ($D_3$) show that he attaches a definite probability to ($D_2$), somewhere in the range $\frac{15}{32}$ to $\frac{1}{2}$? Note that we could narrow the range indefinitely by a sequence of experiments based on longer and longer sequences of tosses.

It was certainly reasonable for the subject to make a choice—he had nothing to lose and something to gain. But this merely shows that for suitable recompense he is guessing. If the stakes are sufficiently high it is foolish not to guess, and so the comparability part (S 1) of the simple order postulate should always be made true in a case like this. But a guess is a guess for all that. That we are willing to simply order our probabilities under suitable forcing does not show that they are really simply ordered.

It seems to me that ($D_2$) is not, strictly speaking, comparable to ($D_1$) and ($D_3$). This suggests that (S'1) does not hold for all probabilities and hence that (S1) does not hold for all acts. We may call (S1) and (S'1)

20 FS, pp. 33, 74.

21 J. M. Keynes, *A Treatise on Probability* (London: Macmillan, 1921) Chap. 3.

22 "The Bases of Probability," *Bulletin of the American Mathematical Society*, **46** (Oct., 1940), 763-774.

comparability principles, so our position is that not all probabilities and expected utilities are comparable.

(S2) and (S'2) are transitivity principles. Do these apply to all probabilities and expected utilities or must they too be dropped? To keep them is to say that probabilities and expected utilities are partially ordered, as did Keynes. Certainly transitivity is not as objectionable as comparability, but I have certain doubts about it too. Why should we seek to make our choices and degrees of partial belief transitive? If one is choosing among closely spaced alternatives, it is pretty arbitrary how one orders them, so it seems doubtful that any harm could come from violating (S2) with respect to them. Also, after choosing $A_2$ over $A_1$ and $A_3$ over $A_2$ and then being presented with $A_1$ and $A_3$, one may notice a common element between $A_1$ and $A_3$ and find it difficult to compare these two. On the other hand, since the numerical values of degrees of partial belief are somewhat arbitrary it may be as easy to make these values transitive as to make them intransitive. Also it may be advantageous to make the same choice in the same circumstances, and this policy will result in a certain amount of uniformity. And of course one shouldn't make a *set* of choices (or adopt a long-run policy) which would place one at a disadvantage because it violates the transitivity condition.[23]

4. It follows from the simple order postulate that there is no fundamental distinction between (1) a partial belief in a nonprobabilistic proposition and (2) a total belief in a probabilistic proposition (Section II,2), since the strength of the partial belief and the amount of probability which is the object of the total belief can both be measured by the technique described in Section III,2. That is, on the pragmatic theory of probability, degree of partial belief and probability are the same thing.

A major consequence of this identification of beliefs of type (1) and (2) is that probable knowledge replaces partial ignorance, and there are no unknown probabilities. All cases of uncertainty are cases of probability, and in the limiting case unbelief becomes identical with a probability of one-half. Doubt and ignorance become a special type of knowledge: knowledge that the probability is one-half. The issue here is bound up with some formulations of the principle of indifference[24] according to which one may assign definite probabilities even in the absence of relevant evidence.

But there are cases of unbelief in a proposition $p$ which are also

---

23 For example, one should avoid a "Dutch book," a set of bets such that one can't possibly win and may lose.

24 But not that of Professor Lewis; see AKV, pp. 301, 307 ff.

cases of unbelief that the probability of $p$ is one-half. At one time I personally was in this state toward the following propositions:

It rained in Jackfield on August 20, 1803.

It snowed in Birdum on December 5th of last year.[25]

I am not saying that there is no connection between unbelief and probabilistic belief in such cases. Thus forced to choose between a probability of $\frac{1}{2}$ and one of $\frac{9}{10}$ I would certainly prefer the former; this point will be discussed further in Section IV. Nor do I wish to maintain that one has no relevant evidence in such cases.[26] Actually I don't think 'relevant evidence' is defined with sufficient precision to make this question meaningful. But all I wish to maintain is that there is at most very little information in such cases, and that then it is reasonable not to believe that the probability is one-half. This is all a matter of degree, of course. Thus after finding from my *Geographical Dictionary* that Jackfield is in West England and Birdum is near the Sandy Desert in Australia, I was willing to make some tentative probability assertions about these propositions.

We conclude then that one must distinguish (1) a partial belief in a nonprobabilistic proposition from (2) a total belief in a probabilistic proposition. This suggests that there are cases of partial beliefs in probabilistic propositions which do not reduce to either (1) or (2). We will discuss these cases later (in Section IV,2).

## IV. *Indeterminate Probabilities*

1. The critical discussion of the preceding section has shown that some probabilities (and expected utilities) are not simply ordered. Of course some probabilities (and expected utilities) are. We will call probabilities (and expected utilities) of the former kind *indeterminate,* and those of the latter kind *determinate.* In this section we will say a few things about indeterminate probabilities and how they are related to determinate ones. We will not, however, attempt to give a complete theory of indeterminate probabilities.

First, some remarks on the name 'indeterminate probabilities'. Determinate probabilities are so-called because each is a single, definite real

---

25 It may be objected that if one is unacquainted with the proper names used here he doesn't understand the statements, and if he is acquainted with these names he knows something about the climate of Jackfield and Birdum. But we can easily replace 'Jackfield' by the 'town called "Jackfield" in Webster's *Geographical Dictionary*' and similarly with 'Birdum'.

26 Professor Lewis argues that there is some relevant evidence in every case (AKV, p. 307 ff.), but I am not sure whether he means 'every case', or 'every case of practical interest'.

number. In contrast, indeterminate probabilities are not determinate numbers, but have an approximate, indefinite, vague, indeterminate character. Indeterminate probabilities might also be called unmeasurable or nonnumerical probabilities, but these terms are misleading because, as we shall see, indeterminate probabilities can be measured and numbers can be applied to them, though this is not such a simple matter as it is in the case of determinate probabilities. Some writers, e.g., von Mises, would not call indeterminate probabilities probabilities at all,[27] but I think indeterminate and determinate probabilities are sufficiently alike to justify classifying them together.

Partial beliefs in nonprobabilistic propositions are said to be determinate or indeterminate according to the nature of the degree of belief involved. The partial belief of the coin example (Section II,1) is determinate, whereas a partial belief that it will rain tomorrow (Section II,2) is indeterminate, as is a partial belief at an intermediate stage of inquiry (Section III,1). Partial beliefs in probabilistic propositions are more complicated. Since a degree of partial belief is also a probability, these involve probabilities of probabilities. We will call the probability which is the degree of belief a *second order probability*, and the probability in the object of belief a *first order probability*. Partial beliefs are classed as indeterminate or determinate according to the nature of their second order probabilities.

Let us next discuss ways in which we can distinguish indeterminate from determinate partial beliefs. For example, how can one tell whether the partial belief in a Red Wing victory (see the example of Section III,3) is indeterminate or determinate? One way is to use memory and introspection: a person can recall what evidence he has and judge directly whether he is guessing or being forced to guess. This is a subjective way of deciding whether a probability is indeterminate or not. Are there more objective manifestations of this difference? I am not sure. There may be less uniformity among the values assigned by rational, reflective individuals in the case of indeterminate probabilities than in the case of determinate probabilities, both within the assignments of different individuals and between assignments of different individuals. Of course there will be some disagreement over determinate probabilities, but perhaps there will be more over indeterminate probabilities. Among rational, reflective people guessing may vary more than knowledge. But whether or not there are objective manifestations of and behavioral tests

27 Richard von Mises, *Probability, Statistics, and Truth*, second revised edition, prepared by Hilda Geringer (New York: Macmillan, 1957). Original German edition published in 1928: First Lecture.

for the distinction between indeterminate and determinate probabilities, the distinction is nevertheless a significant one.

2. It was mentioned earlier that there are cases of partial beliefs in probabilistic propositions (Section III,4), which involve second order probabilities of first order probabilities (Section IV,1). The concept of an indeterminate probability is required for an adequate analysis of some such beliefs, so we will consider them next.

It will be instructive to consider two examples, each containing a sequence of partial beliefs of increasing strengths. In each example the sequence is based upon a series of 101 random selections with replacement (to guarantee independence of the probabilities) from a box of 200 marbles. The sequences of partial beliefs are based on the propositions

(E) The last (101st) draw will be red
(F) The probability of E is one-half.

The subjects observe the first 100 draws, examine the contents of the box after the 100th draw, and then observe the 101st draw. The partial beliefs in each sequence are the partial beliefs in (F) initially, after the first draw, after the second draw, . . ., after the 100th draw, and after the contents of the box have been examined.

In the first example the subject is told nothing about the contents of the box except that it has 200 marbles of various colors, the marbles are all of the same size, the box is regular in shape, etc. (Though the term *chance* is not used in the presentation, the subject would normally conclude from the information given that each marble has an equal chance of being drawn.) In the second example the subject knows all this and in addition that the box before him was chosen by a random process from among three boxes. (Again, the subject is given enough information to conclude that the chance of getting each box is the same, though the term *chance* is not used in the presentation.) He further knows that the contents of these boxes are:

Box 1: 50 red, 150 non-red
Box 2: 100 red, 100 non-red
Box 3: 150 red, 50 non-red.

To complete the description of the examples we stipulate that the subjects know the calculus of probability and use it where applicable, that the box from which the drawings are made has in fact 100 red and 100 non-red marbles, and that in both series of drawings the relative frequency of red marbles approximates closer and closer to ½.

It is perhaps difficult to say just what a normal subject would believe in the first example, but many (including the author) would begin in a state of unbelief towards (F), acquire a weak partial belief in (F), then acquire stronger and stronger partial beliefs in (F), and (after the box of marbles is examined) end with a total belief in $(F)$. Each of these partial beliefs is indeterminate, having an indeterminate secondary probability and a determinate primary probability. The indeterminate probability begins at a minimum (in the initial state of unbelief), gradually increases during the investigation (though not uniformly), and terminates at a maximum (in the final state of total belief).

It should be remarked that both the frequentist and the a priorist in probability theory could agree that the degree of partial belief changes in the way just indicated, but they would account for this change in different ways. The frequentist would say that proposition $(F)$ is empirical, and the subject's degree of belief changes as the proposition becomes confirmed. The a priorist would probably hold that $(F)$ is a priori, but construe it as elliptical for

($F'$) The probability of $E$ relative to the observations made until
       now is one-half,

and account for the changes in partial beliefs by saying that the contents of $(F')$ change as the sequence of draws proceeds.[28]

In the second example the subject, who can use the calculus of probability, would not begin in a state of unbelief. There are three hypotheses about which box is at hand, namely,

($G_1$) It is Box 1
($G_2$) It is Box 2
($G_3$) It is Box 3,

and these respectively imply probabilistic propositions about the last draw, namely,

($H_1$) The probability of red on draw 101 is $\frac{1}{4}$
($H_2$) The probability of red on draw 101 is $\frac{1}{2}$
($H_3$) The probability of red on draw 101 is $\frac{3}{4}$.

Before the first draw these are equally probable, so the subject would have a determinate partial belief in each of them of strength $\frac{1}{3}$. Since in each case the proposition believed involves determinate probabilities, both the first order and the second order probabilities of these partial beliefs are determinate. This is so throughout the example, for the subject can calculate the probability of each of these probabilities after every draw. E.g., if the first 10 draws are half red his degree of partial belief in ($H_2$) would be about $\frac{2}{3}$ and in ($H_1$) and ($H_3$) about $\frac{1}{6}$ each.

Since the probabilities of the three hypotheses ($H_1$), ($H_2$), ($H_3$) are determinate they may be combined to give a single probability about

[28] One could hold that an a priori concept of probability is the fundamental concept involved in $(F)$ and still say that $(F)$ is empirical. See my "Dispositional Statements," *Philosophy of Science*, 22 (1955), 175-193.

the last draw. Initially (and indeed at any time that equal numbers of red and white marbles have in fact been drawn) the effects of $(H_1)$ and $(H_3)$ balance out with the result that the probability of a red is $\frac{1}{2}$. So the subject will have, in a certain sense, total belief in $(F)$. Here, then, is a case of unbelief in a nonprobabilistic proposition $(E)$ which may be replaced by a total belief in a probabilistic proposition $(F)$. This is possible here because both first order and second order probabilities are determinate, and several determinate probabilities may sometimes be combined and reduced (in a sense) to a single determinate probability. But indeterminate probabilities of determinate probabilities do not so reduce, and hence it is not possible in the first example to replace uncertainty about $(E)$ by certainty about $(F)$.

Both examples are models of inquiry about the probabilistic proposition $(F)$, with an evolution of partial belief concerning $(F)$. The first example parallels the process of answering such questions as: what is the probability of a man 40 in condition $\phi$ dying of disease $\psi$? Researchers often begin with practically no specific data, then obtain poor samples, and finally establish a probability value with many samples obtained by careful techniques. In such cases the evolution of partial belief involves an increase of indeterminate probability from an initial minimum through various intermediate strengths to a final maximum (when total belief is reached). In the second example the degrees of belief of $(H_1)$, $(H_2)$, and $(H_3)$ change, but the composite degree of belief in $(F)$ remains the same (at $\frac{1}{2}$). ($F$ and $H_2$ as stated come to the same thing, but their belief contexts are different.)

Perhaps it should be mentioned that our distinction between indeterminate and determinate probabilities is not the same as Lewis' distinction between reliability and probability, even though these two distinctions are related.[29] Lewis applies his distinction to frequency estimates, while our distinction applies to probabilities associated with beliefs, but this difference need not concern us here. Roughly speaking, the reliability of a probability judgment measures the quantity and quality of the data or evidence on which the probability value is based. Lewis' distinction cuts across ours, as may be seen by reference to the two examples just discussed. The secondary probabilities in the first example are indeterminate, while in the second example they are determinate. But in each example the two factors of reliability and probability are present, for as the draws are made the subject acquires more and more evidence relevant to his belief.

[29] Lewis presents his distinction in AKV, pp. 292-306, and the reader is referred to this source for a definitive statement.

3. Let us consider once again the simple order postulate. There is a measure of truth in this principle. Suppose one is forced to act on a proposition $p$ on which he has no opinion. It is often better to guess at a probability for $p$ than to guess that $p$ is true or false. Moreover, in a case like that of the Red Wings (Section III,3) a guess of 0.5 is superior to a guess of, say, 0.8, or 0.9, or 0.99. After all, an average team wins about one-half of its games. In brief, if this state of unbelief or weak partial beliefs is to be represented by a single number then 0.5 is better than 0.9.

But why represent it by a single number? This is just the kind of oversimplification that we have been attacking. A set of numbers (or a function) would give a better representation of a state of unbelief or partial belief. Thus the indeterminate probability associated with an unbelief might be represented by a curve showing a strong preference for the probability one-half and weaker and weaker preferences as the probabilities go to one (and to zero). As the subject gets more information this curve would become sharper and sharper to represent the passage through partial belief to total belief. If the probability shifted away from one-half the center of gravity of the curve would shift accordingly. This quantitative representation of partial belief would be more accurate than that given by the simple order postulate. But even this model would omit one essential feature of partial belief: its approximate, indefinite, unprecise, vague, indeterminate character. Here is a property which distinguishes indeterminate from determinate probabilities.

We see, then, that indeterminate probabilities are basically different from determinate ones. But they are nevertheless closely related. As the considerations of Section III make clear, there are occasions on which it is desirable to measure indeterminate probabilities by single numbers. A principle of indifference operates here: within a certain range of indeterminacy, it is arbitrary and indifferent what precise number is assigned.[30] This being so, it is usually desirable to assign these numbers so they satisfy the laws of probability (are simple ordered, etc.), in other words, to replace the indeterminate probability by a determinate one. How much distortion this replacement involves depends upon the range of indeterminacy; if this range is small an indeterminate probability is not much different from a determinate one.

Determinate probabilities are single numbers, which can be manipulated by the calculus of probability. Insofar as indeterminate probabilities can be replaced by determinate ones they too may be handled

---

[30] This principle is distinct from the traditional principle of indifference, but they both apply to cases where there is very little evidence.

numerically. But because some distortion is involved in this replacement, there are limits to the results one can obtain by using numbers for indeterminate probabilities. To express this difference briefly we shall say that determinate probabilities are *strongly numerical* while indeterminate probabilities are only *weakly numerical*. This limitation in the use of numbers for reasoning about indeterminate probabilities strikes pretty deep. Since indeterminate expected utilities (which are based on indeterminate probabilities) are also weakly numerical, this limitation has implications concerning the extent to which we can use probability to calculate the best policy for acting and investigating.

Let us see first what can be done with determinate probabilities by virtue of their strongly numerical character. One can calculate the best policy for acting and investigating. Suppose that in the second example of Section IV,1 the subject is allowed to guess what the 101st draw will be and will be given a prize if he is correct. Suppose further he is charged at a certain rate for each draw he observes. Given the value of the prize and the cost of gathering information he can determine whether it is better to investigate and then choose or to choose without investigation. Similarly, one can compute how risky the outcomes are, i.e., determine the security of a course of action. By considering larger and larger groups of uncertain events one can often formulate a relatively riskless policy for the whole group. Insurance is an obvious example.

Thus because determinate probabilities are strongly numerical one can often reduce the amount of uncertainty he faces. The resultant certainty may only appear at a high level. For example, the only thing we may be certain of is that we have adopted the best policy. But it is a type of certainty nevertheless, and may be valued because it is. This replacement of uncertainty by certainty is accomplished by means of the traditional calculus of probability. Using this calculus one can compound events indefinitely (even infinitely) and come up with precise methods and strategies for dealing with large classes of cases.

The calculation of probabilities for compound cases clearly depends on the strongly numerical character of the given probabilities. Hence, these computations cannot, in general, be made for indeterminate probabilities, which are only weakly numerical. Since any exact numerical values assigned to indeterminate probabilities are guesses, second order calculations of security and computations for combined cases will not decrease or destroy the guesswork inherent in the situation. Rather, they will tend to amplify or increase it. The penumbras surrounding the degrees of indeterminate partial belief will tend to multiply and may make the result too vague to be significant. Thus though the calculus of probability may be applied to indeterminate probabilities, the results are much less useful than the results of applying it to determine probabilities.

As a consequence the whole utility framework (discussed in Section II) is of limited use in connection with indeterminate expected utilities. What are *the* consequences of each act? How shall the situation be divided into alternatives? If there are alternative sets of alternatives, giving alternative results, how shall we choose among them? To apply the utility framework of acts, consequences, probabilities, and values, one must already have considerable information. Because determinate probabilities are strongly numerical this information is available when the utility framework is applied to them, but because indeterminate probabilities are only weakly numerical this information is often not available with sufficient precision when the utility framework is applied to them.

Statisticians have sometimes contemplated the possibility of forming a policy for one's whole life in advance, that is, reducing all of one's future choices to a single choice of plan or strategy made right now. It is always recognized, of course, that such an action is impractical, but the reasons given are usually not complete. It is not merely that there are so many alternatives to consider that the process of calculation, while finite, is beyond human power.[31] It is also because we do not have sufficient information to divide the situation up into measurable alternatives, to assign values to the outcomes, etc. In short, if my present complete cognitive state is a partial belief, it is an indeterminate partial belief, not a determinate partial belief. Because of this there are severe limitations on the extent to which we can use the calculus of probability to replace uncertainty by certainty.

We conclude, then, that the pragmatic theory takes the analogy between life and gambling too seriously. Life is a gamble, all right, but it is a vague, not a precise one, and this takes away some of the sting.

## V. *The Pragmatic-Humean Theory of Probability*

1. In Section II we outlined the pragmatic theory of probability. That theory is both descriptive and normative: it offers an approximate description of how a person with a partial belief does behave, and it recommends a systematic method for behaving in uncertain situations. By being both descriptive and regulative the pragmatic theory is like the usual philosophical analyses of probability, but it differs from these in that no attempt is made to provide an analysis of '$P(h,e) = x$'

─────────────

[31] Cf. FS, p. 16.

(in the sense of an alternative statement with the 'same meaning'). Rather, the pragmatist describes the ways in which and the circumstances under which the concept of probability is and should be used, with emphasis on the systematic and public aspects of this usage.

In Section III we criticized the pragmatic theory of probability with respect to the simple order postulate and in Section IV we introduced the distinction between determinate and indeterminate probabilities. In retrospect we can see that the assertions of the pragmatic theory of probability are of two quite different kinds. Statements of the first kind relate probability to partial belief, investigation, and action, and delineate the normative and descriptive aspects of probability. These statements are genuinely pragmatic in character. Statements of the second kind imply that all probabilities are strongly numerical; the assertion that probabilities are simply ordered is one such. These statements are not especially pragmatic in tone, though of course they are compatible with pragmatism.

Since the pragmatic theory of probability does not recognize the existence of indeterminate probabilities, it construes statements of both kinds as applying to all probabilities. We can formulate a revised version of the pragmatic theory by recognizing the existence of indeterminate probabilities and making the appropriate modifications in the original formulations of the theory. Statements of the first kind do apply to indeterminate probabilities, and so can be extended to cover them. Statements of the second kind hold for determinate probabilities (which are strongly numerical), but they do not hold for indeterminate ones (which are only weakly numerical), and hence should be restricted to the former.

Though indeterminate probabilities are not strongly numerical, they are governed by rules. Hence, there is, or should be, a logic of indeterminate probabilities. This logic would be more complicated than the logic of determinate probabilities but it would be analogous to the latter and an extension of it. Incidently, the logic of indeterminate probabilities would have practical applications. Attempts are now being made to instruct digital computers to perform some relatively complicated human functions, including that of investigation and inductive inference. Rules of a logic of indeterminate probabilities could be used and tested on these computers.

We will now combine this revised version of the pragmatic theory of probability, some basic doctrines of Hume's philosophy of induction, and a thesis about causal necessity, to make a unified theory which we will call the *Pragmatic-Humean theory of probability*.[32] Because of the unusual status of the theory in the present paper and the danger that its name will be misleading, some remarks need to be made to prevent any possible misunderstanding. First, this theory is not presented as a preliminary to an argument that it is the best theory of probability. Though I think it gives an excellent account of probability, I personally think it does not go far enough in certain directions (see Section V,4). My reason for developing the Pragmatic-Humean theory in this paper is not that I believe it to be the correct theory of probability, but rather that I wish to use it as a basis for analyzing and criticising Professor Lewis' theory of probability (see Section VI). Second, though the Pragmatic-Humean theory includes some Humean doctrines restated in modern terms it does not include all of Hume's philosophy of induction. In particular, the Pragmatic-Humean theory rejects Hume's account of causal necessity (see Section VI,5). I have used the name 'Pragmatic-Humean' in order to give credit to the main sources of the theory, and not because the theory is merely a conjunction of Hume's philosophy of induction with an already existing pragmatic theory of probability.

2. By the 'traditional calculus of probability' I mean a system based on the following axioms: first, the addition rule for exclusive events; second, the general multiplication rule; third, the principle that logical deducibility entails a probability of one; and fourth, the principle that when $p$ and $q$ are logically equivalent, then $P(c, p) = P(c, q)$.[33]

The traditional calculus of probability provides rules for computing some relative probabilities from others. For example, it tells us that if $P(c, d) = 3/4$ then $P(\sim c, d) = 1/4$. But except in trivial cases it does not tell us the value of any single relative probability $P(c, d)$. To see that this is so consider two specific statements,

(G) A total of 100 swans have been observed and all were found to be white

(H) The next swan observed will be white,

and the relative probability assertion $P(H, G) = 1/4$. The traditional calculus of probability does not determine the truth status of this relative probability statement. More generally, if '$c$', '$d$' and 'if $d$ then $c$' are all factual (not logically true or false),

$P(c, d) = x$

is consistent with the axioms for any value of $x$ (in the closed interval zero to one, of course).

---

[32] This is also a theory of induction, of course, but since probability plays the basic role I have used 'probability' in preference to 'induction' in naming the theory.

[33] See Janina Hosiasson-Lindenbaum, "On Confirmation," *The Journal of Symbolic Logic*, 5 (Dec., 1940), 133-148.

This is an exceedingly important fact about the traditional calculus of probability, because it leaves open the possibility that there are additional rules governing the assignment of values to at least some relative probability statements. Are there such rules? This is equivalent to the question: Is (justificatory) inductive logic any more than the traditional calculus of probability and its statistical applications?[34] In the past, inductive logicians have offered such rules: e.g., induction by simple enumeration, Mill's methods.

The question just raised is closely related to the question: To what extent should rational people agree on relative probability judgments? This is one of the moot points in probability theory. Most a priorists say that '$P(c, d) = x$' is an a priori statement of logic, and hence that if we all thought deeply and clearly enough we would agree on it. But this is more a claim of what we should do in a hypothetical idealized situation than what we should do in actual practice. Empiricists generally hold that '$P(c, d) = x$' is an empirical statement, so disagreements about it are traceable to differences in evidence concerning it. The pragmatist's position is not entirely clear here, but he does stress that probability beliefs are subjective and personal, and he seems to include most relative ones along with the nonrelative ones in this characterization.

My own opinion falls between that of the pragmatist and the typical a priorist. I think it is not entirely arbitrary what value we assign to $P(H, G)$ in the example given earlier in this section, but I agree that there is room for much rational disagreement. The distinction between determinate and indeterminate probabilities is relevant here. $P(H, G)$ is an indeterminate probability, and because indeterminate probabilities are more arbitrary and indefinite than determinate ones, there can be more disagreement among rational people on the former than the latter. The amount of agreement there should be on indeterminate probabilities varies with the strength of the evidence. When there is no, or practically no, directly relevant evidence, the situation is fairly summed up by 'one guess is as good as another'. When there is a great deal of directly relevant evidence the logic of indeterminate probabilities will require considerably more agreement among rational people.

We conclude, then, that inductive logic should include more than the traditional calculus of probability and its extensions to cover indeterminate probabilities. It should also contain rules governing the assign-

---

[34] One needs here to distinguish justificatory logic, which is concerned with the validity of arguments (deductive and inductive), from heuristic logic, which contains principles putatively useful in solving problems (inductive or deductive). Hereafter when I use the term 'inductive logic' it will be in the sense of justificatory inductive logic.

ment of values to at least some relative probabilities independently of others. This set of rules determines an *inductive method* which all rational people should use in evaluating inductive arguments. Since there are other logically possible inductive methods (see below) it will be well to have a name for this one; we will call it the *standard inductive method.*

What account shall we give of the rules of the standard inductive method? One way to describe them is the pragmatic way, in terms of norms which rational people use to some extent and ought to use more fully. This amounts to extending Peirce's pragmatic theory of belief and the pragmatic description of determinate partial beliefs given in Sections II and III (of this paper) to cover all partial and total beliefs, including relative partial beliefs and indeterminate partial beliefs. This account of the standard inductive method we define to be part of the Pragmatic-Humean theory of probability. Since Peirce's pragmatic theory of belief and the pragmatic theory of probability have been described extensively here and elsewhere, and since the application of pragmatism to the standard inductive method is straightforward, we need not spell it out in detail here.

The account just given of the role of the standard inductive method in inductive inferences is very much like Hume's. Hume saw that inductive inferences are made in accord with nondeductive principles; in his terms, they are made "by experience," "by habit," "by custom."

Custom, then is the great guide of human life. It is that principle alone which renders our experiences useful to us, and makes us expect, for the future, a similar train of events with those which have appeared in the past. Without the influence of custom, we should be entirely ignorant of every matter of fact beyond what is immediately present to the memory and senses.[35]

There is a negative aspect to Hume's characterization of probability and induction that should be noted: namely, that inductive inference is not reasoning.

Nothing so like as eggs; yet no one, on account of this appearing similarity, expects the same taste and relish in all of them. It is only after a long course of uniform experiments in any kind, that we attain a firm reliance and security with regard to a particular event. Now where is that process of reasoning which, from one instance, draws a conclusion, so different from that which it infers from a hundred instances that are nowise different from that single one? . . . I cannot find, I cannot imagine any such reasoning.[36]

[35] David Hume, *An Enquiry Concerning Human Understanding* (La Salle, Ill.: Open Court Publishing Co., 1949), p. 47 (Sec. V, Part I). See also pp. 44 f. Hereafter cited as ECHU.

[36] ECHU, p. 37 (Sec. IV, Part II).

... it is not reasoning which engages us to suppose the past resembles the future, and to expect similar effects from causes which are, to appearance, similar.[37]

All inferences from experience, therefore, are effects of custom, not of reasoning.[38]

... *even after the observation of the frequent or constant conjunction of objects, we have no reason to draw any inference concerning any object beyond those of which we have had experience;* ...[39]

This refusal to call inductive inference 'reasoning' is not in accord with ordinary usage, for people often do call inductive inference reasoning, and say that good evidence for a hypothesis constitutes a reason for accepting it. More generally, as ordinarily used, words like 'reason', 'evidence', 'justification', and 'probable' involve a commitment to the standard inductive method (see the next subsection). We will make this extended concept of reason (rather than Hume's narrower concept of reason) part of the Pragmatic-Humean theory.

3. An essential doctrine of Hume's philosophy of induction can be formulated in terms of the status of alternatives to the standard inductive method. We have given this formulation elsewhere, so it will suffice here to summarize it.[40]

The standard inductive method includes the rule of induction by simple enumeration: the more often property $\phi$ has been accompanied by property $\psi$, the more likely it is that the next instance of $\phi$ will be accompanied by $\psi$. The other inductive methods include different but related rules. The *inverse inductive method* assigns probabilities according to the rule that the higher the relative frequency with which $\psi$ has accompanied $\phi$ in the past, the lower the probability that the next occurrence of $\phi$ will be accompanied by $\psi$. The *random predictive method* assigns to the proposition that the next occurrence of $\phi$ will be accompanied by $\psi$ a probability which does not depend on the relative frequency with which $\phi$ and $\psi$ have been associated in the past.

We can now give a formulation of Hume's doctrine that there is no noncircular justification of induction. Each of these three inductive methods (as well as many others) is logically consistent, and so there is no purely logical way of deciding among them or justifying a choice of one of them. Moreover, each inductive method constitutes a standard of evidence and of probable predictive success, and hence is impregnable in

37 ECHU, p. 41 (Sec. IV, Part II).

38 ECHU, p. 46 (Sec. V, Part II).

39 *A Treatise of Human Nature*, edited by L. A. Selby-Bigge (London: Oxford University Press, 1946), p. 139 (Book I, Part III, Sec. XII). Hereafter cited as THN.

40 "Presup. Theo. Ind.," pp. 177-188. Secs. II through V of "Signif. Carnap Syst."

the following sense: if a person uses one of these methods he can never find any empirical reason for abandoning or modifying that method. It follows from these two facts that there can be no noncircular justification of the standard inductive method; any attempt to show that the use of the standard inductive method is at least as beneficial as the use of an alternative inductive method is question-begging because it requires the use of some inductive method.

We have not, of course, fully described these inductive methods. Nor can we do so, because no one knows a complete set of inductive rules which are stated with sufficient precision to be mechanically applicable and which are adequate for a large class of actual inductive inferences. Rudolf Carnap has precisely defined some inductive methods and proved theorems about them. His results are instructive, but the methods he considers are applicable only to highly limited formal languages, languages which are adequate for only a portion of qualitative science. Moreover, the application of Carnap's inductive methods presupposes a great deal of empirical information.[41]

The inadequacy of inductive logic in its present state may be shown by considering the following three arguments, which closely parallel the three inductive methods mentioned earlier. First: many swans have been observed, all have been white, therefore probably the next swan observed will be white. Second: this wire has been bent many times and hasn't broken yet, therefore it will probably break soon. Third: though this (fair) coin has turned up heads more often than tails, the probability that it will fall heads next time is still one-half. Prima facie these three arguments conform respectively to the rules of the standard inductive method, the inverse inductive method, and the random predictive method. Actually all three arguments can be accounted for in the standard inductive method by taking into account the relevant background information: we know that bird coloration is often uniform, that wires wear out when bent repeatedly, and that the successive tosses of a fair coin are independent. That is, in actual practice we do not make any inductive inferences merely on the basis of some enumerated instances, but use also our general knowledge about the property under consideration and laws and rules governing it. These considerations show that that formulation of the rule of induction by simple enumeration given earlier is not complete; a condition must be added which allows its application to the swan case but not to the wire and coin cases. Unfortunately we do not know how to formulate this condition in a precise way. This is an example of

41 See my review of Carnap's *Logical Foundations of Probability*, *The Journal of Philosophy*, 48 (August, 1951), 524-535, and Sec. 3 of "Presup. Theo. Ind."

the general point made earlier, that we cannot fully and precisely describe our three inductive methods.

These critical remarks are relevant to our formulation of Hume's thesis that there is no noncircular justification of induction. Since we have not given detailed and precise descriptions of the three alternative methods, we have not proved that they are really logically consistent and not subject to empirical refutation. How do we know, then, that when these methods are fully stated each will still be consistent and empirically irrefutable? The answer is that of course we do not really know, we can only speculate. But I do not see any reason why the situation should change in this respect when the methods are completely described, and no one has given any satisfactory argument that it should.

Hume's doctrine that there is no noncircular justification of induction is to be included in the Pragmatic-Humean theory of probability. To conclude our treatment of this doctrine we will discuss its implications concerning the committive character of the term 'probable' and allied terms (e.g., 'evidence', 'reason'). We will do this by examining two analyses of '$P(h, e) = x$' from the point of view of the Pragmatic-Humean theory of probability.

The first analysis of '$P(h, e) = x$' is:

(J)  $x$ is the value which results when the standard inductive method is applied to the pair $h, e;$ and the standard inductive method is the *correct* method to use.[42]

The second analysis replaces '$P(h, e) = x$' by:

(K)  $x$ is the value which results from applying the *correct* inductive method to the pair $h, e$.

The Pragmatic-Humean theory of probability is like the pragmatic theory of probability in having both descriptive and normative components, and so we should look at these analyses from both points of view. Descriptively, both analyses differ from ordinary usage in making an explicit commitment to and approval of some inductive method. While standards operate in the use of the term 'probable' in the way indicated in Section II,4, one usually only makes an explicit appeal to them if challenged; certainly we don't always have the concept of the standard inductive method explicitly in mind, as the first analysis implies. Normatively, the Pragmatic-Humean theory recommends that we be more explicit, rigorous, and systematic in the use of the standard inductive method. Moreover, if challenged we should express approval of it and commitment to it, while admitting with Hume that there is no noncircular justi-

---

42 This is similar to the analysis in Sec. V, 3 of my "Signif. Carnap Syst."

fication of it. We need not, however, explicitly refer to it every time we use it.

4. Let us now summarize the content of the Pragmatic-Humean theory of probability as we have presented it thus far. The Pragmatic-Humean theory gives a pragmatic account of probabilities (both determinate and indeterminate) which relates them to partial belief, investigation, action, and choices made in conditions of uncertainty, and which is both descriptive and normative. Probabilities are governed by rules, which for determinate probabilities include the rules of the traditional calculus of probability and for indeterminate probabilities suitable generalizations of these rules. There are also rules governing the assignment of relative probabilities; these are the rules of the standard inductive method. There are logically consistent and internally defensible inductive methods other than the standard inductive method, and as Hume said, there is no non-circular way of justifying one over the others. But we do use probability in accord with the standard inductive method and in a certain sense are committed to this.

After discussing Lewis' views on causal necessity we will add to the Pragmatic-Humean theory a thesis about causal necessity (Section VI,5). This will complete the positive content of the Pragmatic-Humean theory of probability. There is in addition a negative or skeptical component, which excludes certain things. The theses of the preceding paragraph are compatible with the essential features of many a priori theories of probability; for example, those of Keynes and Carnap. They are also compatible with postulate theories of induction, such as those of Russell and the writer's own presupposition theory.[43] All these people can say that the positive content of the Pragmatic-Humean theory (with the possible exception of its thesis about causal necessity in Section VI,5) is correct as far as it goes, but that it fails to give a complete analysis of the meaning of probability statements. But these theories are not compatible with the negative thesis of the Pragmatic-Humean theory, which is that its account of probability is complete in its general features (though not in all its details, of course), and that nothing more is to be found in the directions indicated by a priori, postulate, and frequency theories of probability. This negative thesis is in the spirit of Peirce, who intended his pragmatic analyses to give all the cognitive meaning of a proposition, and it is in general accord with Hume's empiricism, though it is not literally compatible with what Hume says about the uniformity of nature

---

[43] A postulate theory holds that the validity of inductive arguments presupposes the truth of some broad factual assumptions about the universe. Cf. "Presup. Theo. Ind.," pp. 177, 189 ff.; also the first few pages of the writer's "On the Presuppositions of Induction," *The Review of Metaphysics*, 8 (June, 1955), 574-611.

(as we will soon see). In any case, I think the Pragmatic-Humean theory of probability is a strong, coherent, well-rounded theory, worthy of serious consideration by pragmatists such as Professor Lewis as well as by philosophers in general.

To clarify this negative component of the Pragmatic-Humean theory we will compare the status of uniformity in it, in the presupposition theory of induction, and in Hume's own philosophy of induction.

5. Various formulations of 'the' principle of the Uniformity of Nature are possible. The one given by the presupposition theory is: Whatever causal connections hold in one region of space-time hold throughout all space-time. According to the presupposition theory this principle is synthetic and factual, there are logically possible universes in which this principle is false, in such universes the standard inductive method may not be the best to use, and so this principle is presupposed in a certain sense by the standard inductive method.[44] By virtue of its negative or skeptical component the Pragmatic-Humean theory holds that the Uniformity of Nature principle and other putative presuppositions are irrelevant to the validity of induction. According to this theory an inductive method is constituted by certain rules, and general synthetic principles about the universe play no role in these rules.

It should nevertheless be noted that the standard inductive method possesses a property quite analogous to the property attributed to the universe by the Uniformity of Nature principle. This is the fact that mere differences in space-time position never affect the probability of an induction. This is of course a verifiable property of the method, and not an unverifiable property of the world as the presupposition theory of induction would have it. But just as the presupposition theory would claim that there are logically possible universes not obeying the Uniformity of Nature principle, so the Pragmatic-Humean theory must admit that there are conceivable inductive methods not having this uniformity property. For example, one could use the standard inductive method before a certain time and the inverse inductive method after that time.

These two theories may be contrasted by saying that the presupposition theory places space-time uniformity in the world (and derivatively in the method), while the Pragmatic-Humean theory places it in the method alone. Hume's own position is closer to the presupposition theory on this point. He speaks of induction "supposing" and being "founded on the presumption" that the future will resemble the past.

For all inferences from experience suppose, as their foundation, that the future will resemble the past, and that similar powers will be conjoined with similar

44 "On the Presuppositions of Induction," *op. cit.*, pp. 589 f.

sensible qualities . . . In vain do you pretend to have learned the nature of
bodies from your past experience. Their secret nature, and consequently all
their effects and influence, may change, without any change in their sensible
qualities. This happens sometimes, and with regard to some objects: Why may
it not happen always, and with regard to all objects?[45]

. . . probability is founded on the presumption of a resemblance betwixt those
objects, of which we have had experience, and those, of which we have had
none; and therefore 'tis impossible this presumption can arise from probability.[46]

Hume's principle that the future will resemble the past is a kind of
uniformity of nature principle. In the following passage Hume argues
that it cannot be demonstrated.

If reason determined us, it would proceed upon that principle, *that instances,
of which we have had no experience, must resemble those of which we have
had experience, and that the course of nature continues always uniformly the
same.* In order therefore, to clear up this matter, let us consider all the arguments, upon which such a proposition may be supposed to be founded; . . .

Our foregoing method of reasoning will easily convince us, that there can be
no *demonstrative* arguments to prove, *that those instances, of which we have
had no experience, resemble those, of which we have had experience.* We can at
least conceive a change in the course of nature; which sufficiently proves that
such a change is not absolutely impossible. To form a clear idea of any thing, is
an undeniable argument for its possibility, and is alone a refutation of any
pretended demonstration against it.[47]

Here Hume is attempting to show that the uniformity principle is not a
logical statement—in his terminology, that it does not express a relation
among ideas. This argument seems to presuppose that the uniformity
principle is a meaningful proposition about the universe, not just a rule
of inductive inference.

Thus Hume seems to agree with the presupposition theory in placing
space-time uniformity in the world, rather than with the Pragmatic-
Humean theory, which (as we have defined it) places space-time uniformity in the inductive method alone. Since an inductive method is a
set of rules used by an inquiring mind, the choice here is, broadly speaking, between holding that uniformity is in the world directly and in the
mind derivatively and holding that uniformity is in the mind only and
not in the exterior world at all. There is a similar choice with regard to
the related concept of causal necessity, and in Section VI,5 we will discuss the stand taken on this issue by the different theories we are concerned with.

45 ECHU, p. 39 (Sec. IV, Part II).
46 THN, p. 90 (Book I, Part III, Sec. VI).
47 THN, p. 89 (Book I, Part III, Sec. VI).

## VI. *Professor Lewis' Theory of Probability and Causality*

1. My aim in developing the Pragmatic-Humean theory of probability has been to have a theory with which to compare Lewis' own theory of probability. It seems to me that the Pragmatic-Humean theory fits well with a pragmatic epistemology like Lewis', and that the Pragmatic-Humean theory avoids many of the difficulties that confront Lewis' a priori theory of probability. I am not, of course, suggesting that because Lewis is a pragmatist in epistemology he ought to adopt a pragmatic theory of probability, and it may well be that he will think such a theory would create more problems for him than it would solve. But in any case I think it is interesting and fruitful to examine Lewis' theory of probability by comparing and contrasting it with the Pragmatic-Humean theory.

We will begin by discussing Professor Lewis' theory of relative probability judgments, and by asking him some questions about it. Let *e* be an evidence statement (e.g., a set of weather data) and *h* an empirical hypothesis (e.g., that it will rain). Is a probability proposition of the form $P(h, e) = x$ analytic a priori or synthetic a posteriori? This question presupposes that the ordinary usage of 'probable' is sufficiently clear to make the question intelligible, that there is only one basic meaning of 'probability',[48] and that the analytic a priori, synthetic a posteriori dichotomy is epistemologically adequate. Lewis says that there is only one basic meaning of probability,[49] and he clearly accepts the analytic synthetic dichotomy as against either a Kantian trichotomy or an Hegelian continuum, so our question is a legitimate one for him.

There are several places where Lewis seems to say that probability propositions of the form $P(h, e) = x$ are a priori. He rejects the frequency theory on the ground that when it attempts to explain the verification process it goes off into an infinite regress. For if a probability assertion *h* is empirical we can ask: Is *e* good evidence of *h*? But the latter question concerns the probability statement '$P(h, e)$ is high', which on the frequency theory is again an empirical statement for which we can demand evidence. Lewis then says that "*no* theory which identifies rational cred-

---

[48] To avoid misunderstanding one might say: there is only one basic *inductive* meaning of 'probability'. This qualification is needed here because there is a well-developed mathematical theory in which 'probability' means the limit of a relative frequency in the long run, and presumably no one (certainly not J. M. Keynes and I assume not Lewis) would deny the existence of this theory or of this use of the word 'probability'. What I am concerned with in this paper is the use of 'probability' in the context of inductive inference, e.g., "this hypothesis is highly probable on that evidence." Whenever I use 'probability' and '*P*' in this paper it is in the inductive, applied sense of the term.

[49] AKV, p. 314.

ibility in general with any kind of empirical objective fact, could be in any better case." And, he says, the only adequate type of probability theory "is one which will identify such probability with some fact which is knowable *a priori* when the data on which it is to be judged are given."[50]

Since Lewis holds that every a priori proposition is analytic,[51] the foregoing quotations seem to establish that he believes $P(h, e) = x$ to be analytic a priori. But Lewis makes other statements about induction which prima facie contradict this interpretation and seem to require that it be qualified. Lewis takes the problem of the validity of memory seriously, devoting a chapter to it.[52] He seems to say that to justify induction one must *assume* that memories are prima facie correct.

It is also necessary, in order to *justify* any empirical judgment . . . that some generalization of the sort derived from past experience should be afforded. In every instance of valid induction from presently given data, there is *required*, over and above these data and the rules of induction, a *general premise* concerning past cases resembling the present one.[53]

He speaks of the *problem* of the validity of memory,[54] and says that "all that is needed is an *initial assumption* that the mere fact of present rememberings renders what is thus memorially present in some degree credible."[55]

The question immediately arises: Is this memory assumption analytic a priori or synthetic a posteriori? If it is synthetic a posteriori, how can an analytic a priori probability proposition depend on it for its justification? On the other hand, if the memory assumption is analytic a priori, it is strange and misleading for Lewis to speak of the *problem* of the validity of memory and to use such words as 'justify', 'require', and 'assumption' in this connection. Moreover, Lewis quotes Hans Reichenbach's justification of induction with approval,[56] and one wonders why, if $P(h, e) = x$ is analytic, any justification of induction is needed.

If Lewis holds that his memory assumption is synthetic a posteriori, his theory of probability is a postulate theory of induction (cf. Sec. V,4). Though there are many different postulate theories, it may be of help to make reference to my own particular form of postulate theory, called 'the presupposition theory of induction'. According to the presupposition

50 AKV, p. 290; cf. pp. 304, 315, 318.
51 AKV, p. 158.
52 AKV, Chap. XI.
53 AKV, p. 327, italics added.
54 AKV, pp. 328, 333.
55 AKV, p. 354, italics added; cf. p. 357.
56 AKV, pp. 278, 325.

theory '$P(h, e) = x$' is to be analyzed into '$P(h, e \cdot \Pi) = x$ & $\Pi$', where $\Pi$ is a conjunction of certain general assumptions about the nature of the universe. Lewis' memory postulate is an assumption of the general kind that goes into $\Pi$, and I'm inclined to agree with Lewis that a memory postulate is needed. According to the presupposition theory '$P$' expresses an a priori concept of probability (not a frequency one), and $P(h, e \cdot \Pi) = x$ is analytic a priori. But $\Pi$ is synthetic, and $P(h, e) = x$, without the $\Pi$, is *not* analytic. The presupposition theory of induction should be contrasted with an analytic a priori theory of probability, which maintains that $P(h, e) = x$ is analytic a priori even when $e$ is an evidence statement which does not include any general memory assumption or other postulate. Carnap seems to hold such a theory in his *Logical Foundations of Probability;* it is noteworthy that he explicitly denies the need to talk about justifying induction by means of postulates.[57]

My original question to Lewis can now be better stated as: Is your theory an analytic a priori theory of probability or a postulate theory of induction? My first impression on reading *An Analysis of Knowledge and Valuation* was that Lewis intended the second alternative, and others have understood him that way.[58] But I now think he intended the first alternative, namely, that $P(h, e) = x$ is analytic a priori even when $e$ contains no presuppositions. I base my interpretation on two points. First, as noted earlier, Lewis says that $P(h, e) = x$ is analytic a priori, never as much as hints that for this to be so $e$ must contain presuppositions, and seems at one place to reject postulate theories of induction.[59] Second, he *closes* his chapter "Probable Knowledge and the Validity of Memory" by saying that "it seems undesirable thus to rest the final validity of empirical knowledge upon an *ad hoc* postulate" and then justifying the memory "postulate" on the ground that it is impossible to formulate a consistent, meaningful concept of reality without this postulate.[60] His

---

[57] *Op. cit.,* pp. 177-182.

I personally do not think Carnap's theory is satisfactory (see my "Signif. Carnap Syst.,") but this is not relevant to the present point. *Added in proof:* Since this paper was written, *The Philosophy of Rudolf Carnap* has appeared; this is Volume XI of the Library of Living Philosophers, edited by P. A. Schilpp, 1963. Carnap's position in this work is considerably different from his position in *Logical Foundations of Probability,* though he still denies the need for presuppositions. See especially his reply to my "On the Significance of Carnap's Inductive Logic for the Philosophy of Induction," pp. 980-983.

[58] Paul Henle, Review of AKV, *The Journal of Philosophy,* 45 (Sept., 1948), 528.

DeWitt H. Parker, "Is There a Third Kind of Knowledge?", *The Philosophical Review,* 59 (April, 1950), 227.

[59] AKV, p. 334.

[60] AKV, pp. 357-362.

procedure here is similar to that of *Mind and the World-Order* where he argues that a form of uniformity of nature principle is a priori.

A certain minimal order is prescribed a priori in the recognition of the real.

... it is impossible to imagine any sort of experience which would not present such statistical stabilities as would validate probable prediction, and such as would represent the experience of things.[61]

Hence I think that Lewis' views on the justification of induction in *An Analysis of Knowledge and Valuation* are basically the same as in *Mind and the World-Order,* and not fundamentally different as has sometimes been thought, though of course the formulation is different.[62]

I will assume that I am correct in saying that Lewis' theory of probability in *An Analysis of Knowledge and Valuation* is an analytic a priori theory. (If I am not correct, some revisions of what I shall say in the balance of this essay would be needed.) A number of further questions immediately arise. Does Lewis give an extended justification of the memory postulate because he thinks that it *appears not* to be analytic a priori, though it really is? I can understand why Kant and J. M. Keynes offer justifications of the presuppositions of induction, since they both believe in the synthetic a priori,[63] but I do not see why a Kantian-like justification[64] is necessary if the memory principle is analytic a priori. Is the Rule of Induction[65] another principle needing the same treatment, and are there still others? Lewis correctly calls attention to Hume's failure "to give sufficient consideration to the question of probability."[66] The Pragmatic-Humean theory of Section V of the present paper is an attempt to remedy this defect in Hume. Does Professor Lewis believe that his treatment of the memory postulate and the Rule of Induction constitutes a refutation of the thesis that there is no noncircular justification of induction as this thesis is formulated in Section V,3 above? If so, how? It seems to me that since there are logically consistent inductive methods which are alternatives (in the sense of Section V,3) to the standard inductive method, there can be

[61] *Mind and the World-Order* (New York: Dover Publications, 1956), pp. 353, 382. Hereafter cited as MWO.

This uniformity of nature principle is *not* the same as the one discussed above in Sec. V,5.

[62] See Henle, *op. cit.,* p. 528.

[63] At least this is the way I read Keynes. See "On the Presuppositions of Induction," *op. cit.,* pp. 605-606.

[64] AKV, pp. 357-362.

[65] AKV, pp. 273 f., 362.

[66] AKV, p. 228.

no analytic a priori justification of the standard inductive method, and hence an analytic a priori theory of probability is untenable.

I shall conclude this subsection with one further criticism of Professor Lewis' theory of probability. There are three main objections to the frequency theory of probability. (1) The frequency concept of probability presupposes the existence of an infinite sequence of events. (2) Application of the frequency concept of probability presupposes that the given infinite sequence of events has a limit. (3) The frequency theory attempts to explain inductive inference by taking the relative frequency $f_1$ in a finite subsequence as evidence for the limit of the relative frequency $f_2$ of the whole infinite sequence, but any value of $f_1$ is logically compatible with any value of $f_2$, so a nonfrequency concept of probability is needed to connect $f_1$ and $f_2$ (i.e., given $f_1$ it is *probable* that the limit of the infinite sequence is $f_2$). Since Lewis does not accept the frequency theory of probability he is not open to objections (2) and (3). But he defines probability to be *"a valid estimate of a frequency from the given data."*[67] Hence objection (1) is applicable to his theory. I do not see how we can construe all data in terms of frequencies, nor does it seem to me advisable to do so. The meaningfulness of 'the probability of a head on a fair toss of this coin is ½' does not depend on there being an infinite sequence of tosses of this coin, all coins, or on there being any infinite sequence at all. It does not help to use the notion of *possible event* here, because (apart from other difficulties) frequency probability applies only to ordered sequences, and there are many possible orderings with different frequency limits. Moreover it is not necessary to define probability in terms of frequencies, since one can make probability statements about relative frequencies by means of a nonfrequency concept of probability, such as a pragmatic concept of probability.

2. I turn next to Lewis' analysis of physical object statements. This might seem to be a digression, but it is not, for Lewis holds that the concept of probability plays an essential role in the analysis of physical object statements. I think he is correct in this general position, though I shall criticize his specific account of the relation of probability to physical object statements.

In his analysis Lewis makes essential use of the idea of an expressive language, or what is sometimes called a sense datum language. But he does not seem to have completely made up his mind about the status of an expressive language.[68] I should like to ask Lewis whether he

---

[67] AKV, p. 291; cf. pp. 303, 304, 311-314.
[68] Cf. AKV, pp. 182, 204.

believes that (1) ordinary language does not contain expressive statements (in this technical sense), but expressive languages do exist, at
least in his writings and the writings of other sense-data philosophers,
or (2) there is no expressive language and there can be no such language.
Peirce advocated the latter alternative,[69] but as we stated in Section II,1
his pragmatic analysis reduces propositions about physical objects to
other physical object propositions. Lewis reduces physical object propositions to propositions about sense data, hence he would seem to be
committed to the existence of sense data propositions. Thus, if there
were no sense data propositions or sense-data statements, there would
be no entity for the knower to be certain about. Hence it seems to me
that Lewis should either hold (1), or hold (2) and in addition say that
there are (private) propositions which cannot be expressed in language.

Lewis holds that a nonterminating judgment (e.g., 'This desk is
solid') should be analyzed into an infinite set of hypotheticals, each a
terminating judgment. A terminating judgment is of the form 'if $p$ then
$q$', where $p$ and $q$ are atomic expressive propositions and 'if . . . then
. . .' expresses what Lewis calls a 'real connection'. A nonterminating
judgment cannot be conclusively verified or falsified. Expressive statements are merely reports of present experiences, and make no predictions, so (barring linguistic error and lying) are not subject to error.
Terminating judgments do make predictions and can be wrong, and
they can in suitable circumstances be conclusively verified or falsified.[70]

Now what exactly is the relation of a nonterminating judgment to
the set of terminating judgments into which it is analyzed? Sometimes
Lewis speaks as if the nonterminating judgment is an analysandum, the
infinite conjunction of the terminating consequences of this nonterminating judgment is the analysans, and analysans and analysandum are
logically equivalent,[71] as on the usual view of analysis. Thus he says
that a "non-terminating judgment must be *translatable* into judgments
of the terminating kind,"[72] and frequently uses the word 'consequence'
in this context. But on this interpretation the nonterminating judgment

---

[69] This was his doctrine of the inexpressibility of Firstness.

[70] AKV, pp. 181, 219, 257; cf. also pp. 184-6, 204.

[71] We will use 'logical implication' to include implications that depend on the
interpretations and meanings of the terms involved, as well as implications which hold
by purely syntactical rules. 'Logical implication' also allows the antecedent to be
clearer and less vague than the consequent, and vice versa, so an analysandum can
logically imply its analysans. This concept of logical implication seems to be what
Lewis calls 'analytic consequence' (AKV, p. 249) and is closely related to his notion
of strict implication.

A logical equivalence is a two-way logical implication.

[72] AKV, p. 181, italics added.

logically implies one of its terminating consequences, the latter can be conclusively falsified, and hence by *modus tollens* the former is conclusively falsified, which contradicts Lewis' thesis that a nonterminating judgment cannot be conclusively falsified.

Perhaps because he is aware of this difficulty Lewis later gives a somewhat different account of the relation between terminating and nonterminating judgments. He seems to say that the connection between a nonterminating judgment and one of its terminating consequences is a probabilistic one, so falsification of the latter does not conclusively falsify the former but only partly disconfirms it.[73] But if this is Lewis' view then by his own admission he has not explicitly analyzed nonterminating judgments into terminating judgments, that is, he has not reduced physical object statements to sense data statements. Hence he is not offering an *analysis* of nonterminating statements, in the ordinary sense of the term. This is so even though on Lewis' view the probability connection between a nonterminating judgment and its terminating judgments would be an analytic a priori one.

These difficulties are not resolved by the technical summary at the end of the chapter on terminating judgments.[74] Here Lewis discusses some relations between physical object propositions and expressive propositions. He says the nonterminating judgment

(L)   A sheet of real paper lies before me

has "the analytic consequence"

(M)   When a visual sheet-of-paper presentation is given and *I move my eyes,* then in all probability a seen displacement of this presentation follows.[75]

The italicized statement "I move my eyes" expresses a nonterminating judgment (since I could dream that I did this without it being so), but even if this is changed to the corresponding expressive judgment it is not clear what Lewis is saying here. He tells us that the 'if . . . then . . .' of statement (M) expresses a real connection, but he does not adequately explain the relation of real connections to probabilities. We will return to this problem in Section VI,5 below, but in the meantime we need to consider two possible interpretations of (M). These are (1) the real connection expressed by the 'if . . . then . . .' is probabilistic[76] and so (M) expresses a *relative* probability proposition, and (2) the real

[73] AKV, pp. 233, 236 f.

[74] AKV, pp. 248-249.

[75] AKV, p. 249. Italics added.

[76] At AKV, p. 229 Lewis specifically states that there are probabilistic real connections.

connection expressed by the 'if . . . then . . .' is nonprobabilistic so (M) is a nonprobabilistic hypothetical whose consequent is the *nonrelative* probability assertion.

(P) In all probability a seen displacement of this presentation follows.

On the first interpretation (M) is analytic, according to Lewis' a priori view of relative probabilities, and hence cannot explicate the *empirical* content of (L); if (M) is analytic it follows logically from every proposition (according to the *so-called* 'paradoxes' of strict implication). On the second interpretation (M) involves *nonrelative* probabilities, so to analyze this interpretation we need to consider Lewis' theory of nonrelative probabilities; we will do this next.

3. Since relative probability judgments are analytic a priori for Lewis they cannot be of much help in analyzing physical object propositions. But Lewis is an empiricist with respect to nonrelative probability judgments,[77] so there is a possibility that Lewis can resolve his difficulties by means of them.

The view that nonrelative probabilities are empirical while relative probabilities are a priori must face the following questions. What is the empirical or pragmatic content of nonrelative probability judgments? If relative and nonrelative probabilities are so different in internal constitution, how can the relations to each other that they obviously do have be explained? I do not find adequate answers to these questions in Lewis' writings. He states that we do not need to withdraw 'probably h' when h turns out to be false, but he does not tell us under what conditions we should withdraw it.[78] Since Lewis wants to ground empirical knowledge on certainty he may think that an expressive nonrelative probability statement is not subject to error, but certainly there must be circumstances under which a physical object probability proposition (e.g., "in all probability it will rain") is falsified.

Lewis says that "a categorical conclusion *asserts the premised data* of the probability determination," adds that 'Probably P' has a significance beyond this data which he cannot explain, and then concludes

For one who should lack a primordial sense of probable events, every attempted explanation of a categorial probability statement must fail.[79]

There are two serious objections to this. First, 'Probably P' cannot assert *the* data 'D' on which it is based, because in general there is no

77 AKV, pp. 249-251, 318 ff.
78 AKV, p. 318.
79 AKV, pp. 319-320.

single datum proposition from which it is derived. Moreover, the same hypothesis may be derived (with the same probability) from contradictory sets of evidence. That is, we may have $P(h, e_1) = P(h, e_2)$, where $e_1$ and $e_2$ are logically incompatible, so '$P(h)$' cannot assert either $e_1$ or $e_2$. One might analyze '$P(h) = x$' into

(Q)   $x$ is the value which results from applying the *correct* inductive method to the pair $h, e$, where $e$ expresses *my* total information.[80]

In other words, one may construe a *nonrelative* probability proposition as *referring to* the evidence on which it is based, even though it cannot explicitly mention this evidence, or else it would be a *relative* probability proposition. But contrary to what Lewis suggests, a nonrelative probability proposition cannot, in general, be equated to the evidence on which it is based.

The second objection is to Lewis' appeal to a "primordial sense" of probability. I do not wish to object to this approach in principle; I have considerable sympathy, for example, with J. M. Keynes's view that probability is indefinable.[81] But Lewis is considerably worse off than Keynes in this respect. Lewis felt it necessary to define the a priori concept of relative probability; he should explain why it is impossible to define the empirical concept of nonrelative probability. Moreover, even if nonrelative probability is undefinable, we are entitled to know something about the rules by which an empirical physical object statement like "it will probably rain" or a sense-datum statement like (P) above is confirmed or disconfirmed.

Whatever these rules may be, it is implausible to suppose that one could *conclusively* verify any *empirical* probability statement in a single instance. Lewis seems to think this is possible,[82] and his theory that terminating judgments can be decided with theoretical certainty requires that this be so. But it seems to me essential that many cases are required for the conclusive verification of an empirical probability statement, if indeed conclusive verification of such statements is possible.[83] This is so on all empirical theories of probability I am acquainted with, and I find an empirical concept of probability which allows conclusive verification in a single case very mysterious.

---

80 Cf. the analysis (J) and (K) in Section V,3.

81 *Op. cit.*, Chap. 1.

82 AKV, p. 322.

83 Note that we are not discussing the issue of the single case versus the long-run, i.e., the problem of whether a probability statement about a single case is meaningful or intelligible.

4. It will be of interest to hear what Professor Lewis has to say in answer to the questions already raised in this section. I should like to suggest now that he could avoid many of the difficulties in his present theory of probability by accepting the Pragmatic-Humean theory of probability, or some variant of it.

To begin with, a pragmatic theory of probability offers a very simple and adequate account of nonrelative probabilities. As we showed in Section II, it treats nonrelative probabilities in terms of choices made in situations of uncertainty, in a way very similar to the way pragmatists have treated nonprobability assertions. Hence a pragmatic theory of probability fits well with the remainder of Lewis' philosophy. Moreover, a pragmatic theory of probability shows how nonrelative probabilities are related to relative probabilities; see Sections III and V. Thus the objections raised in the preceding subsection against Lewis' empirical theory of nonrelative probabilities do not apply to a pragmatic theory of them.

It is true that on a pragmatic theory of probability nonrelative probabilities have a certain personal character. But this is as it should be, because what probability value we assign to a given hypothesis $h$ depends on what evidence $e$ we have, and this evidence certainly varies from individual to individual. (Note in this connection the reference to '*my* total information' in the analysis $(Q)$ of '$P(h) = x$' given in the preceding subsection.) But relative to this evidence, the probability one ought to assign to a proposition depends on rules which to a degree are held in common by all rational people (see Section V). Speaking about probable assurance Lewis says "this degree of assurance is not merely a psychological 'felt intensity' of belief, but the degree to which it is epistemically warranted."[84] The Pragmatic-Humean theory of probability holds this to be true of nonrelative (as well as relative) probabilities.

Let us return now to Lewis' assertion that

(L)  A sheet of real paper lies before me

has the consequence

(M)  When a visual sheet-of-paper presentation is given and I move my eyes, then in all *probability* a seen displacement of this presentation follows.[85]

Lewis is unclear whether (M) expresses a relative probability or not (see Section VI,2), but on either interpretation there are serious objections to what he says about (M) (see Sections VI,2 and VI,3).

84 AKV, p. 324.
85 AKV, pp. 248-49, italics added.

These objections do not apply if (M) is interpreted by a pragmatic theory of probability. On this theory (M) is interpreted as a practical consequence whose consequent is a partial belief. Consider a slight reformulation of (M):

(M') If I experience a visual sheet-of-paper presentation and I move my eyes, then it is highly *probable* that I will experience a seen displacement of this presentation.

The proposal is to accept the Pragmatic-Humean account of 'probable' here. On this theory 'probable' has both a descriptive aspect (it indicates something about my partial expectations, how I would bet, etc.) and a normative aspect (it signifies my willingness to revise my expectations to accord with the norms of probability theory and inductive logic). When (L) is analyzed in this way the result is an analysis of a total belief into partial beliefs. And if "I move my eyes" is replaced by its expressive equivalent, the result is a phenomenalist analysis of physical object beliefs.

Another alternative is to give up the phenomenalist attempt to reduce physical object propositions to sense data propositions and to use pragmatic probability to relate the two kinds of propositions.[86] If sense data propositions exist there are certainly probability connections between them and physical object propositions, and one approach to the problem of knowledge is to describe and codify these. The result would not be an analysis or reduction, but it would be an account of the relation of immediate 'knowledge' to mediate knowledge.

The question 'Are probability judgments analytic a priori or synthetic a posteriori?' is a fundamental one for Lewis' theory of probability, so it is natural to consider it in connection with the Pragmatic-Humean theory of probability. On this theory probability judgments are analyzed into habits of action, and since dispositions to respond are neither a priori nor a posteriori, the question is not an appropriate one as it stands. Of course we can ask whether 'A believes $P(h, e) = x$' is a priori or empirical, and the answer is that obviously it is empirical. But the pragmatist is analyzing the public elements common to the beliefs of rational people, and for him probability is normative. Hence the original question 'Are probability judgments analytic a priori or synthetic a posteriori?' should be replaced by 'what kind of considerations do and should influence the formation and alteration of the probability beliefs of a *rational* man?' As we shall see, the answer of the Pragmatic-Humean theory to this question resembles Lewis' answer to the original question.

86 See my "On the Presuppositions of Induction," *op. cit.*, Sec. 5.

The Pragmatic-Humean theory of probability gives the same kind of account of the acceptance and rejection of nonrelative partial beliefs as of total beliefs. One's nonrelative partial beliefs should be empirically grounded in the evidence. The relative frequencies with which a given type of event occurs is *likely* to be close to the probability of that event, and if it is not we should revise our subjective probabilities accordingly. One's nonrelative probabilities should also depend on his relative probability beliefs, since these provide the link between the evidence and a nonrelative probability belief. Relative probability beliefs in turn should depend strongly on rules of probability and inductive inference (see Sections II,4 and V,2). On the Pragmatic-Humean theory these rules function in an a priori way, since they are definitive of what we mean by 'probable'. They are not, however, a priori in the sense of being the only possible consistent inductive rules (see Section V,3). Thus empirical considerations should play a predominant role in fixing nonrelative probability beliefs, while rational considerations are essential for determining relative partial beliefs.

I think this discussion has shown that the Pragmatic-Humean theory of probability, while quite different from Lewis' theory, is not as different as it might at first sight seem. Lewis repeatedly objects to Hume's skepticism, and he may feel that the Pragmatic-Humean theory is too skeptical. Lewis could of course adopt the pragmatic portion of the theory and reject the Humean part (see Section V,1), but he should note that several of his objections to skepticism are not applicable to the Pragmatic-Humean theory. We will show that this is so for three of Lewis' criticisms of skepticism. (1) Lewis says that the skeptic identifies certainty and knowledge, neglecting probability.[87] The Pragmatic-Humean theory is an attempt to rectify Hume's weaknesses on this point, and to restate Hume's thesis that there is no noncircular justification of induction explicitly in terms of probabilities. (2) Lewis objects to the skeptic's saying that inductive inference rests on 'nonrational' assumptions and that inductive evidence never 'validly' supports empirical propositions.[88] As we noted in Section V,2 Hume is indeed guilty of this fault, and we were careful to make the Pragmatic-Humean theory conform to ordinary usage on this point. All rational people are committed to the standard inductive method, and there is nothing in the Pragmatic-Humean theory which implies that one ought to change this commitment (see Section V,3). (3) Lewis thinks that skepticism is the only alternative to recog-

---

[87] AKV, pp. 228, 259. MWO, p. 381.
[88] AKV, pp. 191, 260. MWO, p. 379.

nizing that there are causally necessary connections in nature.[89] We will discuss causality in the next subsection. It is sufficient to say here that the Pragmatic-Humean theory does not accept Hume's doctrine that causal necessity is subjective.

Lewis may feel that to refute skepticism one must give an analytic a priori justification of induction.[90] This would amount to saying that the only alternative to skepticism is an analytic a priori theory of probability. I am not sure that Lewis intends this, but if he does he would be requiring more of a refutation of skepticism than Kant, since Kant needed the synthetic a priori to refute Hume's skepticism about induction. Moreover, it seems to me that the existence of alternative inductive methods shows that an analytic a priori justification of induction is impossible (see Section VI,1).

5. As Lewis sees, no theory of probability is adequate unless it accounts for causality, so we will conclude with a brief discussion of this subject.

Lewis' view of causal laws is that they are neither mere summaries of actual occurrences nor expressions of logical connections. Hence the 'if . . . then . . . ' of a causal law is stronger than a material implication but weaker than a strict or logical implication.[91] Such an implication expresses what Lewis calls a 'natural connection' or a 'real connection'. The essential difference between an implication expressing a real connection and a material implication is that the former implies (in a suitable context) a contrary-to-fact proposition, while the latter does not.

I believe that Lewis is right in holding that there are implications which express real connections. Moreover, any theory of probability which only accounts for the verification of material implications and not for the verification of these other implications is inadequate. Lewis' theory of probability is superior in this respect to both the frequency theory and Carnap's a priori theory since Lewis does attempt to account for the verification of causal laws. Because of this I should like to ask Lewis some questions concerning his views on causality.

The first question has to do with the relation of causality to probability. It seems to me that there are cases of 'if . . . then . . .' expressing real connections which are not *intrinsically* probabilistic or statistical; let us refer to these as *causal implications*. Any nonstatistical causal law is an example, as is the statement

(R) If he *had* dropped his glasses they *would have* broken.

[89] AKV, p. 228.
[90] See AKV, p. 361. Cf. MWO, Chap. XI.
[91] AKV, pp. 211-229.

My logic of causal propositions[92] treats causal implication and its relations to material implication, strict implication, contrary-to-fact implication, causal necessity, and causal possibility. Let us call an elementary or atomic proposition involving one of these causal notions a *nonprobabilistic causal proposition*. The term 'probability' is not an ingredient of a nonprobabilistic causal proposition, though of course one can ask about the probability of such a proposition relative to given evidence.

It is a significant fact that a nonprobabilistic causal implication cannot be verified by observing one instance. Both sentence (R) and

(S) If he *should* drop his glasses they *would* break

say something about *potentialities* (or *dispositions*) as well as *actualities*, and hence cannot be confirmed by observing a single actuality. Now Lewis says that a terminating judgment "admits of decisive and complete *verification* and falsification,"[93] hence the 'if . . . then . . .' of his terminating judgment cannot express a causal implication in the sense of my logic of causal propositions.

One might hold that there are no nonprobabilistic causal propositions (as I have defined them) but that all causal propositions and expressions of Lewis' real connections are at heart probabilistic propositions. As I understand Lewis he does not hold this. On the other hand, he does wish to say that not all causal propositions are of the nonprobabilistic variety, and cites an example like

(T) If Smith *should* jump out of the window, he *would* probably be hurt.[94]

As Lewis points out, such propositions imply, in suitable contexts, contrary-to-fact assertions which involve probability as an essential intrinsic ingredient. Thus there are *probabilistic dispositions,* expressed by statements like (T), as well as *causal dispositions,* expressed by statements like

(U) This mud is soft.

Lewis seems to think that probabilistic dispositions and causal dispositions are essentially the same, but this does not seem to me to be so. For example, I would analyze (U) by means of causal implication but (T) by means of probability,[95] and though the concepts of casual implication and probabilistic implication are related, I do not believe that

92 "The Logic of Causal Propositions," *Mind*, 60 (July, 1951), 363-382.

93 AKV, p. 181; cf. pp. 186, 204, 226.

94 AKV, p. 229. The example is not exactly the same as Lewis', but it fits what he has in mind.

95 "Dispositional Statements," *Philosophy of Science*, 22 (July, 1955), 175-193.

one is definable in terms of the other.[96] But in any case it seems to me that any *empirical* use of 'if . . . then . . .' which expresses a probabilistic real connection will refer to potentialities as well as actualities, and hence cannot be conclusively verified in one instance, as Lewis' theory of terminating judgments requires.[97]

Let us next explore further Lewis' views about causal implications (as they occur in nonprobabilistic causal propositions). He says (1) that a causal implication is not a material implication and (2) that a causal implication expresses a real connection, which is a "necessary connection of matters of fact."[98] Presumably the second statement says more than the first. What, exactly, does Lewis intend it to add to the first? Since Lewis states his views in opposition to Hume, and since we need to relate Hume's views on causality to the Pragmatic-Humean theory of probability, we will begin with them.

Hume's analysis of causality makes reference to the mind, so let us analyze a belief in a causal proposition rather than the causal proposition itself. Consider

(V) *A believes that in every case C causes E,*
where the implied implication is intended as a causal implication. The following seems to me close to Hume's proposed analysis of (V).

($W_1$) *A believes that every case of C is in fact a case of E*

($W_2$) *A believes that C and E satisfy Hume's rules of spatial and temporal contiguity, temporal sequence, etc.*

($W_3$) *A has a habit of passing from the idea of C to the idea of E.*[99]
The implication implicit in ($W_1$) is a material implication, as is, presumably, the implication needed to symbolize ($W_3$). It is clear from this analysis that Hume could accept Lewis' thesis that a causal implication is not a material implication. Hume also agrees that there is an idea of causal necessity, but he says this necessity is in the mind alone.

There is no internal impression, which has any relation [to necessity], but that *propensity,* which custom produces, to pass from an object to the *idea of*

96 There may be propositions which involve both probabilistic and causal dispositions, for example, the statistical laws of quantum mechanics.

97 Compare the discussion at the end of Sec. VI,3.
The following fact about the Pragmatic-Humean theory of probability is worth noting in this connection. On this theory a person's belief in a probabilistic proposition is described in terms of how he *would act* in specified conditions of uncertainty. Though the conditions involve chance events, the prediction of his behavior is causal and deterministic, not probabilistic.

98 AKV, p. 228.

99 THN, "Rules by Which to Judge of Causes and Effects," Book I, Part III, Sec. XV; also pp. 165-166 (Book I, Part III, Sec. XIV).
ECHU, pp. 81, 82.

its usual attendant. This therefore is the essence of necessity. Upon the whole, *necessity is something, that exists in the mind, not in objects; . . . . . .* the necessity of power, which unites causes and effects, lies in the *determination* of the *mind* to pass from the one to the other.[100]

When any object is presented to us, it immediately conveys to the mind a lively idea of that object, which is usually found to attend it; and *this determination of the mind forms the necessary connexion* of these objects.[101]

'Tis the constant conjunction of objects, along with the determination of the mind, which constitutes a physical necessity . . .[102]

But there is nothing in a number of instances, differing from every single instance, which is supposed to be exactly similar; except only, that after a repetition of similar instances, the mind is carried by habit, upon the appearance of one event, to expect its usual attendant, and to believe that it will exist. The connexion, therefore, which we *feel* in the mind, this customary transition of the imagination from one object to its usual attendant, is the sentiment or impression from which we form the idea of power or necessary connexion. Nothing farther is in the case.[103]

I think Hume is wrong in holding that causal necessity is purely subjective, for the following reason. There are uniformities (constant conjunctions) which satisfy Hume's criteria for cause and effect but which are accidental and not the result of a causal law. An accidental uniformity should not and often does not give rise to a belief in a genuine causal connection. That is, Hume's criteria of causality are relevant signs of causal necessity, but they do not fully characterize it. There must be some means by which we distinguish real causal connections from accidental uniformities. To say that causal necessity is in the mind, as Hume does, is to say that we do make this distinction, but to leave room for no criterion by means of which we can make it. Thus the distinction between accidental or contingent uniformities and genuine causal universals[104] cannot be explained by a purely subjective view of causal necessity.

When Lewis speaks of there being 'necessary connections of matters of fact' he undoubtedly wishes to reject Hume's view that causal necessity is purely subjective. I should like to ask him if he holds the stronger thesis that causal necessities are objective in one following sense. There are 'real connections' or potentialities in nature, and a causally necessary statement is true (i.e., expresses a causal law) only if it properly describes, characterizes, or corresponds to such a real connection or potentiality. The difference between a causal uniformity and an accidental uniformity

100 THN, Book I, Part III, Sec. XIV, pp. 165-166. Italics added.
101 THN, p. 169. Italics added.
102 THN, p. 171.
103 ECHU, p. 81.
104 See "The Logic of Causal Propositions," *op. cit.*, Sec. 2.4.

is that in the former case there is a corresponding objective causal necessity in nature while in the latter case there is not, though of course the accidental uniformity might result from causal laws, together with some
accidental feature of the initial or boundary conditions. The issue here
can be compared with the earlier one concerning space-time uniformity
(see Section V,5). As in that case we can ask: Is causal necessity in the
world directly and in the mind derivatively, or is it in the mind only and
not in the exterior world at all? Hume accepts the latter alternative while
the former seems correct to me.[105] Lewis certainly rejects the latter alternative, but I am not sure he adopts the former. His discussion of 'real
connections' in *An Analysis of Knowledge and Valuation*[106] does not
seem to commit him on this point, but in an article Lewis seems to subscribe to the view that causal necessity is in the world directly and in the
mind derivatively.[107]

If one accepts the view that causal necessities are objective (i.e., that
they are in the world directly and in the mind derivatively) he then has
the problem of explaining the meaning of this concept. Exactly what this
problem is depends on one's theory of meaning, but it is a difficult problem for both empirical and pragmatic theories of meaning. Consider first
the empiricist theory that every genuine concept either has a direct application in immediate experience or is a compound of concepts that do.
I do not think there are any immediate experiences of objective causal
necessity[108] nor do I see how causal necessity can be defined in terms of
concepts derived from immediate experience. On these points I think
Hume was correct.

The difficulty a pragmatic theory of meaning has in accounting for
causal necessity arises out of the fact that potentialities are not observable.
There is no difference in observable predictions between a causal implication such as

(S) If he *should* drop his glasses they *would* break

and the corresponding material implication

(X) Either he doesn't drop his glasses or they do break.

Both say the same about what will actually happen. They differ only
about what might happen, but doesn't, and this is not an observable
difference. Using our earlier terminology we can put the point by saying
that (S) and (X) express the same actualities and differ in meaning only
with respect to potentialities, while all observations are of actualities, not

105 See "On the Presuppositions of Induction," *op. cit.*, p. 582.

106 Pp. 211-229, 249-253, 513-514.

107 Pp. 244-245 of his "Realism or Phenomenalism?", *The Philosophical Review*, 64
(April, 1955), 233-247.

108 See my "Dispositional Statements," Sec. 3. 3.

potentialities. Thus there are no experimental phenomena which distinguish (S) from (X). According to Peirce's version of the pragmatic theory of meaning two propositions differ in meaning only if there are experimental phenomena implied by one and not the other. Hence Peirce's formulation of pragmatism cannot account for the difference in meaning between (S) and (X), and consequently cannot account for objective causal necessity. Now Peirce did believe that causal necessities were objective, so his theory of meaning is inconsistent with his metaphysics at this point.[109] Lewis sometimes speaks as if he shared Peirce's view that two propositions differ in empirical meaning only if they predict different observable phenomena.[110] It seems to me that if Lewis does in fact hold this view, and believes that causal necessities are objective in the sense explained above, his theory of meaning and his metaphysics are also incompatible.[111]

Lewis may not wish to subscribe to the thesis that causal necessities are objective (in the sense stated above), but may feel that there is another alternative to Hume's doctrine that causal necessity is subjective. Such an alternative would fit in well with the Pragmatic-Humean theory of probability, so let us explore the possibility briefly in connection with this theory. It will be recalled that the Pragmatic-Humean theory includes a modern version of Hume's doctrine that there is no noncircular justification of induction (Section V,4), but it rejects Hume's subjective account of causal necessity (Section V,1). The Pragmatic-Humean theory does not use categories like 'in the mind' or 'in nature', so the question 'Is causal necessity in the world directly or in the mind alone?' is not an appropriate question for this theory.[112] But since the Pragmatic-Humean theory rejects Hume's account of causal necessity, we can fairly ask how it would explain the meaning of causal necessity. As noted above, Hume's view that causal necessity is subjective is inadequate because it does not explain how we in fact distinguish accidental uniformities from causal uniformities. We do make this distinction, though of course in any particular case we can make it only with a certain degree of probability. The Pragmatic-Humean theory treats problems like this by considering the practical consequences and the rules of inference involved. Thus it might

109 I have argued this point against Peirce in detail in my introduction to the Peirce selections in *Classic American Philosophers,* edited by Max Fisch (New York: Appleton-Century-Crofts, 1951) , pp. 42-53.

110 AKV, pp. 137, 176-77, 184, 208, 229.

111 In this connection see the controversy between Lewis and E. J. Nelson in *The Philosophical Review,* 63 (April, 1954), 182-196.

112 Compare the treatment of the question 'Are probability judgments analytic a priori or synthetic a posteriori?' in Sec. VI,4 above.

account for the difference in meaning between sentences *(S)* and *(X)* above by finding differences in the procedures which should be used to verify these propositions. There may be differences in the amount and kind of data required to establish each proposition as probable, differences in the proper procedures for gathering this data, and differences in the rules of induction used to pass from the data to the conclusion. Such a way of explaining the meaning of causal necessity would be compatible with the general pragmatic conception of meaning, and if it could be carried out it would avoid the difficulties raised in the two preceding paragraphs. Perhaps Professor Lewis has in mind some such approach as this, for he does not seem to think that there is any conflict between his theory of meaning and his doctrine that causal implications express "necessary connections of matters of fact."

ARTHUR W. BURKS

DEPARTMENT OF PHILOSOPHY
UNIVERSITY OF MICHIGAN

## 17

## C. Douglas McGee

# A DISPOSITIONAL INTERPRETATION OF
# CRITERIA IN MIND

THIS article has two main points: (I) to show how Lewis' notion of 'sense meaning' can be interpreted in dispositional terms; how criteria in mind, as dispositions, can and do function in the application of expressions and in the comparison of meanings; (II) to show that if this dispositional interpretation of 'sense meaning' is right, then Lewis' theory of the certification of the a priori truth of analytic statements is wrong.

The first of these points could be made in either or both of two different ways: (A) One might try to show that Lewis' discussion of criteria in mind in *Analysis of Knowledge and Valuation,* and particularly his account of the role of sense meanings in the application of terms, powerfully suggests, and at one point almost explicitly states, that sense meanings are disposition-like. (B) One might try to describe—at first hand, so to say—his own activities of thinking and meaning and in the application of terms, in an attempt to identify among those activities something which Lewis might be willing to call a 'criterion in mind'. If what was thus identified as a sense meaning turned out to be a classificatory habit, or a linguistic ability, or some particular manifestation of such a disposition, then this would constitute some independent evidence for the dispositional status of criteria in mind.

I have chosen here to take the second of these paths.[1] To do the first in a convincing way would require too copious a use of quotations. I should like, however, immediately to quote the passage where Lewis comes closest to calling sense meanings dispositions:

We have thought it well judged to take sense meaning as criterion *in mind:* but the important character connoted by 'in mind' here is 'entertained in advance of instances of application which are pertinent' rather than any necessary contrast between what is in mind and what would be describable

---

[1] Both avenues are exhaustively explored in my unpublished Ph.D. thesis, "C. I. Lewis' Theory of Sense Meaning," Widener Library, 1956. That thesis, and hence this article, its by-product, owe much to the encouragement given me by Professor C. I. Lewis.

in terms of overt behavior. Common-sense reference to meanings as something 'inwardly observable' when entertained, with an assurance exceeding any which outward observation of another could give, has indeed been intended. But if anyone conceive it important to exclude what is thus inwardly observable only, then that aspect of the matter is dispensable. One may consider such criteria of application, of meanings entertained in advance, in terms of incipient behavior or behavior attitudes if one choose; and the observability of these will then be comparable to the observability of the use of language.[2]

This passage can stand for the others in which Lewis comes close to saying that meanings are disposition-like;[3] it would be uneconomical to repeat all of these and, in the second place, this suggestion thrown forth by Lewis' discussion has already been caught by reviewers and by other commentators.

In the third place, to engage here in a few pages worth of phenomenology, or reflective psychology, may serve the following purpose: it may show that there *are* such things as sense meanings or, better, that there are activities which can plausibly be identified as criteria in mind, and that they do sometimes operate in some of the ways that Lewis says they do. So far as there has been scepticism in regard to this partially factual point, this in part Lewis' own fault; Lewis' direct discussion of the nature of sense meanings is so meager as to be positively offhand. With few exceptions Lewis seems to infer his view of what sense meanings *are* from his views as to what they *must do*. So far as Lewis argues transcendentally *to* the nature of sense meanings *from* the functions assigned them by his epistemological theory, he is liable to the charge of having altered or even invented phenomenological facts or ontological entities to fit that theory.

To confirm or to dispel this suspicion it would seem reasonable to seek some phenomenological evidence as independent as can be from the theoretical specificities and commitments of Lewis' epistemology. Obviously we cannot ask for perfect independence, since we must take from Lewis at least a minimum characterization of sense meaning in order to know what we hope to find. We require, that is, a (sense?) meaning for 'sense meaning' that will beg the fewest possible questions, that will involve the least epistemological commitment consonant with our need to be able to recognize a criterion in mind if we come across one. Let us suppose that we have that minimal characterization expressed in the following words: we shall understand 'sense meaning', or 'criterion in mind', "as a test-schematism and an anticipated result of it, or . . .

2 C. I. Lewis, *An Analysis of Knowledge and Valuation* (La Salle, Ill.: Open Court, 1946), p. 144. Hereafter cited as AKV.

3 Cf. especially AKV, pp. 235-236, 260 f., 355; cf. AKV, pp. 325 f *re* 'beliefs-attitudes' and 'belief-habits'.

conceived in any other manner as a criterion of application which can be entertained in advance of particular occasions of application."[4] Now, if sense meanings as criteria in mind are essential to our use of language, or even if they operate in cognition but are not essential to it, it should be possible for a user of language to describe these operations. At least this will be so to the extent that criteria in mind are capable of envisagement,[5] sense-recognizable,[6] sense-apprehensible,[7] and inspectable.[8] If a sympathetic attempt is made to inspect the inspectable and to describe what is inspected, its results should furnish evidence pertinent to so much of Lewis' position as is predicated on the observable operations of sense meanings.

I

When we try to describe what it is like to approach "an empirical situation with intent to apply or to refuse to apply an expression, or to assert something as evidenced or its falsity as evidenced,"[9] the first thing we are likely to remark about sense meanings is their absence, or at least their failure obviously to be present. The fact is that we are seldom aware of going through any rehearsal of schematic imagery in order to apply terms to experience. To suppose such a performance necessarily or usually to precede our application of 'dog' or 'triangle' would be misleadingly inaccurate: application involves nothing so deliberate, at least not often. To stop and consciously to recall what we mean by 'martlet' or 'lantana' can involve a deliberate 'calling to mind'; this sometimes happens when we are unsure of our meaning or puzzled about whether a term is applicable to some questionable instance. Only then is it likely that one would make himself go through some imaginary test-application, and even then this particular kind of deliberation may not be usual.

Now if this is the case—and on phenomenological grounds it can scarcely be doubted—explicit rehearsal of a meaning is inessential to application. More critically, even to know that we *can* apply most words we do not have to make a trial application in imagination. Knowing that we are able to apply a term is like knowing that we are able to swim: both have to be learned, but after that in neither case do we have to go through

4 AKV, p. 138.
5 AKV, pp. 152, 154, 157, 168, 189.
6 AKV, pp. 154, 157.
7 AKV, pp. 155, 168.
8 AKV, p. 193.
9 AKV, p. 135.

the activity, internally or otherwise, to know that we are able to perform it. To answer "Yes" to the question "Are you able to swim?" it is not necessary kinaesthetically to rehearse dog-paddling or the Australian crawl: it is enough to know that you could swim if you tried. This knowing manifests itself not in the production of imagery, but as a feeling of readiness, or assurance. If some particularly obstinate questioner challenged our assertion that we were able to swim, we might then partially justify our claim even in the absence of a pool by overtly producing the appropriate motions. He or we would probably count this as some evidence that we were able to swim, but we should probably insist that we "knew it all along."

In like fashion, if asked "Do you know what 'cat' means?" or "Can you apply the word 'cat'?" we should probably immediately answer "Yes." In order thus truly to answer we do not have to 'inspect' or entertain in imagery any part of our meaning of 'cat'. It is true that an imaginary rehearsal of the intensional meaning of 'cat', or some trial application in imagination, would probably be counted as some evidence that we could apply 'cat'. On the other hand, an inability consciously so to perform would not be decisive evidence that we could not apply 'cat', though perhaps we should then have to admit that there was present only a very imperfect grasp of the sense meaning of 'cat'.[10] We are able to operate under such imperfect conditions, but these cases may be taken to represent a kind of vanishing point of meaning.

Thus when we try to capture without change what goes on between the question "Do you know how properly to apply 'aardvark'?" or "Do you know what 'zygote' means?" and our true, even our considered, affirmative answer, we ordinarily find no more than a feeling of readiness, of confidence or assurance. The fact that application can take place without the production of explicit imagery shows that the 'inspection' or 'envisagement' of an explicit schematism is inessential to the act of application. To this Lewis would no doubt agree. But the fact that we can know, "in advance of instances of application which are pertinent," but without explicit rehearsal of a sense meaning, that we are *able* to apply a term, would seem to indicate that explicit schemata were inessential to that 'meaning-in-advance' the possibility of which they were adduced to explain.

Now we may be tempted to take a quick and easy way with meanings, producing as a result of our investigations the following truism: what

10 Cf. AKV, p. 133; C. I. Lewis, *Mind and the World-Order* (New York: Charles Scribner's Sons, 1929), pp. 86-89 on Royce on Peirce. Hereafter cited as MWO; C. S. Peirce, *Collected Papers of Charles Sanders Peirce*, eds. Charles Hartshorne and Paul Weiss (Cambridge: Harvard University Press, 1934), 5.151, 5.388-410.

is essential to the ability to apply a term is the ability to apply that term. Meaning in advance of application can take place without reference to explicit schemata and, when we look for something which, so to say, underlies meaning *and* the production of explicit imagery, and which would serve to explain them, all that we can find is our awareness of an ability. We might call such an ability or habit a 'latent' or an 'implicit schema', but this does seem somewhat to smack of the celebrated *virtus dormitiva*, and the notoriety of this could lead us to conclude that "meanings themselves, as obscure intermediary entities, may well be abandoned."[11]

The trouble with this severe verdict is that it ignores the extenuating possibility of taking meaning-in-advance as dispositional, and still using it to explain some of our activities in the use of ordinary language. Students and lovers of the counterfactual will be quick to point out that, even if dispositional statements be translated into contrary-to-fact conditional statements, neither kind of statement is unexceptionably clear. This can be granted, but, as White allows, such translatable references to dispositions do seem less mysterious, less objectionable ontologically than reference to meanings as irreducibly mental or conceptual entities. The fact is that dispositional meaning-in-advance, and the manifestation of such abilities in imagery, can usefully be referred to in the explanation of linguistic practice. I should like here just to sketch two or three ways in which intensional meaning 'in terms of sense' can and does function in the use of language. I am not sure that he would, but I hope Lewis would agree that we are talking about the same thing.

The first point is this: schemata can be made explicit in the form of imagery, and in this form can be 'envisaged', 'inspected', and even 'compared'. It is not easy to describe what it is like to entertain such imagery nor to make clear the character—at once organized and sketchy, patterned and schematic, gestaltish, iconic, and determinable—that it can have. Even at subverbal levels of *expectation,* the precursor of intensional meaning, anticipatory imagery is fairly specific without being entirely determinate, is organized or patterned in such a holistic way that one is led almost inevitably to use phrases like 'picture', or 'pattern', or 'fitting', to say that some class of experiences to come will 'fit into the picture' of expectation and that others will not, trying in this way

11 W. V. Quine, *From a Logical Point of View* (Cambridge: Harvard University Press, 1953), pp. 48, 22. Cf. M. G. White, "Ontological Clarity and Semantic Obscurity," *Journal of Philosophy*, 48 (1951), 373-380; N. Goodman, "On Likeness of Meaning," in *Semantics and the Philosophy of Language*, ed. L. Linsky (Urbana, Ill.: University of Illinois Press, 1952), pp. 67-74.

to call attention to the organized, gestalt-like character even of expectation, and even when expectation is vague.

It is worth pointing out that anticipatory imagery is not exclusively visual, but may be auditory, tactile, kinaesthetic, or even gustatory.[12] Examples of expecting to see something, or the entertainment of visual imagery, bring us closest to Lewis' discussion of sense meaning, but they do involve a certain peculiar risk: the risk of supposing that the entertainment of visual schemata involves the inspection of a static and wholly determinate 'mental picture'. Lewis no doubt hoped to avoid this even by the name 'schemata', but neither he nor Kant has wholly avoided the temptation, especially severe in any attempt to describe visual imagery, to sacrifice descriptive accuracy in the interest of expository clarity. This is understandable; it is frustratingly difficult to describe the entertainment of visual imagery. Visual images in general—not just schemata, but most instances of visual imaging—are less like hard and intractable things and more like manipulatable series of events. To visualize, to 'inspect', 'sensibly to apprehend', in advance or otherwise, is to act, not to be acted upon; it is a performance, not a passive aesthesis; it is more like drawing a sketch than like looking at one; it may leave out unremembered details, or aspects consciously or unconsciously discarded as irrelevant, while still retaining a recognizable iconicity. In the case of expectation, and no doubt in the case of intensional meaning, whatever external or extensional object will subsequently meet or fulfill or disappoint expectation is an entirely determinate and specific individual. But even in the case of visual entertainment it would be misleading to say that the imagery involved had to be completely determinate and specific. It is whatever it is, but what it is has the kind of specificity that a gesture does, and it is determinate as the motion of an artist's hand or eye is determinate.

It is, after all, impossible to duplicate on the printed page any kind of imitative activity—the activity of sketching, or painting, or waving one's hands—and thus to convey the 'open-textured', the at once iconic and diagrammatic character of schematic imaging. (Perhaps for 'triangle' we should have to draw something like this ↗ ↘ ↩, and for 'pentagram' like this ↗↘↖→↙, trying in this way to suggest the significance of motion and direction, how 'triangle' can mean three sides, and 'three sides' can mean three gestures.) To present some finished product in the form of a sketch or a painting would tend not only to subordinate imaging to images, but to overemphasize the importance of visualizing in

---

[12] Cf. William James, *The Principles of Psychology* (New York: Henry Holt and Co., August, 1931), Vol. II, pp. 50-68.

general. Schemata are more like processes than like products. To say that they are 'sense-apprehensible' or 'inspectable' is not false, but it may be a bad way of saying that we can be aware of something that we are doing when we are doing it. A schema can be 'apprehended' more in the way we apprehend ourselves humming or doodling and less in the way we apprehend a photograph in the family album. This is not to press the theoretical argument which says that highly detailed and specific pictures *cannot* do the work of schemata (since what is disclosed in subsequent experience will almost inevitably differ in details from the 'mental picture', and thus render its application either impossible or inexplicable),[13] but rather the phenomenological observation that behavior which involves imagery, even including visual or pictorial imaging, seldom involves the long inspection of a detailed and static mental picture.

While these inadequate words can have at very best suggested some characteristics that imaging can have, it may be possible, by supposing that Lewis would allow that schemata consist of such imagery, to show how reference to sense meanings can help explain the application of terms, and also to show a way in which intensional meanings can be compared. The first point can be made in terms of the relation between 'intension' and 'signification':

As criterion *in mind*, sense meaning is intensional meaning rather than signification: it is that in mind which *refers to* signification. Signification comprises essential properties; and these properties have their being when and where they are instanced, regardless of the association of them with any term or expression. Animality, for example, is a certain property objectively incorporated in animals, which would be just what it is regardless of any linguistic usage associating it with the symbol «animal». It was in order to dispel the subtle ambiguity of the traditional usage of 'intension'—ambiguity as between a meaning in mind and an objective character meant—that it seemed necessary to add signification to the list of fundamental modes of meaning.[14]

Consider first an occasion on which we *do* entertain or imaginatively rehearse some sketchy criterion in advance of an instance of application: say that such entertainment takes place at Time-t, that the word with which we are concerned is 'Q' (for instance, 'book'), and that part of its 'inspectable meaning', that intension which we are entertaining in advance, is characteristic '$\psi$' (for instance, the characteristic of having pages which are strung or bound together). Since '$\psi$' is included in the meaning of 'Q', the question which will arise in the case of any prospective candidate for the application of 'Q' is this: is the candidate

13 Cf. Paul Henle, review of AKV, *Journal of Philosophy*, 45 (1948), 531.
14 AKV, p. 133 n.

characterized by $\psi$ or is it not? The candidate arrives at Time-t-plus-something, and it has whatever characteristics it has. Only if among these characteristics happens to be $\psi$ will 'Q' apply to it. For purposes of the classification at hand, all of its other characteristics are irrelevant, the pertinent question being, "Does the candidate, presenting itself at Time-t-plus-something, in fact have the comprehensive essential character—in this case $\psi$—such that anything which should have this character is correctly nameable by 'Q', and whatever should lack this character, or anything included in it, would not be so nameable?"[15]

That comprehensive essential character—essential for the applicability of a term—which may or may not in fact characterize what happens to be discovered by experience, is what Lewis calls 'signification'. $\psi$ belongs both to the sense meaning and to the signification of 'Q'—it must, since intension determines signification—but as *intension* it is the criterion which we consult at Time-t to determine the sort of thing to which we will apply 'Q', while as *signification* it is that character which does (or does not) characterize the things presented at Time-t-plus which thus do (or do not) belong to that sort. As sense meaning, as criterion in mind, '$\psi$' is an imaginary, hopefully premonitory sketch (tactile, or visual, or motor imagery of feeling, or seeing, or turning pages); to say that we recognize an instance of '$\psi$' in subsequent experience and thus are able to apply 'Q' is to say that we take an experience met at Time-t-plus (the sensations of feeling, or seeing, or turning pages) as similar to the '$\psi$' of Time-t. The relation of imagery to that which it imitates is the rather straightforward relation of similarity, and this felt or taken similarity between intension and signification brings expressions to their application.[16] To put it otherwise, if we are consistently to apply 'Q', we have somehow to relate characteristics given at different times. Unless we are willing to suppose that '$\psi$-at-Time-t-plus' is numerically identical with '$\psi$'-at-Time-t', which would be exactly to ignore the element of time, it is necessary that when '$\psi$-at-Time-t-plus' occurs we should recognize it, or take it as similar to what we had 'in mind' at Time-t. When the characteristics of whatever object turns up at Time-t-plus are taken

[15] The reader will note that it is not necessary in the immediate context to distinguish between the occurrence of qualia as cues for the predication of objective properties, and the use of properties as evidence for the prediction of further properties. For our present purpose we can take it that the recognition of qualia is necessary but not sufficient to the predication of properties, and that properties in turn evidence the application of further terms. The practice of recognition and application does not require that this distinction be made explicit.

[16] There is no claim here that the arbitrary symbol 'Q' is similar to anything; it is exceedingly rare for the connection which we learn to make between 'Q' and '$\psi$', between squiggle and intensional meaning, to have any basis in similarity.

to include the signification of 'Q' then we say that 'Q' applies to what has turned up.

It seems to me that the important difference between intension and signification, as between intension and denotation, has to do with *time,* and this is a point which 'extensionalistic' critics of Lewis have not given its proper bearing. When Lewis says that criteria are *in mind,* what he means by "in mind" is "in advance of instances of application." When Lewis says that "sense meaning as criterion is independent of any question of existence or non-existence of that to which the criterion applies," and when he says that "sense meaning obviously could not be identified with denotation, and is in no wise dependent upon existence of what is meant,"[17] he is not driving toward a metaphysical point, but is calling our attention to the purposes which the activity of meaning serves. He is telling us that if thinking and meaning are to be of any use, it is not sufficient only to be able to recognize an instance of Q when one is encountered: it is necessary also to know what you are going to mean by 'Q'. One could not even recognize a Q, that is to say, recognize an instance of the signification of 'Q' as an instance of the signification of 'Q', unless the characteristics to be significant had been previously determined—as intensional meaning. The priority in time of intensional meaning distinguishes it from signification as well as from denotation. Expecting, intending, meaning: these depend for their usefulness on their possible presence anterior to some particular occasion of their use. The purpose of meaning is to guide conduct, and it is difficult to see how it could serve this purpose were it not an activity which could be carried out in some freedom from actual and urgent instances of its use.[18]

Nor is this point destroyed by the consideration that, more often than not, there is no conscious rehearsal of imagery prior to application. In the first place, it is often extremely useful that there can be. As Price puts it

it is true that we do sometimes cash our words by means of images. . . . When I utter a sentence to myself or to others, I am only using my words understandingly if I know what it would be like for the sentence to be true. Similarly I can only understand another man's sentence which I see or read, if

17 AKV, p. 137.

18 Cf. AKV, pp. 141, 171 f., 256; C. I. Lewis, "Logic and Pragmatism," in *Contemporary American Philosophy,* eds. G. P. Adams and W. P. Montague (New York: The Macmillan Co., 1930), Vol. 2, pp. 31-51; C. I. Lewis, "Experience and Meaning," *Philosophical Review,* 43 (1934), 125-146; C. I. Lewis, "Meaning and Action," *Journal of Philosophy,* 36 (1939), 572-576, especially p. 575; C. I. Lewis, "The Given Element in Empirical Knowledge," *Philosophical Review,* 61 (1952), 174 f.; C. I. Lewis and C. H. Langford, *Symbolic Logic* (New York: Appleton-Century, 1932), pp. 257-262. Hereafter cited as SL.

I know what it would be like for that sentence to be true. This knowledge is dispositional. It is a capacity for recognizing situations which would render the sentence true and for distinguishing them from situations which would render it false. If in a particular case I am doubtful whether I possess it, what shall I do? Sometimes I shall do just what the imagist describes. I shall try to cash the sentence by means of images. I shall try to 'envisage' or 'picture to myself', an example of the kind of situation there would be if the sentence were true. . . . We can now see what the importance of image-cashing is. It is something which we do in the *absence* of the object or situation described.[19]

In the second place, if we can say that intensional meaning is dispositional in character, we need not demand that '$\psi$' have been explicitly rehearsed at Time-t in order that '$\psi$' be considered a part of the sense meaning of 'Q'. For '$\psi$' to belong to the intensional meaning of 'Q' it is enough that '$\psi$' would have been made explicit if the intensional meaning of 'Q' had been explicitly rehearsed. The criterion for the application of a term consists not merely of characteristics or qualities which were entertained prior to application, but of those characteristics which would be made explicit were the meaning explicitly rehearsed. Given the relation of intension to signification, it follows that all qualities but only such qualities as would be thus rendered explicit would, when encountered in subsequent experience, be recognized as belonging to the signification of the term in question, and thus to furnish occasions for its application. For instance, when we encounter at Time-t-plus an object characterized by $\phi$, we will ordinarily apply 'R' to that object if '$\phi$' is a characteristic that would have been rehearsed at Time-t had the sense meaning of 'R' been then rehearsed.

My guess is that this is grossly accurate to the actual mechanics of application: that the ways in which we decide our willingness to apply or to withhold terms, or the ways in which we simply use language without repeated explicit deliberation, can be explained in these terms. But the reader will already sense a difficulty where I say only that the criterion for the application of a term consists of "those characteristics which would be made explicit were the meaning exhaustively rehearsed." I cannot say "could be"; nothing we have remarked so far could guarantee the ways in which a disposition could or could not manifest itself. To talk about what "would be" is to talk about matters of fact, about what, probably, will happen. What as a matter of fact would be made explicit in rehearsing the meaning of a familiar term is probable to the point of monotony, and this is an important fact when an explanation of the uses of language is desired. But probability is not certainty,

---

[19] H. H. Price, *Thinking and Experience* (Cambridge: Harvard University Press, 1953), p. 253.

and this is bound to make trouble when what is desired is necessary truth. Let me try now to show how classificatory habits and their manifestations in explicit imagery can function in the comparison of meanings, and then just why such comparison cannot certify a priori truth.

If the unwary reader is asked abruptly and without preliminaries to mention a term that means the same as 'spinster' or 'male sibling', or asked whether 'All cats are mammals' could be false, there is a good chance that for his immediate answer he will have consulted only his 'sense of language', if that. If we say to the reader—or perhaps, now that the reader is alerted, to some ordinary user of ordinary language, Mr. Z—that our cat catches mice as well as ever, though she is now 98 years old, he will probably conclude that we are exaggerating, or just plain lying. However kindly, he will accuse us of misrepresenting the facts. If we say instead "Our cat is a feathered biped, and warbles sweetly," or "Our cat has gills and fins and scales and lives under water," the reader as Z will first clear up the difficulty about catbirds and catfish, and then very likely accuse us of misusing the *words*, at least the word 'cat'. "That," he will say, "is simply not what is meant by 'cat'!" Of course the matter is not simple—among other things, it is not clear if we are being accused of misapplying the word 'cat' or of contradicting ourselves in some stronger sense—but in either case it is often not difficult to remark the difference between Z's practice in the rejection of what he takes to be an intelligible lie, or an inaccurate but understandable statement of fact, and his reaction to what he takes to be an abuse of language, an aberrant or improper use of words; or between our own tactics when, as ordinary Z's, we have to meet the disparate challenges of 'That is false' and 'I beg your pardon?'[20]

In the first sort of case Mr. Z may feel that he "knows what to expect," even if he does not expect it. Z can set about planning the disconfirmation of the claim that our cat was born before 1860, complicated and extensive though such a plan will be; this need not involve explicit envisagement in advance, although it can. But when he tries to entertain the latter proposals, to form some relatively clear expectation against which to measure any presented situation, Z does not find merely that those habitual patterns which inform his use of 'cat' cause him not to expect feathers and two feet (as they led him to expect less fantastic feline longevity): he comes up against something that feels even harder. He finds that the expectation of fur and four feet is so fixed in his use of

[20] Often, but not always. Compare "Our cat is 8000 years old and speaks fluent Sumerian." Cf. V. C. Aldrich, "Pictorial Meaning and Picture Thinking," reprinted in H. Feigl and W. Sellars, *Readings in Philosophical Analysis* (New York: Appleton-Century-Crofts, 1949), pp. 175-181.

'cat', that the relevant patterns of classification have such clarity and depth as to make the expectation expressed by "a cat which is at the same time a feathered biped" one that Z in one sense cannot entertain, and in another sense *will not* entertain. The latter locution is probably to be preferred. Z, as it happens, is a fellow of most excellent fancy; he can imagine almost anything you will. He is able not only to envisage the sort of thing to which he would be willing to apply 'cat', and the sorts of things to which he would consider 'singing' and 'feathered biped' applicable, but he may even be able to depict, in imagination or on paper, some monstrous Papageno with a feline face. But this uncanny creature however met will at most convince him that life and art are strange, and that once again he needs a new word. "I know what I mean by 'cat'," he may say, not without consternation, "and *that* is *not* a 'cat'." Or, perhaps, hedging in significant fashion, "That is not the sort of thing *I* would call 'a cat'!"

Such response, such not unusual decisions and discriminations, may follow an experiment in imagination. But suppose we take the meaning as disposition-like, and as the implicit ground of explicit imagery: then we shall have to conclude that the results produced by Z's imaginary experiments are to be found less in his discovery of what conjunctions of characteristics he can and cannot in fact imagine, and more in his making explicit some pattern of characteristics in whose presence he is willing to apply a term, or willing to include some item in a specific classification. This process will ordinarily be as much one of decision as discovery, and it might almost be better to say that what is 'fixed', what is determined, is one's *willingness*. Those habitual organizations of expectation and of imagery which inform Z's use of 'cat' are not such that they will have or can have only one explicit manifestation—they would be of far less use in application if they did. What one determines as a result of imaginary test-applications is which of the variety of manifestations of a disposition that can be made explicit he will in practice use as exemplary, will require to characterize any item, imagined or real, before he calls it 'cat'. Such decision as to what will be used as 'essential to application', and what is in this sense the intensional meaning of a term, will *feel* more like discovery in cases where the 'decision' has been firmly and perhaps unconsciously fixed by training or by teaching: where the use of that term has been originally very frequent and indiscriminate, but has been narrowed and restricted in the face of a variety of slightly different experiences, or where the use of a term has been very carefully and explicitly taught. In such cases the patterns of habit which guide his use have been so disciplined and so sharply organized that Z takes what he does in fact make explicit as that which must be made explicit, and takes the particular manifestations that he considers exemplary as the inevitably essential meaning of the term.

Whatever their limitations for more sophisticated purposes, imaginary experiments in this sense do furnish one usual and wonderfully accessible source of a variety of slightly differing experiences. In the safe, imaginary fire of their variety it can be determined or decided which characteristics will and which will not or should not be used as the nominal essence of a term.[21] Given the frequent crudity and the inevitable ambiguity of ostensive definitions, such experimentation is an invaluable adjunct, perhaps even an indispensable technique. It is true that one usually begins his learning by confrontation with actual instances of the kind of object a term denotes. But this can be only the beginning: if we are subsequently to use the terms, we must also begin to discriminate what the presented instances are presented as instances of. This is a business of trial runs and false starts: some tentative determination is fixed, and then by subsequent decisions that some prospective instance, actual or imagined, is not one to which we are willing to apply the term, we progressively narrow that set of characteristics in whose presence we are willing to apply the term. Actual instances must furnish a final control if the expression is usefully to be applied, but imagined instances are not only immediately available in greater profusion, but their flexibility, their naturally 'abstract' or sketchy character, and the minute variations which we can consider through their entertainment are most useful in determining what we shall mean in advance of application.

Another point to be made is this: those determinations which more or less fix the pattern of characteristics which $Z$ takes as essential to his application of a term will likewise fix $Z$'s willingness to substitute expressions for one another. If $Z$ 'discovers' or decides that it will be just characteristics '$\psi$' which are his criterion for the application of term '$Q$', he may likewise discover or decide that '$\psi$' is also his criterion for the application of '$R$', or is included in that set of characteristics which is the sense meaning informing his use of '$R$'. If in such cases $Z$ tries to tell us that '$Q$' and '$R$' have the same meaning, or that he cannot consistently assert ' "$Q$" that is not an "$R$" ', we should be able to understand what he is trying to convey.

Often those dispositional organizations of expectation and imagery which are the original grounds of $Z$'s ordinary linguistic practice will be relatively fixed and relatively stable in their relationships. Perhaps

21 Cf. John Locke, *An Essay Concerning Human Understanding* (New York: E. P. Dutton & Co., n.d.), pp. 220, 224 f., 250. Cf. pp. 201 ff. Book III, Chap. 2, Sec. 3 of the *Essay* gives a Lockean account of the refinement of the sense meaning of 'gold'.

more often Z's particular and explicit judgment that two terms are alike
in meaning will not so much report a relation of meanings as decide
one. If it were said that Z thus "determines necessary relations of
meaning," we and Z should have to recognize that the 'necessity' involved
pertains primarily to Z and only derivatively to the relations, and that
'determine' here is not only ambiguous but is something of a pun. The
only locus of the only 'necessity' that can be found in any context we
have so far considered is in Z's determination—and determination in
the sense of fixed resolve—to apply 'Q' under all and only those circumstances under which he would also be willing to apply 'R', or not to
apply 'Q' except when he would also be willing to apply 'R'. That this
is the ground of what must pass for necessity in such contexts will be
observed when we see the particular way in which the ordinary user
of language is likely to hedge or to qualify his position (as Z did a
few pages back). Z may assert that 'man' and 'rational animal' have
the same meaning, but if we substitute what now appear to be synonyms
for synonyms in 'All S is S', and then ask Z "Is it necessarily true that
all men are rational animals?", Z may retreat to a defense of his use of
'man' and 'rational animal' before, or even instead of, answering the
question. He will defend his decision to use certain characteristics as
prerogative on grounds that are doubly pragmatic—the general utility
of meaning in advance of application, and the particular virtues of the
characteristics he has fixed upon as reliable symptoms of the presence
of some sort of thing whose behavior is known; his willingness to
exchange the relevant terms will have just so much fixity as is established
by this prior determination. But that this kind of fixity is sufficient to
justify a claim of necessary truth Z himself may doubt. He may be
unwilling to claim that, having applied 'man' to something, he could
never be induced to withdraw his application of 'rational animal'. He
may say that he finds such a situation unimaginable or unthinkable
or inconceivable, but, if he is very cautious, he may refuse to move from
this inability to a claim of logical impossibility. Or say that Z tries
experimentally to put together in imagination the meanings of 'round'
and 'square'. This attempt can be made, and it produces a violent
phenomenological flutter, and a squinting, twisting feeling of uneasiness
or vexation. Z may well be led by this to say that "it is intuitively
evident that these two constituents cannot be so compounded,"[22] but
at the same time hold that it would go beyond the evidence that any
such experience could provide to base upon it a claim so momentous
as that of necessary truth. He might even carry his caution so far as

[22] AKV, p. 115 n.

to tell us that "psychological undeniability, even if it exist, would not be a proof of truth."[23]

But there are degrees of evidence that are short of 'proof' and truth does not have to be necessary to be useful, even when it is truth about the relations of meanings. Granting caution its full due, it remains true that from such imaginary experiments do come many or even most judgments by the users of a language that two terms in their language are alike in meaning (more or less alike or probably alike in meaning), and likewise many decisions or discoveries in regard to one's ordinary-linguistic commitments in the application or substitution of terms. Those patterns of imagery through which a linguistic habit or ability can be made manifest, what can thus be rendered explicit and 'inspected', can have the sense-apprehensible relations of 'inclusion' or 'incompatibility' of which Lewis speaks. If, for instance, we ask Mr. Z what he means by 'pentagram', that pattern of gestures he may perform will not only express what he takes to be the sense meaning of the term, but is such that he might claim discovery of an 'incompatibility' between it and that which would inform his meaning of 'circle'. Since the former performance is evoked also by 'pentacle', Z will judge that 'pentagram' and 'pentacle' are in this sense synonymous. Should he ever find it necessary to trap a devil at his study's door, his knowledge that 'Solomon's Key' and 'Wizard's-foot' have also this same meaning will be invaluable.

If it is said that in such cases one can only suppose the determination of synonymy in a natural language to rest on the 'sense of language' of its users, the answer is "of course." The only peculiarity here is not that this is so, but that anyone should think it peculiar. One is minded to say that were synonymy not thus determined in a natural language, it would not in a natural language be determined at all. Yet indignantly to ask "What more, in a natural language, is wanted or required?" would be, rhetorically speaking, a very poor move, since the question can be answered. It is easy to show that even Mr. Z does not remain satisfied with such loose and uncertain determinations. The relations of dispositions of which we have spoken remain the genetic and causal grounds of the ordinary use of language, and continue to function in Z's judgments about the language he uses, but if we were able further to follow the fortunes of Mr. Z, we should see how he uses dictionary definitions, and also what can be called 'ad hoc linguistic rules' to codify and more strictly to regulate his practice in the use of his natural language. There is space enough here to follow only one suggestion to which the question "What more is wanted or required?" may call our attention: the sense in which such objections and demands can be peculiarly, distinctively philosophical.

## II

What the philosopher, Professor McP, wants, obviously, is necessary truth, a priori truth, or a relation of synonymy so strictly defined that the substitution of synonyms for synonyms can transform a logically true sentence, containing only the variables and constants of the vocabulary of formal logic, into an analytic sentence of equal necessity. The particular purposes for which philosophers of the empirical and analytic persuasion have needed the notion of analyticity could not be served by anything less, and this may have induced in them a certain intolerance toward humbler purposes. Thus if Professor McP claims that judgments of relations of criteria, of likeness of meaning, or of inconsistency, are never made, or that the distinctions which they purport to mark do not exist, we shall have to reply that, as a description of actual practices in the use of language, his claim is simply false. But if by stigmatizing such distinctions as 'unreal' McP is trying to tell us that they do not meet philosophically specified standards of certainty or exactitude (or if, as is sometimes the case, he is saying that the means of decision employed is not explicable or even mentionable in some preferred metalanguage), then that is a different story, and makes a different claim with which we might have to agree.

I think that Lewis and some of his critics may have fallen into a misconceived and sterile pattern of disagreement, that their arguments may be aborted by a mutual, or rather a resembling mistake, one which can be displayed in like-sounding sentences, with italics marking the difference in emphasis. Critics of Lewis can be thought to say: "Unless *necessary* relations of meaning exist implicit in a natural language, it makes little sense to talk about relations of meaning in a natural language. We fail to find any necessities implicit in linguistic use, therefore we conclude that it is senseless to talk about relations of meaning in a natural language." Lewis can be thought to say: "Unless necessary relations of meaning exist *implicit* in a natural language, it does little good to talk about necessary relations of meaning. But the purposes for which analytic sentences are needed must be served; they can only be served if there are necessary relations of meaning already implicit in the uses of language; necessary relations of meaning *must* therefore exist implicit in natural language."

Both Lewis and his critics, it would seem, will be satisfied only with relations of meaning which are both implicit and necessary. Lewis' opponents fail to find necessity, and seem almost to conclude that nothing can be implicit, that the whole notion of meaning is a sham. Lewis insists that necessity must be found, and seems almost as a consequence to find necessity implicit in the meanings of ordinary language.

It seems to me that the critics of Lewis—supposing that I have fairly represented a position opposed to his—err in disregarding the pragmatic purposes which are served by sense meaning in advance of application, and served even by the comparison of such meanings. Here Lewis is fine. But when it comes to implicit certainties, when it comes to the certification of a priori truth, then I fear that the critics of Lewis are closer to the right, and that Lewis is the one who has erred. What is most peculiar to Lewis' theory of a priori truth as he explains it in *Analysis of Knowledge and Valuation* is the way in which he takes explicitly analytic statements to have the status of reports, or to have as their function merely the expression of a necessity already fully established. Our knowledge of a priori statable truth purportedly depends on the inspection of antecedently fixed intensional meanings, and of their relations. We may wonder how 'fixed' such meanings can be, *prior* to the imposition of an explicit and extrinsic linguistic or semantical rule, but Lewis tells us that "Normally it is our sense meanings which are first definite, and our verbal formulations which are supposed to conform."[24] According to Lewis we can "start from sense-recognizable characters, taken as essential for the application of terms and as constituting our criteria of classification" and then we *"find the allowable modes of definition and the truly analytic relationships determined by the fact of the inclusion of one test of application by another; the entailment of one essential character by another, or the incompatibility of one sense-apprehensible character with another."*[25] Presumably all of this is implicit in knowing what we mean, in the sense of being able to recognize instances to which our meaning is applicable.[26]

It is true that a person can 'find' that he means something that he did not know he meant, or 'discover' that something he has said has implications of which he was not momentarily aware. "Every logician from Plato down has found occasion to point out how liable we are to accept as definition some formulation which covers readily thought of instances but fails to elicit and include characters which we should nevertheless require to be present where we apply the term defined."[27]

24 AKV, p. 164.
25 AKV, p. 146, italics added.
26 AKV, pp. 236-242.
27 AKV, p. 163.

Quite so, but before we go down the garden path with Euthyphro there is something we should like to know: how, short of Platonism, are we to explain the sense in which we 'discover' that some quality or character not explicit in a definition is nonetheless essential or necessary to the meaning in question? Lewis wants us to stop short even of Aristotelianism, and yet he seems to ask us to suppose that there are, before explicit verbal definition is accomplished, and hence before those relationships can be said to be those of formal, logical entailment, inexplicit relations of sense meanings which are nonetheless necessary.[28]

Any character in the absence of which we should refuse to apply a term is of the essence. It is included in the signification of the term; and any definition which does not entail such an essential character represents a faulty analysis of the meaning in question. . . . A connection of meanings is recognized as intrinsic; hence statement of it as holding *a priori* for all things comprehended by the term in question. But our verbal expression of these meanings may omit the ground of this intrinsic connection of them. And thus, through failure of analysis, the appearance of synthetic judgments *a priori* can arise.[29]

Not only do such 'intrinsic connections' *not* depend on explicit, verbal formalization—and I think that 'intrinsic' here means what I earlier meant by 'implicit'—it is rather the other way around:

The fact of such relationships is what rules our acceptable definitive statements and renders them significant of something more than verbiage. Such analytic connections *become* amenable to formal derivations when the properties signified, or the things to which the properties are essential, are defined conformably to relationships which they actually have.[30]

The trouble is that in his attempt to show that analyticity is grounded in a priori relations of sense meanings, and that verbal rules are derivative from these, Lewis is led to suppose that implicit criteria of application have an incredible degree of clarity and fixity. The assumption that implicit sense criteria are so fixed and clear, are intrinsically so well-regulated prior to the imposition of extrinsic, semantical rules, is an unfortunate one: peculiar in such an unlikely Platonist as Lewis, and in its failure subversive of his theory of analyticity. Both the peculiarity and the poignancy of its failure can be seen in one sentence at the end of Book Two of *Analysis of Knowledge and Valuation*.

Since language was not in fact brought down from heaven, but is a product of human devising, the important question relates to this norm or antecedent

---

28 Cf. AKV, p. 166.
29 AKV, p. 163.
30 AKV, pp. 165-66; cf. AKV, p. 379.

criteria controlling acceptability of statements put forward as definitive and the admissability of rules put forward for guidance of deductive derivations.[31]

Unfortunately it seems likely that the norm or antecedent criteria 'in terms of sense' may be less clear cut than those statements or rules of which they purport to be the norm.[32]

The inadequacy of unaided sense meanings to certify a priori truth can be most sharply shown if we continue to suppose that sense criteria are disposition-like, and then set Lewis against Lewis. Purportedly it is

relations between sense meanings, ascertainable by comparison of them as such criteria, and independently of particular empirical occasions, [which] is the source of our analytic knowledge. Such knowledge, like the meanings it concerns, is essentially independent of linguistic formulation, though the modes of linguistic expression are a frequent and more or less reliable clue to the relationships of meaning so expressed.[33]

Now, if phenomenological examination had disclosed that, antecedent to each intelligent application of a term, or as a necessary condition of knowledge in advance of application that he did have the particularly relevant ability, the user of language consulted a clear, explicit criterion of application, then there would have been no need to distinguish between 'implicit meanings' and 'explicit schemata'. Once this distinction is made, however, it becomes necessary to inquire into the relation between what is implicit, and what is *made* explicit. Lewis raises a related question in regard to memory:

Once such questions are raised, it becomes necessary to observe that much of what is commonly—and with sufficiently good reason—called 'our knowledge' is not explicit judgment at all. Rather it represents habitual attitude, acquired by reason of past judgments and past trials of them, which becomes the basis of present decision and action, without any explicit revival of those contents of previous experience which are the basis of it. . . . For the same reasons that animal activities would be impossible without habit, human life also, so far as it is governed at all by conscious cognition, would still be impossible without belief-habits which become effective without conscious revival or re-examination of their bases. . . .[34]

---

31 AKV, p. 168.

32 I think it possible and desirable to separate (1) the explanation of the origin and the justification of the utility of analytic sentences, from (2) the justification of their necessity. Lewis in AKV tries to accomplish both by the same reference to sense criteria. But while an answer 'in terms of sense' is appropriate to the former, the latter requires also a reference to explicit and extrinsic rules. Reference neither to sense alone nor to rules alone is sufficient fully to account for necesssary analytic truth, since the former mistakes the source of their strength, and the latter overlooks the ground of their use.

33 AKV, p. 168.

34 AKV, pp. 325-26.

The really critical question for the validity of empirical knowledge is not whether grounds sufficient for the justification of belief are actually contained in the explicit psychological state called judgment: rather it is the question whether the knower's situation in empirical belief is such that *sufficient grounds* could be elicited upon enquiry, or whether it is such that this is even theoretically impossible.[35]

One could scarcely doubt the pertinence of these citations to meaning, but the question raised by the second is in this connection troublesome. If that which can be elicited in making explicit a meaning can never be equivalent to its implicit ground, then one can never directly inspect or express such ground. If what can be made explicit is always different to what is implicit, then an analytic statement cannot claim as its justification the status of a direct report or an unconventionalized expression of an observed a priori relation of intensional meanings. If, to speak roughly, clear and explicit schemata were what we ordinarily started with, there would be no problem; or if we knew with certainty that what we ended with, what was *made* explicit, was an exact logical duplicate of what we started with, there would likewise be no problem. But phenomenological reflection in showing that the former is not ordinarily true leads one to say that the latter could not be true, for the implicit ground of meaning seems to be dispositional.

Perhaps the simple statement that a disposition is not the sort of thing (if one can call them 'things') that can be inspected *an sich* makes as strong an objection as need be made. It is possible, however, to give two final turns to this screw, by showing that what can be made explicit and can be inspected cannot, according to Lewis' own arguments, sufficiently ground a priori truth.

It is plausible to assert that sense meaning underlies and gives structure to linguistic meaning: in terms of intensional meaning, dispositionally construed, one can give a fair account of the patterned organizations of habits and abilities whereon the uses of language rest. But Lewis' theory of analyticity would seem to require the additional and stronger assertion that there exists a precise parallelism between the logical relationship codified in explicitly analytic statements and certain specific and inspectable relations of sense meanings. If this were not the case, it is difficult to see how the latter could stand as antecedent criteria for the former. But it is more difficult to see how this could be known to be the case. In the first place, if what is inspected has to be made explicit, it follows that what is inspected will have been selected. This raises the possibility that what is made explicit has to its implicit

35 AKV, p. 329, italics added; cf. AKV, pp. 355-56.

ground a relation of only 'conventionalized likeness'.[36] While the determinability of sense meanings is all but indispensable to the practice of application, the same determinability that makes it possible for one implicit schema to be fulfilled by a range of determinate objects, makes it necessary that whatever is rendered explicit, is envisaged or inspected, is perforce a selection, or a specification of the meaning in question. The fact that what is made explicit to be inspected has been selected means that the relations of explicit schemata to each other could not be known to parallel relations among implicit schemata, or sense meanings. If an analytic statement reports a relation of explicit schemata—which can, indeed, be envisaged and inspected—what is expressed in an analytic statement will represent some narrowing down or sharpening up of an originally loose and usefully indeterminate pattern of meaning, and the statement itself and hence its 'likeness' to its implicit ground will be to a degree 'conventionalized'.

If it constitutes an objection to Lewis' theory to note that it is only selected instances of a meaning-as-disposition that can be inspected, the fact that it is selected *instances* which alone can be 'simply and directly inspected' means, according to Lewis, that the justification of universal and necessary applicability or impossibility could not be accomplished by such inspection. That which can be made explicit and inspectable, or can be expressed by an explicitly analytic statement, is but one manifestation of an implicit schema. At any one moment, or over any indefinite amount of time, one can inspect or state only a finite number of the infinite set of manifestations of a sense meaning *qua* disposition. And, whether a test-application or any experimental manipulation of an explicit schema is actual *or* imaginary, whether we are observing the linguistic behavior of another or 'inspecting' the particular exemplifica-

---

36 Cf. Peirce, *op. cit.*, 2.27. "When a man endeavors to state what the process of his thought has been after that process has come to an end, he first asks himself to what conclusion he has come. That result he formulates in an assertion, which, we will assume, has some sort of likeness—I am inclined to think only a conventionalized one— with the attitude of his thought at the cessation of the motion. That having been ascertained, he next asks himself how he is justified in being so confident of it; he proceeds to cast about for a sentence expressed in words which shall strike him as resembling some previous attitude of his thought, and which at the same time shall be logically related to the sentence representing his conclusion, in such a way that if the premiss-proposition be true, the conclusion-proposition necessarily or naturally would be true."
There is even psychological evidence for the assertion that the likeness of an explicit to an implicit schema is always 'conventionalized'. Cf. Jean Piaget, *Judgement and Reasoning in the Child* (New York: Harcourt, Brace & Co., 1928), p. 56; Jean Piaget, *Language and Thought in the Child* (New York: Harcourt, Brace & Co., 1932), p. 159; Jean Piaget, *Psychology of Intelligence* (New York: Harcourt, Brace & Co., 1950), p. 32; James, *op. cit.*, I, p. 243 ff.

tions of our own intended meanings—and particular exemplifications are all we can thus envisage—

whichever of these two aspects of meaning one would emphasize, it will be essential to that clarity and precision required in logic and like problems, that a meaning should be something which is determined beyond what any number of observed occasions of the use of expressions will assure with theoretical certainty. No classification can be completely fixed by observation that such and such items are accepted as subsumed under it. Always theoretical alternatives with respect to instances of some specifiable type, not yet examined, will remain over, and leave any *criterion* of the classification in like measure indeterminate—this quite apart from any question of the persistence of behavioral attitudes observed to date.[37]

Whatever the relations of explicit schemata—and they can have relations of 'inclusion' or 'incompatibility'—neither the observation nor the 'observation', neither the examination nor the 'examination' of what is thus rendered explicit can with theoretical certainty fix a relation of intensional meanings with that clarity and precision required in logic and like problems, such as the determination of analytic truth—at least not in Lewis' sense of 'analytic truth'. (Mr. Z's nonphilosophic needs are more easily met.) This is not simply to say that '"*P*" is analytic' or '"*P*" is necessarily true' could be asserted only as probable; on the present interpretation this *is* the case, but it is not altogether clear that Lewis would disallow this possibility.[38] Be this as it may, the really crucial difficulty is that, on the basis of all that is in fact available of what Lewis insists must be its justifying ground, one cannot even know that an analytic statement is *true*. For an explicitly analytic statement supposedly asserts that a relation of intensional meanings is logically necessary, but the only relation that can be made fully explicit, all that can be directly expressed or reported in '*P*', is not a relation

---

[37] AKV, p. 145.

[38] Continuing from the citation immediately above, Lewis says that ". . . our evidence of what another person means, in the mode of intensional meaning, can be inductive only and will fall short of theoretical certainty. Whether we have better assurance of our own meanings, and if so on what grounds, is perhaps a question just as well omitted." AKV, p. 145. Cf. AKV, p. 155. On pages 89-95 of AKV, Lewis is concerned to argue that one can 'discover' the analyticity of a statement only by discovering the *truth* of an explicitly analytic statement, that is, the truth of a statement which asserts the logical necessity of a relation of criteria. But whether what is necessarily true must be necessarily true; whether the assertion of the analyticity of '*P*' requires not only that ' "*P*" is an explicitly analytic, necessary statement' be known true, but itself in turn known to be *necessarily* true; whether the attribution of analyticity to '*P*' is itself an analytic statement; these questions seem to be left open. Cf. SL, pp. 240 ff., 497-502; R. Carnap, *Meaning and Necessity* (Chicago: University of Chicago Press, 1947), pp. 173-177, 196 f.; Quine, *op. cit.*, pp. 150 ff.; W. V. Quine, "Three Grades of Modal Involvement," Proceedings of the XIth International Congress of Philosophy, Vol. 14 (Amsterdam: North-Holland, 1953), pp. 74-76.

of uniquely privileged criteria, but merely of individual instances, of the always particular manifestations of dispositions. To suppose that one had discovered a relation of logical necessity among *the* intensional meanings of expressions, or to argue that he had justified an attribution of analyticity to such peculiarly prerogative criteria by reference to some relation of particular exemplifications of them would thus, by Lewis' reasoning, be to commit an *ignoratio elenchi*.

There are symptoms of this difficulty throughout *Analysis of Knowledge and Valuation*. There seems to pervade the book a kind of strain or tension between the two different jobs that Lewis wants sense meanings to do: to serve as the link between language and its application, and to certify a priori truth.[39] To take sense meanings as disposition-like does not destroy their utility in the explanation of application, but the matter is otherwise for the certification of a priori truth. If the interpretation of intensional meanings as dispositions is adequate, then Lewis' account of the certification of analyticity is not. One cannot simply and directly observe a disposition, but only particular manifestations. Where the determination of logical necessity is in question, Lewis himself insists that a meaning must be more clearly and completely fixed than it could be 'by observation that such and such items are accepted as subsumed under it'; the 'observation' and acceptance of particular imaginary items has no apparent advantage in this respect. A claim that a logically necessary relation exists between sense meanings cannot be based on observation of actual *or* imaginary instances, which are in either case necessarily finite and particular.

C. Douglas McGee

Department of Philosophy
Vassar College, 1957

[39] For instance, if the criterion for the application of an objective statement is just a set of actual and possible terminating judgments, what is the criterion for the inclusion of particular terminating judgments in the set? If a sense meaning is simply equivalent to a set of terminating judgments, it cannot serve as the privileged criterion for membership in that set, and yet it is purportedly by comparison of sense meanings as 'criteria of possible confirmations' that a priori truth is certified. Cf. AKV, pp. 136-37, 192-195, 211, 237, 249 ff.

Roughly, the set of terminating judgments can be identified with the set of manifestations of a disposition, and 'the' criterion of possible confirmations must be identified with 'the' disposition, if it is to be identified at all. The application of objective statements is thus explicable, but obviously this explanation subverts Lewis' theory of a priori truth.

## 18

*Stephen C. Pepper*

# LEWIS' THEORY OF VALUE

L EWIS' theory of value is concerned mainly with the judgment ascribing value to an object. His central thesis is that a value judgment
of this sort is an empirical judgment, no different from any other empirical judgment such as that of attributing physical or sense property to an object. To assert that a nugget of pure gold has a specific
gravity of 19.3 and to assert that it has beauty, are both empirical judgments, true or false, open to the same sort of verification or confirmation.

The present paper will be confined entirely to Lewis' development
of this thesis in his *An Analysis of Knowledge and Valuation,* and here
what he says about empirical knowledge in Book II can well be
considered as simply an introduction to his analysis of valuation in
Book III.

A brief summary of his conclusions regarding empirical statements
in Book II is thus relevant. He classifies empirical statements under
three headings: (1) formulations of given experience (sometimes called
'expressive judgments'), (2) terminating judgments, (3) nonterminating judgments.

On Lewis' view, immediately given experience in sense presentation
is indubitable and is the content referred to in the first class of statements. Lewis observes that there is some difficulty in describing such
statements. As soon as they are made they seem to contain more
than they are defined as asserting. Outside of discussions in theory
of knowledge they are seldom made and seldom needed. "If, for example,"
he writes,

one say, "I see a red round something," one assumes but does *not* assert, "The
words 'red' and 'round' correctly apply to something now given." This last is
not a given fact of present experience but a generalization from past experience
indicating the customary use of English words. But one does not have to know
English in order to see red; and that the word 'red' applies to this presently
given appearance, is not a fact given in that experience.

Lewis goes on to say that

knowledge itself might well get on without the formulation of the immediately given: what is thus directly presented does not require verbalization. But the *discussion* of knowledge hardly can, since it must be able somehow to refer to such basic factualities of experience.[1]

Included in Lewis' description of this class of statements is an assumption, not shared by all philosophers, that a man cannot be mistaken about what is given in a sense presentation. If a man's formulation in a statement is in error, it is because he has *lied* about what he is perfectly well aware was given in his experience. This assumption of Lewis' is going to be so important in a parallel formulation for his theory of value that his explicit statement of the assumption at this point should be quoted:

Apprehensions of the given which such expressive statements formulate, are not judgments; and they are not here classed as knowledge, because they are not subject to any possible error. Statement of such apprehension is, however, true or false: there could be no doubt about the presented content of experience as such at the time when it is given, but it would be possible to tell lies about it.[2]

For those who cannot accept this conception of statements referring to immediate experience, the difficulty is how a person (including the person who makes the statement) can ever be sure he is not (unintentionally) lying. In order to check up on this possibility he would apparently have to resort, in part, to some other kinds of empirical judgments to confirm his attributions of immediacy. We shall have to return to this problem later in its application to Lewis' value theory.

Terminating judgments, Lewis' second class of empirical judgments, represent some predication of further possible experience. They find their cue in what is given: but what they state is something taken to be verifiable by some test which involves a way of acting. For a terminating judgment, a hypothesis is entertained, and, if true, it terminates in a specific experience of immediacy which, as given, is for Lewis indubitable and hence final in its verification of the judgment.

Nonterminating judgments, the third class, assert objective reality, some state of affairs as actual. They contain nothing that is not intrinsically verifiable, but they cannot be completely verified because they apply to such a large number of occasions for specific verification. That gold has a specific gravity of 19.3 cannot be verified for all pieces of gold, nor even for one nugget through all the instants of its presumed existence. Such judgments can, however, be warranted by their

---

[1] C. I. Lewis, *An Analysis of Knowledge and Valuation* (La Salle, Ill.: Open Court Publishing Co., 1946), p. 183. Hereafter cited as AKV.

[2] AKV, p. 183.

probability. When warranted, they justify objective beliefs in the properties of things in the world about us.

Now, according to Lewis, these three classes of empirical judgment apply equally to values. There are (1) formulations of the immediate experience of value, (2) terminating judgments of value, and (3) nonterminating judgments concerning the value properties of valuable objects. His main concern is with the third class of judgments which, however, he would hold depend upon the other two. For specific confirmations of a nonterminating judgment of the value of an object are made by a number of terminating judgments, which are verified by experiences of indubitable immediacy, which in turn are formulable as immediate experiences of value. All value judgments pivot on formulations of value immediacies.

Since all value judgments for Lewis pivot on a formulation of an indubitable immediate experience of value, this experience is the ultimate criterion of value for Lewis. This point Lewis acknowledges in these words:

It is essential for a naturalistic view to maintain that the quality or character by reference to which, ultimately, all things are to be judged valuable or disvaluable is a quality unmistakably identifiable in the direct apprehension of it in immediate experience. It must hold that such immediately apprehensible value-quality or value-character constitutes the criterion by reference to which, eventually, those value-predications which are subject to possible error and need confirmation are to be attested.[3]

Whatever this unmistakably identifiable quality in immediate experience is, by reference to which, ultimately, all things are to be judged valuable or disvaluable, *it constitutes the criterion* that eventually attests the value or disvalue of any object or act to which value is attributed. The identification of this quality is thus evaluatively basic to Lewis' theory of value.

Notice that this basic criterion for Lewis is a type of factual occurrence. A *formulation* of the immediate experience of value may then become the ultimate *verbal criterion* in discourse, since it expresses symbolically and for communication the factual criterion of value in immediate experience, but the verbal formulation or expressive judgment is not itself the basic criterion. The basic criterion is a fact. This is an important point to notice, for it shows the method by which Lewis establishes values as facts, and consequently value judgments as statements of fact, empirical judgments subject to error and so true or false in reference to fact. Even formulations of immediacy may be false, since a man may lie in stating them.

3 AKV, p. 400.

The pivotal question then as regards the ultimate criterion of value is the identification of the immediate experience of value. This is the most precarious and difficult feature of Lewis' theory. So let us postpone consideration of it until the general structure of the theory can be brought out. Lewis' general term for the immediate experience of value is "satisfaction," and in building up the superstructure of Lewis' theory we may use this term wherever he does as if for the nonce it did not contain difficulties.

The structure of Lewis' theory is essentially revealed in a set of distinctions he makes within his field of values. These may be schematical as:

I. Intrinsic Values (satisfactions)
                  (A)  Inherent
II. Extrinsic Values  (B)  Instrumental
                  (C)  Contributory

The intrinsic values are the ultimate immediate experiences of satisfaction on which all other classes of value are based. They are to value judgments what sense data are to other empirical judgments about the world. One cannot be in error about them as had. The awareness of them he calls *prizing*.

Extrinsic values are those attributed to objects conducive to intrinsic values. One may always be in error in one's judgment of extrinsic value. Such judgments Lewis calls *appraisals*.[4] An appraisal may be in error not only in its judgment that an object is conducive to intrinsic value when in fact it is not, but also in respect to the kind or degree of intrinsic value attributed. An error of appraisal occurs if an object is judged conducive to satisfaction when upon verification it is discovered to give pain, or to give not as much satisfaction as anticipated. All values attributed to objects are extrinsic values.

The reader can now see how Lewis can affirm on his view that

evaluations are a form of empirical knowledge, not fundamentally different in what determines their truth or falsity, and what determines their validity or justification, from other kinds of empirical knowledge.

Just as other kinds of empirical knowledge are judgments about objects, true or false, which must ultimately find their justification in data of immediacy, so with evaluations. The only difference, and not an essential one, is that the data of immediacy for other kinds of knowledge are sense data, while for evaluations, they are satisfactions.

4 AKV, p. 398.

Lewis devotes a section to the question why value judgments should so often be considered different from other empirical judgments. This is due, chiefly, he thinks, to a shift of the criteria for justifying a large class of other empirical judgments, particularly most of those central to the physical sciences. In evaluations there is a more direct relation to data of immediacy than in other empirical judgments. If we make a judgment that something is hard, we may confirm it by feeling it and sensing directly that it is hard, but for precision we are likely to consider the ultimate criterion as some external test, such as dropping on it a sharp pointed instrument, having a certain weight, from a certain height. Here visual data from pointer readings have been substituted for the immediate sense datum of the feeling of hardness. The substituted criterion is for precision purposes regarded as superior to the criterion of tactile immediacy. But in value judgments the immediate data of felt satisfaction or dissatisfaction are regarded as superior to any correlated criteria as yet known. Lewis summarizes this contrast neatly by an illustration:

The most nearly decisive confirmation of the thing's being really round will not be experiences of 'looking round' or 'feeling round' but the results determined by precision instruments. But for value-predications, this relation between the expressive and the objective meanings appears to be reversed: a thing *is* valuable according as it may *appear* valuable.[5]

In further support of Lewis' point here, it is worth remarking that if precision correlates should turn up for immediate experiences of satisfaction comparable to those employed in the sciences as precision criteria for hardness, shape, color, sound, and the like, this last distinction between evaluations and other empirical judgments would vanish. And with the rapid developments in psychology and physiology, the likelihood of such a discovery appears rather high. It seems to be only an accident of scientific development that supports for the time being any marked distinction between evaluations and other empirical judgments.

Having established the comparability of appraisals to other empirical judgments, Lewis is prompt to show that such value judgments are as objective as other empirical judgments. To speak of an object as good is to appraise it as conducive to satisfactions. This is a judgment about a property of the object just as much as one about its hardness, shape, or color. It is true or false and open to confirmation in essentially the same way as other empirical judgments.

5 AKV, p. 381.

There are three main modes of being conducive to satisfactions. The first of these is that in which an object acquires extrinsic value by being so constituted as to induce satisfactions (or dissatisfactions) by direct presentation. Such objects have in Lewis' terms *inherent* value. In his phrasing:

Those values which are resident in objects in such wise that they are realizable in experience through presentation of the object itself to which they are attributed, we propose to call *inherent values.*[6]

Those objects of extrinsic value, however, to which values are attributed on the ground that they are conducive to the attainment of other objects which yield intrinsic values, possess *instrumental value.* These values attributed to a thing "consist in an instrumentality to some *other object,* in presentation of which a value is directly realizable in experience."[7] In this formulation it seems to be intended that there should be no *satisfaction* in an instrumental value. The satisfaction lies in the *other object* to which the object of instrumental value leads. A judgment of instrumental value is essentially a judgment of causal connection with an object of inherent value. Of course, there are objects which have both instrumental and inherent value.

Lewis' contributory value is not quite parallel with his inherent and instrumental values. What Lewis is isolating here is a judgment of the value of an object or experience in so far as it contributes to the total value of a person's life. He is seeking to analyze the criterion of Prudence. "Human life is permeated," he says, "with the quality of concern."[8] This 'concern' has to do with making the best of one's life; and thereby a norm is instituted that a man ought to make the best of his life. This norm is that of being "rational instead of foolish or perverse" in respect to one's values, "to be capable of constraint by prevision of some future good or ill; to be amenable to the consideration 'you will be sorry if you don't,' or 'if you do.' "[9] And "the basis of this imperative is a datum of human nature."

The criterion for this imperative is the temporal whole of a good life.

If in one sense [he wrote] the determination of values must be eventually in terms of the value-qualities of direct experience, still in another sense no immediately experienced good or bad is final, but rather is further to be evaluated by its relation to the temporal whole of a good life.[10]

[6] AKV, p. 391.
[7] AKV, p. 391.
[8] AKV, p. 429.
[9] AKV, p. 480.
[10] AKV, p. 483.

The object evaluated for a contributory value is evidently any object or experience (including even experiences of intrinsic value) in regard to the degree in which they contribute to a norm of rational Prudence which Lewis describes as "the temporal whole of a good life." And then Lewis adds a comment, important for the dynamic sanctioning of this value, that "this imperative is a datum of human nature."

I think Lewis means here as regards Prudence that it is a descriptive feature of a man's personality structure to make choices in such a way as will always seem to him to maximize his values and, whenever he finds he has made an error, to try to correct the error so as to maximize his values again. If so, this would appear to me also, with just a few qualifications so far as Prudence is concerned, to be essentially true of human motivation. And I shall not press this point further. However, it is possible that Lewis is referring to a sort of a priori rationality, such as emerges in his ethical views. If so, that would be another issue.

At this point Lewis is faced with the problem of quantitative evaluations. For the judgment of contributory value is one which states the degree in which an object or experience will maximize a person's "temporal whole of a good life." Having committed himself to the view that the ultimate datum of value is satisfaction as immediately experienced, and having oriented his reader to considering his view as one in the tradition of hedonism,[11] Lewis surprises his reader by repudiating the typical hedonistic quantification of satisfactions in terms of intensity, duration, and perhaps number or extent. Instead, he offers a vigorous destructive criticism along typical organistic lines, of Bentham's proposed calculus of pleasures and pains, culminating in an organic or Gestalt conception of value integration. A Gestalt-like quantification is, to be sure, not necessarily contrary to the hedonistic tradition. That a combination of experiences which taken separately would yield little satisfaction or none can, if properly composed, yield great satisfaction is a result entirely harmonious with a hedonistic type of theory. But the quantity of satisfaction in the two sets of experiences is customarily gauged by the intensity, duration, and extent of the resulting satisfaction. And if in a total experience there are some dissatisfactions, these in some degree detract from the total positive value of the experience. With Lewis pivoting his value theory on the immediate experience of satisfaction, one would think that he would also accept the immediate experience of a satisfaction's quantification in terms of intensity,

11 "Hedonism in general represents one expression of this type of view; since pleasure is a kind of good which is immediate and concerning which finding or not finding is conclusive." AKV, p. 397.

duration, and extent. That these are not measurable with precision (or by precision instruments such as can be used for degrees of hardness or the size of a circle) is to be expected on Lewis' own analysis of the difference in the criteria employed in the two types of terminal judgment. Yet if comparative preferences among goods as better or worse are not based on the *quantity of satisfaction* which the goods can yield, then Lewis would necessarily be pivoting his value theory on acts of preference and not on immediate feelings of satisfaction as first indicated. He appears to fall into Mill's classic dilemma, resulting from an espousal of the doctrine of 'qualities' of pleasure—except that for Lewis, every satisfaction would be qualitatively different from every other. Every value experience would appear to be qualitatively unique, and acts of preference alone would be left for Lewis as indices of value.

Indeed, this seems to be just what Lewis is willing to adhere to when he is finally faced with the problem of comparative evaluations of better or worse. His most detailed statement of the method for reaching the total value of an object is his proposed mode of determining the social value of an objective existent. He defines the social value of an object as that which includes all the inherent and instrumental values of the object realizable by whatever persons would be affected by the existence of the object in question. This, he observes, is the sort of value judgment required whenever there is question of public policy before us—a proposal to remodel a school, or to reelect a mayor, or to commission a statue for a park. Lewis' proposed method is to proceed as follows: consider each value that the object has in respect to the satisfactions derivable.

Each such satisfaction derivable from the object enhances the value of it in accordance with the degree of satisfaction to be derived. A degree of satisfaction of such immediate value is determined by the place of that value in the series of satisfactions in general, arranged in order of better and worse; that is, in order of preference. The conjunction of two such value-potentialities in the object give[s] value to it in accordance with the principle that the conjoint value of two satisfactions, A and B, is determined by the place of (A and B both) in our series of immediate values in general, as determined by direct preferring.[12]

And so on. The most illuminating thing to notice in this passage is that "degree of immediate value" is described as "the place of that value in a series of satisfactions in general, arranged . . . in the order of preference." Intensity of satisfaction as a person appears to find it in immediate experience is thus reduced (it would seem) to an item of prefer-

12 AKV, p. 550.

ence, a place in an order of preferences, respecting "a series of satisfactions in general."

There is nothing theoretically wrong with such a reduction. But in terms of what many readers would think Lewis was referring to as 'immediate satisfaction', this would seem to be the conversion of an intensive quantity as immediately felt, into a distensive quantity, which is not what seems to be immediately felt. It would look like trying to tell a person that the degrees of loudness of a tone are not differences of intensity but differences of distensity, such as the degrees of distance of pitches from one another on a pianoforte keyboard. Or has Lewis all the while been referring to something quite different by 'satisfaction' than most readers would take the term to mean?

Contributory values are, then, to be appraised for their degree of contribution to "the temporal whole of a good life" by a method of direct preference in paired comparison. The whole good life comes out by this process to be terminus as well as the norm of the series of paired comparisons, and can be made out to be qualitatively different from any of its components, which also may be qualitatively different from each other. The whole life is

a temporal Gestalt of experience in the sense of being its included and mutually qualifying parts . . . in just this organic relationship to one another. If the particular constituent experience is reassessed from the point of view of the consummatory whole, such reassessment nevertheless does not displace or cancel the value immediately found in it in passing: quite the contrary, it attributes to it a value of it as related to and qualifying and qualified by other constituents.

Lewis concludes that if this principle of the organic whole (as it applies to the value of a whole of experience) emerges as a paradox, nevertheless "it expresses a fundamental fact."[13]

Lewis also states in this context that

wholes of experience take precedence to distinguishable and momentary experiences included in them. . . . The final and ruling assessment of value in our experience must answer to the continuing rational purpose directed to the comprehensive and consummatory end of a life found good on the whole. This value characterizing a whole life is also intrinsic.[14]

This is the rational norm of Prudence, the *summum bonum* of empirical valuation.

I should not care to criticize the spirit of Lewis' criteria for evaluating acts of Prudence. But his *summum bonum* seems to me rather the cri-

---

[13] AKV, p. 503.
[14] AKV, p. 486.

terion by which one evaluates a life after it is done than the criterion for the myriad practical decisions of Prudence a man makes in a day or a year. One rather considers the predictable consequences of a proposed act for the situation at hand. The practical criterion is the situation. And the extent of the situation is limited to the probable range of important consequences. A decision to light a cigarette or tie a shoelace ordinarily involves a very limited situation. A decision to take a degree in medicine involves a much larger situation. Only rarely does the situation reach the full extent of a man's life. However, this latter would indeed be the final appeal for difficult decisions within the bounds of Prudence. So, this comment is not one of basic disagreement.

And here with the description of the ultimate norm for acts of Prudence the strictly empirical formulation of valuations stops for Lewis. Beyond this point comes ethics, the study of 'right' and 'justice' in interpersonal relations. The last sentences in *An Analysis of Knowledge and Valuation* are: "Valuation is always a matter of empirical knowledge. But what is right and what is just can never be determined by empirical facts alone."[15]

Since Lewis stops his empirical value theory at this point, a critic of his value theory had best respect, however regretfully, this boundary too.

As regards Lewis' fully empirical approach, and his thesis that "valuation is always a matter of empirical knowledge," the present critic is in complete accord. And, as regards the opposed view, that value-predications are not matter-of-fact statements, but merely expressions of emotion and hence neither true nor false, I deliberately align myself with Lewis' classic comment that "this is one of the strangest aberrations ever to visit the mind of man."[16] The ultimate answer to the emotive school is, of course, to do what they say cannot be done—constructively build up an empirical theory of value. This is just what Lewis is in process of doing.

The form an empirical theory of value naturally takes is that of first indicating or defining the basic value data, and then proceeding to relevant matters bearing upon these data, such as the judgments that can be made about them, the objects to which they can be directly or indirectly attributed, and the criteria in terms of which they can be evaluated.

Lewis follows this form of exposition. He indicates satisfactions as the data of value, then analyzes in great detail certain important

15 AKV, p. 554.
16 AKV, p. 366.

types of objects that yield satisfaction, and gives some attention to the criteria and methods for evaluating these objects.

My chief difficulties with Lewis lie in his mode of indicating the data of value and the inadequacy of this indication. He names the datum for the immediately good as 'satisfaction' and says it is indubitable, and suggests a few illustrations. As one man who has puzzled over this problem a good deal, I can only honestly say that I am not sure just what Lewis means. "Everybody," Lewis says, "knows what it is; and if anyone should not, we could hardly tell him." He adds that here he realizes "that between words and what they signify there is a gap; and more words will not build a bridge across it."[17] As empiricists, both he and I, it would seem that we could make words serve us rather than be blocked by them. What is involved here is not a problem of finding more words, but of finding out some facts. Once the facts are indicated we can easily get words to refer to them. I think Lewis is using an ineffective method to reach the value-facts—namely, the method of appealing to an indubitable experience.

In Lewis' doctrine of indubitable experience, he appears to me to have become the victim of an ambiguity between 'whatever is' an experience and 'what one takes' as his experience. 'What one takes' as his experience may or may not be 'whatever is' the experience. Lewis admits that an expressive statement formulating an immediate experience may be a lie. He implies that such a statement can be a lie only if a man does it intentionally with an awareness of the difference between what his statement reports and the experience it refers to. Considering the disputes over the content of immediacy among many discriminating and scrupulous philosophers in the history of cognition, I believe the evidence is very much against Lewis' thesis that some of these men must have been lying. It seems more likely that many of them must have been mistaken.

So, I have no confidence in Lewis' method of appealing to certainty regarding the content of data of immediacy. These are matters of hypothesis as much as grosser matters, and require every available device of corroboration to establish their probable nature.

Nor do I think his giving up the notion of the certainty of immediacy will undermine seriously his appeal to probability for empirical judgments. Experience gives a very high reliability to certain types of perception—such as the perception of the six-sidedness of a die and the perception of the number of dots on each face. For purposes of prob-

17 AKV, p. 400.

ability theory these perceptions may be reliably taken as practically certain. And that is enough for practical purposes.

Lewis' vagueness when he tries to indicate the nature of satisfactions increases my conviction that he himself does not know exactly what he is talking about in this connection. It is "not so much one quality as a dimension-like mode," he says, "more like color in general or pitch or hardness in general,"[18] and so on.

Now, if we do not restrict ourselves to searching for indubitable immediacies of value data, but are willing to take advantage of a variety of evidences to pin-point experiences which might reasonably be taken as value data, we come upon a number of such data. There is conation with the attributes favor-disfavor; there is achievement with the attributes success-frustration; there is affection with the attributes pleasure-pain. These may be converged upon behavioristically through studies of purposive structures, and of movements in a consummatory field or in a riddance field. Introspective correlations may be made with these and connections found among them. But these various discriminable qualities cannot profitably be gathered up under a general heading of satisfactions-dissatisfactions. Such a heading discourages discrimination where discriminations are most urgently needed.

And another thing. Suppose satisfaction were discriminable as a general quality. Why should that be taken as the value quality in immediacy? Because it has an opposite—dissatisfaction? So likewise has white an opposite—black. A quality of immediacy is not labeled value in addition to being the quality it is. Evidently something is required in a value quality which is not to be found in other qualities of immediacy. This other thing is plentifully referred to in Lewis' treatment of valuation. It is the dynamic selective action of value qualities. It is the fact of decision. The pleasures of consummatory satisfactions occur in consummatory fields in which organisms are motivated to maneuver so as to maximize these pleasure qualities. The quality of success emerges in the selective action of purposive structures which operate according to the laws of learning to minimize frustrations and maximize the successes of achievement. Here among others are qualities that enter into decisions and are selectively regulated by their own structural relationships for maximization or for minimization. These qualities are shown to be values by the dynamic selective structures in which they are embedded.

This sort of dynamic selective sanction for values I miss in Lewis' 'satisfaction' so far as he ventures to describe or indicate it. I wonder

18 AKV, p. 401.

if his appeal to certainty as a sanction for 'satisfaction' as a value quality is not to compensate for not finding (or, at least, not utilizing) the empirical sanction of dynamic selective structures available for isolating value qualities.

And when finally Lewis has to face the problem of quantitative evaluation of better or worse among his satisfactions, he abandons his satisfactions and resorts to *preferences*. Preferences, of course, are dynamic acts. But then why restrict preferences to satisfactions rather than just as well to colors, and pitches, and hardnesses? Why bring satisfactions in at all? Yet, of course, I should not recommend this drastic measure. For preferences in general are just as empty of discriminating experiential content as satisfactions in general.

In short, Lewis' 'satisfactions' are just abstract counters. They symbolize whatever it is, or whatever they are, that are the empirical data of value. Lewis could just have postulated them. That would have been much more consistent as an empiricist than to have tried to certify them as indubitables. For whenever an empiricist resorts to an a priori, he is that much the less of an empiricist. And, as is usual when resort is made to an a priori, Lewis gained nothing by it. When he calls his critic a liar, however discreetly, what can a critic do but discreetly reply in kind, giving, nevertheless, as an empiricist, some empirical reasons for disagreement.

That Lewis' shortcomings in indicating the basic value-facts for his theory have so little damaging effect on the empirical analyses of the objects of value which follow, is due to the circumstance that these analyses would stand essentially as they are whatever the basic value-facts turn out to be. Whether the basic value-facts are pleasures, or fulfilments of desires, or requirednesses, or organic integrations of experience, provided only there are such, the distinction he elaborates between inherent and instrumental and contributory values would still hold. It is for these analyses that Lewis' book will long be highly 'appraised'.

Minor queries about details of these analyses can be raised. But the big principles elaborated stand, once basic value-facts of some kind are admitted. Objects of inherent and instrumental value are objects of potential value. They are objects which have a probability of inducing satisfactions (to use Lewis' term) in view of their causal relationships. Accordingly, judgments attributing values to them are empirical judgments usually of the nonterminating kind open to confirmation like any other empirical judgments.

Lewis' analysis of the esthetic object, the work of art, for instance, as a relatively enduring object of inherent value is masterly in all its details. He clearly distinguishes the vehicle from the often inadequate particular presentation and both of these from "what is actually there for [the subject's] apprehension," namely, the object of inherent esthetic value. He brings out the important factor of relevancy for determining the details attributable to the esthetic object. He notices how closely bound these relevant details are to the physical vehicle in objects like pictures, how relatively remote in others like poems. In very few pages he has encompassed practically all the pertinent factors. In doing this he sets up the esthetic object as an object for empirical description on a par with any other object of perception.

The same applies to the various other objects of potential value Lewis analyzes. To my mind, he has made his principal point that value judgments are empirical judgments, true or false.

STEPHEN C. PEPPER

DEPARTMENT OF PHILOSOPHY
UNIVERSITY OF CALIFORNIA

## 19

*Robert W. Browning*

# HUMAN NATURE IN LEWIS' THEORY OF VALUE

LEWIS makes unmistakably clear his conviction that human nature is somehow the datum which grounds prudence and rationality as immanent norms of action, and that human nature as expressed in its distinctive sort of living will find certain imperatives of believing and doing to be nonrepudiable.

Propaedeutic to the question of how human nature grounds the validity of imperatives is the inquiry we wish to make in this paper: what is the relation of the conception of human nature to the modes of value, particularly to inherent value?

Since, on Lewis' account, human nature is relationally involved in predications of human inherent values and of instrumental values connected thereto, we wish to ask how it is involved and more particularly what conception of it is tacitly in mind when sound evaluations are made. There are many connected questions to which we do not address ourselves. Two large clusters of adjoining inquiries are: How do men know values? and when a man does make a sound comparative evaluation how does he act upon it? The second of these will be completely ignored, leaving prudential and other imperatives and theory of action for treatment elsewhere. In passing we will touch upon the first of these, however, for it is indeed interesting that a man does not simply issue valuations relative to himself. He may evaluate for animals; he evaluates socially in many modes among his fellows; if he is a connoisseur perhaps he evaluates aesthetic objects for them; and, as concerned citizen and as statesman, he estimates the social value of alternative possibilities. We will be looking for what relationship some of these assertions of value presume to hold between the value and one or other notion of 'human nature' as a relatum.

Whatever human beings do obviously represents a capacity of human nature, and we shall not dwell on this patent point, although exactly what it is that one is doing when he exercises powers familiar in acquaintance is not at all obvious. It would have to be acknowledged, furthermore, that men, out of deference to attractive theory, sometimes distort or deny what they do. Of course human nature makes human knowledge possible. This would lead to more than a truism if one went into the details of what factors external and internal, and of what ingredients, material and a priori, are involved. But this is not our objective here, where our concern is with the tacit relational reference to some conception of human nature in certain attributions of value. The general powers of human cognition which are equally manifest in more or less neutral science and in valuation will receive no attention, but where special qualifications of the human nature of the knower seem to be more particularly requisite for the adequacy of valuational judgment it must be duly noted. This is expressly the case in the judgments of the connoisseur, and it is by direct implication the case in judgments of social value.

All things done by men are in the comprehensive sense 'human', and in this wide sense human nature might correlatively be used to comprise the propensities of any and all men. More frequently 'human nature' is used to denominate some 'normal' range of propensities, capacities and behavior-tendencies found in members of the species, with deviants excluded. Different but in one way wider and in another way narrower is the use of 'human nature' as naming an inferred matrix and limiting notion as manifest when one says that (native) human nature is fairly plastic, permitting conditioning for a great variety of cultural formations; but no one supposes that this genetic human nature is utterly amorphous and infinite in its capacity of absorbing conditioning. The inferred 'raw' human nature sets limits to what can be done to and with it. This notion does not include actual behaviors, and is in this sense narrower than the previous meaning; but it permits a great lot of varieties of 'cooked' human nature, including all the deviants in the first meaning, who get excluded in the second. Indeed, actual uses of the second will very likely be culture-bound; this may not be inherent to the root idea, but surely it is very difficult to frame the empirical notion which will not be tied up with the sociological data which are accidental to one's own culture. The idea of an intercultural normal human nature is one for which presumably content is still being gathered; it is a notion which centers about an ideal of 'health'; and it is complicated by the question of whether a given kind of personality structure might be healthy in one culture and not in another.[1]

I think that something like the second meaning but purged of its limitations to any given culture is a meaning frequently used by Lewis. He is emphatic that when a proponent of the third approach is carefully

---

[1] I will not go on to several other root meanings, one of which is that of some essential core of tendencies requisite for survival of the species.

scrutinizing the individiual human organism to find human nature—and perhaps scrutinizing the new-born infant to find it in purer form—he is likely to leave out much of what is distinctive to human nature.[2] Man is a social being,[3] although perhaps not predisposed to any particular form of society beyond the familial one. Man is a *cultural* social being, although perhaps not—except by what comes through learning[4]—predisposed to any particular sort of culture. Man is a social being with the capacity, through learning and criticism, of participating in a cumulative, dynamic progressive culture. I assume that Lewis accepts the notion that a large portion of human nature is constituted by what is shared with mammalian nature, but his emphasis is certainly upon what is distinctive.

After reminding ourselves of a few general features of Lewis' theory of value, we will briefly introduce five topics and then proceed to a discussion of each in turn. (a) Men living in their distinctive human way, saving their past and engaged in self-government in the present out of deference to expected futures, have now fixed the intension of (intrinsic) 'value'. (b) We shall find that full articulation of the ascription of inherent value in objects involves reference to the kind of being in whom (or in which) immediate value is produced (under proper circumstances) by the presence of the object. A man is not limited to reference to self, or to family, or to class, or to nation or even to mankind in making judgments of inherent value or of instrumental value; however, attention is naturally given to those that are in reference to human beings. Ascribing inherent value as a property to an object definitionally requires a conception of a standard human nature, and the confirmation of the ascription, which is a nonterminating judgment, requires standard conditions. A wider use of 'inherent value' where standard conditions are required but no particular restrictions are placed on the history or conditioning of the subject will be terminologically handled by calling such values 'genuine' (but not objective). Prudence would still be called for if all an agent's value-judgments were egoistic; but morality as we know it is founded in knowledge of values to other beings, human and animal. (c) In societies which have attained a reflective stage, conscientious participants, no less than those delegated with authority, are

2 C. I. Lewis, *The Ground and Nature of the Right* (New York: Columbia University Press, 1955), p. 90. Hereafter cited as GNR.

3 We will not here go into the different senses in which man is naturally social and in which he is *imperatively* social.

4 By what comes through learning, there may be (for Lewis) a tendency toward a best culture for a given natural environment; if so, it would be different in details for Esquimaux and for Trobriand Islanders.

called upon to make judgments of social value, and not just of actual social value but of comparative value of alternative social developments. Lewis believes that he has an empirical meaning for all the concepts used therein; the crucial meaning, I think, requires the supposition that all sapient men would tend to respond with the same preferences. This assumption is open to doubt. (d) Discernment of relatively high inherent values for others is especially typified in the capacities of the critic or connoisseur. The relatum of human nature on the subject side which is involved in the ascription of such properties to the object side does not seem to be average standard human nature but rather an idealized human nature of maximum sensitivity. There is an assumption here again, I think, of the unity of human nature. It is not easy to employ human nature as some kind of touchstone without having the normative use surreptitiously introduce an ideal human nature which is not fully an empirical concept; but I believe that Lewis guards himself with circumspection if 'empirical' is allowed to include idealization of actual capacities. (e) Although 'good' and 'bad' are basically used in a nonmoral reference, without which there would be no conduct and no moral right and wrong, there are, as human nature develops in society, found to be inherent values of disposition and character.

Everyone remembers that Lewis distinguishes valuation from ethics. The former is empirical knowledge, "essential for," and "antecedent to," any concrete application of the principles of ethics; but value determinations are not sufficient by themselves for any solution of ethical problems, in general or in particular."[5] "In order to be distinguished from transcendentalism, from Protagorean subjectivism, from nihilism, all three, it is essential for a naturalistic conception of values to hold that some valuations have the significance of empirical cognition."[6] But, of course, it is not some need of what comes under a particular philosophical banner that constrains Lewis' mind. The notion "that value-predications are not matter of fact statements at all, being mere expressions of emotion and hence neither true nor false" is, he holds, "one of the strangest aberrations ever to visit the mind of man," invalidating (as it does) all action and implying "both moral and practical cynicism."[7] That evaluations are "not fundamentally different in what determines their truth or falsity, and what determines their validity or justification, from other kinds of empirical knowledge," has been "obscured by failure to distinguish mere apprehensions of good or ill in experience from predic-

[5] C. I. Lewis, *An Analysis of Knowledge and Valuation* (La Salle, Ill.: Open Court Publishing Co., 1946), p. 554. Hereafter cited as AKV.

[6] AKV, pp. 319f.

[7] AKV, pp. 365f.

tions of the possible realizations of these qualities in particular empirical contexts, and from appraisals of the objective value-quality resident in existent things."[8]

This three-fold distinction is important, and it is admitted (or, some critics would say, stipulated by the definition of knowledge) that what comes under the first of the three is not knowledge. As with Dewey and others, what is simply 'had' in immediacy is not cognition.[9] It may serve some role in cognition, as when it is assigned the office of constituting evidence for some prediction; but, in itself, it is just a possession. Ultimate "or basic value"[10] is of this sort; it is "directly experienced goodness."[11] All kinds of valuation come back to this, which is "valued for its own sake";[12] ". . . the only thing intrinsically valuable—valuable for its own sake—is a goodness immediately found or findable and unmistakable when disclosed."[13] Valuations other than such value-apprehension of the given, whether predictions of the occurrence of a value-quality under certain specified conditions or whether attributions of inherent or instrumental value to some actual or hypothetical entity or kind of entity, are in principle cognitive, and may be in error. "Inherent values" are those values "which are resident in objects in such wise that they are realizable in experience through presentation of the object itself to which they are attributed." "Instrumental values" are "those values of things which consist in an instrumentality to some *other object*, in presentation of which a value is directly realizable in experience."[14] A work of art is a good example of the residence of an inherent value; a tool is an instance of an instrumental value. In the sequential, cumulative, and Gestalt aspects of conscious living, there are other relationships of these values than arithmetic addition; there are surely enhancements and spoilings—the sort of thing to which G. E. Moore was drawing attention by the label "principle of organic unities." These facts are very important for those summings-up which are requisite for reasonable self-government—as is sharply evident if one entertains

---

8 AKV, p. 365.

9 Cf. AKV, p. 182.

10 AKV, p. 373.

11 AKV, p. 387.

12 AKV, p. 385.

13 AKV, p. 397. "Prizings and disprizings of the presently given content of experience, are formulatable in expressive statements, the reference of which terminates in the immediate and phenomenal. With respect to these, the subject whose experience is in question can make no mistake, unless a verbal one in the manner of expressing what he finds."

14 AKV, p. 391.

a "dictate of rationality" which enjoins "acting and choosing in ways such that the lifetime results of them will conduce, in highest possible degree, to satisfaction on the whole."[15] However, we are not yet ready to speak of either prudence or morality; we are dealing with that without which there would never emerge prudential, technical or moral rightness, namely, goodness and badness and the "variety of modes" in which they are assessed.[16]

Are values restricted to human beings? No, there is presumption that immediate values extend as far as sentience. Nor are men wholly caught by an idol of the tribe so far as cognition of value is concerned. Men can have empirical knowledge of extrinsic values which are in relation to the experience of other species and of their own species and of classes within these. Man apparently can "transcend the limits of what is relative to his human nature."[17] After the manner of Royce and Hocking, Lewis argues:

The self that finds mistake or invalidity inevitably claims superiority over the self that is subject to this error or this fallacy. If we can ask the question *whether* the judgments of worth which we make are merely relative to our subjectivities, then it is already implied that we can determine correctness of an answer to it, and that in such answer we can free ourselves of the subjectivities suspected. Among the superiorities which the self-critical animal inevitably claims for himself is the capacity for just this kind of possible self-transcendence.[18]

Since man "sometimes must decide" he "cannot repudiate the question of a good and bad which is not relative to his inclination merely."[19] And in the context I take this to include goods not only for fellow human beings but for fellow animals. In a hypothetical colloquy of the animals "the real question here is one of worth or value; and no appeal to biological characteristics and capacities or to survival and power to prevail, or even to cosmic history itself, can settle that issue"; "survival in competition does not prove superiority; it proves only the ability to survive. . ." Like James, Lewis holds that in "any attempt we make to affect the future . . . our effort will be empty and irrational without the conviction that the total state of affairs will be infinitesimally better if we succeed."[20]

15 AKV, p. 548; cf. pp. 479, 486ff.

16 GNR, p. 64.

17 C. I. Lewis, *Our Social Inheritance* (Bloomington, Ind.: Indiana University Press, 1957), p. 48. Hereafter cited as OSI.

18 OSI, p. 49.

19 OSI, p. 50.

20 OSI, pp. 46, 47. One may doubt whether many human beings think of, or worry over, this emptiness or irrationality; one admires the moral concern which is revealed in

For a stretch of several pages, Lewis' reader wonders if the exposition will reach a Platonic intuitionism. Perhaps an intuition of 'height' of value (as in Scheler and Hartmann) would be theoretically simpler than the naturalistic alternative. However, Lewis' appeal here as elsewhere is to direct preferring, after the manner of Mill's use of Socrates in relation to the contented pig.[21] Taking the latter consistent course, there is required, it seems to me, empathetic apprehension of the inner life of animals. As our author has said, ". . . wherever there is question of the value of anything relative to another person than oneself" the exercise of "empathetic imagination" is necessarily involved.

We have to 'put ourself in the place of' the other person—whatever the epistemological hazards in so doing—and gauge value as realized by him on the supposition of whatever fundamental likeness to ourself seems justified by the evidence of his behavior and other pertinent circumstances.[22]

The intuitionist will have to intuit the possible values experienced by a species when he is intuiting their relative heights; Lewis will have empathetically to intuit them before he reacts with his 'gradable' degree of preference. In either case I do suppose this to be difficult and hazardous —I do not quite regard it as nonsense in respect to our mammalian relatives. I do get a very pale blur when I attempt to image the value-qualities in the experiences of crustacea or insecta. Using Mill's criterion, Lewis comes out with the same result as Socrates and Mill.

If men account themselves more fortunate than other creatures in their natural endowment, it will be on the ground that, by the critical and self-critical capacities so vouchsafed to them, they are privileged to achieve a life which is a better life to live. And if they are interested in the direction of any continuing process they discover in the cosmos, that interest will, if serious, find its final point in the quality of conscious life which this cosmos will support and perhaps may foster.[23]

the statement. Lewis has just said: "Even in confronting the cosmos, we cannot dismiss it as meaningless to ask whether this be a good world or a bad one in which we live." Assuming that the cosmos is not a moral agent, I presume that this question, for Lewis, translates into the question of whether the universe contains more good than bad. An alternative rendition would ask whether a sufficiently comprehensive and sensitive mind (but nevertheless of a human-type) would, on contemplating the universe, prefer that it exist or not. I see no reasons why one should not ask the parallel question whether human nature is good or bad. I think that Lewis would admit this question as intelligible (complex as it is) if it relates to the preponderant kinds of fruits which are brought about by human agency; he rejects the question if it is asking whether man's native value-reactions are corrupt and require wholesale transformation. Cf. AKV, p. 398. A cognitive intuitionist may believe himself to have a better translation of the meaning of these questions and access to a different mode of answer.

21 OSI, p. 53. Cf. AKV, pp. 542-545.
22 AKV, p. 545.
23 OSI, p. 52.

Granted man's superiority, I do not think that Lewis counts animals as negligible. His application of the "law of compassion" shows that he does not.[24] And his schemata equip him for being ready to judge of, and to accept supermen, should they emerge; but one may feel that these must be just superior men even if their biological ancestry were not in present human form—where 'man' connotes certain powers of rational decision.

Lewis has a naturalistic value-theory, albeit one in which he provides no simple naturalistic analysis of ultimate value terms. It is empirical; it interprets "good and bad as matters of empirical fact and as significant, at bottom, of naturally found qualities of experience."[25] Occurrent value in immediacy is, like other qualities of immediacy, presumably indefinable. Actual value-qualitites are very various, as Lewis in a noteworthy and eloquent passage shows;[26] and if there is any one value-quality it must be a quality of qualities. "Immediate or directly findable value is not so much one quality as a dimensionlike mode which is

---

[24] GNR, pp. 91f.; cf. AKV, p. 531.

[25] GNR, p. 97. His theory is 'naturalistic' also in the sense that it comports with a naturalistic metaphysics. For a few generations to account for value as a natural occurrence has not seemed difficult. This persuasion, I should suppose, has been too facile if one's conception of 'natural' has been taken exclusively from the explanatory patterns of the extant natural sciences and if one has a nonbehavioral definition of value—such as has been common in 'naturalism', where hedonisms, or at least affective theories, have flourished. Conscious processes remain mysterious. But, with a generalized positivistic attitude of taking whatever phenomena one has, free from any initial commitment to 'reduce' it to the behavior of certain hypothetical entities, and accepting causal explanation to consist in the finding of correlations, one acknowledges no 'mysteries' although one may recognize greater and lesser complexities and that many tracts of occurrences have not been resolved into lawful patterns. Alternatively, many naturalists have not forsworn the label but have insisted that their naturalism was nonreductive. Lewis has, I think, taken this latter as so patent as not to require statement. His naturalism has been austerely empirical, but this has not meant that he went along with the narrower stipulations of the so-called empirical criterion of meaning or that he embraced a strict positivistic analysis of causation. The restraints which have held him aloof from doctrinaire empiricism in theory of knowledge and in ethics spring pretty plainly from the feeling that such a view is insufficiently empirical in its approach to human experience.

[26] AKV, p. 405. Whether or not one classifies Lewis as a hedonist—I do not—one must recognize that what is found to be good (in his account) makes very great allowance—uncharacteristic of historical hedonism—for the contribution of striving to value. Again, he lays stress upon other features of what is found in contributory values—uncharacteristic of historical hedonism—such as self-respect and (to borrow from G. E. Moore) various organic unities. Apparently, like Mill, Lewis' sapient man finds greater value, greater satisfaction (whether or not this be greater pleasure), in a life with a large view, with devoted work, even if marked by many defeats than in one with numerically more and intenser organic and sensory pleasures. If Lewis holds an affective theory, as I say, it stands in contrast to what one might figuratively call a 'sedentary' affective theory.

pervasive of all experience."[27] But it is unlike a dimension in certain ways which our author's subtlety registers but which will not be repeated here. Value-disvalue is a "general mode of presentation"; it is subject to comparative notings of degree, but not necessarily with "decisive result" nor such that "non-preference establishes a relation of 'equivalence' that is transitive."[28] By his sort of ostensive method, it is plain enough, I believe, that Lewis means roughly that value is any sort of pleasingness or satisfaction in immediacy, although what is satisfying may be charged with meaning. I class him as ultimately holding an affective theory of primary value. Although he states that value "stands in no invariant context and has no stable correlations, by reference to which we might locate it map-wise through its external relationships,"[29] he does proceed to assert: "Value-disvalue is that mode or aspect of the given or the contemplated to which desire and aversion are addressed; and it is that by apprehension of which the inclination to action is normally elicited."[30] I take this as an identification by a connection, not as a statement of an identity or as an essential connotative definition.

In the sequel, I shall briefly take up, under (A), the question of why Lewis' naturalistic theory of value is affective rather than behavioral and affective rather than conative. The relation of the conative to the affective in human and higher animal life will be seen to be ascribed to a sort of 'inbuilt teleology' which, while not a priori in the traditional sense, serves certain roles analogous to the a priori.

Restricting ourselves to human values—although realizing human moral values will include consideration for animals—it is basic to recognize that man is, as he is, a locus of immediate values, and that ". . . the natural bent of the natural man stands in no need of correction in order validly to be the touchstone of intrinsic value."[31] This is fundamental as against any doctrine of a revelation or of an intuition which allegedly reveals or discerns that man's immediate valuings are not only corrigible

---

27 AKV, p. 401. It is, he continues to remark, "more like color in general or pitch or hardness in general. It is like seen bigness . . . Or more closely; immediate value is related to the quality-complexes of presentations exhibiting it, as seen bigness would be related to visual patterns exhibiting size if the world were so constituted that from description of the *other* aspects of any such pattern we could conclude, with fair safety, as to its apparent bigness." This observation may remind the reader of discussions by deontologists of nonnaturalistic dependent characters; but here we have a naturalistic dependent character mode.

28 AKV, p. 403.

29 AKV, p. 400.

30 AKV, p. 403. "The immediately good is what you like and what you want in the way of experience; the immediately bad is what you dislike and do not want," p. 404.

31 AKV, p. 398.

but ought to be corrected. But perhaps only extreme notions of 'human depravity' have held this. And nothing Lewis says on this point constitutes a denial that man might have a natural egoism which makes him very likely to be unjust, or a natural passionateness which makes him very likely to be imprudent.[32] Lewis could affirm these latter propositions since they relate to the organization and administration of life, not to the ultimate value ingredients.[33]

Of ultimate or basic human values, it is simply to be said that they are portions of human experience; and the bearer of—instance of—human nature in whom a given immediate value arises is surely part-cause of its existence. There might well be considerable treatment of the conditioning or education of the experient as a requisite for his experiencing certain values. And I should suppose that successful training could be classed as instrumental value. Education, religions, and practical philosophies do work at modifying the subject of experience. But most attention has been given to the object-pole, indeed, to the

[32] I make these remarks because some critics, without specifying one or more specific targets, may level a broadside at Lewis' whole conception of human nature as belonging to the Enlightenment and as overlooking the depths of irrationality and evil in man—a great oversight which the Christian Fathers or Darwin or Dostoevsky or Freud should have served to correct. This is not the place to attempt it but I do think the insights of the latter are to be incorporated—Darwin's already are appropriated by Lewis—but I do not think that our author's whole conception will thereby be overthrown. Rather I opine that Lewis' norms can be shown to have an evolutionary role, and can be exhibited as providing a base on which an agent can make a self-appraisal of imprudence and a self-indictment of guilt.

[33] I am not sure that I am happy with this, for, with the acknowledgment of something like a principle of organic unities, there may be individuals who *find* complexes to be good which I do not wish to call 'good', e.g., the enjoyment of sadistic complexes. Of course, I have to admit that the feeling-tone is what it is and that we regard it as such to be good. Perhaps Lewis has provided us with all that we need by our being able to evaluate the act connected with the experience as a 'contributory' value and 'morally'. I want to be able to say of some successful tyrant who was very obtuse in his sensitivities and who rather generously satisfied his own sadistic impulses that his life was not good even if he looks back on it as a whole and pronounces it to have been very good. Now, of course, I do not know that this kind of case can happen; possibly the laws of human psychic nature are such that a tyrant has been so estranged from his fellows that he has had to recognize that he was not really happy. But I am not at all sure that my hypothetical case is impossible, and I rather suspect that in the jungle of human history it has several times been actual. I think that it is only in its socially contributory aspect that Lewis can evaluate the tyrant's life negatively; the bully's summum bonum has been a bonum. I can join Lewis in saying the tyrant's life was one of injustice. Perhaps Lewis can say more—that internally evaluating the tyrant's life from the standpoint of contributory values, one can see that he would have had a *better* summum bonum if he had chosen in ways that maintained more community with his fellows. In this case, is there a tacit appeal to 'normality', that normal human nature is such that it will experience richer immediate values if it chooses the courses which develop fellowship and sense of sympathetic identification than if it chooses the courses which secure fulfillments of predatory impulses, native or acquired?

causes of intrinsic values and hence to instrumental values of the external sort—perhaps because purposes of relatively immediate control focus here. Nevertheless, we do not wish to forget that inherent values, which do possess an objective potentiality, possess it in relation to certain kinds of subjects. The potentiality cannot become actual without them, and the attribution of potentiality is an incomplete statement if it is devoid of reference to—may we call him?—the appreciator. One would wish to ask whether society, by its conditioning of the individual, does not indirectly cause some of his immediate values and also thereby cause what at next remove are his intrinsic values.

I take as obvious that human nature is, or rather individual human beings are, among the causal conditions of the occurrence of their respective values. The interactional or relational status of values would occasion, in the language of many value theorists, attachment of the label 'relative' to values in this theory of value. Further, when this status is not simply ascribed with reference to a generic human nature but with reference to individual human beings, it would occasion attachment of the label 'subjective'. These labels are not in accord with Lewis' usage, and, one suspects, he feels that they are often attached amidst not a little confusion. Perhaps I will add a bit to the confusion, but I am not clear as to what Lewis usually means in ascribing objectivity to a value and as to what his exact context of thought is in explicating predications of value in the mode of simple potentiality. We shall approach by taking hold of the latter first, under (B) below.

The predication of a 'potentiality' alone is a very incomplete formulation, and the addition of the qualification 'simple' is only descriptive and does not make a virtue of the incompleteness. Of course, this is not a complaint itself directed toward Lewis but rather at the slovenly habitudes manifest in our use of the natural language, which habitudes he accurately reports. Attribution in the mode of simple potentiality is actually a very prevalent 'mode of predication'—although not at all frequent as compared with what it might be. Essentially I grasp this handle to ask what values are 'relative to' when predicated in this mode. In doing so, I first inquire whether predication of value as simple potentiality is not an attribution in the mode of relativity to *possible* experients who are not actual, and then whether this unimaginably wide range is not further cut down to some kind of implicit reference to human nature. I believe that Lewis has the vastly wider view in mind but out of deference to use he normally shrinks the application of 'objective inherent value' to values in relation to men and further in relation to normal men. To dignify the status of the class of values which consequently are nonobjective but which are reliable to some individuals because of being relative to their stable idiosyncrasies, the label 'genuine' will be invoked both here and again under (D), later.

Less indefinite is the reference to human nature when (C) human social value is estimated; but most interesting here is the question of the specifications of an instance of human nature who would be qualified to judge of, say, possible alternative courses of a civilization. Lewis seems to concur with Mill on the point that "the judgment of relatively better quality is only to be made by those who are familiar with both terms of the comparison."[34] The best judge will not be a normal man in the sense of an average man; he will be a most unusual man, a superbly sapient man. Would there be an outcome if there are fundamentally different types of sapient men? In the strictest sense it appears that the sapient man does not cognize nor judge 'higher' and 'lower' values—he reacts with preferential ratings after, in principle, as wide a cognition as he can make of the possibilities and after an empathetic review of the values in the careers of the various persons as lived under the different alternatives. If he is not just summing up the values along alternative courses but is reacting to different 'wholes' of life, his own nature would seem to be involved. And the question arises whether different sapient men, selected by sapience on some independent criterion, would tend to concur in preferences as to alternative wholes of cultural life.

(A) Everyone acknowledges the objectivity of instrumental values with the crucial provision that the end is accepted. Lewis affirms the objectivity of inherent values. There is a question here of the propriety of the ascription of 'objectivity' unless the imputation of the inherent value to the object is made in reference to its potentiality with respect to *normal* instances of human nature. On the other hand, it is a fact—redundantly, an "objective fact"—that an object may have "a potentiality for producing experience of a certain quality"[35] in a highly idiosyncratic individual. So far there is only a terminological question, and one might settle it (as we suggested under (B), above) by agreeing to call the former potentialities 'genuine and objective' and the latter 'genuine but nonobjective' (or 'nonpublic'). However, as is most vivid when one comes to deal with aesthetic inherent values of high degree, there seems to be more involved than the distinction which we have already made. (This impression is re-enforced by some of Lewis' discussions of objective properties; he does not take what we may call a 'minimum' view.) Neither the class of 'genuine' (nonobjective) value

34 OSI, p. 53.
35 AKV, p. 389.

properties nor the class of objective properties as previously sketched seem to be a good locus for aesthetic values of high degree. Although critics and connoisseurs are statistically deviant in their possession of their unusual capacities, one would not believe either that they are perverse or that their value-deliverances are wholly the result of indoctrination or idiosyncratic personal history. One suspects that by using semi-sociological tests of value-objectivity based on the twin criteria of public extent and durability as source of immediate value one's results would manifest gradations rather than one neat cleavage. (It may be surmised that although 'masterpieces' of art will not rate high in popular appeal, they may show up well on the durability curve.) As the connoisseur is the test-base, the normal human nature to which reference is implicitly made in ascribing high aesthetic value to selected potentialities is not average normal human nature. Presumably the tacit reference is to an idealized human nature of high healthy sensitivity. Questions of what the connoisseur does and of what the correlative analysis of 'bad taste' is (if it exists) are involved. And the status of the objective potentiality in an art object may be distinctive, not assimilable without further criteria to other previous meanings of objectivity.

(E) Lastly, assuming that there are imperatives of prudence and imperatives of morality—imperatives founded in the nature of man—it is to be noted that, since man is also reflectively self-critical, these account for another level of values, instrumental and inherent. We especially refer to values of moral disposition and character.

In the end we will remark that any teleological ethics requires knowledge in comparative valuation and knowledge of possibilities and probabilities of value-realization. Of itself, such an ethics does not require similarities of valuations of objects. For direction of coherent social policy, however, one does need tendency toward convergence on comparative evaluations of social orders, although the preferred social order will presumptively allow much variation of individual taste in respect to large ranges of inherent value. Whether maximization of immediate value is the criterion for all social action is an ethical question, and one which, I believe, Lewis would answer in the negative.[36] There are generic aspects of social order which Lewis holds to be prescribed by ethics, i.e., specifically by the law of justice, but large areas of determination under the general frame would need be determined by comparative evaluation.[37]

We proceed to a discussion of each of the five topics.

[36] AKV, pp. 551ff.; GNR, pp. 72ff.
[37] GNR, pp. 95ff.; OSI, pp. 96ff.

(A) Why does Lewis take intrinsic value (to which pivot all other forms of value are related) as generically affective rather than behavioral, and why does he take intrinsic value as more specifically affective than consciously conative?

The gist of the answer to the first is brief and, to my mind, definitive.

It is possible to reduce the whole problem of values to behavioristic terms. But so to do is to resign the original problem in favor of another which is more simply soluble theoretically. We should not be willing to identify the experience of another—or of ourself—with behavior; for the simple reason that experience and behavior are not the same thing.[38]

The labels 'value' and 'behavior' (or the name of some portion of the latter) do not have the same denotation; there simply is not equivalence of meaning, value having its locus in experience. It is not denied that one can stipulate behavioral definitions of value terms nor that one can (only to an extent, I should insist) thereafter develop an account parallel to another account which makes the references to consciousness. But this would still leave the account in terms of consciousness—partly achieved and partly to be achieved—and it is this account which is in much more accord with what we do come back to in our concerns with value. It is this account which is requisite "for any understanding of the normative."[39]

Although Lewis, in contrast with traditional hedonists and perhaps typical affective theorists, does recognize 'activity', 'initiative' and the contributory effects of achievement on experienced value, it is plain enough that his view belongs in the large family of affective 'theories' as against conative ones and as against theories of intuited objective value-essences endowed with obligation-entailing authority of a metaphysical ought-to-be. Presumably the whole cluster of considerations which makes him an empiricist and naturalist are responsible for his rejection of the latter—a view which, one may add, is not devoid of support in the feeling of many of us in our culture. However, with the varied sorts of value-attribution in use (and our author manifests admirable powers of ferreting them out),[40] why does he anchor all the

---

[38] AKV, pp. 545n.

[39] OSI, p. 83. In the context he says: "Value terms have their essential significance, finally, by reference to the qualities of consciousness. And to identify what they intend in terms of physical correlates, thus reducing the qualities of conscious life to the status of epiphenomena, is merely to revive old-fashioned materialism in a more sophisticated guise."

[40] The critic must concede that Lewis is acutely sensitive to the wide variety of modes of value-attributions, and that he goes a long way in making a sort of map of them and their conditions. The survey is empirical and the generalized observations of

others in values in immediate experience, and why is not conation-and-achievement given the fundamental role? I suppose generally that there is 'evidence' in the way in which his hypothesis illuminates or brings coherence into the data. I suppose, more crucially, that one's own sense of how one administers his activity and makes judgments expressive of his deliberations points to an anchoring of instrumental value and inherent value in immediate value.[41] As a result of this sort of inspection, some of what the conativist takes as intrinsic is declared to be instrumental. But perhaps this statement is too weak to express Lewis; perhaps it is just as reflectively obvious to him that substituting conscious conation for value is an instance of substituting one thing for another as is substituting bodily movements for value. On this view he would assume that we all do implicitly mean by 'value' what he does, but persons who state other 'theories' simply are offering mistaken renderings of their own meanings. He reminds us that where we have meanings "already fixed by the nature of our interest or by the problem in question," there statements "put forward as analytic may still be false." Where there is "antecedently fixed intension" one should not be misled by "changing of the subject."[42]

Now a consequence of not ascribing synonymy to value and objects of conation[43] is that Lewis then must have a considerable or a complete synthetic connection between affective value and conation. Is this inter-

the conditions are empirically based. The wide variety, it is held, all relate back to immediate value.

[41] A man whose sense of value assigns inherent value a quite different status will probably not be convinced; I should expect this on the part of some intuitionists. There is possibly room for considerable rapprochement on empirical grounds between an affective theorist who, like Lewis, finds conation to be a very important condition of the experience of a great deal of immediate value and one who defines the experience more comprehensively so as to include the conative and its conscious satisfaction together but all under the 'conative' or 'conative-achievement' label. The latter theory does have a hard time with the values which seem to come as 'gifts'—e.g., a pleasing unexpected sight.

[42] AKV, pp. 378f.

[43] There might be identity of denotation between immediate values and objects of conation, but still the nature of the former be quite distinct from the fact that they could be designated by the latter. My interpretation is especially based upon OSI, pp. 79-85. Possibly another case could be made upon a remark like the following, which occurs in Lewis' superlative discussion on immediate value in AKV. "Value-disvalue is that mode or aspect of the given or the contemplated to which desire and aversion are addressed; and it is that by apprehension of which the inclination to action is normally elicited" (p. 403). I take this sentence as a comprehensive way of denoting the value-disvalue aspect "of the given or contemplated"; it is based on a synthetic or material truth; if in the context it is used as a definition one could say that it is a definition by use of a reliable accident; it is not an analytic definition. The teaching of OSI precludes taking the basic linkage as analytic.

pretation precipitate? Is it a priori possible that men prefer the bad? Is it not analytic that what they would pursue would be the good? Since Lewis seems to take the negative, there appears to be a sort of Platonism here, in the loose sense, the meaning of good being independent of the mundane actualities. But immediate good is in experience; it is not transcendent; the mundane actualities of which it could be independent (it is being asserted) are the volitional actualities. In a figurative sense, men could be said to pursue under the form of the good even when they are materially in error, mistaking the content which belongs under the form. But such an error would have to be in reference to inherent or instrumental good, not to immediately had good. (Errors also can be made in comparisons of remembered or entertained immediate goods.) Is the attractiveness of good a priori? No, not in the traditional sense, although it may be affirmed in some extended sense of referring to something antecedent to and serving as a conditioning structure in particular experiences. It is an empirical fact that consciousness is oriented toward the good and bad, and may be ascribed a function of making deployments of behavior with respect to them. Although this is an empirical fact, is it peculiarly some kind of 'necessary' fact? It is not necessary in the logical (or other?) sense that one could not imagine "a world in which conscious beings generally should be so constituted that felt pain automatically induced them to persevere in the act which caused it and to repeat this mode of action on later like occasions. . ." Our actual world is not like this. However, "natural selection" is not invoked as the explanation of why it is not like this; instead, its application on the conscious level depends upon the assumption that "associated felt satisfaction will prompt to the doing of an act, and that associated pain or frustration will prompt to avoidance. . ."[44]

Consciousness at large turns toward the good, and to the bad it literally is averse.[45]

To seek the good and to avoid the bad is the basic bent of conscious life And the laws of learning are laws of ameliorating the quality of living by conserving and adhering to what is good, discarding and avoiding what is bad. When as with ourselves, learning becomes in part a self-directed activity, and the results of action come to be consciously assessed as desirable or undesirable, conducement to the good and avoidance of the bad still remains as the rational criterion of such learning and doing as has any rationale.[46]

[44] OSI, p. 81.
[45] OSI, p. 80.
[46] OSI, pp. 83f. Cf. ". . . the ultimate aim of every sensible action is some realization of positive value-quality in experience . . ." AKV, p. 392.

I take these as assertions of fact; incidentally, in the appeal to learning, they justify a slight amount of optimism. Strictly, I would not call the "bent of consciousness" a priori, but one sees that it is conceived to carry a formative-constitutive role. "Inbuilt," one notes, rather than "a priori," there is "a kind of inbuilt teleology correlative with the functioning of consciousness in vital processes."[47] This teleology is instanced much more widely than in the human species, but where, in the latter, "learning becomes in part a self-directed activity" this basic bent of human nature is the presupposed ground of right and wrong in doing. Whatever refinements may need to be added, justification of choice will be generically by appeal to value. One feels that for Lewis 'perversity' may exist and 'irrationality' may exist, but these furnish no evidence except for perversity and irrationality.

Accordingly, in our author's view the connection of value and conation is not a connection which men ought to follow because of a synthetic a priori proposition linking the ideas. Rather is the linkage a material fact; it is a fact of the nature of sentient docile animals and therewith a fact of human nature. In certain contexts one might make statements 'analytic' of the basic bent of consciousness. Such statements should not be confused with statements analytic of stipulated definitions. Both are arbitrary from the logical standpoint; the former is emphatically not arbitrary from the standpoint of human activity.

(B) When Lewis comes to treat of "value-attributions in the mode of relativity to persons" he explicitly holds these to be "species of ascriptions of value-in-fact." There is no objection to this stipulation; indeed, it seems to me that it is in major correlation with usage. The "relativity to persons" means to Lewis relativity to "actual conditions . . . which are to be found in the nature or circumstances of the person or persons in question, in contrast to conditions affecting the object apart from all relation to persons or to conditions affecting all persons alike."[48]

One observation is to be made. There is no reason why there should not be a category of value-attributions in a mode of relativity to possible persons or to possible sentient beings, but not in the manner of ascriptions of value-in-fact. And it is at least a question worth entertaining whether this is not just the ascription of value in the mode of simple potentiality when the conditions are spelled out a little bit. One may contemplate something of the infinitude of such possibilities if he thinks of the range of existing organisms, conditioned as they are, but in various conceivable circumstances in this world, and perhaps also in

47 OSI, p. 80.
48 AKV, p. 521.

worlds with somewhat different laws than ours. Then there is the range of values relative to organisms basically like those existing but conditioned in different ways than they are now conditioned—this is most important with psycho-physical organisms like man, which are highly malleable by training. Again, is there not a range or ranges of values in this mode constituted by the relation of objects to hypothetical sentient beings which might have evolved but did not? I should think that all these predications thus roughly indicated (although needing further specification) are meaningful and thus legitimate. Some, of course, are much more remote from empirical data than others, and partake of the nature of thought-experiments. It is small wonder, then, that we do not widely predicate in this way—except sometimes vividly in science-fiction—for our economical habits of speech would be simply staggered by both the myriads of such possible predications and the possible details of so many of them. I submit then that two pertinent questions may be put with respect to Lewis' attribution of value in the mode of simple potentiality, and they stand as possible elastic alternatives. (1) Is attribution of value in the mode of simple potentiality an elliptical way of referring to the hosts of value-ascriptions relative to psycho-physical beings, either wholly independent of restriction to fact or belonging to the mode of "ascriptions of value-in-fact" but accepting only very general conditions of fact, say, found by existing organisms in our world? Or, (2), on the other hand, does Lewis not really intend that his value in the mode of simple potentiality be cut down much further, for instance, (a) to causal potentiality of immediate value to human beings, or (b) to this potentiality *with respect to human beings possessed of human nature of some standard sort—not conditioned in any of a great lot of definitionally deviant ways* in which it can and could be conditioned?

It might be said that surely Lewis cannot intend the former, at least in its more latitudinarian forms, out of relation to the laws of our world and probably to the kinds of sentient beings found in it. Well, he can mean whatever he can think of; I incline to suppose that he does not concern himself with anything so wide, at least more than momentarily.[49] And there is textual evidence that Lewis—in a way not incom-

---

[49] Lewis does speak as if we only approach by degrees to predicating "an unqualified *property of the object,* independent of anything which is not an essential character of it . . ." Usually some "hypothetical conditions" are assumed; "hardly any valuation envisages a potentiality so bare as to be free of all such implicit limitations." AKV, pp. 539f.

One might appeal to the parallel Lewis insists upon between ascribing value and ascribing specific gravity, where the latter certainly refers to our world. However, I would not take this as definitive for while it may be granted that science has reference to the actual universe it is a frequent occurrence in science—and often done in thinking

patible with the meaningfulness of the first—does take or stipulate an affirmative line with respect to some improved form of the second question.

I do not refer—at least weightily—to such phrasings as 'conditions affecting all persons' alike in contrast to the conditions relative to persons where both of these are under the genus of value-in-fact. But I do refer, for instance, to the extension of this which more clearly results in a distinction of *objective* value as against even some *genuine* values. Relativity to persons accounts perfectly well for why some persons do not experience actual value under the normal conditions of encounter with objective values; now it also accounts for the fact that "what lacks impersonal or objective value may still be genuinely valuable to an individual or a class."[50] The latter Lewis treats—initially at least—as a problem. "Nobody can realize a value in experience through the instrumentality of an object which has no potentiality for such value-realizations."[51] In answer, he first makes a distinction between 'valuable to S' and 'valued by S' (the latter particularly here to mark the individual's capability of error with respect to the former), and then he offers another distinction, more important (I think) for other purposes than for the immediate one. This latter is the distinction between predicating value comparatively of an object or absolutely. In a positive ascription of comparative value one is saying that the object has more value than disvalue—I suppose in a public or objective sense—or one is saying it is better than some members of its class. In ascribing non-comparative or absolute value, one is saying that the object has "some value; that it is not altogether worthless."[52] "Whatever object can, under some circumstances or other, be instrumental to the realization of satisfaction on the part of anybody, has by that fact just that much of value and is not absolutely worthless."[53] I assume that this statement applies to inherent values when whatever is "instrumental to the

---

up experiments—to consider what would happen under circumstances which have never been observed and possibly have never existed. One speaks of ideal situations: how would helium behave at absolute zero? And physicists have been known even to talk of anti-matter and of the possibility of another universe constituted of ingredients with certain polar relations to those constitutive of our world.

50 AKV, p. 523.

51 AKV, p. 524.

52 AKV, p. 524. The distinction of comparative and absolute, it may be further noted, is one that can be used from a first-personal point of view and with respect to values which are 'relative' to the person. Thus the distinction is not a neat correlation in which 'comparative value' is ascribed only in a public or objective sense and absolute value alone is marked by 'relativity' to person or special group.

53 AKV, p. 525.

realization of satisfaction on the part of anybody" is an object of direct confrontation.

Lewis is recognizing an exceedingly wide meaning of value where genuine values (I suppose) include both objective values and those restrictively local to the situations, endowments, conditioning, etc. of special persons or groups; the latter values—we are saying—are genuine without being objective. Pretty plainly his emphasis—owing to treating inherent and instrumental values of objects as properties of objects and thus as parallel with other public properties—is upon the objective inherent and instrumental values, and for these some notion of the nondeviant public, or of normal human nature or of standard (perhaps ideal) human endowment is required.

I believe that the alternative causal accounts are clearly enough indicated, and that the 'problem' is skeletally solved by making the distinction; the maintenance of the distinction will be helped by marking it with a pair of labels. Whatever is a value is a value and whatever object produces a value is a value and is said to be 'genuine'; if the relationship is idiosyncratic, the stimulating object is not an objective value in one of Lewis' meanings of 'objective'. As will be repeatedly observed, there is one terminological inconvenience resulting: there are two different meanings of 'objective' as opposed to 'subjective' in the relevant discussions of value. But they need not produce confusion. Let us make the threefold distinction as applied to values, where all three are denoting objective facts. At one extreme are 'objective' simple potentialities, which, as we have just been saying, are objective by virtue of their being reliable potentialities for all standard instances of man under standard conditions. At the other extreme are value-apprehensions which are 'subjective', not in the sense of referring to the locus of intrinsic value, for all intrinsic values are in immediacy, but in the sense that the occurrence of value in one subject's experience may be highly unreliable as a sign that other persons, or this subject at other occasions, will find the object valuable. In between these two, there lies (I suppose) a group of values which are relative to the person but the conditions are such that he finds reliable signs indicative of repeatable or enduring satisfactions from the objects. In this sort of case, whatever he takes as a sign is 'objective' in the sense of being reliable in contrast with indicators which are 'subjective' in the sense of being misleading. But since the value in the object does not serve as a value to normal persons under normal conditions (or some variant of this theme) it is not an objective value, although it is a genuine value to the individual. Masterpieces of art are objective values in the first sense. Some sentimental trinket which I or a psychologist may reasonably conclude will continue to be valuable to me, and to me only, is—or something indicative of it is—objective in the second sense. It is to be called 'genuine', but is to be dispossessed of the label 'objective'. If this is Lewis' stipulation, as I think it is, I wonder if it makes a difference if I am normal or if I am abnormal in investing such sentiment in the trinket, although in either case its value is relative to me. And since it is a value-in-fact to me in either case, and this fact is a public fact, I believe it does count as a tiny item in counting up social value. E.g., would not a Puritan or totalitarian regime be insofar wrong if it destroyed this trinket provided devotion to the trinket was noninjurious to others?[54]

Having made the distinction between absolute or noncomparative value and comparative value, Lewis draws the right outcomes, which are impractical and practical respectively. Almost "any mentionable object" has *some* value "in the mode of simple potentiality" where this includes values relative to persons and—shall we add?—to sentient beings. But this shows how trivial is such ascription. What has importance for practice is *comparative value:* ". . . what is commonly meant by calling an object valuable, is its being a desirable existent and comparatively good on the whole."[55] Further, perhaps what is especially important for social practice is the determination of the social value of actual and possible objects. To this we shall turn.

'Social value', one notices is highly complex. The social value of an existent is not the public estimate of some one characteristic of it. In the determination of social value, all the value-potentialities of the object are to be rated; all the persons to be affected are to be considered; the conditions of value-realization are to be envisaged and judgment made concerning those which are beyond control. The restriction to the context of actuality, including recognition of features which we cannot alter, is noteworthy for cutting out references to what might be in other worlds or in other evolutionary developments or even in unrealistic proposed transformations of our own culture. The assessment from an impersonal point of view is not meant to rule out idiosyncratic values, relative to persons, provided these realizations are socially harmless. Although Lewis repudiates for his well-known reasons the calculus of Bentham, he holds that the idea of social value has meaning and that rough estimates can be made of the social value of objects.

---

54 "What is useful to or gratifies any member of a society and brings no harm or distress to any other, has by that fact some measure of impersonal and social value. That is a root thesis of Western civilization, predicated upon respect for each and every individual and his possible achievement of a good life." GNR, p. 71.

55 AKV, p. 529; cf. p. 525.

524 R. W. BROWNING

(C) 'Social value' does not generically denote, at one extreme, all values for all human beings, nor, at the other extreme, only inherent values which are similarly appreciated by everyone. Social values are not restricted to inherent values, and there are myriads of social values (as Hegel or any alert conservative might remind us) of which the average individual is not conscious. Although one is committed to an inquiry which is almost inconceivably complex in its details when one simply seeks to determine the 'social value' of an existent object, Lewis exhibits the principles involved as an illustration of the problems to be encountered in dealing with complex modes of evaluation—especially by anyone who finds that he must reject the notion of quantitative measurement of values. And I shall go on, as I believe is legitimate, to speak of the social value of a policy or of a social order, which are extremely complex 'objects'. Assessments of the social value of objects and arrangements are particularly relevant to political decision and to those individual decisions which may have the same objective. Social values, however, are not exhaustive of the concerns involved in moral decision; and normally an estimate of the social value of objects is made in independence of questions of the merits of persons. "Final imperatives belong to ethics, and no valuation is unqualifiedly final until it is subjected to the ethical critique."[56] Antecedently, at least, Lewis is right in protesting that there is "no reason . . . why an egoist in ethics and an uncompromising social utilitarian should disagree over the questions what *is* in the interest of the individual and what *is* for the best good of all concerned."[57] Their dispute is in ethics not in valuation. The domain of positive social value presumably excludes those positive values of individuals which are generally damaging, and includes what "is useful to or gratifies any member of a society and brings no harm or distress to any other. . ." Broadly speaking, says Lewis, "the social values of things are values which they have for *some* of us, at least, in ways which are not subversive of but may conduce to the interest in a good life for all of us together."[58]

When "any object" is assessed "on the whole," "when the question is whether and how far a thing will be in the public interest and socially desirable," the evaluation will be "highly complex."

First, because it will take account of all the value-potentialities of the object, instead of some one value or type of value only, and will require some collation of these various values and disvalues of it. Second, because it involves

56 AKV, p. 540.
57 AKV, p. 553.
58 GNR, p. 71; cf. AKV, p. 527.

taking account of whatever persons are likely to be affected by this object; their number, and the bearing of it on their realizations of value. Third, because it calls for attention to the circumstances affecting such value-realizations from the object; and with respect to those which are beyond control, the assessment of their probability. Finally, it requires that we bring together all these considerations in one resultant evaluation of the object on the whole.[59]

No Benthamite quantification of value is possible; and, if it were, there is positive reason to doubt that the laws of arithmetic would be found to hold if one quantified the value ingredients and their sum, for instance, in independence of the mathematical operation. But Lewis maintains that "every simple value-modality can be determined in degree" by placing it "in some linear order of values . . ." "Also, while arithmetical operations cannot be applied to the collation of values, nevertheless the conjoint resultant of two values can always be assessed . . . by reference to the criterion of direct preferring."[60] With respect to the second problem, "Value to more than one person is to be assessed as if their several experiences of value were to be included in that of a single person." With respect to the third problem, where occurrence is not subject to control, "A potentiality of value $A$, which is realizable under circumstances the probability of which is $m/n$, gives value to the object according as we should evaluate it if value $A$ were to be realized from it in $m$ instances out of $n$ trials."[61] And preference is to settle the issue between rival values, the higher of which has lower probability of realization.

For example, if ice-cream from one store tastes better than that from another but is more likely to melt before getting it home, then the question which ice-cream is worth more, is to be determined by considering whether the better taste outweighs the more frequent loss by melting or the other way about. And this is to be determined by the criterion of direct and rational preferring. . .[62]

What is to be done if there is a clash of preferences in the family? It would seem that Lewis is assuming concurrence of preferences in the instances of human nature, or is, if there is disagreement, having recourse to the sapient man, after the manner of Mill.

We return to this problem in a moment, and direct our attention toward the evaluation of policy and of alternative kinds of civilization. But first it is to be underscored that Lewis asserts the legitimacy of the question of what is in the public interest and socially desirable and that

59 AKV, p. 542.
60 AKV, p. 543.
61 AKV, p. 550.
62 AKV, p. 548.

in this general sense Bentham had a meaningful problem although, against him, it must be "recognized that values have degree only and are not quantitatively measurable."[63] There is an immanent "standard of correctness"; this is required so that—however loose our estimates—there is "something which is approximated to or guessed at. . ."[64] We are "capable of knowing what we are trying to do in the attempt to ameliorate the conditions of human life and maximize our realizations of the valuable."[65] "However fantastic the supposition that we could in practice arrive at evaluation of an object by carrying out this program in detail," still "the theoretical possibility of such theoretical value-determination is what gives practical significance to our practical estimate."[66]

I want to believe, and am inclined to believe, that 'social value' and what is best 'on the whole' are meaningful. It is possible that these are ideal meanings pointed at by idealized extrapolations from the better and worse which are semi-empirically determined; the attempt at the self-clarification of these determinations calls for the a priori or ideal meaning, and the empiricist's intellectual conscience (of which Lewis has a strong instance) insists that procedures be shown which will achieve something in the way of putting content into the form. Lewis has offered, to my mind at least, the most ingenious 'solutions'—in idea, at least—to a group of knotty problems in social evaluation: how can an empiricist evaluate where there are genuine conflicts of interest? Weird as the application would be, he has suggested procedures for collating values in a manner which manifests 'objectivity'. There is objectivity of procedure and there is presumed to be, ideally, an objectivity of the 'judge'—who does the preferring—grounded in his human nature. We shall raise a query about the latter.

There are other 'solutions' than the one suggested by Lewis. There are nonnaturalistic solutions which, for 'evidence', must appeal to our intuitions. And I think there may be a 'looser' answer along the lines of saying that we may know 'better' and 'worse' without having found the formula of the 'best'. To be sure, there must be some implicit criteria even for the comparative judgments, but we may be groping for fuller criteria. For this scheme and for Lewis' there are doubtless less competent and more competent assessors of the better outcomes of situations of conflict. It would further seem that if we do find gradations of capacities with which we are familiar and do reflectively accept,

63 AKV, p. 551.
64 AKV, p. 542.
65 AKV, p. 543.
66 AKV, p. 551.

and if, so to speak, these all slant toward the same general locus (whether or not this is yet pinpointed), then it is possible and permissible to extrapolate toward (if not exactly to) an ideal assessor. But, as will be seen, I am not absolutely sure that in the present case there is convergence of the types of gradation which are involved.

If combinations of possible values cannot be assessed comparatively except by direct preferring of a given agent, it becomes a very important question whether there is a tendency for normal or competent agents to concur in their preferences. And therewith, especially in relation to weighing social values, emerges the question of whether Lewis really agrees with Mill in having a grading of quality or not. In either case Lewis goes along with Mill in not taking the average man as furnishing the standard response. Rather, he would want the most sapient man, capable of responding to the largest range of possibilities, to be the preferer. There is a distinction to be made, however, as to two different grounds for wanting the most sapient men to do the judging. For either of them one must have recourse to the sapient man—ideally, I will add, to the fully sapient man—because only he can really sympathize with, empathetically take in, the values of different sorts of persons. But what is he to do after he sympathizes with them? What is the nature of his preferring? Is he the gauge which registers the greater (nonmetrical) degree of value, accepting the values of the various lives as their possessors do or would experience these? Or, secondly, does he make a qualitative appraisal which, so to speak, may raise or lower weights of constituent values either because of an apprehension of their qualitative ranking or because of *Gestalt* factors which duller persons do not see?

Now if Lewis means the first, then—questions of the exceedingly complicated mechanism of such knowledge and such preferring to one side—I think the 'objectivity' is preserved. But if he means the second, and still of course avoids an intuitive cognitivism with respect to 'height' of value, then the question of the nature of the being who determines the 'ranking' and who registers the *Gestalten* and their value becomes acute. Textually, there is uncertainty as to the interpretation of Lewis, for I have not noticed that he puts the issue sharply to himself.[67] There are passages which give one 'suggestions' along either of the two

---

[67] Belatedly, I notice a sentence which, though not conspicuous, may refute my statement. "We are to collate value to any other (person) with value to ourselves in the same manner that we should, rationally, if his satisfaction or dissatisfaction were to be included in our own experience, but in such wise as to affect as little as possible any other and like experience of ours." AKV, p. 550f. The provision at the end of the sentence seems intended to rule against getting any 'wholistic' effects from the survey of lives together. Presumably in assessing the pig's pleasure, one must not allow any of his contempt for it to diminish his assessment of its degree of value.

lines. There are various reminders that in our dealings with others we ought to have regard for the sufferings of others in the actual intensity in which these are or would be undergone; this seems to be required by the Law of Objectivity.[68] On the other hand, there is his frequent proper emphasis upon contributory values and organic wholes, which might be extended beyond the individual career to cultures. Although he says "there is no such thing as *the* value of an object or objects,"[69] he does offer his ingenious way of settling, "in terms of direct preferring" the problem of comparing "the values of two objects when one of them offers satisfaction in higher degree but to fewer people, and the other a lower degree of satisfaction but to a larger number."[70] And, although, without context, the "question which is best, a warm overcoat, a Sanskrit dictionary, or a load of hay, has no answer,"[71] still anything can be valued comparatively by being put in a "linear order of values" for "there is one such order of values with respect to which *any* two things can be compared; namely, the value of them as ultimately contributory to some whole of life."[72] Is this "whole of life" only individual or may it be societal?

It is not in the lowest category of utilities but in the highest category of contributory values—the values of things as contributory to some individual life *or to lives in general*—that any two things are comparable as better or worse, and that we may be obliged to assess such comparative values of them.[73]

Contributory "to lives in general" may mean contributory to these lives taken distributively, or it may mean contributory to them as some 'whole of life'. In the latter case, one wishes to know whose perceptions are to be

---

68 Cf., e.g., GNR, p. 91.

69 AKV, p. 530.

70 AKV, p. 546. Perhaps his solution can be construed as supporting the first interpretation by placing a stress on the word *'seriatim'* in the provision that your preference be expressed with respect to alternative objects which affect a number of persons as "if you had to live the lives of each of them *seriatim*." AKV, p. 547. Will this bear the weight of saying that not only must you not carry over any Gestalt-contributory effects from one imagined life to another but you must not use your own actual nature to do the assessing, for it will not take the values in these other lives as they are for their possessors? I do not see how one can get the comparative assessments out of the actual conscious natures of the men who are in conflict. By this default and by some positive textual evidence, I assume that Lewis goes in the direction of recourse to the informed impartial spectator, sapient like Mill's Socrates, omni-sympathetic like James's "moral philosopher." But this judge must not be so impartial that he cannot do any preferring. The determination of what is preferable comes back to the sort of human nature that he is supposed to exhibit when he speaks in the role of preferrer.

71 AKV, p. 537.

72 AKV, p. 543.

73 AKV, p. 537, *italics* added.

trusted as discernments of the cultural organic wholes and whose preferences are to be taken as the authentic ones. It seems to be an assumption
about human beings—which assumption could well be an empirically
mistaken one—that sapient men will tend to agree in their reactions.
One feels no assurance that the actual responses of fairly sapient persons would concur. The criterion of direct preferring will not work to
establish objective assessment of social value, to determine what type of
social order is better, if men selected as most qualified by some independent criterion prove to be very different in their preferrings. I make no
contention one way or the other; I simply do not wish to beg this question, which, as I have said, is *conditionally* an important one.

The essence of these remarks could be brought down illustratively to
preferences between less probable greater value and more reliable lesser
value when, say, alternative courses of public policy are under consideration. One wonders if all sapient persons would manifest the same
degree of timidity or riskiness, determining some optimum between
these. Keynes and others have called the attention of economists to the
plurality of economic motives—and to the supposed fact that men do
not simply prefer in accord with Lewis' "justification of betting according
to the probabilities" which "lies in the fact that by following this rule
we shall win the most money over a lifetime."[74] Some persons, whether
sapient or not, I think 'prefer' a bit more security as against chance of
higher prosperity and some others get an extra thrill out of taking
greater risk. Perhaps Lewis feels that neither deviation is reasonable—no
more than Aristippus' or Bentham's preference for nearer pleasures. That
there are such variations among persons, however, would call for ruling
out some informed men as unqualified judges. Possibly to secure an
unobjectionable meaning of correct evaluation in such complex cases
one will have to make reference to an ideal sapient man. Then it would
be of interest to note what kind of conception of *ideal human nature*
is used to "ideally satisfy the intent of our judgment."[75] And one would
scrutinize the notion to make sure that it was not covertly nonnaturalistic.

*If* Lewis trusts sapient men to evaluate alternative wholes of society
wholistically, and if the supposed concurrence of sapient men should
break down, then it would be an interesting additional question—beyond
our present province—whether an important portion of the program of
his ethics would collapse. He may have an ethic of rights which can
obviate recourse to such determinations of maximization of compossible

[74] AKV, p. 549.
[75] AKV, p. 547.

values; on the other hand, there seem to be important moral decisions where these comparative evaluations are called for.

(D) The ascription of an inherent value to an object—or, for that matter, of an instrumental value or a utility—is an assertion of a potentiality in that object. In what we must remember he calls a "first approximation," Lewis asserts that "we might say that attributing value to an existent, *O*, means that under circumstances *C*, *O* will or would, or probably will or would, lead to satisfaction in the experience of somebody, *S* . . ."[76] This is highly general; indeed, without specifications of 'circumstances *C*' it is a definitional propositional function and not a proposition. As a "first approximation" it allows for possible further restriction as well as for plugging content into the forms. Our chief interest is not in 'circumstances *C*' but in whether further qualifications are going to be placed on 'somebody, *S*'. Have not further conditions been imposed when, a couple of pages later, he writes as follows? "A confirmation which is to be as nearly decisive as possible requires that the test-observation should be made by an expert and under optimum conditions of the test-experience." "That the test of it is by reference to the experience of someone, does not make it relative to persons. . ."[77] He is now talking about something which is to be tested by a connoisseur or expert, not about something which might sporadically lead to satisfaction in the experience of someone. Apparently he is speaking of a genuine 'property'; I do not know whether in his view all potentialities, or only some of them, are properties, but in one aspect all properties are potentialities.

A potentiality is formulatable by some if-then statement or set of such, asserting what we have called a *real connection*, of which causal connections are examples. . . .

When viewed in their relation to experience, all properties of things are such potentialities. This is the significance of the fact that, to be genuine and objective, the property in question must be capable, theoretically at least, of confirmation.[78]

A property of a thing is called *objective* if it is genuinely a property of that object, and not apparent only, or merely relative to incidental relation to a subject; as the redness of a 'really red' object is an objective property, but the redness of one which merely 'looks red' to a particular person or under special conditions, is not objective.[79]

76 AKV, p. 512; cf. pp. 525, 527.
77 AKV, p. 514.
78 AKV, p. 513; cf. pp. 226ff.
79 AKV, p. 392n.

We seem to be getting a valuational realism here, not of course in the sense that the inherent "goodness resident in the object" exists as a good itself but exists "as a potentiality for producing experience of a certain quality."[80] But even then it holds considerably more than Lewis' initial approach would at minimum dictate. First, in scaling down, let it be observed that Lewis calls attention to an important difference between objective value and such objective properties as roundness and hardness: ". . . with respect to value-terms their objective meaning is derivative from and ruled by their expressive meaning; whereas for other terms, their expressive meaning is at least likely to be subordinated to their objective meaning."[81]

The difference is that, with respect to 'hard' and 'round' . . . we have at some point thrown overboard such tests as those of *feeling* hard and *looking* round . . . But with respect to goodness, the mode of feeling remains the head and front of the whole matter, and no 'more precise' test of objective value would be true to our intent.[82]

Again, while "objective roundness is not appropriately defined by relation to the object's being seen as round," the "relation between the objective character of a thing and the possibility of some experience of satisfaction . . . is definitive of and constitutive of the kind of goodness objects have."[83] Secondly, if there is an assumption that the 'goodness' or 'potentiality' exists in the object as a unified differential structure, which (sometimes) elicits a differential qualitied response in a standard percipient subject, may not this be challenged? Is it not conceivable that a plurality of heterogeneous combinations in structures of objects may, as stimuli, yield value-quality as an effect? Thirdly, in allowing for although not necessarily embracing a doctrine of 'plurality of causes', should one not loosen up the requirements on the percipient side of the causation as well as on the stimulus side? Then we come to a minimum statement like the following, still retaining (perhaps objectionably) the phrasing about "the objective character of the thing": since "*value*-property is the objective character of the thing as capable of contributing some satisfaction to direct experience,"[84] this character is shown to be present in *any* stimulus which secures the requisite kind of effect; it is present as a potentiality *in relation to* the sort of percipient who had the requisite kind of effect in immediacy on being

80 AKV, p. 389.
81 AKV, p. 381.
82 AKV, p. 382.
83 AKV, p. 389.
84 AKV, p. 412.

stimulated by the object. The same object-stimulus, however, will not have this potentiality in relation to some other sorts of percipient. Let us call this the 'minimum doctrine'; it is not in accord with Lewis' terminology, and I think he rejects it, although it will linger around.

In our author's favored terminology, inherent values are not called 'relational'. He does pronounce instrumental value and utility to be relational properties.[85] The relation signalized is that of the thing to which the value is ascribed *and* some other *object*—not a subject—and is, of course constituted by a causal relation to the second object. I am talking as if—and Lewis once allows this[86]—inherent values ought also to be labelled 'relational', but here the relation is to a subject or—problematically—to a qualified subject. (In the 'minimum doctrine', special qualifications are not imposed on the subject.)

I shall opine in the end that for predications of human value, requirements are imposed by Lewis on the qualifying subject, and that these may be thought of in their representativeness of one or other notion of 'human nature'. I believe that in Lewis' employment of 'real connection' he rejects, or he does not allow for, the speculative notion of 'plurality of causes'. And, at least in his treatment of the inherent values in objects of high aesthetic worth he will be found to be assuming some kind of unified differential structure in the object which can be responded to wholistically and differentially by the adequate observer. Before tentatively offering such opinions, however, we ought to make further notations in the text.

Lewis means to reject the view that "the kind of goodness which objects and other existents may have is a goodness relative to the individual judgment of it or the particular character of any person's value-findings in the presence of this object . . ."[87] Now for talk of utility or of instrumental goods where the end is assumed, everyone must concur

---

[85] AKV, p. 515. Further, due to certain linguistic habits (for which there are practical reasons) instrumental value is not infrequently predicated in the manner of 'relativity to the actual'—in which one means a categorical-probability statement (unlike statements in the subjunctive about values as simple potentialities) either predicting the probable occurrence of values because of certain conditions which presumably will be utilized in certain ways or predicting the probable nonoccurrence of such values because of the absence of the manageable conditions. Strictly the utility judgment is not directly about the inherent values thus predicted or not predicted, but the assertion of instrumental value requires reference to them. AKV, p. 518.

[86] "Ascription of extrinsic value is, plainly, relative. Or if all value-attribution is relational, then predication of extrinsic value is relative in an additional and special sense . . ." AKV, p. 382. In ordinary use, we simply predicate (inherent) value without mentioning the conditions of its relationality. I think Lewis feels that it is awkward or pedantic to depart from such use.

[87] AKV, p. 407.

in rejecting both parts of the quoted statement. But what about inherent values? As for the first half, I certainly do not suppose that the existence or nonexistence of an inherent value in an object is relative to the individual judgment because, instead, it is whatever way it is; and the way it is is what conscientious judgment is aimed to state. But this acknowledgment is quite compatible with the occurrence or nonoccurrence of immediate value being dependent upon the particular structure or character of the percipient. A critic might urge that from Lewis' naturalistic approach, this is where one ought to begin; to be sure, as one gathers data from many individuals one may revise one's first attributions out of deference to having (as Hume noted) the convenience of similar public predications. Thus, let us say, we find that one individual experiences an intrinsic bad on confrontation with a certain cluster of properties in a certain object but that many other apparently normal persons undergo pleasing passages of experience on confrontation with the same object; then we are likely to ignore, or even explicitly reject as 'false' or 'abnormal' the attribution made by the deviant individual. Let a distinction be made, however, from the standpoint of the deviant individual. He will be concerned, as we implicitly recognized under (B), whether peculiar momentary circumstances in himself or outside prevented him from experiencing a good which others speak about, or whether he may reliably infer that in the case of the object under question what is other men's meat will continue to be his poison. He has learned, or he had better learn, to agree with Lewis' statements:

. . . as regards the objective value-property of a thing observed, immediate liking or disliking may be non-indicative and the basis of a judgment which is false.

. . . on first hearing a piece of music, or first viewing a painting, we cannot be mistaken about our present enjoyment of it, or felt indifference or distaste; but any conclusion we draw from that about this musical composition or this picture as a continuing source of possible enjoyments or dissatisfactions, may later prove to be in error.[88]

One notices the phrase 'continuing source' in conjunction with the notion of 'objective value-property'. Our hypothetical deviant individual may concur, but be interested in what are continuing sources of immediate values to himself, and not be disposed to undergo conditioning in a dubious attempt to make himself similar to others. For him and for Lewis we may rule out the 'minimum doctrine' so far as practical use is concerned; such a maximum attribution of inherent value as the minimum doctrine calls for would be—although perhaps theoretically unob-

[88] AKV, p. 410.

jectionable when one is thinking strictly about causation—most unhelpful and on occasions misleading for practice.[89]

A possible meaning (or possible criterion) of objective value may be brought out by the question: is the "object enjoyed" one which is "genuinely desirable"?[90] But this is not itself yet determinate between certain possible interpretations, for the criteria of 'genuinely desirable' are not specified. One rendering might be that an object the possession, perception or contemplation of which continues to be, or would continue to be, a source of immediate value to an individual is thereby genuinely desirable, no matter how idiosyncratic the subject may be in his response. The object is an enduring source of value to him and he can make assertions about its potentiality in this respect and can frame conditional predictions about future events—predictions which can be objectively confirmed. A quite different criterion is had if one will not allow idiosyncrasy and stipulates that an 'objective' potentiality in an object requires the 'publicity' of being capable of being verified in the experience of many persons and over a long period of time. Obviously, this schema of a criterion can be quantitatively fixed at different points by specifying a certain class of men, all normal adults in one culture, all normal men regardless of culture, all normal men, all men, etc.

Assuming a correlation between potentialities of an object and contents in immediate experience presumably caused by the presence of the objects, I find comments of Lewis which do parallel these approximate distinctions. He is talking about the distinction of 'subjective' and 'objective' as applied to immediate 'prizings and disprizings' (and not

---

[89] In such discussions as occur under (B) and here, one does not wish to confuse terminological differences with real differences in theory. Some differences may be only 'verbal' when viewed from the standpoint of looking at the nonlinguistic phenomena and of the causal relations among them. Still a couple of observations are to be made. Some of the phenomena to be explained are value-predications themselves. Here adequate theory will show the grounds or causes of different modes of predication, even if these causes are only certain loosely recognized distinctions plus the slovenliness or economy of common speech. An additional factor of utility or convenience enters when one is concerned with 'modes of predication' which are to be endorsed and not simply explained; for it is part of the assumed context of value-predication that these be useful in the guidance of practice. Hence some attributions of value which may be theoretically sound may be here discarded. The most obvious class is attributions of value in so low a degree as to be negligible as compared with the high degree of some other values which are at stake. And we have seen that there is exceedingly little use for myriads of the possible predications which could be made in the mode of bare potentiality. There is even very little use—except 'ceremonial'—for public predications of personal values. Advice is normally passed along only where it is presumed to have some currency. To be sure, some attribution of inherent values which are highly idiosyncratic is not only made in soliloquy in one's private administration of his affairs but also in conversation as items of pleasant 'chit-chat' among intimate friends.

[90] AKV, p. 414.

about inherent values in objects, for which I am assuming a parallel relation). After again saying that for value quality in immediacy *esse est percipi,* he remarks:

However, if we should take the fact that on this occasion, a content of experience having such and such character in other respects, is infused with positive value-quality, or with disvalue, as evidence that on another occasion an otherwise similar content of experience will again be marked by this same value-quality, then we might be wrong. . . . Or if we should infer that other persons would, in the same situation in which we find ourselves, be affected with this same value-quality in their experience.[91]

I will call these the first and third sentences, because—between them—is another sentence, which I will denote as 'the middle sentence':

As also we might be wrong if we should infer from this experience that an object the presence of which is witnessed by this given content, is an object having a corresponding value-property; that the presented object is good because the experience is gratifying or bad because the experience is dissatisfying.

Now one of my questions in effect has been: what is the explication of this middle sentence, particularly the phrase "an object having a corresponding value-property"? As Lewis elsewhere observes, (almost) no one thinks value is in the object in the manner of primary properties.[92] If the value-property 'exists' as a 'power' or potentiality, then I wonder if this means more than that the object does or can, when serving as a stimulus to a subject of a certain sort under conditions of a certain sort, produce a value-quality of a certain kind in immediate experience. I would like to know from Lewis if this middle sentence is independent of both the other two. Or, as I have been supposing, do the first and third, *mutatis mutandis* give alternative explications of the middle sentence. Of course, the criteria suggested by the first and third could be put together as a logical sum or as a logical product, as well as be selected alone. Accordingly, making the transition from objectivity of content in experience to objectivity of inherent value as a property of an object, we have suggested the following possibilities. (I will state them for inherent goods; the parallels for inherent bads are obvious.)

(1) There is an inherent value in an object when presence of the object does or would repeatedly give (under appropriate circumstances) immediate positive value-quality to one person.

(2) There is an inherent value in an object when presence of the object (under appropriate circumstances) does or would afford imme-

91 AKV, p. 415.
92 AKV, p. 386.

diate positive value-quality to a number of normal persons. (I believe that "normal" is a reasonable insertion.)

(3) There is an inherent value in an object when presence of the object (under appropriate circumstances) either to one person on repeated occasions or to different (normal) persons on at least one occasion each does or would yield immediate positive value-quality.

(4) There is an inherent value in an object when presence of the object (under appropriate circumstances) does or would *repeatedly* afford immediate positive value-quality to a number of normal persons.

(5), (6), etc. Ditto—when the number of normal persons is increased to all adults in one culture, or all men, etc.

In the last elastic rubric I have intended a number of more restrictive formulations. The parallel of (1) the first does seem to be rejected by Lewis when, of a presentational content, he says it is to be called "subjective" if it owes to one's "personal make-up or personal history."[93] For one's personal make-up or history might determine with marked stability that a certain object will have inherent value for him—but quite idiosyncratically. (We have previously suggested—under (B), above—that such values be called 'genuine but nonobjective'.) Of course, I see no reason why, on Lewis' general approach, we should not give this class of values some such label as objective 'private' inherent values. In at least one place Lewis refers to them as 'personal values'.[94] And Lewis seems to take one of the last very strict formulations when he continues:

where there is no such preponderant influence of what is personal, but the factors responsible are to be found in the objective situation, together with the capacities of apprehension shared by humans generally, the value-quality apprehended as affecting the given content of presentation may be said to be objective.[95]

This is a very restrictive criterion, especially if 'capacities' means 'actual capacities' and doubly so if 'capacities of apprehension shared by humans *generally*' means 'capacities of apprehension shared by humans *universally*'. And then, I feel, it is too strict. Perhaps distinctions of degree may rescue one but it appears to have quite uncomfortable consequences when one is talking about beauty in objects. In fact there Lewis will

93 AKV, p. 416.
94 GNR, p. 70.
95 AKV, p. 416.

emphatically not be impressed in the least by the reactions of majorities nor asking for the common upshot in the responses of all men.

Before turning either to what value-ascriptions issue from the capacities of apprehension shared by all men or to the nature of the ascribings done by a very few men called 'connoisseurs', let us pause a moment in between with the idea that a qualitative experience is 'nonindicative' or 'subjective' if it comes about from, or 'comes through', a constellation of causes which are abnormal in the region of the subject, and that it is 'objective' if it comes about by causes which are normal in the region of the percipient. (This probably needs further qualification to rule out stimuli which would produce illusions in all normal percipients.) Assuming further that most men are normal and assuming the stipulation that sound ascription of 'objective' value in objects requires that the stimulus-structure is an 'enduring' or continuing source of actual or possible immediate value and that it must be such with respect to many persons, what will we find when we come to the actual problems of asserting or denying the presence of objective inherent value? Without intending any unempirical legislation of facts, I confess that—sitting in my armchair—I suppose we will not find the phenomena offering us a clear-cut division between candidate values some of which, on the one hand, stimulate immediate value in nearly everyone and continue to do so, and the remainder of which, on the other hand, stimulate immediate value in a few deviant persons and this most erratically. Instead, I expect that in this sociological type of procedure we will discover for many candidate-values a distribution of attributions resembling a normal probability curve, and that again we will find no sharp cleavage between enduring values and nonrepeatable values but rather varying degrees of stability in various value sources. If I am right in these suppositions, let me parenthetically remark, I do not contend that of itself it upsets Lewis' project of ethics. It is simply corrective of the idea of a clean cleavage between 'objective' inherent values and merely ostensible ones. On the criteria of reliability (or enduringness) and of number of persons yielding favorable response on one occasion or through time, it anticipates that the results will manifest gradation. The 'line' separating objective from nonobjective will be quite arbitrary. It can be drawn by stipulating criteria of the normal man and of a minimum standard of enduringness of objective value. (Now I trust that the way in which human nature is appealed to by Lewis in ethics is different from what I have done here; I have not insisted on reference to any valuation common to all normal men; in basing ethics our author may appeal to factors or capacities, native or social endowments, common to all normal men.)

R. W. BROWNING

Now perhaps this outcome of (expected) gradations in enduringness and in extent of inherent values can be circumvented, either by searching for universal values or by resorting to a test which is independent, so to speak, of 'majority vote'. There are quite surely instrumental values 'common to humans', and there are inherent values ascribed to *kinds* (or within *ranges*) of things, which ascriptions might be tacitly common to humans. All human beings need food, water, oxygen, sunshine or vitamin C, society, affection; perhaps all mature ones have needs related to sex, to ego-status, etc. Lewis, of course, does not define value in terms of needs or of fulfillment of needs, but the process of fulfilling a need is—when conscious—normally a pleasant passage of experience and the object or objects intimately identified with this fulfillment will be ostensibly inherent goods. However, on this kind of meaning of 'objective' which requires commonness to nearly all human beings, one is very hesitant to say that *specific objects* of these kinds or ranges are or contain *objective* inherent values. A given person may be even moderately hungry but not respond favorably to a chunk of blubber, a pot of poi, a piece of limburger cheese. Some sex expression may be a good to a normal adult but a proffered 'sexy' object or solicitation may be repulsive. There is also a problem as to whether the factor of conditioning, which is obviously involved, may not be equally marked in certain ranges of art objects. In the practice that pertains to inherent values in the compass of one's own experience—or in that of persons of one's acquaintance— one deals with what he meets and has reason to suppose he can meet. He does not meet food-in-general, affection-in-general, art-objects-as-such, etc. He buys and prepares definite kinds of food, he encounters concrete persons and may search for men with certain general qualifications, he looks at specific sculptures or observes that he does not like abstract painting. In the administration of life neither, on the one hand, are values intellectually cognized in full concreteness—they cannot be, although experience itself is concrete—nor, on the other hand, are they dealt with on very high levels of abstraction (or, if in some complex long range planning they may be, this is rather rare). Doubtless a search for universal values is useful for some purposes; but as a way of finding a clean cleavage between 'objective value properties' and those that are nonobjective among the concrete objects which one meets and among moderately abstract objects which one judges, it is not serviceable. Here no magic comes out of naming values at such a level of abstraction as may enable one to say they are universal; and physiologically basic values—although universal—do not exhaust all value-objects possessing ostensibly objective inherent values.

So far we are left with our own untested supposition that, using (a) durability of the object as a value-source and (b) extent of sorts of persons favorably affected (actually or potentially) as the criteria of the presence of an objective value property in an object, we probably would run into results showing practically continuous gradations. More hopeful than the previous diversion—if one is unsatisfied with this situation— may be inquiry into the nature of aesthetic criticism with a view to noting whether this field contains suggestions of a different kind of test than resort to promiscuous sociological observation or than appeal to basic physiological needs. When we look at the text of Lewis on this point we find the strongest assertions of "the objective character which is to be discerned and assessed" together with the strongest denials of the competence of majorities of men. Report of value-quality in immediacy, of course, is not a 'judgment'. An aesthetic judgment is about the property of a thing—the "objective character which is to be discerned and assessed." Training and cultivation of the appreciator do not make *these* properties; they help one to discern them.[96]

Remembering that "value in objects is a potentiality of them for conducing to experience of positive value-quality," one asks 'conducing' in whose actual or possible experience? Can the presence of value be asserted and degree of value be assessed out of relation to—so to speak— its clientele? Or, put a little stridently, is not aesthetic value qualitatively assessed by assessing its clientele? Emphatically it is not in reference to everyone's experience or to a majority's experience that Lewis gives his answer in the case of aesthetic values. Here (unlike the domain of economic values, where, as constituting demand, numbers do count), the 'counting of noses' has no relevance. "That a sentimental picture like The Doctor is more widely appreciated than Still Life with Apples, has no bearing on their aesthetic rank." The judgment of the connoisseurs "may stand as against any number of contrary votes gathered indiscriminately, because it is something objective which is judged, and not something relative to the particular and perhaps undiscerning experience."[97]

The phrase 'may stand as against any number of contrary votes gathered indiscriminately' does seem to be exceedingly strong and therewith dubious—unless it means 'any number of contrary votes gathered with discrimination so as to select persons of poor taste'. Elsewhere connoisseurs are pictured as (among other things) making predictions about the possible value-experiences of other persons on confrontation with

96 AKV, p. 461. ". . . the potentiality judged is a property of the object . . ."
97 AKV, pp. 460. Cf. 465, 411f., 458f., 514, 526f.

art objects; here, one feels, the connoisseurs are unlikely to be concerned with any predictions about the conditional future experiences of the Philistines even if the latter could be persuaded, say, to keep looking on and off at certain pictures. Elsewhere there is reference to the durability of an aesthetic object as a source of value to an individual and reference to "most other people."

If it should be asked *why* this picture is one of small artistic merit, one might make such answers as . . . "Because the color-contrasts are bad"; "Because the center of interest is misplaced." And in elaboration of these criticisms, one might refer to observable physical properties of the painting on the one hand and to general principles of pictorial art on the other. But if one who is untutored in art should challenge the principles of criticism advanced and persist in asking *why* these objective characteristics of the painting make it a poor picture, then the critic must eventually be driven to make an answer of a different sort: "You may like it now, but I don't think you would if you should live with it a while"; or the ruder observation, "Apparently your color-perception is faulty: those who are expert in such matters, as well as most other people, do not find that combination and arrangement of colors pleasing."[98]

Although there is no elaboration of how the "general principles of pictorial art" are obtained, one has in brief compass here Lewis' main teaching, and it is sensible. The critic does have skill for conditional predicting of valuational effects; and he is not dealing with a value in an object out of relation to all men or in relation to a little coterie of men. What, however, does the last sentence quoted mean? Does it not mean: 'Either your discrimination of colors and color *Gestalten* is deficient, or your feeling-reaction to the colors and color combinations which you perceive is deviant'? I do not see how he can say 'faulty' or 'wrong' in the latter case except as synonymous with 'abnormal' and 'unfortunate'. Looking sociologically at appreciators, in respect to given art objects, there are a lot of deviants. Normatively, the deviants who are more highly perceptive are praiseworthy; the deviants who are sub-standard in perception are unfortunate; and many otherwise 'average men' tend to go with the latter.

One does not find it plausible to suppose that aesthetic values of high degree are to be placed either in the class of 'personal' or 'genuine' (nonobjective) value properties or in the class of objective properties as determined by average standard human nature. Although perhaps high aesthetic values are not the most popular inherent values and do appeal most strongly to relatively few persons, still one would indeed hesitate to class them as 'genuine' nonobjective values. One does not

98 AKV, pp. 411f.

attribute the restricted intense appeal of 'great art' to the personal idiosyncrasies of the devoted minority; one supposes these works to possess objective value which is inadequately appreciated by the majority of men owing to their personal limitations. The expert is deemed to be more highly discriminating and perhaps somehow to be more appropriately responsive.

Can one be assured that connoisseurs are not a little band of arrogant and similarly deviant men? In some sensory areas of operation there is good empirical evidence that the connoisseur makes better the 'same' discriminations which many others make more feebly and less reliably. I acknowledge that considerable risk is run in accepting with assurance that the same principle holds over the whole range of aesthetic criticism. If a majority of mankind were color-blind, still men would be able to find this out, and would have grounds to refrain from calling the deviants arrogant men obsessed with similar illusions. Lewis holds, I am sure, that on the central point of there being an objective potentiality which some men discern, this case and the case of difficult art are parallel. With respect to the problem of confirmation, however, there is this complicating difference. In the case of light waves and their wave-lengths, an alternative objective mode of determination is possible. Indeed, the physicist—though not the man in the street—may have "thrown overboard such tests as those of . . . *looking*" green. "But," as we have previously quoted Lewis, "with respect to goodness, the mode of feeling remains the head and front of the whole matter, and no 'more precise' test of objective value would be true to our intent."[99] Were the mode of feeling to be confined to a very few persons, one might well guess that—in a given case—we had run into a 'personal value' which happened to be instanced in several persons with similar histories or structure. And were the members of this tiny minority unable in their discussions to relate their immediate positive value quality to certain structures in the phenomenal object, one would have grave doubts that he had run into more than a coincidence of likings from a variety of causes. Neither of these two possibilities fit the situation which obtains with respect to 'classics' and 'masterpieces'. Many persons find values in these objects. And discussion of their features by their appreciators is somewhat intelligible. From this ground, I believe that one could work out to the more controversial areas. It can be determined that some persons are more discerning than others about the nonvalue characteristics and the value-making characteristics of objects. Their reactions on meeting new objects do not present, I suspect, a random distribution. And if, as confessional dis-

99 AKV, p. 382.

cussion between them continues, there is manifestation of a significant amount of agreement, original and developing, there may be fair presumption both of similarity of apperception in the subjects and of recognition of the same properties in the objects. If the individuals with the hyper-sensitive discriminatory capacities also prove to have better-than-average powers of prediction of the future reactions of others, this gives some further support to the hypothesis of their 'expertness'.

Circularity is avoidable; it is not inevitable that one conclude that being an object possessing objective aesthetic value means being an object which under proper circumstances stimulates members of a specially endowed group to have immediate value (perhaps of high degree), and that determination of membership in the specially endowed group is settled by being a person who experiences immediate value (in high degree) on proper confrontation with a special set of objects. On the other hand, one does not prove the generic normalcy of critics (their abnormality being only unusual degree of an endowment or skill shared in lesser degree by almost all others) or the practical continuity among men of degrees of appreciation for given objects or the possible existence of a plenum of objects capable of affording in experience value of any degree. But this is a possible hypothesis; and as a possibility it has for the present the merit of avoiding certain difficulties.

That appreciation of some works of art . . . may be confined to a relatively few, proves nothing; it is possible, even if not probable, that the explanation is to be found in their superior discernment. Relatively few people can hear sounds of 25,000 cycles per second; but those who do, hear a real sound: they prove it in the laboratory. The corresponding proof of objectivity in artistic discernment, is a little hard to come at; but at least we must admit that objectivity of a value-apprehension is not dependent on the statistics of general appreciation; and 'genuinely and objectively valuable' does not mean simply 'conducing to satisfaction on the part of people in general.'[100]

The last clause does not restrict itself to actuality; and—because of the saving word 'simply'—it need not be taken as contradicting the meaning of objectivity of inherent value found elsewhere; besides, the author seems to be going on to make the point again (which unhappily tends to blur two different meanings of objectivity) that what is genuinely and reliably a value to some persons is objectively so, for it is "impersonally valuable and socially desirable" provided it is not hurtful to others. Thus aesthetic values (provided these be socially harmless) could be in this sense objectively valuable even though they were valuable only to a little coterie of similarly deviant individuals. But I do not

100 AKV, pp. 526f.

think this is his proper doctrine of high aesthetic values. I have put in the word 'high' to indicate that the values may stand in one or more continuities instead of exhibiting radical discontinuity. I have suggested that the potentialities which constitute such values are not in relation to average human nature but still are in relation to a standard human nature. Perhaps this standard is that of the *ideally perceptive and healthily sensitive man*. (That this may posit two or more capacities rather than one will receive comment momentarily.) Such a being is still conceived as a man. The notion need not be nonnaturalistic; criticism of critics is not wholly devoid of criteria. Actual connoisseurs whose abilities approach toward the standard are connoisseurs for other men, not just for themselves or for their deviant group. And, while our author's naturalism does not provide a categorical imperative for the average or subaverage appreciator to undergo tutelage in the hope of becoming like his more sapient fellows, there may be a normal presumption that his life will be richer if he can better appreciate what more discerning and sensitive persons do appreciate. Of course, such a development might involve a corresponding loss of other appreciations and then the man of prudence will have to estimate what will probably be most profitable; and it is quite conceivable that he may have reason to suppose that his abnormal conditioning will promise the probability of greater value for him by a continued pursuit of his idiosyncratic values.[101]

[101] Some time ago I wrote: "Suppose an individual rather reliably finds intrinsic values under the stimuli of extrinsic values which are not commonly found to be effective for such purposes, and yet suppose further that these ways are not detrimental socially. Should he try to become normal? According to the emotive intimations of alleged objective values, presumably he should. On the other hand, according to what we regard as Lewis' proper doctrine and his principle of rationality, there is no reason why he should attempt to re-educate himself toward greater normality unless reliable specialists tell him it will make him happier—or he has other reason to believe this will afford him more satisfaction. We assume that, apart from the ethical considerations which may really be involved, these are the relevant alternatives and that Lewis' proper doctrine is the second, despite the overtones of linguistic suggestion that one should attempt to follow the expert in appreciating objective inherent values. Except for effects upon the value-systems of others, the only need that an individual bestir himself to change his private economy of values lies in his own interest in improving that economy—and the improvement for him might go in the direction of further deviation from the normal just as well as toward it." "On Professor Lewis' Distinction Between Ethics and Valuation," *Ethics*, 59 (January, 1949), 103. I suppose that every individual has some genuine personal values; indeed, it is normal to have them in respect to things which, with intimate sentiment, relate to persons and places which importantly figure in that unique habitat in which one's life has been cast. Perhaps there are personal specifications on the more concrete levels of values which, as usually described, are relatively universal. But I do not know whether it is actually possible—as well as theoretically possible—that one might enrich his life as a whole by deliberate conditioning in an abnormal direction.

I have no proof that all men or nearly all men do or could appreciate high aesthetic values. But I do not doubt that the passing of value judgments which sound as if they are simple positive assertions are normally, in the economy of the psycho-physical organism's attention, made from a comparative base.[102] And I would observe that heavy banking upon this fact, plus the assumption that men are similar in root capacities though not in degree of their endowment or of their development, would enable us to make a reconciliation of those passages of Lewis which seem to define objectivity of value properties in relation to "capacities of apprehension shared by humans generally"[103] and those other passages which seem to assert the objectivity of aesthetic values in total indifference to "counting noses" and "any number of contrary votes gathered indiscriminately."[104] (Indeed, I have several times inserted the word 'high' when referring to the aesthetic value of established art objects in order to suggest the relevance of degree.)

Let us see in a little detail the shape of this 'reconciliation' and then turn briefly to the related questions of what is 'bad taste' and 'good taste' and of the nature of the expertness of the expert.

Basically, one takes the properties of the object which are more differentially productive of immediate value to be objective inherent values provided the "factors responsible" are to be found in the objective situation, together with the "capacities of apprehension shared by humans generally" rather than with personal idiosyncratic predispositions. One insists that "capacities of apprehension shared by humans generally" be understood to include capacities that are undeveloped and are shared in very weak degree as well as those shared in strength. Then, the fact that some persons would normally be called 'blind' to certain values can be construed as more strictly meaning that they apprehend these values so feebly that they hardly notice them, and that because these are registered so weakly they do not speak of them—for in practice one tends only to speak of high comparative value. Or, one might even say that the 'capacity' is so undeveloped that it does not function. All of this could be done (ad hoc, or not) compatibly with the material assumption that all men share in some basic aesthetic sensitivity. And the word 'generally', used by our author, need not mean 'universally'; some minority of men might not be equipped to 'register' on stimulation by certain inherent values.

---

[102] Lewis, as I read him, is pointing this out in his distinction between ascriptions of value comparatively and ascriptions of value noncomparatively or absolutely. AKV, pp. 524f.

[103] AKV, p. 416.

[104] AKV, p. 460.

In a supplementary fashion one may observe that not only is valuing for purposes of public utterance tacitly comparative but so also is valuing for personal practical purposes. And there is the point, which may be especially associated with the name of Dewey, that in the eventuation of deliberation the rejected good becomes a "bad" for the situation for which it was a candidate. Additionally, there is the psychological item that negative quality tends to attach to threat of interruption of movement toward a good for which there is mental set—even though the interruption could be held to be for the sake of something else which is good. Because valuing is comparative in one's own career, the more sensitive persons are apt to down-grade below zero renditions of artistic intent which others might find to be fairly good. Perhaps if they were in prison, let us say, and had only a choice between a poor musical performance and none at all, they might value this performance very much for its contribution to their lives; and at the same time they could concede that the artistry was "not very good." The value would be well above a hypothetical zero. Given their freedom, they would find much better sources of value and hence would again look upon the amateur effort as 'bad'—though the hearer must realize that this may be translated: 'though a good, not the right thing to choose'. Similarly, situations may be dreamed up in which persons characterized as having 'poor taste' presumably would give evidence that they do recognize value in the 'high-brow' materials. Under normal circumstances they spurn the works which seem to them so thin and rarified when simultaneously they can turn to such relatively exciting sources as calendar art, Western movies, or prize-fights. The low-brow hates to have his lively experiences interrupted by a request to strain after something which has for him a low yield of immediate value. With this, the high-brow should be able to sympathize, remembering that for himself whenever one's thinking or imagining provides one with better passages of experience than external sources of entertainment can provide, the intrusion of the external stimuli are resented as bad; it is for this very reason that he joins in opposition to forced listening to radio programs in public places.

When two appreciators 'contradict' one another, they may not be divided over the issue which seems to separate them, but rather over some other. (Indeed, the opposition may amount to a difference in degree of certain attitudes.) One may seem to say '$V$ is a value and $W$ is bad', and the other may seem to say '$W$ is a value, and $V$ is bad'. What each might mean is 'The value I have put first is the superior value and it is a mistake to give the second value a higher priority'. (And, of course, it might mean 'Hooray for the value I named first!) ' The 'theory' which we have expressed in the last few paragraphs is one which allows that the persons in dispute might each acknowledge that the item which they name second does have absolute value; it was called bad only because of the thought of its threatening or supplanting the better value.

Now I do not know whether the view sketched is Lewis' teaching, but I incline to believe that it is. Certainly he does not hold that every man has the actual capacity to appreciate every good work of art; and perhaps he does not even hold that every man has the latent capacity. Probably he at least holds that every normally endowed man has considerable latent capacity to appreciate some beauty and some art. I think the persons of superior taste represent a continuity of capacity with that of average men; that they are deemed superior and not simply deviant bespeaks the fact that average men can find illumination and direction (which are felt as education and self-elucidation rather than as external information and imposition) in what the critic may communicate to them. More acute sensory discernment, in which Lewis speculated the superiority might consist, is surely not enough by itself to make a man of excellent taste. What if an individual could make many sensory discriminations of which others are incapable and yet be unable to respond (even in favorable situations) with the having of value in immediacy? He could not even pick out the inherent values among the welter of discriminated structures; to orient his special powers to inherent values he would have to receive direction from others.[105] And what if an individual discriminated the same object as others and noted its structure better than they are able to do but found the object (under standard external circumstances) to be a disvalue instead of a value? After a pause for rechecking, the normal men will deem him somehow disordered or perverse. Accordingly, for expertness or superiority in taste there is at least a negative requirement of not being perverted in quality of value response as well as the positive requirement of being abnormally well equipped in power of discernment. I doubt if this is enough. At least the power of discernment must mean more than sensory acuteness; it must include capacity to apprehend very complex Gestalten. I suspect that we may also want to demand unusual capacities of sensitive response as well as unusual discrimination; but I do not know how to characterize this superior aesthetic appropriateness of response, except to express the assumption that not to be perverse (and in this sense to have 'pro' and

---

[105] Of course to have objects offered as works of art is a form of direction. Further, one expects such objects to have been created with economy; hence its parts and features ideally will each contribute to the 'whole'. But there are departures from the ideal. And, as for beauty in nature, who is to guide? Here one had better be prepared to do some 'framing' and to exercise much selection in getting a good aesthetic object.

'anti' feelings rightly deployed) on occasions of confrontations with objects is the basic but coarsest form of appropriateness. I assume that there are nuances of aesthetic quality, accompanied by sense of their degree of value, present in the responses which are more subtlely appropriate.

The man of good taste presumably has resemblance to an ideal human being along the lines of reliable recognition of aesthetic inherent values, good sense of the comparative ranking of these values (though not necessarily with articulated reasons) and of course normal response to them and possibly supple subtlety of the unanalyzed sort to which we have just made reference. Men of poor taste and of bad taste are presumably deficient in degree, or even totally, with respect to these characteristics. It will be well to distinguish some of the different ways in which one may fail to have good taste, and then to ask further as to any requirement beyond good taste which a competent critic must possess.

We pass over the obvious fact that privation of, or impairment of, a sense through which an inherent value is presented incapacitates the candidate-appreciator for veridical experience and reliable judgment. Deaf Beethoven cannot comment well on a given performance; but one recognizes that such a man might have superlative aesthetic sensitivity but be, so to speak, deprived of the data in a specified case. (1) Assuming the presence of the sensory base, and talking in the milieu of art and beauty, the first deficiency to be noted is value-blindness, inability to locate aesthetic objects. Of course, this occurs as a matter of degree; a person can locate or 'see' some value-objects but not others. (2) Assuming a person can locate aesthetic inherent values, he may be poor in the capacity to differentiate their features and to note the 'motive' power of the various aspects and structures, and he may not feel how these tend toward fusion and integration. (3) One may do rather well in discerning aesthetic inherent values and even in analyzing their structure but he may depart far from what experts say in assessing their comparative worths. One explanation which can be offered is that this situation may derive from the addition of 'personal' values to (and the subtraction of 'personal' disvalues from) standard objective values—with the agent failing to recognize and allow for the private component which skews his results.[106] (4) One can conceive the possibility that an individual might discern some inherent values and deem them to be disvalues. He is not blind with respect to their differential role; his response is perverted, according to one or more standards of normal human nature.

---

[106] Another source of the disparity may be his failure to allow for the way in which basically nonaesthetic factors may affect 'objective' aesthetic value—if they do, as I believe they do (e.g., propaganda or moral considerations).

Although the following are rather difficult to establish empirically, I feel that there are certain other deficiencies. (5) An individual might grossly like the good things, and might rate those which come within his ken in approximately the right order and still be—even under favorable circumstances—deficient in intensity. Since his preferential ratings are 'correct', his judgment affords overt evidence for being accepted as sound, but still his taste may be felt to be too anemic to merit being called 'good'. (6) If there are finer differentiations of appropriateness of response in complementarity to the finer perceptive discriminations, then a person might, as in (5) make the right general kind of response, and, in addition, possibly have sufficient intensity and gusto, but still be deficient in subtlety and fineness of qualitied response.

All six of these, it seems to me, may instance degrees of departure from good taste (I am not so sure of the second and of the last two). The first two plainly occur in degree. I suppose the commonest observed deficiency—perhaps because the evidence for it is so patent—is the third. The fourth, when it occurs, is most vivid of all; but I suspect that most candidate instances are not genuine instances—they are cases of moral or practical disapproval in opposition to, or suspending, the aesthetic engrossment.[107]

---

[107] Parallel with a question raised before one may ask whether it is not desirable to have 'poor taste'. If one were shut up in ugly surroundings would poor taste be a good thing—saving oneself by having areas of blindness if not indeed utilizing perversity also as a diplomatic trick on the environment? Perhaps some persons literally in prison work out protective devices of stolidity which involve (5). But it is especially (3)—along with some sociological facts—which may suggest the prudence of being equipped with bad taste. Suppose that there are many more inherent values available which are rated well by bad taste than there are values rated high by good taste (and I dare guess that this is a fact), will not the prudent hedonist find it wiser to have bad taste, so that he will enjoy life more? Of course if bad taste mean preference for the inferior when the superior is present, no such reason can be given for the retention of bad taste. And there is a serious doubt whether one's standards of taste are a sort of thing which (like a party platform) can be shifted around at the convenience of will. It is a further question of fact how much good taste inhibits appreciation of inferior values; perhaps there are large individual differences on this point.

It is not bad taste to appreciate the values which are available, even if these are lowly. One had better, so far as possible, maintain a flexibility and adaptability to the supply of inherent values. He had better not become like the 'highbrow' whom Candide met in Venice, whose standards were so exacting and whose taste was so refined that he could enjoy nothing. Sensible people do not cut themselves off from appreciation, and they do make allowances for sources—even enjoying as well as praising the work of children. The enjoyment may often be more nonaesthetic than aesthetic, but it is genuine. And it need not corrupt taste. One does feel that corrupting taste, so as to get more fun, would in some way be unworthy of a man.

One wonders if Lewis would posit further material factors with respect to human nature which would deflect any ostensibly prudential temptation to tamper with taste. Lewis is not, I believe, a hedonist in value theory. I assume at the present juncture he would take the route of Mill in invoking Socrates and the sapient man.

By reversal of the deficiencies named, I suppose that we have characteristics of the person of 'good taste' (except he really needs little of the
second capacity; it serves only to assure others that he is a person of taste
since he can give some account of it). Where it seems that the critic
has qualifications which go beyond the possession of good taste is in two
areas of knowledge: (a) analysis of the object, and (b) understanding of
other persons or knowledge of standard human nature in such a way as
to make conditional predictions possible.

(a) Although we here avoid going into any discussion of the distinction between aesthetic inherent values and other inherent values,
or (if all inherent values be broadly classed as aesthetic) between 'high'
inherent values and others, I opine that one criterion of degree is that
the former induce experiences which are quasi-noetic; the object and
human nature are such that there is normally a consummatory effect
rather than an instrumental and transitive one, but this is in part because
the phenomenal object is engrossing enough to keep interest in it rather
than leading away from itself to practice or to some other contemplative
interest. Borrowing a phrase from another tradition, there is an objective
'fittingness' here, not a fittingness as a utility but apparently a fittingness
to the perceptual-emotional apperceptive powers. Not only does one in
appreciation wander around—visually, 'auditorily' or in imagination—
in the object, but it correlatively seems to be a feature of aesthetic
criticism that one attempts to point out in the object the features in
virtue of which the positive aesthetic value is felt. (If there is positive
ugliness, there is presumption that this also can be done; but I believe
that the locus which would be pointed to would be that which is taken
to 'spoil' an otherwise nice effect.) I do believe—whether it is achieved
by some direct raising from the subliminal to the conscious or whether
by a fused rapid use in imagination of Mill's canons of induction—we
are often able to tell in respect of what features of an object we have
certain feelings; we can distinguish in respect to which components we
tend to get the ingredients of certain complex attitudes or emotions.
Competent critics, I do suppose, possess an exceptional amount of this
sort of skill—in reference to their own experience and in a way which
is applicable to many other persons. The critic can, of course, point out
some of these features even when he happens personally not to be feeling
the 'effect'. A few of his references may go back to the physical object,
but the object which is mostly under analysis is a public phenomenal

---

The last item, under (E), below, affords suggestion of the pride man may take in
consistency and, indeed, in moral values. Lewis is certainly not an egoistic hedonist
in ethics. Perhaps when the final evaluation (the ethical evaluation) is rendered, a self-
censorship will be called for out of deference to social health.

550

R. W. BROWNING

object, the publicity of which banks upon fundamental similarities in instances of human nature.[108]

(b) The critic makes some 'law-like' statements relating a certain object and the experiences of men under certain circumstances. The statements may be construed as conditional predictions. This goes beyond the activity of the man who simply exemplifies good taste. The latter may have done well in his private aesthetic assessments, but he may not have attended to the tastes of others or developed any skill at relating the deliverances of his taste to theirs. He may manifest right sensitivity without forecast. He is not a critic. One supposes that he could learn to be a critic. How much would his becoming a critic be a matter of learning to notice and to articulate explicitly what he already inchoately but reliably discerns? How much would it be a matter of his attaining psychological knowledge of others? And in this domain would the psychological knowledge be of the discursive sort such as would be creditable in psychology in virtue of correlations between himself and others in past experiences with objects of specified characteristics, or would it be the product of a skill of an intuitive sort, perhaps such as the novelist or dramatist himself possesses as marked by his descrying how a personality will react to a certain situation? In the latter case, can the skill be learned or quite significantly improved through effort? These questions will be left. I will only opine that the critic goes beyond the man of good taste *both* in the capacity to discern the structure of the aesthetic object, dealing mediately with its structural factors and their integration in the whole, and in capacity to sense how it is likely to affect others, particularly those who are more or less close to exemplifying standard human nature. I find it a bit difficult to suppose that the latter skill is a matter of fusing the results of an almost unconscious rapid use of, say, Mill's canons of induction; on the other hand, I find it difficult to imagine the structure of the skill in any other way, though an inner 'role-taking' plus the deposits of past knowledge seems a little more plausible. I do read Lewis as believing that the skill is greatly subject to improvement

[108] Strictly it is impossible to prove that any two individuals have the 'same' phenomenal object (or highly similar phenomenal objects), but if—as they keep talking about it (or their respective objects)—they find themselves agreeing about relationships in it, this is taken as confirmation. And when they find themselves making almost no sense to each other, this may be taken as negating the supposition. I do suppose that both native ability and previous experience have much to do with an individual's 'making' of a phenomenal object in perceptual experience. Some persons may lack the native endowment which is requisite for effecting certain perceptual discriminations or for integrating certain elements into certain wholes. Primitive art and some forms of abstract art based on sensory elements will (I guess) have more nearly universal appeal than complex dramatic forms which involve a larger concatenation of factors and which for concrete materials draw upon habitudes of a local culture.

if indeed not wholly a product of learning. He speaks of "the necessary discipline of those who would . . . cultivate that discernment by which they may more surely and accurately judge, from a single inspection, the potentialities of an object for their own further value-findings in the presence of it, and those of other persons."[109]

Plainly the critic is engaged in making some large cognitive claims. It is worth reviewing for a moment where the shifts come from experiences which are noncognitive to those that are cognitive. The experiences of immediate value are noncognitive; they happen normally to take place on encounter with the objects possessing inherent value under certain conditions. An inference made that under such-and-such a pattern of particular circumstances an immediate value of certain quality and intensity will accrue is cognitive and formulates a terminating judgment. Cognitive and formulating a nonterminating judgment is the inference that whenever such-and-such general conditions occur for normal subjects encountering a certain object then immediate value will accrue in their experiences; this judgment is equivalent to the usual ascription of inherent value to the object (whether labeled 'aesthetic' or not). A judgment of comparative value will—directly or indirectly—make a reference to two or more immediate values, whether actual or hypothetical. A comparison of two simultaneous immediate values (in one's own experience, of course) will apparently for Lewis be a finding, and not itself be subject to error. One will find his preference. A comparison between an occurrent value and a remembered one or an envisaged one is subject to error. Comparative evaluation of objects has, no doubt, several modes and combinations of modalities.[110] In aesthetic evaluation

109 The alleged skill is a rather shocking phenomenon to an empiricist—is it not? Fancy, making predictions upon the basis of a single encounter! But Lewis, the empiricist, is able to be very empirical here, which involves him in speaking in a manner far removed from usual empirical habitudes. Although the prediction may be made at the first encounter with the object under question, it is not made, of course, simply on the basis of this solitary acquaintance but rather also on the basis of much other experience with different and with somehow 'similar' objects which have stirred many men.

110 One may appraise the objects for their potency as inherent values without regard to social conditions, as I presume we do in aesthetic criticism; or one might assess them with regard also to the social situations (in which case a popular 'song hit' may bulk 'quantitatively' much larger than the Mona Lisa and its reproductions); or, as I should suppose is common when making reference to existence, one may combine the estimates of inherent and instrumental value (in which case the new model of a car, together with its characteristic kinds of 'encounter', may exceed the popular song as a source of value); indeed, one had better consider not only the instrumental aspect but also the Gestalt aspect of contributory values; and if one is doing this in respect to theoretically alternative developments of civilization he may decide that a society richer in sensitivity to values—and possibly attainable through education—would not

the judgment is not about how many people will in fact enjoy the object, nor how much, nor what causes extraneous to the object influence their responses, nor how to get more persons to appreciate it. But the evaluation does relate to how properly qualified persons under appropriate circumstances would react to the given object and, in effect, to how they would preferentially rate it as an object of contemplation.

What is being judged? Overtly, it is a potency of an object. But it is a potentiality of the object to produce certain sorts of experience perhaps for normal men and certainly for a range of deviant men, namely, those who are more perceptive and sensitive (which qualifications probably can be specified—though not easily—in ways that are not circular). Not only is there a reference to human beings, then, but this reference involves itself in a kind of comparative estimation of them. Further, the judgment is comparative in another way, for it indirectly if not directly is rating the potency of the object against other possible objects.

The competent critic, in addition to possessing good taste, is one who (a) can analyze in an illuminating way the component 'motivating' factors in works of art, and (b) can discern the potencies of the objects with respect to qualified subjects in such a manner as to fit him for making conditional predictions about the experiences of the subjects.

Reverting for a moment to our question of whether there is a clean cleavage between 'objective' inherent values and 'genuine but non-objective' inherent values, the answer seems to be negative. In Lewis' sense of 'objective', I do not doubt that there are objective values; nor do I deny that in reference to a considerable elastic range of application the usage is a sensible one.[111] But where one decides to quit calling values 'objective' because they do not (under proper circumstances) affect the right kind of people, or enough people, in the right way, does seem to be quite arbitrary within a considerable range; it is upon this decision—and not some natural gulf in the phenomena—that the division between 'objective' and 'nonobjective' rests. With respect to aesthetic values (or high aesthetic values), the better qualified judges are more or less continuous with those who are slightly expert, who in

evaluate the jazz tunes and motor cars so highly, e.g., this 'possible' civilization, he may determine, would be better than ours. In this last we have the complexities of social evaluation implicitly before us.

[111] We acknowledge that inherent values bear a number of significant analogies with the objective correlates of sensory data. We do not pause to dwell upon important weaknesses of the analogies (besides the chief one discussed by Lewis) —such as relate to the presence in the one case of a discriminable organ, the close similarity of the perceptual organs of different persons, the relative unmodifiability of the datum through teaching, the slowness of fatigue in the case of vision and touch, etc.

turn are continuous with ordinary men, who in turn are continuous with those of inferior discernment. Even were their valuings more homogeneous than I suspect they are, the lower bounds of objects credited with 'high' objective aesthetic value (because of their potency) would still be arbitrary. "How high is 'high'?" Actually, I suspect that some important native factors do make for basic similarity, and a few variations in endowment make for diversity; plainly many cultural factors make for intracultural similarity and for intercultural diversity. I suppose that actual experts do, so to speak, have a limited currency for their expertness, but they are in principle experts for other men and not simply for themselves or for an isolated species of their fellows.

(E) In creating the moral sense, human nature through human living has erected another layer of values, beyond those which man's animal nature (including high-level aesthetic sensitivities derivative therefrom but excluding man's distinctive self-governing powers) could generate. Reflecting on their past uses of the capacity of self-administration, men do re-evaluate their own decisions and life-policies, and these evaluations do enter into their circumspect future conduct, as well as color their estimates of tracts of their own careers. Such coloring—and it is more than coloring—obtains both from prudential and from ethical critique. We have here eschewed a discussion of man's nature as a ground of the dimensions of the normative, for this would have taken us into the large topic of human nature in relation to the forms of rightness. But we do not trespass in noting that the account of human values could not begin to be even a complete inventory of types if it did not make reference to the values which emerge because of the reality of men as self-critical continuants. Nor do the values referred to simply stand alone; they have marked 'contributory' roles. Lewis rightly observes that any name that is "to serve as a synonym for the immediately and intrinsically valuable" will have to be adequate to cover "the wide variety of what is found directly good in life," including "the sense of integrity in firmly fronting the 'unpleasant' " and "the benediction which may come to the defeated in having finished the faith."[112] If in Lewis' account the genesis of the value-aspect of such 'integrity' is that of being first an instrumental good, resident in disposition and personal character, there can nevertheless be no doubt that it is an inherent value in normal human recognition. It has this status to the self-conscious agent—whether he is a prig or not—and it is an inherent value to the impartial spectator.

[112] AKV, p. 405. Cf. GNR, p. 70.

A remark was promised upon the relation of varieties of valuings and a teleological ethics.

In order to get an ethics of any social teleological sort (or for that matter, of certain non-teleological sorts) it is requisite "that some valuations have the significance of empirical cognition."[113] It is not requisite, however, that men have any particular degree of similarity in their values (provided their varied goods can be known) in order for there to be the materials of moral decision. Accordingly, since I opine that Lewis does have recourse to similarities in establishing predications of 'objective' inherent values, I believe that he does on this point an extended work of super-erogation so far as his ethics is concerned; his discussions nevertheless are very interesting for aestheticians and for those concerned with the epistemic status of 'properties'—in this case of value-properties. It is obvious, of course, that similarities of men make value-planning easier than it otherwise would be. And it can be argued that as dissimilarities become great, cognition across the differences becomes increasingly difficult—a difficulty which is rendered more vivid when we are called upon to cognize the values of members of other species.

I will not attempt here to break down into several species what all may go under the general rubric of subjectivistic-relativistic theory of value to see which may permit and which may preclude an objective normative ethics. If moral 'judgment' were wholly assimilated to valuation and valuation were not knowledge, the outcome is obviously negative. But for Lewis valuation is cognitive, and ethics is not valuation. He breaks with the Utilitarians and Dewey, and goes in the direction of Kant here. Lewis' remark that just because I like or dislike oatmeal for breakfast is no moral criterion for legislating what the family will eat epitomizes the distinction between right and value and the possibility of great variety in the latter. If the moral principles (however they be derived or authenticated) do not allow any first personal valuations to determine moral legislation but instead are protective of the value-interests of individuals up to some reasonable point of noninjury (or even small injury) to others, it would seem that objective morality is compatible with a welter of most idiosyncratic valuings. Admittedly, however, things are more neat with regular sorts of human values, particularly if these are nonpredatory and even noncompetitive. The acute practical problems arise over the conflicts. But since one cannot wish them out of existence he may get moral comfort from moral judgments on the valuings themselves—I do, and I wonder if Lewis does

[113] AKV, p. 400.

not also in the form of some tacit supposition that there are healthy as opposed to unhealthy valuings as determined by a norm of human nature which is not an average but a natural ideal. Consider: if one person is made extremely happy by sadistic activity but it can be channeled in ways which hurt others very little (or he can even be fooled into thinking his 'victims' are suffering) is it good on the whole that he be allowed his fun? Or, take the same idea generalized into a possible ideal Utilitarian community: divide the population into a large group and a small group; condition the large group to be sadistic and induce martyr-complexes in the small group; then let there be great happiness as the majority relish their persecution of the minority! True, there are dangers that the majority might pick some of the wrong persons as objects of persecution. But I think we feel a repulsion to the proposal on more grounds than that it might go astray and on more grounds than our opinion that it is impossible. If we have a notion of standard human nature, and take its fulfillment to be the summum bonum, then we can obviate the perverse forms of pleasure and satisfaction which human nature, conditioned in certain special ways, does find or could be made to find in immediacy. We do not have to wait until the evidence of the workings of alternative value-economics are in, and possibly show that sadism, etc., does not pay well individually or socially. Intuitional ethicists can provide themselves with this sort of answer at once—but outsiders question their intuitions. A naturalistic moralist will require elaborate material truths about human psychology to ground his natural norms which are to yield the same moral outcome.

There are problems which have to be left for ethics in seeking the moral basis of a strategy of organizing the flow of value-experiences. The sharper issues here pertain not to the variety of men's valuations but to the rivalries and oppositions among them. Of course, some values enhance other values, some can be teamed up well with others in obvious modes of organizations, and some value-realizations are relatively independent of others. However, of these latter, many possible realizations are to be seen as rather generally 'competitive' in view of the limitations of time and effort, even when these do not exhibit more patent incompatibilities. Certain inherent values may stand in essential antinomic relations to others, as Nicolai Hartmann suggested.[114] Worst of all, some actual and possible valuings stand in a predatory relation to other valuings. The consumption of other animals by the animal man points to a large range of such cases. The values of competitive triumph (many of which are very highly regarded in our culture) as well as the

114 *Ethics*, Vol. II; pp. 219f., 430ff.

values of sadism and cruelty (which are seldom praised under these names but which are more than rarely enjoyed under other labels) are conspicuous cases of predatory valuings. A teleological ethics which utilizes a criterion which turns on quantity of value may discover itself to be possessed of some morally unusual results if certain predatory values are found to be of extremely great value to their experients. Lewis, it may be added, does not endorse a straight Utilitarianism and possesses a formal theory of rights which presumably avoids deciding in favor of the sadist who promises to get a sufficiently great elation.

*Summary.* Valuations of objects, in Lewis' view, are cognitions; they are not the immediate value experiences themselves, which are noncognitive, but they relate to the possibilities of occurrence of such experiences.

Human nature in action has fixed the intension of certain terms, among which is (intrinsic) 'value'. Progress is not made by philosophers or psychologists who give false analyses of its intension, for instance by substituting some formula about behavior or conation for 'value' or 'good'. Human nature (like animal nature) is naturally telic. It has conation attached to actions seen as leading to natural good and to responses seen as avoiding natural evil. Men learn what things cause good and bad in experience, and they are thereby launched upon many sorts of predications of value and upon many comparisons.

Values in objects—values inherent and instrumental—have a status of being potentialities; but this potentiality is with reference to the possibility of producing immediate value in experience. Among the various relationships in which a potency for producing value may stand, attention has been drawn to several. Inherent value may be predicated in relation to any hypothetical (as well as actual) sentient organism; when practically devoid of any further limit, such values may be predicated as almost pure potentialities; since there are myriads of such potentialities, the notion is almost useless except for philosophical purposes, and actual predications in this mode are pretty much restricted to reference to man. Inherent value may be predicated in relation to any actual man; values of this type were called 'genuine' values even though the individual is idiosyncratic in the pertinent respects. Inherent values may be predicated in relation to normal men, over a period of time; values which thus qualify intersubjectively and over a period of time were denominated 'objective'. As evidenced by Lewis' desire to treat inherent (and instrumental) values of objects as properties and as parallel with other public properties, they are tacitly predicated in relation to a standard human nature. The complete parallel of value properties and other properties, however, is not affirmed by Lewis. Although all ascriptions of properties must have commenced with the expressive meaning, in science and to some degree in common sense we have, with respect to some properties, substituted objective tests for their presence. This pattern has not been—and one would think for Lewis will not be—followed in the case of inherent value. He does not advocate—as much as one might expect—the development of a science (or of sciences) of values. Instead of blowing Deweyan trumpets here, he seems to acquiesce in roughly the present demarcation of the sciences, the domain of which does not include much empirical knowledge of values.[115] However, he does consistently assert that aesthetics is an empirical science.[116] In relation to the meaning of 'objectivity' and its application to inherent values, one is troubled about the possibility of other conditionings of man than those with which we are familiar. Presumably there is an attempt to avoid any 'culture-bound' notion of man along with recourse to a conception of standard human nature which recognizes that man is a cultural being.

The assessment of the 'social value' of an object or arrangement is a concern of conscientious members of a self-directing society. This evaluation is an impersonal assessment of the object on the whole and with regard for actual conditions. Despite manifest conflicts of interest, the notion has meaning, Lewis insists. (I suggested the possibility of a 'better' and 'worse' without a formula for the 'best'.) This complex mode of evaluation requires placing the object in a scale by successive acts of finding preferences; and surely, if Lewis allows that there may be a clash of preferences of different persons, he must be having recourse to the sapient man. Strictly, the appeal to the fact of preference must be qualified in an important way. It is not an appeal to actual preference; it is an appeal to what would be the preference of an extraordinarily informed and omni-empathetic person. In so far as one attempts to give actual body to the notion, one is disturbed, for the criterion of direct preferring will not establish objective assessment of alternative courses of social action if men selected as most qualified by some independent criterion tend to be markedly different in their preferrings. I am not sure of the actual convergence of preferences of such men. If preference is allowed in respect to Gestalt properties of whole alternative cultures, I strongly suspect that there will not be convergence of preferences. But I incline to believe that Lewis does not intend to allow his sapient judge to evaluate Gestalt and contributory values beyond individual lives, although he certainly does intend to have these organic factors

115 OSI, p. 69.
116 AKV, pp. 468f.

considered within individual lives. In principle, then, he keeps to objectivity, and the hypothetical sympathetic preferer acts as the agency of nonquantitative 'summing up' of the results. The summing up is, however, itself an act of preference, and hence what sort of human nature is supposed to be exemplified in the preferer is crucial. He cannot be so 'impartial' as to have no preference.

There is recourse to another kind of sapient man in predications of high aesthetic value, which again presumes comparative assessment. Objective values of high aesthetic standing are predicated in relation to (I believe) an ideally perceptive and healthily sensitive man. He is still conceived as a man. Actual connoisseurs and critics are connoisseurs and critics among and for men, and not just for a little deviant group. Aesthetic expertness, although it is directed toward the object, cannot be out of relation to the possible subjects who make the object an aesthetic one. The critic excels his fellows in the discernment of aesthetic objects and of the cooperation of their features toward the integral effect, and he makes 'law-like' statements about the objects which amount to predictions of what certain men would experience under certain conditions. The judgment is doubly a comparative one for it is asserting high aesthetic value and the men who concern him are the men who are appropriately sensitive.

If there seems to be a contradiction between ascriptions of inherent aesthetic value which is discerned in the object and holding that the possibility of some experience of satisfaction in a subject is necessary for the kind of goodness objects can have, presumably these can be reconciled by supposing there to be in the object a differential organized correlate of the possible experience, while this structure would not be an inherent value if it were not for the fact that it makes an immediate experience of value possible. Supposing, contrary to fact, that the same structure existed without the possibility of the experience, it would not be a value. The structure attended to and talked about by the critic is not the physical structure but the phenomenal object. It seems to me that the allegations of its objectivity and of its aesthetic rank are based in reference to human materials which exist in gradations. The allegations are sensible; but they are arbitrary in the sense that the lower limit of 'high aesthetic value' and the lower limit of aesthetic value itself are ultimately matters of arbitrary stipulation in a range of phenomena.

Lastly, we did not totally pass over a deposit which is made in the realm of inherent values by the reflection of men on the discharge of their own moral agency. Human beings "take a hand in conditioning themselves." "The satisfactions so findable in self-determined activity, directed in accord with our convictions of the right" may be called "goods of integrity." Their value, "as contributory to a life to be found good in the living of it, can be preeminent."[117]

ROBERT W. BROWNING

DEPARTMENT OF PHILOSOPHY
NORTHWESTERN UNIVERSITY

[117] GNR, p. 70.

## 20

## D. W. Gotshalk

### C. I. LEWIS ON ESTHETIC EXPERIENCE
### AND ESTHETIC VALUE

LEWIS has not written extensively on esthetics, and what he has written seems to be more an effort to fit a discussion of this field into the prearranged framework of his epistemology than a fresh and independent treatment of esthetical problems. Perhaps, as a result of this, a certain amount of confusion and paradox appears to exist in Lewis' treatment, and it is mainly to an aspect of this that attention will be directed in the following discussion of Lewis' views of esthetic experience and esthetic value. Our primary references will be to Appendix B of MWO entitled "Esthesis and Esthetics," and two chapters in AKV, Chapter XIV: "Inherent Value and the Esthetic" and Chapter XV:"Esthetic Judgment."[1]

### I

The explicit theory of esthetic experience that Lewis develops is briefly that esthetic experience is the absorbed contemplation of directly presented content for its own sake. Thus, Section 3, Chapter XIV, AKV: " 'Esthetic' here connotes, first and foremost, the aboriginal empirical apprehension of what is directly presented and is contemplated in its value-character as given."[2] Further,

'The esthetic' carries with it some connotation of pause, of contemplative release; as 'the moral,' has its connotation of the attitude which looks toward action and which, in its orientation to the present, is preoccupied with what is signalized as further possible. The two are not wholly exclusive of one another or incompatible: nevertheless the esthetic attitude is at odds with the normal active attitude which, like walking, preserves its equilibrium by continually moving forward. The one would appreciate the given in its own given character; the other would make use of it as a cognitive clue. Thus the esthetic apprehension calls for suspension of this forward-moving élan of life and a

---

[1] C. I. Lewis, *Mind and the World-Order* (New York: Chas. Scribner's Sons, 1929), hereafter cited as MWO; *An Analysis of Knowledge and Valuation* (La Salle, Ill.: Open Court Publishing Co., 1946), hereafter cited as AKV.

[2] AKV, p. 438.

recovery from the continual distraction of it from the present. And although all experience is esthetic in the broad sense of being presentation of some quality-complex in which value or disvalue is directly findable, it becomes esthetic in the narrower sense which is more appropriate, only if it becomes object of the esthetic attitude; only if the experience is marked by absorption in the presented content on its own account.[3]

There is a minor discrepancy between Lewis' various descriptions of esthetic experience that should be removed before proceeding. In MWO, Lewis seems to regard what he calls in the above passage 'esthetic experience in the narrower sense' as an abstraction and a fiction. Thus, he writes:

The given, as here conceived, is certainly an abstraction. Unless there be such a thing as pure esthesis (and I should join with the critic in doubting this), the given never exists in isolation in any experience or state of consciousness.[4]

Again: "There is no such thing as 'esthetic' experience," since "all experience has both the aspect of value and the aspect of sign: it is at once esthesis and cognitively significant."[5] The prima facie implication of these views is that the 'forward-moving élan of life' mentioned in the AKV passage above is never absent from experience and the full contemplative pause necessary for the esthetic experience in the narrower sense is never present. Hence, esthetic experience in the narrower sense is a fiction. Perhaps, in the interval between writing MWO and AKV, Lewis came to believe that the esthetic may be not only an *element* in all experience but itself a major type of experience. In any case, the two views are reconcilable by holding that an experience insofar as it is esthetic is contemplative absorption in presented content, and arrest of movement and of interest beyond the present. Whether there is any instance of experience that is wholly this and nothing more need not be decided.

This view of esthetic experience seems at first glance very persuasive not only because it appears to grow naturally and neatly from Lewis' epistemology, but also because it appears to fit into certain views of esthetic experience that have had wide currency. Prall's theory of the 'esthetic surface' mentioned by Lewis himself,[6] Münsterberg's theory of isolation in the present, Bullough's psychical distance, as well as the general belief that the esthetic is the qualitative, the immediate, and the intuitive, are cases in point. However, when one studies Lewis' precise

3 AKV, p. 439.
4 MWO, p. 54.
5 AKV, p. 405.
6 AKV, p. 438.

view more carefully in the special context of his own system, serious difficulties begin to emerge. Indeed, one seems to be confronted with a puzzling dilemma. Lewis wishes to make all immediate apprehension indubitable, noncognitive, final, and infallible, and to construe the 'esthetic' as the form par excellence of immediate apprehension. Yet, if esthetic experience is this, then, on Lewis' system, it becomes impossible to say strictly that one can have an esthetic experience of a work of art or natural object, or even have an esthetic experience of esthetic values as Lewis has defined these. Let me briefly point up this dilemma.

We need not question whether it is psychologically possible or axiologically advisable to contemplate the immediate qualities of experience "for the sake of the value so realizable in immediate experience."[7] Nor need we question whether "There can be no such thing as failure of correctness in the apprehension of a value-quality characterizing immediate experience."[8] The point is that if infallible and noncognitive apprehension or a subform of this is esthetic experience, as Lewis holds, it is not the type of contemplative experience we have of works of art or natural objects, nor the type of contemplative experience we can have of esthetic values in Lewis' sense.

To take the last point first: esthetic values in Lewis' sense are strictly beyond the range of esthetic experience as he describes it. "Esthetic values," Lewis tells us, "are a subclass of inherent values."[9] That is, they are extrinsic values, inherent in things, and consist "in a potentiality of the thing for conducting to realization of some positive value-quality in experience."[10] Thus, esthetic values are values in objects such as natural entities and works of art, and, like all values of this type, are independent of a particular person or subject. A value property of an object

is not relative to any *particular* experience, or to experience of any particular person, but is an independent character of the thing, inasmuch as any particular experience may fail to be indicative of the character of experience in general to which it is capable of conducing.[11]

Now, if esthetic values are a type of extrinsic or inherent value, and if inherent value is a potentiality to generate immediate quality that exists independently in things and that may be misapprehended in any particular experience of things, then it seems clear that an experience

7 AKV, p. 438.
8 AKV, p. 433.
9 AKV, p. 434.
10 AKV, p. 432.
11 AKV, p. 458, italics in text.

that is always infallible and that is limited to immediate quality cannot in itself be said to be an experience of esthetic values in Lewis' sense. This infallible experience limited to immediate quality may be a basis on which you might *infer* the existence of esthetic values as above defined. But in itself it cannot be said to be an experience of these values because these values are independent qualities and are not disclosed infallibly and indubitably, as immediate qualities are, in any particular immediate experience.

Second, regarding works of art (and natural objects) : we often fail to apprehend the values of a work of art correctly. Certainly, it is possible to overrate or underrate an artistic production, not merely in retrospective *judgment* but during the *actual experience* of the production. At least, there is nothing prima facie infallible in any given experiential apprehension of the values of a work of art (or of a natural object). Moreover, the experience of works of art (and natural objects) usually involves cognitive activity, often of considerable range. In listening to a piece of music for its contemplative values, each moment may be filled with expectation, and as the piece proceeds, with remembrance. A whole tissue of cognitive acts may enter into the grasp of the music.[12] Similarly, in apprehending the expressive quality, not of a tone or word or color, but of a vast tonal or verbal or color structure for its own sake, some relating of the diverse expressive elements and organizing them into a totality in one's consciousness, is part of grasping for its own sake what is in these total objects. Thus to limit esthetic experience to a kind of noncognitive and infallible apprehension is to make it just *not* the kind of contemplative *experience* we have of works of art (and extensive natural objects), and is to put these entities themselves, as well as the objective values in them, strictly beyond the range of esthetic experience.

## II

It may be interesting to speculate on why Lewis came to hold a theory of esthetic experience that places works of art and esthetic values beyond the range of esthetic experience. The obvious reason remains the most convincing, viz., that Lewis is simply extending the distinctions of his epistemology to esthetics without realizing the peculiar hazards of this process. In the epistemology, there is a sharp distinction between immediate experience and judgment, presentational certainties and objective probabilities. This type of distinction,

12 Cf. Stuart M. Brown, Jr., "C. I. Lewis' Esthetics," *Journal of Philosophy*, 68, No. 6 (March 16, 1950), 150.

and all it implies, is carried over into the discussion of esthetic phenomena, with the result that esthetic experience is interpreted as a kind of infallible, noncognitive apprehension of immediate quality, and, to balance this, the objects and values in objects recognized conventionally (and by Lewis) as esthetic in the highest degree, are inevitably placed in a mediate, judgmental, probability area, and thus, strictly speaking, beyond the field of esthetic experience.

Perhaps, there is an even deeper source of the difficulties here under consideration. This is a vestigial trace in Lewis of the faculty psychology which stratifies the mental life into layers—esthetical, logical, ethical, utilitarian, and allows no interpenetration of these layers. Lewis makes a very real effort to work free of this compartmentalization of mind and conscious life. He achieves notable success in suggesting that esthetic values are not a special class of values but simply values taken under a certain orientation,[13] and esthetic objects are not exclusive things but simply things as inducing a certain type of mental orientation.[14] But the corollary of this in theory of mind is not fully developed, so that the mind is viewed not as a complex of elements all of which may intermingle with any one in dealing with this one element's object, but is viewed too often as a set of distinct elements each of which operates exclusive of the others: immediate apprehension is noncognitive and cognition is nonimmediate, immediate apprehension is infallible and cognition only probable, etc.

When one turns away from Lewis' esthetic analysis with its background epistemology and psychology to that free and intent experience of works of art and natural objects that gains from them the values imbedded there for contemplation, it seems obvious that this experience involves no exclusive faculty or exclusive type of immediate apprehension but the *whole* self engaged with all of its powers mobilized for contemplation. Even action enters, as when one changes one's position in viewing a picture or natural landscape; and certainly cognition enters, as when one recognizes the developing meaning of a musical theme or dramatic idea, and recalls and anticipates the larger whole of which the moment of the object now before one is a part. Indeed, there is no element of the self useful in following and gaining a grasp of the whole object as it offers itself to us for our intrinsic contemplation, that can be excluded from this contemplation. Moreover, such a type of contemplation on account of its purpose or style of direction—not its

13 AKV, p. 445.
14 AKV, p. 440.

component faculties—is unique among human processes.[15] If one does not wish to give it the name 'esthetic' because one's epistemology forbids this, some other name will do. But in any case it is primarily dominated by a concern for what is in the object of attention for its own sake, and clearly it puts both the object and its esthetic values fully within the range of its operation.

From the account so far given, it might easily be concluded that Lewis' theory of esthetic experience and esthetic values lacks all plausibility. Such is by no means the case. In AKV, Lewis preserves the basic dualism or dichotomy of the immediate and noncognitive versus the mediate and cognitive by devoting two chapters to esthetic problems, the first chiefly to his theory of the esthetic experience as immediate experience, and the second mainly to his theory of esthetic judgment as cognition of esthetic values. But in both chapters are long passages on esthetic objects that soften the 'dualistic' framework within which his esthetic theory is stated. This discussion of esthetic objects gives considerable plausibility to Lewis' theory of esthetic experience and esthetic values. For these objects are conceived, as they well might, as generating intrinsically satisfying experiences. Why should not such objects be assigned the esthetic values when esthetic experience is defined as a type of intrinsically satisfying experience?

The plausibility of this position vanishes, however, when one inquires into what esthetic experience as just defined can really apprehend, and when one learns that on Lewis' premises it can apprehend the immediate only, and that esthetic objects and the values of these objects, as all other things that are objective, are themselves mediate, and matters of inference and judgment, and independent of any particular immediate experience. Then, the paradox of Lewis' position becomes plain, and we see that on this position we have an experience called esthetic that strictly cannot itself be said to grasp esthetic values or esthetic objects, and values and objects called esthetic that, while capable of being judged cognitively, cannot strictly be said to be grasped by esthetic experience.

### III

In the two chapters in AKV devoted to esthetic topics, Lewis' treatment has the range if not the solidity that is characteristic of his handling of other problems. Many themes are introduced, each of which could form the subject of a critical essay. It is true that most of these

15 Cf. *Art and the Social Order* (Chicago: University of Chicago Press, 1947, 1951; New York: Dover Publications, Inc., 1962), Chap. I, II.

themes are treated rather incidentally, while the main discussion concerns esthetic experience, esthetic objects and esthetic values, and their cognition. However, it may be interesting to mention at least one of these themes, before trying to indicate briefly what further Lewis' discussion of esthetics sums up to.

Lewis requires of esthetic objects that they provide an enduring good, as if a momentary rainbow in the sky soliciting a passing interest were not as authentic and complete an esthetic object as a mountain lasting centuries and making an indelible impression on many generations. When he turns to works of art, this specification of the enduring indirectly leads Lewis to speculate as to what *is* the entity which is *the* work of art—what entity is it "which is termed 'Beethoven's Fifth Symphony'?"[16] The problem seems to him especially acute in regard to literary and musical works which are generally reproduced in transient forms and in great quantity, and less so with a cathedral, or a piece of sculpture.[17] The problem leads Lewis to suggest the existence of an esthetic essence, a complexus of common properties, found in all authentic instances of any thing properly bearing the title of that work of art, and to conclude that "the direct object of (esthetic) contemplation is an esthetic essence."[18]

The most obvious comment on this speculation is that the direct object of contemplation in any absorbed esthetic experience is the full concrete diversified and particularized entity before one, and not any "qualitative and abstract essence which is here incorporated, and is theoretically repeatable in some other physical object."[19] Thus, when one is directly contemplating a symphony it is the tone as emitted and structured by this particular band of musicians in all the diversity it has under this particular conductor, that is being really attended to. The ghostly complexus of common properties in it and other such presentations is only incidental in such absorbed contemplation. Where this 'essence' may be of some moment, so far as it is, is in general or critical discussion seeking to make generalizations that might apply abstractly to many presentations. In other words, such a complexus of properties might be a useful point of reference for getting a few *general* cognitions and assertions straight in regard to a work of art. But in direct esthetic contemplation the concern of the perceiving at full tide is with the whole *individualized* perceptual entity not merely an *abstract* essence,

16 AKV, p. 469.
17 AKV, p. 470.
18 AKV, p. 476.
19 AKV, p. 477.

and it is this individualized thing in all its concrete perceptual diversity therefore that *is* the esthetic object, the essence being a kind of interim surrogate useful for general orientation perhaps, but not itself the 'live creature'.

Lewis disclaims that his task in AKV is "to attempt any contribution to the science of esthetics,"[20] and observes "that the science of esthetics remains largely underdeveloped."[21] Yet he states a very interesting conception of a science of esthetics,[22] which is connected with his general theory of scientific knowledge, and has the same merits and limitations of this general theory. Also, he carries his conception of valuation as a form of empirical knowledge into his discussion of esthetic values, and seeks to show that esthetic values are as objective and as open to empirical survey and determination as the factual properties of natural entities explored by the empirical sciences. This conception also has exactly the merits and limitations of Lewis' general theory that valuation itself is a form of empirical knowledge, and is more suitably discussed, as is the other thesis just mentioned, in a critical account of Lewis' general position than in a discussion limited to Lewis' esthetics.

What is perhaps very worthy of remark in this context, apart from the concepts and suggestions previously considered, is Lewis' special regard for the esthetic moment in life. Not only does Lewis show throughout his discussion a quiet yet evident personal relish for the esthetic. In his theory he holds the esthetic to be a self-justifying good of the highest type and possessing the form of good that any other possible self-justifying good exhibits.[23] It is ironic that in a book devoted to an analysis of knowledge and of valuation as a form of knowledge, the supreme value assigned to knowledge is its subservience to action. Lewis regards as merely an occupational disease, the tendency of the scholar to impute an interest in truth for its own sake as "the characteristic *final* purpose of knowing."[24] Insight apparently is not at all a characteristic supreme good, but is mainly a guide to action, although it is somewhat difficult to see to what action AKV might lead, except of course the writing of essays and books on its insights!

In this particular attitude toward the noetic and the esthetic, I believe, Lewis is unconsciously reflecting the conditions of our times rather than stating the nature of the case and its legitimate claims. In

20 AKV, p. 466.
21 AKV, p. 469.
22 AKV, pp. 466-469.
23 AKV, p. 439.
24 AKV, p. 442, italics mine.

our times, the arts and the esthetic exist on the periphery of society, and the arts have little use except as objects of terminal enjoyment. Hence, the esthetic end, supremely embodied in the arts, seems properly conceived not only as a good for its own sake, but as the purest form of such a good. On the other hand, the sciences in our times have an almost overwhelming use in the development of technology, and vast consequences as means to action. Since the sciences in our times present by all odds the most impressive array of knowledge in existence, it seems appropriate to conceive all knowledge as instrumental, directed to action and the future, etc.

In some ways, the present situation of the arts and sciences in our culture is not as bad as it might be. But it does seem unfortunate to canonize this situation. There is so much more that can be legitimately demanded! No doubt, the supreme aim of the arts is the esthetic, conceived as a certain type of terminal experience. But so much more can be combined with this major end coherently and internally, and such a variety of multiple functions infused with the esthetic that the arts might easily move into the center of a society without distorting their major aim.[25] There is no internal reason why the arts must languish on the periphery, as they do at present.

Conversely, the vast service to technology and action furnished by scientific knowledge might well be further developed and certainly should not be disturbed. But the quest for knowledge can also be exciting in its own right, and, one of the great possibilities of value in human life can be ignored or obliterated by a disregard for the intrinsic satisfactions in knowing. Indeed, it is when these two aims—the instrumental and the final—are intimately combined in one operation, and knowledge is, as for instance, in nuclear physics today, a quest with its own exciting internal rewards for the knower as well as a promise of control of actions, that cognitive activity calls forth a maximum of human energy and leads to its greatest achievements.

The characteristic *final* purpose of knowing *is* knowing, or knowing has no final purpose at all, only an instrumental one. The problem in theory and practice is to understand this final purpose in proportion, neither discarding it as an aberration nor elevating it to an exclusive self-sufficient status. To put the whole matter very simply, it seems obvious that all knowing should be interesting, and if possible useful, but preferably both. The Greeks may have exaggerated the intrinsic values of knowing, but it seems no answer to exaggerate the instrumental values. Among human values, in sequestering to the arts and the

25 *Art and the Social Order*, Chap. X, secs. 2, 3.

esthetic terminal status par excellence and to the sciences and the cognitive with other things instrumental status par excellence, Lewis seems not merely to be echoing and perpetuating the exaggerations and deficiencies of our times, but also to be failing to conceive the character of these goods in the perspective of that universal experience, in which alone, according to his own theory of valuation, one grasps the full objective nature of a value.

D. W. GOTSHALK
DEPARTMENT OF PHILOSOPHY
UNIVERSITY OF ILLINOIS

## 21

## Mary Mothersill
## LEWIS AS MORAL PHILOSOPHER

I N the preface to *An Analysis of Knowledge and Valuation,* Lewis
writes:

The first studies toward this book were addressed to topics in the field of ethics.
But in the course of those earlier studies it became apparent that the conceptions
which I wished to develop should not stand by themselves; they required the
support of further considerations relating to values in general. In particular,
they depended on the premise that valuation is a form of empirical knowledge.
And the development of that thesis would, in turn, call for much which
must be antecedent. In consequence, the studies in ethics were put aside for
the time being, and the contents of this present volume may be viewed as
prolegomena.[1]

Lewis goes on to explain that in order to establish the cognitive
validity of value judgments, he found it necessary to work through a
detailed analysis of empirical knowledge in general—the problem of
Book II; and this in turn required the account of meaning and analytic
truth which he gives in Book I. His explanation is more than a piece
of retrospective editorializing; Lewis' preoccupation with ethical questions is manifest on almost every page of *An Analysis of Knowledge
and Valuation.* The order and arrangement of arguments, particularly
in Book III, would be baffling to anyone who did not recognize its propaedeutic function. Conversely, the thesis developed in *The Ground and
Nature of the Right,* while logically independent, would be difficult to
interpret or to appreciate without reference to the earlier work. Taken
together, the two books are to be understood in the light of the author's
announced plan:

We cannot finally escape the fact that ethics and epistemology and the theory
of meaning are essentially connected. And while it is ethics which is the capstone, the foundations must be laid in the examination of meaning.[2]

Philosophical critics of Lewis have concerned themselves chiefly
with the ground-work of the system; both the theory of meaning and

---

[1] C. I. Lewis, *An Analysis of Knowledge and Valuation* (La Salle, Ill.: Open Court
Publishing Company, 1946), preface vii. Hereafter cited as AKV.

[2] AKV, Preface xi.

the account of empirical knowledge have been discussed extensively and in detail. The ethical theory for which these preliminary studies are supposed to prepare the way has been neglected. Partly this is because the actual space which Lewis finally devotes to what he describes as the "peculiarly ethical problem" is rather small. Having completed the "foundations," he discovers, as it were, that the pyramid is all but complete; what has to be added is obvious and as Lewis holds, undiscussable. The 'ethical imperative' as such needs only to be made explicit. The distinction which Lewis observes and which confines ethical investigation to the problem of justice is idiosyncratic. Book III of *An Analysis of Knowledge and Valuation* and in particular the chapter on the summum bonum is taken up with discussion of the question of rational choice, of the "economy of values," of the nature of the "good life" and other topics which traditionally fall within the scope of moral philosophy. The ethical theory which emerges from this work when it is supplemented by the thesis of *The Ground and Nature of the Right* is neither radically new nor obviously implausible. In general outline, it represents a point of view which many contemporary philosophers share; Lewis holds, for example, that all values, economic, aesthetic or moral, have an essential relation to human enjoyment and suffering, that there are no supernatural goods or transcendental sources of authority. He also holds that to judge that an object is good or an action right is, or may be, to make a cognitive claim, one which is either valid or invalid and which is subject to rule-governed testing procedures. To be rational is to make consistent and intelligent choices in the light of one's conception of a life which, taken as a whole, will be found "good in the living." To be moral is to take account of other people's wishes, desires and aspirations as if they were your own and to remember that morally speaking there are no privileged persons: what is right for me must be right for anyone similarly situated. But in order to do what is objectively right, it is not enough to have good intentions; one must carry them out with intelligence and foresight. The concept of moral rightness is autonomous; it cannot be derived from any statements about the good. Nevertheless one can neither know one's duty nor carry it out without knowing what *is* good and how to achieve what is good.

Stated in these general terms Lewis' position is, as I have said, one which commends itself to many. It has historical parallels; Lewis acknowledges his affinity with Bentham (though with important qualifications). The position developed by Sidgwick in *Methods of Ethics* is similar to Lewis' doctrine in a number of important respects. There are contemporary philosophers with whom on disputed points Lewis shares common ground. Like Dewey, he believes that value judgments are continuous with factual judgments and that the attempt to draw a sharp line of separation is not only misguided but in its effects is a positive moral hazard. Like Santayana, he believes that all values are in the last analysis intrinsic and that they are all, just as they occur, democratically self-justifying. One could go on to multiply instances of apparent convergence and agreement. And yet it is peculiarly difficult to assess Lewis' contribution to ethics or to locate his theory within the tradition of American naturalism. This is the more surprising because of the importance which Lewis himself attaches to ethical studies and also because his contributions to logic and epistemology— in his view the 'foundations of ethics'—have been substantial and unquestionably distinguished.

A partial explanation is that Lewis has expressed his views on ethics in a way which raises a great many problems of interpretation. One does not see why he chooses to organize his arguments in the way he does; his manner of exposition is allusive and oblique. Claims which one would suppose to be generally acknowledged are introduced formally and hedged with qualifications while extremely controversial questions are disposed of simply in passing. Theories opposed to naturalism are not merely rejected, they are excoriated. Yet these theories are never specified, and the reader is left to reconstruct the position which Lewis' arguments are designed to refute. These ways of being difficult are certainly not peculiar to Lewis. Anyone who has tried to make an outline summary of *Methods of Ethics* will not be defeated by the involutions of Lewis' argument. And Dewey, whether from habit or policy, addressed his objections to trends, tendencies, 'movements of thought', rather than to identifiable theories. And yet Sidgwick's argument is clear enough if you take it piecemeal and notice at what points he abandons an impasse and tries to make a fresh start. There are clear and cogent passages in Dewey and even what is cryptic and diffuse is often persuasive, through sheer volume and force of repetition. With Lewis, on the other hand, every step offers fresh difficulties. The summary statement of his position which I have given above is not just an abstract. It is the result of interpretation and conjecture. Even if I were to adduce the textual evidence for each sentence of the summary, there would still be ample room for doubts and questions. If my statement *is*, as far as it goes, adequate, then Lewis' ways of expressing himself seems unnecessarily recondite. A utilitarian theory of value which avoids the alleged pitfalls of the naturalistic fallacy by treating moral rightness as an autonomous concept is not free of difficulties, but on the other hand it is not at all *recherché*. The obscurity in which Lewis invests the outlines of the theory has the further disadvantage that it prevents him from coming to grips with the real and obvious problems which must be dealt with. I do not think that this is the result of simple oversight on the part of Lewis. What causes trouble is the attempt to combine epistemological interests with certain moral considerations in a way which will not beg any substantive questions. Since anyone who sets out to deal with moral philosophy in a systematic way must make this attempt, the vicissitudes of Lewis' theory merit analysis. If in what follows I concentrate on the shortcomings of his theory, it is because I believe that for the solution of general problems, they are most instructive.

## I

Here are some of the problems of interpretation which confront anyone who tries to arrive at a clear statement of Lewis' position: (1) What exactly is the rationale of the distinction between ethics and theory of value? At first one thinks that ethics is to be confined to problems affecting criteria for moral decisions or choice and is concerned exclusively with the question 'what ought I to do'. Value theory accordingly would be concerned with exploring logical analogies between judgments to the effect that an object is good and ordinary descriptive statements, or as Lewis calls them, 'judgments of objective belief'. This accords with some of the things Lewis says and allows for the partial dependence of moral judgments on value judgments. He writes:

. . . although any moral judgment will, in application, always presume some value-judgment or judgments as antecedent, no evaluation of an objective existent can ever be sufficient by itself to resolve a question of right conduct.[3]

Ethics has to do with the highest and most general of moral principles, those which Lewis calls the Law of Moral Equality and the Law of Compassion.[4] But in practice, a person who was 'right minded', that is committed to direct his behavior in the light of these principles, would have to be able to act in such a way as to bring about good consequences. This in turn would require him to know, or have a way of finding out, what things *are* objectively good. The Law of Moral Equality does not, as Lewis says, "delineate the *content* of justice."[5] For that one needs a knowledge of empirical values. In the chapter in which he distinguishes the right from the good he notes:

[3] AKV, p. 530.

[4] *The Ground and Nature of the Right* (New York: Columbia University Press, 1955), p. 91. Hereafter cited as GNR.

[5] GNR, p. 95.

The achievement of the good is desirable but conformity to the right is imperative. . . . Nothing is strictly right or wrong except some possible activity or the manner of it, whereas in an equally strict sense anything under the sun may be good or bad.[6]

On this interpretation the distinction is intelligible and not unconventional. Prichard and others have thought that ethics should occupy itself only with questions of obligation and moral rightness. But this interpretation does not square with Lewis' repeated and emphatic contention that *every* valuation has normative import and dictates choices of action. When he says in the passage quoted above that conformity to the right is imperative, whereas the good is only desirable, he seems to overlook the wide range of application he has previously assigned to the notion of 'imperatives'. His fundamental thesis, the assertion of the essential bond between knowing, evaluating and acting is often stated in these terms. As he notes at the outset of *An Analysis of Knowledge and Valuation* "that to which value-terms apply is always characterized by something holding an imperative for action."[7] Or later:

To act, to live, in human terms, is necessarily to be subject to imperatives; to recognize norms. Because to be subject to an imperative means simply the finding of a constraint of action in some concern for that which is not immediate; is not a present enjoyment or a present suffering.[8]

This might be allowable as an extended, quasi-metaphorical use of 'imperative' which does not, except on a verbal level, conflict with the view that Laws of Justice and Compassion are the distinctively ethical and final imperatives. But it is not so easy to dispose of a further command or set of commands which Lewis also calls 'imperatives' and which, according to his account are universal, categorical, indemonstrable and practical. They have all the formal characteristics which are supposed to be peculiar to the ethical imperative. For example Lewis writes:

The final and universal imperative, "Be consistent, in valuation and in thought and action"; "Be concerned about yourself in future and on the whole"; is one which is categorical. It requires no reason; being itself the expression of that which is the root of all reason; that in the absence of which there could be no reason of any sort or for anything.[9]

Or later:

6 GNR, p. 59.
7 AKV, preface x.
8 AKV, p. 481.
9 AKV, p. 481.

The pertinent dictate of rationality will be: So act and so prefer that the manner of your acting and preferring will be that which, if consistently adhered to, you will be permanently best satisfied to have adopted.[10]

Thus the nature of the proposed distinction between value theory and ethics becomes very obscure. It is not that ethics has to do with decisions and value theory with judgments. Granting Lewis' claim that evaluations are a form of empirical knowledge, still, on his view, *every correct judgment of value* is implicitly normative; it "holds an imperative for action," by which, presumably, he means that it suggests or entails a reason for choosing. Moreover the imperative enjoining consistency and concern for one's future is not hypothetical and could not be translated into any kind of testable 'if-then' statement. It is based on a 'real definition', in Lewis' language an 'explicative statement'. It is not arguable: someone who was serious and who repudiated the imperative to be consistent or concerned for the future would, according to Lewis, be incapable of responding to *any* argument. Lewis acknowledges that the 'valuational' imperatives share the status of ethical imperatives.

. . . we may observe that the fundamental dictum of justice, "No rule of action is right except one which is right in all instances, and therefore right for everyone," is likewise [i.e., like the imperative to be consistent] not a principle acceptance . . . argument where natively the recognition of it should be absent. Logically considered, it is a tautology: it merely expresses a formal character of the correct or justified, implicit recognition of which is contained in acknowledgment of the distinction between right and wrong. Given this moral sense, recognition of the principle is mere self-clarification; and where the moral sense should be lacking, argument for this or any other principle of action would be pointless.[11]

What it comes to is this: ethics and value theory are both concerned with imperatives which are categorical rather than conditional and which determine rational decision or choice. But ethics deals only with those imperatives which enjoin, either under the Law of Compassion or the Law of Justice, a concern for other people.

(2) According to Lewis, what are the problems of philosophical ethics? In value theory the philosopher must make explicit the concept of the 'rational imperative', elucidate the claim that valuations are a form of empirical knowledge, and defend this thesis against a variety of objections and criticism. Does the moral philosopher proper have a similar assignment? One would think so: the ethical imperative and its final authority in matters of decision are not, according to Lewis, sub-

10 AKV, p. 548.
11 AKV, p. 482.

ject to question. But the rational imperative, to choose with a view to what will make life good on the whole, is not subject to question either. What does one do in a case of conflict? Presumably Lewis would say that the ethical imperative must prevail. But then what would be the status in such a case of the rational imperative? Would it be temporarily suspended or waived? Or was it all along to be thought of as conditional rather than categorical? Again: granting the validity of the Law of Compassion and the Law of Moral Equality, what is the relation between these highest principles and the traditional catalogue of 'moral duties'—telling the truth, paying one's debts, keeping promises, helping those in distress? Are the latter also beyond question? If they are, then how does one decide cases where by discharging one of these duties one must violate another? If they are not beyond question, then what is the ground of whatever authority they have? These are a few of the questions which Lewis' thesis immediately brings to mind. It would be unfair to object on the grounds that he does not dispose of these issues once and for all; they are extremely difficult. Moreover, *The Ground and Nature of the Right* is not a treatise but a set of lectures, and Lewis does not pretend to offer more than an outline sketch of his views. But the fact is that these questions are never mentioned either in the lectures or in *An Analysis of Knowledge and Valuation*. This omission is puzzling. The problem of moral conflict and the problem of relating the concept of duty in general to particular rules of conduct have been assumed to fall within the province of moral philosophy. If inconsequential, they are not obviously so. Why does Lewis ignore them?

(3) All action which is not reflexive or purely habitual is directed to the attainment of some anticipated good, that is, in Lewis' view, to the apprehension of some immediate value in experience. Such value is not a quality but "a dimensionlike mode which is pervasive of all experience."[12] It is unmistakably identifiable and ranges along a positive-negative axis. Value-disvalue is that mode or aspect of the given or the contemplated to which desire and aversion are addressed; and it is that by apprehension of which the inclination to action is normally elicited.[13] The rational man is he whose decisions and choices are consistently governed by the intention to maximize his experience of positive value over a given temporal span. This view sounds like strict and unqualified psychological hedonism. Lewis says that it is *similar* to hedonism, but he rejects the label. Why? He has given an answer but it

12 AKV, p. 401.
13 AKV, p. 403.

is one which  is relevant at best to ethical rather than psychological hedonism. It is to the effect that the term 'pleasure' suggests satisfactions which are "unsubtle and organic," that while it may be construed in a wider sense by an Epicurus or a Bentham, it is likely to mislead "the unwary and unsophisticated."[14] Now this may be a wise precaution; but the genuine philosophic puzzles which beset traditional hedonism, both as psychological theory and as ethical doctrine, are not of the sort which can be resolved by a change of terminology. The claim that all sensible or purposive action is aimed at securing value as disclosed in immediate experience may be defensible, but its defense would have to take account of the familiar difficulties formulated most succinctly by Butler. It cannot be established by fiat.

Because he holds that the ethical imperatives are autonomous and are not derivable from empirical questions of value, Lewis is not in Bentham's sense an ethical hedonist. But the delineation of the summum bonum, the final criterion of choice short of the ethical imperatives, is a task which falls within theory of value. The moral ideal (subject to the ethical critique) is "the life found good in the living" and is a further claim which is "not to be argued."[15] The summum bonum is the "final touchstone" of value; problems of choice must be referred ultimately to the question of what will contribute to "a life found good in the living." Lewis gives a detailed account of the procedures involved in deciding that question. I shall return to this topic later. A point on which he is most emphatic is that no appeal beyond the intimations of first-personal experience is required and that none is allowable. *A* can ask whether *B* has achieved self-realization, whether he is a useful member of society, whether he is a conscientious and right-minded man, but none of the answers will bear on the question whether *B* has achieved the summum bonum. Only *B* himself can answer that, and while he may not remember things accurately—he may forget, for example, how unhappy he was as a child—still there is no need, even if there were some way, to correct such mistakes. *B*'s life is 'good in the living' if he finds it to be so.

Where should this subordinate or 'pre-ethical' morality be located in the conventional schema for classifying ethical theories? Where *could* it go except under 'hedonism'? How else can one construe the identification of immediate with intrinsic value?

14 AKV, p. 405.
15 AKV, p. 483.

The immediately good is what you like and what you want in the way of experience; the immediately bad is what you dislike and do not want.[16]

. . . the only thing intrinsically valuable—valuable for its own sake—is a goodness immediately found or findable and unmistakable when disclosed: all values of any other sort, including all values attributable to objects, are extrinsic, and valued for the sake of their possible contribution to such realizations of the immediately good.[17]

Intrinsic value, which is that for the sake of which all other things are valued, belongs exclusively to occasions of experience as such; and value in objects consists in their potentiality for contributing goodness to such occasions.[18]

Ethical hedonism has been defended by very able philosophers. Those who admit the possibility of a systematic ethics, as traditionally conceived, and yet who reject hedonism as being patently inadequate are in error. When it is compared with alternative theories which are addressed to the same fundamental questions, hedonism is preeminently plausible. Why does not Lewis acknowledge his allegiance and exploit the resources of traditional doctrine? In order to convey the scope and structure of his own moral perspective he would, it is true, have to introduce qualifications and distinguish among pleasures as 'higher' and 'lower', or 'true' and 'false'. But he has to do that anyway and devotes considerable space to developing such themes as that the good life is preeminently active, "permeated with the quality of concern,"[19] "filled with the anxiety to achieve,"[20] or that the activity of work is "one of the most important values and perhaps the surest."[21] The problem of justifying discriminatory rankings of this sort without rejecting first principles are familiar and have been well-advertised by critics of hedonism since the time of Plato. This problem is genuine and cannot be disposed of by substituting the term 'immediate value' for the term 'pleasure'. For example, what would Lewis say about a person who affirmed wholeheartedly that he found his life "good in the living" but at the same time confessed that he had never been troubled by "anxiety to achieve" or "concern for the future" and had never done an honest day's work in his life?

(4) Why does Lewis insist that the method he proposes for assessing value is different from Bentham's method? It is hard to be sure that it actually *is* different. He rejects the literal interpretation of the cal-

16 AKV, p. 404.
17 AKV, p. 397.
18 AKV, p. 433.
19 AKV, p. 433.
20 AKV, p. 438.
21 AKV, p. 454.

culus on the grounds that intensities are not "extensive or measurable magnitudes which can be added or subtracted."[22] This difficulty has been widely recognized—Sidgwick has a good discussion of it—and Bentham himself suggests that the assumptions underlying the calculus have a quasi-axiomatic status. Lewis discovers an inconsistency in Bentham's account of the dimensions of 'propinquity' and 'remoteness'. Bentham seems to say—although he is not at all clear—that we should pay more attention to pleasures which are relatively close at hand, a notion which, as Lewis points out, is at odds with the fundamental point about being prudent. This too, as Lewis recognizes, is a comparatively minor matter. What he does object to is the suggestion that "the value in any whole of experience is simply the aggregate of the values in the separate experiences which make it up."[23] In one way this remark is puzzling, since, if the calculus is strictly speaking uninterpretable, then it is unclear what it would mean to speak about an 'aggregate of values'. Still it is clear enough what Lewis has in mind. Any temporal span of experience is or may be conceived as a *Gestalt* and the value of the whole is partly a function of the way the ingredient episodes are ordered in sequence. He writes:

... the value of an experiential whole may be affected not only by the values immediately found in its separate and included moments but by the relation of these moments of experience to one another. It may be that a life which begins badly but ends well is better than one which begins well but ends badly, even though the ingredient experiences which make it up should be as nearly comparable as could well be imagined and should differ only by what is involved in the different temporal order of them.[24]

Or later:

The value attaching to a whole of experience is not independent of the values realized in its constituent parts, but neither is it determined by them without reference to the manner of their composition.[25]

There is no reason to dispute this claim, but why does Lewis think that aside from the question of arithmetic procedures it is incompatible with Benthamism? Lewis, like Dewey, wants to stress the organic and consummatory character of experience, the mutual qualification of means and ends. This concern appears in many different passages:

22 AKV, p. 490.
23 AKV, p. 488.
24 AKV, p. 488.
25 AKV, p. 495.

. . . the small boy may work long and hard for the price of a circus ticket, but his labor will be infused throughout with the value-quality of vivid anticipation; and his later satisfaction at the circus may also be enhanced by honest pride in having earned his own enjoyment.[26]

A tramp in the hills is the more enjoyable for having an objective, and the attained objective is the more enjoyed because it has been so reached.[27]

The goodness of pursuing and attaining is not the goodness found in striving, regardless of the end pursued, plus the goodness found in having something desired, regardless of how it is attained. It lies peculiarly in the relationship between the active intent, the conation, and the realization.[28]

There is nothing in traditional hedonism which precludes ranking earned rewards higher than unearned rewards. At times it seems as though the real object of attack for Lewis is something quite different, the Hartleian idiom which Bentham uses in talking about experience. In rejecting the notion of an 'aggregate' Lewis speaks of living as "continuum of immediacy,"[29] one which is self-conscious, self-concerned and self-affecting", and he approves Bergson's concept of life as a "durée characterized by the tension of an élan vital."[30] The experience of listening to music, he believes, offers the best analogy. Now the question of how one should describe phenomenal experience, what should be emphasized, what left out, cannot be answered in the abstract. It depends on what the description is to be used for, what problem one is interested in. William James criticizes the 'Sensationalists' for treating consciousness as if it could be "chopped up in bits" and proposes that instead of speaking of chains or trains of thoughts we should speak of a "stream of thought." The point of this proposal, according to James's argument, is that the revised model will enable us to deal with certain riddles about perception, similarity and the concept of the self—riddles which on the older scheme were evidently insoluble. This is the context within which the merits of James's recommendation must be discussed. The interests which lead one to prefer a certain idiom for describing experience as such need not be technical ones; they may be dramatic and literary. Life, according to Virginia Woolf, is not "a series of gig-lamps symmetrically arranged. It is a luminous halo; a semi-transparent envelope. . . ." She was aware (at least part of the time), that life has, so to speak, its gig-lamp aspects; but she thought them uninteresting as topics for literature.

26 AKV, p. 486.
27 AKV, p. 498.
28 AKV, p. 498.
29 AKV, p. 495.
30 AKV, p. 498.

The question in the case of Lewis is, what is his point in stressing the flights rather than the perches in phenomenal experience? Sometimes, like Bergson, he writes as if to suggest that this is just the way life *is* and that any alternative vocabulary is incorrect or inappropriate. But surely this is a matter on which individual experiences may differ. Perhaps some people experience life as a *durée* animated by the *élan vital*; but for others life in its "phenomenal immediacy" may *be* a series . . . just one damn thing after another. If there are such differences, then Lewis by virtue of his commitment to the finality of first-personal assessments, would be bound to respect them.

The specific problems to which he thinks his concept of experience is relevant are those involving personal decisions and choice. Here his argument becomes very hard to follow. Assuming the correctness of the main thesis—that the objective value of an object lies in its potentiality for conducing to experiences of immediate value for some person or persons—and bearing in mind his contention that whatever is valuable "holds an imperative for action," what one would *expect* him to say is this: When faced by the need for a far-reaching decision—it is this kind that Lewis is primarily concerned with here—one ought to consult one's funded knowledge about what lines of action in the past have proved satisfactory and then, taking into account one's present circumstances and estimating the probabilities of a fortunate outcome as among the available alternatives, decide on that action which seems most likely to maximize one's experience of immediate value in the future and on the whole.

At times it seems that this is the procedure which Lewis recommends. In characterizing Bentham's doctrine he writes:

If an expected consequence of an act or event will have a certain value in case it occurs, then the rationality of the art or desirability of the event, is not measured simply by the value of the consequence, but by this value as qualified by the probability that it will follow, in accordance with what is called in probability theory the mathematical expectation.[31]

This apparently is the part of Bentham that Lewis agrees with since he goes on to say:

So far, there is accord with the dictates of rationality, since one who should act on this principle would in the long run achieve anticipated values in general to the maximum possible extent; just as one who laid his wagers according to mathematical expectations would in the long run win the maximum possible amount of money.[32]

[31] AKV, p. 492.
[32] AKV, p. 492.

This is the account of rational decision which seems to follow from Lewis' theoretical premises and to be in accord with his general position. Nor is there any reason, as I said earlier, why someone carrying out this procedure should not take account of that increment of value which, in Lewis' view, is the product of the interpenetration of means and ends. The strictest Benthamite could admit the fact (if it is a fact) that a walk in the country which has a goal is more agreeable than aimless rambling. He could also carry out what Lewis calls "the final evaluation" which involves a reference to "that overarching temporal *Gestalt,* the purview of a whole life."[33] He would ask himself, on the occasion of important decisions: which of the various things I *could* do, would make my life on the whole most pleasant. But Lewis clearly believes that making such decisions requires something that Bentham either rules out or leaves out. What can it be? A clue, I think, is that, except in the passage I quoted above, Lewis avoids speaking of the summum bonum as the 'maximum' of experienced value during a whole life. Another clue is Lewis' distinction between 'immediate value' and 'contributory' value. He writes:

. . . if in one sense the determination of values must be eventually in terms of the value-qualities of direct experience, still in another sense no immediately experienced good or bad is final, but rather is further to be evaluated by its relation to the temporal whole of a good life.[34]

Any experience may have such instrumental value or disvalue, which is not an intrinsic quality realized within it but is found in the further experience to which it leads. And since experiences in general have both such intrinsic value and such instrumental value, the *final* assessment of the value of any experience must include reference to both.[35]

The simple and obvious fact which calls for recognition is only this: that while the experiences of which life is made up have each its absolute and not-to-be-cancelled goodness or badness when and as realized, the value of *having* that experience has reference *also* to the instrumental effects of it upon the future. Value as immediately found is subject to no critique. But the aim-to-realize it, and the value of *having* that particular experience, are still subject to rational criticism by reference to the value which it may contribute instrumentally to any whole of experience in which it is included.[36]

The point about 'immediate value' is clear enough: at this moment I am drinking coffee; I enjoy it, I can't be mistaken about this and nothing that has happened in the past or could happen in the future can

33 AKV, p. 503.
34 AKV, p. 483.
35 AKV, p. 485.
36 AKV, p. 485.

'cancel' the 'immediate value' which I here and now apprehend. What about the second question? What is the 'contributory value' of my present enjoyment? One would think that since the goal is "life found good in the living" and since during this little 'temporal *Gestalt*' I am finding life good, that my present experience would be pure gain. But Lewis says that my present experience may have disvaluable consequences. This sounds peculiar: what could it mean to talk about the 'consequences' of a *value experience?* The fact that I enjoy coffee, find immediate value in the experience of drinking it, is a good reason for drinking it. (It holds an 'imperative for action'.) The fact that I take the time to drink (and enjoy) this coffee may cause me to be late for class. Drinking coffee in general may be bad for my ulcers or my disposition. These would be reasons for not drinking it. But it is not, as Lewis seems to say in the passage above, the *immediate value experience* that has these causal or consequential properties. What would it mean to ask: What are the probable consequences of my present enjoyment of this coffee? Is my objection pedantic? If it is, and if what Lewis intends to say is that although I am truly and certainly enjoying my coffee now, I will be sorry tomorrow that I drank it, then how does he differ from Bentham? And why do I need to perform a special act of 'synthetic envisagement'? My present value experience does not 'lead to' future experience in any series except the chronological one. The ambiguity which pervades Lewis' discussion is one which Bentham recognizes and avoids. Speaking of the dimensions of 'fecundity' and 'purity' he remarks that these are

scarcely to be deemed properties of the pleasure or the pain itself . . . they are in strictness to be deemed properties only of the act, or other event by which such pleasure or pain has been produced; and accordingly they are only to be taken into account of the tendency of such act or such event.[37]

Perhaps what Lewis means to say and what he thinks Bentham overlooked in this: An immediate value experience contributes to a whole life experience just by being part of it. But its contribution, seen under the aspect of 'synthetic envisagement', *need not be positive.* (Here by hypothesis, reference to the consequences of the *act*, e.g., drinking the coffee, are excluded.) Isn't this paradoxical? How could an experience of immediate value *not* contribute to the positive value of life on the whole? When he tries to convey his sense of how this might come about Lewis has drawn his analogies from music or the drama and since these are not the sort of thing which Bentham or his followers

---

[37] Jeremy Bentham, *An Introduction to the Principles of Morals and Legislation* (New York: Hafner Publishing Co., 1948), Chapter IV.

would have chosen to illustrate deliberative processes, the analogies may be helpful. Lewis writes:

... music offers a kind of example which typifies in certain respects this consummatory character or experiential wholes and the values of them. A musical composition or rendition discloses a kind of value which comes as near to being purely esthetic and directly found in experience of it as one could well discover. But the goodness or badness of a piece of music is not constituted out of the goods and bads of its separate notes or even of its separate phrases. One cannot compose a symphony of sour notes—let us hope—or out of exclusively dissonant passages: the momentarily experienced qualities of constituents are not indifferent for the value which characterizes it as a whole. But neither are they decisive; their temporal and other relations are likewise essential. ... One does not hear the symphony in its opening passage, nor in the middle of the second movement, nor in the finale: one hears it and appreciates it as a progressive and cumulative whole. Yet this value of it as a whole is as directly realized in the progressive experience of it as the beauty of the opening chord was found in that moment. And further, the value disclosed in it is consummatory. ... We find the similar thing exemplified in drama and in the novel. And these examples are the more pertinent in that it has its measure of truth to say that the drama and the novel imitate life, merely emphasizing, by their selectiveness and their exclusion of the irrelevant, the kind of significances and values which life may present.[38]

What is required Lewis holds is "some manner of synthetic apprehension" and continues:

If we borrow an old word and say that what is essential in such cases is a synthetic intuition, it is to be hoped that ... various problems associated with 'intuition' can still be avoided. ... And if it be objected that there is no such thing as synthetic intuition, then let us reply by reference to such envisagement as that by which we hear a symphony, or discover that a [long] journey is comfortable or uncomfortable, or decide that a lengthy undertaking goes smoothly and is a rewarding experience or proves difficult and tedious.[39]

It is not always necessary to make decisions by reference to an intuition of one's life as a whole. Our problem may be simplified:

First, we may break it up into parts. Just as the architect—who likewise recognizes that everything in his plan must be subordinated to the whole and evaluated by relation to it—still does not attempt to devise or judge every detail directly in that relationship, but instead by proximate relation to some lesser and included whole such as this room or this facade; so too we break down our contemplated good life into major components and judge of minor constituents by their contributory effect on these—a good job, a good home, a good vacation, a satisfactory conclusion of the task in hand.[40]

[38] AKV, pp. 496-97.
[39] AKV, p. 506.
[40] AKV, p. 509.

The analogy Lewis invokes has three elements: that which calls for assessment, "life in the living" is like a symphony, a drama or a novel; the act of assessment, based on the "synthetic envisagement" of a temporal *Gestalt*, is like the critic's judgment of a work of art; deliberation about what will contribute to life as a whole is like the problem of the creative artist, e.g., the architect. If this is to be taken seriously then Lewis' "final evaluations" really *are* quite different from the Benthamite procedures which he criticizes. In moments of decision I am to view my life with a quasi-aesthetic detachment and ask myself whether my present value experience, e.g., enjoying my coffee, will harmonize with the whole, whether it is a detail which will enhance the total pattern of values which I envisage. It would be like asking: What would it do to this passage if I changed the *F* to an *F#*? Or: Would an extra syllable spoil the rhythm of this line? My 'life as a whole' would have the status of an abstract particular and would be perhaps akin to those 'aesthetic essences' which Lewis describes in the chapter on aesthetic judgment. On this interpretation it would *not* be paradoxical to say that my present value-experience, though genuine, is not a contributory value. There might have been too much enjoying of coffee in this regional area of my life, creating an effect of monotony; enjoying milk, tea or beer would have been a little more interesting just at this point. Furthermore, if final evaluations are like aesthetic appraisals, then some otherwise puzzling remarks about pain can be accommodated. For example Lewis writes:

If one should, without illusion of memory, find a life worth living though the greater part of it be spent in suffering, there could be no prescribed manner of evaluation which could overrule that finding, or convict one of error in it. And no rule could be of assistance to us in so evaluating a whole of experience beyond the rule that it should be envisaged adequately and truly as a whole, and no part of it omitted from our concern.[41]

The conception I have outlined is coherent and it does justify Lewis' claim to be proposing something different from Benthamism. Still it would be hazardous to conclude that this represents Lewis' serious intention. For one thing, he does not explicitly distinguish prudential judgments (I'm enjoying this coffee but I shouldn't be drinking it; it will keep me awake all night) from judgment of 'contributory value' (Is my present enjoyment a significant contribution to the value structure of my life as a whole?). If, as I have argued, these are different kinds of judgment and if Lewis would wish to defend both, then there are questions about their relations in practice.

41 AKV, pp. 494-95.

For example, what is the 'imperative for action' if on the one hand my drinking coffee (which I enjoy) is likely to have unpleasant consequences and yet on the other hand the temporal *Gestalt* comprising future pain as qualified by present enjoyment is envisaged as being 'good on the whole'? Another difficulty is that Lewis believes that aesthetic experience in general is of secondary importance. Such value is 'passive' rather than 'active'. If a man "bent on good works" and "solid achievement" should be "heedless or even a little disdainful" of the aesthetic, then he would suffer deprivation.

> But still this attitude might have some color of justification in view of 'the necessary and possible character of a life good on the whole. In its repudiation of first claim upon us of esthetic values, it is probably correct.[42]

And Lewis also observes that "life is never dramatic in the living of it: the seriousness of intent would be spoiled by any self-conscious sense of the drama."[43] This observation is not exactly *inconsistent* with the account of "final evaluations"; one could say that an actor must "live his part" while on stage and only during the entr'acte review and assess the quality of his performance. Still there seems to be something incongruous in holding on the one hand that aesthetic values are secondary and on the other that ultimate moral decisions are made on the basis of an aesthetic assessment of the value of life as a whole. Again, perhaps Lewis would deny that 'final evaluations' do have the character of aesthetic judgment. But this would leave the whole process a mystery: they are not (or not exclusively) straightforward prudential judgments designed to maximize experienced value in the future; external standards are specifically ruled out; the ethical imperative has not yet been introduced. In assessing my life I am not asking whether I have experienced as much value as I could have; neither am I asking whether I have done my duty, developed my capacities, made the world a better place to live in: I have just to decide whether my life envisaged as a temporal *Gestalt* of experienced values is, as a whole, intrinsically valuable. If this is not an aesthetic question, what is it?

The puzzles about the summum bonum would be less important if the "ethical imperative" which has the authority to overrule the command to be concerned about oneself "in the future and on the whole" were independent with respect not merely to its form but to its content. But as it turns out, the difficulties of "final evaluations" are simply multiplied on the specifically ethical level. In *The Ground and Nature of the Right* Lewis writes:

42 AKV, p. 455.
43 AKV, p. 497.

The basic imperative for individuals in their relations to one another is simply the socially significant counterpart of what we have observed already: the dictate to govern one's activities affecting other persons, as one would if these effects of them were to be realized with the poignancy of the immediate —hence in one's own person. The dictate is to respect other persons as the realities we representationally recognize them to be—as creatures whose gratifications and griefs have the same poignant factuality as our own; and as creatures who, like ourselves, find it imperative to govern themselves in the light of the cognitive apprehensions, vouchsafed to them, by decisions which they themselves reach, and by reference to values discoverable to them.[44]

That is to say: As far as I am conscientious, I shall be no less concerned with the aim of others to achieve their respective good lives than I am with my own. The problems about first personal assessments cannot, at any rate, be less of a stumbling-block when it comes to assessing the value experiences of others.

## II

Up to now I have not mentioned what Lewis regards as the main thesis of value theory and the most essential part of the foundations of ethics. That is the claim that valuations are a form of empirical knowledge. As far as I understand this claim, I see no reason to dispute it. Assuming the correctness of his analysis of empirical belief—and questions about that are too complicated to go into here—I think Lewis does establish the analogy he wants to establish and shows that one can know that something is objectively good, i.e., that it has potentialities for conducing to value experience for oneself or for others. And this is not the only solid part of Lewis' theory. As I suggested at the outset, *all* of his most general premises, taken independently, are interesting and one would think defensible. There are good reasons—many of them have been stated—for holding that valuations, while they are empirical, hold "imperatives for action," that nothing is genuinely valuable except in relation to some possibility of human experience, that ethical principles cannot be derived from empirical valuations, that ethical principles have supreme authority in matters of decision. Lewis' positive moral doctrine, his idea of what *makes* life good in the living, strikes me as incomplete in some respects, in others, open to question. Still, it is a defensible ideal and one which many people share. The main point which my previous questions were designed to bring out is that Lewis somehow does not do justice to a position which, in outline is certainly sound. Why should this be? Any answer must be speculative but I should like to suggest the following: Lewis is predominantly concerned with

44 GNR, p. 91.

moral issues. He believes like Dewey that the solution of problems in value theory and ethics is a matter of more than theoretical interest. His own view, as he sums it up at the end of *The Ground and Nature of the Right* is 'naturalistic' in its conception of the good and with respect to ethical imperatives it is 'rationalistic'. There are two positions opposed to his; one he calls 'transcendentalism' and the other 'relativism' or 'subjectivism'. He believes that there are genuine issues of philosophic truth and error at stake here and that in this context, as in every context, the question whether one believes truly or falsely has practical consequences. In the Preface to *An Analysis of Knowledge and Valuation* he writes:

. . . if one say, "The good is pleasure," then either his statement explicates correctly the nature of that which gives direction to rational conduct or else it is false and has consequences which may be devastating. And if another assert, "The good is activity befitting the nature of a man," then his divergence from the hedonist is not that he intends something else in using the term 'good' but that, addressing himself to the intrinsically desirable, he reads the nature of it differently. Otherwise, no debatable issue would lie between these [two]. . . .[45]

And in a later passage:

The difference which lies between those who recognize a rational end of action only where some potentiality for human satisfactions can be found and those who would allege, as rationally imperative, ends which are independent of any possible human satisfaction, is a very important moral issue.[46]

On the moral issue Lewis takes a stand, first against 'transcendentalism', the notion that with respect to values

we are natively incompetent, or born in sin, and can discern them justly only by some insight thaumaturgically acquired, or through some intimation of a proper vocation of man which runs athwart his natural bent.[47]

And second against

the errors of Protagorean relativism or scepticism which would destroy the normative by reducing it to merely emotive significance.[48]

Although he believes that relativism and transcendentalism are both wrong and dangerous, Lewis never attacks either position directly. There is nothing to compare with Bentham's incisive polemics against those who claim the authority of revelation or 'natural light', nor does

45 AKV, preface x.
46 AKV, p. 413.
47 AKV, p. 398.
48 AKV, preface viii.

Lewis attempt the sort of sociological analysis and exposé which Dewey undertook in *The Quest for Certainty*. Even relativism, the more dangerous alternative according to Lewis, is never directly criticized. Except for one, oft-repeated charge on which I shall comment later, Lewis has nothing to say about the theories or positive claims of his hypothetical opponents. His argument is purely defensive; he tries to deploy his own position in a way which will make it immune to attack either from the left or from the right. At every stage of the argument I think he is conscious of fighting on two fronts at once: whenever he argues a point designed to block the relativists, he must make certain that in so doing he has not given any grounds to the transcendentalist. Some of the questions of interpretation which I have raised can be clarified if one looks at the theory as a complex piece of defensive strategy.

Consider the discussion of 'immediate' and 'intrinsic' value: Lewis believes that value is essentially linked with liking, enjoyment, satisfaction and pleasure. But these familiar terms have a 'subjectivist' ring and might give aid and comfort to the relativist. In anticipation of his attack, liking and enjoyment must be construed as discovery or recognition of a certain "dimensionlike mode of experience" which will be christened 'immediate value'. In order to satisfy the requirements for empirical knowledge in general one must also assume that no errors are possible at this level. ("Nothing is even probable, unless something is certain.") Thus 'immediate value' becomes "a quality unmistakably identifiable in the direct apprehension of it when disclosed in experience.[49] Given this assumption plus the fact that we can predict what actions or choices will lead to the discovery of 'immediate value', one can go on to define 'objective value'. It is the potentiality an object may have for conducing to value experience for some person or persons. The relativists are those who deny that one can *know* that an object is valuable; now they have been disposed of for the time being. But suppose a transcendentalist should appear; he would support the case against relativism but would then go on to claim that 'immediate value experience' is a minor, subordinate value, that all that is *truly* good is saving one's soul or fulfilling the will of God. The question is how to establish in advance that any such claim must be disallowed. One way would be to ascribe to immediate value experience itself the very characteristics which the transcendentalist ascribes to his 'true good'. So one would be led to say that immediate value experience is the final intrinsic value, "the ultimate aim of every sensible action," "that for the sake of which all other things are valued." The position is

---

[49] AKV, p. 400.

now secured against attacks from either side but what has emerged is something that looks very much like ethical hedonism. But one hesitates to say that *pleasure* is the intrinsic good for two reasons: first because 'pleasure' has misleading connotations and suggests a priority for passive, organic, sensuous enjoyments whereas in the 'economy of value' these rank low;[50] and second, one simply knows of lives that have been really good although not particularly pleasant. But as soon as one begins to talk of an 'economy of values' and lives which, though they consist largely of suffering, are "worth living"[51] then the transcendentalist has his foot in the door again. How can one forestall his contention that the 'economy of values' has a supernatural foundation or that a 'good' life is one devoted to the service of God or humanity? One way would be to insist that the goodness of a good life consists in the total structure of organically related value experiences when they become the object of synthetic envisagement. Suppose the relativist should reappear to claim that there is no such thing as 'synthetic envisagement'. The answer is that there *must* be, just as there must be an imperative to be sensible, consistent, and concerned for the future. To deny this would be to deny "the distinction of what is rational from what is perverse or silly,"[52] "to dissolve away all seriousness of action and intent, leaving only an undirected floating down the stream of time."[53]

Like all such attempts, my reconstruction is hardly more than a caricature. Still it suggests the way in which someone who adopts Lewis' tactics may get caught up in his own dialectic. I believe that his position can be simplified and strengthened but to do so requires a number of basic changes. The most important of these is a general shift of strategy. Lewis approaches his problem in a way which suggests that naturalism in value theory and rationalism in ethics are positions which are extremely precarious and conversely that the alternatives—transcendentalism and relativism—are in their different ways intuitively plausible. But the exact opposite is the truth: one ordinarily assumes that valuations may be correct or incorrect and that the moral law is 'objective'. To say clearly what is involved in these assumptions is a difficult task but certainly much *less* difficult than it is to make out any kind of respectable case for the other positions. Transcendentalism is supported by a fabric of shoddy arguments and poetical clichés; relativism is not

50 AKV, p. 447.
51 AKV, p. 495.
52 AKV, p. 481.
53 AKV, p. 481.

so much a theory—at least one has never seen it clearly stated—but rather a set of overlapping logical confusions. Those who claim to support it observe that opinions differ about right and wrong but what inferences this truism entitles us to make, whether indeed it entitles us to make any inferences, are questions that are left obscure. It seems to me therefore that Lewis should be more stouthearted and should take his stand with the assurance that naturalism, while it needs clarification, does not need an *apologia*.

The second point is procedural and is related to the first: the proper way to deal with objections is to meet them, not to try to forestall them. Lewis sets out to make his position unassailable in advance. His preoccupation with the question, 'What *must* be the case if values are to be truly objective' encourages a prioristic arguments and a consequent neglect of everyday value experience and the language in which it is ordinarily discussed. This works to his disadvantage in a number of ways. For one thing it leads to the proliferation of technical terms. It is crucial for Lewis' argument that one should know what one likes or enjoys. And this is something one *does* know, but to express this fact in terms of the 'apprehension' of 'immediate value' in experience does not make it any more certain; if anything, it makes it sound rather dubious. (How can it be proper to speak of 'apprehension' unless there is the possibility of 'misapprehension'.) 'Liking' and 'enjoying' are relatively clear; 'immediate value' is vague and this vagueness may prevent one from recognizing real logical difficulties. It is hard to tell, for example, whether Lewis believes that the fact that nothing is valuable except in relation to possible human experience provides logical support for the claim that the only intrinsically valuable thing is immediate value experience itself. It certainly does not follow; in fact if conducing to immediate value experience is a necessary condition for being valuable, then it would seem to require another set of conventions to allow one to apply the predicate 'valuable' to experience itself. Perhaps Lewis is not guilty of this confusion; the point is that his terminology makes it difficult to be sure that he is not.

A further point: the belief that relativism must be defeated at all cost may lead to the neglect of questions which are supposed to give a foothold to the enemy. Lewis, as I have noted, does not at any place in his theory of value or in his ethical theory deal directly with the problem of moral conflict. This is a strange omission in a work which is addressed primarily to elucidating the concept of rational choice. To be sure, Lewis is in good company; Kant also refrains from mentioning the fact that in order to discharge one duty one may have to be delinquent in another. But then Kant too was very much concerned about not allowing loopholes for 'subjectivism'. This precaution is needless: we all know that there are difficult choices and situations in which *whatever* one does is wrong but we do not conclude from this that there are no 'valid imperatives' or that morality is a matter of taste.

A somewhat similar point might be raised about Lewis' positive moral doctrine to which I alluded earlier. He has definite views about what makes life worth living and provides a comparative ranking of human values in which he finds a place for hard work, aesthetic experience, physical pleasures and so forth. In this respect Lewis is a traditionalist and his affiinities are with Dewey, Santayana and Hartmann rather than with more recent theorists. He does not claim the immunity of metaethics. But his moral convictions, though candidly avowed, are never systematically organized or defended. It may be that the most important values are 'active' and "imbued with concern for the future." But many people—indeed whole traditions—think otherwise. One cannot dispose of important moral questions in a series of *obiter dicta*. That there are disagreements is not a fact which supports 'subjectivism' and even if it did, it would have to be acknowledged.

What I have been suggesting is that the difficulties of Lewis' theory arise in part from his tendency to provide elaborate arguments in support of claims which, although we may not clearly understand them, most of us would be willing to accept and that this is coupled with the tendency *not* to provide arguments for claims which intelligent and responsible people might want to dispute. As an illustration, consider Lewis' treatment of 'imperatives'. There are, as I have noted, various kinds of imperatives; one thing they have in common is that they are incontrovertible, in Lewis' phrase "not to be argued." There is the imperative which every valuation holds for sensibly taken action; there is the imperative to be concerned for the future; there is the imperative to make important decisions in the light of the summum bonum, 'the life found good in the living'; finally there is the ethical imperative in its dual aspect, the Law of Compassion and the Law of Moral Equality. In the final chapter of *The Ground and Nature of the Right* he summarizes his opinions. There is no need to look for an ultimate ground of moral rightness; it is sui generis. The principles of logic are not themselves subject to logical proof. The "validity of the prudential aim so to act as to maximize the goodness realizable in a whole lifetime" cannot be demonstrated to a convinced Cynic.[54] Now if it is a question here of *logical deduction,* then Lewis is clearly correct; moral laws and logical principles are not entailed by statements which are not

54 GNR, p. 85.

moral laws or logical principles. But Lewis sometimes seems to say something quite different, namely that laws and principles cannot be learned or taught. Here again his language allows of different interpretations, but he does say on a number of occasions both that someone who was a born Cyrenaic could never be persuaded to mend his ways and also that the "fundamental dictum of justice" could not be "inculcated by argument where native recognition of it should be lacking."[55] Either this is a repetition of the logical point or else it is empirically false. If it were true, we would be in a bad way; babies are neither prudent nor moral nor logical but they can learn (and also fail to learn) to be all three. Even if it is not intended seriously, talk about 'native recognition' in such contexts is misleading. It carries the suggestion that acknowledging these imperatives is an all-or-none affair, and this seems to be the assumption which underlies a curious polemical argument on which Lewis frequently relies. It consists of an appeal to the disastrous consequences of 'repudiating' imperatives. To do this is to "dissolve all significance of thought and discourse" and "all seriousness of action and intent."[56] Here I think is a sort of paradigm of the general difficulty I have been trying to describe. Lewis' argument is designed to show us that we *must* acknowledge the imperative to be prudent, and he conjures up a picture of what experience would be like for a witless creature who had no awareness, perhaps, of the passage of time and no ability to learn anything. But in a primitive sense we *are* prudent; we have to be to survive. At a certain stage of sophistication we can grasp the concept of prudence and agree that it is logically involved in the concept of being reasonable. At this level there is nothing that needs to be 'proved'; nor is it clear what would be involved in 'repudiating the imperative'. I cannot simply will myself to become an amoeba. But prudence admits of degrees; beyond the level of survival, one may be concerned about the future to a greater or lesser extent. Some people think prudence a virtue, even the highest virtue; others think not. This *is* a practical issue on which one could take sides and taking a side would mean approving a certain way of educating children, commending behavior and awarding praise and blame in general. Lewis' argument is not adequate to the moral issue; in order to make it so, he would need to examine the alternatives. *Dulce est desipere in loco* and other maxims of imprudence are not the expressions of subhuman intellect. Someone who rejects them as bad advice should have a reason and Lewis does not offer one.

55 AKV, p. 482.
56 AKV, p. 481.

The questions I have raised touch on a difficult problem which affects not only Lewis' theory but any attempt to treat moral philosophy in a systematic way. Stated briefly it is this: how is it possible to discuss the epistemology of ethics without at least *appearing* to have begged substantive moral issues? Unless we know what *is* right, how can we ever get started at the task of explaining how we *know* that something is right? And any categorical statement about what *is* right is either a tautology (One ought to do one's duty) or else it is open to question (One ought to tell the truth). So any theory of moral knowledge must consist simply in showing that we know what is implied by our definitions; if not that, then it must be a disguised plea for a particular moral doctrine. I have no general solution for this problem but I think it is helpful to compare the situation in ethics with what one finds in other fields. Epistemological inquiry of any sort is subject in principle to the same challenge which is so frequently made to moral philosophers. How do we know anything about the physical world? One begins with unanalyzed intuitions and then there is the question of what authority and status they have. Are they the touchstones by reference to which we decide to reject the adequacy of the analysis? As long as this question is undecided, one can construct the various familiar dilemmas which are sometimes treated under the heading of the 'paradox of analysis'. What is interesting is that this paradox, if it *is* a paradox, is not a constant headache in areas outside of ethics. A philosopher working on a theory of perception is not continually harassed by critics who charge him with triviality or special pleading, whereas in ethics, this is perhaps the most familiar and certainly one of the most tiresome objections. Elsewhere, one might say, the paradox of analysis is treated as one among a variety of philosophic problems; in ethics it assumes the status of a sort of superproblem. It would be interesting to know why this should be the case.

On the general issue Lewis himself has had a number of perceptive things to say. In the introduction to *Mind and the World-Order*[57] he writes:

It is—I take it—a distinguishing character of philosophy that it is everybody's business. The man who is his own lawyer or physician, will be poorly served; but everyone both can and must be his own philosopher. He must be, because philosophy deals with ends, not means. It includes the questions, What is good? What is right? What is valid? . . . the question of the ultimately valuable ends . . . remains at once the most personal, and the most general of all questions.

[57] New York, Scribner's, 1929.

And everyone *can* be his own philosopher, because in philosophy we investigate what we already know . . . Philosophy is concerned with what is already familiar. To know in the sense of familiarity and to comprehend in clear ideas are, of course, quite different matters. Action precedes reflection and even precision of behavior commonly outruns precision of thought—fortunately for us. If it were not for this, naive commonsense and philosophy would coincide, and there would be no problem. Just this business of bringing to clear consciousness and expressing coherently the principles which are implicitly intended in our dealing with the familiar, is the distinctively philosophic enterprise.

My criticisms of Lewis' moral philosophy could be summed up by saying that if he had paid more attention to what is familiar in our everyday dealings with the good and the right and less attention to speculative doctrines, his position would have been stronger than it is.

MARY MOTHERSILL

DEPARTMENT OF PHILOSOPHY
BARNARD COLLEGE, NEW YORK

## 22

## A. C. Ewing

# C. I. LEWIS ON THE RELATION BETWEEN
# THE GOOD AND THE RIGHT

THE issue between the utilitarian who makes the right dependent on the good and his opponents is not so prominent in ethical controversy now as it was twenty or thirty years ago, and it is apt to be neglected in face of the still bigger questions whether and in what sense ethics is objective or subjective, a priori or empirical, nonnaturalist or naturalist. But, in whatever way these questions are answered, the question of the relation between good and right will face us within the framework of our ethical philosophy, be this objectivist or emotivist, naturalist or nonnaturalist. And that the question has some practical, and not only theoretical, importance is shown by the frequent disputes as to whether one is entitled to break a general moral law for the sake of the consequences or not. Where does Professor Lewis stand as regards this issue of the relation between the good and the right? It certainly cannot be discussed without going to the roots of his whole ethical theory. We must start with his view of good on which according to him the right is, in the main at least, dependent.

Now Professor Lewis takes what he calls a naturalistic view of value. In doing so he seems to have various things in mind. One (the chief) is that the presence of goodness or badness is known empirically.[1] Another is that naturalism holds "that no action can be determined as right or wrong without reference to consequences of it as good or bad."[2] A third is that

the natural bent of the natural man stands in no need of correction in order validly to be the touchstone of *intrinsic* value. It [naturalism] repudiates the conception that with respect to intrinsic values we are natively incompetent, or born in sin, and can discern them justly only by some insight thaumaturgically acquired, or through some intimation of a proper vocation of man which runs athwart his natural bent.[3]

[1] C. I. Lewis, *An Analysis of Knowledge and Valuation* (La Salle, Ill.: Open Court Publishing Co., 1946), p. viii. Hereafter cited as AKV.

[2] C. I. Lewis, *The Ground and Nature of the Right* (New York: Columbia University Press, 1955), p. 97. Hereafter cited as GNR.

[3] AKV, p. 398.

Now it is clearly only in the first of these senses that 'naturalism' is generally understood. The third is what almost all philosophers assume in dealing with ethics—I suppose the author has in mind Barthian theologians as his opponents here—; the second is also held by many philosophers who would never be called naturalists, indeed by all who have even a moderate inclination to utilitarianism. What is usually emphasized is rather the refusal of naturalism to go beyond what is experienced. Naturalism is however more commonly stated in terms of the analysis of the meaning of ethical words than in terms of the epistemology of their application. I should myself define a 'naturalist analysis' of good as an analysis in terms of concepts of a natural science (usually, though not always, those of psychology). And at least insofar as Professor Lewis defines 'good' in terms of satisfaction or liking, his account would also fall under this definition of naturalistic.

Naturalism, at least as understood by Professor Lewis, entails an objective view of ethics. For in asserting empirical knowledge of the good it is at least asserting *knowledge* of it. He is very hostile to any account of ethics which would involve saying that no ethical judgments are true or that there is no objectively valid way of deciding which are true. His 'naturalistic' view is that

valuations represent one type of empirical cognition; hence that their correctness answers to a kind of objective fact, but one which can be learned only from experience and is not determinable *a priori*. Only if we recognize the truth of that can we avoid the transcendentalist dictum of a moral obligation which is independent of the humanly desirable, without falling into the errors of Protagorean relativism or that moral skepticism which would destroy the normative by reducing it to merely emotive significance. To make it clear that empiricism in epistemology and naturalism in ethics do not imply such relativism and cynicism has been one main objective in the writing of this book.[4]

It is indeed surprising that Professor Lewis has not more to say about the emotive theories that rival naturalism in their appeal to empiricists. And it does not seem to have occurred to him, as it had not occurred to me till a few years ago, that one might combine an emotive theory of ethics, or at least a theory according to which ethical judgments as such do not assert anything that could be true but are purely emotive and practical, not informative, in character with an admission that some ethical attitudes are yet more reasonable, better, more fitting than others in a sense in which that is not analysable either naturalistically or as a mere expression of the speaker's emotional and practical attitude. (To the obvious objection that, if so, the judgment that they are better is itself a true ethical judgment the reply would be made that, although

4 AKV, p. viii.

it is correct English usage to call ethical judgments 'true', the word 'true' means something so very different here from what it does in nonethical cases that it is really misleading.) Certainly we can trace a very strong tendency in the direction of such a view in Great Britain. It would be a reasonable guess that it is either the most generally held ethical view among British philosophers or will be so very soon. I do not hold it myself but, largely because of its possibility, I do not think that the denial of objective truth to ethical judgments can be equated with ethical scepticism or dismissed as cursorily as Professor Lewis dismisses it. He however says that

the denial to value-apprehensions in general of the character of truth or falsity and of knowledge, would imply both moral and practical cynicism. It would invalidate all action; because action becomes pointless unless there can be some measure of assurance of a valuable result which it may realize.[5]

Good in the sense usually signified by 'intrinsically good' is for Professor Lewis a quality apprehended immediately in experience, but this immediate awareness of good is not yet knowledge any more than is the feeling of pain. This is quite an understandable position, but it is backed by an argument which would imply the total repudiation of what the great majority of philosophers in the past have meant by 'knowledge'. For Professor Lewis contends that knowledge implies the possibility of error,[6] which is just what so many philosophers who have written on 'knowledge' have been most concerned to deny. They wished to maintain that there was a certain attitude of mind, knowing, in which error was impossible. However his view of knowledge is more common today, and insofar as this apprehension of good is only an unexpressed feeling, it may reasonably be urged that it should not in any case be called knowledge. He admits that, when we formulate our immediate apprehension of value in words, we may make verbal mistakes, but points out that what a judgment asserts is not the correctness of the language used in it but the truth of what the language is intended to convey. It would follow that a judgment can be altogether wrongly expressed and yet not false, though it would then run the risk of not being understood by anyone. It may be objected that what the language is intended to convey cannot in the case of immediate value judgments be true, since what it is intended to convey is the immediate apprehension of value to which Professor Lewis has just denied truth. The answer seems to be that the content of apprehension is true if judged but it is not already judged when we apprehend it, as the feeling of pain is

5 AKV, p. 366.
6 AKV, p. 397.

distinct from the judgment that I have a pain. Unless this be admitted, I do not see how even predictions that an experience will have value can be true, thus cutting out the rest of Professor Lewis' moral philosophy. For the content of the judgment that, if I do so and so, I shall have a valuable experience is the same as the content of my apprehension that it is good when the experience comes.

What about the quality of good immediately apprehended? Professor Lewis apparently agrees with Moore in regarding it as simple and indefinable,[7] but not in regarding it as nonnatural. And of course, as Moore recognized in his illustration of yellow, an empirical, natural quality may very well be simple and indefinable. Professor Lewis however admits that there are various other words which come near describing what is meant by 'good', especially 'liked' and 'wanted', which he prefers to 'pleasure' or 'pleasant',[8] and in one passage at least he gives a definition in terms of 'satisfaction'.[9] In one respect he makes what I consider an important improvement on Moore's view in regarding value not as a single quality "so much as a dimension-like mode which is pervasive of all experience."[10] Thus good is rather a class of qualities than a specific quality, and similarly bad. He admits, however, that the term 'dimension' is not strictly accurate since "a dimension should be a respect in which things can vary independently of other and similarly dimensional characteristics," whereas the content of experience does not vary normally[11] with respect to value while otherwise being invariant.

Besides the immediate apprehension of goodness there are two other important kinds of evaluation in terms of good, which Professor Lewis recognizes as indisputably judgments. First, there are predictions that a certain value quality will be experienced if a certain mode of action is adopted. And, secondly, there are judgments that certain things (including states of affairs as well as physical instruments) are valuable as being liable in general to produce experiences which are good.[12] These two kinds of judgments differ logically in that the former can be conclusively verified since they relate to a single experience, while the latter cannot be conclusively verified but only more and more strongly confirmed. The relation between the two is the same as the relation between "it will hurt if I cut myself with the knife" and "the knife is sharp" or "steel can make

[7] AKV, p. 400.
[8] AKV, pp. 404-05.
[9] AKV, p. 414.
[10] AKV, p. 401.
[11] I should have said it never possibly could, see below p. 603.
[12] AKV, pp. 375-6.

a keen cutting edge" except that the property of producing valuable experience is more variable than the properties of physical things dealt with by science (at least outside meteorology). In respect of verification the third class of judgments are thus in the same position as scientific judgments about physical things and causal laws, and Professor Lewis assimilates them to these, for after all it is a causal property of an object that it is liable to produce satisfying experience. A priori propositions in ethics, he thinks, are never evaluations but always analytic or alleged analytic corrections of meaning.[13] (This does not apply to principles regarding what we ought to do. Professor Lewis objects to using the term, evaluation, to cover these, and as we shall see later he introduces non-empirical principles in this field.) It will of course be understood that, insofar as 'good' is used of physical things, it does not signify intrinsic value, which can belong only to experiences, but a liability causally to produce intrinsically valuable experiences. A further distinction is made between utility, instrumental value and inherent value.

A thing *A* will never be said to have extrinsic value or instrumental value, unless it is meant to imply that there is some other thing, *B*, to which it is or may be instrumental which has intrinsic value. . . . But we shall say that *A* is useful *for* or *instrumental to B*, or merely that *A* is useful or has *utility*, without implying any certainty that *B* or anything else to which *A* may lead has intrinsic value.[14]

According to this terminology a bomb used for aggressive war would have utility but not extrinsic or instrumental value. And a further distinction is made within 'extrinsic value' between 'inherent value' where the intrinsically valuable experience is produced by the mere presentation of the physical object, as with a work of art, and instrumental value where the mode of production is more indirect.[15] Among the things which have instrumental value will of course be right actions, at least unless they altogether fail of their object in which case perhaps they have only utility, and I suppose they can also be said sometimes to have inherent value, namely, when their contemplation immediately gives rise to an intrinsically valuable experience of admiration. The situation is however complicated by the fact that the mental side of an action is an experience, and so might be intrinsically valuable in the full sense, though Professor Lewis no doubt holds that this point is a subordinate one, the value of right actions lying mainly in their effects.

13 AKV, p. 378.
14 AKV, p. 385.
15 AKV, p. 391.

Naturalism and subjectivism are sometimes confused, but Professor Lewis quite rightly emphasizes that his view need not be subjective because it is naturalistic, unless 'subjectivism' is understood to mean any view which denies intrinsic value to inanimate things.[16] We may add that in the latter case almost every theory of ethics would have to be called subjective. But the quality of intrinsic goodness, though it occurs only in experiences and its *esse* is therefore in a sense *percipi*, is really present in these experiences and is not merely fancied to be so, and the sort of value which can be attributed to physical things is present as objectively in them as is any causal property recognized by science.

This leaves open the possibility of making distinctions between 'objective' and 'subjective' within the framework of Professor Lewis' view. He points out that, where the reason why something in an experience is intrinsically good or bad is peculiar to the individual, we may talk of the goodness or badness as 'subjective', where not as 'objective'.[17] Another distinction between 'objective' and 'subjective' is drawn as regards right action. An act is subjectively right if it is judged to be right by the agent, objectively if it is correctly judged by him to be so.[18] Such differences between subjective and objective must plainly be recognized in any system of ethics. When something is subjectively good or subjectively right in these senses, it will still be objectively true that it is subjectively good or right.

If ethical naturalism can do justice to the objectivity of value-judgments, is there any further objection to it? Here I shall make the following points, hoping that they will lead to an explanation by Professor Lewis. In the first place he gives a naturalistic account of the meaning of 'good', but he does not give any analysis of the meaing of 'right', 'ought', 'duty'.[19] He evidently does not think that they stand for qualities (or relations) immediately given in our experience, as goodness does in his view. Must they not then be complex concepts? And what are the simpler concepts to which these complex ones are to be reduced? The only at all plausible way of answering this question compatibly with Professor Lewis' empiricism of which I can think would be to say that 'the right act' or 'the act which I ought to do' in a given situation just means the

---

16 AKV, p. 407.

17 AKV, p. 416.

18 GNR, pp. 48-9.

19 He does say (GNR, pp. 3-4) that "to say that a thing is right is simply to characterize it as representing the desiderated commitment or choice in any situation calling for deliberate decision," but if 'desiderated' just means 'desired by the agent' any choice one wants to make is right, and if it means 'approved by the person who pronounces it right' the definition is circular if taken as ultimate.

instrumentally best act, but such a definition is certainly not asserted by him. Further, it would make it verbally self-contradictory to deny utilitarianism, and there is no suggestion that this is so. But if rightness is not given directly in experience, and is not analysable in terms of what is, must it not be a nonnatural concept after all? Professor Lewis in fact does, at least in one passage, come very near to admitting the essential point of the contention that rightness is such a concept. "The right is *sui generis:* if the formulation of it be a kind of fact, still it is fact of a kind which is like no other."[20] He concludes that since "what is right cannot be proved right by summoning premises which themselves say nothing about right and wrong," any first principles of right must be indemonstrable,[21] a conclusion which he would hardly have drawn if he had meant to analyse right either naturalistically or in terms of good, for in that case any principles of right would either be capable of being established inductively or be definitions.

Secondly, I contend that there is this important difference between the properties discussed in ethics and other, empirical properties. Wherever we ascribe the property of goodness or badness to an experience or the property of rightness or wrongness to an action, we can see not merely that it actually has the property but that it must have it, its other properties and circumstances being what they are. Value-properties follow from the other properties of what is evaluated and the property of rightness or wrongness follows from the nature of an act and its circumstances in a way in which factual properties do not. Suppose I want to do something that is morally wrong, I could not avoid moral guilt and yet satisfy my desire by contriving to perform an act which had all the other empirical properties that the original act proposed would have had but differed from it in not having the additional property of moral wrongness, as I might contrive that it should be different in some particular empirical respect. We can see that to suppose I could do this would be completely absurd. It is certainly not just a case of causal impossibility. I do not say that value-judgments and judgments as to what is right or wrong involve a necessity of the same kind as that of logic—I believe they do not—but this argument does seem to show that they depend on the empirical facts in a very different way from that in which ordinary empirical judgments do. They are dependent on the empirical qualities and relations of that of which they are predicated, yet they do not just assert additional empirical qualities or relations. Our apprehension of value seems itself to be an apprehension not that what

20 GNR, p. 84.
21 GNR, pp. 84-5.

is valued has in fact an additional empirical property (valuableness) over and above its other properties but that the value somehow follows from the factual nature of what is valued. At least the value judgment has to be justified by reference to the latter and could not be different the latter being what it is. And the same applies to judgments concerning the rightness or wrongness of actions except that here we consider the circumstances rather than the inherent qualities of the latter. However I do not think that this difference is an absolute one. Its circumstances are only relevant to the rightness of an action insofar as they affect its relational properties, and it seems to me (though Professor Lewis might disagree) that the relational properties of an experience can be relevant to its intrinsic value and the internal qualities of an action relevant to its rightness. It seems to me that it is this necessity linking a certain factual nature with a certain value or a character of rightness or wrongness together with the difference in nature between these and factual qualities, and not, as Professor Lewis thinks, a confusion with analytic propositions about meaning, which is the main foundation of the belief in the a priori character of ethics. The properties with which ethics deals are not empirical properties, yet they seem to follow necessarily and so in a sense a priori from empirical properties.

Thirdly, unless at some point or other a breach is made with naturalism, is not the fallacy committed of reducing ought-propositions to is-propositions, i.e., to something of a quite different logical character? I suppose the break might be made with propositions that an act is right or what we ought to do, while accepting the merely factual and empirical character of the propositions which ascribe goodness or badness to experiences, but even with 'good' it seems to me clear that we are not saying only that what we call good has a factual property but also adopting towards it a favourable attitude which we may call commendation and, I should add, saying something such as that it *ought* to be commended. That value-judgments do not merely state facts but also commend is a point made by thinkers of the Stevensonian type, e.g., in Britain especially Hare[22] and Nowell-Smith,[23] against naturalism, though their conclusion is different from mine. They maintain that ostensible value-judgments are not really statements of propositions at all but something else, more like commands or exhortations to adopt certain attitudes; I maintain that they are statements of propositions but not of a purely empirical kind. That it carries with it some sort of obligation to adopt some favourable attitude to what is called good seems to me indeed the only

[22] Richard M. Hare, *The Language of Morals* (Oxford: Clarendon Press, 1952).
[23] Nowell-Smith, *Ethics* (London, Baltimore: Penguin Books, 1954).

property common to everything pronounced good in an ethical context and so still seems to me to have a strong claim to constitute the definition of good. As I have said, I think that value propositions depend on factual propositions, but this is not the same as saying that they are reducible to them. Professor Lewis himself admits that "there is a significance of the rationally imperative in every value-judgment,"[24] but is not this really admitting that the judgment that something is good already includes the notion of ought? If so, goodness cannot be a property just given in feeling but must presuppose reflection, as Professor Lewis admits is the case with 'ought'. Further, is this compatible with holding that intrinsic goodness is a simple and unanalysable quality? And, if it is a constituent of the meaning of good, does not 'ought' become the primary concept of value theory rather than good?

It is plain that explicit answers to the above questions would have made it easier to understand and appreciate Professor Lewis' view of the right, but he cannot be accused of neglecting the concept in his philosophy. He insists that rationality in action and thought only begins with the concept of right or ought.[25] Without admitting that this concept is nonnaturalistic, he does allow a sharp breach of continuity when passing from good to right. The apprehension of good involves only feeling which an animal can have, but the apprehension of rightness is possible only for a rational being. It indeed follows naturally from the apprehension of good and evil for such a being, but it involves thought and is impossible unless the being is able to reflect what causes will produce good results, while "the sense of good and bad, by contrast, is primordial to conscious life at large," it being even plausible to suppose that "mere feeling of euphoria or dysphoria is the most ancient form of consciousness."[26] The reflection is a reflection as to causes, and so falls within the realm of empirical science, but as we shall see, Professor Lewis admits that certain principles not empirically established but bound up with the very nature of rationality and therefore presumably a priori in a very important sense are needed if we are to determine what is right.

He speaks as if his ethical theory were in the main utilitarian, though it certainly is not completely so. He insists that the notion of good and

---

24 AKV, p. 413.

25 Professor Lewis generally uses the term right rather than the term ought and does not state the relation between them. We may no doubt assume in discussing his views that 'the right action' and 'the action that ought to be done' are synonymous, while 'a right action' differs from this simply in that there could be several right actions in a given situation and then, while we ought to do one of them, we could not say of any single one that it was 'the right action' or that we 'ought to do it'.

26 C. I. Lewis, Our Social Inheritance (Bloomington, Ind.: Indiana Univ. Press, 1957), p. 49.

evil is antecedent and that apart from this there could be no right or wrong.[27] Apparently going further, he says that

there hardly could be a rightness or wrongness of any species which attaches to any act without reference to some mode of goodness or badness with which consequences of the act, as predicted, will be affected.[28]

In the closing paragraph of *The Ground and Nature of the Right*, as we have noticed already, he makes it one of the leading features of 'naturalism' in the sense in which he is using the term that it holds that "no act can be determined as right or wrong without reference to consequences of it as good or bad." He is there opposing the kind of a priori ethics which supposes that we can know moral laws apart from the empirically observable effects of action.

He has much sympathy even with utilitarianism of the hedonistic variety, and in one passage he says that "the term 'valuable' is to be applied to objects and other existents solely with the meaning 'capable of conducing to satisfaction in some possible experience.' "[29] He disagrees with the hedonists in thinking 'pleasure' and 'pleasant' not apt designations to cover all intrinsic goods, but he seems to think of their error as one rather of expression than of content. His chief ground of condemnation is that the words suggest passive and sensuous goods rather than the goodness of serious activity, but he admits that hedonists have generally meant by 'pleasure' something much wider than the normal meaning of the word.[30] But is this criticism far-reaching enough? Might it not be objected that it is unjustifiable to assume that all the intrinsic value of a state of mind always lies in the degree in which it is felt, as hedonism implies, and not some also in our cognitions and conations as such? Or, if it is retorted that the three, cognition, conation, feeling, cannot be separated, then it follows for that very reason that there can be no justification for the hedonist doctrine that pleasure is the only good. Even if our experiences and states of mind would have no intrinsic goodness if they never gave any pleasure, as even Moore was inclined to admit, it does not follow in the least that their degree of intrinsic goodness is in strict proportion to the degree of pleasure accompanying them, and if we consider particular cases it seems hardly possible to maintain that it is. But Professor Lewis does not make this point. However, there are at least two other important respects in which he diverges from hedonism (1) in his admission of a principle of

27 GNR, p. 58.
28 GNR, p. 75.
29 AKV, p. 414.
30 AKV, pp. 404 f.

*Gestalt* resembling Moore's principle of organic wholes, (2) in his attitude to justice.

Returning to the question whether he was a utilitarian in the more general sense, it may be said that what constitutes utilitarianism is not just reference to the goodness or badness of the consequences in determining what is right, but the doctrine that what makes an action right is its tendency to produce the greatest good possible under the circumstances of the action. In that sense we shall see it is by no means clear that Professor Lewis is a utilitarian. Indeed he seems almost to rule utilitarianism out as a matter of course in at least one passage.

There is, for example, that outstanding kind of objection to utilitarianism: "But is it *just* to sacrifice an unwilling victim to save the nation from disaster?" The question whether whatever will maximize the social good is forthwith just, is still a moral issue. If there were no other kind of determinant of what it is right to do than merely the preponderant goodness of total results, that issue of justice not only would be already answered, it would be gratuitous to raise it, since the correct answer would be merely tautological. But we could hardly admit that this question about justice is thus gratuitous. Consonantly, we cannot accept any utilitarian account which would make it such, as sufficient on the point raised.[31]

And in the last page of the *Analysis of Knowledge and Valuation* it is asserted that one can hardly expect to resolve "questions of social justice in the distribution of goods according to any principle in terms of the value of them alone" and "that what is right and what is just, can never be determined by empirical facts alone."

Further, even insofar as Professor Lewis is a utilitarian, his mode of applying his utilitarianism cannot but be profoundly affected by his adoption of what we may call the principle of *Gestalt*. The assumption of the earlier utilitarians was that the total good of any whole could be determined, ideally at least, by just summing its parts, thus implying that the value of $A + B$ is always equal to the value of $A +$ the value of $B$ as existing separately. This principle is emphatically repudiated by Professor Lewis, and not merely because we cannot, strictly speaking, sum values, since he says that it might be expressed without the use of mathematical language by saying that "there is nothing in the value of any whole of experience beyond the values found in its experiential constituents severally." Against it Professor Lewis insists that life is not a mere aggregate of separate moments, and that the kind of values realized in it could

never be understood by a creature who could adequately envisage any and every moment of experience, and appreciate any value to be found within a

31 GNR, pp. 72-73.

single specious present, but could never put these experiences together in his mind.

The reason for this is that

for a creature which lives a self-conscious and active life, no experience momentarily given says the last word about itself, because its significance for him is never merely of and for that moment. What is immediately given now, has its own fixed and absolute character, with respect to value as in other ways. . . . But there is no moment whose quality and value fails to have a further significance as contributory to or subversive of further and more inclusive aims and values. . . . One could no more appraise any whole of experience justly without respect to such considerations than one could evaluate a piece of music from hearing it played backwards.

It is not merely that one experience causally affects others thus producing experiences factually different from any that could (causally) have occurred without the earlier one, but that the total value of a stretch of life comprising two parts, *A* and *B*, may be very different from what we should expect from considering the value of *A* and *B* by themselves, as is shown by the circumstance that there are cases where we should value the whole stretch of experience much more if *B* followed *A* than if the same *B* preceded *A*. Progress is better than degeneration, so that, if *A* is better than *B*, it may be highly relevant which comes first, and again can we say that it would make no difference to the total value of the experience of attaining something "if the moment of attained desire came first and then had to be paid for by effort and endurance"? Reversal, if it could occur, might take away the whole point and most of the value of the process. Professor Lewis even says that

if one should, without illusion of memory, find a life worth living though the greater portion of it be spent in suffering, there could be no prescribed manner of evaluation which could overrule that finding, or convict one of error in it.

He admits that we could not imagine a good life as constituted solely of evil experiences or a bad whole as constituted solely of good parts, not being like Bradley's optimist who was supposed to hold that this is the best of all possible worlds and everything in it is a necessary evil, but short of such extremes "no rule could be of assistance to us in evaluating a whole of experience beyond the rule that it should be envisaged adequately and truly as a whole, and no part of it omitted from our concern."[32]

Let us note that although there is nothing in a conscious life except those passages of experience which make it up, nevertheless this statement itself is a near-falsification because a life as lived is not the sum of its separate moments.

[32] AKV, pp. 494-99.

The goodness or badness of a life on the whole is not to be found, as Bentham thought, by adding up the transient gratifications of it and subtracting the sum of its griefs. Life is experienced in some parts, and pervasively, whole-wise or Gestaltwise, much as we hear a symphony which is being played and not merely as a succession of notes or chords one after the other.[33]

This feature of values has a most particular application to life as active, for "the goodness of pursuing and attaining is not the goodness found in striving, regardless of the end pursued, plus the goodness found in having something desired regardless of how it is attained."[34]

The introduction of this notion of Gestalten or organic unities must make a radical difference to utilitarianism, perhaps even more than Professor Lewis realizes. Firstly, it is quite incompatible with hedonism. The view may be interpreted in two ways. It may be held that the intrinsic value of a particular experience is actually altered by what occurs subsequently, or it may be held that it always remains the same whatever happens afterwards but that the value of a whole set of varied experiences may acquire an additional increment over and above the value of the experiences themselves (or incur a loss) because of the relation in which they stand to each other. (I think the latter is Professor Lewis' view.) [35] But on neither interpretation can it be reconciled with the reduction of the goodness of something to its pleasantness. The pleasantness of yesterday as lived through cannot possibly be altered by anything that happens today; the pleasure with which I look back upon it might, but that would be today's pleasure, not yesterday's. And the second interpretation would also be incompatible with hedonism because it would make goodness dependent not only on pleasure but on the relation between pleasures. There cannot be a pleasure in a whole experience over and above the pleasure enjoyed in the successive phases of it. Now one may certainly be a utilitarian without being a hedonist, but this seems to me to raise a special difficulty for Professor Lewis' view. For, if his quality of goodness is not pleasantness, what is it? It is a recognized and very general objection to Moore's view that most philosophers find it impossible to discover a single simple quality, goodness, on inspection. Moore's good is of course *nonnatural*, but is it any easier to find a single, simple *natural* quality of goodness present in everything that can be pronounced intrinsically good, when we have set aside pleasantness, the one tolerably promising candidate for the position? I doubt it.

33 GNR, p. 68.
34 AKV, p. 498.
35 AKV, pp. 479, 503.

Secondly, the *Gestalt* theory destroys the possibility of determining the goodness or badness of the total consequences of an act by any system of inferences. The value of a Gestalt cannot be inferred from its parts but only seen at a glance.

Thirdly, it raises serious difficulties about the conception of the *greatest* good. On Professor Lewis' theory this conception loses its numerical character and seems to become simply the good which it would be rational to prefer. This seems to me an improvement, but if 'best' is understood as meaning 'rationally to be preferred over all alternatives', ought not 'good' also to be defined in terms of rational choice, so that it should mean, not indeed 'rationally to be preferred' since this implies comparison, but 'rational object of choice or pursuit for its own sake, other things being equal'? We cannot define the superlative of an adjective in one way and the positive in a quite different way, unless we hold that 'best' really does not mean the same as 'most good'. If this view, which is incidentally mine apart from certain minor reservations, were adopted, right would be prior to good, thus destroying utilitarianism in the ordinary sense.

Since we cannot arrive at the value of a whole by summing its parts, we can only discern its value by what Professor Lewis calls 'synthetic apprehension'. This is not a case of intuitive knowledge of an a priori proposition but the imagining of a whole complex set of experiences in order to enable us to realize what it would feel like to have them, or the simpler task of remembering a past experience or phase of our life as a whole and so getting an idea of its goodness or badness. This problem of how to evaluate goods is of course of the greatest importance for determining what acts are right as long as we hold consequences to be relevant at all. Where we have to determine the rightness or wrongness of an action affecting various other persons, ideally we should need, Professor Lewis thinks, to imagine the experiences of the different people as all belonging to ourselves in succession and then try to view them as a whole in a single span of attention so that we may have an adequate impression of the value of them all taken together. We should further have to allow for probability by the ingenious method of imagining for a probability of $m/n$ what it would be like to have the value $m$ times in $n$ successive trials.[36] At least

however fantastic the supposition that we could in practice arrive at evaluation of an object by carrying out this program in detail and collating all the possible satisfactions it may contribute to human life, in the manner indicated, still our actual and practical estimates of the value which a thing has to society at large,

---

[36] AKV, p. 550.

will be more or less accurate according as they approximate more or less closely to the total evaluation which would be so arrived at. And the theoretical possibility of such theoretical value-determination is what gives practical significance to our practical estimate.[37]

Professor Lewis speaks in terms of the evaluation of objects, but I do not see how he could but apply what he has said to the determination of the rightness of actions.

There are a number of difficulties here of which I shall mention two.

(1) To imagine the experiences of the persons affected by my actions as if they were to occur successively to myself would on occasion distort their ethical significance. There are, e.g., ethical objections to the infliction of suffering on a man for the benefit of somebody else which would not arise if it were for the man's own undisputed benefit.

(2) I might like one kind of life very much more than another and yet on moral grounds pronounce the former less good intrinsically and not only instrumentally for its effect on other people. Would people of all temperaments really like a life of continuous heroic moral effort and self-sacrifice better than a moderately selfish one? Even if moral wrongness is relative to consequences (or at least the consequences the kinds of action in question generally tend to have), morally wrong actions are also intrinsically bad, yet people often enjoy doing them.

But Professor Lewis admits that the rightness of an action cannot be determined by reference to the goodness or badness of its consequences without introducing also some principle of a nonempirical kind. It may be noted that in this respect he agrees with Sidgwick, the man who has probably given the most detailed philosophical exposition and defence of hedonistic utilitarianism. It will be plain to any who have read my discussion up to this point that I agree with him there. It seems obvious that the mere assertion that there is a simple empirical quality of any kind present in some set of results or present in it in greater degree than in any possible alternative is not already to say that the action with these results ought to be performed. Nor could the connection between the two be established inductively unless the quality of obligatoriness were also regarded as empirically discoverable. Besides there is the question whose good we ought to take into account. There is no strictly empirical refutation of egoistic hedonism unless we mean by 'wrong' disapproved by most people or productive of unhappiness on the whole, which is certainly not Professor Lewis' view. And he realizes the validity and importance of Kant's two principles, the principle of universalization and the principle that men ought to be treated as

37 AKV, p. 551.

ends-to-themselves, or at least of something like what Kant was trying to
express when he formulated these. We must for these reasons regard
Professor Lewis' ethical philosophy as an attempt at a synthesis between
naturalism and rationalism, and he would certainly wish it so regarded.
In the last paragraph of *The Ground and Nature of the Right* he de-
clares that ethical naturalism and ethical rationalism are complementary
and not antithetic. One might perhaps sum up his view by saying that
he appeals to experience to determine what things are good and to
rationalism to determine the principles on which the good is to be distributed, a not prima facie unreasonable division of labour. And he
insists on assimilating rationality in action to rationality in thought in
opposition to very much contemporary moral philosophy. An attempt by
a philosopher of Professor Lewis' standing to build up a view of this
type is an important event in the history of the subject, and without
thereby committing myself to 'naturalism' in ethics I venture to express
the hope that he will be followed by many others. It is one of the most
promising philosophical circumstances of today that at least in my own
country (I am not sufficiently familiar with the situation in the United
States to judge) the prevailing tendency is to seek to build a bridge over
the yawning chasm which a little while ago seemed to separate the nonnaturalist and rationalist or intuitionist from the empirical and naturalist
or subjectivist schools. Everyone should welcome the accession of Professor Lewis to the bridge-builders. Nor have I much criticism to make
of his account of the rational principles determining right action. My
chief complaint is that his view is not worked out more fully.

For what purposes are rational principles needed in his ethics? In the
first place, it seems, we must have a principle which connects right and
good. Otherwise there would be no reason why he ought to do anything.
Professor Lewis, as we have seen, insists that right and good are essentially connected, and he does not make this either a definition or an
empirical proposition. He further notes that there is an element in the
right which is not present in the good. "The achievement of the good
is desirable but conformity to the right is imperative."[38] In his general
theory of knowledge he rejects synthetic a priori propositions,[39] but the
above admission seems to imply that any proposition connecting right
and good is synthetic in the sense which most advocates of synthetic
a priori propositions have had in mind. But he does not dwell on this
principle as much as on certain others in his account of rationality in
ethics.

[38] GNR, p. 59.
[39] AKV, pp. 158 ff.

Granted that the right depends on the good, whose good is relevant? Professor Lewis admits that he cannot logically refute egoism, or even an egoist of the present moment who should see no point in considering even his own future welfare, but he insists that at any rate a man who took such views would certainly not be rational. So far as we are concerned with prudence, Professor Lewis thinks, "to be rational means only to value a satisfaction not presently realized as we should value it if and when experienced," with the implication that similarly, when we go beyond prudence, rationality requires us to treat other people's satisfactions as just as important as our own.[40] So in *The Ground and Nature of the Right* he suggested that

what lies at the root of all the imperatives of our thinking and doing [is] the Law of Objectivity; so conduct and determine your activities of thinking and of doing, as to conform any decision of them to the objective actualities, as cognitively signified to you in your representational apprehension of them, and not according to any impulsion or solicitation exercised by the affective quality of your present experience as immediate feeling merely.[41]

The Law of Objectivity, he suggests, should be divided into two principles.[42] One of these is the Law of Compassion which affirms that we should take account of the happiness and suffering of others. One might have expected that the statement of it as an offshoot of the Law of Objectivity should be to the effect that we ought to be as much influenced in our action by the good of others as by the equal good of ourselves (and similarly with evil), but it is actually stated here in a weaker and less precise form. The second principle, the Law of Moral Equality, "dictates respect for others not only as ends in themselves but as entitled to full self-determination of their individual action, to some privacy of decision, and to freedom from coercion in their decisions taken, so long as they bring no harm to others and accord to others a like freedom."[43] In *An Analysis of Knowledge and Valuation* Professor Lewis seems to be expressing the same kind of view when he identifies rationality with consistency.[44] Consistency requires that I should treat the good of others as of equal importance with my own and that I should treat other men qua rational beings as subject to the same freedom and entitled to the same rights as I claim for myself on account of my capacity as a rational being. From the Law of Moral Equality is derived a principle of universalization like that of Kant. The basis of

40 AKV, p. 550.
41 GNR, p. 89.
42 GNR, p. 91.
43 GNR, p. 92.
44 AKV, p. 480.

this lies for Professor Lewis in the fact that a rational being must have reasons for his decisions, and a reason that is valid once will *always* be valid in similar circumstances. Since we must take account of all relevant circumstances, this does not mean that there is necessarily any class of acts signifiable simply by a general rule which are always wrong or always right. And it is stated negatively, not positively.

An act is wrong if it contravenes *any* rule of right doing. And it is right only if it contravenes *no* rule of right doing.[45] . . . Thus, logically viewed, the significance of "Do right" is "Do no wrong"; "Do nothing you would call upon others universally to avoid."[46]

It is not claimed that there is any logical self-contradiction in denying these principles. We can, if we like, act just according to our momentary desires without rational justification, but if we wish to be guided by reason in our actions, we must follow them. A reason valid under certain circumstances must always be valid under the same ethically relevant circumstances, i.e., if it is applied in some cases and not in others, a ground for this must be found in a difference in the circumstances. It might be thought that the principle of objectivity already entails strict utilitarianism. It seems to imply that I ought to consider everybody's good as of equal value with my own, and if so it may seem to follow that our duty is always to produce the greatest good irrespective of who has it. But Professor Lewis draws no such inference: even the egoist, he holds, might accept these principles.[47] What the consistent egoist would say presumably is:—Every man's good is equally important, and everybody has an equal right to pursue his own, but nobody has any obligation to help anybody else or even, if it suits his own interest, to abstain from bringing on him evil. That is not logically self-contradictory. All we can say is that the egoist is justifying a course for himself which he in practice could not help condemning in others if they pursued it in defiance of his interests. It would in any case be very odd if such a conclusion as universalistic utilitarianism could be established simply by a priori deduction from the nature of reasonableness. If so, the principle of objectivity would conflict not only with egoism but with the ethics of most people, for most people hold that they are not under an equal obligation to promote the good of everybody. It is generally recognized that a man has a stronger obligation to promote the good of

[45] The conception of prima facie duties expounded by Sir David Ross is unfortunately ignored by Professor Lewis. Of course a right act can be in some respect prima facie wrong.

[46] GNR, pp. 94-95.

[47] GNR, p. 95.

his children or parents than to promote that of a complete stranger. But presumably all the principle of objectivity does is to lay it down that another man's good has as much claim on me as my own equal good, other things being equal. It may be maintained that the existence of certain relations between me and some men which do not exist between me and others is a circumstance often ethically relevant so that, where it is a question of a man choosing between producing a certain good for his child and an equal good for a stranger, other things are not equal. Without already covertly assuming the utilitarian principle it does not commit one to saying that degree of goodness is the only criterion relevant to determining what has a claim on one and the degree of force of the claim. Indeed the principle of objectivity, as it is stated, seems no more than the tautology that reason requires one to decide on the merits of the case and not to let ourselves be led astray by our emotions and prejudices, or at least if we once make the assumption that there is a reasonable way of deciding practical questions, the principle adds nothing to this but a tautology.

I should add that it is self-evident that the mere fact that a good belongs to somebody other than myself does not cancel all obligation to produce the good, but that is a synthetic proposition.

Besides the very general principles mentioned, Professor Lewis evidently thinks there are others dependent on some reference to empirical facts and yet not deducible simply from the goodness of the results of carrying them out.[48] They are needed to determine what is just by bringing in considerations of individual desert. But he does not make any attempt to formulate or discuss them. His attitude, however, is significant as showing that he does not think utilitarianism the right view, since he is not prepared to identify the useful with the just and evidently regards it as at least probably false to hold that justice is only right when it is compatible with the production of the best possible results. Here two points strike me as very relevant.

(1) A theory of ethics can conflict with utilitarianism only if it disagrees with the principle that the rightness of an action is determined by the *quantity* of good it will produce (allowing for probability or improbability where necessary), compared to that producible by alternative actions. But any strictly quantitative way of looking at good has been rejected by Professor Lewis in favour of the view that the best alternative is just that which, if experienced by us *in toto* with proper attention to all its parts, we should on rational consideration find preferable. How would he answer the objection that, if this is what 'the

[48] AKV, p. 554; GNR, pp. 72-73.

greatest good' means, it is self-contradictory to say that we ought not to choose the course which will produce it? Is it not saying that it is in some cases irrational to choose what we rationally ought to choose?

(2) Might not the situation be met by a reference to the *Gestalt* principle without any divergence from utilitarianism? The principle of justice lays it down that the rightness of an act depends not only on the total good it produces but also on the way in which that good is distributed, but to a utilitarian who accepts the *Gestalt* principle need there be any difficulty about this? All he need say is that in the acts required by justice we are still producing the greatest good but in determining what this is we must consider not only the amount of good enjoyed by the different individuals concerned but also the relation between their goods, which, if the distribution is unfair, may be so undesirable as to outweigh the advantage gained by greater individual enjoyment. What the Gestalt theory of Professor Lewis just says is that the value of a whole is not necessarily in proportion to the value of its several parts but depends also on the relations between them.

Professor Lewis holds that these principles, though not themselves empirical, have an essential reference to experience as determining how they are to be applied in particular.

It takes two things to determine the rightness of action: a rule or directive of right doing or something operative in the manner of a rule, and a judgment of goodness to be found in the consequences of the act in question . . . Observation that it takes both these things to constitute an act right is, I think, often overlooked, and one or the other of them may be cited as if it alone were a sufficient ground of such rightness. Possibly that helps to explain the opposition between those who emphasize goodness and consequences and those who emphasize conformity to principle and moral perfection.[49]

The rule is that the major premise, through empirical consideration of consequences determines the minor. Thus, in order to apply the Kantian principle of universalization, we must ask whether the consequences of universalizing a particular rule of action would be good or bad; to apply the law of objectivity in considering the effects of an action we must rely on our empirical sense that this kind of effects in the past have been satisfying or dissatisfying.

The justification of the nonempirical principles [I do not think they are called a priori till the lecture on *Social Inheritance*] presents our last problem. Professor Lewis admits that they are not strictly demonstrable,[50] but he does suggest ways of argument which without being

[49] GNR, pp. 75-76.
[50] GNR, pp. 84-85.

demonstrative show the irrationality of the ethical sceptic. He argues that the necessity to make decisions and to make them rationally, and so the essential ethical attitude, is rooted in human nature. We cannot help deciding, for not to decide is itself a decision, and we must decide for some assignable reason, but if we accept the reason as valid in one case we commit ourselves to acting and thinking consistently with it hereafter. He, however, also produces a further argument which it might be contended was demonstrative, since he thinks that the ethical sceptic is bound logically to be also a sceptic as to all knowledge, and to show that a view leads to complete theoretical scepticism has often been regarded as equivalent to demonstrating its falsity. It has been said that to prove that you must either accept a certain proposition or accept nothing, is the only way of completely proving anything. But Professor Lewis does not think that he has achieved complete demonstration in this way. In any case I do not think that ethical scepticism need involve theoretical scepticism. Professor Lewis argues that, if general scepticism as to values were accepted, it would entail that all knowledge was futile because valueless.

. . . those who would deny the character of cognition and the possibility of truth to value-apprehensions, must find themselves, ultimately, in the position of Epimenides the Cretan who said that all Cretans are liars. Either their thesis must be false or it is not worth believing or discussing; because if it should be true, then *nothing* would be worth believing or discussing.[51]

But the argument seems to me open to the objection that there is a distinction between saying that nothing is worth discussing and saying that there is no ground for holding any proposition to be true. The ethical sceptic can still discuss if he wants to do so, although the discussion is on his view of no objective value, and arguments could still have a logical connection with their conclusion even if there were never any ethical obligation to use them or value to be produced by doing so. And they might lead to true beliefs, psychologically and logically, even if it did not matter in the least whether we had true beliefs or not. I cannot agree with Professor Lewis that value judgments are prior to logic itself.[52]

Yet the 'must' of Professor Lewis' argument is not merely a psychological must. It seems to be a logical must of a hypothetical character. If we are to act rationally, or insofar as we do act rationally, we must accept his principles. As we all know to our cost, a man may very well act irrationally, and there is no self-contradiction per se in ignoring

51 AKV, p. 373, Cf. p. 366.
52 AKV, p. 480.

the principles in action and even in denying them in theory, but we all aim at being rational in our actions at least for part of the time, and insofar as we are rational at all we assume the principles in question. If we are to be rational, we must consider all circumstances fairly and not be prejudiced by our present feelings (the law of objectivity), and we must not accept a reason for or against an action without being prepared to admit its validity also in any other similar case. We may thus say that these principles owe their validity to being deduced a priori from the nature of rationality. Their necessity is only hypothetical, but it has a binding force on us insofar as we cannot help aspiring to rationality. This is the function of the argument for Professor Lewis. It is not a mere appeal to intuition, and if valid at all, it must like Kant's ethic be valid, though Professor Lewis does not, I think, mention this point, not for the human race only but for all rational beings. But the limits of what one can establish in this a priori way are very narrow. The argument can only give the most general formal conditions of right ethical thought. Neither the principle of objectivity nor the universalization principle tells us anything about the concrete goods which their application presupposes. Of these we must learn by a unique mode of apprehension which Professor Lewis, I think, has assimilated too closely to sensation, while it has been assimilated too closely to a priori logical thinking by other writers (including, I fear, myself in the past) but which is really very different from either.

A. C. EWING

DEPARTMENT OF PHILOSOPHY
CAMBRIDGE UNIVERSITY

## 23

## William R. Dennes
# LEWIS ON THE MORALLY IMPERATIVE

IN *An Analysis of Knowledge and Valuation* (1946), *The Ground and Nature of the Right* (1955), and *Our Social Inheritance* (1957), Clarence Irving Lewis has given us what seems to the present writer to be the most thorough and enlightening examination presently available of leading historical and contemporary positions in value theory, in ethics, and in theory of knowledge, and of the fundamental relations of these to one another. While he accepts in large part the position of philosophical naturalism in value theory, he goes a long way towards showing that insights essentially Kantian with respect to moral imperatives are not only compatible with such naturalism but are an indispensable supplement to it. "If," he writes in the concluding chapter of his Woodbridge Lectures,

we look briefly to the general character of any ethic which should conform to the general conclusions here reached, we may observe that it would be of that type usually called naturalistic, so far as it is classified by reference to the thesis that no act can be determined as right or wrong without reference to consequences of it as good or bad. Also, it would be naturalistic in its interpretation of good and bad as matters of empirical fact and as significant, at bottom, of naturally found qualities of experience. It would, however, have a character frequently taken to be antithetic to naturalism; namely, in the thesis that right and wrong are nevertheless indeterminable except by reference of rules or principles—principles themselves including reference to the good and bad as essential to determining what specifically they dictate. It would likewise be liable to classification as antithetic to naturalism in its conclusion that these imperatives of right, and the validity of them, have no other determinable and final ground than that character of human nature by which it is called rational. However, if a view incorporating both sets of these features can be consistently maintained, then what so appears is that ethical naturalism and ethical rationalism (if "rationalism" is the right word here) are not in fact antithetic but complementary. Perhaps they are antithetic only for a naturalism which connotes nature short of human nature, or for a rationalism which interprets rationality as non-natural and significant of some transcendent world.[1]

---

[1] C. I. Lewis, *The Ground and Nature of the Right* (New York: Columbia University Press, 1955), p. 97. Hereafter cited as GNR.

Other sections of this book deal in detail with Lewis' theory of value; but it would be impossible to discuss his account of the morally imperative without some explicit reference to that theory since he regards judgments of value as indispensable to, and in certain senses antecedent to, judgments of duty. "There are," he holds, "two main forms of such critical judgment: appraisals of the good and bad, and assessments of the right and wrong. As between these two, it is the sense of good and bad which must be antecedent, and the sense of right and wrong which presumes that and is built upon it."[2]

While Lewis makes good use of the work of Aristotle[3] and of Hume,[4] as well as of more recent writers, in what he says about the nature of value he addresses himself primarily and directly to the subject matter itself. His analysis is fresh, straightforward, and in the best sense empirical. It depends much less upon philosophical 'isms'—even those he mentions with respect—than any brief account of it can suggest. He develops what seems to me a definitive analysis and criticism of Benthamite utilitarianism,[5] emphasizing the fact that "the value of an experiential whole may be affected not only by the values immediately found in its separate and included moments but by the relation of these moments of experience to one another."[6] He corrects the notion that the fallacy which G. E. Moore has made famous is either "peculiar to naturalistic theories of ethics or characteristic of all theories of that class."[7] He gives a thoroughgoing (and to me decisive) cricitism of all dogmas that attempt to specify *the* single and absolute value of any object or objects.[8] His writings offer scores of wise and genial opinions about values in various areas of experience and the factors that determine them—opinions that are illustrated by concrete examples, homely or

2 C. I. Lewis, *Our Social Inheritance* (Bloomington, Ind.: Indiana University Press, 1957) , p. 78. Hereafter cited as OSI.

3 E.g., in his theory of objective potentiality, *An Analysis of Knowledge and Valuation* (La Salle, Ill.: Open Court Publishing Co., 1946), hereafter cited as AKV, pp. 433, 511, and elsewhere; in his emphasis on "a whole life" as the subject of moral concern, AKV, p. 485 and Book III, *passim;* and his doctrine that the worth of intrinsic values is not discursively demonstrable or derivable (although Lewis bases his position on considerations very different from Aristotle's doctrine of essence) .

4 E.g., in his warning (AKV, p. 484) against the "tendency to wayward sacrifice of a possible good life to immediate desire."

5 AKV, esp. pp. 488-497.

6 AKV, p. 488.

7 Cf. OSI, p. 82 n.

8 Cf. AKV, pp. 529 f. ". . . there is no such thing as *the* value of an object or objects, which is either relative or absolute, subjective or objective. Instead there are all these various modes in which the value of objects commonly is—and for good reasons must be—assessed; each having its own specific meaning and corresponding criteria of correctness."

recondite, and that make the study of Lewis' books an intellectual feast. But for his doctrine of imperatives the crucial considerations are his distinctions between extrinsic and instrumental values, inherent values, and intrinsic values;[9] his insistence that all intrinsic value is realized as immediate felt satisfaction in the experience of living;[10] his argument that such values may be objective as potentialities in the sense that we can rely upon certain sorts of occurrent transactions to produce experience of them with a probability logically similar to (if of lower degree than) the probability with which we can rely on certain sorts of occurrences to produce experience of shapes, weights, and colors, and also in the sense that some of them are very widely appreciated by many people in quite diverse cultures; his doctrine that where values are compared, felt preference among them and among the consequences of enacting them is the deciding arbitrator;[11] and that the summum bonum for man is a whole of experience—a life as satisfying as one can conceive and can devise reasonable steps to achieve.[12]

Throughout his development of these doctrines Lewis regards value as a quality, or a "dimension-like mode"[13] or determinable (?), that is recognized and appreciated; and he argues that if there were not such a quality (or mode) there would be no sense in the arguments of those who differ about the intrinsically good, and no theoretical conflict between them. Like Spinoza,[14] Lewis recognizes that there is no object or act that may not under some circumstances have value, intrinsic or extrinsic. Many who have followed the work of Santayana, Prall, R. B. Perry, J. R. Reid, and C. L. Stevenson will ask whether it is satisfactory to say (except tautologically) that there is a common value quality in all things that may delight or satisfy (or a common mode quantified and exemplified), or whether the common factor (or dimension-like

9 AKV, pp. 382-392, 432, and Book III, *passim.*

10 AKV, p. 397 ". . . the only thing intrinsically valuable—valuable for its own sake—is a goodness immediately found or findable and unmistakable when disclosed." (P. 407.) ". . . nothing has really intrinsic and ultimate value except such goodness as might characterize a life found good in the living of it . . . ."

11 AKV, p. 544 "Any two of them [i.e., values directly realized or realizable] may be valued comparatively; any two together may be valued in comparison with any third; and so on. The degree of any one of them is fixed by its place in the whole order of possible values in experience; by the total facts of what we should prefer it to and what we should prefer to it."

12 AKV, p. 483 ". . . if in one sense the determination of values must be eventually in terms of the value-qualities of direct experience, still in another sense no immediately experienced good or bad is final, but rather is further to be evaluated by its relation to the temporal whole of a good life."

13 AKV, p. 401.

14 *Ethics,* III, Prop. XXXIX, Scholium, and Prop. XV.

mode) is not the relation of being liked, enjoyed, approved, delighted in, loved. This relation (or family of relations) is one, they would say, into which *any quality*, quite as much as any object, may either enter or not. Whether it does or does not is a contingent fact to be empirically determined. It is not entailed by any factor that could satisfactorily be described as a value quality.

One wishes that the late David Prall were still with us to discuss with Lewis problems about values as quality *vs.* values as objects of positive motor-affective attitudes. He would, I think, welcome Lewis' insistence on taking seriously as conscious awareness (and not merely as behaviorally manifested or reported) processes of imagining, remembering, planning, expecting, enjoying as experienced in one's own life and as we suppose them in the careers of others. And although those who agree with Prall would welcome all that Lewis says about the need for great (and ever-developing) ranges of carefully tested knowledge if we are to predict reliably the consequences of actions, and effectively execute actions that are intelligently deliberate, or at least amenable to thoughtful decision, and would probably welcome also Lewis' insistence on the notion of a whole life as satisfactory as we can conceive as the summum bonum, they would raise the question whether any serious judgment that a given pattern of life is best must not, so far as it is a value judgment, express the felt preference of him who 'envisages' the pattern of life in question and makes the judgment. And this experience of felt preference would be no accidental or dispensable factor, but essentially the factor that makes the difference between even the most informed description or prediction and an actual valuation. In characterizing some recent (mostly naturalistic) philosophical positions as 'emotive',[15] Lewis sometimes belabors straw men. He writes as if those (they are unnamed) who hold such views are themselves merely expressing, and pretending to limit all of us to expressing, casual or momentary and unconsidered whims or velleities. But the able among the naturalists Lewis probably has in mind have recognized as fully as he has the differences between informed carefully considered judgments of wide scope on the one hand, and careless opinions and casual preferences on the other. What they consider constitutive of value is the relation of liking which need not be emotive as that term is used in ethics. What they interpret as 'emotive' statements are another and also an important matter: statements that are used in order to express delight or interest and to induce them in others. Also they would be bound to ask whether there is anything sacrosanct (let alone self-evident) about the notion that a whole life, or the lives

15 E.g.: AKV, p. 413; GNR, pp. 57, 71, 88.

of many generations of men or of all mankind, is the proper object of concern and approval. There is no *principium individuationis* that will determine how extensive a context, or how complex an imagined object, ought to be considered for serious approval or disapproval. Let us remember the ". . . lady, fair and kind; was never face so pleased my mind. I did but see her passing by, and yet I love her till I die." If anybody would advise more caution and fuller knowledge before making such a commitment, would he not be expressing a preference for more scope and wider comparison, and for the probable consequences of these, and recommending these, but in no sense doing something different in logical type from what the poet-lover reports he had done?

Is there an imperative of reason that with another kind of authority enjoins us to consider "wholes of experience"? Lewis' eloquent and often moving account of the factors that enter into what he approves as concern for such wholes—for other men's (and even other animals') experience, and our own future experience and theirs—I find enlightening and very largely persuasive. But is his account thus persuasive, as naturalists would say, as confirming and inducing such attitudes as he recommends? In general Lewis' remedy for the faults of naturalistic philosophies is more thorough and critical, but still essentially naturalistic analysis. Some of those who owe him most will probably judge that his notion of value quality is one that needs such further examination.

Even if one were satisfied that a particular conception of human living, so far as our best (though of course only probable) knowledge goes, had the structure, the scope, and the flexibility to enable mankind to achieve the maximum good (as Lewis understands good) in experience, would it follow that we *ought* to bring such a pattern of living into existence? Not as Professor Lewis interprets these matters. All that would follow would be that in fact the conception in question would be the conception of the most satisfactory life for men. If we are to understand adequately the imperative: Act in such ways as will produce the best life for men; it is indeed necessary to recognize another factor, and Lewis argues that this other factor is the factor of rule or principle which reflects a categorical rational obligation to be consistent. An act may, on Lewis' interpretation be good, and an agent's intentions may be good, in terms of the actual or probable experienced values of them and of their consequences.[16] But the rightness of an act is another matter. "It takes two things, then, to determine the rightness of action: a rule or

---

[16] *Vide*: GNR, p. 63. One of the most instructive of Lewis' contributions is his analysis of the content of an act in terms of the consequences of the agent's commitment to effect it, and the basis of judgment of intentions and purposes as such consequences, expected or actually occurrent. GNR, pp. 47 ff.

directive of right doing, or something operative in the manner of a rule, and a judgment of goodness to be found in the consequences of the act in question."[17]

For Lewis the root of all rules of right—of right thinking and of right doing—lies in the natural rationality of human beings which demands consistency. "Rationality," he writes,

in this sense, is not derivative from the logical: rather it is the other way about. The validity of reasoning turns upon, and can be summarized in terms of, consistency. And consistency is, at bottom, nothing more than the adherence throughout to what we have accepted; or to put it in the opposite manner, the non-acceptance now of what we shall later be unwilling to adhere to. We are *logically* consistent when, throughout our train of thought, or our discourse, we nowhere repudiate that to which we anywhere commit ourselves. Thinking and discoursing are important and peculiarly human ways of acting. Insofar as our actions of this sort are affected with concern for what we may later think or wish to affirm, we attempt to be consistent or rational; and when we achieve this kind of self-accord, then we are logical, and what we think or say, whether true or not, has logical validity.

The conception of *principle*, as implying, at one and the same time, a consistency in what we think and consistency in what we do, and consistency between our thinking and our doing, reflects this same consideration; this same attempt to avoid any attitude of thought or action which later must be recanted or regretted.

Consistency of thought is for the sake of and is aimed at consistency in action; and consistency in action is derivative from consistency of willing—of purposing, of setting a value on. If it were not that present valuing and doing may later be a matter of regret, then there would be no point and no imperative to consistency of any kind. No act would then be affected by relation to any principle, and no thinking by any consideration of validity. Life in general would be free of any concern; and there would be no distinction of what is rational from what is perverse or silly.

To act, to live, in human terms, is necessarily to be subject to imperatives; to recognize norms. Because to be subject to an imperative means simply the finding of a constraint of action in some concern for that which is not immediate; is not a present enjoyment or a present suffering. To repudiate normative significances and imperatives in general, would be to dissolve away all seriousness of action and intent, leaving only an undirected floating down the stream of time; and as a consequence to dissolve all significance of thought and discourse into universal blah. Those who would be serious and circumspect and cogent in what they think, and yet tell us that there are no valid norms or binding imperatives, are hopelessly confused, and inconsistent with their own attitude of assertion.[18]

No one has been clearer than Lewis on the point that the self-consistency of a body of beliefs or of statements, while necessary to their

17 GNR, p. 75.
18 AKV, pp. 480-481.

asserting anything simultaneously or in a single system, is nevertheless perfectly compatible with their being false. It is part of his definition of rationality that those who possess it, if they entertain beliefs and make assertions, as men in fact do, should not commit themselves to mutually contradictory beliefs or assertions. But is this obligation categorical or is it hypothetical because conditioned by the occurrence of the wish to believe or assert something? That there exist members of the class of beings who wish to believe or assert, there can be no doubt. But the fact that the protasis of a hypothetical statement is frequently, or even invariably, true does not make its apodosis a necessary truth. There is some inclination to define 'man' as naming a class of beings that believe and assert. If we adopt such a definition our ascent from a hypothetical and contingent statement to a statement of necessity: "Any member of the class man must believe consistently," is trivial except as it may express (and even induce) a zeal to cultivate and promote among men a respect for such consistency. To render the imperative, 'Be consistent', as categorical we should have to make out as categorical some imperative such as 'Think', or 'Explain', or 'Make statements'. Certainly most men engage to a greater or less extent in such activities; but if we say of any who does not think, or to all of us in moments when we may not be thinking, that we are insofar not human, we are merely illustrating a highly restrictive definition of the term 'man'.

Similar questions rise with respect to Lewis' reliance upon a 'moral sense' of which the recognition of the obligation to be consistent is said to be a clarification, expression, or formulation. "Given this moral sense, recognition of the principle is mere self-clarification; and where the moral sense should be lacking, argument for this or any other principle of action would be pointless. This moral sense may be presumed in humans; and creatures who lack it can only be lured by some kind of bait or driven by some kind of pain."[19]

Lewis' insistence that it is an imperative of reason that our decisions as to how we shall act must be consistent with our best attested knowledge of the probable consequences of our actions seems to me basic to a rational ethics and quite unimpeachable. The question that faces us is the question how far the imperative is tautological. If genuinely to will an action is to commit ourselves to carrying it out successfully, and if our only way to determine how this can best be done is by means of the best available knowledge of relevant cause-effect relations, then (by definition) we are not genuinely willing an action if we attempt to carry

[19] AKV, p. 482.

it out in ignorance of, or in violation of, what we can learn of relevant causal relations. Lewis formulates the relevant imperative as the

. . . Law of Objectivity: So conduct and determine your activities of thinking and doing, as to conform any decision of them to the objective actualities, as cognitively signified to you in your representational apprehension of them, and not according to any impulsion or solicitation exercised by the affective quality of your present experience as immediate feeling merely.[20]

If we accept this imperative and are to proceed consistently, there is no way by which we can pretend that what may be experienced as good in the careers of other men or in our future will be any less good than what we may experience here and now as beautiful, delightful, or otherwise satisfying. Hence Lewis' corollary:

Conduct yourself, with reference to those future eventualities which cognition advises that your activity may affect, as you would if these predictable effects of it were to be realized, at this moment of decision, with the poignancy of the here and now, instead of the less poignant feeling which representation of the future and possible may automatically arouse.[21]

[And]

. . . to govern one's activities affecting other persons, as one would if these effects of them were to be realized with the poignancy of the immediate—hence, in one's own person.[22] . . . so far as is here concerned, to be rational means only to value a satisfaction not presently realized as we should value it if and when experienced.[23]

Students of Lewis' writings will remember that he divides the "most general of moral principles" into two: "The Law of Compassion" and "The Law of Moral Equality."[24] And many will think that he has given his best summary formulation of the moral imperative in the words:

So act and so prefer that the manner of your acting and preferring will be that which, if consistently adhered to, you will be permanently best satisfied to have adopted. Presumably that means acting and choosing in ways such that the lifetime results of them will conduce, in highest possible degree, to satisfaction on the whole.[25]

No brief account of Lewis' theory of the moral imperative can begin to do justice to the genial insights and interpretations he brings to bear to flesh out his conception of the temporal whole of a good life as the

20 GNR, p. 89.
21 GNR, p. 89.
22 GNR, p. 91.
23 AKV, p. 550.
24 GNR, pp. 91-96.
25 AKV, p. 548.

summum bonum; to his clear exemplifications of the respects in which imperatives are formal, cannot dictate specific duties and yet are indispensable; to his successful avoidance of suggestions of a puritanical or pedantic loss of spontaneity in what a brief summary must seem to imply by emphasis on interminable 'concern' about the theoretically illimitable consequences of choices. Lewis' writing, like his *viva voce* teaching, admirably obeys his own wholesome advice to "hold fast to our sense of the real and the reasonable."[26] And no brief summary can suggest the deep understanding with which he explains the contribution made by what he interprets as rational consistency to the continuity, enrichment, and transmission of man's social inheritance. Indeed, many would judge that the literature of philosophy contains no comparably rich discussion of the force and the limits of the requirement of consistency in human activity, both cognitive and practical.

Questions about Lewis' doctrine of imperatives, if briefly put, are likely to be as inadequate as must be any short exposition of his position. Many who agree fully with him in his doctrine that knowledge of the doings and prizings of men and of their conditions and consequences cannot of itself determine what we ought to do, and that the formal imperative: Act in those ways which, if generally followed, would produce for men the most satisfactory life on the whole, is admirable advice, must still raise questions about the status of the formal imperative as a priori, and about the sense in which it is enjoined by 'reason'. If the good for man is conceived, not as a particular quality but as a complex pattern of living experience preferred to any other, i.e., genuinely loved, then is the obligation to do all that is possible to promote such experience something that we should call a dictate of reason, or is it part of what is meant by genuine love that we are committed to effort to bring into existence, to maintain and to nurture what we genuinely love? Insofar as we do not make this effort, is not our pretense of love hypocritical?

What do we accomplish if we assert that rationality, as respect for consistency, is rooted in human nature? That it is obligatory upon a man to evince such respect since if he did not he would not be a man—he would lack 'that character of human nature by which it is called rational' —a character that needs no justification or defense since these would have to assume it and employ it? Would we thus be engaged in empirical investigations in psychology, sociology, political economy and history? These would yield us probable knowledge of what men and their doings are like, but could yield no imperatives—no conclusions as to how we

26 AKV, p. 543.

ought to live or what we ought to do. Or would we be rendering the imperative necessary but wholly empty by insinuating a definition of man as in this sense rational? Or would we be expressing, what I should certainly like to see much more widely prevalent, a profound approval of and commitment to consistency, enlightenment, fairness, and justice as Lewis has interpreted these? It is now perfectly feasible, as everyone knows, for men so to blast, roast, and poison their fellows and themselves that human life will disappear from the face of the earth. Does any categorical imperative command that there be men in existence? That human life must never disappear from the universe? And that consequently consistency of thought and of action is an absolute moral obligation? Do the judgment that the human race ought not to be extinguished, and the judgment that human well-being ought to be enhanced—do these judgments derive their authority as illustrations of, or as derivatives from, definitions of man or of human nature? Or from sociological, economic, and psychological knowledge about patterns of living that will probably satisfy men's needs and use fruitfully and not destructively the tensions generated by inevitable conflicts? Or are they expressions of love for life that might be so lived and shared? Is such love merely, as some say, the *motivation* for efforts to ascertain by scientific study the lineaments of what is satisfying, and for efforts to find the grounds of obligation in something that could suitably be called an imperative of reason? Or is such love the essential factor, over and above information, expressed in any serious moral imperative?

Lewis is right. More than knowledge of probable consequences of alternative actions is required to constitute a judgment of duty. Is the more that is required the imperative of rational consistency? Or is it the imperative of love, without which St. Paul (whom I cite here as moralist rather than as theologian) judged knowledge and power to be worthless. It may be that an even fuller synthesis of the factors of value and of constraining principle can be achieved, and that it would do even fuller justice to moral experience and to moral judgment. It may be that the love, the positive motor-affective attitude, which lifts qualities, objects, and acts out of mere neutral self-identity and makes them values is also the factor that operates essentially when we respect consistency in thought and action. Actually such consistency is in itself something that we can "take or leave"—and some men at all stages of history have certainly chosen pretty thoroughly to leave it. There is little theoretical significance in classifying them as not human, although such a step may express a strong, and sometimes persuasively influential, affective attitude. The price of neglecting consistency (perhaps as much as mankind is now neglecting it) might well be the disappearance of the human race. But is not the judgment that that should not be allowed to happen an expression, not of the recognition of the intrinsic authority of consistency, but of love for human life and for the illimitable range of values it is capable of producing and nourishing? May not the final authority of the imperative and the decisive constituent of values be of the same nature?

WILLIAM R. DENNES

DEPARTMENT OF PHILOSOPHY
UNIVERSITY OF CALIFORNIA

## 24

*Karl H. Potter*

## TERMINATING JUDGMENTS OR TERMINAL PROPOSITIONS?

THIS paper deals with a number of related topics in Lewis' epistemology. In Part I his troublesome doctrine of expressive statements is considered. In this section I try to show that the sources of this doctrine are (1) an unnecessary feature of Lewis' terminating judgments, and (2) an ambiguity in the word 'certain'. I argue that by reformulating terminating judgments as terminal propositions the difficulties over sense-reports can be avoided without harming the remainder of Lewis' system.

In the second part I attempt to suggest that the reformulation proposed in Part I fits well with the sort of solution to the problem of counterfactuals being pioneered by Nelson Goodman. This line of attack involves replacing counterfactual statements with dispositional terms. I try to show that several Lewisian insights are reconstructable along these lines, although his appeal to modal logic as a means of explicating 'real connections' must be rejected.

My approach to these problems is biased toward extensionalism. However, some concessions to nonextensional modes of analysis appear to be necessary, and some of the places where this is so are pointed out in Part II. In Part III, by way of conclusion, I suggest that the search for one basic mode of meaning—either intension or extension—is misguided, and that different types of analysis are appropriate with respect to different types of problems.

### I

In Book Two of *An Analysis of Knowledge and Valuation,* hereafter cited as AKV, C. I. Lewis introduces the notion of an 'expressive language'. This language, he claims, is needed in order to talk about the given elements of sense without attributing to those elements objective properties, an attribution which is clearly subject to doubt and to withdrawal if subsequent evidence proves to be contrary.

More fully, Lewis' argument comes to something like this.

    (1) If anything is to be probable, something must be certain.

(2) Only statements can be certain.

(3) Something is probable.

Thus,          (4) There must be some certain statements.

(5) These statements cannot be analytic, for they must contain references to data which are to serve as evidence for the probabilistic assertions of ordinary discourse.

Thus,          (6) There must be nonanalytic, certain statements about data.

Now            (7) In ordinary discourse all nonanalytic statements are probabilistic, since synthetic and a posteriori, and therefore they are always uncertain.

Therefore (8) The statements about data, in order to be certain, cannot be statements in ordinary discourse at all. They have a special kind of character, and need to be framed in a special kind of language, which may be dubbed 'expressive language'.

Developing this line of thought, Lewis distinguishes three kinds of judgments: (a) nonterminating judgments, which are assertions about matters of fact such as 'the cat is on the mat'; (b) terminating judgments, which are hypothetical assertions of the form 'if $S$ and $A$ then probably $E$', where $S$, $A$, and $E$ are reports of given data of sense; and (c) expressive statements, reports of the given which function as the $S$, $A$, or $E$ of terminating judgments. To give examples of statements in expressive language, Lewis admits, is difficult if not impossible; perhaps the closest one can come is to appeal to the language of appearing: thus: 'green appears now to be presented' might be an approximation as satisfactory as any we can arrive at.

However, it is of the essence for Lewis' theory that even expressive statements like 'green appears now to be presented' must be understood in such a way that the terms in them are identifiable. To use Lewis' own language, 'green', in order to function appropriately, in this context, must have *intension* (in his technical sense[1]); we must have a "criterion in mind" for distinguishing green presentations from those that aren't, since if we had no such criterion, terminating judgments would predict nothing recognizable.

Now trouble looms. Surely we may make mistakes in applying our criterion in mind, in identifying presentations as green. But if we can

---

[1] Lewis distinguishes four 'modes of meaning', of which signification is one. Thus the denotation of 'green' is the class of green objects, the comprehension of 'green' is the class of possible green objects, the signification of 'green' is greenness, and the intension of 'green' includes all properties which anything must have if it is green. This is overly simple; see *An Analysis of Knowledge and Valuation* (La Salle, Illinois: Open Court Publishing Co., 1946), Part I, Chap. III. Hereafter cited as AKV.

make such mistakes, the statement presupposing identification of a datum cannot be certain, since it may be based on such a mistake.

Perhaps, then, we must formulate an expressive statement as 'apparent green is presented now', but this hardly helps. The same problem recurs concerning 'apparent green'. Does it have intension or doesn't it? If it does, expressive statements aren't certain. If it doesn't, what use is the statement? It can't be used to replace the symbol $S$, $A$, or $E$ in terminating judgments, for the function of terminating judgments is to make predictions which may be verified or falsified, and to verify or falsify a judgment presupposes our ability to identify what is predicted as well as the conditions under which the prediction is claimed to apply.

Something has gone wrong here, it would seem. But what? Surely we do want to say that we have criteria in mind, conceived as broadly as is necessary, for identifying the items to which terms refer. Whether intension is logically prior to extension (as Lewis claims) or vice versa, even the hardiest extensionalist hardly wants to deny that we do in fact identify things by appealing to the characteristics which they appear to possess. Rather he suggests that what we in fact do must not be uncritically construed, and that the characteristics we commonly appeal to in identifying are not to be granted existential status, but to be counted as expedient devices, shorthand for more complicated relationships among particular individuals. But even these more complicated relationships, supposing we were clever enough to be able to grasp them, could and should then be appealed to as criteria for identification.

The trouble, then, must lie in the premises of the original argument. Perhaps it lies in Lewis' rejection of the category of synthetic a priori. But I doubt it. Reports of the given data of sense are not usually counted among synthetic a priori statements even by those who defend such a category. It is hard to see on what meaning of 'a priori' one would want to claim that 'green appears to be presented now' is a priori; surely there is no necessary connection between being or appearing green and being or appearing to be presented now, nor vice versa.

We are left, then, with the first two premises: (1) if anything is to be probable, something must be certain; and (2) only statements can be certain. Both these premises involve the word 'certain'. Perhaps the trouble lies in an ambiguity here.

Goodman has suggested distinguishing indubitability from certainty in this connection.[2] His point is that it is one thing to say "if anything is probable, some *datum* must be certain" and another to say "if anything is probable, some *statement* must be certain." The only kind of certainty appropriate to data consists in doubt being inapplicable to them; they are not the sort of thing that can be doubted. The kind of certainty appropriate to statements is of a different order. Statements *are* the kind of thing one can doubt, and if we say that a statement *p* is certain, we mean that, although it is the *kind* of thing one can doubt, it has certain characteristics which guarantee that the doubt is unjustified—*p* will never fail us. Goodman suggests to Lewis that probability requires the indubitability of data but not the certainty of any statement. If Lewis could accept this distinction, he would not be led to the doctrine of expressive language and the trouble that has been indicated, since (1) will now read 'if anything is probable, something must be indubitable', and (2) would be irrelevant to that.

Unfortunately, Lewis cannot easily accept this resolution (or avoidance) of the problem, at least without dispensing with some of the characteristic features of his epistemological theory. For what 'if anything is probable, something must be certain' means for him is this: if any terminating judgment is to be probable, *its* terms must be certain. That is, Lewis' concern is with the probability of terminating judgments of the form 'If *S* and *A* then probably *E*', and he fears that unless *S*, *A*, and *E* are sometimes certain, there will be a regress of probabilities which will defeat the reckoning of any definite probability of the terminating judgment and so render the judgments of fact for which it is evidence unverifiable in principle. The point to note is that, for Lewis, the symbols '*S*', '*A*', and '*E*' stand for *statements,* not data. It is therefore *statements* which must be certain: the sense of 'certainty' which is in question *is*, after all, not indubitability of data but certainty of statements.

Nevertheless, Goodman's line of resolution still seems promising. Our attention is now called to the *structure* of Lewis' terminating judgments. Perhaps they can be reconstrued in such a way that their elements are not statements. Our interest in this possibility may be whetted the more by recalling that Lewis himself confesses difficulty in understanding the nature of the 'if-then' relation in his terminating judgments. He suggests calling these 'real connections', but what he means by this never becomes entirely clear, although it is clear enough that there are several interpretations of them (material implication, formal implication) which he rejects on the grounds that the relation must hold between possible as well as actual cases.

To sum up what has been said so far: Goodman argues that if Lewis could settle for indubitable data he would not need an expressive language. Lewis, however, may reply that such a settlement is not open to him, for he needs the certainty of the statements which are to serve as the antecedents and consequents of his terminating judgments. We must now ask why Lewis' terminating judgments need be statements at all. If we could discover a way to construe them as nonstatemental, we might be able to find a way out of the predicament of 'expressive language'.

Fortunately, the question we need to ask now can be asked very neatly in Lewis' own terminology, and in the pragmatic spirit he so successfully espouses. Lewis distinguishes between two elements in any judgment. One of these elements is the proposition which is asserted; the other is the asserting of it. Thus, 'Mary is baking pies now' is composed of two elements, the proposition *Mary's baking pies now* and the asserting mood. (In what follows, propositions will, as here, be italicized.) Lewis argues that a proposition is a kind of term, differing from simpler terms (like 'green') only in their degree of complexity.

The pragmatic aspect of this distinction may be put thus: we can entertain propositions in various moods, of which the asserting mood is but one. We might command, exhort, suggest, etc., *Mary's baking pies now*. Which one of these moods we entertain a proposition in depends on our purposes at the moment. In all the moods I have mentioned explicitly, one of the purposes that is in point is the purpose of communicating. If we assert or deny or command or exhort or suggest *Mary's baking pies now*, we do it partly because we wish to communicate something to someone, whether it be Mary or some third party.

Now I suggest that, properly speaking, language is a tool which we have developed primarily for the purpose of communication. No doubt it has turned out to serve many other purposes as well, frequently as a result of its function in effecting communication, sometimes in quite remote ways. We have come to use the term 'language' of music, painting, and mathematics, and of philosophically 'ideal' or 'artificial' languages. These must be considered as metaphorical extensions if we accept the thesis I suggest, that language is primarily a tool of communication. For music, painting, and mathematics, as well as the calculi called 'ideal languages', although they may communicate, do so only in a secondary sense: their primary purpose is something else. Music and painting are primarily media of expression; numbers are primarily useful for counting and measuring. And those who have considered themselves to be constructing 'ideal languges' cannot for a moment suppose that their constructions are intended primarily for use in communication—if they seem to be under this illusion sometimes, they can be quickly disillusioned by being asked whether their artificial languages are better or worse than Esperanto. The purposes that reconstructionist philosophers are after are rather the satisfaction of standards of clarity and consistency in *mapping* the structure of some portion or aspect of things.

To be sure, 'mapping' is also metaphorical. 'Reflecting' the structure might be a less picturesque term. However, 'mapping' (which is Goodman's expression) is helpful in reminding us that the purpose of philosophical reconstructions is not primarily communication, since a map is primarily a tool which can be used to reflect structure but not to communicate. As a tool of communication, a map is in itself almost totally defective; a map without a legend or an explanation (in language) communicates little.

Though all this would seem to be clear enough, philosophers persist in linking their activities closely with language, which suggests that there is more to the link than merely a failure to make an obvious distinction. There is of course a great deal more, although it does seem to me that the distinction between communication and mapping as purposes must not be allowed to be forgotten in considering what more is involved. The additional point of critical importance is that if we leave aside those elements in linguistic episodes (normally sentences) which indicate the moods of the episodes, the remaining elements, the propositions, have a structure—and it is exceedingly tempting to identify the structure of those propositions with the structure of a successful map. As a result, philosophers who seek maps—reflections—of the structure of things are constantly confusing that structure of things with the structure of the propositions we use in communicating about that structure. The error is to confuse the material under investigation with our ways of speaking, or more precisely to confuse the structure of the material under investigation with the structure of those ways of speaking. At best, the ways of speaking may provide clues. The mistake of much contemporary linguistic philosophy is to suppose that the clues are identical with what they are clues *for*.

Now let us return to Lewis' terminating judgments. What is the primary use to which he proposes to put them? Is it communication? I think not. Rather I suspect it is mapping, or reflecting, the structure of the relations among the given elements of sense themselves—and that, as was just argued, is a different purpose.

This may not be altogether clear. What we are inclined to say, I suppose, is that the primary purpose of terminating judgments for Lewis is to make predictions. Unfortunately, 'making predictions' is a way of describing a purpose which is particularly ambiguous as between mapping and communicating. However, I think it can be shown that in fact mapping *is* the primary purpose intended when we say we are interested in making predictions, and that communication is only secondary. A simple way to suggest this is to ask whether the theory of terminating judgments is successful only if it communicates something to people, or is it rather that the theory is successful only if it reflects testable sequences? Surely Lewis' answer must be the latter. A theory intended merely to enable us to communicate, but without requiring that what is communicated be tied down to identifiable experiences, is of little philosophical interest. The philosopher aims for accuracy, adequacy, clarity, and consistency; the purpose of providing a tool for communication can be met without any of these being satisfied, as witness the fact that we can and do talk inaccurately, inadequately, unclearly, and inconsistently and still communicate perfectly well.

If I am right, then, it may be possible to replace Lewis' terminating judgments with some other tool for mapping testable sequences, and to effect this change without necessitating the sacrifice of any of Lewis' aims except possibly his aim—if he has it—of discovering a method of *communicating* more successfully.

The source of Lewis' difficulty, as we have come to see it now, lies in his insisting that the evidence for nonterminating judgments must be further statements of a hypothetical sort. The reason why this is troublesome is that the phrase 'if . . . then . . .' requires statements in the blanks, and this forces Lewis to invent a kind of statement to fill out the blanks in his terminating judgments. But Lewis only need appeal to 'expressive language' if indeed he has no alternative to formulating the evidence for nonterminating judgments as statements. And in particular he does have an alternative provided he does not need his evidence to be entertained in any mood, such as the assertive mood. That is to say, Lewis may perfectly well remove the asserting element from his terminating judgments, leaving us with the proposition it asserts, provided that his purpose does not primarily involve communication.

The question seems to be whether predictions can be thought of apart from their formulations as statements, and if so whether such non-asserted predictions can properly stand as evidence for nonterminating judgments, which are categorical assertions. The second part of the question seems to be answerable in the affirmative. We think of evidence for assertions in nonstatemental form frequently, and this is evidenced (though not demonstrated) by the way we sometimes talk. E.g., we can easily say 'this substance's solubility is evidence that it is salt'—just as easily as its assertive equivalent 'that this substance is soluble is evidence that it is salt', or even 'the fact that if this substance were placed in water it would dissolve is evidence that it is salt'. And this way of speaking suggests an affirmative answer to the first part of our question too. For

'this substance's solubility' seems to be predictive without being formulated as a statement.

This suggests that the solution to Lewis' difficulty may be effected
by replacing *terminating judgments by terminal propositions.*

Such a line of solution has already been pioneered in part by Goodman.[3] He suggests that we systematically replace puzzling counterfactual
hypotheticals by dispositional statements, so that 'if this substance were
placed in water it would dissolve' becomes 'this substance is water-
soluble'. If we then remove the assertive element of such a statement,
we are left with a dispositional term, 'this substance's water-solubility'.

This reform of Lewis' way of speaking has a communicative drawback.
Although 'water-solubility' is straightforwardly understandable, in the
cases Lewis is concerned with the result of the reform is barbarism. For
example, take the evidence for 'this is a doorknob', one of Lewis' examples. One of the terminating judgments which stands as evidence for
'this is a doorknob' may be 'if visual data of a brown sort are presented
and kinaesthetic hand-moving data are also presented, then a sensation
of hardness will result'—this being a way of expressing our familiar
experience of touching the doorknob with our hand. Our reformed procedure replaces this statement with the following term: 'brown-hand-
moving-hardable'! This is highly inconvenient if we want to communicate easily. But as a way of distinguishing the elements involved in the
evidence for 'this is a doorknob'—leaving aside communication as a
purpose and concentrating on mapping—it differs from the statement in
only two important respects: it replaces the statemental 'if . . . then . . .'
by the suffix 'able', and it leaves aside any reference to a mood.

Does this reformulation of terminating judgments into terminal propositions help Lewis escape his predicament? We saw that Goodman suggests that it is the indubitability of data that Lewis needs to ground
probability, and not the certainty of any statement, and we saw further
that Lewis has to reply that he needs *both*, since it is statements which
stand as the terms in his terminating judgments. The reformulation
proposed allows Lewis to get along without certain statements by
getting along without terminating judgments. And this is effected in
two steps: (1) replacing 'if . . . then . . .' by '-able', and (2) removing
the mood-indicator and leaving the proposition standing alone.

But it may well be objected at this point that I have hardly done
justice to the full scope of Lewis' difficulty, and that the proposed
reformulation does not really meet the problem. For essentially what

[3] Nelson Goodman, *Fact, Fiction and Forecast* (Cambridge, Mass.: Harvard University
Press, 1955), Chapter Two.

has happened is this: Goodman offers two alternative senses of 'certain', one applicable to things such as data, the other applicable to statements. Since Lewis' commitment to statements leads him into hot water, we replace the statements with terms. But this is only successful, it may be argued, just as long as we avoid inquiring into the nature of the third sense of 'certain', the sense applicable to *terms*.

There is an easy answer to this objection, and that is that there is no sense of 'certain' which applies to terms. I think in fact this answer is sufficient. But the objector has something of importance on his mind. What he is worrying about is not the certainty of terms, but the certainty of our identification of a thing as properly named by a term. His point is of the following sort: if Lewis is right, every term, including propositions, has a criterion of application. Now it is a judgment on our part that a given term '$D$' applies to a specific item in our experience $x$, and this judgment is open to error and subject to withdrawal. We may be wrong in applying '$D$' to $x$, since we may have misunderstood the criteria governing the term's use.

Before dealing with this objection, let me point out something encouraging about it in comparison with a parallel sort of criticism which Lewis himself tries to meet. The objection which Lewis has to meet is similar to the one just described, but there is one important difference; the critic who argues that the $S$, $A$, and $E$ of Lewis' terminating judgments are always only dubiously applicable appeals to at least two sources of error: (1) our not understanding which criteria govern the use of the term in question, and (2) the possibility that we are under some undetected illusion in thinking that a datum of that sort appears or has appeared to be presented. To explain: an $S$, $A$, or $E$ which can fit into Lewis' terminating judgment must have a minimal structure involving at least one quale-term and the phrase 'appears to be presented' or 'seems to appear' or some such predicate; thus, e.g., 'datum $D$ appears to be presented' might be an $S$. Now it is open to a critic to suggest, not only that in a given instance we may be under a misapprehension about the proper use of the term '$D$', but also that even if we are right in our classificatory procedures we may be quite mistaken in thinking that that kind of experience has appeared to be presented. This possible line of criticism gives Lewis a great deal of trouble, leading him, among other things, into the backwaters of the trustworthiness of memory.[4] The encouraging thing about our reform and the criticism with which we now have to deal is that only one of the two sources of error can arise on our account, since a term or proposition by itself can make no claim

[4] AKV, particularly pp. 357 ff.

that anything is presented. Thus our removal of the assertive component
of Lewis' terminating judgments removes one source of difficulty, indeed
the source Lewis himself finds the most serious of all.

We are left with the other part, the objection, even on our view of
terminal propositions, that we may not understand which criteria govern
the use of '*D*'. But supposing we make such a mistake, we may reply:
what harm is there? Suppose people normally use '*D*' to apply to red
things, and we, beset by color-blindness, use it to apply to green things?
Clearly communication with normal people may be considerably dis-
rupted. But we have already dissociated ourselves from any claim to be
serving the ends of communicative expediency.

There may be thought to be some harm, however, to the purposes we
*are* committed to. For (to make use again of the mapping metaphor) if
our map identifies elements in the terrain ambiguously or too vaguely,
this will disrupt the usefulness of the map. And confusion on our part
about the criteria governing the use of '*D*' as a mapping term will
therefore defeat the end being sought.

The obvious answer to this is that, after all, it is up to us whether
'*D*'—as a *mapping* term—functions properly or not. The only way to
make a term more precise or unambiguous is to indicate precisely what
criteria we intend 'D''s proper application to involve. If it be now
objected that this involves an appeal to ordinary language and sets up
a regress of possible misunderstandings, we again point out that this
may be disturbing for communicative purposes but is logically distinct
from the primary purpose of the map itself. *This* regress is irrelevant to
questions of evidence, and does not undermine the probability of terminal propositions.

However, it might be thought that by throwing out terminating
judgments I have also thrown out probabilities altogether, which is
surely too drastic a way of solving Professor Lewis' problems! But this
is not the case, for I insist below that the probability factor be kept in
the terminal proposition, whatever complications in formulation that
may involve. We shall next turn to some of the problems about the
proper analysis of terminal propositions, and consider how probabilities
can be incorporated into them.

## II

So far our task has been confined to providing Lewis with a way of
grounding probability without committing himself to the paradoxical
doctrine of 'expressive language'. But it was pointed out earlier that
there is an additional reason why our interest may be whetted at the

prospect of replacing terminating judgments by terminal propositions. Lewis tells us his view requires a peculiar kind of 'if . . . then . . . ' relation which he dubs 'real connection' or 'strict implication' and contrasts with the 'if-thens' of material and formal implication as in *Principia Mathematica*. In short, Lewis' epistemological theory not only suffers under the difficulties of expressive language; it also has difficulties with the problem of counterfactual propositions or, otherwise phrased, the status of possibilities.

It will be immediately recognized, surely, that the solutions to both Lewis' problems—expressive language and real connections—seem to lie along the same path, if Goodman is right. The 'if . . . then . . .' form of judgments is unnecessarily opaque, and the results of this obscuring formulation become evident when we observe the two unsatisfactory doctrines to which it leads Professor Lewis. That both difficulties can be avoided at once by the same expedient is, I think it can hardly be denied, a welcome discovery if true.

My thesis in the remainder of this paper is that Lewis provides us in AKV with sufficient reason to reject his own proposed line of solution to the counterfactual problem and to accept something resembling Goodman's.

Lewis, following Frege and anticipating Hare, suggests that we systematically analyze judgments by separating the proposition entertained from its mode of entertainment. He also suggests that a proposition is a kind of *term* and has the same varieties ('modes') of meaning as other terms. What this amounts to is a suggestion about an appropriate method of philosophical analysis. Let us try to see how this method can benefit us.

It seems clear that we are helped in understanding the structure of a proposition if we remove the misleading aspects pertaining to the mood in which the proposition is entertained. This is to say that we wish to refrain from counting doubt as part of what is entertained in 'I doubt that $p$', for example. Likewise, in 'I assert that $p$', my asserting is not to be counted as an element in $p$. So far so good.

The more interesting questions begin when we ask, for example, which parts of the structure of (1) 'Mary runs and Sally runs' we wish to count as part of the proposition asserted, and which as part of the asserting. I might translate (1) as either

(1a) *'Mary's running and Sally's running, yes'*

or as

(1b) *'Mary's running, yes and Sally's running, yes'*.

In (1a) the conjunction is part of the proposition asserted—the phrastic, to borrow Hare's expression—whereas in (1b) the conjunction is part of the mode of asserting—the neustic. Or compare (2) 'Suppose that Mary and Sally are both running', which is equally ambiguous between

(2a) *'Mary's running and Sally's running,* suppose'

and

(2b) *'Mary's running,* suppose and *Sally's running,* suppose'

or (3) 'Mary and Sally, run!', which might be either

(3a) *'Mary's running and Sally's running,* do!'

or

(3b) *'Mary's running,* do! and *Sally's running,* do!'

Is there any good reason to choose one of these translations rather than the other? It rather depends on what one proposes to do next. If one intends to try to find a referent, or a map-location (so to speak), for *every* element in the translation, whether in the phrastic or the neustic, then it doesn't matter. If, on the other hand, one proposes to treat only the phrastic as the referential component of the judgment, then it does matter, since on interpretation (a) we shall have to look for something for *and* to refer to whereas on interpretation (b), since the *and* has been exported to the neustic, we are not obliged to find a referent for it.

Actually, we might well have judgments which have conjunction-elements in both the phrastic and the neustic. Thus, e.g., (4) 'Mary and Sally, run along, and Jacky, you run along too!' might well be rendered as

(4a) *'Mary's running and Sally's running,* do! and *Jacky's running,* do!'

It could also, however, be rendered as

(4b) *'Mary's running,* do! and *Sally's running,* do! and *Jacky's running,* do!'

or as

(4c) *'Mary's running and Sally's running and Jacky's running,* do!'

The above examples make it clear, I think, that conjunction is phrastic-neustic-ambiguous, i.e., that it could, without violating our understanding what is going on here, be exported to the neustic or left in the phrastic.

If we are going to choose among these translations, it will therefore be on grounds of our intentions in utilizing the distinction between phrastic and neustic. The intent should be evident: it is tempting to try to formulate the phrastic in such a way that every element in it refers, or better, identifies a location on the map which is our aimed-for reconstruction. If we accept this plan of procedure, we may then wish to choose from among the translations offered above those which system-atically export the conjunctive element into the neustic—namely, (2b),

(3b), and (4b). And in general we might decide to follow the principle 'export to the neustic whenever possible', with the aim of simplifying our reconstruction as much as possible.

Parallel considerations affect negation and disjunction. Let us illustrate. (5) 'Mary is not running' might be translated as either

(5a) *'Mary's not running,* yes'

or

(5b) *'Mary's running,* no'.

If we accept the principle of exporting to the neustic wherever possible, we should choose (5b).

Likewise, (6) 'Either Mary runs or Sally runs' might be translated as either

(6a) *'Mary's running or Sally's running,* yes'

or

(6b) *'Mary's running,* yes or *Sally's running,* yes'.

In (6a) we are affirming a disjunction; in (6b) we are disjoining two affirmations. The neustic in (6b) might also have been written 'one or the other or both, yes'. (If the disjunction is exclusive, we could rewrite the neustic of (6b) as 'one or the other but not both, yes'.) Again, the disjunctive element seems phrastic-neustic-ambiguous. It might, without violating our understanding, be kept in the phrastic or placed in the neustic. If we choose (6b) we do so because of our intent to find map-referents for each element in the phrastic coupled with our dismay at the prospect of trying to find such a referent for 'or'.

Now let us try (7) 'either Mary doesn't run or else Sally does run'. This combines negation and disjunction. But the possibilities are easily identified. We may say

(7a) *'Mary's not running,* yes or *Sally's running,* yes',

or

(7b) *'Mary's not running or Sally's running,* yes',

or

(7c) *'Mary's running,* no or *Sally's running,* yes'.

Again, if we accept the principle of exporting to the neustic whenever possible, we shall choose (7c).

But (7) is equivalent, logicians tell us, to (8) *'Mary's running* ⊃ *Sally's running'.* If this is the case, then (7c) may also serve as a translation for (8).

We have studied the application of the method of exporting to the neustic in relation to the basic logical connectives. We have seen that they are phrastic-neustic-ambiguous, and that the justification of the method of exportation to the neustic lies in our plan to frame the phrastic so that each element in it satisfies some criterion of isomorphism with the universe it maps. So far, then, we have not seen any compelling reason to export to the neustic. Although the prospect of mapping in this fashion may appear attractive, we certainly cannot claim that the procedure is unavoidable, and there well may be reasons, not considered here, why it is inadvisable.

However, the advisability of exporting to the neustic becomes more evident when we turn from logical connectives to quantification words. Consider (9) 'All cows give milk'. This may be translated as

(9a) 'for every x, *cow$_x$*, no or *milk-giving$_x$*, yes',

if we are to follow our practice of exporting everything possible to the neustic. Likewise (10) 'some cows give milk' becomes

(10a) 'at least one x such that *cow$_x$* and *milk-giving$_x$*, yes'.

But if we did not export to the neustic, we would have

(9b) '*all cows' giving milk*, yes'

and

(10b) '*at least one cow's giving milk*, yes'.

Again, it looks as if neustic-exporting translations are superior to non-neustic-exporting translations only if we have mapping plans of the sort already described.

In the case of quantification, however, there are *additional* reasons for exporting to the neustic. Take (11) 'the Queen is handsome'. This may be translated as either

(11a) '*The existent-now Queen's handsomeness*, yes'

or

(11b) 'one and only one x such that *present Queen$_x$* and *handsome$_x$*, yes'.

That (11b) is a preferable translation can be seen when we compare the following: (12) 'the golden mountain doesn't exist'.

(12a) '*the existent-now golden mountain's existence*, no'

(12b) 'the one and only one x such that *present golden mountain*, no'

or (13) 'the present king of France is bald'—

(13a) '*the presently existent king of France's baldness*, yes'

(13b) 'one and only one x such that *present king of France$_x$*, yes and *bald$_x$*, yes'.

Exportation to the neustic is an essential part of the analytic solution to these famous puzzles. We must reject 'existence as a predicate', i.e., reject *existence* as an element in any phrastic, or court serious paradox.

So far, we have considered analyses of statements whose elements can, consistently with the general rules covering phrastic and neustic formation, be incorporated into either the phrastic or the neustic. In some cases, we have argued, the only consideration guiding us to place the elements in question (e.g., logical connectives) in the neustic is the trouble that would be caused if we tried to find elements in the world for these connectives to reflect. In other cases (e.g., quantification-words) there are more positive considerations related to the puzzles generated if we leave the elements in the phrastic. Still, even in these cases, one can, consistently with the sense of the distinction between phrastic and neustic, leave such items as 'existence' in the phrastic; this is not precluded in principle, and only is avoided because of the anomalies it produces in practice. Quantification, then, is phrastic-neustic-ambiguous.

However, there are other cases where it is plainly *incorrect* to place an element in the neustic. Let us consider first temporal signals. E.g., in (14) 'Mary is baking pies now', 'now' is a temporal signal. This might be translated as

(14a) *'Mary's baking pies now*, yes'

or as

(14b) *'Mary's baking pies,* yes now'.

However, it is clear that the former properly represents the sense of the sentence we set out to translate, but not the latter. The point may be made clearer with another example: (15) 'I said (thought) then that Mary had been baking pies'. This *must* be rendered (in part) as

(15b) *'Mary's baking pies previously to $t_1$*, yes at $t_1$' (where $t_1$ represents the time at which this utterance or thought occurred).

There are two time signals in (15), and both must be represented, one in the phrastic, the other in the neustic. Returning to (14), then, it will be clear that (14b) says that *'Mary's baking pies'* is being asserted at the present time, but does not say at what time Mary was, is or will be baking. Thus its phrastic may be said to lack a time signal. (14a) on the other hand specifies that the baking is now going on, but leaves vague when the assertion takes, took or will take place. Its neustic lacks a time signal. Any proper translation of (14) should include two time signals. In thinking of neustics and phrastics we should always think of them as involving a blank—one for each—which must be filled in by a time signal—either a specific one or a null one. Thus if I said at 10 o'clock on the 28th of November 1961 'Mary is baking pies now', that time and date will fill the blanks in both the phrastic and neustic of the translation. On the other hand, if I say at 10:01 on the same date (16) 'freely-falling bodies fall at $\frac{1}{2}gt^2$', this will be represented as

(16a) *'freely-falling bodies' fallability at $\frac{1}{2}gt^2$ null-time,*
yes 10:01-11-28-61'.[5]

---

[5] Not 'freely-falling bodies falling. . . .', since this, together with the neustic specified, would indicate that at no time are freely-falling bodies falling at that rate.

Null time signals in the phrastic, then, indicate generalizations—in fact, are symptoms of lawlike relations. Null time signals in the neustic, on the other hand, mean that this sentence has not been, is not and will never be uttered.

Neustic-deportation, then, is a practice with definite limitations. The time signal that indicates when the state-of-affairs reflected in the phrastic occurs *cannot* be deported to the neustic without losing the sense of what is to be translated.

Now let us circle back into the vicinity of Lewis' problems. Next, consider (17) 'Mary is probably baking pies now'. Lewis himself suggests what the proper analysis of this has to be, and in the translation offered here I follow his suggestion. The suggestion is that it is important to differentiate the probability of a proposition from the reliability with which we assert it.[6] For phrastic-neustic talk, this means that we must consider probability analogously to the fashion in which we have just finished considering time. Thus (17) is correctly rendered as

(17a) *'Mary's baking pies now with probability m/n on data D,*
yes now with reliability *R* of data *D'*.

As with the time signal, we provide, in effect, blanks in both the phrastic and the neustic, the former for the probability, the latter for the reliability estimated. Again, it is flatly incorrect to attempt to export the probability coefficient into the neustic; the reason is that the probability is what we assert, while reliability relates to the grounds for our conviction in asserting it.[7]

And now at last we are ready to address the problem of real connections and Lewis' attempt to characterize them through modal logic. The point to be made is quite simple in the light of what has gone before.

---

[6] This matter is taken up below. For Lewis' discussion of the distinction between probability and reliability, see AKV, particularly pp. 292 ff.

[7] The reader may be disturbed by the appearance in both the phrastic and the neustic of the phrase 'data *D'*. But there is no particular basis for disturbance; the appearance of this phrase in the phrastic corresponds to the ground which Lewis rightly insists must be recognized in order to give probability to any judgment (or, for us, proposition), while its appearance in the neustic corresponds to that whose reliability is estimated. At worst, the formulation here is guilty of redundancy; the situation might better be pictured by means of some mechanism for tying parts of the neustic to parts of the phrastic in various appropriate ways. But since it is not a part of the intent of this study to devise completely accurate ways of formulating phrastics (or neustics), we need not digress here to indicate such a mechanism. All that italicizing means in this paper is that the material so italicized must be adequately and accurately mapped in a reconstruction. (In Goodman's phrase, they are propositions "we care about," "for which we . . . insist that any systematic translation preserve their truth value" (Nelson Goodman, *The Structure of Appearance* [Cambridge, Mass.: Harvard University Press, 1951], p. 21). The problem of how successfully to map what we care about, i.e., the choice of elements of propositions, is another story.

It is this. Just as there are two time signals, one belonging in the phrastic and the other in the neustic, and just as there are two 'probability' factors, one belonging in the phrastic and qualified as probability proper, the other belonging in the neustic and perhaps to be called 'reliability'—just so there are two kinds of necessity, one which belongs in the phrastic, the other in the neustic. Necessity is like time and probability, *not* like logical connectives and quantification. That, in substance, is why the material conditional cannot exhaust the meaning of the counterfactual conditional. But it is also why modal logics cannot solve the problem Lewis hopes they can.

Let us take, then (18) 'if that piece of salt had been placed in water it would have dissolved'. Suppose one were to propose solving the problem this conditional poses by exporting the necessity of the relation to the neustic, thus:

(18a) 'Necessarily *that piece of salt's being placed in water,* no
or *that piece of salt's dissolving,* yes'.

This would be a mistake. The temptation to make it derives from the analogy with the ways in which problems about logical connectives and quantification words can be solved by exporting them to the neustic. But as we have seen, there are other cases where one cannot so export, and this is one of those cases. That this is one of those cases is evident if we reflect that necessity is the upper limit of probability; it is, so to speak, a probability of 1. But just as there are two kinds of probability, so there are two kinds of necessity. The 'necessarily' that appears in the neustic of (18a) is the necessity which represents the highest possible reliability coefficient for data D. That is, these data give us complete assurance, so (18a) says, that the probability characteristic of what is in the phrastic is whatever we have estimated it to be. But (18a) hasn't estimated it to be anything. So (18a) is incomplete, since it doesn't fill the probability blank which we have provided for all empirical statements—and that blank is a blank in the phrastic.

If we take account of the probability blank in the phrastic, we can see that this might be filled by a probability-coefficient of any size, together with reference to a body of data (e.g., *'with probability 4/5 on data D'*), and that a special case of this coefficient would be *'with probability 1 on data D'*. This phrase correctly represents the kind of necessity which the counterfactual is supposed to have: we know that the given piece of salt would have dissolved in water because of our knowledge of past correlations. The kind of necessity that is in question is not the kind which is characteristic of analytic or logical truths. And the difference between the two kinds of necessity—the empirical kind and the logical kind—is reflected in the fact that logical necessity is neustic-phrastic-ambiguous, but empirical necessity is not.

It is clear, then, that we cannot export the relevant kind of necessity from the phrastic. It must remain there. For this very reason modal logic solutions of the counterfactual problem are mistaken. For the essence of such solutions is to find a modal operator such as the square, to treat it as neustic-phrastic-ambiguous, and to proceed to export the necessity of the counterfactual link into the neustic. But the word 'necessarily' in the neustic indicates something different; it indicates that our grounds for asserting this proposition are absolutely reliable. Analytic necessities have this character; they are absolutely reliable on the evidence involved, since there is no such evidence. But counterfactual conditionals cannot have this degree of reliability, since their reliability *is* based on evidence. That is one mistake. And even if they did have absolute reliability, to say so would not adequately explain what is meant by saying that being placed in water that piece of salt must necessarily have dissolved. That is a second mistake. So we see that modal logic 'solutions' are completely misleading. The mistakes involved in appealing to them are analogous to the mistakes involved in confusing truth with warranted assertability.

So there must be a probability factor in the phrastic, and in the case of law statements that probability will be high, so high as to warrant our saying it approximates necessity. Clearly we have not explained what is involved in this kind of necessity, but we have at least ruled out a line of analysis which has been tempting to Lewis, among others, and we have done so without falling back into an analysis broached solely in terms of truth-functional connectives such as the horseshoe; in fact we have indicated why no such solution will do.

It remains to inquire how we are to frame the phrastic which results. The phrastic of (18a) has two parts, disconnected. This is awkward. Where shall we put the blank which the probability (or necessity) factor is to fill? We are reminded that the phrastic itself has a structure, and that we have no rules as to how to proceed in organizing the words so as to reflect that structure. Specifically, if we put the 'necessarily' with the first of the two components of (18a)'s phrastic, it will be natural to suppose that 'salt's being placed in water' is necessary, while if we put it with the latter component we might suppose that 'that piece of salt's dissolving' is necessary. But in fact neither is necessary; what is necessary is that one is followed by the other. For clarity's sake we need to collapse the two disjoined segments of the phrastic into one, and Goodman's formula, mentioned before, provides an easy way of doing so. We may then rewrite (18) as

(18b) *'that piece of salt's water-solubility necessarily on data D, yes'*,
or if we wish to indicate temporal signals and reliability as well:

(18c) *'that piece of salt's water-solubility at time $t_0$ necessarily*

*on data D,* yes $^{t_0}_{\text{now}}$ with reliability *R* of data *D'*

where $t_0 =$ the null time signal, data *D* are relevant data, $m/n$ is the measure of reliability of the probability-estimate with respect to *D*, and the choice between the 'now' or '$t_0$' in the neustic is to be made depending on whether the sentence is uttered or not.

Lewis' terminating judgments can then be translated analogously.

(19) 'If *S* and *A* then probably *E*' becomes

(19a) *'S - A - E able at time $t_0$ necessarily on data D,* yes

$^{t_0}_{\text{now}}$ with reliability *R* of data *D'*.

### III

I have tried to suggest that by carefully following out Lewis' suggestion about distinguishing the proposition entertained from the various aspects of its entertainment—the phrastic from the neustic—we can find a line of solution to two of his most serious difficulties, expressive language on the one hand, real connections on the other. There may be, in addition, beneficial by-products.

For example, Lewis spends a good deal of time in AKV attacking what he calls 'extensionalism', which is the view that extension, i.e., denotation, is the basic mode of meaning. The relevance of the extensionalism-intensionalism issue to his epistemology, however, is located mainly within the level of judgments of his terminating and nonterminating varieties; the issue of the interpretation of the relatively noncontroversial logical connectives such as 'and', 'or', and 'not', as well as the issue over the interpretation of quantification words, do not arise in any important way from his epistemological concerns. However, Lewis feels he must refute extensionalism in general in order to justify the particular mode of solution he proposes for problems pertaining to real connections, probability and so forth. To put it another way, he feels the need of a general account of meaning, not one limited to the levels on which one happens to be operating in the context of a specific problem. Our analysis here, on the other hand, would tend to suggest that, while extensional (truth-functional) methods are inappropriate at the level of time signals, probability, and necessity, they are as appropriate at the levels of logical connectives and quantification as the intensionalist alternative, and have, in the case of quantification, considerable advantages. Furthermore, the proper translation of most sentences involves activities on many of these levels, most frequently the levels of logical connectives and quantification, and for purposes of mapping there is a gain for us if we systematically export to the neustic whenever possible. All these are reasons for not throwing out neustic-exportation for logical connectives and quantification words merely in order to have the elegance of one theory of meaning for all levels. As far as can be told, what is advantageous at one level is not necessarily so at others.

In fact, the intensionalist-extensionalist issue on the present analysis has a very different look from what it had before. For on the present account, 'taking extension as the basic mode of meaning' comes to proposing solutions for all problems by exporting the troublesome terms to the neustic. This is, I think, precisely what Lewis has in mind and it is the extensionalists' inability to treat the sickness of counterfactuals by neustic-exportation that leads him to reject that view. However, accepting that extensionalism, so understood, is untenable, and that therefore we must accept its contradictory, the question remains whether we must accept its contrary as well. The contradictory of extensionalism is *not* intensionalism, if by 'intensionalism' is meant 'taking some mode of meaning other than extension as the basic mode of meaning'; rather it is merely 'not taking extension as the basic mode of meaning'. The question remains open whether we should light upon some alternative 'basic mode', or whether we should instead agree upon what is indicated by the present analysis, that while one may export to the neustic wherever possible, and therefore one may accept truth-functional accounts of meaning ('extensional') at those levels of analysis where it is possible, at other levels exportation to the neustic is impossible and so at those levels one must appeal to non-truth-functional accounts of meaning.

Lewis is right that extensionalists cannot explain counterfactuals. He is wrong, however, in concluding that therefore we must everywhere reject extensionalist analyses. The acceptance of intensionalism does not follow from the rejection of extensionalism.

For a variety of reasons, then, the theory of knowledge which Lewis pioneers benefits greatly from the replacement of terminating judgments by terminal propositions (and for that matter by replacing non-terminating judgments by nonterminal propositions). The resulting theory avoids expressive language; it precludes the modal logic solution to the counterfactual problem, which has been, I think, shown to be mistaken on other grounds[8]; and it suggests that the correct view concerning the

[8] See Gustav Bergmann, "The Philosophical Significance of Modal Logic," *Mind*, 69 (October, 1960), 466-485.

relationships between extension and intension is a kind of compromise. It does not in itself, granted, solve the counterfactual problem. But it is compatible with all that Lewis has to say about the nature of real connections, while locating the issue within a context of mapping which promises, through such work as Goodman's, to yield instructive insights where other methods have failed.

KARL H. POTTER

DEPARTMENT OF PHILOSOPHY
UNIVERSITY OF MINNESOTA

## C. I. Lewis
## REPLIES TO MY CRITICS

APOLOGY for not attempting any proper response to the compliment I receive from contributors to this volume:

Since receiving your papers—all in one parcel—I have spent a month reading them and making notes of the sort called marginalia. Allow me to express my gratification in the high order of importance and value I find in them. That the discussion is here oriented upon my own work is largely accidental to the value of them. And in my opinion, it would be better to print them with no comments from me whatsoever. But our Editor does not agree to that; and, though unconvinced, I conclude that I shall best support my opinion by sending him such unsatisfactory remarks as I can manage within limits which I must observe. If he sends these to print, the responsibility will be clear. But I could not allow that to happen without apology to the authors for the kind of comment to which I shall restrict myself.

These remarks must be brief: on that point I am obdurate. Some of these papers include discerning summaries of my views on this or that topic which are better than I could have made myself. That calls for no comment beyond my thanks. And a number of them have used something in my work as a point of departure for constructive development of conceptions going quite beyond my own or wholly independent. That I would acclaim; but I do not, in such cases, think it in point for me to comment here. But, whatever the main intent of the papers, and whatever the manner of their presentation, there are few amongst them which are not, on some point or on many, critical of some thesis which I have advanced. That, again, is as it should be, and nothing different would be gratifying. But I fear that it is such critical portions of the papers that I am here supposed to 'answer'. And that, I must decline to attempt. It will go without saying that, in most instances, I shall think there is something which might be offered in rebuttal; I believe what I believe, in spite of believing also that it could not be the case that everything which I believe is true. But, my critic being an acute person, his points raised are matters of real difficulty; and any answer which I think I have could be made good only if it should run to comparable length. To attempt such counter-observations on all the points on which I have been challenged here, would expand this book to inadmissible dimensions. And my circumstances do not allow me that much time. Either I must answer some only, allowing it to be thought that I do not sufficiently respect the others—or that there is nothing to say in defense—or I must answer none.

I happily choose this last alternative. Perhaps if I merely stand aside and look helpless, half my critics will take after the other half. In any case, I have had fifty years in which to present what I have to say as well as I can. If my ideas cannot now stand up under criticism, then they must fall on their faces. I have neither the ambition nor the conceit to protect them further. Remaining moot points must now pass into the domain of the philosophy-reading public; and another generation will take over. I sincerely hope they may do better than mine.

In what follows, I confine myself to informal and unguarded reactions, not to be taken as more than that. Certain small matters, connected with my writing, which may have incidental explanatory value, will be included, along with acknowledgment of certain ways in which, and points on which, I have not done as well as should be done—though I doubt that I am able to do better—and other observations which it will be permissible for me to set down here without argument.

(Since the above, and all that follows, was written and sent to the Editor, we have had the grievous news of the passing of Arthur Pap and of Paul Henle. I leave my references to them in the form in which they had been written and transmitted.)

Victor Lowe is one who is able to penetrate beyond what I have put down for print to something of the animus behind it. I take pleasure in his discerning observations. Particularly it pleases me that he ventures the word 'simplicity' in connection with me. I do not—I hope—stray far from common sense; and I do not attempt to go much beyond it. For me, it is a large enough task if I can follow it, and in measure make explicit what is implicit in it, in these last and difficult questions gathered together under the name 'philosophy'.

Lowe chides me gently for not leaving room, in my conception of philosophy, for metaphysics of the speculative sort. I think I know just what he has in mind, and should like to re-quote here something which, in the Whitehead volume in this Library, A. D. Ritchie quotes from Whitehead:

Speculative Reason seeks with disinterested curiosity an understanding of the world. Naught that happens is alien to it. . . . Also, so long as understanding is incomplete, it remains to that extent unsatisfied. It thus constitutes itself the urge from the good to the better life. . . . the Speculative Reason is in its essence untrammelled by method. Its function is to pierce into the general reasons beyond limited reasons. . . . This infinite ideal is never to be attained by the bounded intelligence of mankind. (*The Function of Reason*, 29, 30 and 51.) [1]

The genius for such speculation, I do not have. In my own workaday conception of metaphysics, it mainly concerns the basic categories of the real; the base-concepts which serve as criteria for our over-arching classifications of what we encounter in experience, and our fundamental ways of understanding it. But my intent in this has been positive, not negative; to illustrate the fact that, like the man who had spoken prose all his life without realizing it, we are making metaphysical assertions as often as we ascribe actuality to any object or to any objective event, or repudiate anything as being content of mistaken apprehension only.

But I have my own sense of the vastly deep beyond the point where my vision terminates. I should adopt a Kantian conception of the Unknowable if it were not for two things: First, I conceive that, the nature of our possible knowledge being itself understood, knowledge is a veridical, though always incomplete, apprehension of the real as it is in itself. And second, there seems to be little one can say about the unknowable without the hazard of a kind of contradiction. My sense of what is ultimate I do not put into words. There is a favorite haunt, in an almost uninhabited wilderness, to which I go as often as I can. I hope there will always be such wilderness spots remaining. And I hope there will always be, included in philosophy, a kind of literature which I could not by any possibility write.

Paul Henle's paper on Meaning and Verification represents the *beau ideal* of one type of contribution to a volume such as this. His topic concerns something which stands exactly at the crux of the theory of empirical knowledge which I would offer—the topic of Chapter VIII in AKV. He presents first the turning points of that discussion, with citations in support. Then he puts his finger on a main issue, noting also certain others connected with it. His examination of these leads him to conclude that the theory as it stands cannot hold. But he does not leave it at that. Turning to a certain divergence of what I have said from what Charles Peirce, the originator of this type of theory, has said, Henle seeks to reinstate this general pragmatic conception by amendment of my procedure.

Confronting Henle's paper, I could not feel my predicament here more sharply. I am reminded of a passage in the letter Whitehead wrote to our Editor on a similar occasion: "Thus my own reaction to this book

---

[1] Cited in Paul A. Schilpp (ed.), *The Philosophy of Alfred North Whitehead* (New York: The Tudor Publishing Co., 1951), pp. 336f. Now published by The Open Court Publishing Co., LaSalle, Illinois.

should consist in devoting some years to rewriting my previous works. Unfortunately this is impossible."[2]

I do not have Whitehead's sublime humility; but I *should* rewrite this chapter in AKV. I doubt that anyone has given more careful or better attention to it than Henle has. But on the critical point he considers, he misconstrues what I thought I had said clearly enough. And this misconstruction, I allow, is at the bottom of the issue he discusses. What am I to do?

First, I shall make a general remark about the 'verification theory' of meaning—it should be called 'confirmation theory'. Then I shall offer an example of the critical point. Finally, I shall mention a subordinate but implicated point on which I am aware that my discussion failed of clarity.

The confirmation theory of meaning affords, upon reflection, a theory of empirical knowledge; a pragmatic theory that our empirical knowledge consists in justified expectations of testable eventuations in experience the accrual of which will confirm what we say we know. I have attempted to implement this theory by spelling out a little the logic of it. Unfortunately this logic is complex, because it turns out that it must include not only the logic of intensional meaning (which is deductive logic) but also the logic of probability. It must so extend to probability because the connection between any (supposed) objective factuality and the experiences confirmatory of it is one of (presumably high) probability, not one of theoretical certainty.

Is this a dagger that I see before me? If so, then I can grasp it with my hand; If I look again, I shall in all probability see it again; and if I feel the edge it will feel sharp. Ah, no, Macbeth; you are in no condition to trust what you see or even to test it. The probability that what you see is really there, is measured by the *im*probability of your seeing something if it is *not* there. And in your present state, that is not high.

The probability of a real dagger, established by 'seeing' a dagger, is measured by the improbability of 'seeing a dagger' if there is no real dagger there to see. (This statement is not completely accurate, but it will do.) But this probability-relation, both ways, does *not* depend on the truth or falsity of Macbeth's, or anyone else's, having this visual experience. The probability statement, "If, under circumstances like those of Macbeth in the play, A 'sees' a dagger, then, with probability $p$, there is a real dagger where A 'sees' it"—whatever that probability $p$ may be—is true or false, regardless of Macbeth's, or any other, actually having this experience, or of there being or not being a dagger before him. It is a probability generalization established by past experience which is relevant; and it holds in a hypothetical case, such as our fictional example, as much as in any which is actual. The 'realism' of Shakespeare's play depends on that. However, though the probability-statement, if true, is true for actual and examined cases, and actual but unexamined cases, and fictional cases, and for future and merely guessed at cases—and this is essential to our having any knowledge of the future—it is a different point altogether that the probability of a *real dagger* where someone 'sees a dagger', *does* depend on the *reality* of this visual experience. And here at last we have got something to bite on: the 'seeing' in our example is either an actual experience or a fictional experience. Fictions afford no probability of objective facts; *actual experiences do*. Otherwise no empirical knowledge would be possible.

The surbordinate and involved issue is one which arises because of an ambiguity of language used in Chapter VIII concerning the logical relation between objective-fact statements and probability-consequences of them in terms of experimental activities and experiential results. I observed this ambiguity when the galley proof came to hand, and somewhat hastily added the last section, numbered 17, hoping to dispel it.

I shall say enough here (or anyhow half-enough) so that any reader who has read AKV, and now has section 17 before him, will be in position to decide whether Henle is right and the book is wrong or the book is right and Henle has misunderstood something.

The ambiguity in question relates to expressions of the form "the probability that if A then E." This is not an ambiguity which I gratuitously committed, but one which affects common useage. Consider, for example, the rule for assessing compound probabilities: "The probability of A and B both, is the probability of A multiplied by the probability that *if A then B*." It is this italicized last clause whose intent is in question. We are in no danger of misinterpreting this in a concrete case. For example, if there are two white balls and two black ones in a bag, and they are withdrawn one at a time, and we wish to determine the probability that the first two drawn will both be white, we think as follows: "The probability that the first drawn will be white is $1/2$. And *if the first one drawn is white* (and those remaining are one white and two black), *the probability that the second one drawn will also be white* is $1/3$. So the answer is $1/6$." Compare the italicized part of this last with the italicized portion of the rule. "The probability that if A then B" is a common but misleading locution which really means "the probability of B when, or if, A."

Now observe the location of (h), to be read "in all probability," in the paradigms in Section 17. Is it where it ought to be or not?

Now please read Note 3 in this section.

There is another point involved—or which can appear to be involved. "The probability of B when A" suggests that A has to be true, or you have to know A, in order to determine the probability so meant. Is that, in fact, the case or not? Did we have before us the bag of balls mentioned above? Did anyone draw them? Did we observe any results? Or was the whole thing hypothetical? But were we or were we not able to determine a correct answer—the *truth* about the 'if . . . then . . .' probability in question, 1/3?

It is further in point that, in all these paradigms, 'P' represents an objective statement, but 'A' and 'E' represent expressive statements in terms of the directly experienced. 'A' represents the experience of initiating a specific act, something which we can make true, and are certain about when we do so; and otherwise is false. And 'E' stands for an expected or predicted eventuation in experience, recognizable and certain if or when it eventuates. And the whole expression, "If A then E," represents a terminating judgment, completely verifiable or completely falsifiable by making the experiment of initiating act A. There could be endless questions and endless discussion of these matters; but these are the antecedent presumptions, antecedently explained, with which the symbolism is used.

Henle is quite right in observing that a more complex symbolism in terms of propositional functions would have been more adequate. It would not have been more *accurate,* because where such relations as figure here obtain for functions, they correspondingly obtain for corresponding propositions. I thought the simpler notation might suit my readers equally well.

I leave the rest of this matter to the reader—or better still, I leave it to Henle—to straighten out.

And I shall not—cannot—be even so inadequately explicit as this in response to all the other papers.

Professor Karl Dürr and W. T. Parry have summarized everything essential concerning my system of the logic of Strict Implication. Dürr authoritatively sets my work in proper relation to predecessors. And Parry's article is a succinct indication of its contents by one who understands the technical points of it, and commands the presently relevant literature better than I do. I would remind the reader also that, as acknowledged in Appendix II of Lewis and Langford, *Symbolic Logic,* and in Appendix III of the new edition, Parry's own work has been made available to me, beginning in 1930. The content of Appendix II just referred to, is at least as much his as mine.

Asher Moore's paper on the A Priori sets me thinking of the developments touching that topic which have taken place within my lifetime. By the time I became concerned with matters of logic and epistemology, it was beginning to be the predominant philosophic conviction that the Kantian doctrine of a synthetic a priori must be abandoned. But this was replaced by a firm conviction that the a priori must coincide with the analytic and logically certifiable; the a posteriori with that which requires empirical premises and is based ultimately upon the perceptually learned. Particularly after Russell's *Principles of Mathematics*, this firm distinction between the logical, mathematical and analytic on the one side, and the synthetic, natural-scientific and empirical on the other, became widely regarded as one of our clearest and best-substantiated philosophic insights. I found myself in agreement.

But hindsight is better than foresight. I should have observed that, though *Principia Mathematica* played the role of exhibit A in support of this conviction, nevertheless the exclusively extensionalist logical theory which is built into that work is incompatible with taking this distinction as finally valid; and that those who carry forward this exclusively extensionalist conception of the logical, and refuse to recognize any significance in the logic of intension, are bound eventually to challenge the validity of this distinction between the analytic and the synthetic. And in result, barring some alternative notion which has not yet been put forward, they are then left with no ground for distinguishing a priori from a posteriori, and no clear conception of the foundation of logic and mathematics as distinct from physics and psychology.

Exactly this process of attrition has now begun; though perhaps the consequences, for logic and for theory of knowledge, have not yet been squarely faced. So far as the history of thought suggests, there is no theory of the possible validity of knowledge which is compatible with such a radical empiricism as is implied by repudiation of analytic truth. Even Hume did not challenge 'necessary connections of ideas', but only 'necessary connections of matters of fact'—the synthetic a priori. The suggestion is that we are back with the Sophists; or if not, must at least begin all over again, and from scratch.

For my own part, I wish to acknowledge that the whole body of my philosophic conceptions, in logic, epistemology, theory of value, and even ethics, depends on the validity of this distinction; and if that plank is pulled from under me, the whole structure will come tumbling down. But if that should happen, I still hope it will be observed that I do not saw off anything without first looking to see if I shall have something else left to stand on.

All this has nothing to do with Asher Moore, of course. I but take advantage of an association of ideas, set off by his title, to unload it here. Moore does not concern himself with my foundations, but with certain items of the structure I have built on them. Or so I take it. He makes finer distinctions within the analytic than I have remarked. My distinction between 'analytic meaning' and 'holophrastic meaning' is perhaps in point, but it does not coincide with any of his.

I think his distinctions are mainly valid: I should have a few quibbles along the way.*

Charles Baylis is minded to pin a theory of fact on me, taking advantage of a momentary lapse of my verbal defense-mechanisms in an old article. I account this pure wickedness on his part; he knows that 'fact' is one of the trickiest words in any language; and he knows that I know it. But I shall foil him yet: I shall now pronounce the final and authoritative Lewis theory of fact. A fact is an actual state of affairs. But 'fact' is a crypto-relative term, like 'landscape'. A landscape is a terrain, but a terrain as seeable by an eye. And a fact is a state of affairs, but a state of affairs as knowable by a mind and stateable by a statement.

On second thought, however, perhaps this is just what Baylis is here spelling out. In that case I now have a theory of fact, shorter version and longer version. But if either one of them runs into trouble, I shall, of course, blame Baylis.

In response to Roderick Chisholm's contribution on the Ethics of Belief, I shall be less than relevant to the contents of his paper. That title, all by itself, is indicative of basic conceptions which I think that he and I share, and upon which I set great store.

That knowing, like deliberate doing, is subject to critique, and knowledge is a normative category; that the vital function of knowledge is the normative function of guiding our activities in accord with our justified convictions and warranted expectancies; that the capacity so to govern himself, in thinking and believing, and in the doing which is consequent upon it, is the distinctive capacity of the human animal; that logic and ethics represent two major and correlative aspects of the human critique of such self-governable procedures; that intention in doing and intention in thinking-before-doing represent the directive character of such critique, and are intrinsically connected; these convictions come

* *Editor's note*: In his original MS at this point Professor Lewis inserted a note to the Editor stating that "something more specifically responsive should be added here in final draft." However, since Professor Lewis did not live to see the galleys of his book the addition was not made.

near to being what I have most wanted to bring to attention in all that I have written—in logic or epistemology or in ethics.

Extension and intension—throughout the whole sweep of what philosophy concerns—are cognate; the two sides of one coin. But it appears that, at the moment, that fact has been lost from view, and even denied, by those who would emphasize the extensional exclusively. The reminder of the intensional, which I take to be a continuing motif in what Chisholm has to say, encourages me to think that this present one-sidedness in philosophic thinking may, before too long, find its needed counterpoise, and the balance will be redressed.

The article of Bernard Peach on Analytic Statements is notable for its accuracy concerning my procedures, and touches a number of critical considerations affecting this whole question of the distinction between the analytic and a priori and the synthetic and empirical element in knowledge.

As already indicated, I think this distinction must be final and is essential, both for any satisfactory theory of logic and for an acceptable account of knowledge altogether. I doubt that I could approach the issues Peach raises without going back to fundamentals. But I would agree that no full settlement of these is likely to emerge without observation of considerations largely omitted in my main discussion in Book I of AKV, but briefly discussed in my earlier article "A Pragmatic Conception of the A Priori."

An analytic statement is merely explicative of a concept, or concepts, entertained; not the formulation of any objective factuality, determinable antecedently to experience and merely by thinking. And a concept entertained must be a 'fixed' meaning—fixed for the time being at least and precisely formulatable if not formulated. Without such fixed meanings, there could be no clear questions asked, and no truth or falsity to be found out by experience or experiment.

Concepts, however, are entertained for purposes of application. And they are subject to modification—'replacement' would be a more accurate word—according as we find them useful to apply and contributory to the understanding of objective facts. In any science, for example, there must, at any moment, be base concepts, precisely formulatable. But the development of any science will itself plainly show progressive alteration or substitution among these base concepts in terms of which it is formulated. It will be as much by such alteration of concepts—e.g., 'quanta' in physics—as by new observation and experimental results that better understanding is achieved. In a sense, therefore, our concepts are ideas we *learn to entertain*. They cannot be, in any clear sense 'dictated' by experience. But the general course of experience and our success or failure in attempts to formulate disclosed empirical fact in terms of them exercises a directive influence. Concepts which we successfully apply with consequent understanding survive, and those which pragmatically fail become obsolete. They take the initial form of hypotheses of theory. They become 'confirmed' by substantiations of such theory as correct, applicable, contributory to right knowing. 'Phlogiston' does not alter its meaning; it becomes forgotten. 'Quantum' (with its exact physical sense) will retain precisely that meaning which it has unaltered, but the fate of it as a physical concept will be experimentally determined. But we must forever keep separate the analytic explication of a concept, as a statement whose truth or falsity is necessarily antecedent to any attempted application of it, and the truths of objective fact which are forever at the mercy of empirical findings, and theoretically never established as better than probable—as probable, let us say, as the presently determined facts of physics.

I recognize also that my own general conceptions here pertinent, which are conceptualistic and connected with a basic logic of intension, represent a definitely minority position, confronting a predominantly nominalistic and extensional theory of logic, in current logical studies. But on that point, I cannot change my spots.

These too general remarks hardly relate themselves in any direct way to Peach's comments. I could wish that he had allowed himself more space and more fully presented his own underlying conceptions which eventuate in the specific issues which appear to lie between us.

When Lewis W. Beck explains Kant to those who think in English, I believe him because he knows better than I do. And when he does me the honor of explaining my views to German Kant-scholars, I know he is right by a kind of intuition Kant does not discuss. So when he compares my thinking with Kantian doctrine, I know he must be right, both ways, even if I have a little difficulty in following the development.

I think I detect one point where I stub my toe: it concerns meanings as 'ready made' (my 'Platonism') and yet as choosable for entertainment and application. While we socially inherit most of our meanings, or come by them as result of psychological associations established by experience, still we are responsible for correcting and refining them, and for considered and critical application of them. Also we do, on occasion, invent them and then try them on for fit—as the physicists are now doing, a little frantically, with some very fundamental physical concepts, like 'meson' and 'antimatter'.

Fitting concepts to data, for the purpose of understanding—to see if they will 'work'—is a kind of trial and error process; and one in which no outcome could, all by itself, 'compel' either continued adherence or complete abandonment of a concept in question. But results may make it very difficult to retain 'ether'; comparatively easy to accept 'quantum'. Commitment or alteration or rejection, as a consequence of such pragmatic tests of the usability of concepts, represents a sort of second-order type of induction.

I have nowhere reverted to this topic since the article "A Pragmatic Conception of the A Priori." Probably I should have done so. Whether what is so suggested fits in with, or is ruled out by, what Beck has to say here, I am not sure. But I suspect it to be a missing link, the absence of which now hampers me in following his acute discussion.

R. W. Sellars is the only contributor here who is strictly my contemporary. I am too deeply pleased by his participation, and too much absorbed in reminiscences which it arouses, to be able to direct proper attention upon the circumstantial contents of his paper. I summon pictures of the time when Idealism, New Realism, Critical Realism and Pragmatism confronted each other as the main tendencies of philosophic thinking in America; and contrast it with the present absorption in technical details and relative absence of emphasis on fundamentals, and of definite lines of demarcation. In those days we recognized clearly that one could not discuss epistemology without reference to metaphysics, or metaphysics without reference to epistemology. Sellars has stood sturdily by that conviction, and here re-emphasizes it. I have not done so well. Whenever I make attempt on metaphysics, it always comes out epistemology. But that represents no decision I make or conviction I have; simply I seem unable to do otherwise.

Both of us, I am sure, speculate upon what the next turn of the wheel may bring. It would be no matter for surprise if it should include a clearer recognition that the metaphysical questions are basic and inescapable, and that some answer to them, otherwise than by linguistic and semantic indirection, is required for attack upon further questions in philosophy.

W. H. Hay writes a vigorous and interesting article on relation between my views and Neopositivism. So far as concerns the developmental, I think his historical perspective may be a little bit askew, and that he sometimes surmises where I can remember. Perhaps an alternative first sentence could have been: "The main outline of Lewis' philosophic position is already determined in MWO which went to print in the same year that the Vienna Circle was founded." But Hay is a good detective.

It is quite true that in the early documents of the neopositivists—particularly in Carnap's *Der logische Aufbau der Welt,* but also in the writings of Schlick and Reichenbach—I found an empiricism and an analytic method which were congenial to my own persuasions. I still find them so. But if the younger and present protagonists of neopositivism should re-read these, I think that they might be a little startled, not only by the overlapping of them with pragmatic empiricism but also by the extent of their own removal from this first phase of the movement.

To be sure, the second phase—if I may so call it—came rather soon, and is hardly marked off by any notice given of the shift. But when the phenomenal analysis of the *Aufbau,* squarely based on direct experience, and including summary projection of a parallel empiricistic account of valuations, became replaced by physicalism, and Carnap could write, "The Viennese Circle does not practice philosophy" (*Unity of Science,* 21), and any retained empiricism became reduced to a semantic ghost of direct experience—protocol or observation statements—my sense of the congenial suffered a like attenuation.

And now that I seem to see a third wave coming in, with emphasis upon a behaviorist vocabulary, in order to lay even this ghost of experience which still haunts them, I find nothing for it but the other side of the street. To my jaundiced eye, this behaviorist dialect is a somewhat muscovite methodology for disallowing any mention of the obvious facts of life which they perversely refuse to recognize. Hay says I 'flirt' with behaviorism. That comment is deserved. But I hope my indiscreet gesture will not be misinterpreted.

The same writers who figure in this movement have made and are making other contributions of first importance to philosophy. But I regard physicalism as an unsound metaphysical and epistemological doctrine and—where it touches the valuational and normative—one which can be demoralizing. I happily conjecture that recent developments in physics itself will soon enforce the conclusion that the physical is altogether too metaphysical to represent any *pou sto* for philosophy.

If the Editor had been minded to choose a contributor for the topic of the Given who would not only be most perspicuous about it but thoroughly at home with, and well-disposed toward, what I have said concerning it, he could not have done better than to assign it to Roderick Firth. But as those who have read my autobiographic notes, written earlier, will have noted, I have reached the point of exasperation about this topic. As it appears to me, no conscious being capable of self-observation and of abstract thinking, can fail to be aware of that element in his experience which he finds, willy-nilly, as it is and not otherwise; or to recognize that, without this, he could have no apprehension of an external world at all. In grandfather's day, the word for it was 'sense data'. And anyone who, whatever he wished to say about it, did not understand what was so denoted, would have been regarded as a candidate for the booby hatch. We have since found out that 'sense data' is something of a misnomer: there is no perfect correlation with the state of the sense-organ. But with respect to what grandfather was talking about, there has not been and could not be any change at all. I have chosen this name, 'the given', as having minimal implications of anything beyond the character of it as datal and immediate. Let anyone who will, choose some other name. But let us not abdicate to those crypto-materialists who think that if we can be prevented from using any word which applies to immediate experience, or any factor in it, we may eventually forget that there is such a thing.

However—as you observe—it will be well for me not to write further on this topic: I should only repeat myself, or do worse.

In his paper on Contrary-to-Fact Conditionals, Arthur Pap summarizes what I have had to say on this topic with complete accuracy and notable penetration. Not only does he understand what I have said, and why I expressed it as I did, but he acutely discusses the exact nature of the problem to be met.

At the point where it enters my discussion (Chapter VIII in AKV), there were many things which needed to be said all at once, and if I were to achieve any measure of clarity. And they could not be said all at once. I left this topic, later discussed under this head 'contrary-to-fact-conditionals', dangling; perhaps saying clearly enough what the if-then relationship in question is *not*, but offering no clear explication of what it *is*, beyond indicating that it is the kind of relation which is in question in any prediction of an eventuation (as probable) on the basis of observational premises. I spoke of "matter of fact connections or natural connections or real connections" (borrowing this last phrase, 'real connection', from Wilfrid Sellars). 'Nomological implications' is a more indicative name.

Pap's discussion goes quite beyond anything which I found it possible to set down, and in a way which arouses my enthusiasm. I agree completely.

And let us observe that it is the same problem which is central in Henle's paper; and that it is also basically involved in the questions discussed by Arthur Burks; since whatever else may be in doubt, it is clearly a relation between data (whether actual or hypothetical) and something predictable on such ground as probable.

One main point here is that truth-to-factness or contrary-to-factness or mere hypotheticalness makes no difference to this *relation* between the 'if' and the 'then'. The ground of our *knowledge* of this relationship is another question altogether; whether it be question of this relation holding in a particular instance, or the general question (posed by Hume) whether there are any cases of such relationship.

And a related but different point is that if there are any assurable statements of the general form "If (or whenever) data D, then, with probability $h$, P," the truth of such a statement is, as observed above, independent of the truth or falsity of its hypothesis. This will hold, in spite of the fact that, for any given value of (substitution for) 'D' and 'P' and '$h$'—that is, for any particular statement of this form, its truth is *not* independent of our antecedent knowledge: a *probability* statement is an *epistemic* statement; it asserts something as cognitively justified on antecedent grounds; it is *not* a statement of existential fact in any other sense. And a contrary-to-fact conditional is likewise.

But I must not run on: I leave it to Henle and Pap and Burks.

E. M. Adams' paper is, again, a perfect example of the reason why I could not hope to reply here to essays which are critical. It is an important and trenchant challenge not only to my epistemological conceptions but to pragmatic empiricism in general. To make any attempt to meet it in briefer span than the article itself, would be to take it lightly. I can only make certain observations which will be inadequate but, I hope, pertinent.

First, I would point out that his paragraphs numbered (1) and (3), taken together, set the problem: How is it possible for a conscious individual, confined to data comprised within his own experience as a means of knowing, to have any veridical knowledge of what lies beyond his experience and exists independently of his knowing it? Perhaps this may justly be said to have been *the* problem of knowledge ever since Empedocles.

Adams' paragraph numbered (2) simply indicates that he here limits himself to the task of showing that a *pragmatic* theory (or specifically that of C. I. Lewis) cannot resolve this problem.

But I would point out that the challenge is not to pragmatic theories only, but to almost any theory of knowledge ever heard of—with two exceptions. The first such exception is represented by epistemological theories based on metaphysical idealism. (Monistic materialism affords no solution, since it is equally problematic how one lump of mud can know another.) For me, some of Adams' arguments are curiously reminiscent of those I heard from my revered teacher, Josiah Royce; addressed by him to the conclusion that the only metaphysical conception which is compatible with the validity of knowledge is Absolute Idealism. The other exception is the New Realist conception that an idea, so far as that idea is a knowing of this object in question, and this object so far as it is known by that idea, simply coincide. (This thesis was recommended by another highly regarded teacher, Ralph Barton Perry, who likewise failed to save me from the error of my ways. We students sometimes called this the 'light-house theory of knowledge'. Its main difficulty is to account for the possibility, not of knowledge, but of error.)

Second, I would point out—without any attempt to meet Adams' specific points against my specific theses—that it is essential, in considering any criticism directed upon a pragmatic theory, to recognize what a pragmatist thinks knowledge *is*. Otherwise the critic may embarrass somebody else but leave the pragmatist unscathed. A pragmatist does not accept any copy theory, or think that any such has any clearly-explicable significance. He likewise repudiates any coincidence-theory or inclusion-theory, whether of the new-realist type or in the form of a Bergsonian empathy-theory that, in order to really know a tree or a mosquito, one must think oneself into the role of a tree in the landscape or feel like an insect. And a pragmatist considers a coherence-theory inadequate to empirical knowledge in measure as logical consistency and systematic interconnection may still fall short of what is requisite to assuring empirical truth or justified belief. A pragmatist takes empirical knowledge to exercise the vital function of offering guidance for our governable ways of doing, in the form of justifiable expectancies of the results of such activity, if or when these results of acting supervene. And he emphasizes that knowledge is, by definition, *successful* knowledge; cognition which fails of this pragmatic aim is error. Knowing as such correct anticipation does everything which knowledge, however conceived, conceivably could do. And that is the right way—or at least *a* right way—to delineate it.

Such a meticulously drawn challenge as Adams presents, to so wide a segment of historic theories of knowledge, could only presage some fundamentally novel conception. I hope that I shall some day find before me this epistemological theory which Adams has in mind.

It pleases me that Charles Hartshorne gives attention to the little that I have set down concerning memory; but I value his paper strictly on account of what he has to say himself. I have hardly done more than to recognize that, without memorial knowledge, no other knowledge would be possible at all. And if anyone observe that I merely postulate that what we find ourselves recollecting must, by that fact, be assigned some minimal probability as representing past fact, I shall not be in position to demur. This is a rather sorry way to treat so important a factor in empirical knowledge. If I should ever find myself free of other tasks, I should like to try to do better, in the form of an essay on the ultimate bases of induction. Though minded to think that any of us will, on whatever ground, be obliged to agree with my minimal assumption above, I am minded to learn what I might further and better say from such essays as Hartshorne's.

I would applaud the paper of A. W. Burks on the Pragmatic-Humean Theory of Probability as one which makes a notable contribution to the topic of it and, while making contact with what I have written which may be relevant, is oriented upon further and constructive ideas.

By intention, I confined myself in Chapter X of AKV to basic and elementary considerations concerning probability. There are many conceptions of probability-judgments which, if interwoven with what I otherwise had to say, would have been incompatible with my intended account of empirical knowledge in general and wrecked it. The way to preclude these was to offer outline, so far as necessary, of those conceptions touching the point which were in fact in my mind and unavoidably involved in the working out of this general theory. This limitation to essentials also comported with the fact—noted in the Preface—that, though I stand by so much as I have written, I do not fancy myself an expert in probability theory.

The earlier literature on probability (before Keynes's *Treatise* and Reichenbach's *Wahrscheinlichkeitslehre*) was mostly concerned with probability procedures as a tool for dealing with matters which permit of statistical treatment. The newer literature reflects realization that this topic is of immensely wider significance and is involved with the basic problems of inductive inference and empirical generalizations at large. That calls for very considerable reorientation, now attempted and forwarded by such studies as Burks's.

I do not expect to participate. But I would hazard the opinion that it will still be possible, and possibly advantageous, to separate what pertains to the validity of inductive inference and the probability of conclusions generally, and is thus a basic epistemological problem, from what concerns specifically the valid paradigms of an eventually satisfactory inductive logic or calculus of probability and confirmation. The question suggested by Burks's title would appear to belong under the former category, and represent a topic in epistemology or *theory* of inductive logic—bound to affect any logic which comports with it but likely to be metalogical rather than something *in* a logic which satisfies it. I do not know whether this is Burks's conception of the matter or not, but should be intrigued to find out.

C. Douglas McGee writes to show that (1) my notion of 'sense meaning' can be interpreted in dispositional terms; and (2) if this dispositional interpretation is right, then my manner of attempted certification of analytic truth is wrong.

The notion of 'sense meaning' in AKV is inadequately developed; in particular the bearing of what is said about it in Book I upon topics dealt with in Book II is insufficiently covered. I think that McGee may be struggling with the consequences of that lacuna in my exposition.

Also, if he charges that, on certain relevant points, I am prone to argue from 'must be' to 'is', I plead guilty. I think imagery must be involved in any recognition of objects, or of properties of objects, as falling under concepts—being unable to imagine any other way in which it could be determined that a presented object has a certain (abstract) attribute. (Except as having certain attributes, objects cannot be classified, and hence cannot be recognized.) So I think that this *is* the case, though I have some trouble to say *how* it is the case; somewhat as I have trouble to say how my being disposed to wiggle my finger results in finger wiggling; but am nevertheless convinced that I can induce this result at will. I am not too ashamed of such a *solvitur in ambulando*.

It must surely be allowable to interpret sense-meaning in dispositional terms. Almost any character, predicable of any sort of thing, can be interpreted as a disposition of the thing which has it. That is incident to the likewise general fact that almost any character which anything really has will still be such that it does not always manifest this character, but exhibits it only under specifiable circumstances which do not universally obtain.

But whatever is classifiable in one way—interpretable in one way— will be classifiable and interpretable in other ways as well. Perhaps I unconsciously realized that interpreting sense meanings as dispositional traits would have no explanatory value in substantiation of their giving rise to analytic truths as explication of concepts; and so did not attempt that. In any case, I am surer that concepts, as intensional meanings, do exercise this function as ground of analytic truth than I am of what I have said about sense meaning.

But it would be a slightly different point that if sense meanings *can* be interpreted in dispositional terms, then they *cannot* exercise this function as ground of analytic statements. And on this crucial point, it may be that these remarks amount to no more than confessing that I have somewhere lost the thread of McGee's argument. If so, then I am sorry to exhibit this disability; but confession is good for the soul.

Robert Browning acutely discerns that, in much of what I have written on valuation and ethics—the whole topic of the normative—I must appeal to conceptions regarding human nature. Something pertinent to this has already appeared in *Our Social Inheritance*. But there is much more, and much with which I should be happy to agree, which Browning sets down here. I shall hope to profit by it if, or when, I am able to present something further on the subject of ethics.

The discussion of matters relevant to aesthetics, in Browning's later pages, as well as the whole of Gotshalk's treatment of aesthetics, make me happy that I acknowledged my strictly amateur standing in aesthetics in the Preface of AKV. The main intent of Chapters XIV and XV is to mark the separation, consistently with the included general theory of value, between presentational aesthetic quality and the report of it, and any critical appraisal of aesthetic experience, as a contributory good, or— more important—any critical appraisal of aesthetic objects as such. To this, I added, as a kind of afterthought, a hazarded identification of 'objects', and the different kinds of objects, to which aesthetic judgment is characteristically addressed. In the literature of aesthetics, I have been most influenced by the writings of David Prall and Stephen Pepper. I have no apology to offer for what I have written about aesthetics, but I do not venture to speak up in the company of experts. I wish to thank Professor Gotshalk but shall not comment.

Stephen Pepper, A. C. Ewing, Will Dennes, and Mary Mothersill have covered the whole area of my discussions concerning the normative; a general topic which has been for some years, and continues to be, my final objective. And they have brought perspective on what I have so far sent to print in a way which I should not be able to achieve. There is little for me to say here beyond expressing my appreciation. My comments will be desultory, not well ordered, and sometimes less than directly pertinent.

Stephen Pepper can write authoritatively of my Theory of Value because, more nearly than any other, he is able to view it from the inside. Though he and I were no longer in the same place during those years in which our publications concerning the normative have appeared, I think that we have been, so to say, continuously aware of each other, and of a common background of thought. He preceded me in this field, having begun with such topics, whereas I have moved toward them.

The approach is different, in our two cases, and the emphasis is different. He writes with awareness and command of the psychology of purposive behavior, and with attention directed upon the dynamic. My approach is from the side of the logical and epistemological, and the emphasis falls upon questions of validity. But his contextualism and my observance of the *gestaltisch* are two ways of remarking the same characteristic of the valuational. And my voluntarism likewise correlates with his dynamicism. I should like to think that our respective views, both in theory of value and in ethics, are mutually supplementary rather than rival theories.

In what he writes for this book, he sets aside any difference of outcome and presents a straightforward and best possible resume of my conceptions.

I think that Dr. Mothersill likes plain English and plain issues. After a brief introduction which seems to me markedly judicious and well-put, she proposes to delineate my point of view further by examination of its shortcomings.

I shall not answer the objections; but I find myself stimulated to state where I stand on some of the issues, and some of the reasons; perhaps in plainer language than I have used before.

I think Dr. Mothersill is impatient with me because I will not break down and admit that I am just another hedonist and utilitarian. Perhaps I should: certainly my views follow more closely those of John Stuart Mill's *Utilitarianism* than any other historic model. But I decline to do that, for one principal reason, because I think that 'pleasure' and 'pain', as synonyms for what makes human life good or bad, represent a gross caricature. 'Achievement' and 'frustration' would come equally near to the mark, and 'self-realization' would come nearer. Naming the good as 'pleasure' reflects a failure to observe that the root of the moral sense does *not* lie in the euphoric-dysphoric gamut of consciousness (if it did, pigs would have such moral sensibility as much as men), but in the human capacity for deliberate self-government. And the concern for that which is not immediate, but is objective, must profoundly alter the sense of good and bad, by making it something to be *judged,* and not simply felt.

Some appreciation of this kind of fact is reflected in Bentham's recognition of the dimensions of 'purity' and 'fecundity' in his hedonic calculus; and in Mill's introduction of better and less good *quality.* But this still fails to go to the root of the matter. Human deliberate and objective *judgment* of good and bad qualifies what is directly experienced as good or bad. The creature with a moral sense is likewise affected by a sense of the imprudent and of the sinful—if I may use that ancient term—and his satisfactions and dissatisfactions found are deeply colored by that fact. It is for such reason the uncriticized life is not worth living: the creature endowed with the critical faculty cannot enjoy what affronts his critical judgment; he cannot take satisfaction in concluding or believing in contravention of the dictates of logic; and he cannot find happiness by acting in disregard of the principles of morals.

I am a hedonist—or would be—if that means only (1) that what is right can never be determined without reference to what is good, and (2) that what is good, in any of the legion of other senses in which 'good' is predicated, can never be determined except by some ultimate reference to good or bad as directly findable in experience; and to the manner in which transient goods and bads 'compose' and mutually qualify one another in the complex relationships they enter into as constituents in the larger wholes of experience. But on this second point, the gestalt-like character of any whole of experience must be observed: the attempt to depict a good life, or one which fails to be such, by applying arithmetic to our transient gratifications and disgratifications is, as of today, a little too naïve to call for serious consideration.

I am a social utilitarian—or would be—if that should mean only (1) that the justification of an act is to be determined by reference to the consequences of it (actual or intended) for good or ill; and (2) that no act is morally justified if the decision of it deliberately leaves out of account the effects it may have upon any individual life affected by it. But I am not a utilitarian if that implies supposing that 'the greatest good of the greatest number' offers any sufficient criterion, even theoretically, for the solution of the immensely serious and deadly practical problems of social justice.

Also, I am neither hedonist nor utilitarian if these names imply acceptance of the supposition that any conclusion that so and so is morally right is derivable from the single premise that the consequences of doing it will be good—or be better or be best—in any sense of 'good' whatever. Indeed, I think that the most signal failure of historic utilitarianism is its failure to offer any clear ground for determining whether 'enlightened egoism' is or is not the moral ideal—on which issue Bentham and Mill disagreed. It fails to establish any logical elenchus between "So and so is good" and "Such and such is morally right." In point of fact, there is no such elenchus without an additional and major premise of another kind.

The best brief characterization of my ethical position which I remember seeing (and I regret to have forgotten who made the remark) is that I am a naturalist with respect to the good but a rationalist with respect to the right. But if my 'rationalism', and the manner in which I would combine this with a 'naturalist' account of the good, has failed to be noticed, that is my own fault: I have not yet been able to present a sufficient account of these matters.

I could not well express my appreciation of the careful, objective, and penetrating review which A. C. Ewing gives of my studies in ethics. It represents a kind of lucid and detailed accuracy which I would emulate but am too impatient to achieve—with regard to the writings of any other or even my own. Particularly I am appreciative of his understanding and meticulous discussion of my approximation to or divergence from historic hedonism. I should also like to record the fact that, though there may be little or no evidence of it in my writing, Ewing's *The Definition of Good* is one of the books which is never far from my elbow and to which I have given most careful attention.

I wish to remark also one criticism he makes in passing which I think is justified; criticism, namely, of my saying that what expressive statements like 'I now suffer pain' formulate, is certain (unless a prevarication) but not knowledge and not a judgment. That convention—excluding, as not 'knowledge' and not a 'judgment', what admits of no present doubt—does too much violence to the common usage of these words to be well taken. I should wish to cover the facts in point— e.g., that in such cases there is nothing needing to be *judged*—by some more judicious use of language, if I were to do it over. I think, however, that, granted my own vocabulary, I make no error as to fact and commit no inconsistency.

Concerning the larger issues, I specially regret not to be appropriately responsive to Ewing's discussion and his incidental queries. I should, however, find myself hampered with respect to some of these by the fact that, coming to close quarters with our problems in the way he always does, I should have trouble to locate myself in terms of his frame of reference. For example, I cannot, with intent to be precise, answer categorically the question whether the intrinsically good is, as G. E. Moore would have it, a simple and indefinable property. I cannot because, first, I should have to guess what, exactly, 'simple' means here. Second, remarking that it is the intrinsically good only which is in question (that instrumental goodness or utility is simple or indefinable would have no plausibility), I cannot draw the line between intrinsic and extrinsic goodness where Moore draws it, and I cannot draw it anywhere by reference to his criteria.

I think I can discern the character which distinguishes qualities Moore would call 'simple'. They are those denoted by words (e.g., color names?) whose intended signification could not, by any use of language, be conveyed to one who would not be sensibly acquainted with instances of what they denote (e.g., to those born without sight?). I should be prepared to think that any intrinsic good, and indeed the good in general, would be 'simple' in this sense; impossible to convey to an otherwise human being with no sense of the euphoric and dysphoric. But this has nothing to do with definability. I can define 'ultraviolet' though I can neither see nor imagine what it denotes. And Miss Helen Keller could doubtless define 'red' accurately. And regardless of any supposed 'simplicity', 'good' is definable as 'desirable, valuable, the opposite of bad'. In this connection, I should agree with Ewing that 'desirable' means 'worthy to be desired'; and that nothing is proved desirable—as Mill would suggest—by being desired by somebody, or even by being such as is naturally desired by everybody. However, I should probably disagree with Ewing concerning the criterion of the worthiness in question, thinking that such worthiness to be sought for and cherished is something to be verified or confirmed in experience, and that the criterion of it is relation to qualitative characters findable in experience.

As a fact, this category of 'simple and unanalyzable' ('indefinable') is a relic of the rationalistic epistemology of Leibnitz, in which it is supposed that, in a really correct dictionary, such 'simple' predicates would have to be listed first, and in terms of these there would be just one correct 'real' definition of any other term. I feel sure that neither Ewing nor I could get on with that.

I should have worse difficulties over 'natural or nonnatural'; hoping to be able to understand what others intend by statements in which these terms occur, and even to use them conformably, but unable to think that any distinction so expressed is clear or well-taken.

I deliberately choose here examples which are no more than peripheral to any material issue involved in Ewing's careful paper; hoping thereby to illustrate the fact that I do not attempt any appropriate response, but also to indicate the kind of reason or account which I do not find possible here. If circumstances were otherwise, I should find his discussion exactly of that sort on the basis of which profitable consideration of issues could be initiated. But in any such discussion, I should have to go back to epistemology and logic: I cannot arrive at any theory of ethics in which I could have confidence without such prolegomena. Indeed, I think that theory of ethics has, as principal subdivisions, logic of ethics, epistemology of ethics, and metaphysics of ethics.

If I should be less than completely content with the entirely accurate summary which Will Dennes gives of Lewis on the Morally Imperative, and with the pro-attitude he evinces, I should indeed be impossible to satisfy. But in order to show myself impossible to the very end, I choose for comment the one point on which he is critical and the one point on which I think he is less than one thousand percent discerning. He thinks that in belaboring emotivism in ethics, I overlook the plausibility that the one thing common to what men value is not any objective property in the things valued but the attitude of liking or approving which these things evoke. He also thinks my arguments may be directed against a straw man, and suggests the desirability of observing that the emotivists are good people with moral sentiments like the rest of us.

Let me first illustrate my point. I have lately read some writings on philosophy on which I set high value. But I shall insist to the end that I like and approve these *because* of certain objective characteristics which they demonstrably have; their consistency and cogency, their truth to fact, their intellectual discernment and understanding, and so on. And I shall likewise insist to the end that it is these provable or disprovable characters characterizing them which makes them good; and my attitude of approval is justified or mistaken according as they have or do not have these properties which I attribute to them, and on account of which I approve them. It is not my emotive attitude so much as my judgment which is in point; and this judgment of mine, in evaluing them, is either correct or incorrect, true or false, according as these things assessed do or do not have the characteristics which I believe they do.

These properties are the typical goodnesses of the kind of thing here to be assessed. Other kinds of things, e.g., foods, would be assessed by reference to other attributes, such as pleasing taste, digestibility, and calorie content. Some call these 'good-making' properties; and this is apt language. But the distinction is unnecessary: whatever makes good, is itself good—good instrumentally or contributorily.

And—for example—the supposition that these writings toward which my attitude is pro, are by that attitude of mine made any better; or the supposition that when I call them good, I intend by that to indicate my emotive response and not my judgment of determinable fact; both these suppositions are false. For example, these writings *are* consistent and cogent, or they are not. It is the criteria of logic according to which they must be *judged* on that point; and by reference to which my value-assessment is a correct or incorrect judgment. My assessment is valid or not valid, true or false, by reference to the logical facts of the matter. And I find it *imperative* to judge them by such logical criteria, regardless of my gratification or disgratification in the facts as so found. Emotive attitudes are, as Aristotle observed, to be governed by knowledge of empirically demonstrable facts and by rationality. Any other attitude is subjective and of no validity.

*If* the emotivists should clearly agree that insofar as what is assessed as good or bad is something short of the final end in itself, goodness *is* thus to be attested by judgments which are provably true or false; and it is only with respect to the summum bonum—a life to be found good in the living of it—that attitude of approval or affective-finding-so is a sufficient criterion, then the remaining issue would be tenuous. But they seldom seem to acknowledge this. And short of that, their doctrine appears to me to be a revival of that skepticism and subjectivism with respect to the good and the right, whose root significance has not altered since the first expression of it by the Sophists.

That I argue against a straw man, is in part a question whether, in insisting upon this kind of consideration as being the root issue in point, I am justified or not. But I admit to a tendency to "argue against straw men," or—let me rationalize it—to criticize philosophic theses, not philosophers. It is also doubtful if I ever have, or ever shall, spin out any argument in which I take the negative to that length which is requisite for thorough consideration of all aspects of the view I reject. I have a—probably inexcusable—desire to curtail such negative writing and get back to what I wish to defend. Perhaps what I am most negative to is negativism; and what I am most emotive about is emotivism.

I confess to being a little frightened by emotivism in ethics, because it seems to me to negate all the validities; all possible standards of the good and all principles of the right. The alarming implication of that is, that it leaves no recourse for those who disagree over what is good and what is right but the arbitrament of force. And this relativism which emotivist doctrine implies, is also that type of view least fitted to survive in a world in which we have to meet opponents who are convinced that their side is provably right on grounds of history and of objective fact, and that their cause is worth fighting for. I hope that such skeptics of the objectively valuable and objectively right among us, will lose the argument before all of us lose our liberty of thought and action. There is nothing else which so deeply engages me as this matter of valid standards of the good and valid principles of the right.

MENLO PARK, CALIFORNIA
MARCH 11, 1961

# PREFACE TO THE BIBLIOGRAPHY

The preparation of the Lewis bibliography has been an easier task than some in this series, for his writings, although numerous, have been limited to strictly philosophical subjects, and his articles have appeared, for the most part, in a small set of technical journals. Furthermore, Professor Lewis has been most cooperative in providing an almost complete list of his publications. Consequently, my labors have consisted largely of checking the exhaustiveness of his list and the references for bibliographical details. Although I may have omitted some items in his more than fifty years of professional writing, the list is as complete as he and I have been able to make it.

Professor Lewis spent his last years on the problems of ethics. He left extensive manuscripts in this field, including the unpublished papers listed below. At his instructions, they will be edited by William Frankena and Charles Baylis. They plan to publish them in two volumes under the title, "Essays on the Foundations of Ethics."

I am indebted to Professor Lewis for his extensive help and to Mrs. Doris Calhoun for her secretarial assistance in compiling this bibliography.

E. M. ADAMS

UNIVERSITY OF NORTH CAROLINA AT CHAPEL HILL

## THE WRITINGS OF C. I. LEWIS
(With selected reviews of his books)

### 1910

The Place of Intuition in Knowledge. Ph.D. thesis. On file in the Harvard University Archives, Widener Library Building, Cambridge, Massachusetts.

Contents: I. Introduction—II. Radical Actionism—III. Radical Intuitionism—IV. Intuition and Purpose—V. Intuition and Relations—VI. Idea and Object—Appendix: Intuition and the Non-Euclidean Geometrics.

### 1912

Professor Santayana and Idealism. *The University of California Chronicle,* Vol. XIV, No. 2, pp. 192-211.

(A footnote reads: "A lecture before the Philosophical Union of the University of California. The above title was prearranged; a more appropriate one would perhaps, have been 'Naturalism and Idealism'.")

Implication and the Algebra of Logic. *Mind.* n.s., Vol. XXI, No. 84, pp. 522-531.

## 1913

Realism and Subjectivism. *The Journal of Philosophy, Psychology and Scientific Methods,* Vol. X, No. 2, pp. 43-49.

Interesting Theorems in Symbolic Logic. *The Journal of Philosophy, Psychology and Scientific Methods,* Vol. X, No. 9, pp. 239-242.

A New Algebra of Implications and Some Consequences. *The Journal of Philosophy, Psychology and Scientific Methods,* Vol. X, No. 16, pp. 428-438.

> (Read in brief before the American Mathematical Society, San Francisco Section, October 26, 1912.)

The Calculus of Strict Implication. *Mind.* n.s., Vol. XXIII, No. 90, pp. 240-247.

## 1914

Bergson and Contemporary Thought. *University of California Chronicle,* Vol. XVI, No. 2, pp. 181-197.

> (An address before the Philosophical Union of the University of California, January 16, 1914.)

The Matrix Algebra for Implications. *The Journal of Philosophy, Psychology and Scientific Methods,* Vol. XI, No. 22, pp. 589-600.

Review of A. N. Whitehead's and B. Russell's *Principia Mathematica,* Vol. II. In *The Journal of Philosophy, Psychology and Scientific Methods,* Vol. XI, No. 18, pp. 497-502.

## 1915

A Too Brief Set of Postulates for the Algebra of Logic. *The Journal of Philosophy, Psychology and Scientific Methods,* Vol. XII, No. 19, pp. 523-525.

## 1916

Types of Order and the System $\Sigma$. *The Philosophical Review,* Vol. XXV, No. 3, pp. 407-419.

## 1917

The Issues Concerning Material Implication. *The Journal of Philosophy, Psychology and Scientific Methods,* Vol. XIV, No. 13, pp. 350-356.

## 1918

A SURVEY OF SYMBOLIC LOGIC. Berkeley: University of California Press, 1918. Pp. iv + 406.

> Contents: Preface—I. The Development of Symbolic Logic—Section I. The Scope of Symbolic Logic. Symbolic Logic and Logistic. Summary Account of their Development—Section II. Leibniz—Section III. From Leibniz

to De Morgan and Boole—Section IV. De Morgan—Section V. Boole—Section VI. Jevons—Section VII. Peirce—Section VIII. Developments since Peirce—II. THE CLASSIC, OR BOOLE-SCHRÖDER ALGEBRA OF LOGIC—Section I. General Character of the Algebra. The Postulates and their Interpretation —Section II. Elementary Theorems—Section III. General Properties of Functions—Section IV. Fundamental Laws of the Theory of Equations— Section V. Fundamental Laws of the Theory of Inequations—Section VI. Note on the Inverse Operations, "Subtraction" and "Division"—III. APPLI- CATIONS OF THE BOOLE-SCHRÖDER ALGEBRA—Section I. Diagrams for the Logical Relations of Classes—Section II. The Application to Classes—Section III. The Application to Propositions—Section IV. The Appli- cation to Relations—IV. SYSTEMS BASED ON MATERIAL IMPLICA- TION—Section I. The Two-Valued Algebra—Section II. The Calculus of Propositional Functions. Functions of One Variable—Section III. Proposi- tional Functions of Two or More Variables—Section IV. Derivation of the Logic of Classes from the Calculus of Propositional Functions—Section V. The Logic of Relations—Section VI. The Logic of *Principia Mathematica* —V. THE SYSTEM OF STRICT IMPLICATION—Section I. Primitive Ideas, Primitive Propositions, and Immediate Consequences—Section II. Strict Relations and Material Relations—Section III. The Transformation (—/∼)—Section IV. Extensions of Strict Implication. The Calculus of Con- sistencies and the Calculus of Ordinary Inference—Section V. The Meaning of "Implies"—VI. SYMBOLIC LOGIC, LOGISTIC, AND MATHEMATI- CAL METHOD—Section I. General Character of the Logistic Method. The "Orthodox" View—Section II. Two Varieties of Logistic Method: Peano's *Formulaire* and *Principia Mathematica*. The Nature of Logistic Proof— Section III. A "Heterodox" View of the Nature of Mathematics and of Logistic—Section IV. The Logistic Method of Kempe and Royce—Section V. Summary and Conclusion—Appendix. Two Fragments from Leibniz—Bibli- ography—Index.

Reviews: Norbert Wiener, *The Journal of Philosophy, Psychology and Scientific Methods,* Vol. XVII, No. 3, January 29, 1920, pp. 78-79; Henry M. Sheffer, *The American Mathematical Monthly,* Vol. XXVII, July-Sep- tember, 1920, pp. 309-311.

German Idealism and Its War Critics. *University of California Chronicle,* Vol. XX, No. 1, pp. 1-15.

(Read before the Philosophical Union of the University of California, September 28, 1917.)

## 1920

Strict Implication—an Emendation. *The Journal of Philosophy, Psychol- ogy and Scientific Methods,* Vol. XVII, No. 11, pp. 300-302.

Review of Rupert Clendon Lodge's *An Introduction to Modern Logic.* In *The Journal of Philosophy, Psychology and Scientific Methods,* Vol. XVII, No. 18, pp. 498-500.

## 1921

The Structure of Logic and Its Relation to Other Systems. *The Journal of Philosophy,* Vol. XVIII, No. 19, pp. 505-516.

(Read, with omissions, at the twentieth meeting of the American Philosophical Association, at Columbia University, December 29, 1920.)

## 1922

La Logique de la Méthode Mathématique. *Revue de Métaphysique et de Morale,* 29ᵉ anné, No. 4 (numéro exceptionnel), pp. 455-474.

Review of John Maynard Keynes's *A Treatise on Probability.* In *The Philosophical Review,* Vol. XXXI, No. 2, pp. 180-186.

## 1923

Facts, Systems, and the Unity of the World. *The Journal of Philosophy,* Vol. XX, No. 6, pp. 141-151.

A Pragmatic Conception of the a priori. *The Journal of Philosophy,* Vol. XX, No. 7, pp. 169-177.

> Reprinted in Herbert Feigl and Wilfrid Sellars, *Readings in Philosophical Analysis.* New York: Appleton-Century-Crofts, Inc., 1949, pp. 286-294.
> (Read at the meeting of the American Philosophical Association, December 27, 1922.)

Review of D. Nys's *La Notion d'Espace.* In *The Journal of Philosophy,* Vol. XX, No. 10, pp. 277-278.

## 1924

Review of *Chance, Love, and Logic;* Philosophical Essays by the late Charles S. Peirce; edited with an Introduction by Morris R. Cohen; with a Supplementary Essay by John Dewey. In *The Journal of Philosophy,* Vol. XXI, No. 3, pp. 71-74.

## 1925

Review of C. D. Broad's *Scientific Thought.* In *The Philosophical Review,* Vol. XXXIV, No. 4, pp. 406-411.

## 1926

The Pragmatic Element in Knowledge. *University of California Publications in Philosophy,* Vol. VI, pp. 205-227. (Howison Lecture, 1926)

> Reprinted by University of California Press and by Cambridge University Press, 1926.
> Reviewed by F. C. S. Schiller in *Mind.* n.s., Vol. XXXVI, No. 143, July, 1927, pp. 377-379.

Review of Harold R. Smart's *The Philosophical Presuppositions of Mathematical Logic.* In *The Journal of Philosophy,* Vol. XXIII, No. 8, pp. 220-222.

## 1927

Review of N. O. Losokij's *Handbuch der Logik, autorisierte übersetzung von Prof. Dr. W. Sesemann.* In *The Journal of Philosophy,* Vol. XXIV, No. 24, pp. 665-667.

### 1928

Review of A. N. Whitehead and B. Russell's *Principia Mathematica*. In *The American Mathematical Monthly*, Vol. XXXV, April, 1928, pp. 200-205.

### 1929

MIND AND THE WORLD-ORDER: OUTLINE OF A THEORY OF KNOWLEDGE. New York: Charles Scribner's Sons, 1929. Pp. xiv + 446.

> Reprinted: New York: Dover Publications, 1956.
> Contents: I. Introduction: About Philosophy in General and Metaphysics in Particular. The Proper Method of Philosophy—II. The Given Element in Experience—III. The Pure Concept—IV. Common Concepts and Our Common World—V. The Knowledge of Objects—VI. The Relativity of Knowledge and the Independence of the Real—VII. The A Priori—Traditional Conceptions—VIII. The Nature of the A Priori, and the Pragmatic Element in Knowledge—IX. The A Priori and the Empirical—X. The Empirical and Probable—XI. Experience and Order—Appendices: A. Natural Science and Abstract Concepts—B. Esthesis and Esthetics—C. Concepts and "Ideas"—D. Mind's Knowledge of Itself—E. The Applicability of Abstract Conceptual Systems to Experience—F. The Logical Correlates of the A Priori and the A Posteriori—Index.
> Reviewed by C. A. Baylis in *The Journal of Philosophy*, Vol. XXVII, No. 12, June 5, 1930, pp. 320-327; Hugh Miller in *The Philosophical Review*, Vol. XL, No. 6, November, 1931, pp. 573-579; G. Watts Cunningham in *The International Journal of Ethics*, Vol. XL, No. 4, 1929-30, pp. 550-556; William Stetson Merrill in *The New Scholasticism*, Vol. IV, No. 4, October, 1930, pp. 393-396; F. C. S. Schiller in *Mind*. n.s., Vol. XXXIX, No. 156, October, 1930, pp. 505-507.

### 1930

Pragmatism and Current Thought. *The Journal of Philosophy*, Vol. XXVII, No. 9, pp. 238-246.

> (Among papers in honor of John Dewey read at the meeting of the American Philosophical Association, December 30, 1929, New York City.)

Logic and Pragmatism [autobiographical]. In *Contemporary American Philosophy*, ed. by G. P. Adams and W. P. Montague. New York: The Macmillan Company, 1930, Vol. II, pp. 31-51.

Review of John Dewey's *The Quest for Certainty: A Study of the Relation of Knowledge and Action*. In *The Journal of Philosophy*, Vol. XXVII, No. 1, pp. 14-25.

### 1932

SYMBOLIC LOGIC (with C. H. Langford). New York: The Appleton-Century Company, 1932. Pp. xii + 506.

> Reprinted: New York: Dover Publications, 1951. Chapter I under title, "History of Symbolic Logic," in James R. Newman, *The World of Mathematics*. New York: Simon and Schuster, 1956, Vol. III, pp. 1859-1877.

Contents: I. Introduction—II. The Boole-Schröder Algebra—III. The Logic of Terms—IV. The Two-Valued Algebra—V. Extension of the Two-Valued Algebra to Propositional Functions—VI. The Logistic Calculus of Unanalyzed Propositions—Section 1. General Properties of the Elementary Functions of Propositions—Section 2. Material Implication—Section 3. Further Theorems—Section 4. Consistency and the Modal Functions—Section 5. The Consistency Postulate and Its Consequences—Section 6. The Existence Postulate and Existence Theorems—VII. Truth-Value Systems and the Matrix Method—VIII. Implication and Deducibility—IX. The General Theory of Propositions—X. Propositions of Ordinary Discourse—XI. Postulational Technique: Deduction—XII. Postulational Technique: Deducibility—XIII. The Logical Paradoxes—Appendix: I. The Use of Dots as Brackets—II. The Structure of the System of Strict Implication—Index.

Reviewed by Daniel J. Bronstein and Harry Tarter in *The Philosophical Review*, Vol. XLIII, No. 3, 1934, pp. 305-309; Harry Bradford Smith in *The Journal of Philosophy*, Vol. XXX, No. 11, May 25, 1933, pp. 302-306; John Wisdom in *Mind*. n.s., Vol. XLIII, No. 169, January, 1934, pp. 99-109.

Alternative Systems of Logic. *The Monist*, Vol. XLII, No. 4, October, 1932, pp. 481-507.

## 1933

Reply to Mr. Ushenko. *The Monist*, Vol. XLIII, No. 2, pp. 292-293.

(This is a reply to "Note on Alternative Systems of Logic" by A. Ushenko, *The Monist*, Vol. XLIII, No. 2, pp. 290-291, which criticizes Lewis' "Alternative Systems of Logic," *The Monist*, Vol. XLII, No. 4, October, 1932.)

Reply to Mr. Ushenko's Addendum. *The Monist*, Vol. XLIII, No. 2, pp. 295-296.

(This is a reply to "An Addendum to the Note" by A. Ushenko, *The Monist*, Vol. XLIII, No. 2, p. 294.)

Note Concerning Many-Valued Logical Systems. *The Journal of Philosophy*, Vol. XXX, No. 14, p. 364.

## 1934

Experience and Meaning. *The Philosophical Review*, Vol. XLIII, No. 2, pp. 125-146.

Reprinted in Herbert Feigl and Wilfrid Sellars, *Readings in Philosophical Analysis*. New York: Appleton-Century-Crofts, Inc., 1949, pp. 128-145; also in James L. Jarrett and Sterling M. McMurrin, eds., *Contemporary Philosophy*. New York: Henry Holt and Co., 1954, pp. 277-291.

(The Presidential address to the Eastern Division of the American Philosophical Association at Amherst College, December 29, 1933.)

Paul Weiss on Alternative Logics. *The Philosophical Review*, Vol. XLIII, No. 1, pp. 70-74.

## 1936

Emch's Calculus and Strict Implication. *The Journal of Symbolic Logic*, Vol. I, No. 3, pp. 77-86.

## 1939

Meaning and Action. In a Symposium of Reviews of John Dewey's *Logic: The Theory Of Inquiry.* In *The Journal of Philosophy,* Vol. XXXVI, No. 21, pp. 572-576.

## 1941

Some Logical Considerations Concerning the Mental. *The Journal of Philosophy,* Vol. XXXVIII, No. 9, pp. 225-233.

Reprinted in Herbert Feigl and Wilfrid Sellars, *Readings in Philosophical Analysis.* New York: Appleton-Century-Crofts, Inc., 1949, pp. 385-392.

(Read, with omissions, at the meeting of the Eastern Division, American Philosophical Association, Philadelphia, December 26, 1940.)

Logical Positivism and Pragmatism. (Unpublished. Written for *Revue Internationale de Philosophie* but not printed because of the German invasion of Belgium.)

## 1943

The Modes of Meaning. *Philosophy and Phenomenological Research,* Vol. IV, No. 2, 1943-44, pp. 236-249.

Reprinted in Leonard Linsky, ed., *Semantics and the Philosophy of Language.* Urbana, Illinois: The University of Illinois Press, 1952, pp. 50-63.

## 1946

AN ANALYSIS OF KNOWLEDGE AND VALUATION. La Salle, Illinois: The Open Court Publishing Company, 1946. Pp. xxi + 567.

(The Paul Carus Foundation Lectures. VII.)

Part of Chapter XV is reprinted under the title, "Esthetic Judgment," in James L. Jarrett and Sterling McMurrin, eds., *Contemporary Philosophy.* New York: Henry Holt and Co., 1954, pp. 310-316.

Contents: Preface—INTRODUCTION: I: Knowledge, Action, and Evaluation—1. To know is to apprehend the future as qualified by values which action may realize—2. The meaning of 'action'—3. The meaning of 'knowledge' —4. Knowledge and meaning—5. Only an active being could have knowledge —6. Empirical knowledge predicts experience as consequence of action—II: Knowledge, Experience, and Meaning—1. The two types of knowledge—2. Usual requirements of knowledge—3. Three types of apprehension—Book I: MEANING AND ANALYTIC TRUTH—III: The Modes of Meaning—1. The *a priori* and the analytic—2. Summary of theses in Book I—3. The four modes of the meaning of terms—4. The meaning of propositions and statements—5. Modes of propositional meaning—6. Propositional functions and statement functions—7. Intensional meaning and extensional meaning—IV: Meaning and Language—1. Broader aspects of meaning—2. Symbols and expressions—3. Elementary and complex expressions—4. All words have meaning—5. Analytic meaning—6. Synonymous expressions—7. Holophrastic meaning and analytic meaning—8. Implicitly analytic and explicitly analytic statements—9. Analytic statements impose no restrictions on the actual—V: Definitions, Formal Statements, and Logic—1. The conventionalist view—2. Types of definitive statement—3. Symbolic conventions, dictionary definitions,

induction—9. Congruence by itself is not sufficient to validate belief—10. Congruence and memory—11. 'Deduction' of the basic validity of memory and of induction—Book III: VALUATION—XII: Knowing, Doing, and Valuing—1. Valuations are a form of empirical knowledge—2. Action and valuation—3. Practical justification of action—4. The cognitive content of valuations—5. Types of value-apprehension—6. *A priori* value-predications are not valuations—7. Objective value and immediate value—8. Intrinsic value, instrumental value, and utility—9. Values in objects are extrinsic—10. Inherent values—11. Summary as to terminology—12. **Further explanatory remarks**—XIII: The Immediately Valuable—1. Values immediately realized are intrinsic—2. Naturalism in value-theory—3. The problem of characterizing the immediately valuable—4. Value-disvalue as a mode of presentation —5. 'Pleasure' a poor name for the immediately valuable—6. Is value in direct experience subjective?—7. Immediate value as a quality of appearance —8. All value in objects is extrinsic—9. Value in objects is potentiality for some realization of value in immediate experience—10. Subjectivity of value as relativity to what is personal—11. Are value-qualities more subjective than sense qualities?—12. Subjective value-apprehension and error in value-judgment—13. Immediate value as attaching to presentation—14. Immediate value as affected by the context of the presentation—15. An example—XIV: Inherent Value and the Esthetic—1. Intrinsic value and inherent value—2. Esthetic values are a subclass of inherent values—3. The active, the cognitive, and the esthetic attitudes—4. The broad meaning of 'esthetic'—5. The narrower meaning of 'esthetic'—6. Interests subsidiary to the esthetic—7. Esthetic values and values found in activity—XV: Esthetic Judgment—1. Esthetic judgment concerns a property of objects—2. Comparative evaluations of the esthetic in experience—3. The esthetic character of experience may be judged—4. Esthetics and esthetic theory—5. Types of esthetic objects—6. The esthetic actuality and its context—7. The variety of things esthetically valued —XVI: The Moral Sense and Contributory Values—1. Value-effects of one experience upon another—2. The imperative of rationality and the good life—3. Values contributory to the good life—4. Critique of the Benthamite calculus of values—5. Value in experiential wholes—6. The consummatory character of value in an active life—7. An implication for our relation to others—8. A life to be found good in the living of it—9. Synthetic apprehension of value in experiential wholes—10. Difficulties of such appraisals of value—11. Practical simplifications of the problem—XVII: Value in Objects—1. Various modes of predicating value to objects—2. Value as simple potentiality—3. Value as relative to actual conditions—4. Value relative to persons—5. Absolute value and comparative value—6. Relative value and ethics—7. Value as relative to humans in general—8. Bare utility and instrumental value—9. Value-significance of names—10. Values as relative to control —11. Distinctive modes of evaluation—12. Social value—13. The assessment of social values—14. Socal values and ethics—Index.

Reviewed by Paul Henle in *The Journal of Philosophy*, Vol. XLV, No. 19, September 9, 1948, pp. 524-532; C. J. Ducasse in *The Philosophical Review*, Vol. LVII, No. 3, 1948, pp. 260-280; J. W. Robson in *Ethics*, Vol. LVIII, No. 2, January, 1948, pp. 140-143; W. T. Stace in *Mind*. n.s., Vol. LVII, No. 225, January, 1948, pp. 71-85.

## 1948

The Meaning of Liberty. *Revue Internationale de Philosophie,* Tome 11, No. 6, août 1948, pp. 14-22.
Professor Chisholm and Empiricism. *The Journal of Philosophy,* Vol. XLV, No. 19, pp. 517-524.

## 1949

Practical and Moral Imperatives. Unpublished. (Cooper Foundation Lecture, Swarthmore College, 1949.)

## 1950

The Empirical Basis of Value Judgments. Unpublished.
    (Read before the Yale Philosophy Club, 1950.)
"Kant, Immanuel," *Colliers Encyclopedia.* New York: Collier & Son, 1950, Vol. XI, pp. 519-523.

## 1951

Notes on the Logic of Intension. In *Structure, Method and Meaning: Essays in Honor of Henry M. Sheffer;* edited by Paul Henle, Horace M. Kallen and Susanne K. Langer. New York: The Liberal Arts Press, 1951, pp. 25-34.

## 1952

The Given Element in Empirical Knowledge. *The Philosophical Review,* Vol. LXI, pp. 168-175.
"Ethics in the Age of Science." Unpublished.
    (Read before the American Philosophical Society, Philadelphia, 1952.)
Turning Points in Ethics. Unpublished.
    (Three lectures on the Machette Foundation, Wesleyan University, Connecticut, 1952.)
Review of Royce's Logical Essays, edited by Daniel S. Robinson. In *Philosophy and Phenomenological Research,* Vol. XII, No. 3, March, 1952, pp. 431-434.

## 1953

The Rational Imperatives. In *Vision and Action: Essays in Honor of Horace M. Kallen;* edited by Sidney Ratner. New Brunswick, N.J.: Rutgers University Press, 1953, pp. 148-166.
Paul Carus—1852-1919. *Proceedings of the American Philosophical Association,* Vol. XXVI, 1953, pp. 62-63.
The Nature of Value. Unpublished.
    (Read at New York University, 1953.)

## 1954

Santayana at Harvard. *The Journal of Philosophy,* Vol. LI, No. 2, pp. 29-31.

(Spoken at the Memorial Meeting for George Santayana held in Room D of Emerson Hall, Harvard University, Friday, January 30, 1953.)

A Comment on "The Verification Theory of Meaning" by Everett J. Nelson. *The Philosophical Review,* Vol. LXIII, No. 2, pp. 193-196.

Turning Points in Ethical Theory. Unpublished.

(Read before the Harvard Philosophy Club, 1954.)

## 1955

THE GROUND AND NATURE OF THE RIGHT. New York: Columbia University Press, 1955. Pp. vi + 97.

(Woodbridge Lectures, V, delivered at Columbia University in November, 1954.)

Contents: Preface—1. Modes of Right and Wrong—2. Right Believing and Concluding—3. Right Doing—4. The Right and the Good—5. The Rational Imperatives.

Reviewed by Charner Perry in *Ethics,* Vol. LXVI, No. 2, 1956, pp. 137-139; Rollo Handy in *Philosophy and Phenomenological Research,* Vol. XVIII, No. 2, 1957, pp. 273-274; A. C. Ewing in *Philosophy,* Vol. XXXII, No. 122, 1957, pp. 279-280; J. D. Mabbott in *Mind,* Vol. LXVII, No. 265, 1958, pp. 109-111.

Realism or Phenomenalism? *The Philosophical Review,* Vol. LXIV, No. 2, pp. 233-247.

(Read at the annual meeting of the Pacific Division of the American Philosophical Association, September 9, 1954.)

## 1957

OUR SOCIAL INHERITANCE. Bloomington, Indiana: Indiana University Press, 1957. Pp. 110.

Contents: Preface—1. The Background—2. The Principal Ingredients—3. The Critical Factors.

(Presented as public lectures at Indiana University in the spring of 1956 under the auspices of the Mahlon Powell Foundation.)

Some Suggestions Concerning Metaphysics of Logic. In *American Philosophers at Work;* edited by Sidney Hook. New York: Criterion Books, Inc., 1957, pp. 93-105.

(Read before the Association for Symbolic Logic, Clark University, Worcester, Massachusetts, 1949; abstract in *Journal of Symbolic Logic,* Vol. XV (1950), p. 76.)

Ralph Barton Perry. *Philosophy and Phenomenological Research,* Vol. XVII, No. 4, pp. 579-582.

## 1958

Philosophy. *The Encyclopedia Americana.* New York: Americana Corporation, 1958, Vol. 21, pp. 769-777.

Critique of Pure Reason. *The Encyclopedia Americana.* New York: Americana Corporation, 1958, pp. 212-213.

Professor John D. Goheen of Stanford University has kindly brought to my attention some additional bibliographical notes which reached us too late to be incorporated chronologically into the Adams bibliography. These include the report that a volume of essays is now being prepared for publication by Stanford University Press, and some notes on unpublished papers not reported in the Adams bibliography, as follows:

### 1968-1969

VALUES AND IMPERATIVES (STUDIES IN ETHICS BY C. I. LEWIS); edited and with an Introduction by John Lange. Stanford: Stanford University Press, 1968 or 1969. Pp. c. 250.

Contents: Introduction—I. Foundations of Ethics—1. Ethics and the Present Scene—2. The Right and the Good—3. Doubts about Ethics—4. An attempted Answer. II Selected Papers—1. Values and Facts—2. Pragmatism and the Roots of the Moral—3. Practical and Moral Imperatives—4. The Meaning of Liberty 5. The Rational Imperatives—6. The Categorical Imperative.

(The lectures "Foundations of Ethics" were delivered at Wesleyan University in 1959. "Values and Facts" (approximately 1952) was prepared for a cooperative volume on value to be edited by Professors Roy Wood Sellars and Sidney Hook, but the volume never appeared. "Pragmatism and the Roots of the Moral," a paper read to the Claremont Philosophical Discussion Group, Dec. 5, 1956. "Practical and Moral Imperatives" was delivered at Swarthmore College in 1949. "The Meaning of Liberty" appeared in the *Revue Internationale De Philosophie*, No. 6, in 1948. "The Rational Imperatives" appeared in 1953, in the anthology *Vision and Action: Essays in Honor of Horace M. Kallen on his 70th Birthday*, edited by Sidney Ratner, and published by Rutgers University Press. "The Categorical Imperative" was originally delivered at Michigan State University in 1958.)

### 1933-1960: Supplementary Notes

(a) A published article not listed in "The Writings of C. I. Lewis": "Categories of Natural Knowledge." (An essay printed in *The Philosophy of Alfred North Whitehead,* ed. by P.A. Schilpp. Tudor Publishing Company, New York, Second Edition, 1951.) Now published by Open Court Publishing Company, LaSalle, Illinois.

(b) Unpublished papers not listed in "The Writings of C. I. Lewis";
1. "Scientific Prediction and Practical Meanings." (Paper read at the University of Chicago for the Symposium, "Philosophic Procedures in the Arts and Sciences," Sept. 24, 1933.)
2. "Judgments of Value and Judgments of Fact." (Paper read to Harvard Philosophy Club, 1936.)
3. "Verification and the Types of Truth." (Lewis notes: "Read at Yale and Princeton, 1936-1937."
4. "The Objectivity of Value Judgements." (Paper read to the Brown University Philosophy Club—1941.)

5. "The Conceptual and the Material in Logic and Philosophy." (Read before the Harvard Philosophy Club, 1948.)
6. "Subjective Right and Objective Right." (A paper written in 1952. No indication as to where it was presented.)
7. "Pragmatism and the Roots of the Moral." (Paper read to Claremont Philosophy Club, 1956.)
8. "The Categorical Imperative." (Paper read at Michigan State, July 24, 1958.)
9. "Foundations of Ethics." (Wesleyan Lectures, 1959.)
10. "Persuasive Definition and Scientific Theory." (Unpublished. Prefaced with a 1960 note by Lewis saying that he does not remember when or why the paper was written.)
11. "Our Active Nature and the World We Live In." (Mary Whiton Calkin Lecture, read at Wellesley. No date.)
12. "Values and Facts." (Lewis notes: "Written for a cooperative volume projected by Hook and Sellars. But the project failed of fruition." No date.)

# INDEX

## (Arranged by P. S. S. RAMA RAO)

### A

abilities, 287

absolute, 187

accidents, 402

acquaint (ed) , 315f, 318, 325

acquaintance, 158, 164n, 165n, 166, 405

act, 230, 240f; meaning of, 223ff; cognitive, 290, 293f; mental, 326; and responsibility, 224

action, imperative for, 587f; norms of, 503; right, 601, 610f, 614f

activity, 225, 227

actualities, 402ff, 458f, 461

Adams, G. P., 26, 40, 115n, 273n, 473n

Adams, E. M., Lewis' reply to, 666f

addition, arithmetic, 108; logical, 108

adjunction, 132, 134

aesthesis, 470

aesthetic, experience, 587, 670; Prall and Pepper's influence on Lewis', 670

agnosticism, 295

Alban, M. J., 137n

Aldrich, Virgil C., 475n

Alexander, Samuel, 57

algebra—Boolean, 12, 141; and strict implication, 142f; —Schröder, explained, 110f; dyadic, distinguished from numerical, 105; matrix, 128f; operations in, 100; two-valued, criticised, 111f

alogical, 178

America, 103

American philosophy, 287; Philosophical Association, 312

analogy, of feeling, 409; grammatical, as misleading, 359

*Analysis,* 150n

analysis, 33, 155, 187, 194n, 243, 277ff; goes in circles, 190n; conceptual, 29, 278; linguistic, 284; logical, 181n, 276; phenomenological, 276; philosophical, 28, 641; paradox of, 156n, 187, 595; reflective, 44

analysts, 272, 274; critics, 272f, 275; pragmatic, 284

analytic, 15, 31; defined, 155f; as determined by language rules, 275; synthetic, 280, 358; synthetic distinction, Lewis on, 659ff

analytical movement, 274

analyticity, 243, 264, 267n, 281, 480, 482, 484, 487

Anderson, A. R., 141

Anglo-American culture, 103

antecedent reality, 287, 297, 301f

*Annales de l'Institut Henri Poincaré,* 415n

antilogism, 148, 151

antinomies, Kant's, 3

a posteriori, 158, 267n, 445f, 659

appear, meaning of, 235; —statement, 64, 236f

appearance (s) , 65, 76, 289, 299, 305f, 330, 377, 383ff; and reality, 6; as created, 332; as a function, 288; kinds of, 389f; primacy of, 300; role of, 236f; subjective, passage to objective reality, 378; uniformity of, 287

application, criterion of, 467

appraisals, error of, 492

apprehension, 329, 334, 336, 377, 386, 490, 502, 544, 592; meaning of, 335; non-cognitive, 563, 565; synthetic, 585

a priori, 15, 31, 52, 243, 263, 273f, 277, 518f, 633, 659, 661; analytic, 157, 159f, 167, 284, 445ff; cognitive and non-cognitive, 168f; conveys something novel, 188; copulative, 159; epistemic function of, 275; Lewis' conception of, 44; linguistic, 275; meaning of, 167, 284; nature of, 25; probability judgments as, 68; rationalist theory of, 158n; synthetic, 277, 448, 457, 519, 612; synthetic, Lewis' rejection of, 633, 659

apriorism, 271

Arabic, 258

*Archivio di Filosofia: Semantica,* 327

Aristippus, 529

Aristotle, 90, 118, 126n, 241, 304, 396, 620, 676; *Prior Analytics,* 90, 96, 99, 102

Arrow, Kenneth J., 419n

assertion, 131, 244, 252, 257, 351

procedure, philosophical, 24
process, 30; inner-bodily, 405f; neural, 404, 412; physical, 403f
properties, dispositional, 299, 303, 346; objective, 530; relational, 604
proposal, as substituting 'proposition', 217ff
propositions, 33, 96, 101, 131, 201ff, 244ff, 352, 357, 368, 374, 380, 397, 451, 658; analytic, 155f, 168, 176, 276, 284; a priori, 157ff, 162, 168, 178ff; as a kind of term, 205, 210f, 255, 635, 641; atomic, 458; calculus of, 14; copulative, 156, 176, 178, 184, 199; counter-factual, 641; denote facts, 201f, 206, 210f; entertaining of, 635, 649; hypothetical, 118; intension and extension of, 205; iterative, 156, 173, 178, 182, 185; logic of, 115; MacColl's conception of, 122; Megaric logic of, 117; modal, *de re* and *de dicto*, 118; necessary, as based on equivocation, 277; non-probabilistic, 426, 428, 431; physical object, 417, 450, 452, 455; pronomial, 246; probabilistic, 426, 428ff, 445; sense-data, 417, 450, 455; signifying a state of affairs, 204f, 211, 214, 217; structure of, 641f; synthetic, 156, 176n, 445; terminal, 631, 638, 640
propositional, 335
prosaic fallacy, the, 408
proscriptive principle, 151f
protocol sentences, 77
prudence, 503, 505, 508, 515, 594, 613; criterion of, 494f, 497f
*Psychological Review*, 296
psychologism, 272
psychology, 240, 292, 332
public interest, 524
punishment, 227
purity, 671
purposes, human, 48

## Q

*quale*, 323, 330, 336, 404; as a sign, 387
qualia, 164n, 167, 377, 384, 386, 472n
Quincy, Massachusetts, 7
Quine, W. V., 144, 351, 363, 469n, 486n
quantification (s), 104, 131, 142, 246, 356, 361f, 644f, 647, 649f
quantifiers, 104f, 110, 113, 135, 316, 362; difficulties with Lewis' account of, 318f; existential, 112, 142n; sense meanings of, 319ff; universal, 112, 131, 360, 366

## R

Ramsey, Frank, 415f, 415n

rational, explained, 572
rational reconstruction, 310
rationalism, 158, 167, 288, 591, 612, 619, 673; critical, 324; objective, 299
rationality, 503, 507; meaning of, 613, 624f
rationalist (s), 162, 166, 185, 282; Lewis as a, 672f
real, 19, 38ff, 333; ambiguity of, 38ff; and unreal, 38f, 177; as constituted of facts, 201; as epistemic, 40; categories of the, 655
realism, 42, 167, 274, 287f, 297, 301, 303, 378, 380, 382f, 388, 390, 407, 657; causal, 333; common-sense, 297; compatible with subjectivism, 378f; critical, 289f, 301, 663; Dewey's reaction to, 300ff; direct, 289f, 294f; naive, 292, 297, 299, 301, 303, 403; the New, 10, 663; physical, 297, 305; Platonic, 158n; presentational, 301; principle of, explained, 377, 392f; rationalistic, 158n, 161, 165, 168, 198f; representative, 299; valuational, 531
realist (s), 158, 160, 166, 169n, 188; American, 271; British, 271; Critical, 296, 298, 300, 302, 306; critics, 271f, 274f; New, 298, 300, 302, 306, 667; movement, the New, 10; physical, 307; rationalistic, 185
reality, 38ff, 80, 158, 162; judgments about, 82; Lewis' theory of, 39, 410; objective, 65, 83, 331; statements about, 77; Platonic, 162, 164n, 165; relation to ideal, 43; senses of, 176f; social view of, 407, 410
reason, 165, 439, 627; imperative of, 623; natural light of, 377; sufficient, 230f, 343, 349; speculative, 654
reasoning, calculus of, 93ff
recollection, 398, 412; guessing in, 399, 406
reference class, 370, 372f, 373n
reflection, connotation of, 28; critical, 52; metaphysical, 26
relation, 38, 45, 97; asymmetrical, 403, 405f; De Morgan's theory of, 106; dyadic, 220; internality of, 206; logic of, 106; of ideas, 283; subject-object, 42; symmetrical, 403, 405f; triadic, 220
relatives, defined by propositional functions, 110; logic of, 91, 96f, 108, 112; Peirce on logic of, 109f; Schröder's logic of, 111
Reichenbach, Hans, 67, 310, 312n, 315, 326f, 371, 373, 446, 633n, 664, 668
Reid, J. R., 621
Reid, Thomas, 331
relative frequency, 370ff, 439, 449, 456
relativism, 243, 589ff, 598, 676